GRONINGEN

Groningen

Leeuwarden

FRIESLAND

Assen

DRENTHE

Emmen

Lelystad

LAND

Zwolle

OVERIJSSEL

Apeldoorn

Enschede

GELDERLAND

Arnhem

Nijmegen

Eindhoven

LIMBURG

Maastricht

0 kilometres 20

EYEWITNESS TRAVEL

THE NETHERLANDS

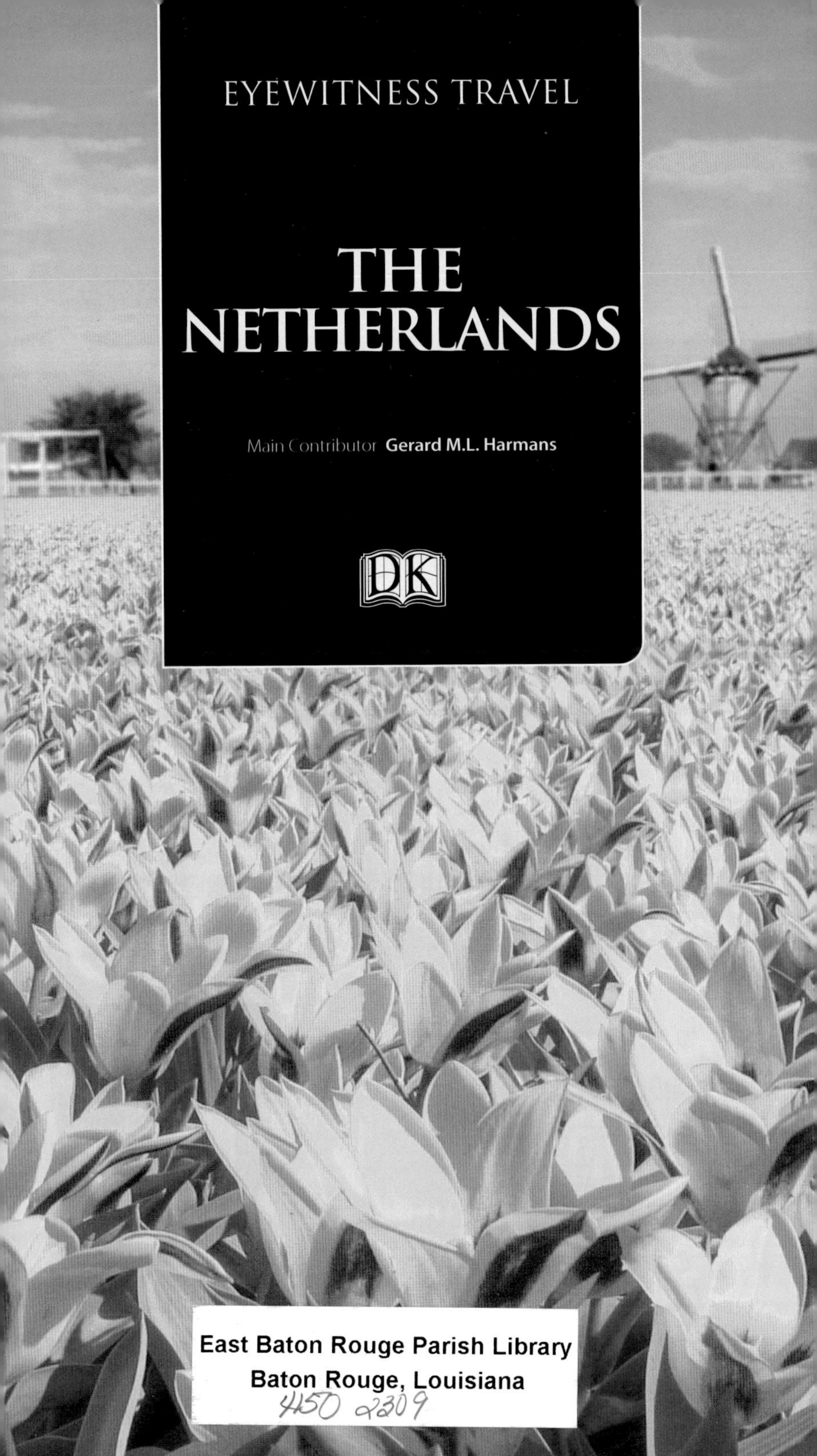

EYEWITNESS TRAVEL
THE NETHERLANDS
Main Contributor Gerard M.L. Harmans
DK

LONDON, NEW YORK,
MELBOURNE, MUNICH AND DELHI
www.dk.com

Produced by Van Reemst Uitgeverij/Unieboek bv

Main Contributor Gerard M.L. Harmans

Design Studio Putto, De Rijp

Art Editor Dick Polman

Editorial (Dutch original) *de Redactie*, boekverzorgers, Amsterdam

Photographers
Max Alexander, Anwb Audiovisuele Dienst (Thijs Tuurenhout), George Burggraaff, Jurjen Drenth, Rubert Horrox, Kim Sayer, Herman Scholten

Illustrators
Hilbert Bolland, Jan Egas, Gieb van Enckevort, Nick Gibbard, Mark Jurriëns, Maltings Partnership, Derrick Stone, Khoobie Verwer, Martin Woodward

Cartography
Jane Hanson, Armand Haye, Lovell Johns Limited (Oxford, UK), Phil Rose, Jennifer Skelley, Peter de Vries

Picture Researcher Harry Bunk
Production Sarah Dodd

English-language adaptation produced by International Book Productions Inc., 25a Morrow Ave, Toronto, Ontario M6R 2H9, Canada

Managing Editor Barbara Hopkinson
Editor Judy Phillips
DTP Designers Dietmar Kokemohr, Sean Gaherty

Printed and Bound by L.Rex Printing Company Limited

First American edition 2003

14 15 16 17 10 9 8 7 6 5 4 3 2 1

Published in the United States by DK Publishing, 345 Hudson Street, New York, New York 10014

Reprinted with revisions 2005, 2008, 2011, 2014

A CIP catalogue record is available from the Library of Congress.

ISSN 1542-1554

ISBN 978-1-46541-195-2

Floors are referred to throughout in accordance with European usage; ie the "first floor" is the floor above ground level.

The information in this DK Eyewitness Travel Guide is checked regularly.

Every effort has been made to ensure that this book is as up-to-date as possible at the time of going to press. Some details, however, such as telephone numbers, opening hours, prices, gallery hanging arrangements and travel information are liable to change. The publishers cannot accept responsibility for any consequences arising from the use of this book, nor for any material on third party websites, and cannot guarantee that any website address in this book will be a suitable source of travel information. We value the views and suggestions of our readers very highly. Please write to: Publisher, DK Eyewitness Travel Guides, Dorling Kindersley, 80 Strand, London, WC2R 0RL, UK, or email: travelguides@dk.com.

Front cover main image: Windmill de Vlieger, in the Dutch town of Voorburg

◀ Tulip fields with a windmill in the background

CONTENTS

Zeeland's coat of arms

Introducing the Netherlands

Girl with a Pearl Earring (1665) by Johannes Vermeer

Amsterdam

Thialf fans *(see p304)*

Western Netherlands

Northern and Eastern Netherlands

The 15th-century Koppelpoort by Amersfoort

Southern Netherlands

Travellers' Needs

Survival Guide

The imposing Sint Jan in 's-Hertogenbosch *(see p364–5)*

HOW TO USE THIS GUIDE

This guide helps you get the most from your stay in the Netherlands. The first section, *Introducing the Netherlands,* places the country on the map and puts it in its historical and cultural context. Chapters on the provinces and the capital, Amsterdam, describe the most important sights and places of interest. Features cover topics from architecture to tulip growing. They are accompanied by detailed and helpful illustrations. *Travellers' Needs* gives specifics on where to stay and where to eat and drink, while the *Survival Guide* contains practical information on everything from the public transport system to personal safety.

Amsterdam

Amsterdam is divided into five tourist areas. The corresponding chapters all begin with a list of numbered sights and places of interest, which are plotted on the Area Map. The information for each sight follows this numerical order, making sights easy to locate within the chapter.

1 Area Map

This map is numbered to show the most important attractions. They are also given in the Street Finder section on pages 154–63.

A locator map places the district in the context of the rest of the city.

Sights at a Glance groups the sights by category: historical buildings and monuments, streets, squares and gardens, museums and churches.

A recommended route covers the most interesting streets in the area.

All pages about Amsterdam are marked in red.

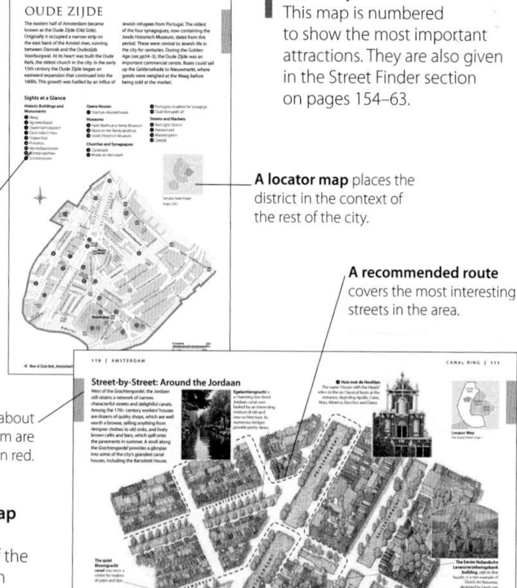

2 Street-by-Street Map

This map gives a detailed summary of the heart of the five main tourist areas of the city.

Stars indicate sights that should not be missed.

3 Detailed Information

All main attractions are described individually, including their addresses, opening hours and other practical information. Keys to the symbols used are on the rear flap of this book.

The Netherlands Area by Area

The Netherlands is divided into 12 provinces. Each of these provinces, Amsterdam and the Wadden Islands are dealt with in separate chapters. The most interesting towns, villages and places are shown on the Regional Map.

1 Introduction
The scenery, history and character of each province are outlined here, showing how the area has changed through the centuries, and what it has to offer today's visitor.

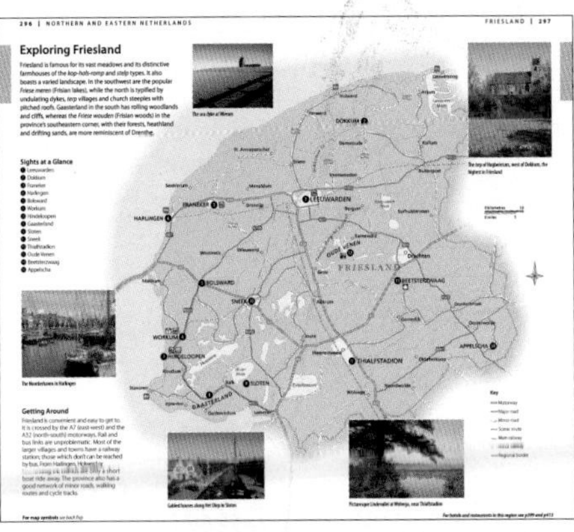

2 Regional Map
This map shows the main roads and the main tourist attractions of an area, and also gives useful information about driving and rail travel.

Colour tabs are used to colour-code each province a different shade for easy reference.

3 Detailed Information
Major sights and attractions are described in detail in the order in which they are numbered on the Regional Map. Within each entry is detailed information on buildings, parks, museums and other sights.

Story boxes explore specific topics.

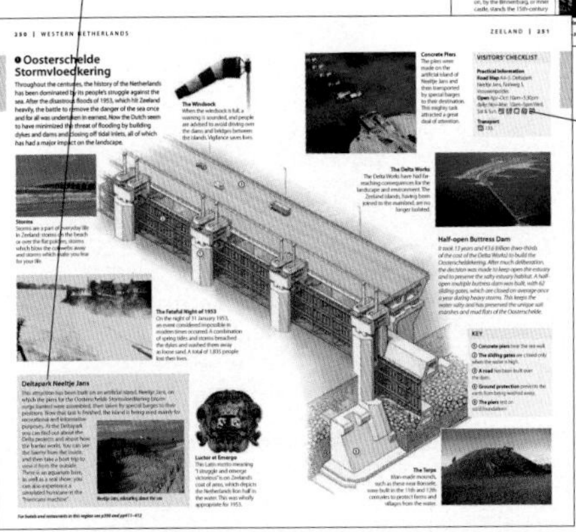

Visitors' Checklist gives practical information to help you plan your visit.

4 The Top Sights
These sights are described on two or more pages. Cutaway illustrations and floor plans show the most important buildings, museums and other sights.

INTRODUCING THE NETHERLANDS

DISCOVERING THE NETHERLANDS

The following itineraries have been designed to include as many of the country's highlights as possible, while keeping long-distance travel manageable. First come three, two-day tours of the Netherlands' most important cities: Amsterdam, The Hague and Utrecht. Visitors can combine these into a single six-day tour by catching a train to the next city. Next come four, seven-day tours. The first of these covers the principal cities in the south, while the second ventures further north to the more rural province of Friesland and the islands that lie just offshore. The third suggested itinerary is a circular tour beginning and ending in Amsterdam, which takes in the quiet towns on the eastern side of the country. The fourth tour is a linear cycle route threading through the towns and countryside along the River Ijssel; this last itinerary can also be followed by car. Pick, combine and follow your favourite tours, or simply dip in and out and be inspired.

A Week in the South

- See beautiful paintings displayed at Haarlem's **Frans Hals Museum**.
- Learn about the ancient culture of the Egyptians at **Rijksmuseum van Oudheden** in Leiden.
- Admire the wonderful blooms of the **Keukenhof** gardens near **Leiden**.
- Visit the handsome old houses of the **Delfshaven**, Rotterdam's earliest harbour.
- See the superb stained-glass windows in Gouda's **St Janskerk**.
- Don't miss the spectacular sight of 19 vintage windmills at **Kinderdijk**.

Keukenhof Gardens, Lisse
Colourful blossoms at the Keukenhof flower gardens, located near the small town of Lisse in South Holland

◀ *View of Delft* (1660) – a masterpiece by Johannes Vermeer

A Week in the North and the Islands

- Explore the culture of the Zuiderzee at the **Zuiderzeemuseum** in Enkhuizen.
- Drive along the 32 km **Afsluitdijk**, built between 1927 and 1933, and enjoy the spectacular views.
- Relax in one of the country's prettiest villages – tiny **Hindeloopen**.
- Cycle the quiet byways of the island of **Vlieland**.
- Visit the **Groninger Museum**, the finest art gallery in Groningen.

A Circular Tour from Amsterdam

- Learn about the strong seafaring traditions of the Dutch at the pretty little village of **Urk**.
- Don't miss the **Schokland Museum**, which showcases the remains of the former Zuiderzee island.
- Take a boat ride among the peaty canals of beautiful **Giethoorn**.
- Saunter the streets of the well-preserved historic town of **Elburg**.
- See the **Mondriaanhuis**, where Dutch painter Piet Mondriaan was born.

A Cycling Tour of the River Ijssel

- Explore the heaths and woods of the **National Park de Hoge Veluwe** by bicycle.
- See the splendid collection of Dutch art at the **Kröller-Müller Museum** near Arnhem.
- Enjoy the small-town charms of **Zutphen** and the medieval library at **St Walburgskerk**.
- Wander the streets of **Zwolle**, one of the country's most beguiling cities.

Two Days in Amsterdam

Known as home to Anne Frank and Van Gogh, Amsterdam is brimming with sights and beautiful canals to explore.

- **Arriving** Schiphol Airport is a 20-minute train journey from the city centre. Amsterdam also has good train connections with the rest of Europe.

View of a canal in the Jordaan, Amsterdam

Day 1

Morning Begin the tour in Dam Square, a bustling open space at the heart of the city, and visit the **National Monument** *(p90)*, an evocative war memorial erected in 1956. Then, pop into the **Nieuwe Kerk** *(p90)*, one of Amsterdam's most beautiful Gothic buildings. Stop next at the imposing **Koninklijk Paleis** *(p92)*, built in the 17th century as the Stadhuis (Town Hall) when the city was at its richest. Afterwards, detour south to the **Begijnhof** *(p91)*, a set of pretty medieval almshouses grouped around a small green.

Afternoon Take a stroll along the Singel, the first of the four canals that make up the **Grachtengordel** *(p99)*, or 'girdle of canals'. With a string of hump-backed bridges spanning olive-green canals, this is Amsterdam at its most beautiful. Pop into the **Museum van Loon** *(p119)* for an insight into the life and times of the Dutch merchant elite, and then head for **Westerkerk** *(p114)*, with its soaring spire and cavernous interior. From there, slip along the street to the city's most popular attraction, the **Anne Frank Huis** *(p112)*.

Day 2

Morning Dedicate this day to explorimg some of the city's best museums. Expect to spend at least a couple of hours at the **Rijksmuseum** *(p126)*, Amsterdam's principal art museum, which features a fabulous collection of Dutch paintings, most notably the wonderful Rembrandts. Then, proceed to the superb **Van Gogh Museum** *(p130)*, devoted to the greatest of all Dutch painters. After all this art, take a break at a local café or go for a stroll amid the greenery of the neighbouring **Vondelpark** *(p124)*.

Afternoon After lunch, visit the city's third major museum, the **Stedelijk Museum** *(p132)*, whose excellent collection of contemporary art is housed in a lavishly refurbished gallery. Or, if museum fatigue is setting in, venture out of the tourist zone to explore the maze-like streets of the **Jordaan** *(pp110–111)*, or rest your legs on a **canal boat trip** *(p117)*.

The 15th-century Nieuwe Kerk, located on Dam Square in Amsterdam

Two Days in The Hague

An important political centre since the 13th century, The Hague is a fascinating city with aristocratic charm.

- **Arriving** The Hague has good train connections with the rest of the Netherlands. The nearest airport is Rotterdam, 21 km (13 miles) away, while Schiphol airport is 48 km (30 miles) away.

Day 1

Morning Stroll the streets of **The Hague** *(p222)*, pausing on Lange Vijverberg for a panoramic view of the **Binnenhof** *(p223)*, a long and elegant series of high-gabled buildings that now house the Dutch parliament. Venture into the Binnenhof and take a guided tour of the **Ridderzaal** *(p224)*, the Hall of the Knights, which dates back to the 13th century. Continue onto the **Mauritshuis** *(p226)*, an outstanding art gallery with a wonderful collection of Dutch paintings, including several exquisite paintings by Johannes Vermeer.

Afternoon Visit the **Museum Bredius** *(p224)* to enjoy a connoisseur's collection of Dutch art. Wander along the tree-lined Lange Voorhout, which is framed by handsome old mansions, one of which, the **Escher in Het Paleis** *(p224)*, exhibits the startling compositions of the graphic artist Maurits Escher. Then, head north towards the unusual **Panorama Mesdag** *(p228)*, where a massive circular canvas depicts the beach at Scheveningen as it was in the late 19th century.

Day 2
Morning Spend the morning at the **Gementeemuseum Den Haag** *(p228)*, whose vast permanent collection includes a wonderful display of Delft pottery and an extravagant collection of modern Dutch artists, with special reference to the austere Piet Mondriaan. Be sure to pop next door to the **Fotomuseum** *(p228)*, which has built up an international reputation for its temporary exhibitions of photography.

Afternoon If the weather is good, take the tram or cycle through the woods to **Scheveningen** *(p229)*, a popular seaside resort where the main attraction is a sandy beach that stretches out as far as the eye can see. You can also take your chances at the casino, enjoy high tea at the **Kurhaus** *(p229)*, stroll along the pier and, finally, admire the outdoor sculptures of the **Museum Beelden aan Zee** *(p229)*.

Two Days in Utrecht

Home to many superb museums, Utrecht is a lively city with magnificent canalside houses.

- **Arriving** Served by Schiphol airport, Utrecht also has good road and train connections. Apeldoorn is just 40 minutes by train and there are departures every 20–30 minutes. There are regular buses from Apeldoorn train station to the Paleis Het Loo.

Day 1
Morning Begin your tour of **Utrecht** *(p204)* at the **Domtoren** *(p206)*. At 112 m (368 ft), this is the highest bell tower in the country and a symbol of the city. The panoramic view from the tower is worth the climb. Next, drop by the **Domkerk** *(p206)* with its fine Gothic stonework. Continue west to the **Nationaal Museum van Speelklok** *(p207)* to explore its fascinating and most unusual collection of mechanical musical instruments, from fairground organs to musical boxes.

Afternoon Continue your tour by walking along the prettiest stretch of the **Oude Gracht** *(p204)* near the Stadhuis, where bars, cafés and restaurants occupy the old cellars and street level is one storey up. Follow the Oude Gracht south to **Museum Catharijneconvent** *(p206)*, which displays an excellent collection of medieval art and religious sculpture. Pushing on, walk to the **Centraal Museum** *(p206)*, noted for its fine art dating from the 16th century onwards.

Fish-eye view of the ceiling of the Domkerk in Utrecht

Day 2
Morning Don't miss the remarkable **Rietveld Schroderhuis** *(p208)*, one of the most influential pieces of modern architecture in Europe, designed by Gerrit Rietveld, a leading member of the De Stijl movement. Allow at least an hour to explore the house. In particular, look out for the retractable, shape-changing windows in the dining room. .

Afternoon Take the train from Utrecht to **Apeldoorn** *(p340)*, a modest country town, on the outskirts of which is the **Paleis Het Loo** *(p338)*, a lavish palace built in the 17th century and occupied by the Dutch royals until the 1970s. Admire the palace's magnificent dining hall, gawp at the extravagant bedroom of William III, enjoy the paintings in the picture gallery, and wander through the lovely formal gardens to finish the tour.

Intricately designed gardens of the Palais Het Loo

A Week in the South

- **Arriving** Start in Haarlem, accessed easily from Amsterdam's Schiphol airport.
- **Transport** Most of this itinerary can be completed using local trains and buses, but a car will give added flexibility. The Kinderdijk windmills are only accessible by car or bicycle.

A row of windmills at Kinderdijk in Dordrecht

Day 1: Haarlem
Explore the centre of **Haarlem** *(p186)*, one of the country's prettiest towns, with a cluster of old and distinguished buildings framing the expansive Grote Markt. Be sure to visit the **Grote Kerk** *(p188)*, a huge and imposing structure with a magnificent nave. Afterwards, admire the potpourri collections displayed at the **Teylers Museum** *(p189)* and then head over to the town's key attraction – the outstanding **Frans Hals Museum** *(p190)*, which features the paintings of Golden Age artist Frans Hals.

Day 2: Leiden and Keukenhof
Start the day by strolling through the lovely old streets of **Leiden** *(p218)*, where a maze of cobbled lanes conceals a string of excellent attractions. This includes the **Rijksmuseum van Oudheden** *(p221)*, which houses an outstanding ancient Egyptian collection, ranging from mummies to temples. Look out also for the sterling Gothic architecture of **St Pieterskerk** *(p221)*, the handsome **Korenbeursgrug** *(p219)* and Leiden's much praised botanical gardens, the **Hortus Botanicus** *(p220)*. In the afternoon, catch the bus or drive out of Leiden to the nearby **Keukenhof** *(p217)*, the largest flower garden in the world, famed for its tulips.

Day 3: The Hague
Pick a day from the city itinerary on *p12*.

Day 4: Delft
Delft *(p230)* is a charming little town with an especially fine Grote Markt (main square), with the Stadhuis at one end and the splendid **Nieuwe Kerk** *(p231)* at the other. Explore the town's network of narrow lanes and visit both the **Oude Kerk** *(p232)* and the **Stedelijk Museum Het Prinsenhof** *(p232)*, where a hired assassin murdered the heroic William of Orange – the bullet holes can still be seen in the wall.

Day 5: Rotterdam
Enjoy the big city feel of **Rotterdam** *(p234)*, a pulsating metropolis of lively bars, great restaurants and a bustling street life. Take a detour to see the modernist architecture of the famous cube houses or **Kubus Paalwoningen** *(p235)*, stroll along the old city harbour of **Delfshaven** *(p236)* and take a trip up the **Euromast** *(p236)* for the panoramic view. Finish the day at the outstanding **Museum Boijmans Van Beuningen** *(p238)*, which houses an internationally famous collection of Dutch art.

Day 6: Gouda
Enjoy the small town atmosphere of **Gouda** *(p243)* with its cobbled streets, slender canals and handsome main square, the Grote Markt, where you can admire the magnificent **Stadhuis** *(p243)*. Try to visit on a Thursday morning in the summertime to enjoy the town's famous cheese market with its fancily-dressed porters. Be sure to drop by **St Janskerk** *(p242)*, a distinguished Gothic structure with a breathtakingly beautiful set of stained-glass windows dating from the late 16th century.

Day 7: Dordrecht
Spend the morning exploring **Dordrecht** *(p244)*, an ancient port that nudges up against one of the busiest waterways in the world. Highlights here include the ornate and rather fanciful **Grote Kerk** *(p244)* and the **Museum Simon van Gijn** *(p244)*, with its period rooms and magnificent Brussels tapestries. Venturing out of Dordecht, cycle or drive over to the **Kinderdijk** *(p245)*, where no fewer than 19 vintage windmills line up along a canal, looking proudly out over the surrounding polders.

Colourful buildings in the pretty town of Haarlem

For practical information on travelling around the Netherlands, see pp432–49

A Week in the North and the Islands

- **Arriving** Head from Amsterdam to Alkmaar.
- **Transport** Hoorn, Enkhuizen, Leeuwarden, Harlingen and Groningen are easy to reach by train, and there are regular daily ferries from Harlingen to Vlieland, Holwerd to Ameland, and from Harlingen and Vlieland to Terschelling. However, to complete this itinerary, hiring a car is essential.

Day 1: Alkmaar
Heading north out of Amsterdam, stop at **Alkmaar** *(p184)*, whose charming old centre is encircled by olive-green canals. On Friday mornings, the main square comes alive with the town's famous cheese market. Afterwards, be sure to visit **Hoorn** *(p182)*, an old Zuiderzee seaport with a fine ensemble of old buildings, as well as the **Westfries Museum** *(p182)*. Moving along the coast, you soon reach **Enkhuizen** *(p182)*, another handsome former seaport and the home of the outstanding **Zuiderzeemuseum** *(p180)*.

Day 2: Friesland
Drive north from Enkhuizen to cross the Waddenzee via the **Afsluitdijk** *(p174)*, thus reaching the province of **Friesland** *(pp295–305)* at a point near the exquisitely pretty waterside hamlet of **Hindeloopen** *(p302)*. Proceed northeast from here to reach **Sneek** *(p303)*, a relaxing little village famous for its sailing clubs, and **Leeuwarden** *(p300)*, a good-looking town well worth an afternoon's wanderings. Admire the wonderful ceramic collection at **Het Princessehof** *(p300)*, and allow some time for the **Fries Museum** *(p300)* with its displays on all things Frisian.

Day 3: Harlingen to Vlieland
Begin the day amid the maritime atmosphere of **Harlingen** *(p297)*, an ancient seaport where vintage sailing boats crowd the harbour. Then, catch the ferry over to **Vlieland** *(p273)*, the smallest of the Waddenzee islands, whose sand dunes stretch out along its northern shore. Take a hike or a bike ride along one of the many trails, or hunker down in the island's one and only village, **Oost-Vlieland** *(p273)*, where there is an interesting museum, the **Tromp's Huys** *(p273)*.

Day 4: Terschelling
Take the ferry from Harlingen or Vlieland to **Terschelling** *(p278)*. The first port of call will be **West-Terschelling** *(p278)*, a lovely little village that houses the **Museum 't Behouden** *(p278)* . Wander through the village, a popular summer resort, and then cycle out across the island, either to the dunes and beaches of the north coast or to the woods and mud flats of the south.

Day 5: Ameland
Catch the ferry from Holwerd to **Ameland** *(p278)* and arrive in the village of **Nes** *(p278)*. Here, choose between the mud flats, marshland and bird reserves of the south coast and the sand dunes of the north, but be sure to visit tiny **Hollum** *(p279)*, a picturesque hamlet of old seafarers' cottages and thatched farmhouses fanning out from a delightful country church.

Day 6: Dokkum to Pieterburen
Head to **Dokkum** *(p300)*, an ancient town where the Christian missionary St Boniface met a grisly end. Explore the town centre with its pretty canals and

Transporting cheeses at Alkmaar cheese market, North Holland

old houses, and then push on to **Lauwersoog** *(p290)*, a tiny village deep in the countryside, and **Uithuizen** *(p291)*, where you can sign up for a guided walk across the mud flats (an activity known as *wadlopen* in Dutch). Also visit Pieterburen for its Seal Sanctuary, the **Zeehonden-crèche** *(p291)*.

Day 7: Groningen
Don't miss out on **Groningen** *(p280)*, a bustling city flush with excellent restaurants and a busy nightlife. Spend the morning exploring the city centre; highlights include the imposing **Martinikerk** *(p282)* and the delightful **Prinsenhof Gardens** *(p283)*. The big attraction, however, is the **Groninger Museum** *(p284)*, where a wide-ranging art collection is housed in a splendid modern building designed by Alessandro Mendini and opened in 1994.

Spritsail barges in Sneek, Friesland

A Circular Tour from Amsterdam

- **Duration** Seven days – if travelling by bike, consider building in extra rest stops and extending to 10 days.
- **Arriving** This tour starts and ends in Amsterdam.
- **Transport** The towns in this itinerary are readily accessible by train, but local buses are unreliable, so visitors will need a car to travel to the villages. For the energetic visitor, this tour can be done by bike.

Day 1: Marken to Volendam
See the famous stilt houses of **Marken** *(p178)*, a tiny village perched on an island in the Markermeer. Learn more of the island's heritage at the **Marker Museum** *(p178)*, which occupies six old island houses. Continue up the coast to **Volendam** *(p178)*, where a dyke still protects the village.

Day 2: Edam and Enkhuizen
Edam *(p178)* is extremely pretty, its cluster of ancient houses huddled around a network of narrow canals and swing bridges. Allow an hour to explore Edam and then move on to **Enkhuizen** *(p182)*, a handsome old seaport with a splendid harbour in the lee of a mighty, defensive tower, the **Drommedaris** *(p182)*. Finish the day at Enkhuizen's excellent **Zuiderzeemuseum** *(p180)*.

Day 3: Urk
Cross the Markerwaarddijk from Enkhuizen to reach the outskirts of **Lelystad** *(p331)*, a modern town whose main pull is the replica 17th century sailing ship on the **Bataviawerf** *(p331)*. Pushing on, it's a short haul to **Urk** *(p330)*, an intriguing little place and one-time island fishing village now attached to the mainland. Grab a plate of seafood before continuing on to the delightful **Schokland Museum** *(p330)*. Just like Urk, Schokland was once an island and the remains of the old fishing village are fascinating.

Day 4: Vollenhove and Giethoorn
Traversing the polder landscape, visitors soon reach minuscule **Vollenhove** *(p321)*, once an important seaport. Allow an hour to explore the village, and then push on east to **Giethoorn** *(p322)*, one of the country's most unusual villages, with a string of old thatched farmhouses dotting a network of peaty canals. Take a boat ride here; spare some time to explore the unspoiled wetlands of **De Weerribben** *(p321)* conservation area.

Day 5: Staphorst to Zwolle
Take a detour south from Giethoorn to **Staphorst** *(p324)*, an old-fashioned village whose elongated main street is flanked by thatched farmhouses. Visit on Sunday morning when the locals head off to church in traditional costume (note: taking photos is considered impolite). Continue to **Zwolle** *(p320)*, a distinguished city whose star-shaped fortifications encase a centre of narrow lanes, elegant squares and attractive old buildings. Visit the **Grote Kerk** *(p320)* for its splendid interior, the **Stedelijk Museum** *(p320)* for its Golden Age period rooms, and the **Paleis aan de Blijmarkt** *(p320)* for its exhibitions of contemporary art. Last but not least, stroll along the harbour, where vintage canal boats are polished and scrubbed to delightful effect.

Day 6: Elburg
Discover the gentle charms of **Elburg** *(p340)*, a former Zuiderzee seaport that now sits beside the Veluwemeer, the narrow waterway separating the mainland from reclaimed polder lands. See the medieval town gates, pop into the St Nicolaaskerk and drop by the **Gementeemuseum Elburg** *(p336)*, where pride of place goes to a fine collection of silverware, once the property of the local guild of sailors.

Boat travelling along the waterways of Giethoorn, Overijssel

Day 7: Amersfoort
Head southwest along the Veluwemeer waterway towards **Amersfoort** *(p206)*, a medium-sized town whose ancient centre is still encircled by canals. Visit the key attractions: the splendid Koppelpoort, one of three surviving medieval gates; the soaring Onze Lieve Vrouwetoren (the Tower of the Church of Our Lady); and the **Mondriaanhuis** *(p206)*, a museum in the former home of artist Pier Mondriaan. Allow an hour or so to cover the 50 km (31 miles) back from Amersfoort to Amsterdam.

The medieval gate of Koppelpoort in Amersfoort

For practical information on travelling around the Netherlands, see pp432–49

A Cycling Tour of the River Ijssel

- **Duration** Seven days.
- **Arriving** Arnhem, at the start of this itinerary, is easy to reach by train, bus and car, as is Kampen at the end of the itinerary.
- **Transport** To complete this itinerary, hire a bike in Arnhem or take one with you on the train or by car.

Cycling trail in the National Park de Hoge Veluwe, Gelderland

Day 1: Arnhem
Begin the tour with a stroll through the centre of **Arnhem** *(p344)*, a lively city that suffered terribly during the Battle of Arnhem in 1944. It now hosts a vibrant restaurant and nightclub scene. Pause to admire the imposing edifice of the **Eusebiuskerk** *(p344)*, restored after wartime damage – as were the neighbouring **Stadhuis** *(p344)* and **Duivelshuis** *(p344)*, both of which are fine examples of Dutch Renaissance architecture. Then, go down to the Rijnkade, where there is a walking and cycling path along the bank of the River Rhine.

Day 2: National Park de Hoge Veluwe
Pedal out to the **National Park de Hoge Veluwe** *(p342)*, a chunk of mixed woodland, heath, marshland and sand dunes that stretches north of Arnhem. Explore the park's maze of cycling trails, and be sure to visit the **Museonder** *(p342)*, a subterranean museum that offers a picture of what the natural world looks like below ground level – from how roots grow to the animals that burrow there. Afterwards, head for the park's crowning highlight – the **Kröller-Müller Museum** *(p342)*, with its world-famous art collection and open-air sculpture garden, Beeldentuin. Return to Arnhem for the night.

Day 3: Bronkhorst to Zutphen
Head out of Arnhem to **Bronkhorst** *(p345)*, a tiny but immensely pretty little place with a cluster of immaculate cottages. Then, continue to **Zutphen** *(p345)*, a beguiling country town with a huddle of ancient buildings and the remnants of medieval walls. Look out for **Drogenapstoren** *(p345)*, a fortified tower dating from the 15th century, and drop by **St Walburgskerk** *(p345)*, a splendid Gothic church with a medieval library, where the books are still chained to the desks.

Day 4: Deventer
Cycle onwards and relax in **Deventer** *(p324)*, a small and historic town that nudges up against the River Ijssel. Watch the heavily-laden barges ploughing up and down the river, and then wander along the main square, the Brink, as it curves past the town's intriguing **Historisch Museum** *(p324)*, which occupies the old and very ornate weigh house, the Waag. Don't leave town without trying the local speciality, Kruidkoek, a tangy spice cake.

View of the Deventer skyline across the River Ijssel

Day 5: Sallandse Heuvelrug
From Deventer, travel northeast to the partly wooded, sandy heathlands of the **Sallandse Heuvelrug** *(p324)*, now protected as a national park. At the Bezoekscentrum (Visitor Centre), visitors can get their bearings and pick up maps of the park and its myriad cycling routes. While wandering through the park, look out for the black grouse – this is its last remaining breeding ground in the whole of the Netherlands.

Day 6: Zwolle
Cycle to Zwolle *(see p16 for details on Zwolle)*.

Day 7: Kampen
Approach **Kampen** *(p320)* from the east across the River Ijssel to appreciate the town's fine riverside setting and soaring spires. Once in town, make a beeline for the unusual **Ikonenmuseum** *(p321)*, with its substantial collection of Russian and Greek icons, and get the low-down on the town's long history at the intriguing **Stedelijk Museum** *(p321)*. Finish the day by wandering through the town centre, admiring its handsome old buildings, most memorably the Oude Raadhuis and the three remaining town gates, which date back to the 14th century.

Putting the Netherlands on the Map

The Netherlands is situated in Western Europe, bordering Belgium to the south and Germany to the east. To its north and west is the North Sea. The country is popularly known as Holland, although the provinces of North and South Holland form only part of the Netherlands in reality. Since the completion of the Deltawerken (Delta Works), the coastline is some 800 km (500 miles) in length. The country's major waterways and excellent road and rail systems make it an important gateway to the rest of Europe, and to Germany in particular. Approximately one-sixth of its total area is covered with water. The Netherlands has a population of about 16 million.

For map symbols see back flap

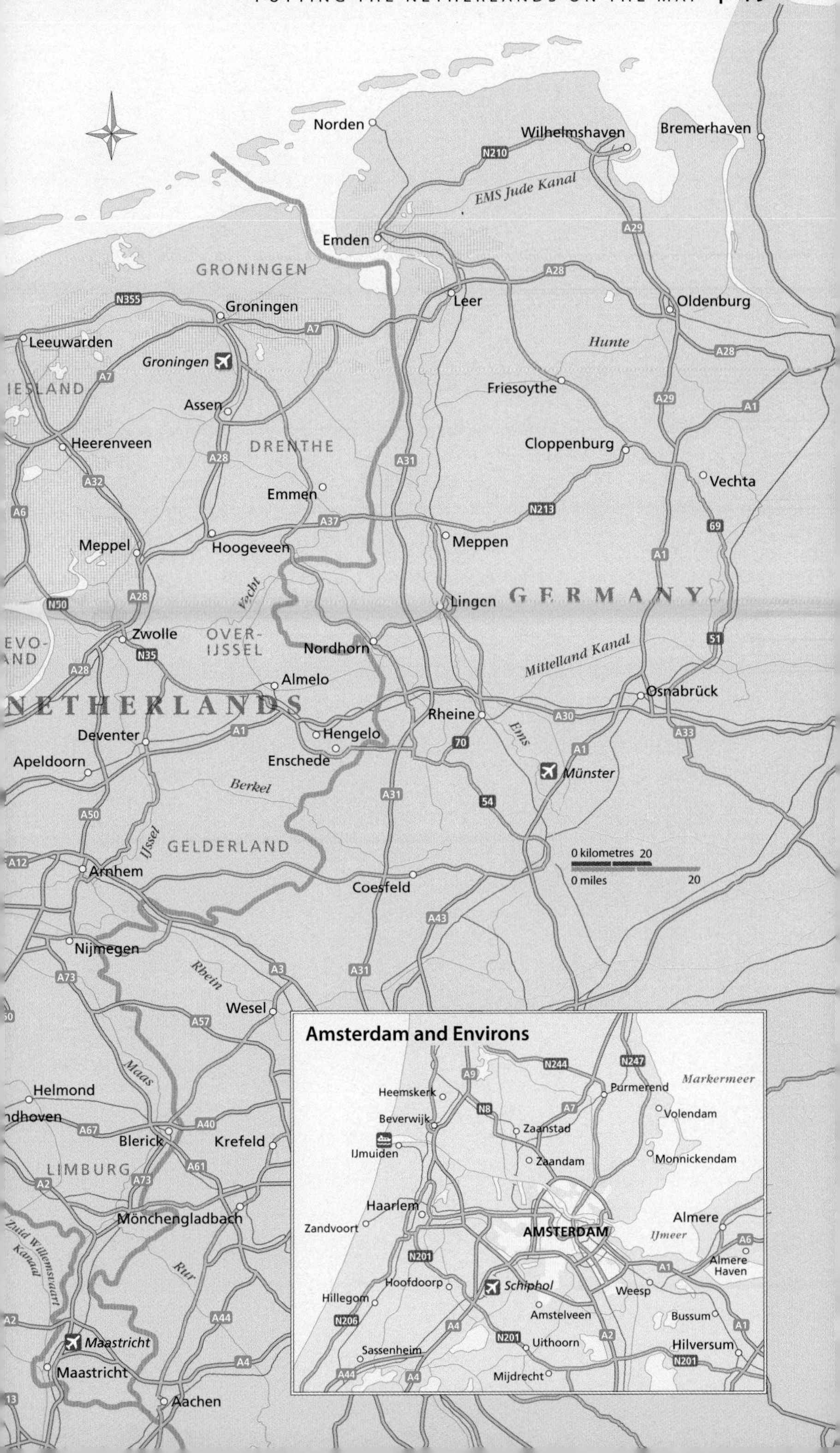
Norden
Wilhelmshaven
Bremerhaven
N210
EMS Jude Kanal
A29
Emden
GRONINGEN
A28
N355
Groningen
Leer
Oldenburg
A7
Leeuwarden
Hunte
Groningen
A28
IESLAND
A7
Friesoythe
A29
A1
Assen
Heerenveen
DRENTHE
Cloppenburg
A28
A31
A32
Vechta
Emmen
A6
N213
A37
69
Meppel
Hoogeveen
Meppen
A1
A28
Vecht
N50
Lingen
GERMANY
Zwolle
OVER-
IJSSEL
Nordhorn
51
EVO-
AND
N35
Mittelland Kanal
A28
Almelo
Osnabrück
NETHERLANDS
Rheine
A30
Deventer
A1
Hengelo
Ens
A33
70
Apeldoorn
Enschede
A1
Münster
Berkel
A31
A50
54
IJssel
GELDERLAND
0 kilometres 20
0 miles 20
A12
Arnhem
Coesfeld
A43
Nijmegen
A73
Rhein
A3
A31
Wesel
A57
Maas
Helmond
ndhoven
A40
A67
Blerick
Krefeld
LIMBURG
A61
A2
A73
Mönchengladbach
Zuid Willemsvaart Kanaal
Rur
A44
Maastricht
A4
Maastricht
Aachen
Amsterdam and Environs
N244
N247
A9
Purmerend
Markermeer
Heemskerk
N8
A7
Volendam
Beverwijk
Zaanstad
IJmuiden
Zaandam
Monnickendam
Haarlem
Almere
Zandvoort
AMSTERDAM
IJmeer
A6
N201
A1
Almere Haven
Hoofdoorp
Schiphol
Weesp
Hillegom
Amstelveen
N206
Bussum
A4
N201
A2
A1
Uithoorn
Hilversum
Sassenheim
N201
A44
A4
Mijdrecht

A PORTRAIT OF THE NETHERLANDS

From the Frisian Islands in the north to Zeeland in the south, the Netherlands is a place of contrasts, with fine sandy beaches, picturesque villages and vibrant towns with multilingual and outward-looking people. The mighty river Rhine bisects the country, bringing trade and prosperity from far and wide.

The landscape of what is now the Netherlands has changed considerably over the past 2,000 years. Since Roman times, large tracts of land have been swallowed up by the sea in areas such as Zeeland and the former Zuiderzee. Old maps show that during the Middle Ages almost half of today's provinces of North Holland and South Holland were under water. Since then, large parts of this land have been reclaimed. The constant battle with the sea reached its height with the Delta Works. This massive hydraulic engineering achievement *(see pp250–51)* was designed to protect the southwestern part of the country against flooding. The project was started after the disastrous floods of 1953, in which more than 1,800 people died.

The Netherlands covers an area of 41,547 sq km (16,040 sq miles), about one-tenth the size of California. With some 16 million inhabitants, this means a population density of around 380 per sq km (1,000 per sq mile), making it the third most densely populated country in Europe after Monaco and Malta. However, this is not something that is readily noticeable to visitors outside the main cities, as the flat landscape seems anything but crowded.

Dutch people are friendly, outgoing and direct. They care about social issues and the environment and almost everyone speaks English, many fluently. They live in a country that is neat and tidy, where there is excellent public transport and where visitors find it easy to get around.

The pier, the focus of social life on the beach at Scheveningen

◀ Flowers in the Keukenhof garden near Lisse, the largest flower garden in the world

Holland's dunes, a natural barrier against the sea and an important water catchment area

Introducing the Netherlands

Although the Netherlands is this country's official name, most of the rest of the world calls it Holland. This book uses both names. However, Holland actually comprises only two of the 13 Dutch provinces. North and South Holland contain the country's three main cities of Amsterdam, Rotterdam and Den Haag (The Hague), which together with the cities of Dordrecht, Utrecht, Leiden and Haarlem form a horseshoe-shaped conurbation known as the Randstad, literally, "rim city" *(see pp170–71)*.

When people ask, "What is the capital of the Netherlands?", the smiling Dutch tend to reply: "Our capital is Amsterdam, and the government sits in The Hague." Amsterdam is the most cosmopolitan of these three cities, as well as the country's centre for cultural life. Rotterdam, home to the Europoort, one of the world's largest ports, is the Netherlands' industrial centre. The Hague is the seat of government and quarters many prestigious institutions, including the International Court of Justice. With its neighbouring seaside resort of Scheveningen, The Hague is where most of the foreign embassies and consulates are situated.

Holland can be roughly divided into the Protestant north and Catholic south, separated by the great rivers flowing into the North Sea: the Rhine, the Waal and the Maas (Meuse). The people in the north of the country tend to be more sober and matter-of-fact, whereas those of the south tend to be much more flamboyant in their lifestyles.

Shoppers at the Albert Cuypmarkt in Amsterdam

Society and Politics

Social life in the Netherlands was for many years based on the idea of *verzuiling*, wherein different sections of society rested their beliefs on four pillars *(zuilen)*: Protestantism, Catholicism, liberalism and socialism. At one time, these groups had almost no contact with one another. Catholics would always vote for the *Katholieke Volkspartij*, join Catholic trade unions, base their social lives on Catholic societies and send their children to Catholic schools. The Protestant "pillar", on the other hand, was formed of two main factions: the Dutch Reformed Church and the Calvinist Church. Both had their own political parties, their own trade unions and their own schools and societies. As for socialism and liberalism, the division was less explicit, though the gap between the world of the "workers" and that of the "entrepreneurs" was huge.

A major step towards unity came in 1980, when the three largest religion-based political parties united in the CDA, a Christian Democratic alliance that went on to dominate government coalitions for the next 20 years. The gap between the other parties closed in 1994, when the Labour Party (PvdA) and the small D66 formed a coalition with the conservative Liberal Party (VVD). This resulted in a tripartite "purple" cabinet, which appeared so successful that the coalition was continued in 1998.

View of the picturesque Dordrecht marina

A hollow post mill in the polder landscape

The Dutch elections of May 2002 surprised everybody as the country moved to the right of the political spectrum. The assassination, nine days before, of the popular, flamboyant and openly gay Pim Fortuyn had shocked the entire country. With his unyielding views on Muslims and immigration, and his criticism of the establishment, Fortuyn

The de Geul river at Epen in Zuid Limburg

Football fans sporting orange costumes

was the antithesis of the Dutch tradition of consensual politics. Despite the loss of their charismatic leader, LPF became the second largest party in the Lower House; only the Christian Democrats (CDA) did better. The coalition parties of the former government lost 43 seats between them, making this the biggest shake-up in Dutch politics since World War II.

Since 2010, the Dutch political climate has changed completely. Dissatisfied with the coalition between PvDA, CDA and conservative Christen Unie, the Dutch voted en masse for VVD and Geert Wilder's Party for Freedom (PVV). However, in 2012, the VVD, CDA and PVV government resigned when the PVV refused to sanction the austerity measures. New elections were held, resultingin a VVD-PvDA government.

A herring stall in Amsterdam

Language and Culture

Dutch, a Germanic language, is used by more than 20 million people in Holland, Flanders and parts of the former Dutch colonies. Afrikaans, a language of South Africa closely related to Dutch, is a separate language, as is Frisian, which is spoken by more than 400,000 people in the province of Friesland. Dutch has many dialects, each of which has numerous regional differences. However, these differences are gradually disappearing because of the far-reaching influences of radio and television.

Culturally, Holland has plenty to offer. The country's colourful history is reflected in its many old buildings and large number of valuable museum collections. Exhibits range from those with local themes to world-famous art such as the collections in Amsterdam's Rijksmuseum *(see pp126–7)* and the Mauritshuis in The Hague *(see pp226–7)*. In addition to the major museums of the cities, contemporary art can be seen in galleries all over the country, and in the profusion of works displayed in the streets and at numerous local markets. As for the performing arts, more variety is available today than ever before. Holland boasts a number of renowned orchestras and is an established name in ballet. Stage and theatre have recently marked a shift from experimental to more conventional performances.

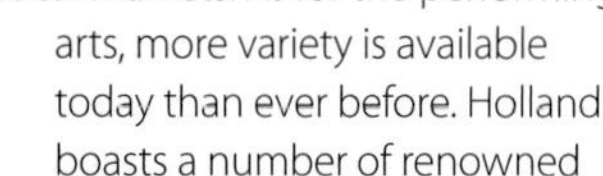

Dutch beer, fresh from the tap

The Dutch Way of Life

The German poet Heinrich Heine (1797–1856) described Holland as a place where "everything happens 50 years later than anywhere else". But today, anyone who reflects on the tolerant Dutch attitude towards drugs, the country's relaxed laws regarding euthanasia and the popular opposition to the deployment of nuclear weapons will come away with a different picture. In fact, the Netherlands was the first country to legalize gay marriages, regulate prostitution, officially sanction euthanasia and tolerate the over-the-counter sale of marijuana. Even the attitude of the Dutch towards their monarchy is modern – they are regarded with an affection more commonly extended to family members than to rulers.

A Dutch production of *The Three Musketeers*

Since the depredations of the Second World War, much has changed in the way the Dutch live their lives. Thrift and moderation, the two traditional virtues of Calvinism, are no longer writ large in society. A measure of flamboyance is slowly but surely making its way into the Dutch lifestyle. Today the Dutch eat out enthusiastically as well as often. Restaurant and cooking columns are now featured in newspapers and magazines, and there are also many cookery programmes aired on television.

Dutch drinking habits have also changed. On fine-weather days, people throng the pavement cafés to end the working day with a beer or a glass of wine. They also drink a great deal more wine with meals than once was the case. The renowned Dutch gin, *jenever* *(see p420)*, is still popular, though younger people prefer cocktails. As in a lot of countries, there are concerns about youngsters and binge-drinking.

As soon as they have spare time, Dutch people head outdoors, often on bicycles, which are enormously popular. Love of the environment is a strong Dutch characteristic. Outdoors, there are hundreds of organized rambling and cycling tours, funfairs and theme parks, as well as a wide assortment of festivals and other events held throughout the year *(see pp36–9)*. And wherever you are, you will always find a flea market – with items ranging from flowers to antiques for sale – not far away.

De Waalkade, the promenade of Nijmegen

The new-found *joie de vivre* of the Dutch reflects the general trend evident in Western European countries. This is the result of a new leisure culture, one which is more "sensory". Less time is devoted to reading and contemplation as food, drink, sport and the arts all take on increasingly prominent roles. Politically, socially and culturally, the Dutch are embracing the 21st century with confidence.

Holding Back the Water

Recent floods in the Netherlands' river valleys, particularly the one which occurred in 1995, when 200,000 people needed to be evacuated from the area, have shown what a threat water continues to pose to the Netherlands. The only way the sea can be held back is by dams, but in order to contain rivers at high tide, the country is adopting a new approach, that of "controlled flooding".

Flooded farm in Gelderland (1995)

Since the 11th century, increasing areas of land have been reclaimed from the sea. Countless dykes were built over the centuries using elementary tools, such as spades and "burries", a kind of stretcher. The illustration shows a breached dyke being filled.

At the Hook of Holland, the sea is not held back by dunes, as it is along the entire coast of North Holland and South Holland, but by a dyke.

The lowest point in Holland is the Zuidplaspolder at Gouda, 6.74 m (22 ft) below sea level.

At Krimpen, the IJssel discharges into the Nieuwe Maas.

The Krimpenerwaard, between the IJssel and the Lek, consists of high-quality hayfields and pasture.

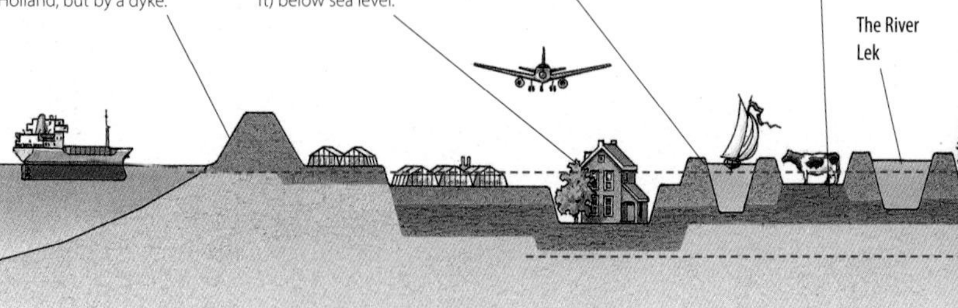

Key

Above sea level

Below sea level

A large part of the Netherlands (blue on the map) is below sea level. These areas have been called "laag-Nederland", or the "low Netherlands", and have only come into being over the past 10,000 years.

Cross-section of the Netherlands

This cross-section of the Netherlands follows a straight line from the Hook of Holland to Achterhoek *(see Locator Map)* and shows clearly how low much of the land is. Only some 65 km (40 miles) inland, at Neder-Betuwe, does the ground rise above sea level. The lowest point in the Netherlands is the Zuidplaspolder, which is more than 6.74 m (22 ft) below sea level. Comparatively elevated areas like the Betuwe have nothing to fear from the sea, but this does not mean that they are not at risk of flooding: the Waal River, which runs more or less parallel to this cross-section, may flood at unusually high tides or after a heavy rainfall.

Floods in the river valleys in 1993 and 1995 led to the implementation of large-scale dyke reinforcement projects, known as the "delta plan for the large rivers". Old flood channels were also repaired as a matter of priority to allow more water to drain off.

The Story of Hans Brinker

The tale of the little boy who held his finger in a leak in a dyke to hold back the sea is not a figure from Dutch folklore but probably originated in the book *Hans Brinker, or, The Silver Skates*, by American writer Mary Mapes Dodge (1831–1905). It tells the story of a poverty-stricken boy who helps his ailing father. Hans and the doctor in the book (Boerhaave) are historical figures. The story was published in over 100 editions in Dodge's lifetime.

Statue of Hans Brinker in Spaarndam

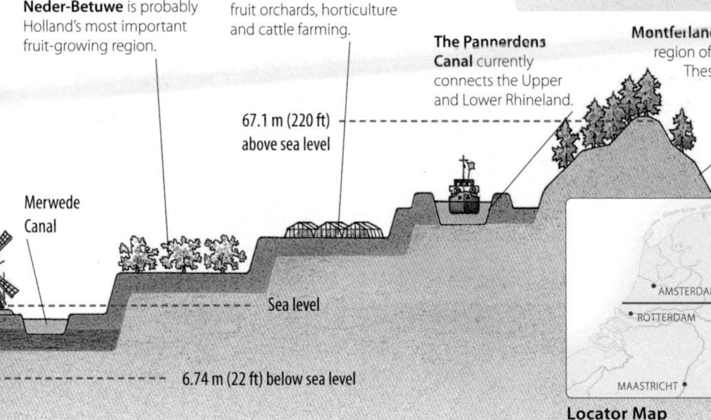
Neder-Betuwe is probably Holland's most important fruit-growing region.
Over-Betuwe is an area of fruit orchards, horticulture and cattle farming.
The Pannerdens Canal currently connects the Upper and Lower Rhineland.
Montferland is an important region of lateral moraines. These moraines were formed by the actions of glaciers.
67.1 m (220 ft) above sea level
Merwede Canal
Sea level
6.74 m (22 ft) below sea level
AMSTERDAM
ROTTERDAM
MAASTRICHT

Locator Map

Cross-section of a Modern River Dyke

Blocks of boulder clay protect the dyke from the wash of the river. The water seeps through the water-resistant clay layer slowly, draining off quickly only once it reaches the sand layer. This way the body of the dyke stays dry and hard.

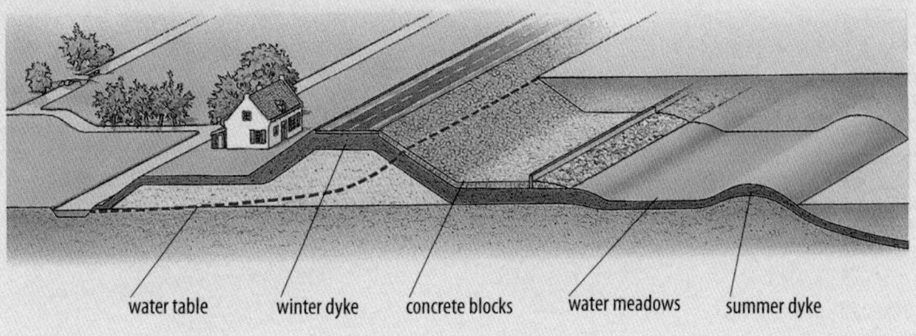
water table
winter dyke
concrete blocks
water meadows
summer dyke

Farmhouses and Windmills

In the mainly flat landscape of the Netherlands , farmhouses always stand in the shelter of trees. Windmills, on the other hand, needing as much wind as they can get, usually stand in very exposed areas. Both are highly valued because they are so picturesque, and it is easy to forget that they actually belong in the category of functional architecture. How a windmill works is explained on page 179.

In the farmhouses of North Holland, the barn, threshing-floor and house are all tunder one pyramidal roof.

This Drenthe farmhouse is a modern version of what has been known since the Middle Ages as a *los hoes* (detached house).

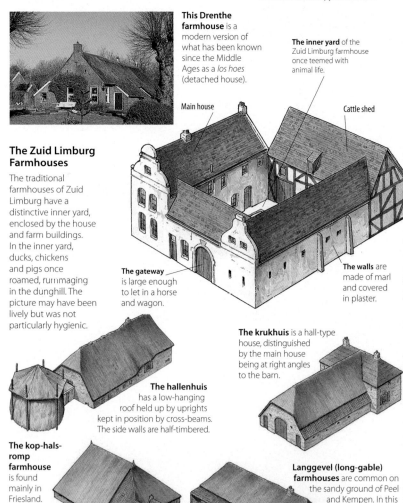

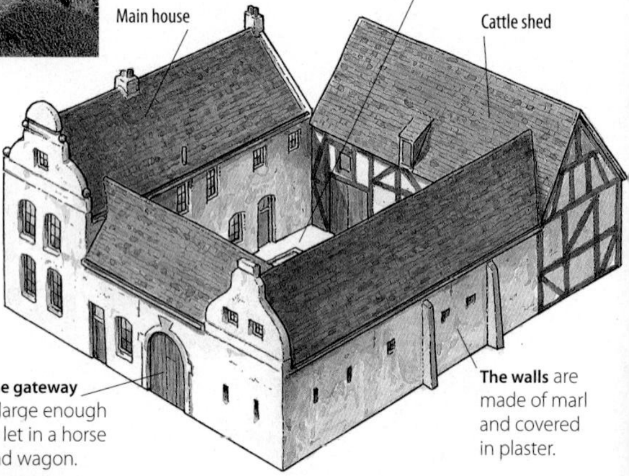

The inner yard of the Zuid Limburg farmhouse once teemed with animal life.

Main house

Cattle shed

The Zuid Limburg Farmhouses

The traditional farmhouses of Zuid Limburg have a distinctive inner yard, enclosed by the house and farm buildings. In the inner yard, ducks, chickens and pigs once roamed, rummaging in the dunghill. The picture may have been lively but was not particularly hygienic.

The gateway is large enough to let in a horse and wagon.

The walls are made of marl and covered in plaster.

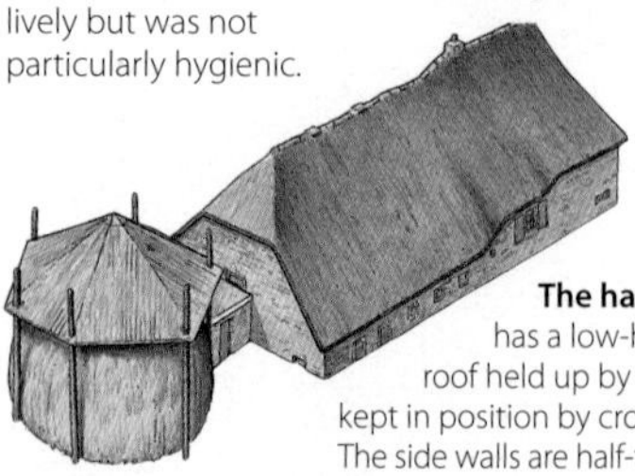

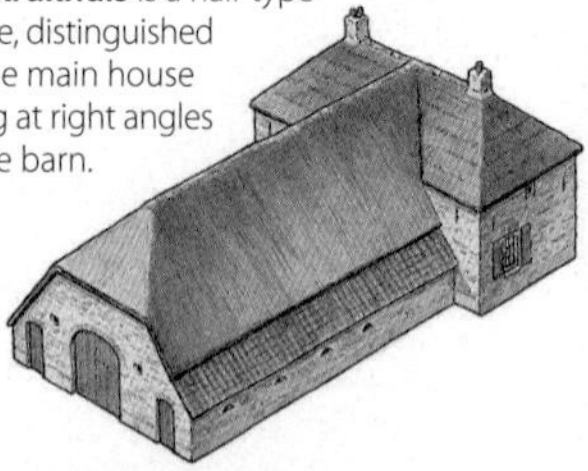

The krukhuis is a hall-type house, distinguished by the main house being at right angles to the barn.

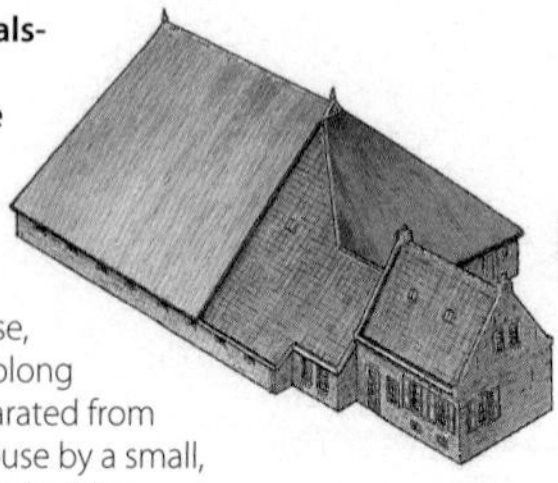

The hallenhuis has a low-hanging roof held up by uprights kept in position by cross-beams. The side walls are half-timbered.

The kop-hals-romp farmhouse is found mainly in Friesland. In this type of farmhouse, the long, oblong barn is separated from the mainhouse by a small, intermediate building.

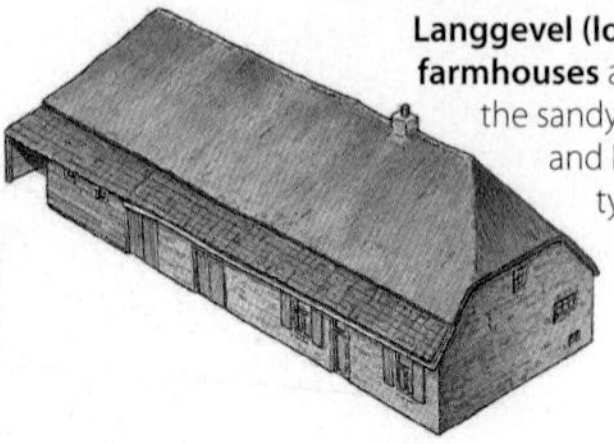

Langgevel (long-gable) farmhouses are common on the sandy ground of Peel and Kempen. In this type of farmhouse, the living accommodatio and farm buildings are arranged in a ro

Paltrok Mills

Paltrok, or smock, mills were developed for use as sawmills around 1600. They were so called because of their resemblance to the paltrok, a smock that was commonly worn at the time. These windmills were mounted on a circular track, allowing them to rotate in their entirety. Generally, smock mills were used to saw *wagenschot* – entire oak trunks that had been split in two.

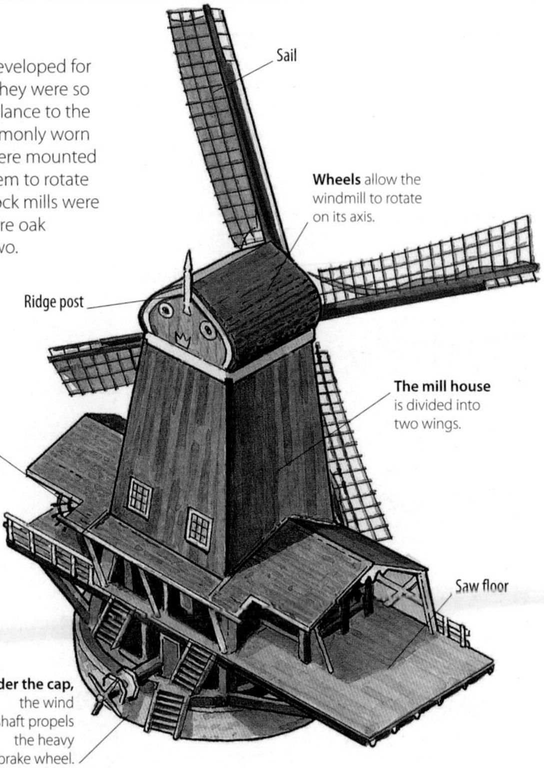

Sail

Wheels allow the windmill to rotate on its axis.

Ridge post

Underneath the porch is a crane for lifting the tree trunks from the water.

The mill house is divided into two wings.

Saw floor

Under the cap, the wind shaft propels the heavy brake wheel.

Belt or berg mills have an extra-high body because of surrounding buildings or trees. A mound (berg) made at the base of the mill provides access to the sails.

Stander (post) mills are the oldest type of mill in Holland. The entire wooden body rotates on a central wooden post. Most post mills were used to grind corn.

Wipmolen are a later version of the stander mills and were designed to pump water. The smaller body rotates on a fixed, pyramidal base.

Stellingmolen, like the belt mill, has an extra-tall body. This type was used to produce dye, oil or paper. An encircling platform halfway up the body enables the mill to be rotated and the sails to be reefed on the wings.

Toren mills (tower mills) have a brick cylindrical body and a cap that can be rotated from inside. Only four survive in Holland today. The oldest one can be seen at Achterhoek near Zeddam.

The tjasker was used to drain small areas of water. It consisted of a sloping axle with sails at one end and an Archimedes' screw at the other.

The Dutch Masters

The proliferation of painting in the Netherlands during the 17th century – the country's Golden Age – corresponded with the great demand for paintings among newly rich townspeople. The lack of major royal and ecclesiastic patrons meant that there was no official school of painting, which left artists free to specialize in particular fields, such as historical subjects, portraits, landscapes and still life, as well as genre painting.

Willem Heda (1594–1680) was one of the masters of still life. The painter's simple compositions reflect his signature use of sober colours.

Frans Hals (c.1580–1666) left an oeuvre of some 200 portraits and more than 50 genre paintings. He painted not only regents and wealthy townsmen but also peasants, soldiers, fishermen, publicans and drunkards. No sketches for his paintings are known, and it is assumed that he painted *alla prima,* that is, straight onto the canvas without sketches. *The Fool,* shown above, dates from around 1623.

Rembrandt Van Rijn

Rembrandt van Rijn is regarded by many as the greatest Dutch painter of all time. He was born in Leiden in 1606 but lived in Amsterdam from 1632 until his death in 1669. Rembrandt was a master in the use of light and shadow. *The Jewish Bride* (painted around 1665) is regarded as one of the best portraits of his later period.

Jacob van Ruisdael (1628–82) was an unrivalled landscape painter. In his *View of Haarlem* depicted here, the low horizon is dwarfed by an imposing sky with clouds.

The silversmith Adam van Vianen (1569–1627) was famous for his ornamental style, which was known as *kwabstijl*, or "flabby style", and distinguished by flowing ornamentation and the use of various fantasy elements. This gilded silver jug is an example of his style. Much of the silver work from this time has been lost because pieces have been melted down in order to trade in the metal for cash.

Jan Steen (1625–79) was a prolific painter with a variety of works, 800 of which survive today. They include everything from altar pieces to landscape paintings to works with mythological themes. However, Steen is known primarily for his genre painting, which gives a detailed, humorous picture of 17th-century society. *The Family Scene,* shown above, is a typical "Jan Steen household" – one in disarray. Tavern scenes were another of the artist's favourite subjects.

Gerard van Honthorst (1590–1656) was greatly influenced by the works of Caravaggio. As well as historical scenes and portraits, he painted genre pieces such as *The Merry Fiddler* (above). His famous nocturnal scenes lit by candle-light led to his being nicknamed "Gherardo delle Notte" in Italy.

Johannes Vermeer (1632–75) spent his entire life in Delft. Only 40 of his works are known today, but even this modest oeuvre plays a prominent role in the history of painting. His balanced compositions appear very modern. Long before the Impressionists, Vermeer succeeded in conveying light through colour. The street depicted in *View of Houses in Delft* (c.1658), left, has become known as "Vermeer's street".

Pottery and Tiles

When in 1620 exports of porcelain from China to Europe fell because of the troubles in China, Dutch potters seized the opportunity and started to produce their own wares, imitating the Chinese style on a large scale. The quality of the Dutch blue-white pottery was excellent. The city of Delft became one of the prime centres for the production of this china, which reached its height between 1660 and 1725. During the Art Nouveau and Art Deco periods, Dutch potters regained their international renown. The best known of them was TAC Colenbrander.

Tulip vase

De Porceleyne Fles is the only Delftware shop which has managed to survive throughout the centuries. The business was bought in 1876 and revived by Joost Thooft, whose initials can still be seen on the workshop's mark. The exquisite painting on the porcelain continues to be done by hand, although the rest of the manufacturing process no longer involves the craft's traditional methods.

Stylized flowers reflect the Italian majolica tradition.

Delftware

Although tin-glazed earthenware was also made in other parts of the Netherlands, "Delft" came to describe almost all earthenware made in the Netherlands during this period. Any piece made after 1650 will always have a workshop mark. Later, the glazer's initials, as well as a code denoting the year and a serial number, were added.

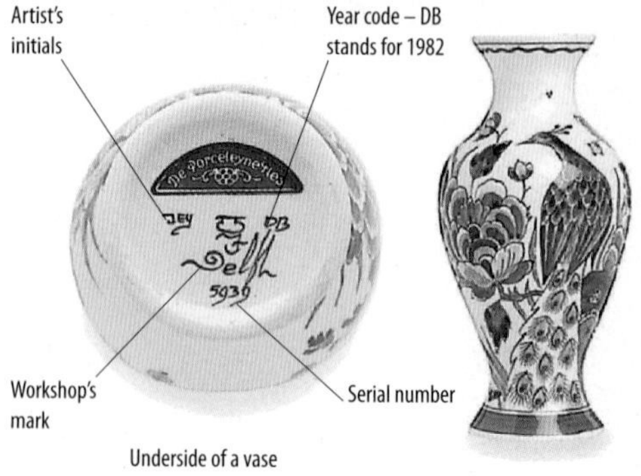

Underside of a vase

This set of four tiles features a pattern of pomegranates, grapes, rosettes and lilies.

The first Dutch porcelain was made in 1759 in the North Holland town of Weesp. At the time, it was second in quality only to Meissen porcelain. However, production was halted after 10 years because of financial difficulties. In 1774, a new factory was opened in Loosdrecht, which was moved to Ouder-Amstel in 1784. This large vase from 1808 is a typical example of the Amstel china that was produced there.

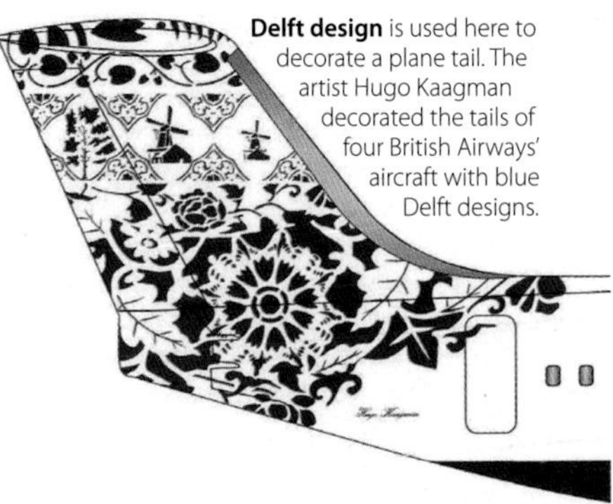

Delft design is used here to decorate a plane tail. The artist Hugo Kaagman decorated the tails of four British Airways' aircraft with blue Delft designs.

Tiles

Majolica wall tiles – decorated earthenware on a tin-glazed background – were made for the first time in the Netherlands during the 16th century, with production reaching its peak in the 17th century. Until 1625, polychrome decoration predominated, after which the majority of tiles were painted in blue on white. Major centres were Makkum – where in the 17th century the Tichelaar family firm, which operates to this day, was established – as well as Harlingen, Delft, Gouda, Amsterdam, Utrecht and Haarlem. The tiles depicted here are from Haarlem. See also page 419.

The lily often features as a corner motif on Dutch tiles.

Tac Colenbrander

One of the biggest names in Art Nouveau pottery is TAC Colenbrander (1841–1930). Originally an architect, he became known for his fanciful floral-based designs for the Rozenburg earthenware and porcelain factory in The Hague, where he was chief designer from 1884 to 1889. As celebrated as his designs were, the ceramics had limited commercial success. One reason for this was their expense, a reflection of the labour-intensive production. In 1912–13, Colenbrander worked for the Zuid-Holland pottery in Gouda. In addition to pottery, he designed wallpaper and carpets, and worked as a graphic and interior designer.

"Day and Night" set by Colenbrander, 1885

The Art Nouveau plate by WP Hartgring was made in 1904, the same year as this master potter won a gold medal at the world exhibition at the St Louis World's Fair. Hartgring worked for 20 years at the Rozenburg factory in The Hague and for 10 years at the Zuid-Holland pottery. His works reflect the Japanese style.

The Netherlands in Bloom

The Dutch love affair with flowers began rather unromantically in homes during the 17th century, when flowers were used to keep bad smells at bay. The aesthetic aspect soon developed, and today the Netherlands is one of the world's most important flower-growing countries. It has an unrivalled distribution system, keeping Holland ahead of competition from countries such as Israel, Spain, Colombia, Kenya, Zimbabwe and Zambia. The Netherlands has a 92 per cent share of the world market for flowers.

Fields of flowers are not confined to the west of the country. These rose fields are outside Lottum in the north of the southern province of Limburg, where every year a special rose competition is held.

Tulips were introduced to Holland from Turkey in the 17th century. They became the subject of an unparalleled speculative bubble which has become known as "tulip mania". Today the tulip is considered a quintessentially Dutch product, with innumerable varieties.

The annual flower competition *(bloemen corso)* in the bulb-growing region is a grand event *(see p36)*.

Cut Flowers From Dutch Nurseries

As consumers have become increasingly demanding, the number of flower species and varieties is constantly on the rise. Consumer tastes vary from place to place: in France, gladioli are very popular, whereas in Great Britain, it is lilies and carnations. In Asia, tulips are in great demand. A small sample of the flowers grown commercially in the Netherlands is shown here.

The iris *(Iris)* flower and bulb are in demand.

The chrysanthemum *(Chrysanthemum)* originated in China.

The sandy soil in the high areas behind the dunes of Holland is known as "geest soil" and is very well suited for cultivating bulbs.

Not all daffodil bulbs can survive the winter.

Crocus bulbs should be planted in September.

Hyacinth bulbs range in colour from violet red to white.

Tulip bulbs are highly resistant to disease and pests.

Iris bulbs should be dug up after flowering.

Flower Sellers

Flower sellers are part and parcel of the Netherlands' street scene. They can also be found indoors, in places such as stations or shopping centres. In most countries, cut flowers are considered expensive and a luxury. In the Netherlands, however, they are practically a daily shopping item and quite cheap. The Netherlands is indeed the land of flowers *par excellence*.

Dahlias *(Dahlia)* come in 20,000 varieties.

The lilac *(Syringa)* is often bought for its fragrance.

The carnation *(Dianthus)* is loved as a spray.

The rose *(Rosa)* is known as "the queen of flowers".

THE NETHERLANDS THROUGH THE YEAR

The Netherlands has much to offer in the way of holidays, festivals and other events. The choice of cultural events is greatest in summer – several cities host theatre festivals in June. Some festivals, such as Leiden's 3-Oktoberfeesten, have deep historical roots, whereas others, such as the multicultural Zomercarnaval in Rotterdam, are much more modern. Many of the events are held to honour navigation and fishing, such as Flag Day (Vlaggetjesdag), held each May in Scheveningen. Music, too, plays a prominent role. The world-renowned North Sea Jazz festival brings the genre's greats to Rotterdam.

Spring

In March, daffodils and crocuses burst into bloom in the country's towns and villages. From mid-April onwards, when the tulips are in flower, the bulb fields along the Dutch coast are a spectacular sight to see.

March

Meezing Matthäus *(Easter)*, Amsterdam and elsewhere. Concert-goers are welcome to sing along during many performances of Bach's *St Matthew's Passion*.

Keukenhof *(end Mar to mid-May)*, near Lisse. These 32 ha (79 acres) of landscape gardens demonstrate the best of all the flowers Holland has to offer. This open air exhibition was started in 1949, and has become internationally renowned.

April

First of April Celebrations, Brielle. Dressed in 16th-century-style clothing, the inhabitants of Brielle (Den Briel) re-create the 1572 recovery of the city from the Spaniards.

A young street musician on King's Day in Amsterdam

Blossoming fruit tree in de Betuwe

Foto Biënnale *(Apr to Jul)*, Amsterdam and other cities. Biannual international photography exhibition takes place in even-numbered years.

Bloemen Corso (Flower Competition) *(late Apr)*, Bollenstreek. Floats with floral sculptures travel a 40-km (25-mile) route through Haarlem, Hillegom, Lisse and Noordwijk.

Koningsdag (King's Day) *(27 Apr)*. The birthday of King Willem-Alexander sees festivities throughout the land; the biggest event is held in Amsterdam.

May

Landelijke Fietsmaand (National Cycling Month) *(all month)*. Cycling activities throughout the country.

Nationale Moldendag (National Windmill Day) *(second Sat in May)*. Some 600 of the 1,000 windmills in the country are opened up to the public.

Vlaggetjesdag (Flag Day) *(May)*, Scheveningen. The arrival of the first herring catch of the season is celebrated with demonstrations of traditional fishing-related crafts, music and a race.

Aspergerie Primeur (Ascension Day), Venlo. In a festive atmosphere on a re-created old-time village green, visitors can tuck into deliciously cooked asparagus.

Keidagen *(around Ascension Day)*, Lochem. Five days of

Flag Day, the start of the new herring fishing season

music, funfairs, street fairs and performances by international artists.
Sloepenrace (Boat Regatta). A regatta from Harlingen to Terschelling.
Jazz in Duketown *(around Whitsun)*, 's-Hertogenbosch. Four days of open-air high-quality jazz and blues bands at various venues in town. The beer flows freely.

The increasingly popular boat race to Terschelling

Summer

Summer in the Netherlands is a time of major cultural events. These include the Holland Festival in Amsterdam, the Theater a/d Werf in Utrecht, the Parade (Amsterdam, Utrecht, The Hague, Rotterdam), and the Haagse Zomer in The Hague. And if theatre is not your favourite pastime, there are plenty of other activities to keep you entertained.

June

Holland Festival *(3 weeks of Jun)*, venues throughout Amsterdam and major cities. A varied programme of concerts, plays, opera and ballet.
Aaltjesdag (Eel Day) *(second Sat in Jun)*, Harderwijk. Major fishing celebration in this former harbour on the Zuider Zee.
Oerol Festival *(mid-Jun)*, Terschelling. This alternative cultural festival lasts for ten days, with clowns, street theatre, acrobats, pop concerts and music from around the world.

Herring-eating by hand

Poetry International *(mid-Jun)*, Rotterdam. Prestigious poetry festival featuring an international programme, in Rotterdam's Doelen district.
Pasar Malam Besar *(second half of Jun)*, The Hague. This festival of Indonesian music and dance, shadow puppets, cooking demonstrations and colourful eastern market takes place at Malieveld in The Hague.
Nationale Vlootdagen (Navy days) *(end Jun/early Jul)*, Den Helder. A chance to see frigates, submarines, torpedo boats and mine hunters belonging to the Netherlands Navy, with spectacular shows put on by the Netherlands Marines.

July

Oud Limburgs Schuttersfeest (Marksman's Festival) *(first Sun in Jul)*. Annual tournament by the marksmen of Limburg is a colourful folk event held in the hometown of the previous year's winner.
North Sea Jazz *(mid-Jul)*, Rotterdam. A three-day spectacle widely acknowledged as the world's largest jazz festival, with performances by the biggest names in jazz.
Tilburgse kermis (Tilburg Fair) *(end Jul)*. One of the biggest and most exuberant fairs in Holland, with a special gay Pink Monday.
Zomercarnaval (Summer Carnival) *(last Sat in Jul)*, Rotterdam. A lively Caribbean carnival with exotic music, plenty to eat and drink and a swirling procession.

August

Gay Pride *(first weekend in Aug)*, Amsterdam. One of the very best Prides in the world; the highlight is the Canal Parade.
Mosselfeesten (Mussel Festivals) *(third Sat in Aug)*, Yerseke; *(last weekend in Aug)*, Philippine. Harvest festival presenting the new crops of Zeeland.
Preuvenemint *(last weekend in Aug)*, Maastricht. Flamboyant festival of food and drink at the historical Vrijthof.
Uitmarkt *(last weekend in Aug)*, Amsterdam. Festive opening of the theatre season with performances and information booths. There is also a book fair, where literary publishers are represented.

North Sea Jazz, one of the world's major jazz events

The Nijmegen Fair, a popular tradition dating back centuries

Autumn

As the cold weather starts slowly but surely to set in, indoor events become more prominent. In autumn, the theatres are full in the evenings, and museums are routinely busy. However, open-air events are still held, the golden light of dusk and magnificent clouds adding to the atmosphere.

September

Monumentendag (Monument Day) *(second Sat in Sep).* Private historic buildings open to the public.
Fruitcorso *(second weekend in Sep)*, Tiel. Spectacular parade of floats with gigantic fruit sculptures.

An elaborate fruit sculpture at the Tiel Fruitcorso

Vliegerfeest (Kite Festival) *(mid-Sep)*, Scheveningen. For two days, hundreds of strange creations hover over the beach.**Jordaanfestival** *(second and third weeks in Sep)*, Amsterdam. Fairs, street parties, talent contests and live music are held in the southern part of the picturesque former working-class district of Jordaan.
Prinsjesdag *(third Tue in Sep)*, The Hague. Accompanied by high-ranking government officials and with a guard of honour, the king rides in his golden carriage from Noordeinde Palace to the Binnenhof (Parliament Building), where he makes his Royal Speech in the Ridderzaal (Hall of the Knights) in order to open the Dutch Parliament.
Nijmeegse kermis (Nijmegen fair) *(end Sep/early Oct)*. Held every year since the 13th century, the fair stretches ribbon-like through the centre of the city. On Mondays and Tuesdays are the "piekdagen", when children can visit the attractions for the entrance price of 50 cents.

October

3-Oktoberfeesten, Leiden. A large public festival to commemorate the relief of Leiden from its siege on 3 October 1574. Permanent fixtures in the festivities are the distribution of herring and white bread to the townspeople, as well as the procession and funfair.
Eurospoor *(mid-to late Oct)*, Utrecht. Europe's biggest model train show takes place in the Jaarbeurs

Soldiers accompanying the King before he makes his Royal Speech in the Ridderzaal

November

Sint-Maarten *(11 Nov)*, Western and Northern Netherlands. In the early evening, children equipped with lanterns walk from door to door, singing songs, for which they are given sweets.
Intocht van Sinterklaas (arrival of St Nicholas)

(second or third week in Nov). St Nicholas is celebrated in every town and village in Holland. He arrives by ship near St Nicholasskerk *(see p95)* and then rides on his grey horse through town. Until 5 December, children traditionally sing Nicholas carols in the evenings, and every morning find sweets in their shoes.

The distribution of white bread in celebration of the relief of Leiden

Winter

December aside, there are not as many events in the winter calendar as there are for the rest of the year – perhaps to the relief of those who need January to recover from St Nicholas, Christmas and the New Year.

December

Sinterklaasavond (St Nicholas' Day) *(5 Dec)*. St Nicholas ends with St Nicholas' Eve on 5 December. Both young and old are brought gifts, more often than not in person by (a hired) Santa Claus. Friends give poems caricaturing each other.

Cirque d'Hiver *(between Christmas and New Year's Eve),* Roermond. Four days of world-class circus acts in the Oranjerie theatre hotel, in the historic town centre.

New Year's Eve *(31 Dec)*. The Dutch spend the last evening of the old year in festive surroundings at home or with friends. Fritters and apple turnovers are eaten and, in many houses, the champagne corks pop at midnight. Afterwards, people walk the streets to see in the New Year with organized firework displays.

January

Nieuwjaarsduik (New Year's Dip) *(1 Jan),* Scheveningen. Every year, at noon on New Year's Day, a starting-gun is fired on the pier in

The latest boats on display at the annual Hiswa

Scheveningen, and hundreds of people in swimsuits run down the beach to take a dip in the ice-cold water.

Leidse Jazzweek *(mid-Jan),* Leiden. Throughout the week, jazz of all styles is played in the halls and cafés of the old town.

February

Hiswa *(Feb or Mar),* Amsterdam. Boat show in the RAI *(see p141)*, featuring all types of crafts, from dinghies to yachts.

Carnival *(Feb or Mar)*. Officially three, but in practice five, days before Lent, the Catholic south celebrates wildly. There are processions with colourful floats, and costumed people sing and dance in the cafés and in the streets.

The arrival of St Nicholas, attracting a great deal of attention

The Climate in the Netherlands

The Netherlands has a maritime climate, characterized by cool summers and mild winters. In summer, the average maximum temperature is around 20°C (68°F), while in winter the average minimum temperature is around 0°C (32°F). It is slightly warmer south of the country's big rivers than north of them, and there are slightly more hours of sunshine on the coast than inland. Because of the temperature difference between the land and the sea, there is a constant westerly sea breeze on the coast in summer.

WEST FRISIAN ISLANDS
Leeuwarden
FRIESLAND
NORTH HOLLAND
Lelystad
FLEVOLAND
Haarlem
Amsterdam
The Hague
Utrecht
UTRECHT
SOUTH HOLLAND
Rotterdam
Nijmegen
's-Hertogenbosch
ZEELAND
Middelburg
NORTH BRABANT
Eindhoven
Maastricht

DEN HELDER

month	Jan	Mar	May	Jul	Sep	Nov
Max °C/°F	5/41	7/45	14/57	19/66	18/64	9/48
Min °C/°F	1/34	2/36	9/48	14/57	13/55	5/41
Sunshine	48 hrs	111 hrs	227 hrs	212 hrs	145 hrs	50 hrs
Rainfall	76 mm	45 mm	32 mm	67 mm	76 mm	79 mm

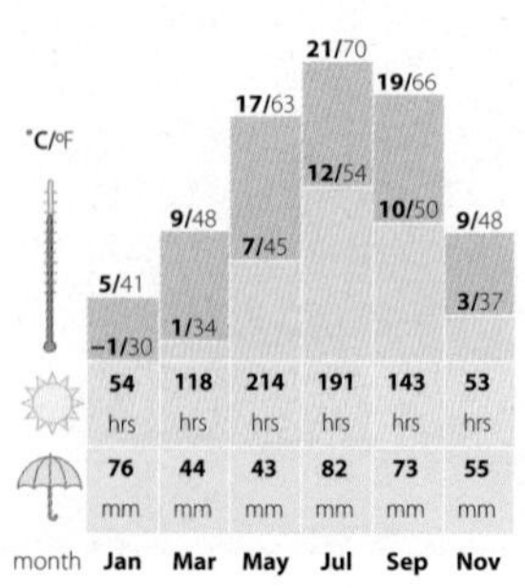

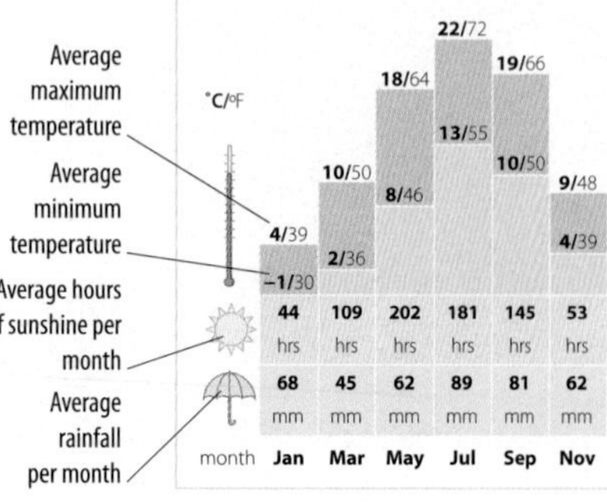

GRONINGEN

Groningen

Assen

DRENTHE

Zwolle

OVERIJSSEL

Enschede

Apeldoorn

GELDERLAND

Arnhem

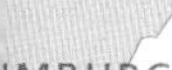

IMBURG

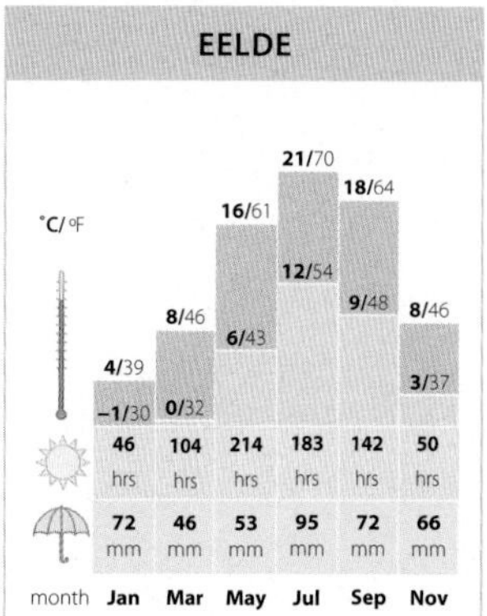

EELDE

month	Jan	Mar	May	Jul	Sep	Nov
°C/°F (high)	**4**/39	**8**/46	**16**/61	**21**/70	**18**/64	**8**/46
°C/°F (low)	**–1**/30	**0**/32	**6**/43	**12**/54	**9**/48	**3**/37
sunshine	**46** hrs	**104** hrs	**214** hrs	**183** hrs	**142** hrs	**50** hrs
rainfall	**72** mm	**46** mm	**53** mm	**95** mm	**72** mm	**66** mm

Spring

Summer

Autumn

Winter

THE HISTORY OF THE NETHERLANDS

In 12 BC, the Romans conquered southern Holland, and in AD 50 they declared the Rhine the northern border of their empire. The region north of this was conquered by the Frisians. At the end of the 4th century, the Romans withdrew from the Low Countries, which were taken over by the Frisians, Franks and Saxons. In the 8th century, the Franks ruled the region alone. The introduction of Christianity, begun by the missionary Willibrord in 695, was completed under Charlemagne.

After the disintegration of the Frankish Empire, the Netherlands fell under German rule. Actual power was exercized by the vassals, of whom the Bishop of Utrecht was the most powerful – until the Concordat of Worms in 1122, when the German king lost the right to appoint bishops. In the course of the 12th century, the Count of Holland was the most important figure in the region.

In the 14th and 15th centuries, the dispute between the two factions – the Hooks and the Cods – marked, in a certain sense, the end of the feudal age. When at the end of the 16th century the Northern Netherlands liberated itself from the Habsburg Duke Philip II, it enjoyed a period of unprecedented economic and cultural flowering. By the mid-17th century, it had become the greatest trading nation in the world, a status gradually relinquished during the 18th century.

The different independent regions making up the republic were joined together under Napoleon, with William I becoming king in 1815. However, unification with Belgium proved unsuccessful and was officially ended in 1839, although it had already ended *de facto* in 1830.

In the 20th century, Holland maintained neutrality during World War I, but suffered greatly during World War II. Invaded by the Nazis in May 1940, the country was not liberated entirely until May 1945. It subsequently developed into one of the most prosperous states within the European Union. Today, the country remains a constitutional monarchy, the royal family enjoying great popularity among the Dutch.

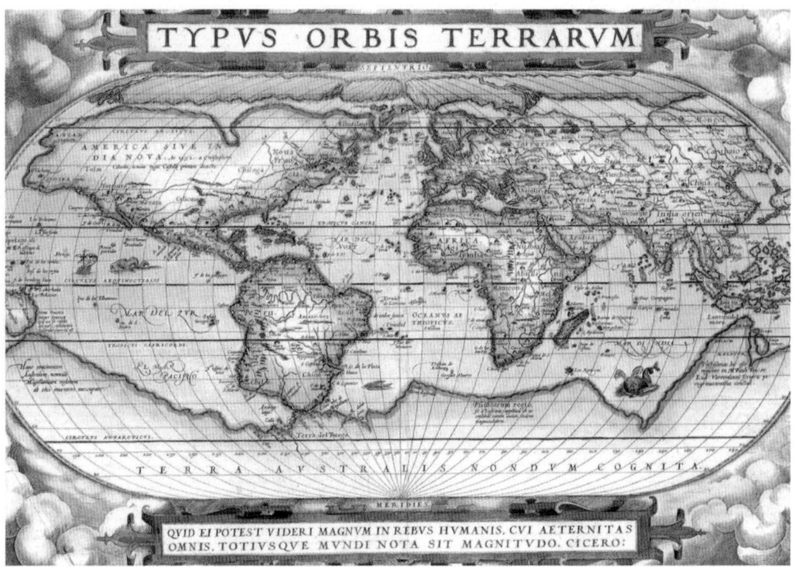

Map of the world from 1564 by the cartographer Ortelius of Antwerp

◄ *The IJ at Amsterdam, Viewed from the Mussel Quay,* painted by Ludolf Backhuysen (1631–1708)

Rulers of the Netherlands

In the Middle Ages, the Netherlands were run by local feudal dukes, as well as by the counts of Holland and the bishops of Utrecht. They were all officially vassals of the German king. In the 15th century, the region came under the rule of the House of Burgundy through marriage alliances, after which it was incorporated into the Habsburg Empire. In 1581, the Northern Netherlands freed itself from the Habsburgs. Since then – with some interruptions – the House of Orange has ruled over parts of what are today called Holland, initially as stadholders, but from 1815 as monarchs.

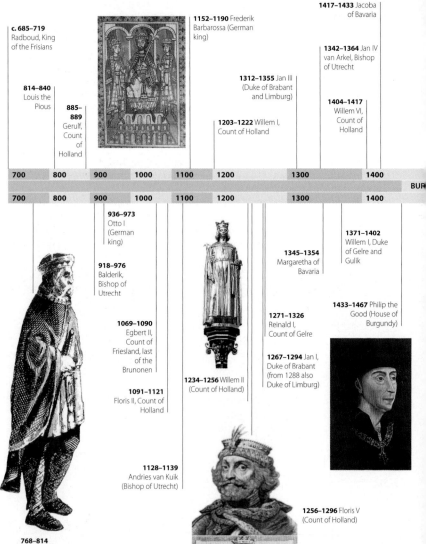

c. 685–719 Radboud, King of the Frisians

814–840 Louis the Pious

885–889 Gerulf, Count of Holland

1152–1190 Frederik Barbarossa (German king)

1203–1222 Willem I, Count of Holland

1312–1355 Jan III (Duke of Brabant and Limburg)

1342–1364 Jan IV van Arkel, Bishop of Utrecht

1404–1417 Willem VI, Count of Holland

1417–1433 Jacoba of Bavaria

700 800 900 1000 1100 1200 1300 1400

BUR

700 800 900 1000 1100 1200 1300 1400

768–814 Charlemagne

918–976 Balderik, Bishop of Utrecht

936–973 Otto I (German king)

1069–1090 Egbert II, Count of Friesland, last of the Brunonen

1091–1121 Floris II, Count of Holland

1128–1139 Andries van Kuik (Bishop of Utrecht)

1234–1256 Willem II (Count of Holland)

1256–1296 Floris V (Count of Holland)

1267–1294 Jan I, Duke of Brabant (from 1288 also Duke of Limburg)

1271–1326 Reinald I, Count of Gelre

1345–1354 Margaretha of Bavaria

1371–1402 Willem I, Duke of Gelre and Gulik

1433–1467 Philip the Good (House of Burgundy)

1559–1567 and 1572–1584 William of Orange, "The Silent" (stadholder of Holland, Zeeland and Utrecht, under Philip II until 1581)

1567–1573 Ferdinand, Duke of Alva (viceroy under Philip II)

1467–1477 Charles the Bold

1477–1482 Maria of Burgundy

1482–1506 Philip the Handsome (House of Habsburg)

1585–1625 Maurits

1625–1647 Frederick-Hendrik

1647–1650 William II

1672–1702 William III

1687–1711 Johan Willem Friso, stadholder of Friesland (1696), Prince of Orange (1702)

1806–1810 Louis Napoleon (French viceroy, king of Holland)

1815–1840 William I (king)

2013 Willem-Alexander (king)

1890–1898 Emma (regent)

1898–1948 Wilhelmina

1500	1600	1700	1800	1900	2000

DY HABSBURG HUIS VAN ORANJE

1500	1600	1700	1800	1900	2000

1559–1567 Margaretha of Parma (governor under Philip II)

1849–1890 William III

1840–1849 William II

1795–1806 Batavian Republic

1751–1795 William V

1948–1980 Juliana

1506–1555 Charles V

1555–1581 Philip II

1747–1751 William IV

1980–2013 Beatrix

Holland and its Monarchy

The Dutch royal family is extremely popular. The former queen, Beatrix, was the fourth queen in a row. The present king, Willem-Alexander, is the country's first king since 1890.

Prehistoric and Roman Times

About 13,000 years ago, the Low Countries emerged from under the ice of the last Ice Age. Temperatures gradually rose, turning the tundra into areas of forest and marshes, inhabited by nomadic hunters. In the Early Stone Age (4500–2000 BC), farming communities were established here and there. The megalith builders were the best known of these settled inhabitants. Around 600 BC, Germanic and Celtic tribes settled in the Low Countries. They were here when the Romans conquered the southern part of the region, in the 1st century BC. In AD 50, the Romans finally declared the Rhine as the Roman Empire's northern frontier, establishing Roman settlements in Utrecht and Maastricht.

The Low Countries (AD 50)

- Germanic peoples
- Roman territory
- Coastline in 3000 BC

Megaliths
Between 3400 and 3200 BC, the inhabitants of the Drenthe plateau built some 100 megaliths. Of these, 54 have survived into the present *(see pp310–11)*. These impressive tombs were once concealed beneath a mound of sand.

Urns
These urns date from 1150–800 BC.

The dark rings in this picture are of the ditches that originally surrounded the urn-mounds. The rings are interrupted at their southeastern edge, possibly to represent the symbolic entrance to the tomb.

55,000 BC Small groups of Neanderthal people inhabit the surroundings of Hijken and Hoogersmilde. A few hand axes and two campsites have been found

11,000 BC Reindeer hunters of the Hamburg Culture inhabit Drenthe

4500 BC Farmers settle on the loess land of Zuid Limburg. They have been referred to as "Bandkeramikers", or the Linear Pottery Culture, after their striped pottery

3400–3200 BC Farmers of the Beaker Folk build megaliths at Drenthe, Overijssel and Groningen

1900 BC Start of the Bronze Age in the Low Countries

10,000 BC | 7500 BC | 5000 BC | 2500 BC | 2000 BC

Wheel from 2700 BC

The Simpelveld Sarcophagus
In the 1930s, a Roman burial urn was excavated at Simpelveld near Limburg. The interior of the urn is decorated with reliefs depicting the exterior and the furnishings of a Roman house.

The Urnfield

In 1991, an urnfield dating from 600 BC was discovered at Someren near Brabant. It had been ploughed under by farmers during the Middle Ages. The dead were cremated in southern Holland from 1500 BC, and in northern Holland from 1000 BC. The burial mounds of Someren were arranged closely together, and each contained its own urn.

Where to See Prehistoric and Roman Holland

In addition to the megaliths of Drenthe and the Someren urnfield, prehistoric graves have been discovered at Almere, Hilversum, Vaassen, Lunteren, Goirle and Rolde, and at Toterfout/Halfmijl in Brabant, where 16 burial mounds have been restored to their original condition, complete with trenches and rings of stakes. The urnfield on the Bosoverheide, a couple of kilometres west of the Weert, was, around 800 BC, one of the largest burial grounds in northwestern Europe. Roman finds can be seen in places like Oudheden in Leiden *(see p221)* and the Valkhof museum in Nijmegen *(see p347)*. The Archeon archaeological theme park in Alphen a/d Rijn *(see p426)* is highly informative and entertaining, for adults and children alike.

Glass Flasks
These Roman flasks from the 2nd century AD were excavated at Heerlen.

Roman Mask
This mask was found near Nijmegen, which was once the camp of a Roman legion.

Farmer with Plough
The plough was used in the Iron Age.

Bronze Age sacrificial dagger

750–400 BC First Iron Age in the Low Countries

450 BC Start of the Second Iron Age, or La Tène Age

55–10 BC Batavians settle in the river area, the Cananefates in the coastal area and the Frisians in the north

Roman temple in Elst

1500 BC | 1000 BC | 750 BC | 500 BC | 250 BC | AD 1

1300 BC The Exloo necklace is made from tin beads from England, Baltic amber and Egyptian pottery beads

300–100 BC The Germans expand southwards across the Rhine, clashing with Celtic tribes

57 BC Caesar conquers the Belgae, who inhabit present-day Belgium

AD 69–70 Batavian Uprising, followed by the re-establishment of Roman rule

Frisians, Franks and Saxons

When the Romans withdrew at the end of the 4th century, the Low Countries, like the rest of Europe, experienced a great migration of peoples. By around 500, the Frisians had spread their territory southwards to the great rivers, while the Saxons lived east of the IJssel and the Franks had settled in the area south of the great rivers. Approximately two centuries later, the Franks took over the whole region as far as the Lauwerszee. With the spread of Christianity and under Charlemagne, the entire area of the Netherlands became Christian. After Charlemagne's death, the region belonged first to the Middle Kingdom of Lothair, and then, from 925, to the German Empire.

The Low Countries (AD 700)

Frisians
Franks
Saxons

Widukind
In 785, Charlemagne defeated the Saxons led by Widukind. This event led to the east of Holland finally being incorporated into Charlemagne's empire.

The Life of St Boniface

Two episodes in the life of the Anglo-Saxon missionary Boniface are illustrated here: on the left, he is shown baptizing a convert; on the right, his martyrdom is depicted. In 716 and 719, Boniface went on missionary expeditions to Friesland. He was subsequently made bishop and later archbishop. In 753, he embarked on a further missionary expedition to Friesland, which resulted in his death the following year.

The staff is one of Boniface's constant possessions. He was reputed to have used it to make a spring well up.

A convert being baptiz

Early Medieval Pottery
For the Frisians, pottery was an important barter good, along with cattle and dye.

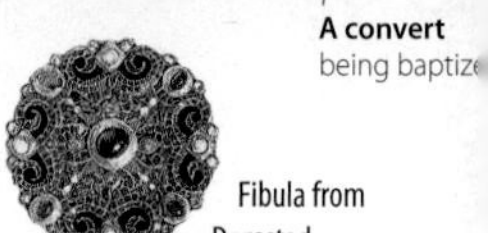

Fibula from Dorestad

Relief showing a Roman galley

295 Constantius Chlorus defeats the Franks at the battle of the Rhine delta, but allows them to remain in the Betuwe, where they are used to defend the frontiers

600–700 Dorestad becomes an important trading settlement

AD 200 | **400** | **500** | **550** | **600** | **650**

350–400 Romans leave the Low Countries

500 The territory of the Frisians stretches from the Zwin in Zeeland Flanders to the mouth of the Weser in Germany

Frankish denarii

Radboud, King of the Frisians
The Frisian king Radboud was forced to capitulate to the Frankish ruler Pippin II. He later regained the land he had lost, and with his army marched on Cologne. In 734, the Frisians under Count Bubo were again defeated at the de Boorne River, allowing Charles Martel to extend Frankish domain up to the Lauwerszee.

Pagan ceremonial axe

Boniface uses his Bible to protect himself from the sword.

Viking Sword
This sword, dubbed "Adalfriid's sword", was found in the Waal.

Dorestad

Situated at the confluence of the Lek and the Kromme Rijn (by present-day Wijk bij Duurstede, *see p211*), Dorestad was the most important trading settlement in northern Holland during the Early Middle Ages. It was the centre of Frisian trade in the 7th century and afterwards under the Merovingians and Carolingians. In the 9th century, Dorestad was repeatedly plundered by marauding Vikings, who sailed up the rivers in their longboats in search of booty. The settlement's decline, however, was due to the damming of the Rhine against flooding rather than because of the Viking raids. There is no reference in historical records to Dorestad after 863. During the 10th century, Dorestad's functions were taken over by Tiel, Deventer and Utrecht. In Wijk, the Museum Dorestad (tel. 0343-571448) gives an excellent idea of what life must have been like here during the Early Middle Ages through its various displays of archaeological finds from that period, as well as its informative diorama, complete with models of port houses.

689 Pippin II defeats the Frisian king Radboud at Dorestad and gains the river region and Utrecht

695 Willibrord becomes bishop of Frisia and establishes his see in Utrecht

700

750

754 Boniface is killed at Dokkum by pagan looters

768–814 Rule of Charlemagne. Holland is divided into *pagi* (cantons), each of which is ruled by a count

800

834–837 Dorestad plundered at various times by Vikings

900

925 Holland is taken over by the German Empire

1000

1007 Last Viking invasion of the Low Countries

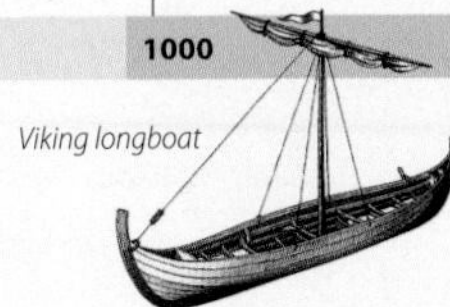

Viking longboat

The Emergence of Towns

In the 13th century, towns started to acquire considerable economic power. At that time, the Low Countries were nominally under the rule of the German king, but in practice local nobles ran things themselves. In the north, the counts of Holland were the most powerful. In the mid-14th century, their territory fell into the hands of the House of Bavaria. Disunity between Margaretha of Bavaria and her son William marked the beginning of the dispute between the Hooks and the Cods, which split towns as well as noble families for one and a half centuries.

The Low Countries (1300)

German Empire

France

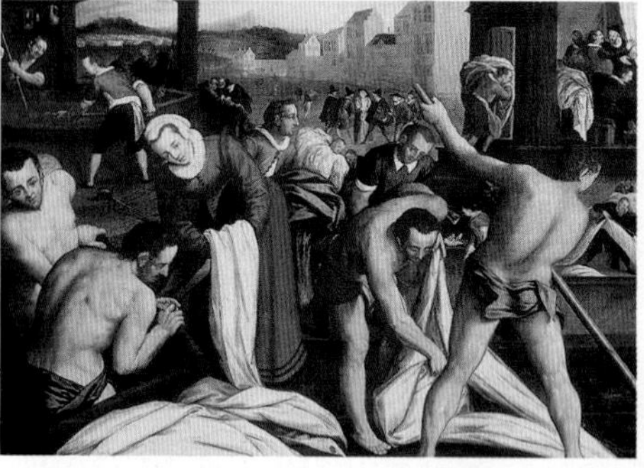

The Fulling Industry
During the 15th century, the cloth industry flourished in Leiden and 's-Hertogenbosch. This painting by IC Swanenburgh shows the fullers and dyers at work. In the background to the right, inspectors are checking the quality of the cloth.

Minting Coins
Minting rights lay not only with the sovereign. Local rulers, both church and secular, were entitled to mint coins.

Pilgrims who had visited Santiago de Compostela, well established as a place of pilgrimage by the 11th century, wore the scallop shell of the apostle St James on their hats.

The sheriff, with his distinctive chain of bells, was the representative of the sovereign. Here he is on the way to pronounce a death sentence, which is shown by the red pole, the "rod of justice", carried by an executioner.

c.1050 The first dykes are built

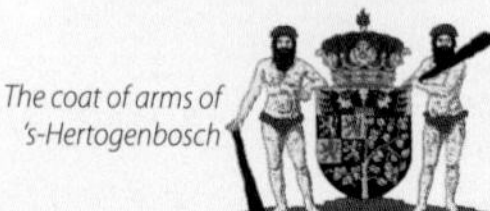

The coat of arms of 's-Hertogenbosch

1185 's-Hertogenbosch is granted its town charter

1247 William II of Holland is appointed king of Germany by the pro-Papal party

1000 | 1050 | 1100 | 1150 | 1200 | 1250

1076–1122 Investiture dispute between the German king and the Pope on the right to appoint bishops

1165 Frederick Barbarossa places Friesland under the joint rule of the Bishop of Utrecht and the Count of Holland

Cruel Punishment
In the Middle Ages, barbaric punishments were often meted out. This cask on the wall of the waag in Deventer was once used to immerse counterfeiters in boiling oil.

Grain brought by farmers to the towns was inspected by officials. Produce in the meat and fish markets was also inspected daily. An excise tax was charged on the basis of the inspection.

A Medieval Town

Demands of trade and industry meant that towns were given all kinds of privileges from the 13th century onwards. Often important allies for the counts of Holland against local feudal lords, Dutch towns were more powerful than in other countries during this period because of the lack of a powerful central authority.

Where to See the Late Medieval Netherlands

Famous monuments from this period are the Oude Kerk in Amsterdam (14th century, *see pp80–81*) and the Begijnhof, which has the city's oldest house (1420, *see p91*); the Cathedral Tower (1382) and the Catharijneconvent (15th century) in Utrecht *(see p206)*; the Onze-Lieve-Vrouwebasiliek (11th–12th centuries) and the St-Servaasbasiliek (11th–15th centuries) in Maastricht *(see p381)*; the 13th-century Ridderzaal and the 14th-century Gevangenpoort in The Hague *(see p224)*; the Pieterskerk (15th century) and the town walls of the 12th-century castle in Leiden *(see p221)*; the Lange Jan (14th century, *see p253*) and the restored abbey (11th–15th centuries) in Middelburg *(see p254)*; the centre of Deventer around the Brink and Bergkerk, including the oldest stone house in Holland *(see p324)*; and the Martinitoren in Groningen (1469, *see p284*).

Silver Chalice
As guilds prospered, they attached increasing importance to appearances. This chalice is decorated with a picture of St George defending a maiden against the dragon.

The Guild of St George (1533)
This painting by Cornelis Antonisz shows marksmen at a meal. Originally, each guild was responsible for protecting a part of the city walls; later, special guilds were set up.

296 Floris V s assassinated y the nobles

Willem Beukelsz

c.1380 Willem Beukelsz. invents the herring-gutter

1421 The Biesbosch is built as a result of the St Elizabeth Day flood

1477 Marriage of Maria of Burgundy and Habsburg Maximilian I brings together Holland and Zeeland under the House of Habsburg

1550 Charles V introduces the death penalty for all forms of heresy

1300	1350	1400	1450	1500	1550

1306 Amsterdam gains city status

1345 Dispute between the Hooks and the Cods begins. At first a disagreement over the successor to William IV, it develops into a struggle between the feudal barons and the cities

1428 Philip the Good of Burgundy forces Jacoba of Bavaria to withdraw from Holland, Zeeland and Hainaut

1517 Luther publishes the 95 theses

Luther

The Dutch Trading Empire

The early 17th century marked a period of expansion worldwide for northern Holland. Within a few decades, the Levant, the Gulf of Guinea, the Caribbean, North and South America, the East Indies, Persia, Arabia, Japan, India and China were all on the Dutch trading routes. The republic's merchant fleet became the world's largest. The powerful Dutch East India Company (VOC), established in 1602, dominated trade with Asia, with a monopoly on all profits from trade east of the Cape of Good Hope, while the Dutch West India Company, established in 1621, concentrated on the New World and the slave trade.

Dealers on the Stock Exchange
With its market traders and exchange, Amsterdam was the undisputed trading centre of Europe.

Purchase of Manhattan
Pieter Minnewit bought Manhattan Island in 1625 from the Delaware Indians for 60 guilders, 10 guns and a brass cauldron.

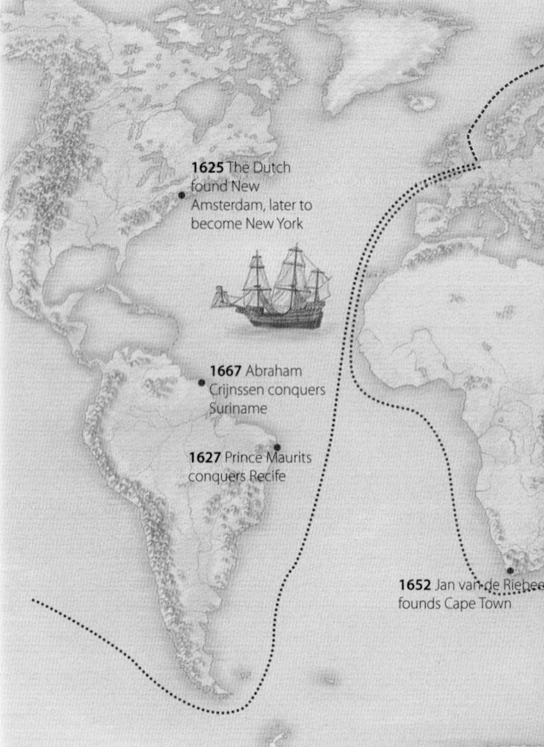
1625 The Dutch found New Amsterdam, later to become New York
1667 Abraham Crijnssen conquers Suriname
1627 Prince Maurits conquers Recife
1652 Jan van de Riebeec
founds Cape Town

The Dutch on Desjima
The Dutch trading office on the island of Desjima was in 1854 the main conduit between Japan and the world.

Key

- **1595–7** De Houtman and Keyzer
- **1596–7** Barents and Heemskerck
- **1616** Le Maire and Schouten
- **1642–3** Tasman

V.O.COMPAGNIE

VOC Plaque
The Dutch East India Company (VOC) obtained sole rights to trade for the republic in Asia. It had the authority to make treaties with other powers and even to declare war.

GENERAEL PIETER PIETERSZ HAYN

The Silver Fleet
In 1628, Piet Hein captured the Silver Fleet of Spain off the north coast of Cuba.

Surviving the Winter in Novaya Zemlya (1596–97)
During an attempt to find a northern route to the Indies, an expedition led by W Barents and J van Heemskerck ended up on the coast of Novaya Zemlya. The group survived in the Behouden Huys, a hut built from pieces of ships.

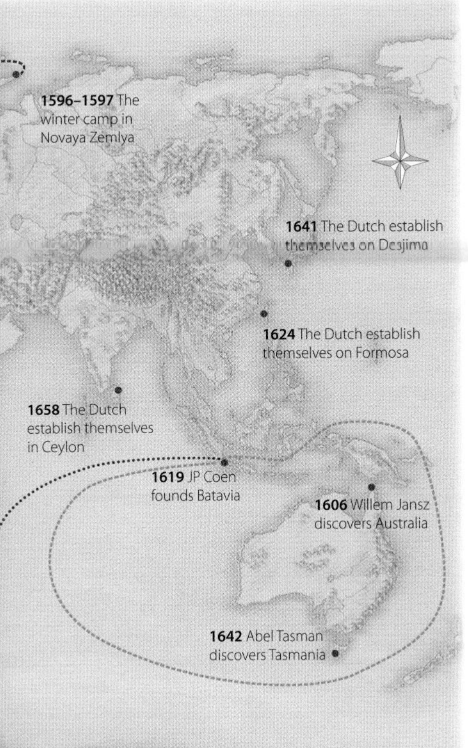
1596–1597 The winter camp in Novaya Zemlya
1641 The Dutch establish themselves on Desjima
1624 The Dutch establish themselves on Formosa
1658 The Dutch establish themselves in Ceylon
1619 JP Coen founds Batavia
1606 Willem Jansz discovers Australia
1642 Abel Tasman discovers Tasmania

The 80 Years War

In the second half of the 16th century, Holland officially belonged to the Spanish branch of the House of Habsburg. In 1567, Philip II sent troops to put down Protestant unrest in Flanders and halt the Protestant Reformation sweeping through northern Europe; this led to a revolt against Spanish rule in northern Holland and resulted in years of civil war and religious strife. The 80 Years War ended in 1648 with the Peace of Münster.

Statesman Johan van Oldenbarnevelt and the Count of Nassau, Prince Maurits, were the main Dutch figures in the conflict with Holland's Spanish rulers during the 17th century.

Johan van Oldenbarnevelt

Prince Maurits

The Great Voyages

While Willem Barents was exploring the Arctic seas, de Houtman and Keyzer set off on the "first voyages" to Java. In 1606, Willem Jansz discovered the north coast of Australia, and in 1616, Jacob le Maire and Willem Schouten were the first to sail around Cape Horn. Abel Tasman discovered Tasmania and New Zealand in 1642–3.

Three-Master Ship
These top-of-the-line 17th-century Dutch merchant ships required only a small crew.

The Golden Age

The 17th century was for the north of Holland a time of unprecedented flowering in trade, art *(see pp30–31)* and science. While elsewhere in Europe economies were in stagnation, the republic's merchant fleet brought great prosperity, particularly to the towns of Amsterdam and Utrecht. The Amsterdam Exchange (Amsterdamse Wisselbank), which was founded in 1609, ensured that Amsterdam became the financial centre of the world. Trade was protected by a powerful navy, which enjoyed significant victories under Michiel de Ruyter.

The Low Countries (1650)

- Republic
- Spanish possessions
- Germany

Johan de Witt
At the time known as the first stadholder-free period (1650–72), the political scene in the republic was dominated by the provincial governor Johan de Witt. This brilliant, impeccable statesman was murdered along with his brother Cornelis by Orange supporters in 1672.

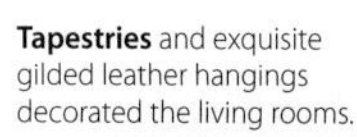

Tapestries and exquisite gilded leather hangings decorated the living rooms.

Oriental carpets were too valuable to put on the floor and so were draped over a table or bench.

Colourful cloths came into fashion in the second half of the 17th century and became a widespread object of study for portrait painters.

View of the Weigh House in Haarlem
In the 17th century, Holland became Europe's main commodities market, with strategic logistic and financial advantages. Products from the Baltic Sea, southern Europe, the Levant and Asia were loaded into the holds of merchant ships which came from all over the world.

1559 Philip II names Margaretha of Parma the governor of the Netherlands

1566 Iconoclastic riots

1567 Duke of Alva arrives in Holland

1572 The "Beggars of the Sea" take over Den Briel

1574 The relief of Leiden

Spanish stew-kettle recovered after the relief of Leiden

1581 Northern Holland declares independence from Spain

1584 Assassination of William of Orange

1585 Fall of Antwerp

1588 The States General proclaim the Republic of the Seven United Netherlands

1602 Dutch East India Company founded

1550 | 1565 | 1580 | 1595 | 1610

Caricature painting of the Pope as a pontiff and devil

Antonie van Leeuwenhoek

The Enlightenment

The Enlightenment, or the "Age of Reason", has its roots in the 16th century. In Holland, this emerged in the work of the natural scientists Swammerdam and Van Leeuwenhoek, and the thinker Spinoza. The jurist Hugo de Groot was the first to formulate a rational – as opposed to a theological – basis for what he called "natural law", that is, a universal law applicable to all humans everywhere, which was one of the great themes tackled by thinkers of the Enlightenment.

Where to See the Netherlands' Golden Age

Good examples of 17th-century architecture are the Trippenhuis in Amsterdam *(see p82)*, the Lakenhal in Leiden *(see p220)* and the Mauritshuis in The Hague *(see pp226–7)*. Vlissingen has the Arsenaal *(see p255)*; Haarlem, the Grote Markt *(see p186)*. Outstanding merchant houses can be seen in the major trading towns of the time, such as Delft*(see pp230–33)* and Utrecht (for example, the Oudegracht, *see p204)*.

Wan-Li China Porcelain, also known as egg-shell porcelain, served as a model for blue Delft pottery.

Michiel de Ruyter
The admiral of the Dutch fleet during the Second and Third English-Dutch Naval Wars was a great tactician held in high esteem by his sailors. His nickname "Bestevaer" meant "Grandfather".

The Muider Circle
The artists and scholars who met at the home of the poet PC Hooft at Muiderslot Castle are now known as the members of the "Muiderkring" (Muider Circle).

Interior of a Patrician Home

This painting by Pieter de Hooch, Portrait of a Family Making Music *(1663), shows the wealth of a patrician residence in the second half of the 17th century. Around 1660, portrait painting shifted in style from sobriety to opulence, a reflection of the flourishing economic prosperity.*

Prince of Poets
Joost van den Vondel (1587–1679), depicted here by HG Pot as a shepherd, is widely regarded as the greatest Dutch poet and playwright of the 17th century.

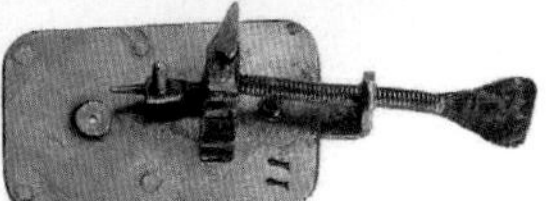

17th-Century Microscope
Antonie van Leeuwenhoek made numerous important discoveries with his home-made microscope.

1625 | 1640 | 1655 | 1670 | 1685 | 1700

1625 Frederick-Henry becomes stadholder of Holland, Zeeland, Utrecht, Gelderland and Overijssel

1642 Rembrandt completes *The Night Watch*

1648 The Peace of Münster marks the end of the 80 Years War

1650–1672 First stadholder-free period starts when the states fail to name a successor after the death of William II

1665–1667 The Second English-Dutch Naval War. Michiel Adriaansz. de Ruyter scores legendary victories (Four Days' Battle, The Battle of Chatham)

1672–1702 Rule of stadholder William III

1689 William III becomes king of England

1698 Tsar Peter the Great visits Amsterdam and Zaandam

Calvinism

From the end of the 1500s, Calvinism took hold in the Netherlands as Protestant opposition to Spanish Catholic rule. Amsterdam, which had sided with Spain, switched loyalties in 1578 to become the fiercely Protestant capital of an infant Dutch Republic. Reformed Church doctrine was to have a profound influence on Dutch history. Strict living and industriousness became ingrained in the character of Calvinists as well as of Catholics and agnostics and was instrumental in the country's prosperity during the Golden Age.

Gold and paintings decorated all churches.

The Statenbijbel was the translation of the Bible officially recognized by the Synod of Dordrecht (1618–19). The language used in it helped to standardize Dutch. The New Translation (Nieuwe Vertaling) did not appear until 1957.

The iconoclasts use combined efforts to topple a huge religious image from the wall.

The Iconoclastic Riots

Underground Calvinist preachers goaded troublemakers into the Iconoclastic Riots of 1566, when the decorations of Catholic churches were destroyed with great violence. Invaluable works of religious art were lost in this way. The interiors of Dutch churches were no longer given the Baroque ornamentation that characterizes churches in the rest of Europe. After all, according to the Ten Commandments in the Bible, "Thou shalt not make graven images" and " Thou shalt not worship nor serve them".

Traces of the damage caused by the iconoclasts can still be seen today in some places, such as this retable in Utrecht.

Pieter Saenredam (1597–1665) painted unrivalled pictures of the plain Calvinist churches – this one is *Interior of the Sint-Odolphuskerk in Assendelft.*

Priceless stained-glass windows are systematically smashed to pieces.

The leaders of the iconoclast riots came from all classes of the population. In addition to fervent Calvinists, there were also paid helpers and all kinds of hangers-on who used the opportunity to do some plundering.

Where to See Calvinist Netherlands

Strict Calvinism can be found in the Netherlands'"Bible belt" which stretches from Zeeland and southeastern South Holland via the Veluwe to the cape of Overijssel and Drenthe. The strict Sunday worship, black clothes and head coverings when attending church, as well as abstinence from modern developments (such as television and vaccinations), are gradually disappearing. However, when visiting such areas, do remember that photography and driving are still not looked upon kindly in Reformed Church villages. These communities are closed, with strong social controls. Calvinist villages worth visiting are Goedereede *(see p245)*, in South Holland, and Staphorst *(see p321)*, in Overijssel, as well as the former Zuiderzee island of Urk *(see p330)*, where older people continue to wear traditional dress.

Early to Church by A. Allebé

Ons' Lieve Heer op Solder

Clandestine Churches

When, in 1597, the Union of Utrecht proclaimed mandatory Calvinist services throughout the Netherlands and Zeeland, a blind eye – in return for payment – was turned to other confessions. Catholics, Remonstrants and Mennonites held their services in secret churches, which were unrecognizable as such from the outside. They were generally held in town houses, although later they were held in secret churches that were built for the purpose, particularly in Amsterdam, with De Zon and De Rode Hoed. The St Gertrudiskapel (1645) in Utrecht and Ons' Lieve Heer op Solder (1663, now the Amstelkring Museum) in Amsterdam are the finest surviving early examples of these institutions.

From Republic to Kingdom

After the death of the powerful stadholder William III, the republic no longer played an important role within Europe. Britain took over as most important maritime and trading power. At the end of the 18th century, a long dispute began between the House of Orange and democratically minded patriots, which was resolved in favour of the latter with the founding of the Batavian Republic (1795). After the Napoleonic era, the House of Orange returned to power, this time not as stadholder but as monarch. In 1839, the borders of the present-day Netherlands were finally established.

The Low Countries in 1800

Batavian Republic

French territory

William I Landing at Scheveningen

In 1813, almost 20 years after the House of Orange had been ousted by the patriots, Prince William returned to the Netherlands. He landed on the shore at Scheveningen, the same place where his father had departed for England. Two days later, he was inaugurated as sovereign. In 1815, he also claimed possession of present-day Belgium and pronounced himself king of the Netherlands.

The British ensign flying on the English warship the *Warrior*, the boat which brought William I back to the Netherlands.

The prince is lowered from the ship in a rowboat, but a farmer's wagon from the beach picks him up to take him ashore through the surf.

Goejanverwellesluis
In 1785, the patriots took power, and the stadholder William V and his wife Wilhelmina of Prussia fled from The Hague. Wilhelmina attempted to return in 1787 but was stopped at Goejanverwellesluis. It was at this point that the Prussian king decided to send troops to restore the power of the stadholder.

1702–1747 Second stadholder-free period

1747 William IV "the Frisian" becomes hereditary stadholder of all provinces

1756–1763 The great powers of Europe become embroiled in the Seven Years War. The republic remains neutral

1791 Abolition of the Dutch West India Company

1700 | 1720 | 1740 | 1760 | 1780

1713 The Peace of Utrecht marks the end of the republic as a great power

The city hall of Utrecht, where the Peace of Utrecht was signed

1786 The patriots take hold of power in various towns. The rule of stadholder William V is restored in 1787 with the help of Prussia

1795–1806 The Batavian Republic

The Siege of Bergen op Zoom
During the War of Austrian Succession, the French occupied the Southern Netherlands, which had been a possession of Austria. In order to strengthen their hand at the peace negotiations vis-à-vis the republic, in 1747 they also annexed Zeeland Flanders and the fortified town of Bergen.

The Schools Controversy

The 19th-century schools controversy between liberals and denominational supporters was over the inequality between independent education and public education. Under HJAM Schaepman and Abraham Kuyper, Catholics and Protestants joined forces and in 1889 laid the foundations for government subsidies for independent education.

Dr Schaepman

Dr Kuyper

The church of the fishing village of Scheveningen is visible in the background.

The people of The Hague were overjoyed at the return of the prince. Celebrations were held throughout the town. The times during which the House of Orange had been regarded as a "clique of tyrants" were definitely over.

Child Labour
The Industrial Revolution led to social deprivation in the towns. In 1875, Van Houten's child law was passed, prohibiting children under age 12 from working as paid labourers.

1800 | 1820 | 1840 | 1860 | 1880 | 1900

1798 Abolition of the Dutch East India Company

1806 Louis Napoleon, brother of Napoleon I, becomes king of Holland

1815 The Northern and Southern Netherlands are united under William I

1830 The Belgian Revolution. Nine years later, the Netherlands and Belgium separate

1839 Haarlem-Amsterdam railway opens

Steam train

1848 Revision of the constitution and introduction of parliamentary system

1863 Abolition of slavery

1870 Abolition of the death penalty

Domela Nieuwenhuis

1885 Van Gogh paints *The Potato Eaters*

1886 Parliamentary enquiry reveals dire conditions in factories

1888 First socialist, Domela Nieuwenhuis, elected to Parliament

Colonialism

Dutch colonial history started in the 17th century when trading settlements were established in Asia, Africa and America. Many colonies were lost during the course of time, but the Dutch Indies (Indonesia), Suriname and the Dutch Antilles remained under Dutch rule until far into the 20th century. In the Indonesian archipelago, Dutch power was for a long time limited to Java and the Moluccas. It was only in 1870 that a start was made on subjugating the remaining islands. Indonesia gained independence in 1949 and Suriname in 1975. The Antilles, Aruba and the Netherlands are now equal parts of the Kingdom of the Netherlands.

Tortured Slave
Rebellion was cruelly punished.

Jan Pieterszoon Coen
Appointed governor-general in 1618, Jan Pieterszoon Coen devastated the Javanese settlement of Jakarta in 1619, founding in its place the new administrative centre of Batavia. He bolstered the position of the Dutch East India Company on the spice islands (the Moluccas) and is considered one of the founding fathers of Dutch colonialism.

Selling female slaves half-naked at auctions was condemned by Holland.

Slave Market in Suriname

In total, over 300,000 slaves were shipped to the Dutch colony of Suriname to work the plantations. The slave trade was abolished in 1819, though slavery itself was not abolished until 1863, making Holland the last Western European power to do so.

Session of the Landraad
This landraad, or joint court, is presided over by the assistant resident. The landraad was the civil and criminal common-law court for native Indonesians and all non-European foreigners in the Dutch Indies. The court could, with government approval, inflict the death penalty.

Batavia During the 17th Century
This painting by Andries Beeckman shows the fish market with the "Kasteel" in the background, from which the Dutch ruled over the strategic Sunda Strait.

Multatuli
The writer Multatuli, in his novel from 1860 *Max Havelaar*, condemned colonial rule in the Dutch Indies. In the book's final chapter, the author directly addresses King William III, in whose name the people of the Indies were being exploited.

The auctioneer sits taking notes at the table. The slaves whom he is selling were delivered by special traders. Until 1734, slaves were auctioned exclusively by the Dutch West India Company, which had the monopoly on the slave trade.

The Establishment of Cape Town
In 1652, Jan van Riebeeck set up a supply station for ships of the Dutch East India Company en route to the Indies. The settlement soon grew into a Dutch colony, which was settled by immigrants from the republic, and to a lesser extent from France (Huguenots) and Germany. Those who moved farther inland were later to become the Boers ("farmers") or Afrikaaners. In 1806, the Cape Colony was taken over by the British Empire.

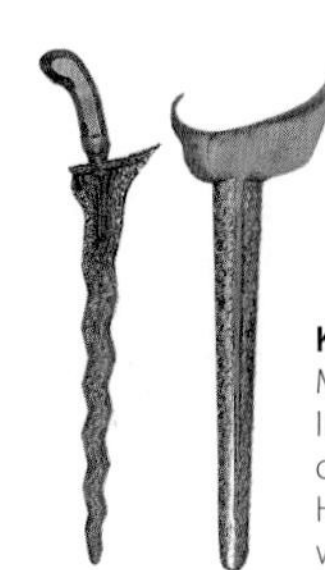

Kris from Java
Many travellers to the Indies brought back characteristic items to Holland. The Javanese kris was a favourite souvenir.

Colonial Wares
From the end of the 19th century, a number of Dutch grocers offered for sale "colonial wares" such as coffee, tea, rice, sugar and various exotic eastern herbs and spices, including the much-prized peppercorns, cloves, nutmeg, mace and cinnamon.

The Modern Netherlands

Neutrality during World War I meant that the Netherlands survived the first decades of the 20th century relatively unscathed. However, the economic crisis of the 1930s and particularly World War II left deep wounds. In 1957, as the country was rebuilding, it became one of the six founding members of the European Economic Community (EEC). The Dutch welfare state flourished in the 1960s and 1970s, and Amsterdam's tradition of tolerance made it a haven for the hippy culture. In a survey carried out by the United Nations in 2012, the Netherlands ranked fourth in the list of best countries to live in.

The Netherlands Today

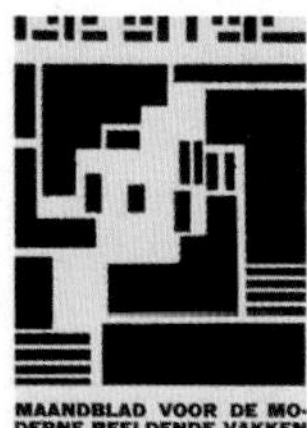

1917 The magazine *De Stijl* is set up by figures from the movement of the same name, such as Theo van Doesburg, Piet Mondriaan and JJP Oud

1930–1940 During the economic crisis of the 1930s, hundreds of thousands of Dutch were on the dole

1949 Holland recognizes the Independence of its former colony Indonesia

1953 On 1 February, storms cause severe flooding in Zeeland and South Holland, drowning more than 1,800 people

1910	1920	1930	1940	1950	1960

TIMELINE

1910	1920	1930	1940	1950	1960

1918 German kaiser Wilhelm II flees to Holland, where he is given asylum

1926 Road tax introduced. Approximately 10,000 lorries and 30,000 cars are on the roads of Holland

1934 KLM's plane "Uiver", a DC-2, wins the handicap section in the London-Melbourne air race

1948 Willem Drees Sr becomes prime minister of four successive Catholic socialist Drees cabinets and lays the foundations of the Dutch welfare state

1940 On 10 May, Nazi troops enter Holland. Rotterdam capitulates on 14 May. Despite this, the city is bombed

1962 The release of Jan Vrijman's film *De werkelijkheid van Karel Appel* brings the postwar Dutch painter to the attention of the general public. Karel Appel (b. 1921) caused a sensation with his statement: "I'll just mess something up"

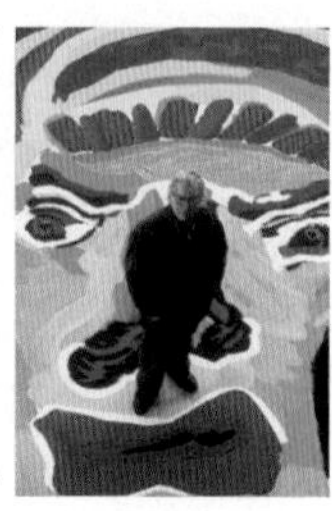

1975 Holland recognizes the independence of its former colony Suriname

1985 A government decision to deploy 48 NATO cruise missiles on Dutch territory causes a storm of opposition. The Komité Kruisraketten Nee (anti-cruise coalition) submits a petition of 3.5 million signatures to Prime Minister Lubbers in October

1995 Paul Crutzen is awarded the Nobel Prize for Chemistry for his ground-breaking investigations of the ozone layer

2000 The Dutch team at the Sydney Olympics wins a record 25 medals, including 12 golds

2002 On 2 February Crown Prince Wilem-Alexander marries Argentinian Máxima Zorreguieta in Amsterdam's Beurs van Berlage

2010 Geert Wilders' PVV gains the most seats in the elections

1970 | 1980 | 1990 | 2000 | 2010 | 2020

1970 | 1980 | 1990 | 2000 | 2010 | 2020

1971 Ajax wins the First Division European Cup at Wembley Stadium in London with star player Johan Cruijff. The club continues as champion in 1972 and 1973

1980 The KVP, ARP and CHU combine to form the CDA, the large Christian Democratic Party

1980 The coronation of Queen Beatrix on 30 April is accompanied by heavy battles between police and anti-monarchy demonstrators and squatters

1992 Under Dutch presidency, the European partners sign the draft Maastricht Treaty in 1991. In 1992, the treaty, under which the European Community becomes the European Union, is ratified

2001 The Netherlands is the first country to legalize same-sex marriages

2002 Right-wing politician Pym Fortuyn is assassinated on 6 May

2004 On 2 November, controversial filmmaker Theo Van Gogh is murdered by a radical Islamist, spurring a national debate on immigration

2013 Willem-Alexander becomes king of the Netherlands

AMSTERDAM

Amsterdam's Best: Canals and Waterways

From the grace and elegance of the waterside mansions along the Grachtengordel (Canal Ring) to the rows of converted warehouses on Brouwersgracht and the charming houses on Reguliersgracht, the city's canals and waterways embody the very spirit of Amsterdam. They are spanned by many beautiful bridges, including the famous Magere Brug *(see pp118–19)*, a traditionally styled lift bridge. You can also relax at a canalside café or bar and watch an array of boats float by.

Brouwersgracht
The banks of this charming canal are lined with houseboats, cosy cafés and warehouses.

Bloemgracht
There is a great variety of architecture along this lovely, tree-lined canal in the Jordaan, including a row of houses with step gables.

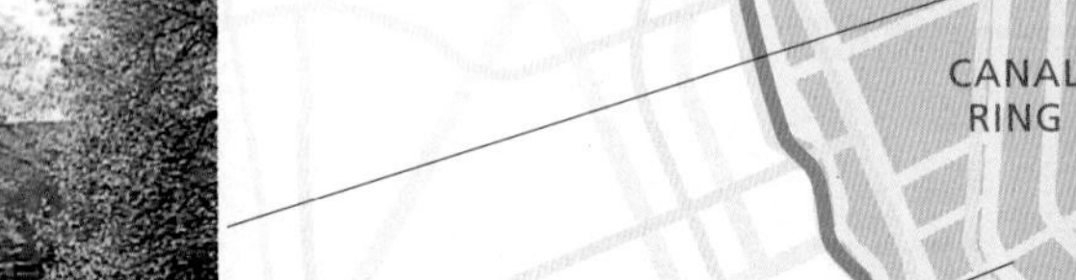

Prinsengracht
The best way to see all the beautiful buildings along Amsterdam's longest 17th-century canal is by bicycle.

Leidsegracht
Relax at a pavement café along the exclusive Leidsegracht.

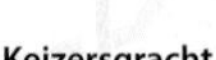

Keizersgracht
A view of this canal can be had from any of its bridges. If frozen in winter, this canal is used for ice skating by many Amsterdammers, both young and old.

◀ Façades of buildings along the Damrak canal

Singel
The *Poezenboot*, a boat for stray cats, is just one of the many sights to be found along the Singel, whose distinctive, curved shape established the horseshoe contours of the Canal Ring.

Entrepotdok
The warehouses on the Entrepotdok *(see p138)* were redeveloped in the 1980s. The quayside is now lined in summer with lively café terraces that overlook an array of houseboats and pleasure craft.

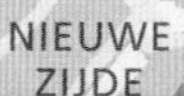

OUDE
ZIJDE

Herengracht
Known as "the twin brothers", these matching neck-gabled houses at Nos. 409–411 are two of the prettiest houses on the city's grandest canal.

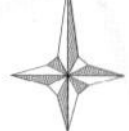

0 metres 500
0 yards 500

Reguliersgracht
Many crooked, brick buildings line this pretty canal, which was cut in 1664. The statue of a stork, located at No. 92, is symbolic of parental responsibility and commemorates a 1571 bylaw protecting this bird.

Amstel
This river is still a busy thoroughfare, with barges and, above all, many sightseeing boats.

The Golden Age of Amsterdam

The 17th century was truly a Golden Age for Amsterdam. The population soared; three great canals, bordered by splendid houses, were built in a triple ring round the city; and scores of painters and architects were at work. Fortunes were made and lost, and this early capitalism produced many paupers, who were cared for by charitable institutions – a radical idea for the time. In 1648, an uneasy peace was formalized with Catholic Spain, causing tension between Amsterdam's Calvinist burgomasters and the less-religious House of Orange, which was dominant elsewhere in the country.

Spice Trade
In this old print, a VOC spice trader arrives in Bantam.

Self-Portrait as the Apostle Paul (1661)
Rembrandt *(see p82)* was one of many artists working in Amsterdam in the mid-17th century.

Livestock and grain trading

The new Stadhuis (now the Koninklijk Paleis) was being constructed behind wooden scaffolding.

Nieuwe Kerk, 1395 *(see p90)*

Dam Square in 1656

Money poured into Amsterdam at this time of civic expansion. Holland was active overseas, colonizing Indonesia, and the spice trade brought enormous wealth. The Dutch East India Company (VOC), the principal trade organization in Holland, prospered – gold seemed almost as common as water. Dutch painter Jan Lingelbach (c.1624–74) depicted the city's Dam square as a busy, thriving and cosmopolitan market, brimming with traders and wealthy merchants.

The Love Letter (1666)
Genre painting *(see p127)*, such as this calm domestic interior by Jan Vermeer, became popular as society grew more sophisticated. Jan Steen, Honthorst and Terborch were other famous genre painters.

Delft Tiles
Delicate flower paintings were popular themes on 17th-century Delft tiles *(see pp32–3)*, used as decoration in wealthy households.

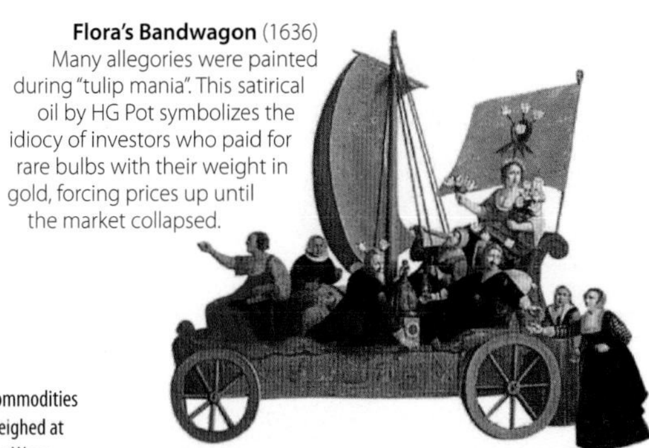

Flora's Bandwagon (1636)
Many allegories were painted during "tulip mania". This satirical oil by HG Pot symbolizes the idiocy of investors who paid for rare bulbs with their weight in gold, forcing prices up until the market collapsed.

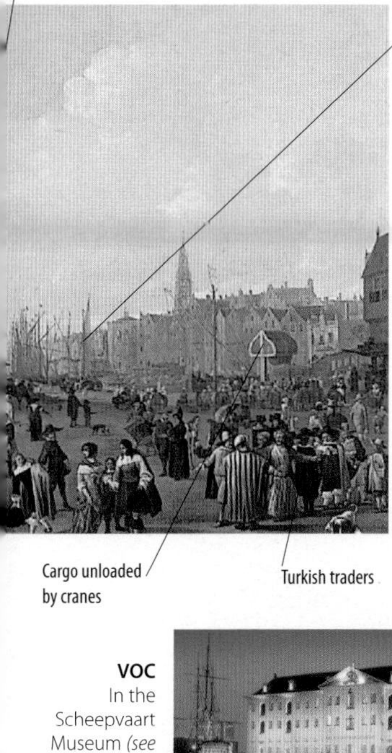

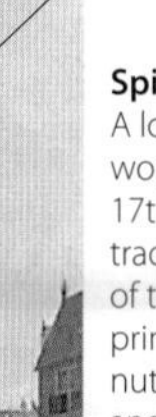

Commodities weighed at the Waag

Ships sailing up the Damrak

Cargo unloaded by cranes

Turkish traders

Spices
A load of spices was worth a fortune in the 17th century. The VOC traded in a great variety of these costly spices, primarily pepper, nutmeg, cloves, mace and cinnamon. As early as 1611 the VOC was the largest importer of spices.

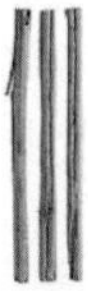

Pepper, nutmeg, cloves, mace, cinnamon

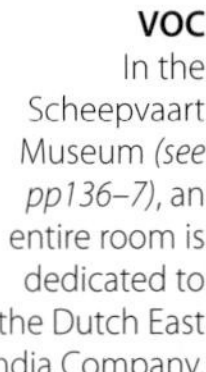

VOC
In the Scheepvaart Museum *(see pp136–7)*, an entire room is dedicated to the Dutch East India Company.

Giving the Bread
This painting by Willem van Valckert shows the city's needy receiving alms. A rudimentary welfare system was introduced in the 1640s.

Where to See 17th-century Amsterdam

Many public buildings, such as churches and palaces, sprang up as Amsterdam grew more wealthy. The Westerkerk *(see p114)* was designed by Hendrick de Keyser in 1620; the Lutherse Kerk *(see p94)* by Adriaan Dortsman in 1671. Elias Bouman built the Portugees-Israëlitische Synagoge *(see p84)* in 1675 for members of the city's immigrant Sephardic Jewish community.

Apollo (c.1648) Artus Quellien's statue is in the South Gallery of the Koninklijk Paleis *(see pp92–3)*. Construction of the place, a masterwork by Jacob van Capenwhich, began in 1648.

Museum het Rembrandthuis (1606)
Jacob van Campen added the pediment in 1633 *(see p82)*.

Amsterdam's Best: Museums

For a fairly small city, Amsterdam has a surprisingly large number of museums and galleries. The quality and variety of the collections are impressive, covering everything from bibles and beer to shipbuilding and space travel. Many are housed in buildings of historical or architectural interest. The Rijksmuseum, with its Gothic façade, is a city landmark, and Rembrandt's work is exhibited in his original home.

Anne Frank Huis
Anne Frank's photo is exhibited in the house where she hid during World War II.

Amsterdam Museum
A wealth of historical information is on display here. Once an orphanage for boys, it is depicted in *Governesses at the Burgher Orphanage* (1683) by Adriaen Backer.

Rijksmuseum
An extensive collection of paintings by Dutch masters can be seen in the country's largest national museum. Jan van Huysum's *Still Life with Fruit and Flowers*, dating from about 1730, is a fine example *(see pp126–9)*.

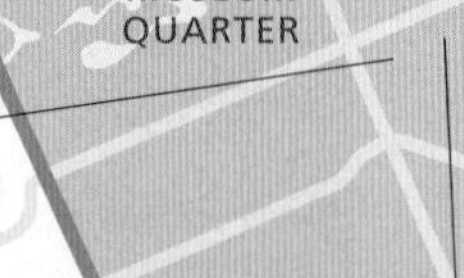

Stedelijk Museum
Gerrit Rietveld's simple Steltman chair (1963) is one of many exhibits at this modern art museum *(see pp132–3)*.

Van Gogh Museum
Van Gogh's *Self-portrait with Straw Hat* (1870) hangs in this large, stark building, built in 1973 to house the bulk of his work.

Koninklijk Paleis
The royal palace on the Dam, a former town hall designed in 1648 by Jacob van Campen, is still regularly used today by the queen on official occasions *(see pp92–3)*.

Science Center NEMO
This amazing building, designed in the form of a ship, overhangs the water by 30 m (99 ft) and houses an educational centre for science and technology *(see pp140–41)*.

NIEUWE ZIJDE

OUDE ZIJDE

Scheepvaart Museum
This maritime museum is decorated with reliefs relating to the city's maritime history. Moored alongside is a replica of the East Indiaman, *Amsterdam*, which is open to the public.

0 metres 500

0 yards 500

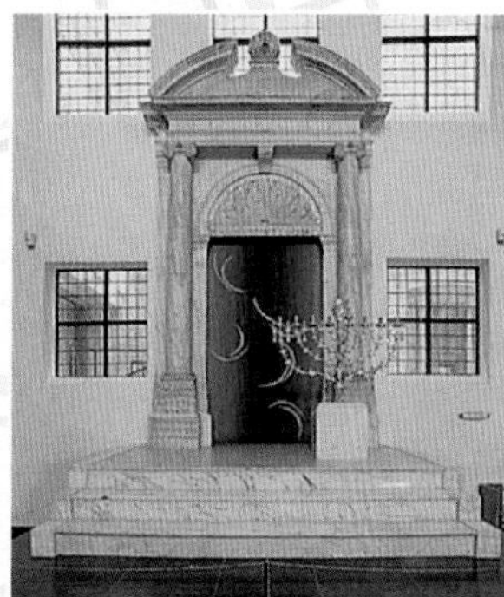

Joods Historisch Museum
Four adjoining synagogues are linked to form this museum.

Verzetsmuseum
Located in the Plantage, this museum documents and commemorates the activities of Dutch Resistance workers in World War II *(see pg145)*.

Amsterdam's Best: Cafés

Amsterdam is a city of cafés and bars, about 1,500 in all. Each area has something to offer, from friendly and relaxed brown cafés – a traditional Dutch local pub characterized by dark wooden panelling and furniture, low ceilings, dim lighting and smoke-stained ceilings – to lively and crowded designer bars. Each café and bar has some special attraction: a large range of beers, live music, canalside terraces, art exhibitions, board games and pool tables or simply a brand of *gezelligheid*, the unique Dutch concept of "cosiness".

De Drie Fleschjes
In one of the oldest pubs (1650) of Amsterdam, you can choose from a wide variety of gins.

Café Chris
This brown café, allegedly the oldest café in the Jordaan, is patronized by regular customers (artists and students).

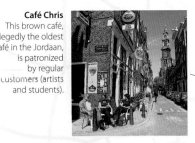

Walem
This designer eatery, one of Amsterdam's oldest cafés, has a sunny canal terrace and is popular with the international crowd.

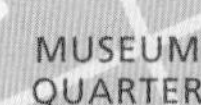

Groot Melkhuis
Originally a farm dating back to 1874, this modern café is very popular, especially on warm summer days.

Hoppe
The dark wooden interior and tang of cigar smoke in the air are the essence of this classic brown café, situated on the lively Spui.

Karpershoek
This lively café (the oldest café in Amsterdam) is close to the Centraal Station and is frequented by travellers looking for a cup of coffee.

Kapitein Zeppos
This café, frequented by trendy Amsterdammers, often hosts live concerts on Sunday afternoons.

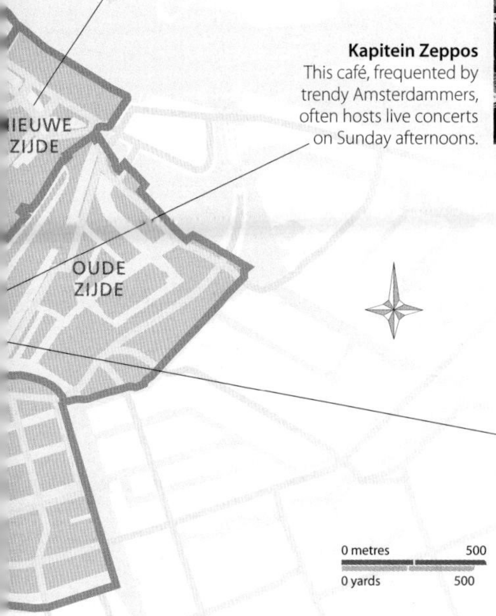

IEUWE ZIJDE

OUDE ZIJDE

De Jaren
Popular with students, this trendy two-storey café has a superb view of the Amstel and a wide selection of newspapers.

0 metres 500

0 yards 500

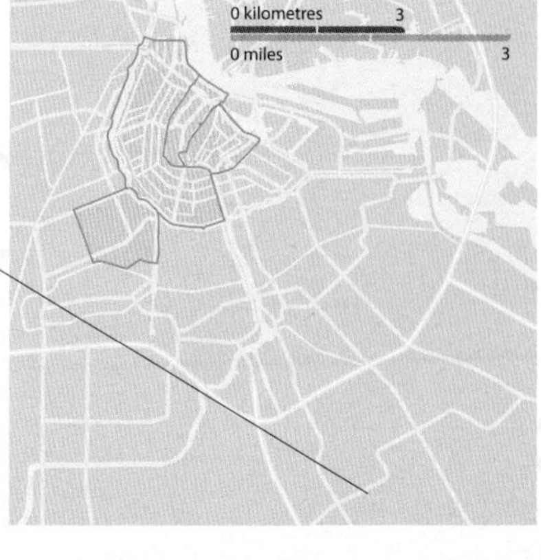

Grand Café Soccerworld
In the café of the arena you can admire the football shirts of the famous Ajax team.

OUDE ZIJDE

The eastern half of Amsterdam became known as the Oude Zijde (Old Side). Originally it occupied a narrow strip on the east bank of the Amstel river, running between Damrak and the Oudezijds Voorburgwal. At its heart was built the Oude Kerk, the oldest church in the city. In the early 15th century the Oude Zijde began an eastward expansion that continued into the 1600s. This growth was fuelled by an influx of Jewish refugees from Portugal. The oldest of the four synagogues, now containing the Joods Historisch Museum, dates from this period. These were central to Jewish life in the city for centuries. During the Golden Age *(see pp54–5)*, the Oude Zijde was an important commercial centre. Boats could sail up the Geldersekade to Nieuwmarkt, where goods were weighed at the Waag before being sold at the market.

Sights at a Glance

Historic Buildings and Monuments

2 Waag
5 Agnietenkapel
6 Oudemanhuispoort
7 Oost-Indisch Huis
8 Trippenhuis
16 Pintohuis
17 Montelbaanstoren
18 Scheepvaarthuis
19 Schreierstoren

Opera Houses

11 Stadhuis-Muziektheater

Museums

4 Hash Marihuana Hemp Museum
10 Museum het Rembrandthuis
14 Joods Historisch Museum

Churches and Synagogues

9 Zuiderkerk
13 Mozes en Aäronkerk
15 Portugees-Israëlitische Synagoge
21 *Oude Kerk pp80–81*

Streets and Markets

1 Red Light District
3 Nieuwmarkt
12 Waterlooplein
20 Zeedijk

◄ View of Oude Kerk, Amsterdam's oldest building

For map symbols *see back flap*

Street-by-Street: University District

The University of Amsterdam, founded in 1877, is predominantly located in the peaceful, southwestern part of the Oude Zijde. The university's roots lie in the former Athenaeum Illustre, which was founded in 1632 in the Agnietenkapel. Beyond Damstraat, the bustling Red Light District meets the Nieuwmarkt, where the 15th-century Waag evokes a medieval air. South of the Nieuwmarkt, Museum Het Rembrandthuis gives a fascinating insight into the life of the city's most famous artist.

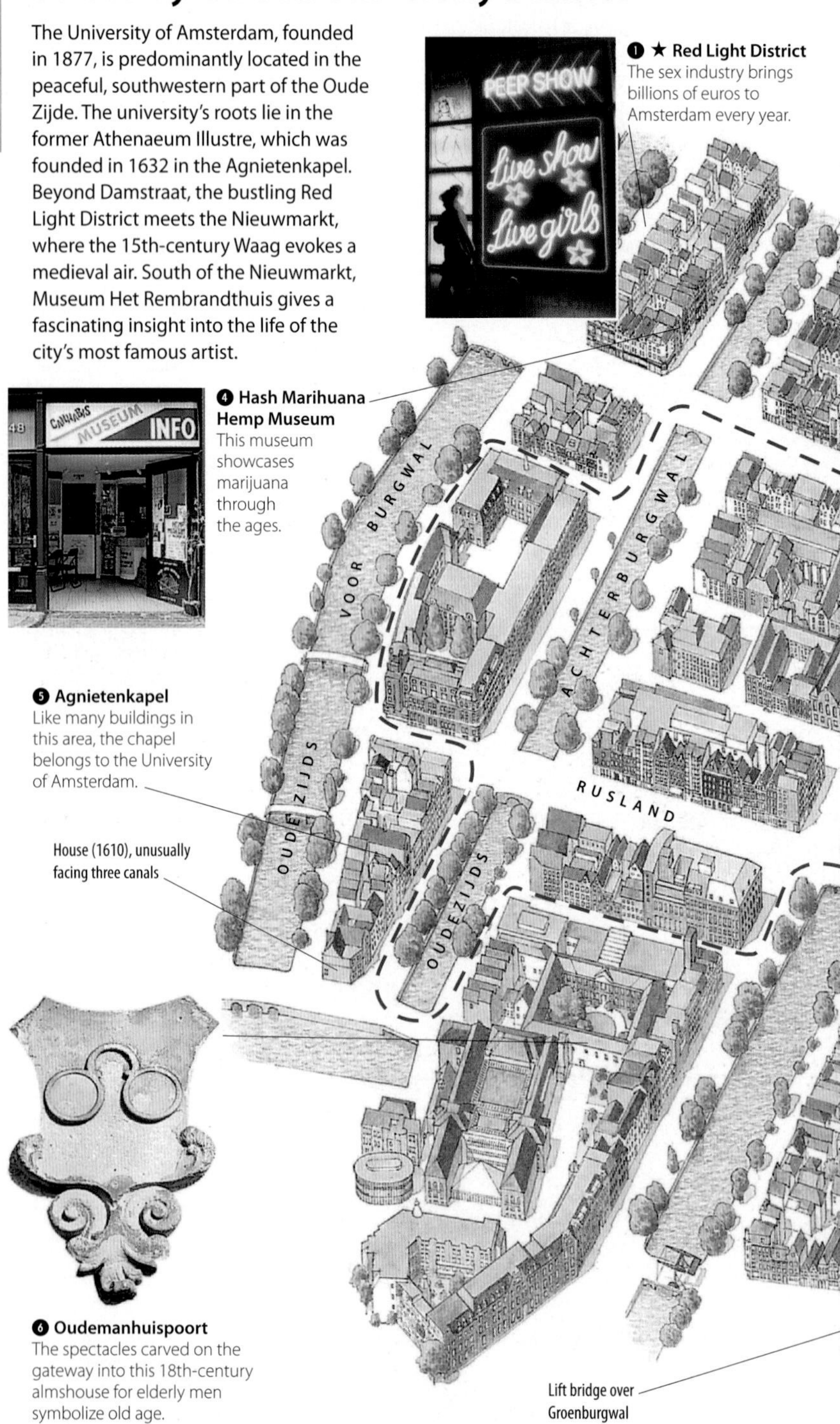

❶ ★ Red Light District
The sex industry brings billions of euros to Amsterdam every year.

❹ Hash Marihuana Hemp Museum
This museum showcases marijuana through the ages.

❺ Agnietenkapel
Like many buildings in this area, the chapel belongs to the University of Amsterdam.

House (1610), unusually facing three canals

❻ Oudemanhuispoort
The spectacles carved on the gateway into this 18th-century almshouse for elderly men symbolize old age.

Lift bridge over Groenburgwal

For hotels and restaurants in this region see pp396–397 and pp406–409

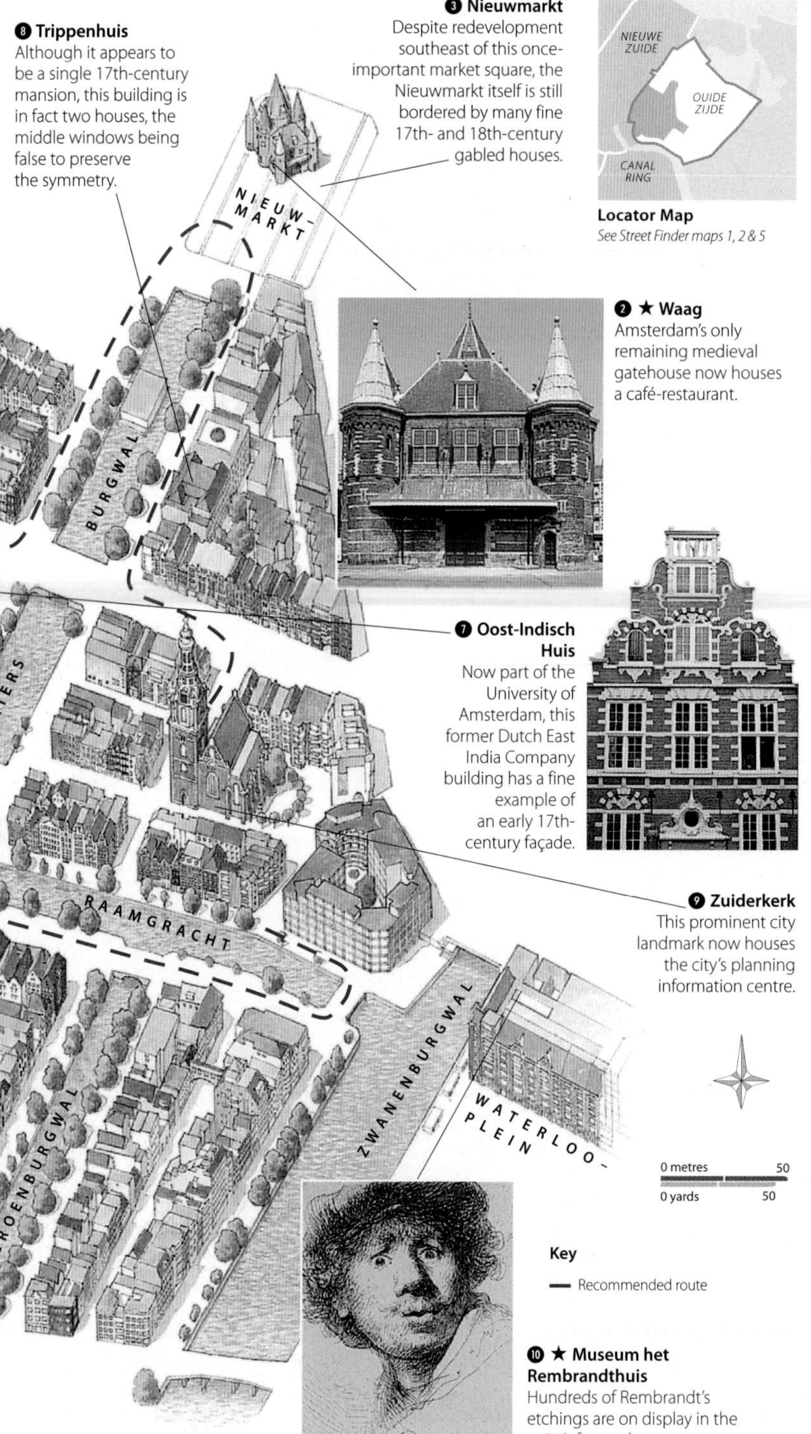

8 Trippenhuis
Although it appears to be a single 17th-century mansion, this building is in fact two houses, the middle windows being false to preserve the symmetry.

3 Nieuwmarkt
Despite redevelopment southeast of this once-important market square, the Nieuwmarkt itself is still bordered by many fine 17th- and 18th-century gabled houses.

Locator Map
See Street Finder maps 1, 2 & 5

2 ★ Waag
Amsterdam's only remaining medieval gatehouse now houses a café-restaurant.

7 Oost-Indisch Huis
Now part of the University of Amsterdam, this former Dutch East India Company building has a fine example of an early 17th-century façade.

9 Zuiderkerk
This prominent city landmark now houses the city's planning information centre.

Key
— Recommended route

10 ★ Museum het Rembrandthuis
Hundreds of Rembrandt's etchings are on display in the artist's former home.

❶ Red Light District

Map 5 A1. 🚋 4, 9, 16, 24, 25.

Barely clad prostitutes bathed in a red neon glow and touting for business at their windows is one of the defining images of modern Amsterdam. The city's Red Light District, referred to locally as de Walletjes (the little walls), is concentrated on the Oude Kerk *(see pp80–81)*, although it extends as far as Warmoesstraat to the west, the Zeedijk to the north, the Kloveniersburgwal to the east and then along the line of Damstraat to the south.

Prostitution in Amsterdam dates back to the city's emergence as a port in the 13th century. By 1478, prostitution had become so widespread that attempts were made to contain it. Prostitutes straying outside their designated area were marched back to the sound of pipe and drum.

A century later, following the Alteration, the Calvinists *(see pp56–7)* tried to outlaw prostitution altogether. Their attempts were half-hearted, and by the mid-17th century prostitution was openly tolerated. In 1850, Amsterdam had a population of 200,000, and more than 200 brothels.

Entrance to one of the clubs in the Red Light District

Today, the whole area is criss-crossed by a network of narrow lanes, dominated by garish sex shops, seedy clubs and unsavoury characters. At night, the little alleys assume a somewhat sinister aspect, and it is unwise to wander away from the main streets. But by day, hordes of visitors generate a festive buzz, and amid the sleaze there are interesting cafés, bars, restaurants and beautiful canalside houses to be discovered. The city council is trying to make the area more culturally attractive by cutting down on window-prostitutes, closing the seediest clubs and encouraging non-sex-industry businesses.

❷ Waag

Nieuwmarkt 4. **Map** 2 E5. 🚋 4, 9, 16, 24, 25. Ⓜ Nieuwmarkt. **Closed** Upper Rooms: closed to the public.

The multi-turreted Waag is the city's oldest surviving gatehouse. Built in 1488, it was then, and often still is, called St Antoniespoort. Public executions were held here, and condemned prisoners awaited their fate in the "little gallows room". In 1617, the building became the public weigh house *(waaggebouw)*. Peasants had their produce weighed here and paid tax accordingly. Various guilds used the upper rooms of each tower. From 1619 the Guild of Surgeons had a meeting room and anatomy theatre here. They added the central octagonal tower in 1691. Rembrandt's *Anatomy Lesson of Dr Nicholaes Tulp*, now in the Mauritshuis *(see pp226–7)*, and *The Anatomy Lesson of Dr Jan Deijman*, in the Amsterdam Museum *(see pp96–7)*, were commissioned by guild members and then hung here.

The weigh house closed in the early 19th century and the Waag has since served as a fire station and two city museums. It is now home to the restaurant In de Waag.

The 15th-century Waag dominating the Nieuwmarkt, with an antique market on the right

Part of the commemorative photo display in Nieuwmarkt metro station

❸ Nieuwmarkt

Map 2 E5. 4, 9, 16, 24, 25. M Nieuwmarkt. Antiques market: **Open** May–Sep: 9am–5pm Sun. Organic farmers' market 9am–5pm Sat.

An open, paved square, the Nieuwmarkt is flanked to the west by the Red Light District. With the top end of the Geldersekade, it forms Amsterdam's Chinatown. The Waag dominates the square, and construction of this gateway led to the site's development in the 15th century as a market-place. When the city expanded in the 17th century *(see pp68–9)*, the square took on its present dimensions and was called the Nieuwmarkt. It retains an array of 17th- and 18th-century gabled houses. True to tradition, an antiques market is held on Sundays during the summer.

The old Jewish Quarter leads off the square down St Antoniesbreestraat. In the 1970s, many houses here were demolished to make way for the metro, sparking off clashes between protesters and police. The action of conservationists persuaded the council to adopt a policy of renovating rather than redeveloping old buildings. Photographs of their protests decorate the metro station.

❹ Hash Marihuana Hemp Museum

Oudezijds Achterburgwal 148. **Map** 2 D5. **Tel** 020-6248926. 4, 9, 14, 16, 24. M Nieuwmarkt. **Open** 10am–11pm. **Closed** 27 Apr.

This museum, which has a branch in Barcelona, charts the history of hemp (marijuana). Exhibits refer back 8,000 years to early Asiatic civilizations, which used the plant for medicines and clothing. It was first used in the Netherlands, according to a herbal manual of 1554, as a cure for earache.

Until the late 19th century, however, hemp was the main source of fibre for rope, and was therefore important in the Dutch shipping industry. Other exhibits relate to the psychoactive properties of this plant. They include an intriguing array of pipes and bongs (smoking devices), along with displays that explain smuggling methods. The museum also has a small cultivation area where plants are grown under artificial light. Police sometimes raid and take away exhibits, so there may be occasional gaps in displays.

❺ Agnietenkapel

Oudezijds Voorburgwal 231. **Map** 2 D5. 4, 9, 14, 16, 24. **Closed** to the public.

The Agnietenkapel was part of the convent of St Agnes until 1578 when it was closed after the Alteration. In 1632, the Athenaeum Illustre, the precursor of the University of Amsterdam, took over the building and by the mid-17th century it was a centre of scientific learning. It also housed the municipal library until the 1830s. The Agnietenkapel itself dates from 1470, and is one of the few Gothic chapels to have survived the Alteration. During restoration from 1919 to 1921, elements of the Amsterdam School architecture were introduced *(see pp146–7)*. Despite these changes and long periods of secular use, the building still has the feel of a Franciscan chapel. The large auditorium on the first floor is the oldest in the city. It has a lovely ceiling, painted with Renaissance motifs and a portrait of Minerva, the Roman goddess of wisdom and the arts. The walls are hung with forty portraits of European humanist scholars, including one of Erasmus (1466–1536). The Agnietenkapel once housed the University of Amsterdam Museum, but the museum's collection can be seen in Oude Turfmarkt 129 (next to the Allard Pierson Museum). A conference centre has taken its place.

Entrance to Agnietenkapel, now a university conference centre

❻ Oudemanhuispoort

Between Oudezijds Achterburgwal and Kloveniersburgwal. **Map** 2 D5. 4, 9, 14, 16, 24. Book market: **Open** 10am–5pm Mon–Sat.

The Oudemanhuispoort was once the entrance to old people's almshouses (Oudemannenhuis), built in 1754. Today the building is part of the University of Amsterdam.The pediment over the gateway in the Oudezijds Achterburgwal features a pair of spectacles, a symbol of old age. Trading inside this covered walkway dates from 1757 and today there is a market for second-hand books. Although the building is closed to the public, visitors may enter the 18th-century courtyard via the arcade.

Crest of Amsterdam, Oudemanhuispoort

㉑ Oude Kerk

The origins of the Oude Kerk date from the early 13th century, when a wooden church was built on a sand bank. The present Gothic structure is 14th century and has grown from a single-aisled church into a basilica. As it expanded, the building became a gathering place for traders and a refuge for the poor. Paintings and statuary were destroyed after the Alteration in 1578, but the gilded ceiling and stained-glass windows remain. The Great Organ was added in 1724, and there are two other fine organs in this lovely church , also home to the tomb of Rembrandt's wife, Saskia.

The Oude Kerk Today
The old church, surrounded by shops, cafés and houses, remains a calm and peaceful haven at the heart of the frenetic Red Light District.

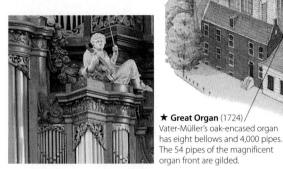

★ Great Organ (1724)
Vater-Müller's oak-encased organ has eight bellows and 4,000 pipes. The 54 pipes of the magnificent organ front are gilded.

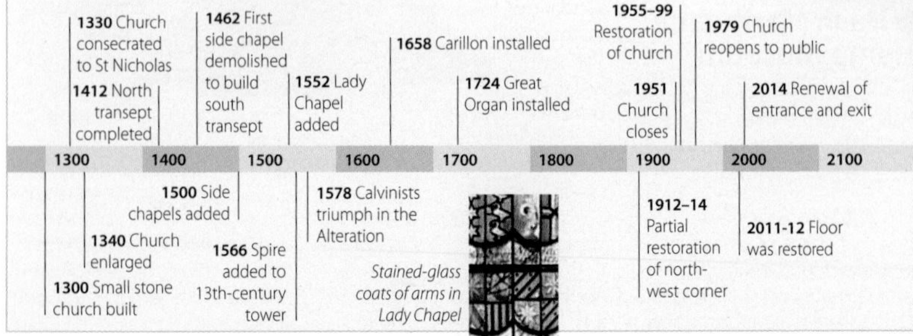

1300 Small stone church built
1330 Church consecrated to St Nicholas
1340 Church enlarged
1412 North transept completed
1462 First side chapel demolished to build south transept
1500 Side chapels added
1552 Lady Chapel added
1566 Spire added to 13th-century tower
1578 Calvinists triumph in the Alteration
1658 Carillon installed
1724 Great Organ installed
1912–14 Partial restoration of north-west corner
1951 Church closes
1955–99 Restoration of church
1979 Church reopens to public
2011-12 Floor was restored
2014 Renewal of entrance and exit
1300
1400
1500
1600
1700
1800
1900
2000
2100

Stained-glass coats of arms in Lady Chapel

For hotels and restaurants in this region see pp396–397 and pp406–409

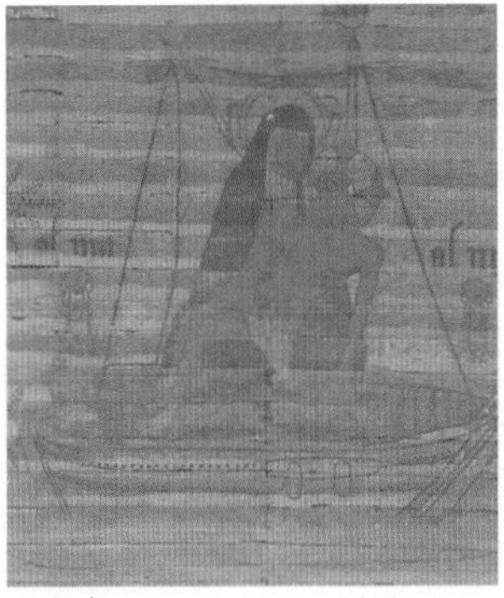

★ Gilded Ceiling
The delicate 15th-century vault paintings have a gilded background. They were hidden with layers of blue paint in 1755 and not revealed until 1955.

VISITORS' CHECKLIST

Practical Information
Oudekerksplein. **Map** 2 D4.
Tel 020-6258284.
oudekerk.nl
Church: **Open** 11am–5pm Mon–Sat, 1–5pm Sun. 11am Sun.
Tower: **Open** Apr–Sep: 1–5pm Thu–Sat; Oct–Mar: phone 020-6892565 to arrange a visit.

Transport
4, 9, 16, 24.

★ Lady Chapel
(1552)
The Death of the Virgin Mary by Dirk Crabeth is one of three restored stained-glass windows in the Lady Chapel.

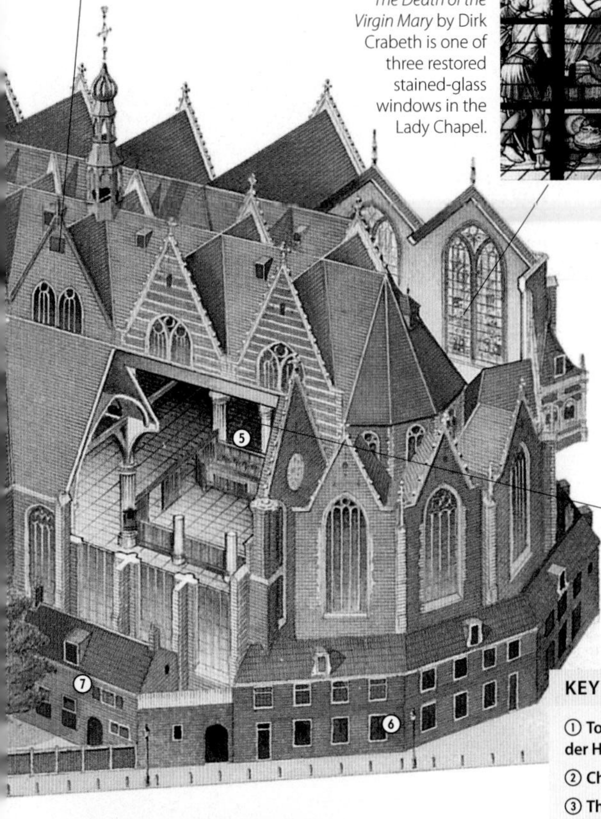

Brocaded Pillars
Decorative pillars originally formed niches holding a series of statues of the Apostles, all destroyed by the iconoclasts in 1578.

The Red Door
The inscription on the lintel above the door into the former sacristy warns those about to enter: "Marry in haste, repent at leisure".

KEY

① **Tomb of Admiral Abraham van der Hulst (1619–66)**

② **Christening chapel**,

③ **The spire** of the bell tower was built by Joost Bilhamer in 1565. François Hemony added the 47-bell carillon in 1658.

④ **Tomb of Saskia, wife of Rembrandt** **(see p82)**

⑤ **Tomb of Admiral Jacob van Heemskerk (1567–1607)**

⑥ **17th- and 18th-century houses.**

⑦ **Former sacristy**

7 Oost-Indisch Huis

Oude Hoogstraat 24. **Map** 2 D5. 4, 9, 14, 16, 24. M Nieuwmarkt. **Open** 9am–7:30pm Mon–Thu, 9am–5pm Fri. **Closed** during graduation ceremonies.

The austere Oost-Indisch Huis, former headquarters of the Dutch East India Company *(see pp52–3)*, is part of the University of Amsterdam. Built in 1605, it was expanded several times to house spices, silk and porcelain from the East Indies. Little original interior decoration remains, but the meeting room has been restored to its 17th-century grandeur.

Ornate balustrade of the Oost-Indisch Huis

8 Trippenhuis

Kloveniersburgwal 29. **Map** 2 E5. 4, 9, 14, 16, 24. M Nieuwmarkt. **Closed** to the public.

Justus Vingboons designed this ornate Classical mansion, completed in 1662. It appears to be one house: it is in fact two. The façade, outlined by eight Corinthian columns, features false middle windows. The house was designed for arms merchants Lodewijk and Hendrick Trip; the chimneys look like cannons. The city's art collection was housed here 1817–85, when it moved to the Rijksmuseum *(see pp126–9)*. Trippenhuis now houses the Dutch Academy. Opposite at No. 26 is the Kleine Trippenhuis (1698). Only 2.5 m (7 ft) wide, it has detailed cornicing, including two carved sphinxes.

9 Zuiderkerk

Zuiderkerkhof 72. **Map** 2 E5. **Tel** 020-5527987. 9, 14. M Nieuwmarkt. W **zuiderkerk.amsterdam.nl**

Designed by Hendrick de Keyser in 1603 in the Renaissance style, the Zuiderkerk was the first Calvinist church to open in Amsterdam after the Alteration. The spire has columns, decorative clocks and an onion dome.

The spire of the Zuiderkerk, a prominent city landmark

The Zuiderkerk ceased to function as a church in 1929. It was restored in 1988 and is now a commercial venue for events and private dinners. The surrounding community housing includes the "Pentagon" by Theo Bosch.

10 Museum het Rembrandthuis

Jodenbreestraat 4-6. **Map** 2 E5. **Tel** 020-5200400. 9, 14. M Nieuwmarkt. **Open** 10am–6pm daily. **Closed** 1 Jan, 27 Apr, 25 Dec. W **rembrandthuis.nl**

Rembrandt worked and taught in this house from 1639 until 1660. He lived in the ground-floor rooms with his wife, Saskia, who died here in 1642, leaving the artist with their only surviving child, a baby son, Titus.

Many of Rembrandt's most famous paintings were created in the first-floor studio. Lessons were conducted in the attic. A fine collection of Rembrandt's etchings and drawings includes various self-portraits. There are also landscapes, nude studies, religious and crowd scenes, and sketches of the artist with his wife. The house has undergone historically accurate restoration and a further wing has been opened to the public.

Self-portrait by Rembrandt with his wife, Saskia (1636)

⓫ Stadhuis–Muziektheater

Waterlooplein 22. **Map** 5 B2. 4, 9, 14. Ⓜ Waterlooplein. Stadhuis: **Tel** 020-6241111. **Open** 8:30am–4pm Mon–Fri (free concerts Sep–May: 12:30pm Tue). Muziektheater: **Tel** 020-6255455. See Entertainment: *pp146–7.* **hetmuziektheater.nl**

Few buildings in Amsterdam caused as much controversy as the new Stadhuis (city hall) and Muziektheater (opera house). Nicknamed the "Stopera" by protesters, the plan required the destruction of dozens of medieval houses, which were virtually all that remained of the original Jewish quarter, and the temporary relocation of a popular market. This led to running battles between squatters and the police.

The building, completed in 1988, is a huge confection of red brick, marble and glass. A mural illustrating the Normaal Amsterdams Peil is shown on the arcade linking the two parts of the complex. The complex has the largest auditorium in the country, and it is home to the Netherlands' national opera and ballet companies.

⓬ Waterlooplein

Map 5 B2. 9, 14. Ⓜ Waterlooplein. Market: **Open** 9am–5pm Mon–Fri, 8:30am–5pm Sat.

The Waterlooplein dates from 1882, when two canals were filled in to create a market square. The site was originally known as Vlooyenburg, an artificial island built in the 17th century to house Jewish settlers. The original market disappeared during World War II when most of the Jewish residents of Amsterdam were transported by the Nazis. After the war, a popular flea market grew up in its place, and today the northern end of the square still hosts a lively mix of stalls.

⓭ Mozes en Aäronkerk

Waterlooplein 205. **Map** 5 B2. **Tel** 020-6221305. 9, 14. Ⓜ Waterlooplein. **Closed** to the public except for exhibitions.

Designed by Flemish architect T Suys the Elder in 1841, Mozes en Aäronkerk was built on the site of a hidden Catholic church. The later church took its name from the Old Testament figures depicted on the gable stones of the original building. These are now set into the rear wall.

The church was restored in 1990, its twin wooden towers painted to look like sandstone. It is now used for exhibitions, public meetings and concerts.

Eclectic goods on offer at the Waterlooplein market

The central hall in the Grote Synagoge, which opened in 1671

⓮ Joods Historisch Museum

Jonas Daniel Meijerplein 2–4. **Map** 5 B2. **Tel** 020-5310310. 9, 14. Muziektheater. Ⓜ Waterlooplein. **Open** 11am–5pm daily. **Closed** 27 Apr, Jewish New Year, Yom Kippur. on request, incl. for the visually handicapped. **jhm.nl**

This complex of four synagogues, built by Ashkenazi Jews in the 17th and 18th centuries, opened as a museum in 1987. The synagogues were central to Jewish life here, until the devastation of World War II left them empty. Restored in the 1980s, they are connected by internal walkways. Displays of art and religious artifacts depict Jewish culture and the history of Judaism in the Netherlands.

Highlights include the Grote Synagoge, its hall lined with galleries; and the Holy Ark (1791) from Enkhuizen *(see p178)* which dominates the Nieuwe Synagoge and holds two 18th-century silver Torah shields and three velvet mantles. Also not to be missed is the 1734 Haggadah containing the Passover order of service.

The buildings were renovated in 2006, when a basement print room was created, and one of the synagogues turned into a children's museum.

⓯ Portugees-Israëlitische Synagoge

Mr Visserplein 3. **Map** 5 B2. **Tel** 020-6245351. 9, 14. Waterlooplein. **Open** Apr–Oct: 10am–4pm Sun–Fri; Nov–Mar: 10am–4pm Sun–Thu, 10am–2pm Fri. **Closed** Jewish hols, 27 Apr. call 020 5310380 to book **esnoga.nl**

Elias Bouman's design for the Portugees-Israëlitische Synagoge is said to be inspired by the Temple of Solomon in Jerusalem. Built for the wealthy Portuguese Sephardic community of Amsterdam and inaugurated in 1675, the huge brick building has a rectangular ground plan with the Holy Ark in the southeast corner facing towards Jerusalem, and the *tebah* (the podium from which the service is led) at the opposite end.

The wooden, barrel-vaulted ceiling is supported by four Ionic columns. The interior of the synagogue, with its pews made of mahogany, is illuminated by more than 1,000 candles and 72 windows.

Italianate façade of the 17th-century Pintohuis, now a library

⓰ Pintohuis

Sint Antoniesbreestraat 69. **Map** 2 E5. **Tel** 020-6243184. 9, 14. Nieuwmarkt. **Closed** to the public.

Isaac de Pinto, a wealthy Portuguese merchant, bought the Pintohuis in 1651 for the then enormous sum of 30,000 guilders. He had it remodelled over the next decades to a design by Elias Bouman, and it is one of the few private residences in Amsterdam to follow an Italianate style. The exterior design was reworked from 1675 to 1680. Six imposing pilasters break up the severe, cream façade into five recessed sections, and the cornice is topped by a blind balustrade concealing the roof. Inside, the painted ceiling is decorated with birds and cherubs.

In the 1970s, the house was scheduled for demolition because it stood in the way of a newly planned main road. Concerted protest saved the building and, until 2012, it housed a branch of the Amsterdam Public Library..

⓱ Montelbaanstoren

Oude Waal/Oudeschans 2. **Map** 5 B1. 9, 14. Nieuwmarkt. **Closed** to the public.

The lower portion of the Montelbaanstoren was built in 1512 and formed part of Amsterdam's medieval fortifications. It lay just beyond the city wall, protecting the city's wharves on the newly built St Antoniesdijk (now the Oudeschans) from the neighbouring Gelderlanders.

The octagonal structure and open-work timber steeple were both added by Hendrick de Keyser in 1606. His decorative addition bears a close resemblance to the spire of the Oude Kerk, designed by Joost Bilhamer, which was built 40 years earlier *(see pp80–81)*. In 1611, the tower began to list, prompting Amster-dammers to attach ropes to the top and pull it right again.

Sailors from the Dutch East India Company would gather at the Montelbaanstoren before being ferried in small boats down the IJ to the massive East Indies-bound sailing ships, anchored further out in deep water to the north.

The building appears in a number of etchings by Rembrandt, and is still a popular subject for artists. It used to house the offices of the Amsterdam water authority but is currently unoccupied.

One of many stone carvings on the Scheepvaarthuis façade

⓲ Scheepvaarthuis

Prins Hendrikkade 108. **Map** 2 E4. 1, 2, 4, 5, 9, 13, 16, 17, 24. Centraal Station. **Open** Sun. call 020 4182885 to book **hetschip.nl**

Built as an office complex in 1916, the Scheepvaarthuis (shipping house) is regarded as the first true example of Amsterdam School architecture *(see p146–7)*. It was designed by Piet Kramer (1881–1961), Johan van der May (1878–1949) and Michel de Klerk (1884–1923) for a group of shipping companies which no longer wanted to conduct business on the quay.

The imposing triangular building has a prow-like front and is crowned by a statue of Neptune, his wife and four

The medieval Montelbaanstoren, with its decorative timber steeple

female figures representing the four points of the compass. No expense was spared on the construction and internal decoration of the building, and local dock workers came to regard the building as a symbol of capitalism. The doors, stairs, window frames and interior walls are festooned with nautical images, such as sea horses, dolphins and anchors. Beautiful stained-glass skylights are also decorated with images of sailing ships, maps and compasses.

The Scheepvaarthuis is now a luxury hotel, the Grand Hôtel Amrâth, which offers guided tours on Sundays.

⓳ Schreierstoren

Prins Hendrikkade 94–95. **Map** 2 E4. 🚋 1, 2, 4, 5, 9, 11, 13, 16, 17, 24. Ⓜ Centraal Station.

The Schreierstoren (weepers' tower) was a defensive structure forming part of the medieval city walls, dating from 1480. It was one of the few fortifications not to be demolished as the city expanded beyond its medieval boundaries in the 17th century. The distinctive building now houses a basement café that offers tastings of genuine sailors' gin.

Popular legend states that the tower derived its name from the weeping (*schreien* in the original Dutch) of women who came here to wave their men off to sea. It is more likely, however, that the title has a less romantic origin and comes from the tower's position on a sharp (*screye* or *scherpe*), 90-degree bend in the old town walls. The earliest of four wall plaques, dated 1569, adds considerably to the confusion by depicting a weeping woman alongside the inscription *scrayer hovck,* which means sharp corner.

In 1609, Henry Hudson set sail from here in an attempt to discover a new and faster trading route to the East Indies. Instead, he unintentionally "discovered" the river in North America which still bears his name. A bronze plaque, laid in 1927, commemorates his voyage.

The Schreierstoren, part of the original city fortifications

⓴ Zeedijk

Map 2 E4. 🚋 1, 2, 4, 5, 9, 13, 16, 17, 24. Ⓜ Nieuwmarkt, Centraal Station.

Along with the Nieuwendijk and the Haarlemmerdijk, the Zeedijk (sea dyke) formed part of Amsterdam's original fortifications. Built in the early 1300s, some 30 years after Amsterdam had been granted its city charter, these defences took the form of a canal moat with piled-earth ramparts reinforced by wooden palisades. As the city grew in prosperity and its boundaries expanded, canals were filled in and the dykes became obsolete. The paths that ran alongside them became the streets and alleys which bear their names today.

One of the two remaining wooden-fronted houses in the city is at No. 1. It was built in the mid-1500s as a hostel for sailors and is much restored. Opposite is St Olofskapel, built in 1445 and named after the first Christian king of Norway and Denmark. By the 1600s, the Zeedijk had become a slum. The area is on the edge of the city's Red Light District, and in the 1960s and 1970s it became notorious as a centre for drug-dealing and street crime. However, following an extensive clean-up campaign in the 1980s, the Zeedijk is much improved. Architect Fred Greves has built a Chinese Buddhist temple, Fo Kuang Shan.

Plaques on the gables of some of the street's cafés reveal their former use – the red boot at No. 17 indicates that it was once a cobbler's.

The Zeedijk, today a lively street with plenty of restaurants, bars and small shops

NIEUWE ZIJDE

The western side of medieval Amsterdam was known as the Nieuwe Zijde (New Side). Together with the Oude Zijde it formed the heart of the early maritime settlement. Nieuwendijk, today a busy shopping street, was originally one of the earliest sea defences. As Amsterdam grew, it expanded eastwards, leaving large sections of the Nieuwe Zijde, to the west, neglected and in decline. With its many wooden houses, the city was prone to fires and in 1452 much of the area was burned down. During rebuilding, a broad moat, the Singel, was cut, along which warehouses, rich merchants' homes and fine quays sprang up. The interesting Amsterdams Historisch Museum, which is now housed in a splendid former orphanage, has scores of maps and paintings charting the growth of the city from these times to the present day. One room is devoted to the Miracle of Amsterdam, which made the city a place of pilgrimage, and brought commerce to the Nieuwe Zijde. Nearby lies Kalverstraat, Amsterdam's main shopping street, and also the secluded Begijnhof. This pretty courtyard is mostly fringed by narrow 17th-century houses, but it also contains the city's oldest surviving wooden house.

Sights at a Glance

Historic Buildings, Monuments and Bridges

2 *Koninklijk Paleis pp92–3*
4 Nationaal Monument
9 Torensluis
10 Magna Plaza
12 Centraal Station
15 Beurs van Berlage

Streets and Squares

5 Nes
7 Begijnhof

Churches

1 Nieuwe Kerk
11 Lutherse Kerk
13 St Nicolaaskerk

Museums

3 Madame Tussauds Scenerama
6 *Amsterdam Museum pp96–7*
8 Allard Pierson Museum
14 Museum Ons' Lieve Heer op Solder

◀ Visitors at the Amsterdam Museum on Kalverstraat

For map symbols *see back flap*

Street-by-Street: Nieuwe Zijde

Although much of the medieval Nieuwe Zijde has disappeared, the area is still rich in buildings that relate to the city's past. The Dam, dominated by the Koninklijk Paleis and Nieuwe Kerk, provides examples of architecture from the 15th to the 20th centuries. Around Kalverstraat, narrow streets and alleys follow the course of some of the earliest dykes and footpaths. Here, most of the traditional gabled houses have been turned into bustling shops and cafés. The messy Rokin, and nearby Damrak, are destined to become the 'red carpet' entry to the city, once the new Noord-Zuidlijn metro is completed.

Kalverstraat
This busy tourist shopping area took its name from the livestock market which was regularly held here during the 15th century.

6 ★ Amsterdam Museum
Wall plaques and maps showing the walled medieval city are on display in this converted orphanage that dates from the 16th century.

7 ★ Begijnhof
Two churches and one of the few remaining wooden houses in the city nestle in this secluded, tree-filled courtyard.

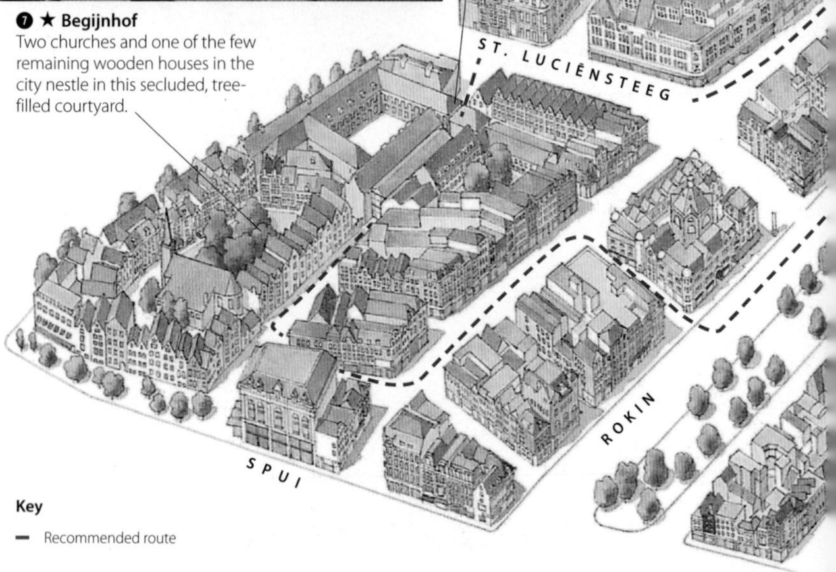

Key

– Recommended route

For hotels and restaurants in this region see pp396–397 and pp406–409

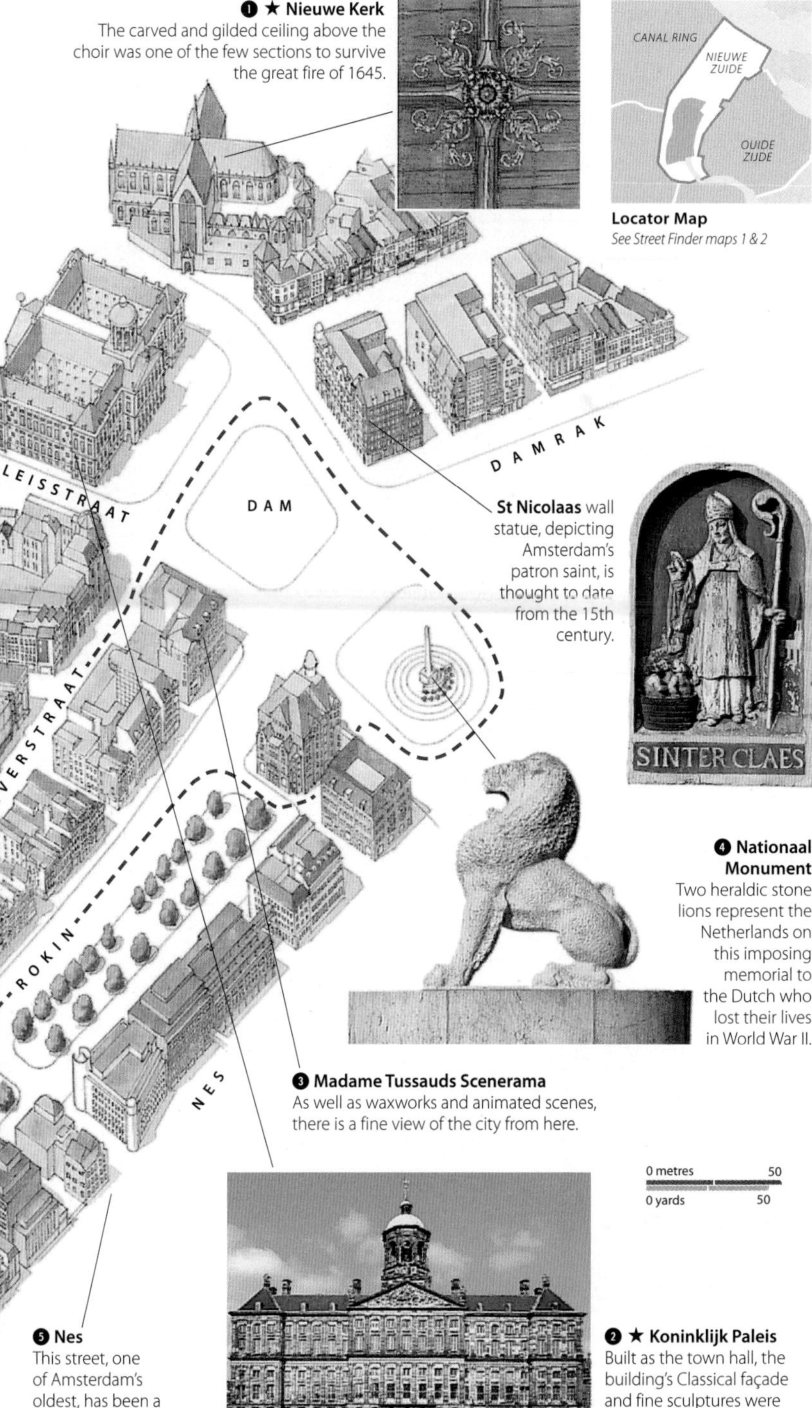

1 ★ Nieuwe Kerk
The carved and gilded ceiling above the choir was one of the few sections to survive the great fire of 1645.

Locator Map
See Street Finder maps 1 & 2

St Nicolaas wall statue, depicting Amsterdam's patron saint, is thought to date from the 15th century.

4 Nationaal Monument
Two heraldic stone lions represent the Netherlands on this imposing memorial to the Dutch who lost their lives in World War II.

3 Madame Tussauds Scenerama
As well as waxworks and animated scenes, there is a fine view of the city from here.

5 Nes
This street, one of Amsterdam's oldest, has been a centre for theatre for over 150 years

2 ★ Koninklijk Paleis
Built as the town hall, the building's Classical façade and fine sculptures were intended to glorify the city and its government.

❶ Nieuwe Kerk

Dam. **Map** 1 C4. **Tel** 020-6386909. 1, 2, 4, 5, 9, 13, 14, 16, 17, 24. **Open** during exhibitions only *(phone to check)*. **Closed** 27 Apr. **nieuwekerk.nl**

Dating from the late 14th century, Amsterdam's second parish church was built as the population outgrew the Oude Kerk *(see pp80–81)*. During its turbulent history, the church has been destroyed several times by fire, rebuilt and then stripped of its finery after the Alteration. It reached its present size in the 1650s.

The pulpit, not the altar, is the focal point of the interior, reflecting the Protestant belief that the sermon is central to worship. The carved central pulpit, unusually flamboyant for a Dutch Protestant church, was finished in 1664 and took Albert Vinckenbrink 15 years to carve. Above the transept crossing, grimacing gilded cherubs struggle to support the corners of the wooden barrel vault. Magnificent three-tiered brass candelabra were hung from the ceilings of the nave and transepts during restoration work following the fire of 1645. The colourful arched window in the south transept was designed by Otto Mengelberg in 1898. It depicts Queen Wilhelmina surrounded by courtiers at her coronation. In the apse is Rombout Verhulst's memorial to Admiral De Ruyter (1607–76), who died at sea in battle against the French.

Stained-glass window at the Nieuwe Kerk in Amsterdam

❷ Koninklijk Paleis

See pp88–9.

Scene by Vermeer, in Madame Tussauds Scenerama

❸ Madame Tussauds Scenerama

Gebouw Peek & Cloppenburg, Dam 20. **Map** 2 D5. **Tel** 020-5221010. 4, 9, 14, 16, 24. **Open** 10am–6:30pm daily (to 8:30pm Jul & Aug). **Closed** 27 Apr. **madametussauds.com**

Madame Tussauds offers an audio-visual tour of Amsterdam's history, as well as projected future developments. Some of the displays, such as the animated 5-m (16-ft) figure of "Amsterdam Man", are bizarre, but the wax models of 17th-century people give an insight into life in the city's Golden Age. Current celebrities and pop stars also feature.

❹ Nationaal Monument

Dam. **Map** 2 D5. 4, 9, 14, 16, 24.

Sculpted by John Raedecker and designed by architect JJP Oud, the 22-m (70-ft) obelisk in the Dam commemorates Dutch World War II casualties. It was unveiled in 1956 and is fronted by two lions, heraldic symbols of the Netherlands. Embedded in the wall behind are urns containing earth from all the Dutch provinces as well as from the former Dutch colonies of Indonesia, the Antilles and Suriname.

❺ Nes

Map 2 D5. 4, 9, 14, 16, 24.

This quiet, narrow street is home to several theatres and good restaurants. In 1614, Amsterdam's first pawnshop opened at Nes No. 57. A wall plaque marks the site, and pawned goods continue to clutter the shop window. At night, Nes can prove to be dangerous for the unguarded visitor.

❻ Amsterdam Museum

See pp96–7.

❼ Begijnhof

Spui (but public entrance at Gedempte Begijnensloot).
Map 1 C5. 1, 2, 5, 9, 14, 16, 24.
Open 9am–5pm daily.

The Begijnhof was originally built in 1346 as a sanctuary for the Begijntjes, a lay Catholic sisterhood who lived like nuns, although they took no monastic vows. In return for lodgings, these women undertook to educate the poor and look after the sick. Nothing survives of the earliest dwellings, but the Begijnhof, cut off from traffic noise, retains a sanctified atmosphere. Among the houses that overlook its wellkept green is the city's oldest surviving house at No. 34. On the adjoining wall there is a fascinating collection of wall plaques taken from the houses. In keeping with the Begijntjes' religious outlook, the plaques have a biblical theme.

The southern fringe of the square is dominated by the Engelse Kerk (English Church), dating from the 15th century. Directly west stands the Begijnhof Chapel, a clandestine church in which the Begijntjes and other Catholics worshipped in secret until religious tolerance was restored in 1795. Stained-glass windows and paintings depict scenes of the Miracle of Amsterdam. Public tours are not allowed. Also, visitors are requested to be quiet and not visit the Begijnhof in large groups.

Plaque on the Engelse Kerk

Begijnhof Houses
These are still occupied by single women.

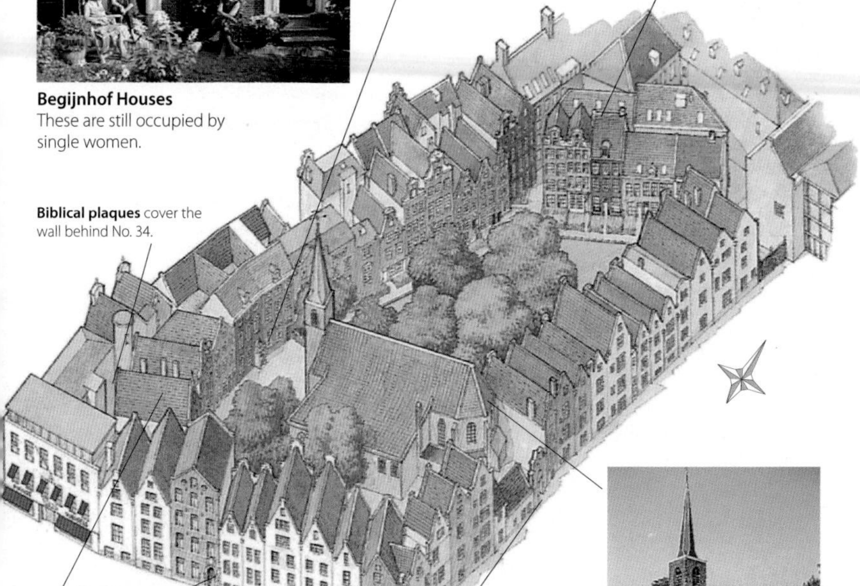

The Begijnhof Chapel, a clandestine church (Nos. 29–30), was completed in 1680. It contains many reminders of Amsterdam's Catholic past.

No. 19 has a plaque depicting the exodus of the Jews from Egypt.

Biblical plaques cover the wall behind No. 34.

Spui entrance

Main entrance from Gedempte Begijnensloot

Houten House
No. 34 is Amsterdam's oldest house, dating from around 1420. It is one of the city's two wooden-fronted houses; timber houses were banned in 1521 after a series of catastrophic fires. Most of the Begijnhof houses were built after the 16th century.

Engelse Kerk
This church was built around 1419 for the Begijntjes. It was confiscated after the Alteration and rented to a group of English and Scottish Presbyterians in 1607. The Pilgrim Fathers may have worshipped here.

❷ Koninklijk Paleis

Formerly the town hall, the Koninklijk Paleis (Royal Palace) is still regularly used by the Dutch royal family on official occasions. Construction of the sandstone building began in 1648, at the end of the 80 Years War *(see p53)*. The Neo-Classical design of Jacob van Campen (1595–1657) reflected Amsterdam's new-found self-confidence after the victory against the Spanish. When not in use by members of the Royal House, the Paleis is open to the public.

★ Burgerzaal
The Burgerzaal (citizens' hall) has an inlaid marble floor depicting the two hemispheres (western and eastern).

★ Sculptures
The palace is decorated with a large number of sculptures of mainly allegorical figures.

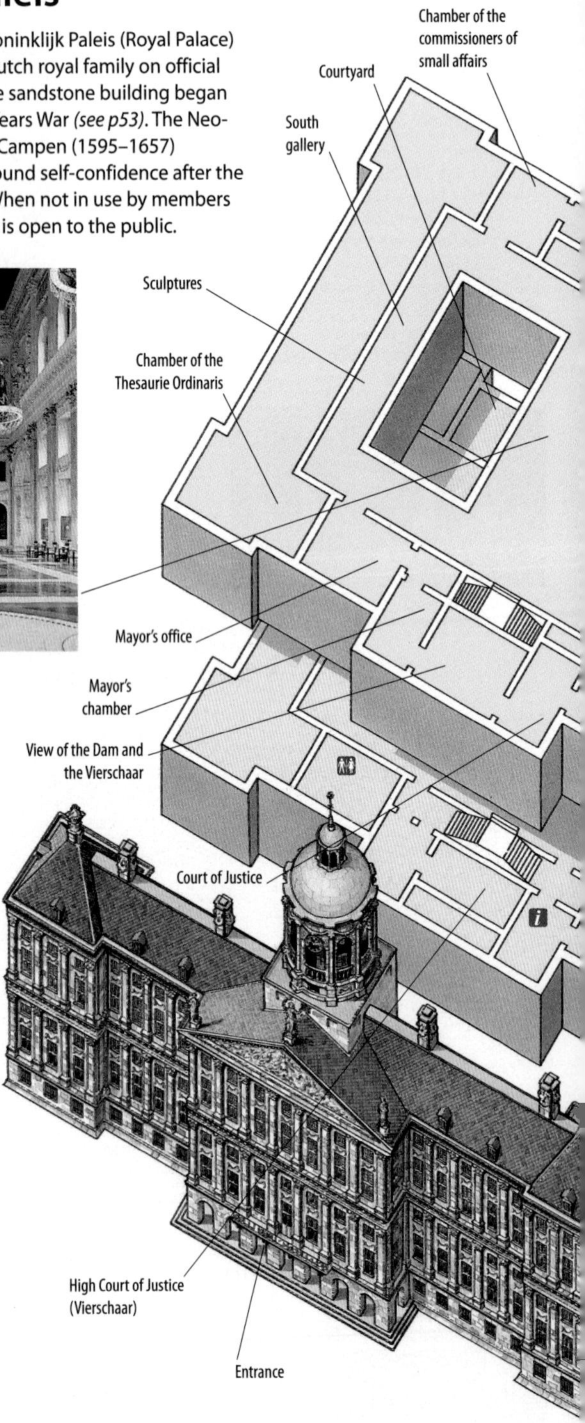

Key to Floorplan

- Ground floor
- First floor

Chamber of the commissioners of small affairs

Courtyard

South gallery

Sculptures

Chamber of the Thesaurie Ordinaris

Mayor's office

Mayor's chamber

View of the Dam and the Vierschaar

Court of Justice

High Court of Justice (Vierschaar)

Entrance

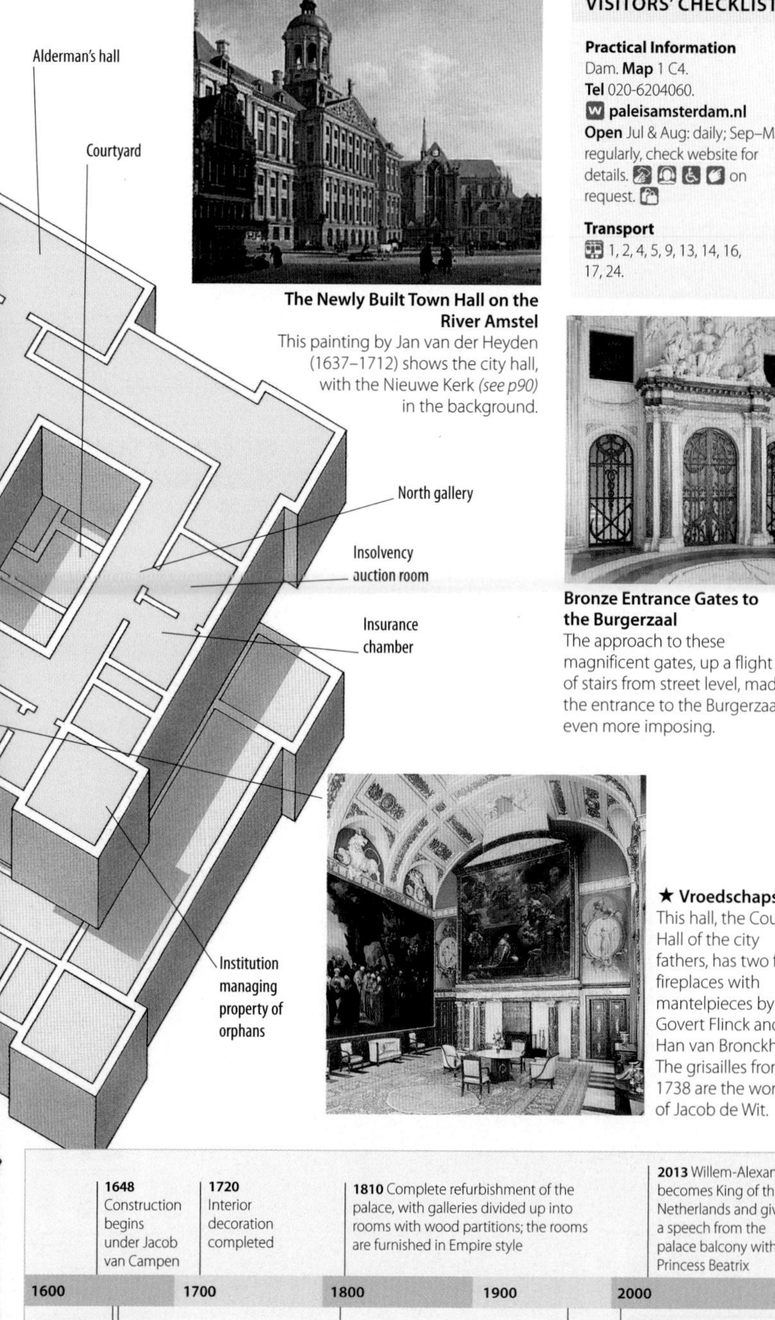

The Newly Built Town Hall on the River Amstel
This painting by Jan van der Heyden (1637–1712) shows the city hall, with the Nieuwe Kerk *(see p90)* in the background.

Bronze Entrance Gates to the Burgerzaal
The approach to these magnificent gates, up a flight of stairs from street level, made the entrance to the Burgerzaal even more imposing.

★ Vroedschapszaal
This hall, the Council Hall of the city fathers, has two fine fireplaces with mantelpieces by Govert Flinck and Han van Bronckhorst. The grisailles from 1738 are the work of Jacob de Wit.

VISITORS' CHECKLIST

Practical Information
Dam. **Map** 1 C4.
Tel 020-6204060.
paleisamsterdam.nl
Open Jul & Aug: daily; Sep–May: regularly, check website for details. on request.

Transport
1, 2, 4, 5, 9, 13, 14, 16, 17, 24.

1600 – **1700** – **1800** – **1900** – **2000**

1648 Construction begins under Jacob van Campen

1655 Ceremonial inauguration of the building

1665 Building completed

1720 Interior decoration completed

1808 Louis Napoleon converts the town hall into a palace

1810 Complete refurbishment of the palace, with galleries divided up into rooms with wood partitions; the rooms are furnished in Empire style

1960 Thorough restoration work throughout the 20th century undoes the building work of Louis Napoleon

2002 Crown Prince Willem-Alexander kisses his bride, Maxima, on the palace balcony

2013 Willem-Alexander becomes King of the Netherlands and gives a speech from the palace balcony with Princess Beatrix

❽ Allard Pierson Museum

Oude Turfmarkt 127. **Map** 5 A2. **Tel** 020-5252556. 4, 9, 14, 16, 24. **Open** 10am–5pm Tue–Fri, 1–5pm Sat, Sun & public hols. **Closed** 1 Jan, Easter Sun, 27 Apr, Whitsun, 25 Dec.
allardpiersonmuseum.nl

Amsterdam's only specialist archaeological collection is named after Allard Pierson (1831–96), a humanist and scholar. The collection was moved into this handsome Neo-Classical building in 1976.

The museum contains Cypriot, Greek, Egyptian, Roman, Etruscan and Coptic artifacts.

❾ Torensluis

Singel, between Torensteeg and Oude Leliestraat. **Map** 1 C4. 1, 2, 5, 13, 14, 17.

The Torensluis is one of the widest bridges in the city. Built on the site of a 17th-century sluice gate, it took its name from a tower that stood here until demolished in 1829. Its outline is marked in the pavement. A lock-up jail was built in its foundations.

In summer, café tables on the bridge offer pleasant views down the Singel.

Allard Pierson Museum's Neo-Classical façade of Bremer and Bentheimer stone

❿ Magna Plaza

Nieuwezijds Voorburgwal 182. **Map** 1 C4. **Tel** 020-6269199. 1, 2, 5, 13, 14, 17. **Open** noon–7pm Sun, 11am–7pm Mon, 10am–7pm Tue–Sat. **Closed** 27 Apr, 25 Dec, 1 Jan. See Shopping: p148.
magnaplaza.nl

A post office building has been sited here since 1748. The present building was completed in 1899; CP Peters, the architect, was ridiculed for the extravagance of its Neo-Gothic design. Redeveloped but well preserved, in 1990 it opened as the city's first shopping mall.

⓫ Ronde Lutherse Kerk

Kattengat 2. **Map** 2 D3. **Tel** 020-6212223. 1, 2, 5, 13, 17.

This church, also known as Nieuwe Lutherse Kerk, was designed by Adriaan Dortsman (1625–82) and opened in 1671. It is the first Dutch Reformed church to feature a circular ground plan and two upper galleries, giving the whole congregation a clear view of the pulpit.

In 1882 a fire destroyed everything but the exterior walls. When the interior and entrance were rebuilt in 1883, they were made more square and more ornate. A vaulted copper dome replaced the earlier ribbed version. Falling attendance led to the closure of the church in 1935. The building is now used by Renaissance Amsterdam Hotel as a business centre. Concerts are sometimes held here.

⓬ Centraal Station

Stationsplein. **Map** 2 E3. **Tel** 0900-9292. 1, 2, 4, 5, 9, 13, 16, 17, 24. M Centraal Station. **Open** daily.

When the Centraal Station opened in 1889, it replaced the old harbour as the symbolic focal point of the city and effectively curtained Amsterdam off from the sea. The Neo-Gothic red-brick railway terminus was designed by PJH Cuypers and AL van Gendt. Three artificial islands were created, 8,600 wooden piles supporting the structure. The twin towers and central section have architectural echoes of a triumphal arch. The imposing

An outdoor café on the Torensluis bridge overlooking the Singel canal

façade's decorations show allegories of maritime trade, a tribute to the city's past. Although currently undergoing a major renovation until 2015, it still handles 250,000 train travellers daily.

Neo-Renaissance façade of the Sint-Nicolaaskerk

⓭ Sint-Nicolaaskerk

Prins Hendrikkade 73. **Map** 2 E4. **Tel** 020-6248749. 1, 2, 4, 5, 9, 13, 16, 17, 24. Ⓜ Centraal Station. **Open** noon–3pm Mon & Sat, 11am–4pm Tue–Fri. 12:30pm Mon–Sat, 10:30am & 1pm (Spanish) Sun. **W nicolaasparochie.nl**

Sint Nicolaas was the patron saint of seafarers, and so was an important icon in Amsterdam. Many Dutch churches are named after him, and the Netherlands' principal day for the giving of presents, 5 December, is known as Sinterklaasavond *(see p35)*.

Completed in 1887, Sint-Nicolaaskerk was designed by AC Bleys (1842–1912). It replaced some clandestine Catholic churches set up in the city when Amsterdam was officially Protestant.

The exterior is forbidding, its twin towers dominating the skyline. The monumental interior has squared pillars and coffered ceiling arches.

Ons' Lieve Heer op Solder, which dates back to the 17th century

⓮ Museum Ons' Lieve Heer op Solder

Oudezijds Voorburgwal 40. **Map** 2 E4. **Tel** 020-6246604. 4, 9, 16, 24. **Open** 10am–5pm Mon–Sat, 1–5pm Sun & public hols. **Closed** 1 Jan, 27 Apr.

Tucked away on the edge of the Red Light District is a restored 17th-century canal house, with two smaller houses to the rear. The combined upper storeys conceal a secret Catholic church, known as Ons' Lieve Heer op Solder (Our Dear Lord in the Attic), built in 1663. Following the Alteration, when Amsterdam officially became Protestant, many such hidden churches were built in the city.

The lower floors of the building became a museum in 1888 and today contain elegantly refurbished and decorated rooms, as well as a fine collection of church silver, religious artifacts and paintings.

Work due to be completed in 2015 will link the church to the house opposite, providing much-needed space for more exhibitions, a shop and a café. The museum will remain open during this work.

⓯ Beurs van Berlage

Damrak 243. **Map** 2 D4. **Tel** (box office) 020-5304141. 4, 9, 16, 24. **Open** only during exhibitions. **Closed** 1 Jan. **W beursvanberlage.nl**

The clean, functional appearance of Hendrik Berlage's 1903 stock exchange marked a departure from late 19th-century revivalist architecture. Many of its design features were adopted by the Amsterdam School. An impressive frieze shows the evolution of man from Adam to stockbroker. The building now serves as a venue for exhibitions, concerts and shows.

Decorative brickwork on the façade of the Beurs van Berlage

❻ Amsterdam Museum

The convent of St Lucien was turned into a civic orphanage two years after the Alteration of 1578. The original red brick convent has been enlarged over the years; new wings were added in the 17th century by Hendrick de Keyser and Jacob van Campen. The present building is largely as it was in the 18th century. Since 1975 the complex has housed the city's historical museum, charting Amsterdam's development.

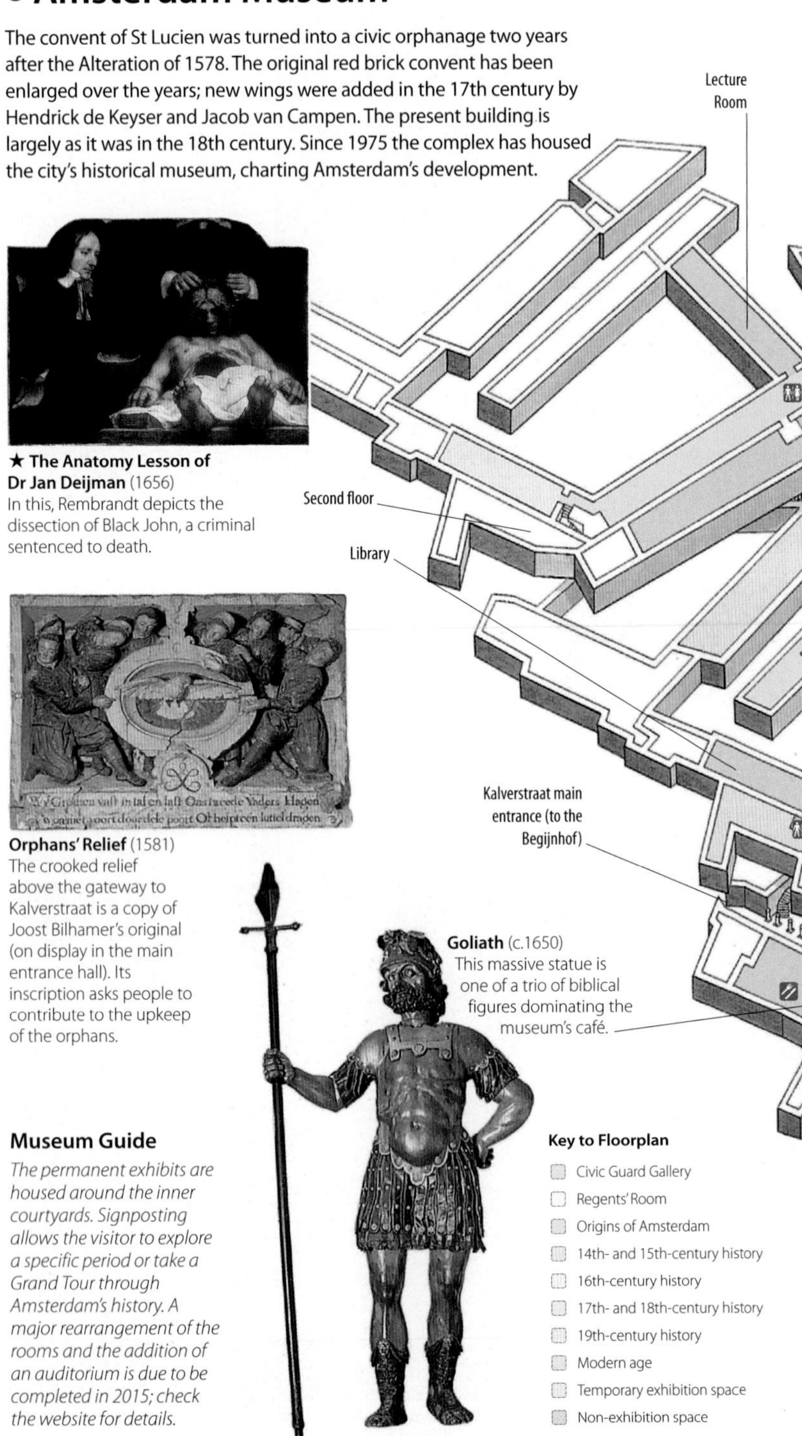

★ The Anatomy Lesson of Dr Jan Deijman (1656)
In this, Rembrandt depicts the dissection of Black John, a criminal sentenced to death.

Orphans' Relief (1581)
The crooked relief above the gateway to Kalverstraat is a copy of Joost Bilhamer's original (on display in the main entrance hall). Its inscription asks people to contribute to the upkeep of the orphans.

Goliath (c.1650)
This massive statue is one of a trio of biblical figures dominating the museum's café.

Museum Guide

The permanent exhibits are housed around the inner courtyards. Signposting allows the visitor to explore a specific period or take a Grand Tour through Amsterdam's history. A major rearrangement of the rooms and the addition of an auditorium is due to be completed in 2015; check the website for details.

Key to Floorplan

- Civic Guard Gallery
- Regents' Room
- Origins of Amsterdam
- 14th- and 15th-century history
- 16th-century history
- 17th- and 18th-century history
- 19th-century history
- Modern age
- Temporary exhibition space
- Non-exhibition space

For hotels and restaurants in this region see pp396–397 and pp406–409

★ The Flower Market and Town Hall
Gerrit Berckheijde (1638–98) painted this scene (1673) showing the site of Amsterdam's original flower market on the Nieuwezijds Voorburgwal, which was filled in at the end of the 19th century. In the background is the Koninklijk Paleis.

VISITORS' CHECKLIST

Practical Information
Kalverstraat 92, NZ Voorburgwal 357, St-Luciënsteeg 27
Map 1 C5.
Tel 020-5231822.
W ahm.nl
Open 10am–5pm Mon–Fri, 11am–5pm Sat & Sun.
Closed 1 Jan, 27 Apr, 25 Dec.

Transport
1, 2, 4, 5, 9, 13, 14, 16, 17, 24.

Keys to the Town of Amsterdam (1810)
These two silver keys were presented to Napoleon upon his entry into Amsterdam.

First floor

★ Civic Guard Gallery
This painting (1557) shows 17 soldiers of the Civic Guard who belonged to *Rot F* (F squad).

Ground floor

17th-century red brick façade

Entrance in girls' courtyard

Entrance on Nieuwezijds Voorburgwal

St Luciensteeg entrance

Hunting Day (1926)
Johan Braakensiek's illustration shows the lively carnival atmosphere in Zeedijk during the celebrations for this day, which took place every Thursday throughout August.

CANAL RING

In the early 1600s, construction of the *Grachtengordel* (canal ring) began and the marshy area beyond these fashionable canals, later called Jordaan, was laid out for workers whose industries were prohibited in the centre. Immigrants fleeing religious persecution also settled here. Historically a poor area, it now has a bohemian air. As the major canals were extended, the merchant classes bought land along the Herengracht, Keizersgracht and Prinsengracht to escape the city's squalor. In the 1660s, the richest built houses on a stretch known today as the Golden Bend. The canal ring was also extended east to the Amstel. Houses here, like the Van Loon, convey a sense of life in the Golden Age. In 2010, the canal ring was declared a UNESCO World Heritage Site.

Sights at a Glance

Historic Buildings and Monuments

4 Huis met de Hoofden
6 Haarlemmerpoort
10 American Hotel
15 Stadsarchief Amsterdam
18 Magere Brug
21 Munttoren

Museums

1 *Anne Frank Huis* *see pp112–13*
2 Homomonument
13 Bijbels Museum
17 Museum Willet-Holthuysen
19 Museum Van Loon

Churches

3 Westerkerk
5 Noorderkerk
12 De Krijtberg

Markets

5 Noordermarkt
14 Looier Kunst en Antiekcentrum

Theatres

11 Stadsschouwburg
20 Tuschinski Theater

Canals and Squares

7 Brouwersgracht
8 Western Islands
9 Leidseplein
16 Rembrandtplein

See also Street Finder maps 1, 2, 4 & 5

◀ View along one of the city's canals

For map symbols *see back flap*

A Guide to Canal House Architecture

Amsterdam has been called a city of "well-mannered" architecture because its charms lie in intimate details rather than in grand effects. From the 15th century on, planning laws, plot sizes and the instability of the topsoil dictated that façades were largely uniform in size and built of lightweight brick or sandstone, with large windows to reduce the weight. Canal house owners stamped their own individuality on the buildings, mainly through the use of decorative gables and cornices, ornate doorcases and varying window shapes.

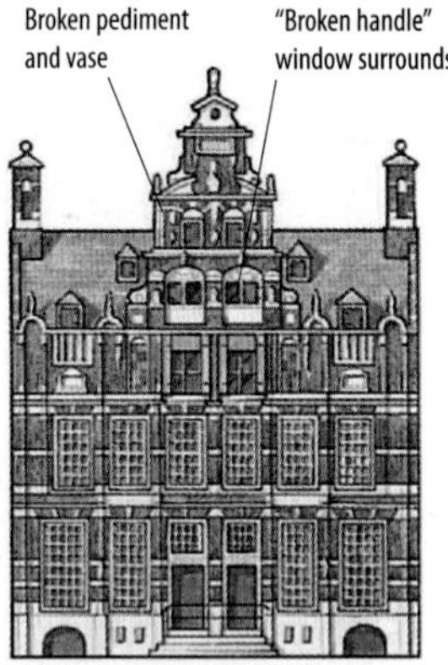

Bartolotti House (1617)
The contrasting brick and stone, flamboyant step gable, with its marble obelisk and scrolls, is typical of the Dutch Renaissance style of Hen-drick de Keyser *(see p114)*.

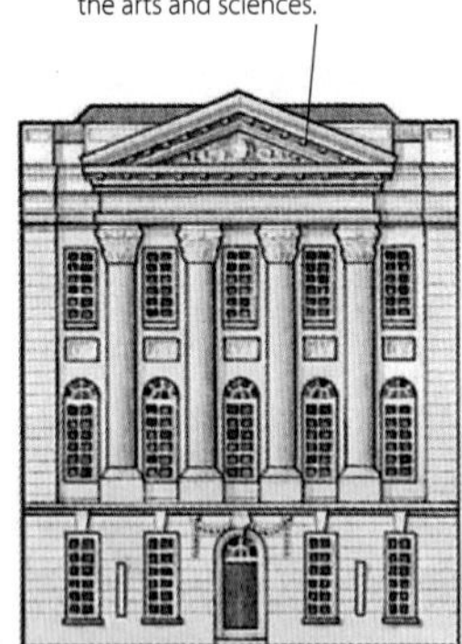

Felix Meritis Building (1778)
The Corinthian columns and triangular pediment are influenced by Classical architecture. This marks the building by Jacob Otten Husly as Dutch Classical in style.

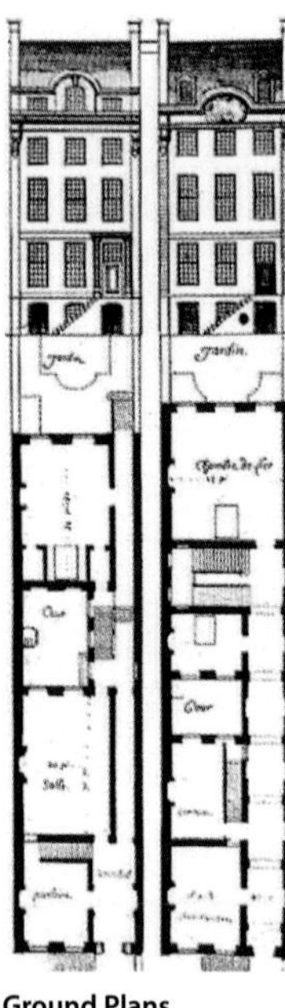

Ground Plans
Taxes were levied according to width of façade, so canal houses were often long and narrow, with an *achterhuis* (back annexe) used for offices and storage.

Cornices

Decorative top mouldings, called cornices, became popular from 1690 onwards when the fashion for gables declined. By the 19th century, they had become unadorned.

Louis XV-style with rococo balustrade (1739)

19th-century cornice with mansard roof

19th-century dentil (tooth-shaped) cornice

Gables

The term "gable" refers to the front apex of a roof. It disguised the steepness of the roof under which goods were stored. In time, gables became decorated with scrolls, crests, and even with coats of arms.

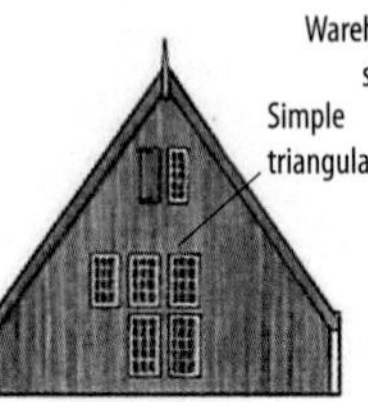

No. 34 Begijnhof (c.1420) is one of the few remaining timber houses.

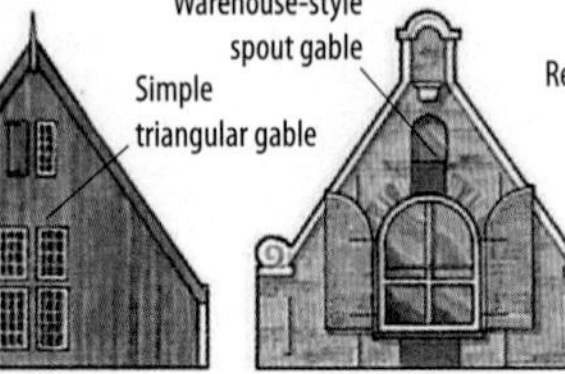

The style of gable on No. 213 Leliegracht (c.1620) was used for warehouses.

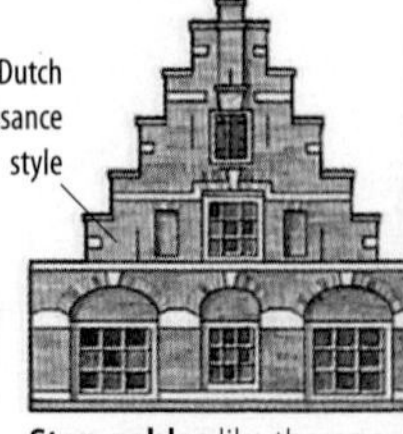

Step gables like the one on No. 2 Brouwervvsgracht were in vogue between 1600–65.

Leaning Façades
Canal houses were often built with a deliberate tilt, allowing goods to be winched up to the attic without crashing against the windows. A law dating from 1565 restricted this lean to 1:25, to limit the risk of buildings collapsing into the streets.

Golden Bend

The stretch of the Herengracht between Leidenstraat and Vijzelstraat was first called the Golden Bend in the 17th century, because of the great wealth of the ship-builders, merchants and politicians who originally lived here. The majority of the buildings along this stretch are faced with imported sandstone, which was more expensive than brick. An excellent example is house No. 412, which was designed by Philips Vingboons in 1664. He was also responsible for the design of the Witte Huis at Herengracht No. 168 as well as Bijbels Museum at Herengracht 366. Building continued into the 18th century, with the Louis XIV style predominating. The house at No. 475, with its ornate window decoration, is typical of this trend. Built in 1730, it is often called the jewel of canal houses. Two sculpted female figures over the front door adorn its monumental sandstone façade.

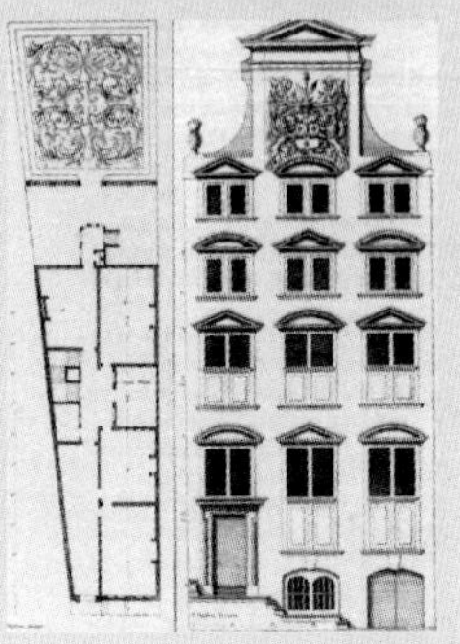

Ground plan and façade of the building at Herengracht 168

Dutch *Hofjes*
Almshouses *(hofjes)* were built throughout the Netherlands by rich benefactors in the 17th and 18th centuries. By providing accommodation for the elderly and infirm, the *hofjes* marked the beginning of the Dutch welfare system.

Sign of a sailors' hostel

Symbol of a dairy producer

Noah's Ark – a refuge for the poor

Wall Plaques

Carved and painted stones were used to identify houses before street numbering was introduced in the 19th century. Many reflect the owner's occupation.

No. 419 Singel has a neck gable, a common feature from 1640 to around 1840.

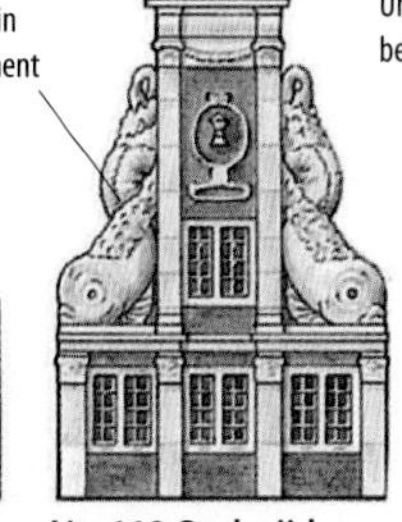

No. 119 Oudezijds Voorburgwal has an ornate 17th-century neck gable.

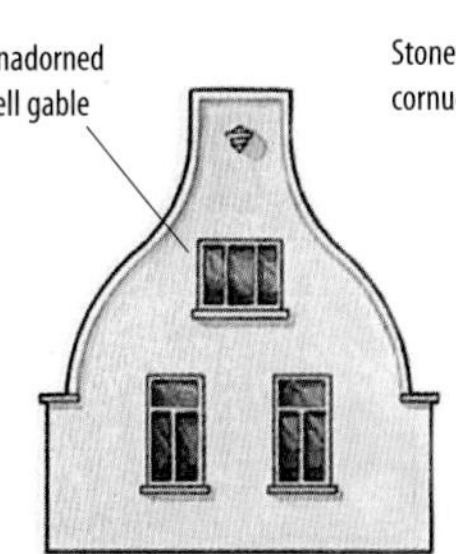

No. 57 Leliegracht has a plain bell gable, popular from the late 17th century.

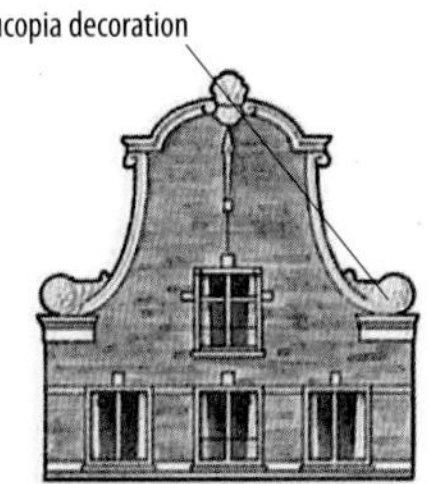

No. 298 Oudezijds Voorburgwal has a bell gable dating from the 18th century.

Dam Square to Herengracht 487

The walk along Amsterdam's finest canals begins in Dam square *(see pp92–3)*. Following the grey dots on the map, leave the square past the Koninklijk Paleis *(see pp88–9)*, cross Nieuwezijds Voorburgwal and Spuistraat down Paleisstraat, and turn left along the left bank of Singel, marked by purple dots. Further directions are incorporated into the route below.

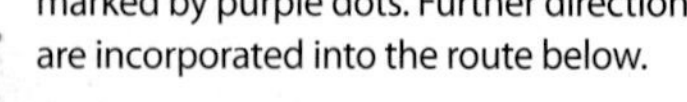

Locator Map

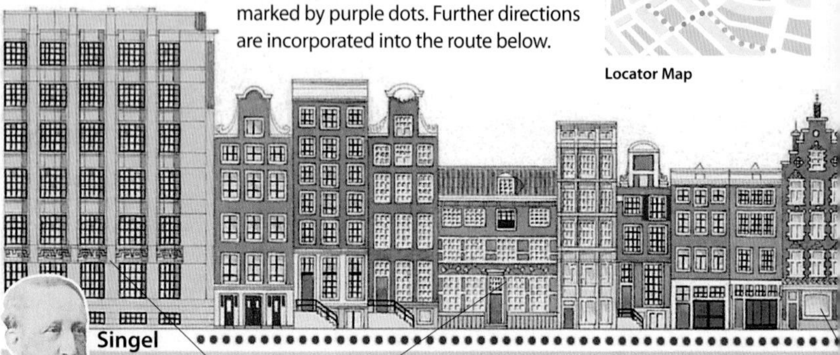

Singel

No. 239 Singel AL Van Gendt designed this massive stone office block for trader Julius Carle Bunge. Known as the Bungehuis, it was completed in 1934.

The double-fronted 17th-century canal house at No. 265 Singel has been rebuilt several times since it was first constructed.

The step gable at No. 279 Sin dates from the 19th century – most along this canal were bu between 1600–65.

The three neck gables on Nos. 353–7 Keizersgracht date from the early 18th century.

Huidenstraat

No. 345a Keizersgracht is a narrow house sharing a cornice with its neighbour.

In 1708, No. 333 Keizersgracht was rebuilt for tax collector Jacob de Wilde. It has been converted into apartments.

The Sower at Arles (1888)
In March 1878, Vincent van Gogh *(see pp130–31)* visited his uncle, who ran a bookshop and art dealership at No. 453 Keizersgracht.

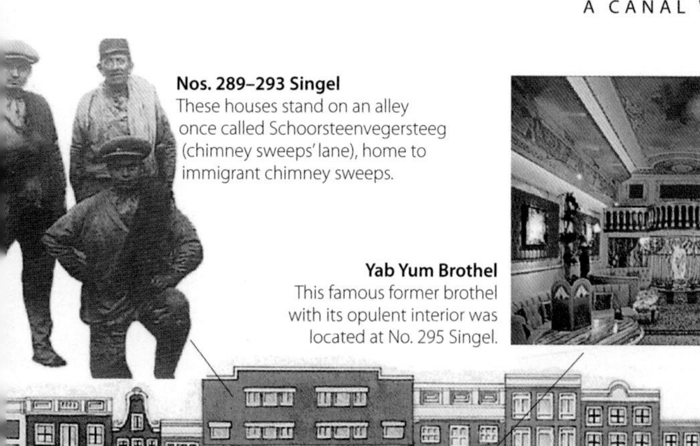

Nos. 289–293 Singel
These houses stand on an alley once called Schoorsteenvegersteeg (chimney sweeps' lane), home to immigrant chimney sweeps.

Yab Yum Brothel
This famous former brothel with its opulent interior was located at No. 295 Singel.

No. 365 Keizersgracht
The doorway was taken from an almshouse on Oudezijds Voorburgwal in the 19th century.

Jacob de Wit
The artist *(see p119)* bought Nos. 383 and 385 Keizersgracht, living in No. 385 until his death in 1754.

34–6 Leidsestraat
...uses the county's first ...ercrombie and Fitch ...thing shop.

Gerrit Rietveld
Rietveld designed the glass cupola on Abercrombie and Fitch, and a line of plain, inexpensive furniture for the store.

De Vergulde Ster
(gilded star), at No. 387 Keizersgracht, was built in 1668 by the municipal stone-masons' yard. It has an elongated neck gable *(see pp100–101)* and narrow windows.

Directions to Herengracht

Turn left on to Leidsestraat, and walk to Koningsplein, then take the left bank of the Herengracht eastwards towards Thorbeckeplein.

Herengracht

Tsar Peter *(see p105)* stayed at No. 527 Herengracht, home of the Russian ambassador, after a night of drunken revelry at No. 317 Keizersgracht in 1716.

Herengracht (1790)
A delicate watercolour by J Prins shows the "gentlemen's canal" from Koningsplein.

The asymmetrical building at Nos. 533–7 Herengracht was built in 1910 on the site of four former houses. From 1968–88 it was the Registry of Births, Marriages and Deaths.

The façades of Nos. 37 and 39 Reguliersgracht lean towards the water, showing the danger caused by subsidence when building on marshland.

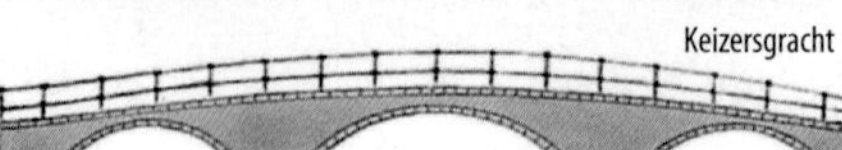

Keizersgracht

Reguliersgracht Brid
Seven arched stone bridges cross the cana which was originally designed to be a street

os. 1059 and 1061 Prinsengracht
ave tiny basement entrances, rare amid e splendour of the Canal Ring, where e height of the steps was considered 1 indication of wealth.

The sober spout-gabled building at No. 1075 Prinsengracht was built as a warehouse in 1690.

My Domestic Companions
Society portraitist Thérèse van Duyl Schwartze painted this picture in 1916. She owned Nos. 1087, 1089 and 1091 Prinsengracht, a handsome row of houses where she lived with her extended family.

Keizersgracht
This photograph of the "emperor's canal" is taken at dusk, from the corner of Leidsegracht. The Westerkerk *(see p110)* is in the distance.

Behind the 18th-century façade at No. 319 Singel is a second-hand bookshop, which is well worth browsing through.

Directions To Keizersgracht

At Raamsteeg, cross the bridge, take the Oude Spiegelstraat, cross Herengracht and walk along Wolvenstraat to the left bank of Keizersgracht.

Keizersgracht

No. 399 Keizersgracht dates from 1665, but the façade was rebuilt in the 18th century. Its *achterhuis (see p96)* has been perfectly preserved.

No. 409 Keizersgracht Built in 1671 on a triangular piece of land, this house contains a highly decorated wooden ceiling.

The wall plaque on No. 401 Keizersgracht shows a bird's-eye view of the port of Marseilles.

The plain, spout-gabled building *(see pp100–101)* at No. 403 Keizersgracht was originally a warehouse, a rarity in this predominantly residential area.

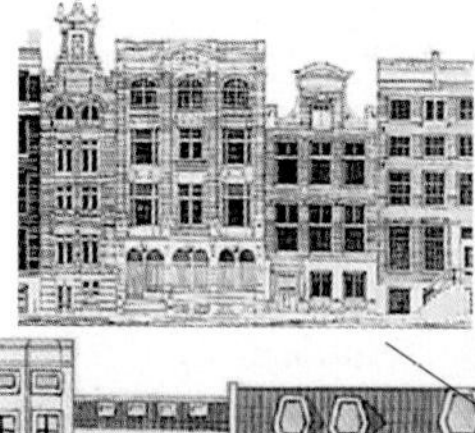

No. 469 Herengracht
The modern office block by KL Sijmons replaced the original 18th-century houses in 1971.

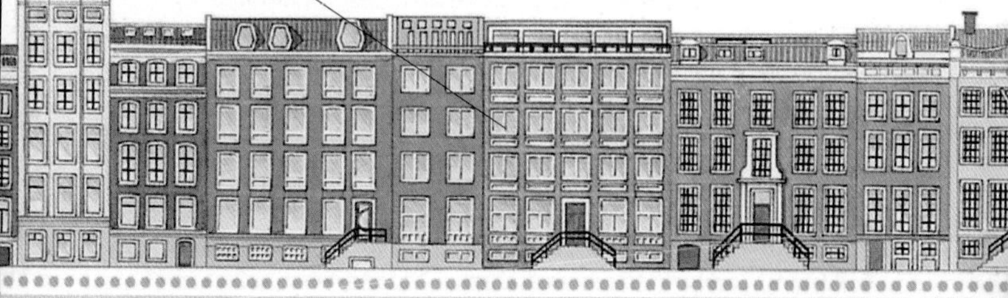

Jan Six II
The façade of No. 495 Herengracht was rebuilt and a balcony added by Jean Coulon in 1739 for burgomaster and artexpert Jan Six.

Riots in 1696
No. 507 Herengracht was the home of mayor Jacob Boreel. His house was looted in retaliation for the burial tax he introduced into the city.

Three houses boasting typical neck gables, at Nos. 17, 19 and 21 Reguliersgracht, are now much sought after as prestigious addresses.

The Nieuwe Amsterdammer
A weekly magazine aimed at Amsterdam's Bolshevik intelligentsia was published at No. 19 Reguliersgracht from 1914–20.

The spout-gabled *(see pp100–101)* 16th-century warehouses at Nos. 11 and 13 Reguliersgracht are called the Sun and the Moon.

Houseboats on Prinsengracht
All registered houseboats have postal addresses and are connected to the electricity mains.

Café Marcella, at No. 1047a Prinsengracht, is a typical local bar which has seating outside in summer.

The unusual office block at No. 313 Keizersgracht was built in 1914 by CN van Goor.

No. 319 Keizersgracht was built by the architect Philips Vingboons (1608–78) in 1639. It has a rare, highly decorated façade covered with scrolls, vases and garlands.

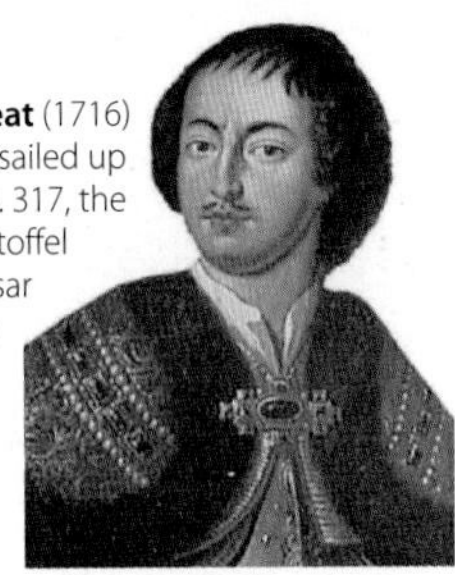

Peter the Great (1716) The Russian tsar sailed up Keizersgracht to No. 317, the home of his friend Christoffel Brants. Legend says the tsar got drunk and kept the mayor waiting while at a civic reception.

Leidsegracht This canal marked the end of Daniel Stalpaert's city expansion plan of 1664. It has a mixture of fine 17th- and 18th-century canal houses.

The Louis XIV-style house at No. 323 Keizersgracht was built in 1728. It has a raised cornice embellished with two hoisting beams, one functional and the other to provide symmetry.

No. 475 Herengracht Art patron Jan Gilde-mester bought this house in 1792. Attributed to Jacob Otten Husly, it has a stuccoed entrance hall.

Jan Corver Burgomaster of Amsterdam 19 times, Corver built No. 479 Herengracht in 1665.

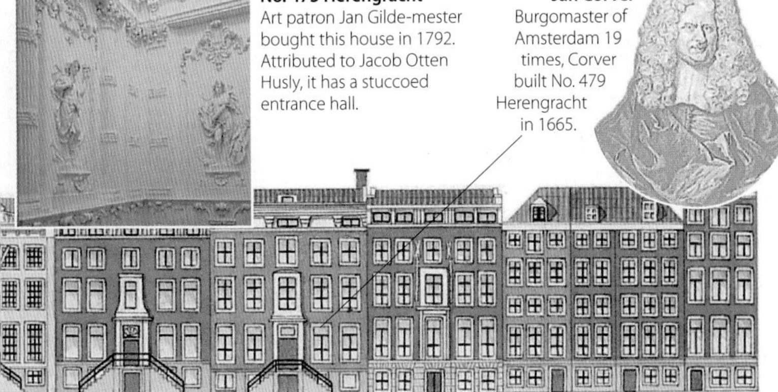

Turn over to continue walk at top of page 102

Herengracht 489 to the Amstel

The second half of the walk takes you along Herengracht, winding past grand, wide-fronted mansions. It then follows Reguliersgracht and Prinsengracht down to the Amstel. Many of the fine houses have been converted into banks, offices and exclusive apartment blocks.

Locator Map

The house at No. 491 Herengracht was built in 1671. The façade, rebuilt in the 18th century, is decorated with scrolls, vases and coats of arms.

No. 493 Herengracht
This 17th-century house was given a Louis XV-style façade in 1767 by Anthony van Hemert.

The Kattenkabinet at No. 497 Herengracht was created by financi B Meijer in 1984. It is devoted to exhibits featuring the cat in art

Directions to Reguliersgracht

At Thorbeckeplein, take the bridge to the right, which marks the beginning of Reguliersgracht. Follow the left bank.

Amstelveld in the 17th Century
This etching shows the construction of a wooden church at Amstelveld, with sheep grazing in front of it.

Restaurant Nel
The Amstelkerk (Amstel Church) now houses a restaurant and offices, while the square is a popular playground for children from the surrounding area.

Directions to Prinsengracht

Turn left by the church, take the left bank of Prinsengracht and walk to the Amstel river.

Prinsengracht

Herengracht (c.1670)
GA Berckheijde's etching shows one side of the canal bare of trees. Elms were later planted, binding the topsoil, to strengthen the buildings' foundations.

No. 543 Herengracht was built in 1743 under the supervision of owner Sibout Bollard. It has a double-fronted façade with an ornate balustrade and decorated balcony.

The small houses at the corner of Herengracht and Thorbeckeplein contrast with the grand neighbouring buildings.

Isaac Gosschalk
The architect designed Nos. 57, 59 and 63 Reguliersgracht in 1879. They have ornate stone, brick and woodwork façades.

Reguliers Monastery
This engraving by J Wagenaar (1760) shows the monastery that once stood on the canal.

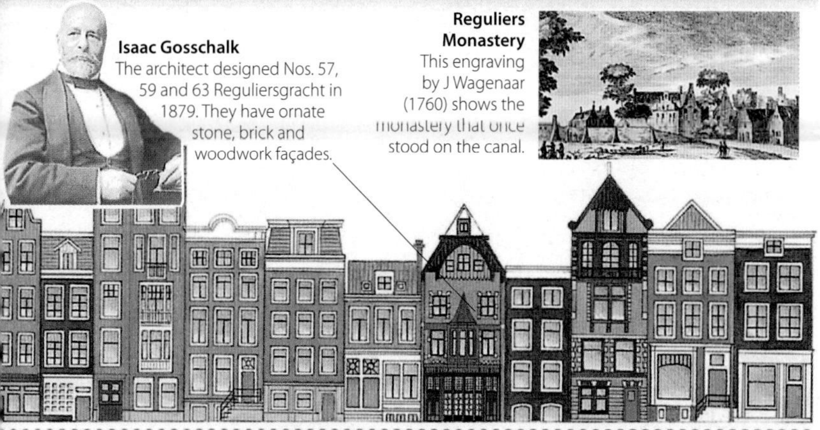

The Amstel
Turn left and follow the broad sweep of the Amstel river, up past the Magere Brug on up Rokin and back to the Dam, where the walk began.

Street-by-Street: Around the Jordaan

West of the *Grachtengordel*, the Jordaan still retains a network of narrow, characterful streets and delightful canals. Among the 17th- century workers' houses are dozens of quirky shops, which are well worth a browse, selling anything from designer clothes to old sinks, and lively brown cafés and bars, which spill onto the pavements in summer. A stroll along the *Grachtengordel* provides a glimpse into some of the city's grandest canal houses, including the Bartolotti House.

Egelantiersgracht is a charming tree-lined Jordaan canal over-looked by an interesting mixture of old and new architecture. Its numerous bridges provide pretty views.

The quiet Bloemgracht canal was once a centre for makers of paint and dye.

❸ ★ Westerkerk
Hendrick de Keyser's church is the site of Rembrandt's unmarked grave and was the setting for the wedding of Queen Beatrix and Prince Claus in 1966.

❶ ★ Anne Frank Huis
For two years, the Frank family and four others lived in a small upstairs apartment that was hidden behind a revolving bookcase *(see pp112–13)*.

❹ Huis met de Hoofden
The name "House with the Heads" refers to the six Classical busts at the entrance, depicting Apollo, Ceres, Mars, Minerva, Bacchus and Diana.

Locator Map
See Street Finder map 1

The Eerste Hollandsche Levensverzekeringsbank building, with its fine façade, is a rare example of Dutch Art Nouveau, designed by Gerrit van Arkel in 1905.

Key
— Recommended route

❷ ★ Homomonument
The pink triangle used to "brand" homosexual men during World War II influenced the design of this memorial to oppressed gay men and women everywhere. It was unveiled in September 1987.

❶ Anne Frank Huis

On 6 July 1942, to avoid their Nazi persecutors, the Jewish Frank family moved from Merwedeplein to the rear annexe of the house at Prinsengracht 263. Anne; her mother, Edith; her father, Otto; and her older sister, Margot, lived here, along with the Van Pels family and dentist Fritz Pfeffer. It was here that Anne wrote her famous diary. On 4 August 1944, the annexe was raided by the Gestapo. All those hiding here were arrested and taken to Nazi concentration camps.

The Secret Entrance
Behind the hinged bookcase was a small suite of rooms where the eight hideaways lived.

Anne in May 1942
This photograph was taken in 1942, when Anne started writing in the now-famous diary that she had been given on 12 June 1942, her 13th birthday. Less than one month later, the Frank family went into hiding.

KEY

① **Bathroom**

② **Anne's bedroom**

③ **Frank family bedroom**

④ **Van Pels family's room**

⑤ **Attic**

⑥ **The annexe**

⑦ **Façade of Prinsengracht 263**

⑧ **Main building housing offices**

View of the Annexe
The rear annexe of the house adjoined the main building, which housed the offices of Otto Frank's herb and spice business The museum website offers a virtual 3-D tour of the annexe.

For hotels and restaurants in this region see pp396–397 and pp406–409

Anne and Fritz Pfeffer's Bedroom
Anne and Fritz slept on the first floor of the annexe. On Anne's bedroom walls were photos of film stars, which she collected. Anne wrote most of her diary at the table here.

VISITORS' CHECKLIST

Practical Information
Prinsengracht 267. **Map** 1 B4..
Tel 020-5567105.
annefrank.org
Open 15 Mar–14 Sep: 9am–9pm daily; 15 Sep–14 Mar: 9am–7pm daily. **Closed** Yom Kippur.
book ahead to avoid queues.

Transport
13, 14, 17.

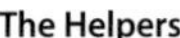

The Helpers
The people in hiding were wholly dependent on their helpers, all of whom were close colleagues of Anne's father, Otto Frank. From left to right: Miep Gies, Johannes Kleiman, Otto Frank, Victor Kugler and Bep Voskuijl.

Museum Guide

The rear annexe is accessible via the reconstructed offices of Otto Frank. The building beside Anne Frank Huis holds various exhibitions. It also houses a café, shop and information desk

The Diary of Anne Frank

Otto Frank returned to Amsterdam in 1945 to discover that his entire family had perished: his wife, Edith, in Auschwitz and his daughters, Anne and Margot, in Bergen-Belsen. Miep Gies, one of the family's helpers while they were in hiding, had kept Anne's diary. First published in 1947, it has since been translated into 55 languages, with some 20 million copies sold. For many, Anne symbolizes the six million Jews murdered by the Nazis in World War II. The diary is a moving portrait of a little girl growing up in times of oppression.

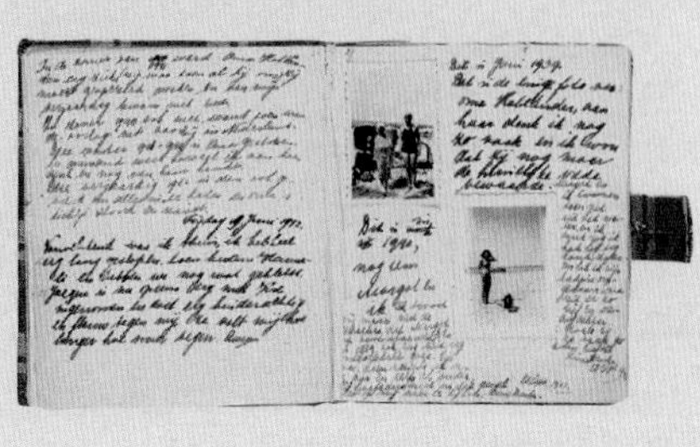

School children visiting the Homomonument

❷ Homomonument

Westermarkt (between Westerkerk and Keizersgracht). **Map** 1 B4. 13, 14, 17. Prinsengracht & Keizersgracht. **homomonument.nl**

This monument to the homosexual men and women who lost their lives during World War II provides a quiet place of contemplation amid the bustle of the Westermarkt. The pink triangular badge that gay men were forced to wear in Nazi concentration camps later became a symbol of gay pride, and provided the inspiration for Karin Daan's 1987 design. The monument consists of three large pink granite triangles, one of which bears an engraving from a poem by Jacob Israël de Haan (1881–1924). On Remembrance Day (4 May), hundreds of gay men and women from all over the Netherlands join delegates from the city council, police, the military and social organisations to lay wreaths and flowers.

❸ Westerkerk

Prinsengracht 281. **Map** 1 B4. **Tel** 020-6247766. 13, 14, 17. Church: **Open** 11am–3pm Mon–Fri, 11am–3pm Sat. Tower: Apr–Sep: hourly 10am–6pm Mon–Sat (to 8pm Jul & Aug); Oct–Nov: hourly 11am–4pm Mon–Sat. Phone 020-6892565 to book. **Closed** Dec–Mar.

Built as part of the development of the Canal Ring, this church has the tallest tower in the city at 85 m (279 ft), and the largest nave of any Dutch Protestant church. It was designed by Hendrick de Keyser, who died in 1621, a year after work began. Rembrandt was buried here but his grave has never been found. The organ shutters (1686) were painted by Gerard de Lairesse, with lively scenes showing King David and the Queen of Sheba. The tower carries the crown bestowed on Amsterdam in 1489 by Maximilian, the Hapsburg emperor. The stunning views justify the climb.

❹ Huis met de Hoofden

Keizersgracht 123. **Map** 1 C4. 13, 14, 17. **Closed** to the public.

Built in 1622, the Huis met de Hoofden (house with the heads) is one of the largest double houses of the period. It has a fine step gable and takes its name from the six heads placed on pilasters along the façade. Legend has it that they commemorate a housemaid who, when alone in the house, surprised six burglars and cut off their heads. The sculptures are in fact portrayals of six Classical deities (from left to right): Apollo, Ceres, Mars, Minerva, Bacchus and Diana. The design of the building is sometimes attributed

The Westerkerk in the 18th century, a view by Jan Ekels

For hotels and restaurants in this region see pp396–397 and pp406–409

to Pieter de Keyser (1595–1676), son of Hendrick de Keyser. Huis met de Hoofden, which has housed a business school, a conservatoire and the Bureau Monumenten en Archeologie, has been bought by JR Ritman, owner of the Bibliotheca Philosophica Hermetica.

❺ Noorderkerk and Noordermarkt

Noordermarkt 44–48. **Map** 1 C3. **Tel** 020-6266436. 🚋 3, 10, 13, 14, 17. **Open** 10:30am–12:30pm Mon, 11am–1pm Sat. ✝ 10am & 7pm Sun. General market: **Open** 9am–1pm Mon; Boerenmarkt: **Open** 9am–5pm Sat.

Built for poor settlers in the Jordaan, the North Church was the first in Amsterdam to be constructed in the shape of a Greek cross. Its layout around a central pulpit allowed the congregation seated in the encircling pews to see and hear well.

The church, designed by Hendrick de Keyser, was completed in 1623, in time to hold its inaugural service at Easter. It is still well attended by a Calvinist congregation. By the entrance is a sculpture of three bound figures, inscribed: "Unity is Strength". It commemorates the Jordaan Riot of 1934. On the south façade, a plaque recalls the 1941 February Strike, protesting the Nazis' deportation of Jews.

Since 1627, the square that surrounds the Noorderkerk has been a market site. At that time, it sold pots and pans and *vodden* (old clothes), a tradition that continues today with a flea market. Since the 18th century, the area has been a centre for bed shops. Bedding, curtains and fabrics are still sold on Monday morning along the Westerstraat; you can buy anything from net curtain material to buttons. On Saturday mornings, the *vogeltjes* (small birds) market sells chickens, pigeons, small birds and rabbits. At 10am, the *boerenmarkt* takes over, selling health foods, ethnic crafts and candles.

Stone plaque on the *hofje* founded in 1616 by the merchant Anslo

❻ Haarlemmerpoort

Haarlemmerplein 50. **Map** 1 B1. 🚋 3. **Closed** to the public.

Originally a defended gateway into Amsterdam, the Haarlemmerpoort marked the beginning of the busy route to Haarlem. The present gateway, dating from 1840, was built for King William II's triumphal entry into the city and named Willemspoort. However, as the third gateway to be built on or close to this site, it is still called the Haarlemmerpoort by Amsterdammers.

Designed by Cornelis Alewijn (1788–1839), the Neo-Classical gatehouse was used as tax offices in the 19th century and was made into flats in 1986. Traffic no longer goes through the gate, since a bridge has been built over the adjoining Westerkanaal.

❼ Brouwersgracht

Map 1 B2. 🚋 3.

Brouwersgracht (brewers' canal) was named after the breweries established here in the 17th and 18th centuries. Leather, spices, coffee and sugar were also processed and stored here. Today, most of the warehouses, with their spout gables and shutters, are residences that look out on moored houseboats.

❽ Western Islands

Map 1 C1. 🚋 3.

This district comprises three islands built on the IJ in the early 1600s to quarter warehouses and shipyards. Some of these are still in use and many period houses have survived.

Merchant and developer Jan Bicker bought Bickerseiland in 1631. Today, the island is a mix of colourful apartment blocks and a jumble of houseboats.

Realeneiland has the pretty waterside street of Zandhoek. A row of pretty 17th-century houses built by the island's founder, Jacobsz Reaal, overlooks the moored sailboats.

Prinseneiland is dominated by characterful warehouses, many now apartments.

The "house with the writing hand" (c.1630) in Claes Claeszhofje

Dutch Hofjes

Before the Alteration, the Catholic Church often provided subsidized housing for the poor and elderly, particularly women. During the 17th and 18th centuries, rich merchants and Protestant organizations took on this charitable role and built hundreds of almshouse complexes, which were planned around courtyards and known as *hofjes*. Behind their street façades lie pretty houses and serene gardens. Visitors are admitted to some but asked to respect the residents' privacy. Many *hofjes* are found in the Jordaan and some still serve their original purpose.

Star-lit façade of De Melkweg near Leidseplein

9 Leidseplein

Map 4 E2. 1, 2, 5, 7, 10.

Amsterdam's liveliest square, Leidseplein is also a busy tram intersection and centre of night-time transport.

The square developed in the 17th century as a wagon park on the outskirts of the city – farmers and peasants would leave their carts here before entering the centre. It takes its name from the Leidsepoort, the massive city gate demolished in 1862, which marked the beginning of the route out to Leiden.

During the day, the square is buzzing with fire-eaters, buskers and other street performers playing to café audiences. It is also popular with pickpockets. At night, it is the focal point for the city's youth, who hang out in the many bars, cafés, restaurants, nightclubs and cinemas in and around the square.

10 American Hotel

Leidsekade 97. **Map** 4 E2. **Tel** 020-5563000. 1, 2, 5, 7, 10.

Leidseplein was fast becoming a fashionable entertainment area when the American Hotel was built overlooking it in 1882. The hotel got its name because its architect, W Steinigeweg, studied hotel design in the United States, and adorned his Neo-Gothic creation with a bronze eagle, wooden figures of native Indians and murals of American landscapes. Within 20 years it was deemed *passé* and the hotel was demolished.

The present building is by Willem Kromhout (1864–1940) and was completed in 1902. His design marked a radical departure, interpreting the Art Nouveau style in an angular Dutch fashion. The building's turreted exterior and elaborate brickwork anticipated the progressive Amsterdam School *(see pp146–7)*.

The Art Deco-style Café Americain is one of the most elegant in Amsterdam. It retains its period furnishings and stained-glass windows. The rest of the hotel was redecorated in the 1980s. Samples of the original furnishings are in the Rijksmuseum *(see pp126–9)*.

11 Stadsschouwburg

Leidseplein 26. **Map** 4 E2. **Tel** 020-6242311. 1, 2, 5, 6, 7, 10. Box office: **Open** 10am–6pm Mon–Sat. See Entertainment: p428.
stadsschouwburgamsterdam.nl

This Neo-Renaissance building is the most recent of the city's three successive municipal theatres, its predecessors having burned down. The theatre was designed by Jan Springer and AL van Gendt, who was responsible for the Concertgebouw *(see p124)* and for part of the Centraal Station *(see p904)*. The planned ornamentation of the theatre's redbrick exterior was never carried out because of budget cuts. This, combined with a hostile public reaction to his theatre, forced a disillusioned Springer into virtual retirement. Public disgust was due, however, to the management's policy of restricting use of the front door to patrons who had bought expensive tickets.

The former home of the Dutch national ballet and opera companies, the theatre today stages plays by local drama groups such as the resident Toneelgroep, as well as international companies, including many English-language productions. The foyer houses a popular restaurant.

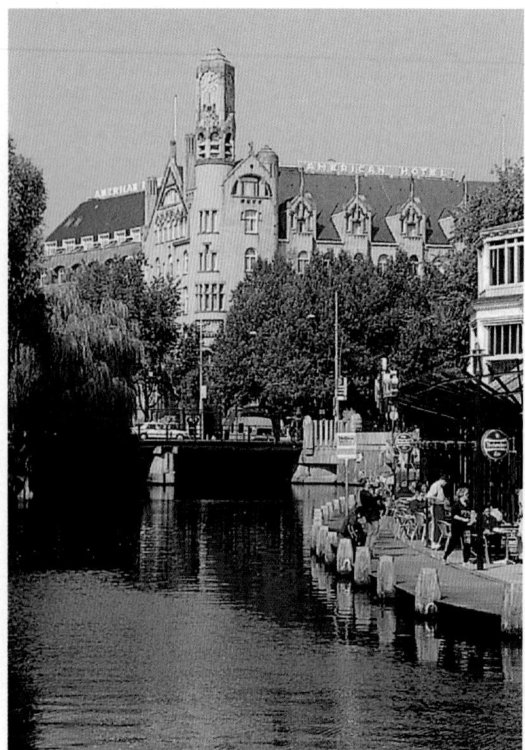

The American Hotel seen from Singelgracht

⓬ De Krijtberg

Singel 448. **Map** 4 F1. **Tel** 020-6231923. 1, 2, 5. **Open** 1–5pm Tue–Thu & Sun. 12:30pm, 5:45pm Mon–Fri, 12:30pm, 5:15pm Sat, 9:30am, 11am, 12:30pm, 5:15pm Sun. **krijtberg.nl**

An impressive Neo-Gothic church, the Krijtberg (or chalk hill) replaced a clandestine Jesuit chapel in 1884. It is officially known as Franciscus Xaveriuskerk, after St Francis Xavier, one of the founding Jesuit monks.

Designed by Alfred Tepe, the church was built on the site of three houses; the presbytery beside the church is on the site of two other houses, one of which had belonged to a chalk merchant – hence the church's nickname. The back of the church is wider than the front, extending into the space once occupied by the original gardens. The narrowness of the façade is redeemed by its two magnificent, soaring, steepled towers.

The ornate interior of the building contains some good examples of Neo-Gothic design. The stained-glass windows, walls painted in bright colours and liberal use of gold are in striking contrast to the city's austere Protestant churches. A statue of St Francis Xavier stands in front and to the left of the high altar; one of St Ignatius, founder of the Jesuits, stands to the right.

Near the pulpit is an 18th -century wooden statue of the Immaculate Conception, which shows Mary trampling the serpent. It used to be housed in the original hidden chapel.

⓭ Bijbels Museum

Herengracht 366–368. **Map** 4 E1. **Tel** 020-624-2436. 1, 2, 5. Herengracht/Leidsegracht. **Open** 10am–5pm Tue–Sat, 11am–5pm Sun & public hols. **Closed** 1 Jan, 27 Apr. **bijbelsmuseum.nl**

Reverend Leendert Schouten founded the Bible museum in 1860, when he put his private artifact collection on public display. In 1975, the museum moved to its present site, two 17th-century houses designed by Philips Vingboons. Highlights are a copy of the Book of Isaiah from the Dead Sea Scrolls and the Delft Bible (1477).

⓮ Looier Kunst en Antiekcentrum

Elandsgracht 109. **Map** 4 D1. **Tel** 020-6249038. 7, 10, 13, 14, 17. **Open** 11am–6pm Mon–Fri. **Closed** public hols. **looier.nl**

The Looier antiques centre is a vast network of rooms in a block of houses near the canal. Its 100 stalls sell everything from glassware to dolls.

Grand façade of the Stadsarchief

⓯ Stadsarchief Amsterdam

Vijzelstraat 32. **Map** 4 F2. **Tel** 020-572 0202. 16, 24. **Open** 10am–5pm Tue–Fri, noon–5pm Sat & Sun. **Closed** Mon & public holidays. (with permission). **stadsarchief.amsterdam.nl**

The Stadsarchief, the city's municipal archives, moved from its former location in Amsteldijk to this monumental building. Designed by KPC de Bazel, one of the principal representatives of the Amsterdam school of architecture, the edifice was completed in 1926 for the Netherlands Trading Company. In spite of much renovation work at the end of World War II and in the 1970s, the building retains many attractive original features, such as colourful floor mosaics (designed by de Bazel himself). There is a permanent display of treasures from the archives in the monumental vaults.

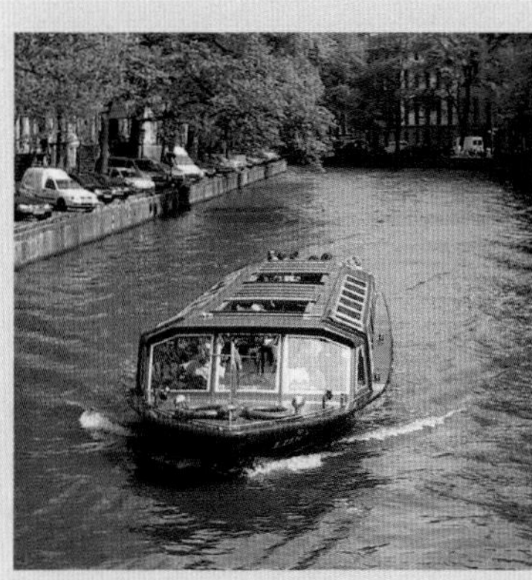

On the Canals

Though Amsterdam's canals were built for moving goods, today they provide a marvellous means of viewing the city's sights and its everyday life. There are many operators in the city offering canal tours with foreign-language commentaries; boats depart from an embarkation point, mainly from opposite Centraal Station, along Prins Hendrikkade, the Damrak and along the Rokin. Another canal-sightseeing option is the popular canalbus which runs along three routes, with 14 stops near the major museums, shopping areas and other attractions. If you feel energetic, try a canal bike, which is really a two- or four-seater pedal-boat that can be picked up and left at any of the canal-bike moorings in the city centre.

⓰ Rembrandtplein

Map 5 A2. 4, 9, 14.

Formerly called the Botermarkt, after the butter market held here until the mid-19th century, this square acquired its present name when the statue of Rembrandt was erected in 1876.

Soon afterwards, Rembrandtplein developed into a centre for nightlife with the opening of various hotels and cafés. The Mast (renamed the Mille Colonnes Hotel) dates from 1889, and the Schiller Karena hotel and the Café Schiller both opened in 1892. De Kroon, which epitomizes a typical grand café, dates from 1898. The popularity of Rembrandtplein has endured, and the café terraces are packed during summer with people enjoying a pleasant drink and watching the world go by.

Two of the many outdoor cafés on Rembrandtplein

⓱ Museum Willet-Holthuysen

Herengracht 605. **Map** 5 A2. **Tel** 020-5231822. 4, 9, 14. **Open** 10am–5pm Mon–Fri, 11am–5pm Sat & Sun. **Closed** 1 Jan, 27 Apr, 25 Dec. **willetholthuysen.nl**

Named after the building's last residents, the museum now housed here allows visitors a glimpse into the lives of the merchant class who lived in luxury along the Grachtengordel (Canal Ring). The house was built in 1685 and became the property of coal magnate Pieter Holthuysen (1788–1858) in 1855. It passed to his daughter Louisa and her art-connoisseur husband, Abraham Willet – both fervent collectors of paintings, glass, silver and ceramics. When Louisa died childless in 1895, the house and its many treasures were left to the city. Room by room, the house is gradually being restored to appear as it did during the time when Abraham and Louisa lived here.

Interior of Willet-Holthuysen museum, on the Herengracht canal

The Blue Room, hung with heavy blue damask and boasting a chimney piece by Jacob de Wit, was the exclusive preserve of the men of the house.

The wallpaper in the dining room today is a careful copy of the 18th-century silk original. The elaborate 275-piece Meissen dinner service provided up to 24 places.

The 18th-century kitchen has been restored using items salvaged from similar houses, including the sink and pump.

On the second floor is a full-length portrait of Willet.

⓲ Magere Brug

Amstel. **Map** 5 B3. 4.

Of Amsterdam's 1,400 or so bridges, Magere Brug (skinny bridge) is the best-known. The original drawbridge was built in about 1670. According to legend, it was named after two sisters called Mager, who lived either side of the Amstel. It is more likely that the name comes from its narrow *(mager)* design.

Magere Brug, a traditional double-leaf Dutch drawbridge

The present drawbridge was put up in 1969 and, though wider than the original, it still conforms to the traditional double-leaf style. Constructed from African azobe wood, it was intended to last 50 years. The bridge is opened a few times every day. It has been featured in many films, most notable being the James Bond film - *Diamonds are Forever.*

⑲ Museum Van Loon

Keizersgracht 672. **Map** 5 A3. **Tel** 020-6245255. 16, 24. **Open** 11am–5pm Wed–Mon. **Closed** public hols.
museumvanloon.nl

The Van Loons were one of Amsterdam's most prestigious families in the 17th century. They did not move into this house on the Keizersgracht, however, until 1884. Designed by Adriaan Dortsman, No. 672 is one of a pair of symmetrical houses built in 1672 for Flemish merchant Jeremias van Raey. In 1752, Dr Abraham van Hagen and his wife, Catharina Elisabeth Trip, moved in.

In 1973, after many years of restoration, it opened as a museum, retaining the house's original character. Its collection of Van Loon family portraits stretches back to the early 1600s. The period rooms have fine pieces of furniture, porcelain and sculpture. Outside, the 18th-century coach house has been restored and houses the van Loon carriages and servants' livery.

⑳ Tuschinski Theater

Reguliersbreestraat 26–28. **Map** 5 A2. **Tel** 0900-1458. 4, 9, 14. Box office: **Open** 11:30am–10pm.

Abraham Tuschinski's cinema and variety theatre caused a sensation when it opened in 1921. Until then, Amsterdam's cinemas had been sombre places; this was an exotic blend of Art Deco and Amsterdam School architecture *(see pp146–7)*. Built in a slum area known as Devil's Corner, it was designed by Heyman Louis de Jong and decorated by Chris Bartels, Jaap Gidding and Pieter de Besten. In its heyday, Marlene Dietrich and Judy Garland performed here.

Now a six-screen cinema, the building has been meticulously restored, inside and out. The best way to appreciate its opulence is to see a film. For a few extra euros, you can take a seat in one of the exotic boxes that make up the back row of the huge semi-circular auditorium.

View of the medieval Munttoren at the base of Muntplein

㉑ Munttoren

Muntplein. **Map** 4 F1. 4, 9, 14, 16, 24. Munttoren: **Closed** to public. Gift shop: **Open** 10am–6pm Mon–Sat.

The polygonal base of the Munttoren (mint tower) formed part of the gate in Amsterdam's medieval wall. Fire destroyed the gate in 1618, but the base survived. In 1619, Hendrick de Keyser added the clock tower; François Hemony, the set of bells in 1699. During the 1673 French occupation, the city mint was housed here.

How the Magere Brug Works

The arched wooden portal provides a pivot for the balance.

Mechanical chain-drive

Steel cables

The balance is made up of two counter-weighted beams.

Each deck has a span of about 5 m (16 ft).

MUSEUM QUARTER

Until the late 1800s, the Museum quarter was little more than an area of farms and small-holdings. At this time, the city council designated it an area of art and culture and plans were conceived for constructing Amsterdam's great cultural monuments: the Rijksmuseum, the Stedelijk Museum and the Concertgebouw. The Van Gogh Museum followed in 1973, its striking extension being added in 1999. The Museumplein has two memorials to the victims of World War II. The *plein* is still used today as a site for political demonstrations. To the north and south are late 19th- and early 20th-century houses, where the streets are named after artists and intellectuals, such as the 17th-century Dutch poet Roemer Visscher. To the west, the Vondelpark offers a pleasant, fresh-air break from all the museums.

Sights at a Glance

Museums and Workshops

1. *Rijksmuseum pp126–9*
2. Coster Diamonds
3. *Van Gogh Museum pp130–31*
4. *Stedelijk Museum pp132–3*
9. Vondelparkpaviljoen

Concert Halls

5. Concertgebouw

Historic Buildings

7. Hollandsche Manege
8. Vondelkerk

Parks

6. Vondelpark

See also Street Finder map 3 & 4

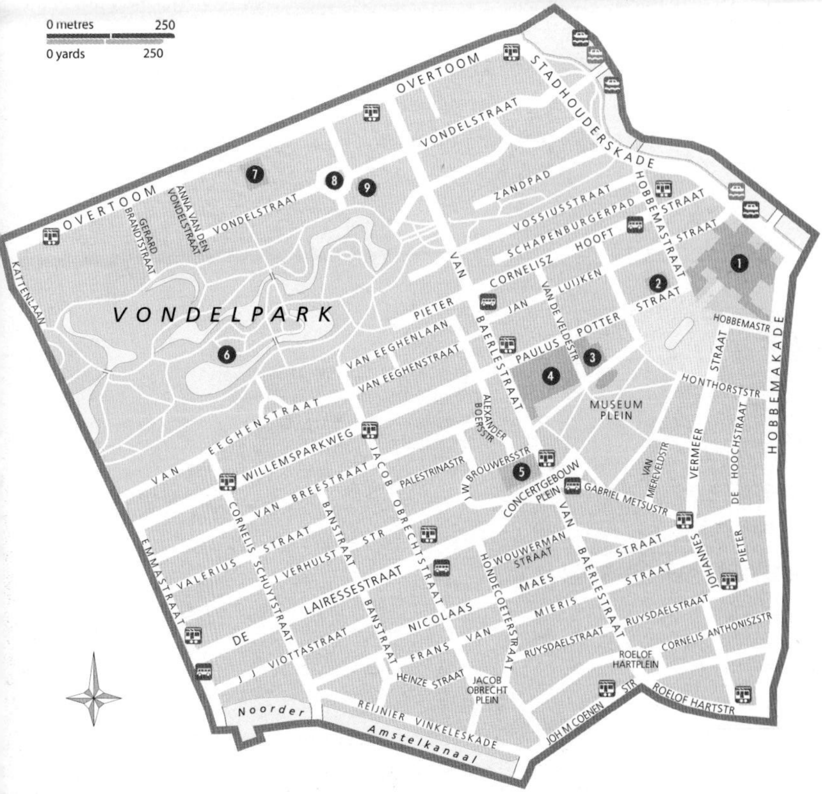

Street-by-Street: Museum Quarter

The green expanse of Museumplein was once bisected by a busy main road known locally as the "shortest motorway in Europe". But dramatic renovation between 1996 and 1999 has transformed it into a stately park, fringed by Amsterdam's major cultural centres. The district is one of the wealthiest in the city, with wide streets lined with grand houses. After the heady delights of the museums, it is possible to window-shop at the many up-market boutiques along the exclusive PC Hooftstraat and Van Baerlestraat, or watch the diamond polishers at work in Coster Diamonds.

3 ★ Van Gogh Museum
The new wing of the museum, an elegant oval shape, was designed by Kisho Kurokawa and opened in 1999. It is dedicated to temporary exhibitions of 19th-century art.

Van Baerlestraat
contains exclusive clothing shops *(see p148)*.

4 ★ Stedelijk Museum
Housing the civic collection of modern art, this museum also stages controversial contemporary art exhibitions. A sculpture garden is behind the building.

5 Concertgebouw
Designed by AL van Gendt, the building has a Classical façade and a concert hall with near-perfect acoustics.

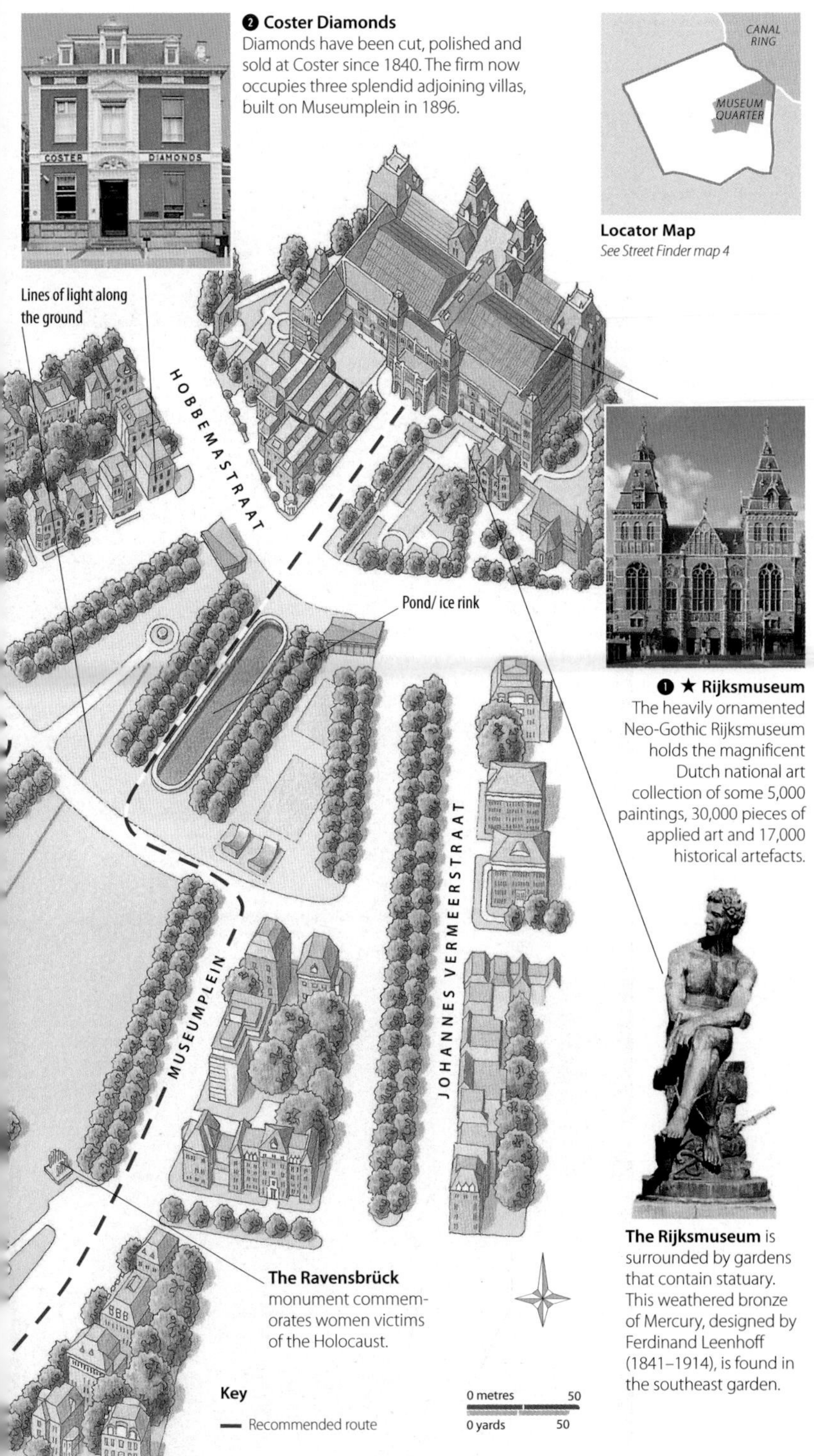

❷ Coster Diamonds
Diamonds have been cut, polished and sold at Coster since 1840. The firm now occupies three splendid adjoining villas, built on Museumplein in 1896.

Locator Map
See Street Finder map 4

❶ ★ Rijksmuseum
The heavily ornamented Neo-Gothic Rijksmuseum holds the magnificent Dutch national art collection of some 5,000 paintings, 30,000 pieces of applied art and 17,000 historical artefacts.

The Rijksmuseum is surrounded by gardens that contain statuary. This weathered bronze of Mercury, designed by Ferdinand Leenhoff (1841–1914), is found in the southeast garden.

The Ravensbrück monument commemorates women victims of the Holocaust.

Key

— Recommended route

❶ Rijksmuseum

See pp126–7.

❷ Coster Diamonds

Paulus Potterstraat 2–8. **Map** 4 E3. **Tel** 020-3055555. 2, 5. **Open** 9am–5pm daily. **Closed** 1 Jan, 25 Dec. **costerdiamonds.com**

One of Amsterdam's oldest diamond factories, Coster was founded in 1840. Twelve years later, Queen Victoria's consort, Prince Albert, honoured the company by giving them the task of repolishing the enormous *Koh-i-Noor* (mountain of light) diamond. This blue-white stone is one of the treasures of the British crown jewels and weighs in at 108.8 carats. A replica of the coronation crown, which incorporates a copy of the fabulous stone, is found in Coster's spacious entrance hall.

More than 1,000 people visit the factory each day to witness the processes of grading, cutting and polishing the stones. The goldsmiths and diamond-cutters work together in the factory to produce customized items of jewellery, in a range of styles, which are available over the counter. In the Diamond Museum, the history of the diamond is traced, from its creation deep in the earth to the dazzling stones that are a girl's best friend.

Glistening diamonds at Coster Diamonds

❸ Van Gogh Museum

See pp130–31.

❹ Stedelijk Museum

See pp132–3.

Façade of the award-winning Concertgebouw (1881) by AL van Gendt

❺ Concertgebouw

Concertgebouwplein 2–6. **Map** 4 D4. **Tel** 0900-6718345. 2, 3, 5, 12, 16, 24. Box office: **Open** 1–7pm Mon–Fri, 10am–7pm Sat & Sun. by arrangement. 5pm Mon, 12:15pm Sun. **concertgebouw.nl**

Following an open architectural competition held in 1881, AL van Gendt (1835– 1901) was chosen to design a vast new concert hall for Amsterdam. The resulting Neo-Renaissance building boasts an elaborate pediment and colonnaded façade, and houses two concert halls. Despite van Gendt's lack of musical knowledge, he managed to produce near-perfect acoustics in the Grote Zaal (main concert hall), which is renowned the world over.

The inaugural concert at the Concertgebouw was held on 11 April 1888, complete with an orchestra of 120 musicians and a choir of 600. A resident orchestra was established at the hall seven months later.

The building has been renovated several times over the years, most recently in 1983, when some serious subsidence threatened the building's entire foundation. To remedy this, the whole superstructure had to be lifted up off the ground while the original supporting piles, which rested on sand 13 m (43 ft) underground, were removed and replaced by concrete piles sunk into the ground to a depth of 18 m (59 ft). A glass extension and new entrance were added by Pi de Bruijn in 1988. The original entrance was relocated round to the side of the building. Though primarily designed to hold concerts, the Concertgebouw also hosts business meetings, exhibitions, conferences, political meetings and occasional boxing matches.

Bandstand in Vondelpark

❻ Vondelpark

Stadhouderskade. **Map** 4 E2. 1, 2, 3, 5,12. Park: **Open** 24hrs daily. Open-air theatre: **Open** Jun–last week Aug: Wed–Sun.

In 1864, a group consisting of prominent Amsterdammers formed a committee with the aim of founding a public park, and they raised enough money to buy 8 ha (20 acres) of land. JD and LP Zocher, a father-and-son team of landscape architects, were then commissioned to design the park in typical English landscape style. They used vistas, pathways and ponds to create the illusion of a large natural area, which was opened to the public on 15 June 1865, as the Nieuwe Park. The park's present name was adopted in 1867, when a statue of Dutch poet Joost van den Vondel (1587–1679) was erected on the grounds. The committee soon began to raise money to enlarge the park, and by June 1877 it had reached its current dimensions of 47 ha (116 acres). The park now supports around 100 plant species and 127 types of tree. Squirrels, hedgehogs, ducks and garden birds mix with a huge colony of greedy, bright green parakeets, which gather in front of the pavilion every morning to be fed. Herds of cows, sheep, goats and even a lone llama graze in the pastures.

Vondelpark welcomes about 8 million visitors a year, and is popular with the locals for dog-walking, jogging, or just for the view. Free concerts are given at the *openluchttheater* (open-air theatre) or at the bandstand during summer.

Façade of the Hollandse Manege, the Dutch riding school

7 Hollandsche Manege

Vondelstraat 140. **Map** 3 C2. **Tel** 020-6180942. 1. **Open** 9am–11pm Mon–Fri, 9:30am–6pm Sat & Sun.

The Dutch riding school was originally situated on the Leidsegracht, but in 1882 a new building was opened, designed by AL van Gendt and based on the Spanish Riding School in Vienna. The riding school was threatened with demolition in the 1980s, but was saved after a public outcry. Reopened in 1986 by Prince Bernhard, it has been restored to its former glory. The Neo-Classical indoor arena boasts gilded mirrors and moulded horses' heads on its elaborate plasterwork walls. Some of the wrought-iron stalls remain and sound is muffled by sawdust. At the top of the staircase, one door leads to a balcony overlooking the arena, another to the café.

8 Vondelkerk

Vondelstraat 120. **Map** 3 C2. 1, 3, 12. **Closed** to the public.

The Vondelkerk was the largest church designed by PJH Cuypers, architect of the Centraal Station. Work began in 1872, but funds ran out by the following year. Money gathered from public donations and lotteries allowed the building to be completed by 1880. When fire broke out in November 1904, firefighters saved the nave by forcing the burning tower to fall away into Vondelpark. A new tower was added later by the architect's son, JT Cuypers. The church was deconsecrated in 1979 and converted into offices in 1985.

Built in 1880, the striking Vondelkerk now houses a number of offices

9 Vondelpark-paviljoen

Vondelpark 3. **Map** 4 D2. **Closed** to the public, renovations underway.

Vondelpark's pavilion was designed by the architects PJ Hamer (1812–87) and his son W Hamer (1843–1913), and opened on 4 May 1881 as a café and restaurant. After World War II, it reopened as a cultural centre. In 1991, the pavilion was renovated once more. The complete Art Deco interior of the Cinema Parisien, Amsterdam's first cinema, built in 1910, was moved into one of the rooms. At one point, it housed an important national film museum, EYE that screened more than 1,000 films a year. However, the museum, which also has a lovely film poster collection, has been shifted to a new building on Badhuisweg. The Vondelparkpaviljoen underwent extensive renovations again over the past year and now functions as a TV and radio media centre, complete with a café and restaurant. The surrounding garden has been beautifully re-landscaped.

❶ Rijksmuseum

The Rijksmuseum, an Amsterdam landmark, possesses an unrivalled collection of Dutch art, begun in the early 19th century. The huge museum opened in 1885 to bitter criticism from Amsterdam's Protestant community for its Neo-Gothic style. After a 10-year renovation to strip the building of its later additions and to restore Cuypers' vision, the museum finally reopened completely in 2013.

Second floor

Winter Landscape with Skaters (1618)
Painter Hendrick Avercamp specialized in intricate icy winter scenes.

★ The Kitchen Maid (1658)
The light falling through the window and the stillness of this scene are typical of Jan Vermeer.

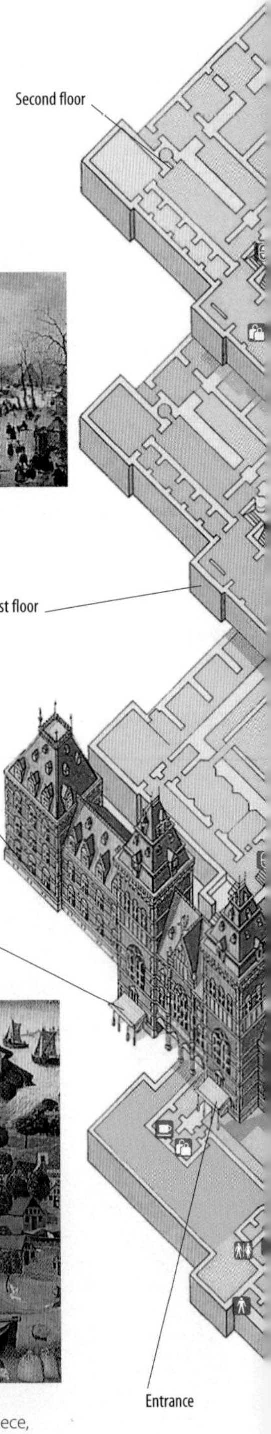

First floor

The Gothic façade of PJH Cuypers' building is red brick with elaborate decoration, including coloured tiles.

Entrance

Gallery Guide

The basement of the museum houses its Special Collections and Asian Pavilion. The ground floor features works from the 18th and 19th centuries, the first floor has works from the Golden Age, while the second floor features works from the 20th century.

★ St Elizabeth's Day Flood (1500)
An unknown artist painted this altarpiece, showing a disastrous flood in 1421. The dykes protecting Dordrecht were breached, and 22 villages were swept away by the flood water.

Entrance

Key to Floorplan

- Special collections
- Medieval and Renaissance art
- Golden Age
- 18th-century art
- 19th-century art
- 20th-century art
- Asian Pavillion
- Non-exhibition space

For hotels and restaurants in this region see pp396–397 and pp406–409

VISITORS' CHECKLIST

Practical Information
Museumstraat 1. **Map** 4 E3.
Tel 020-6747000.
W **rijksmuseum.nl**
Open 9am–5pm daily.

Transport
2, 3, 5, 7, 10, 16, 24.
Stadhouderskade.

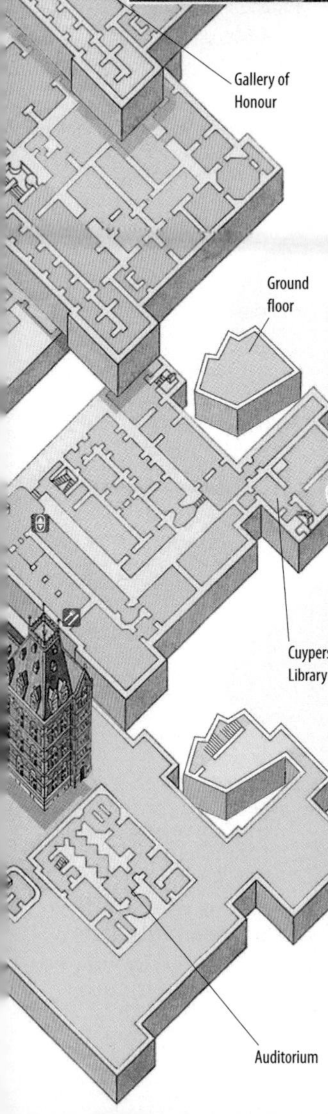

★ The Night Watch (1642)
The showpiece of Dutch 17th-century art, this vast canvas was commissioned as a group portrait of an Amsterdam militia company.

Gallery of Honour

St Catherine (c.1465)
This sculpture by the Master of Koudewater shows the saint stamping on Emperor Maxentius, who allegedly killed her with his sword.

Ground floor

Cuypers Library

Basement

Auditorium

Jan Steen's *Woman at her Toilet* was painted in about 1660

Genre Painting

For the contemporaries of Jan Steen (1625–79), this cosy everyday scene was full of symbols that are obscure to the modern viewer. The dog on the pillow may represent fidelity, and the red stockings the woman's sexuality; she is probably a prostitute. Such genre paintings were often raunchy, but nearly always had a moral twist *(see p227)* – domestic scenes by artists such as ter Borch and Honthorst were symbolic of brothels, while other works illustrated proverbs. Symbols like candles or skulls indicated mortality.

Exploring the Rijksmuseum

The Rijksmuseum is almost too vast to be seen in a single visit. It is famous for owning probably the best collection of Dutch art in the world, from early religious works to the masterpieces of the Golden Age. However, the applied art and sculpture sections, and the Asiatic artefacts, are equally wonderful. In total, 8,000 pieces of art are on display in 80 wings. The selected pieces demonstrate the enormous prosperity of Holland's Golden Age in the 17th century. Rembrandt's *The Night Watch* is one of the masterpieces on display.

Dutch History

The turbulent history of the Netherlands is encapsulated in this section. In the opening room is the medieval altar painting of *St Elizabeth's Day Flood (see p126)*. The central room has 17th-century ship models, artefacts salvaged from shipwrecks and paintings of factories and townscapes from the days of the Dutch Empire. Later displays recall battles in naval history; exhibits from the 18th century deal with the impact of revolutionary France on Amsterdam, ending in 1815 after the Napoleonic Wars.

Early Painting and Foreign Schools

Alongside a small collection of Flemish and Italian art, including portraits by Piero di Cosimo (1462–1521), are the first specifically "Dutch" paintings. These works are mostly religious, such as *The Seven Works of Charity* (1504) by the Master of Alkmaar, Jan van Scorel's quasi-Mannerist *Mary Magdalene* (1528) and Lucas van Leyden's triptych, *Adoration of the Golden Calf* (1530). As the 16th century progressed, religious themes were superseded by pastoral subjects; by 1552, paintings like Pieter Aertsen's *The Egg Dance* were full of realism, by then the keystone of much Dutch art.

17th-century Painting

By the alteration in 1578, Dutch art had moved away completely from religious to secular themes. Artists turned to realistic portraiture, landscapes, still lifes, seascapes, domestic interiors, including genre work *(see p127)*, and animal portraits. Rembrandt *(see p82)* is the most famous of many artists who lived and worked around Amsterdam at this time. Examples of his work hanging in the Rijksmuseum include *Portrait of Titus in a Monk's Habit* (1660), *Self- Portrait as the Apostle Paul* (1661), *The Jewish Bride (see pp30–31)*, as well as *The Night Watch (see p127)*. Look out too for the work of his many pupils, who included, among others, Nicolaes Maes and Ferdinand Bol.

Don't miss Jan Vermeer's (1632–75) serenely light-filled interiors including *The Kitchen Maid (see p126)* and *The Woman Reading a Letter* (1662). Of several portraits by Frans Hals *(see pp190–91)*, the best known are *The Wedding Portrait* and *The Merry Drinker* (1630). *The Windmill at Wijk* by Jacob van Ruisdael (1628– 82) is a great landscape by an artist at the very height of his power. Other artists whose works contribute to this unforgettable collection include Pieter Saenredam *(see p57)*, Jan van de Capelle, Jan Steen *(see p127)* and Gerard Terborch.

Feeding the Hungry from a series of panels by the Master of Alkmaar

The Wedding Portrait (c. 1622) by Frans Hals

18th- and 19th-century Painting

In many ways, 18th-century Dutch painting merely continued the themes and quality of 17th-century work.

This is particularly true of portraiture and still lifes, with the evocative *Still Life with Flowers and Fruit* by Jan van Huysum (1682–1749) standing out. A trend developed later for elegant "conversation pieces" by artists such as Adriaan van der Werff (1659–1722) and Cornelis Troost (1696–1750). Most had satirical undertones, like *The Art Gallery of Jan Gildemeester Jansz* (1794) by Adriaan de Lelie (1755–1820), showing an 18th-century salon whose walls are crowded with 17th-century masterpieces.

Hague School and the Impressionists

The so-called Hague School was made up of a group of Dutch artists who came together around 1870 in The Hague. Their landscape work, which earned them the alternative title the "Grey School" for their overcast skies, captures the atmospheric quality of subdued Dutch sunlight. One of the prizes of the Rijksmuseum's 19th-century collection is *Morning Ride on the Beach* (1876) by Anton Mauve (1838–88), painted in soft pearly colours. Alongside hangs the beautiful polder landscape *View near the Geestbrug* by Hendrik Weissenbruch (1824–1903). In contrast, the Dutch Impressionists, closely linked to the French Impressionists, preferred active subjects such as *The Bridge over the Singel at Paleisstraat, Amsterdam* (1890) by George Hendrik Breitner (1857–1923).

Sculpture and Applied Arts

Beginning with religious medieval sculpture, this section moves on to the splendour of Renaissance furniture and decoration. Highlights that capture the wealth of the Golden Age include the exquisite collections of glassware and Delftware *(see pp32–3)*, and diamond jewellery. A late 17th-century, 12-leaf Chinese screen incorporates European figures on one side, a phoenix on the other; and two dolls' houses

Still Life with Flowers and Fruit (c.1730) by artist Jan van Huysum (1682–1740), one of many still lifes exhibited in the Rijksmuseum

are modelled on contemporary town houses. Some outstanding 18th-century Meissen porcelain and Art Nouveau glass complete the collection.

Prints and Drawings

The Rijksmuseum owns about a million prints and drawings. Although the emphasis is on Dutch works (most of Rembrandt's etchings as well as rare works by Hercules Seghers (c.1589–1637) are here), there are prints by major European artists, including Dürer, Tiepolo, Goya, Watteau and Toulouse-Lautrec, as well as a set of coloured Japanese woodcuts. Small exhibitions are held on the ground floor of the museum, but particular prints can be viewed with special permission from the Study Collection in the basement.

Late 7th-century Cambodian *Head of Buddha*

Asiatic Art

Rewards of the Dutch imperial trading past are on show in this department, which has a separate entrance at the rear of the museum. Some of the earliest artefacts are the most unusual: tiny bronze Tang dynasty figurines from 7th-century China and gritty, granite rock carvings from Java (c.8th century). Later exhibits include a lovely – and extremely explicit – Hindu statue entitled *Heavenly Beauty*, luscious Chinese parchment paintings of tigers, inlaid Korean boxes and Vietnamese dishes painted with curly-tailed fish. This is a veritable hoard of delights and, above all, a monument to the sophistication and skill of craftsmen and artists in early Eastern cultures.

❸ Van Gogh Museum

The Van Gogh Museum is based on a design by De Stijl architect Gerrit Rietveld *(see pp 208–9)* and opened in 1973. A new wing, designed by Kisho Kurokawa, was added in 1999. When Van Gogh died in 1890, he was on the verge of being acclaimed. His younger brother Theo, an art dealer, amassed a collection of 200 of his paintings and 500 drawings. These, combined with around 850 letters by Van Gogh to Theo, and selected works by his friends and contemporaries, form the core of the museum's outstanding collection.

★ Vincent's Bedroom in Arles (1888)
One of Van Gogh's best-known works, this was painted to celebrate his achievement of domestic stability at the Yellow House in Arles. He was so delighted with the colourful painting that he did it twice.

★ Sunflowers (1889)
The vivid yellows and greens in this version of Van Gogh's *Sunflowers* have been enriched by broad streaks of bright mauve and red.

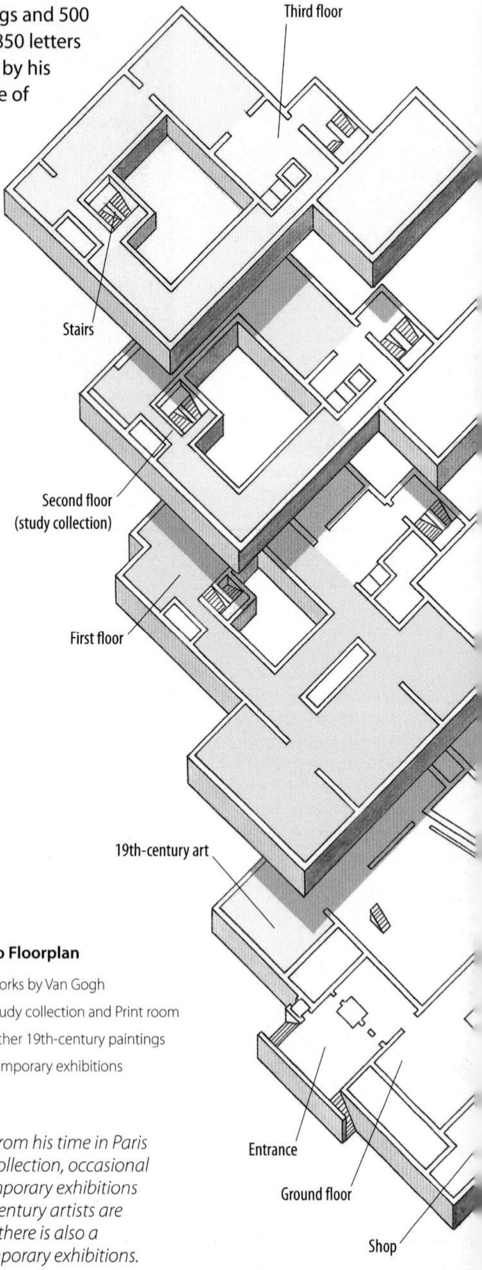

Third floor
Stairs
Second floor (study collection)
First floor
19th-century art
Entrance
Ground floor
Shop

Key to Floorplan

- Works by Van Gogh
- Study collection and Print room
- Other 19th-century paintings
- Temporary exhibitions

Museum Guide

Paintings from Van Gogh's Dutch period and from his time in Paris and Provence are on the first floor. The study collection, occasional exhibits of Van Gogh's drawings and other temporary exhibitions are on the second floor. Works by other 19th-century artists are on the third floor and the ground floor, where there is also a bookshop and café. The new wing houses temporary exhibitions.

An Artist's Life

Vincent van Gogh (1853–90), born in Zundert, began painting in 1880. He worked in the Netherlands for five years before moving to Paris, later settling in Arles. After a fierce argument with Gauguin, he cut off part of his own ear; his mental instability forced him into a psychiatric hospital in Saint-Rémy. He sought help in Auvers, where he shot himself, dying two days later.

Van Gogh in 1871

VISITORS' CHECKLIST

Practical Information
Paulus Potterstraat 7. **Map** 4 E3.
Tel 020-5705200.
W vangoghmuseum.com
Open 10am–5pm daily, 10am–10pm Fri. **Closed** 1 Jan.

Transport
2, 3, 5, 12.

Pietà (after Delacroix) (1889)
Van Gogh painted this work while in the hospital at Saint-Rémy. The figure of Christ is thought to be a self-portrait.

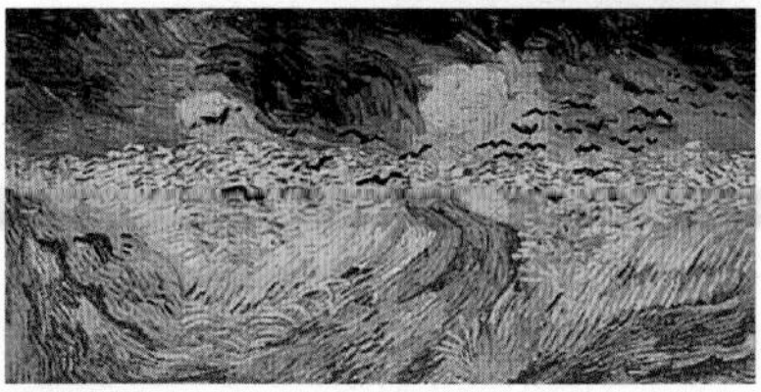

★ **Wheatfield and Crows** (1890)
The menacing crows and violence of the sky in one of his last paintings show the depth of Van Gogh's mental anguish.

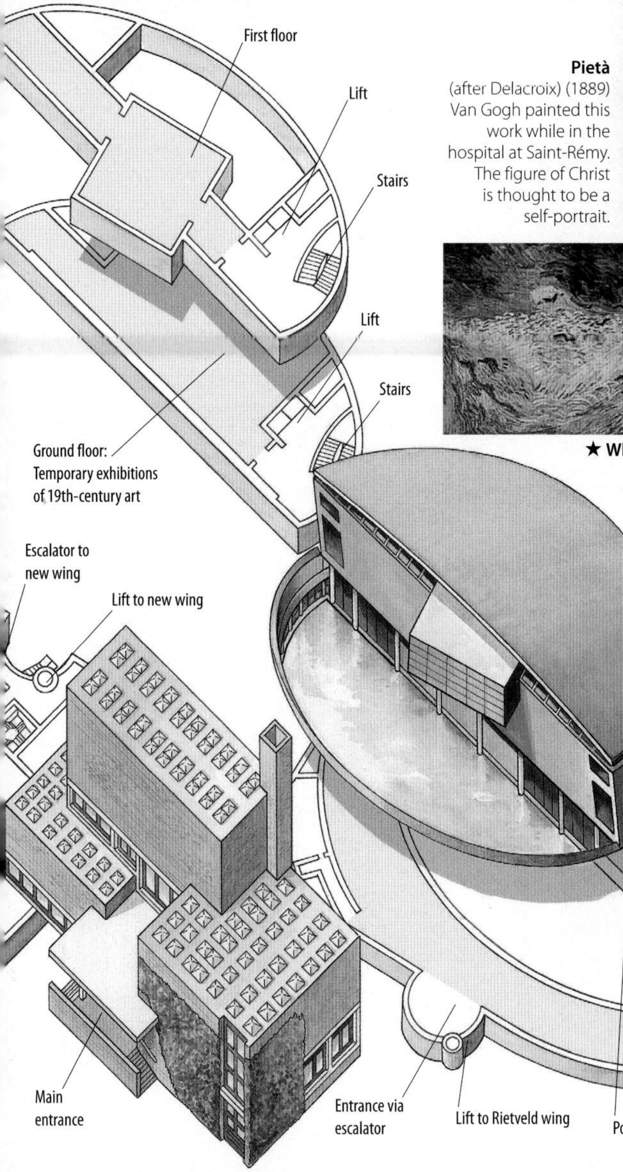

First floor
Lift
Stairs
Lift
Stairs
Ground floor: Temporary exhibitions of 19th-century art
Escalator to new wing
Lift to new wing
Basement
Lift
Stairs
Main entrance
Entrance via escalator
Lift to Rietveld wing
Pool

❹ Stedelijk Museum

The Stedelijk Museum was built to house a personal collection bequeathed to the city in 1890 by art connoisseur Sophia de Bruyn. In 1938, the museum became the national museum of modern art, displaying works by artists such as Picasso, Matisse, Mondriaan, Cézanne and Monet. The building's new wing (nicknamed "the bath tub") is an art piece in itself. The museum also organizes workshops, events and themed guided tours.

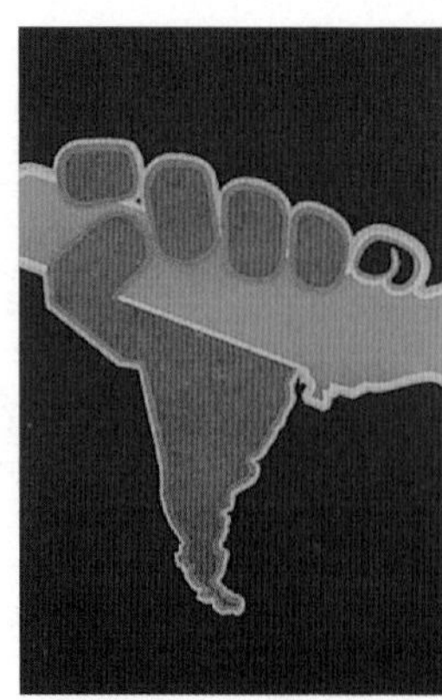

Solidaridad con America Latina (1970)
The Stedelijk's collection of rare posters comprises some 17,000 works, including this graphic image by the Cuban human rights campaigner Asela Perez.

Portrait of the Artist with Seven Fingers (1912)
Marc Chagall's self-portrait is heavily autobiographical; the seven fingers of the title allude to the seven days of Creation and the artist's Jewish origins. Paris and Rome, the cities Chagall lived in, are inscribed in Hebrew above his head.

The Museum Building

The Neo-Renaissance building was designed by AW Weissman (1858–1923) in 1895. The façade is adorned with turrets and gables and with niches containing statues of artists and architects. It makes a striking contrast with the spectacular new wing by Benthem Crouwel that houses a restaurant on the ground floor which is also open for dinner.

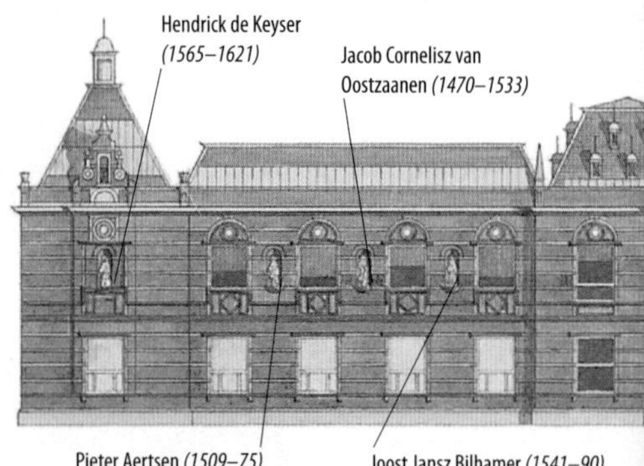

De Stijl Movement

The Dutch artistic movement known as De Stijl (The Style) produced startlingly simple designs which have become icons of 20th-century abstract art. These include Gerrit Rietveld's famous *Red Blue Chair* and Piet Mondriaan's *Composition in Red, Black, Blue, Yellow and Grey* (1920). The movement was formed in 1917 by a group of artists who espoused clarity in their work, which embraced the mediums of painting, architecture, sculpture, poetry and furniture design. Many De Stijl artists, like Theo van Doesburg, split from the founding group in the 1920s; their legacy can be seen in the work of the Bauhaus and Modernist schools which followed *(see pp208–9)*.

Gerrit Rietveld's *Red Blue Chair* (1918)

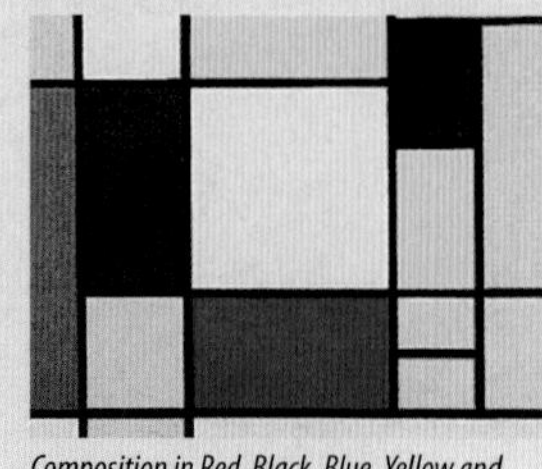

Composition in Red, Black, Blue, Yellow and Grey by Mondriaan

For hotels and restaurants in this region see pp396–397 and pp406–409

Dancing Woman (1911)
Ernst Ludwig Kirchner (1880–1938) was inspired by the primitive art of African and Asian cultures, and by the natural qualities of the materials he worked with.

Man and Animals (1949)
Karel Appel (b. 1921) was a member of the short-lived experimental Cobra movement *(see p193)*. The human figure, dog fish and mythical creature are painted in the naive style of a child.

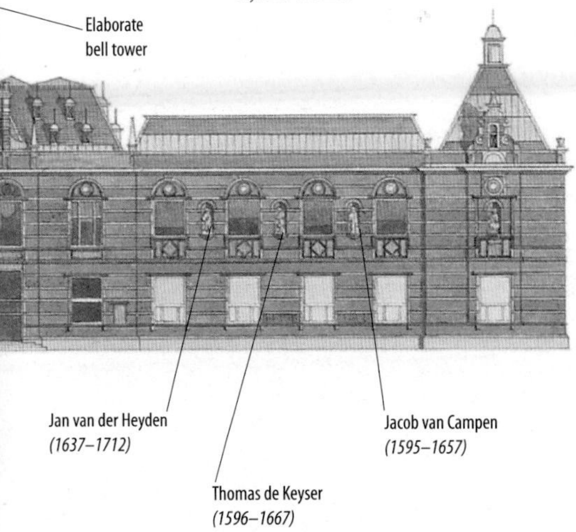

Untitled (1965)
Jasper Johns (b. 1930) believed viewers should draw their own conclusions from his work. This huge canvas, with its bold rainbow (red, blue and yellow streaks and slabs), invites the viewer to think about the symbolism of colour.

VISITORS' CHECKLIST

Practical Information
Museumplein 10.
Map 4 D3. **Tel** 020-5732911.
W **stedelijk.nl**
Open 10am–6pm daily, 10am–10pm Thu.

Transport
2, 3, 5, 12.

★ Kazimir Malevich (1878–1935)

The Russian visual artist Kazimir Malevich can be counted, along with Piet Mondriaan, as one of the founders of abstract art. As well as paintings, Malevich created posters, sculptures, furniture, interior decoration and costumes.

After studying Futurism and Cubism in Moscow, he formulated a new art form called Suprematism, an abstract movement known for its experimentation with colour. Suprematism's central element is the theory of unlimited pre-eminence of free invention in the artistic process. Up until his 20s, Malevich painted abstract geometric forms. The square was his "supreme element". The Stedelijk Museum owns the largest part of the paintings and sketches from Malevich's Suprematist period. One of the most important works, *Suprematisme 1920–1927*, was defaced by a visitor to the museum in 1997.

In 1999, a conflict arose between the Malevich estate and the Stedelijk Museum over the ownership of the dozens of Suprematist works from the Stedelijk's collection.

Self-portrait by Malevich

AMSTERDAM

OUTSIDE THE CENTRE

Great architecture and good town planning are not confined to central Amsterdam. Parts of the Nieuw Zuid (New South) bear testament to the imagination of the innovative Amsterdam School architects *(see pp146–7)*. Many fine buildings can be found in De Dageraad Housing complex and the streets around the Olympic Quarter. The area known as the Plantage (plantation) was once green parkland beyond the city wall, where 17th-century Amsterdammers spent their leisure time. From about 1848, it became one of Amsterdam's first suburbs. The tree-lined streets around Artis and Hortus Botanicus are still popular places to live. From the Werf 't Kromhout, once a thriving shipyard, there is a fine view of De Gooyer Windmill, one of the few in Amsterdam to survive. The national maritime collection is kept at Scheepvaart Museum, a former naval storehouse. NEMO, an educational science centre, is nearby. Fine parks are just a short tram ride from the city centre and offer a host of leisure activities.

Sights at a Glance

Historic Buildings and Structures

2 Entrepotdok
3 Java-eiland and KNSM-eiland
4 Muiderpoort
5 De Gooyer Windmill
7 Koninklijk Theater Carré
8 Amstelsluizen
11 Frankendael
14 Heineken Experience
15 Huizenblok de Dageraad
17 Amsterdam RAI

Markets

18 De Pijp/Albert Cuypmarkt

Museums and Zoos

1 *Scheepvaart Museum pp136–7*
6 Werfmuseum 't Kromhout
9 *Science Center NEMO pp140–41*
10 *Artis Amsterdam Zoo pp142–3*
13 Hermitage Amsterdam
12 Tropenmuseum
16 Verzetsmuseum

Key

Central Amsterdam
Motorway
Main road
Minor road
Railway

0 kilometres 1
0 miles 1

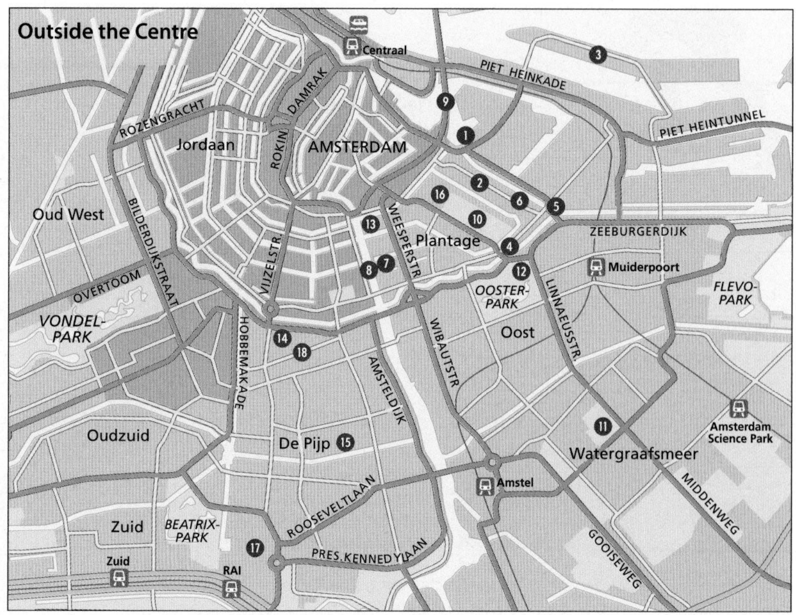

◀ Replica of the *Amsterdam*, an East Indiaman, moored alongside the Scheepvaartmuseum

For map symbols *see back flap*

❶ Scheepvaart Museum

Once the arsenal of the Dutch Navy, this vast Dutch Classical building was designed by Daniël Stalpaert in 1655. Constructed around a massive courtyard, it was supported by thousands of piles driven into the bed of the Oosterdok. The navy occupied the building until the 20th century, and in 1973 it became the Netherlands Maritime Museum. After a major renovation it reopened in 2011; the courtyard, now covered by a vast glass roof, forms the heart of the new exhibition space.

★ Golden Age
Seven characters welcome you to this exhibition covering the golden era of Dutch exploration and trade in the 16th and 17th centuries.

First floor

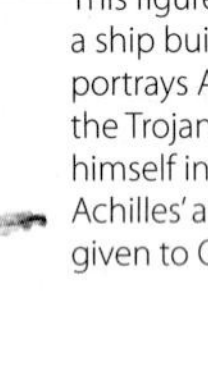

Ajax
This figurehead is from a ship built in 1832. It portrays Ajax, a hero of the Trojan War, who killed himself in despair when Achilles' armour was given to Odysseus.

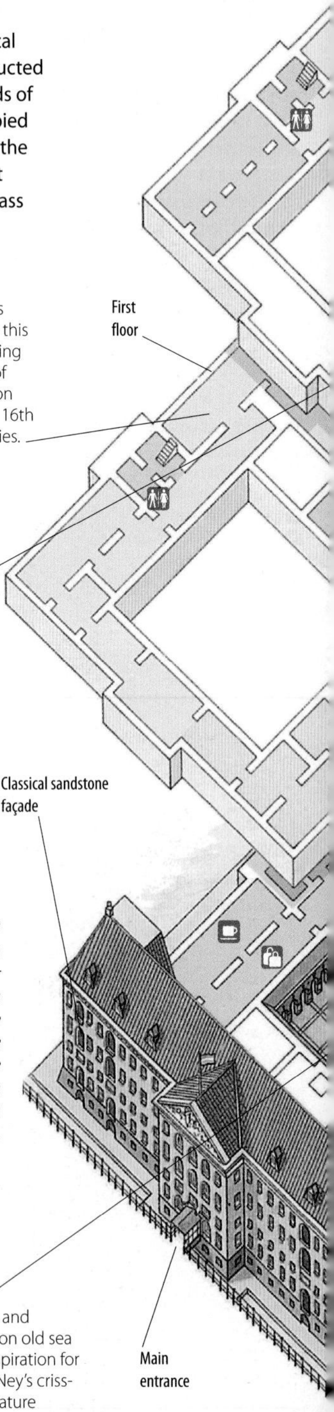

Classical sandstone façade

Museum Guide

This museum's exhibits reveal Dutch maritime history. On a Virtual Sea Trip or aboard the East Indiaman Amsterdam *you can relive the past; other exhibits tell the stories of whaling, the Golden Age and the port of Amsterdam. Objects on Stage showcases the museum's superb collection of nautical paintings, navigation instruments and antique globes.*

Glass Canopy
The compass rose and navigational lines on old sea maps were the inspiration for architect Laurent Ney's criss-crossing steel armature supporting the glass roof.

Main entrance

For hotels and restaurants in this region see pp396–397 and pp406–409

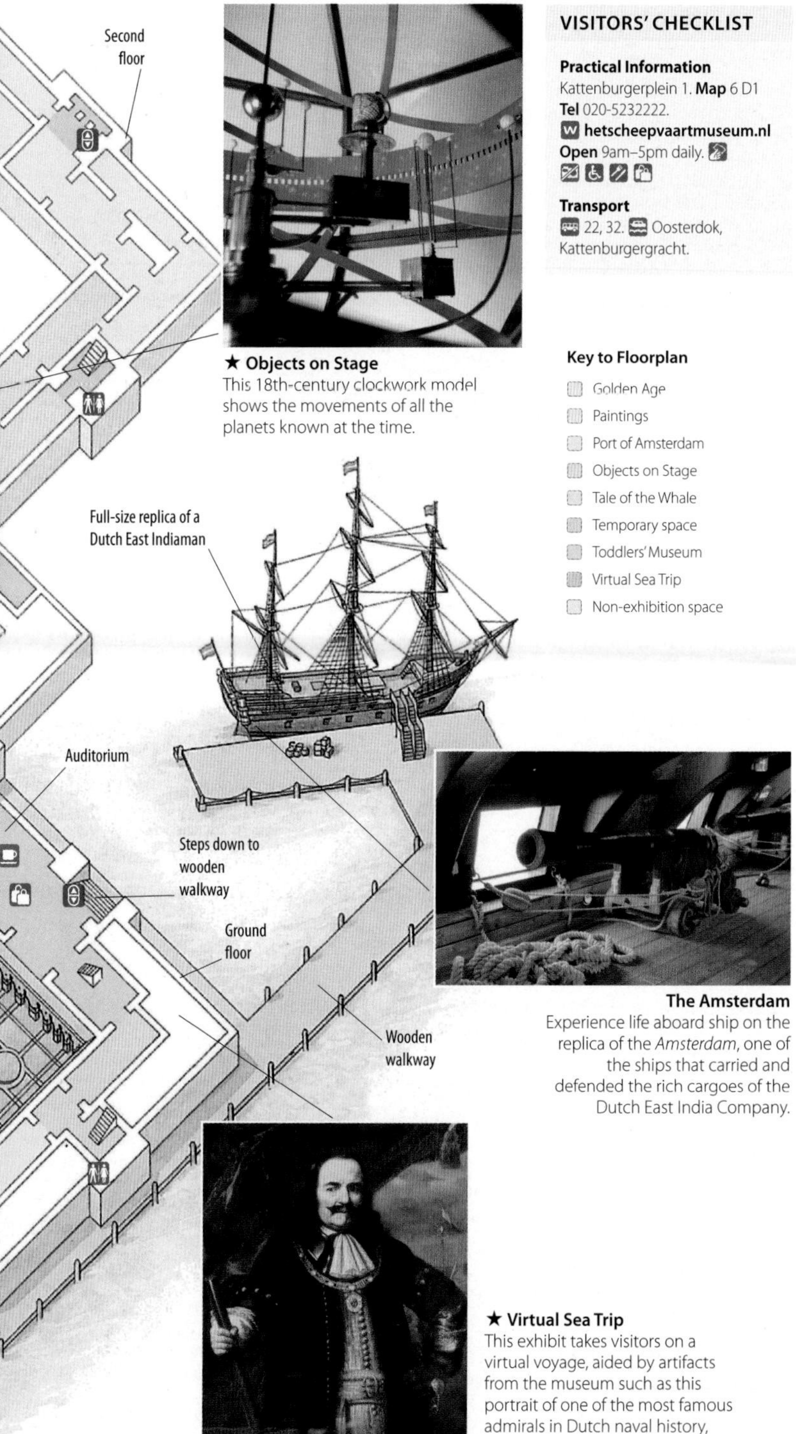

★ Objects on Stage
This 18th-century clockwork model shows the movements of all the planets known at the time.

The Amsterdam
Experience life aboard ship on the replica of the *Amsterdam*, one of the ships that carried and defended the rich cargoes of the Dutch East India Company.

★ Virtual Sea Trip
This exhibit takes visitors on a virtual voyage, aided by artifacts from the museum such as this portrait of one of the most famous admirals in Dutch naval history, Michiel de Ruyter (1607–76).

VISITORS' CHECKLIST

Practical Information
Kattenburgerplein 1. **Map** 6 D1
Tel 020-5232222.
hetscheepvaartmuseum.nl
Open 9am–5pm daily.

Transport
22, 32. Oosterdok, Kattenburgergracht.

Key to Floorplan

- Golden Age
- Paintings
- Port of Amsterdam
- Objects on Stage
- Tale of the Whale
- Temporary space
- Toddlers' Museum
- Virtual Sea Trip
- Non-exhibition space

❷ Entrepotdok

Map 6 D2. 🚋 9, 14, 32. 🚌 22, 43.

The redevelopment of the old VOC warehouses at Entrepotdok has revitalized this dockland area. During the mid-19th century, it was the greatest warehouse area in Europe, being a customs-free zone for goods in transit. The quayside buildings are now a lively complex of homes, offices and eating places. Some of the original façades of the warehouses have been preserved, unlike the interiors, which have been opened up to provide an attractive inner courtyard. Café tables are often set out alongside the canal. On the other side, brightly coloured houseboats are moored.

❸ Java-eiland and KNSM-eiland

Map 6 D2. Java-eiland and KNSM-eiland 🚌 41, 42. 🚋 10.

Situated side by side in the eastern docklands of the city are the islands of Java-eiland, which is long and narrow, and the broader KNSM-eiland. Java-eiland, designed by Sjoerd Soeters during the 1990s, demonstrates a wide variety of architectural styles. By combining these styles with a number of canals across the island, the architect succeeded in creating a very credible

The 18th-century De Gooyer windmill, with its renovated balcony

Amsterdam canal atmosphere. This is compounded by the many shops and small cafés. KNSM-eiland is slightly broader, giving architect Jo Coenen the space to create a central avenue flanked on either side by tower blocks.

❹ Muiderpoort

Alexanderplein. **Map** 6 E3. 🚋 7, 9, 10, 14. **Closed** to the public.

Formerly a city gate, the Muiderpoort was designed by Cornelis Rauws (1732–72) in about 1770. The central archway of this Classical structure is topped with a dome and clock tower. Napoleon entered the city through this gate in 1811 and, according to legend, forced the citizens to feed and house his ragged troops.

❺ De Gooyer Windmill

Funenkade 5. **Map** 6 F2. 🚋 10, 14. **Closed** to the public.

Of the six remaining windmills within the city's boundaries, De Gooyer, also known as the Funenmolen, is the most central. Dominating the view down the Nieuwevaart, the mill, built around 1725, was the first corn mill in the Netherlands to use streamlined sails.

It first stood to the west of its present site, but the Oranje Nassau barracks, built in 1814, acted as a windbreak, and the mill was then moved piece by piece to the Funenkade. The octagonal wooden structure was rebuilt on the stone foot of an earlier water-pumping mill, demolished in 1812.

By 1925, De Gooyer was in a very poor state of repair and was bought by the city council, which fully restored it. Since then, the lower part of the mill, with its neat thatched roof and tiny windows, has been a private home, though its massive sails still creak into action sometimes. Next to the

Spout-gable façades of former warehouses along Entrepotdok

For hotels and restaurants in this region see pp396–397 and pp406–409

KNSM-eiland: a thriving modern city district

mill is the IJ brewery, with its own tasting room (www.brouwerijhetij.nl).

❻ Werfmuseum 't Kromhout

Hoogte Kadijk 147. **Map** 6 E2. **Tel** 020-6276777. 9, 10, 14. 22, 43. Oosterdok or Artis. **Open** 10am–3pm Tue and by appointment. **Closed** public hol.
machinekamer.nl

The Werfmuseum 't Kromhout is one of the oldest working shipyards in Amsterdam and is also a museum. Ships were being built here as early as 1757. In the second half of the 19th century, production changed from sailing ships to steamships. As ocean-going ships got bigger, the yard, due to its relatively small size, turned to building lighter craft for inland waterways. It is now used only for restoration and repair work.

In 1967, the Prince Bernhard Fund bought the site, saving it from demolition. The Amsterdam Monuments Fund later became involved to safeguard the shipyard's future as a historical site and helped turn it into a museum.

The museum is largely dedicated to the history of marine engineering, concentrating on work carried out at the shipyard, with steam engines, maritime photographs and ephemera. Another point of interest is the shipyard's forge featuring a variety of interesting tools and equipment. Some impressive historical ships are moored at the quayside. The museum's eastern hall is sometimes used for receptions and dinners.

The Werfmuseum 't Kromhout museum, located not far from the inner city

❼ Koninklijk Theater Carré

Amstel 115–125. **Map** 5 B3. **Tel** 0900-2525255. 4, 7, 9, 10. Weesperplein. Box office: **Open** 12am–6pm daily. See Entertainment: p147. 11am Sat *(phone in advance)*.
theatercarre.nl

During the 19th century, the annual visit of the Carré Circus was a popular event. In 1868, Oscar Carré built wooden premises for the circus on the banks of the Amstel river. The city council considered the structure a fire hazard, so Carré persuaded them to accept a permanent building modelled on his other circus in Cologne. Built in 1887, the new structure included both a circus ring and a stage. The Classical façade is richly decorated with sculpted heads of dancers, jesters and clowns.

The Christmas circus is still one of the annual highlights at the theatre, but for much of the year the stage is taken over by concerts and blockbuster musicals.

Pillar decoration on Theater Carré

❽ Amstelsluizen

Map 5 B3. 4, 7, 9, 10, 14. Weesperplein.

The Amstelsluizen, a row of sturdy wooden sluice gates spanning the Amstel river, form part of a complex system of sluices and pumping stations that ensure Amsterdam's canals do not stagnate. Four times a week in summer and twice a week in winter, the sluices are closed while fresh water from large lakes north of the city is allowed to flow into Amsterdam's canals. Sluices to the west of the city are left open, allowing the old water to flow, or be pumped, into the sea.

The Amstelsluizen date from 1673, and were operated manually until 1994, when they were mechanized.

9 Science Center NEMO

Science Center NEMO, an educational centre for science and technology, is housed in a striking modern building by the Italian architect Renzo Piano. Designed in the form of a ship, it overhangs the water by 30 m (99 ft): the view from the roof is breathtaking. There are five floors of constantly changing things to do and discover including interactive exhibitions, theatre shows, films, workshops and demonstrations.

Amazing Constructions
Discover why buildings and bridges are so strong and see a scale model of Rotterdam's Erasmus Bridge.

★ The Search for Life
Discover how life began on our world, and explore the possibilities of alien lifeforms.

Bubble-blowing
Can you fit inside a giant bubble? Experiment with giant rings and vats of soapy water.

KEY

① **The motorway** approach to the tunnel under the IJ is beneath the building.

② **Machine Park** focuses on technology.

③ **In NEMO's Wonderlab** you can use real laboratory equipment to do experiments.

④ **In Little NEMO's** Bamboo House you can learn how a house is built.

⑤ **Bridge to the Centraal Station**

★ Chain Reaction
This entertaining show demonstrates cause and effect and action and reaction, with plenty of audience participation.

Nemo: the Philosophy

The word "nemo" is Latin for "no one" and refers to a world between fantasy and reality. At NEMO visitors can become a scientist or technician for a day. The name has been used by a number of important writers over the centuries to describe events and people who find themselves on the thin line between reality and fantasy. For example, Nemo turns up in the Latin translation of Homer's *Odyssey*, when the protagonist Ulysses adopts the name to deceive the Cyclops. And Jules Verne, in his 1870 novel *20,000 Leagues Under the Sea*, enlists Nemo as the mystical captain of the underwater *Nautilus*, which journeys in the shadowy world between reality and fantasy. He crops up again in 1905, when American cartoonist Winsor McCay creates *Little Nemo*, a young boy whose dreamland adventures once again suggest a mingling of fact and fiction.

VISITORS' CHECKLIST

Practical Information
Oosterdok 2. **Map** 5 C1.
Tel 020-5313233
(groups 020-5313118).
W **e-nemo.nl**
Open 10am–5pm Tue–Sun; during school holidays: 10am–5pm daily. **Closed** 1 Jan, 27 Apr, 25 Dec.

Transport
1, 2, 4, 5, 9, 13, 14, 16, 17, 24, 26. 22, 42, 43.

★ View from the Roof
The view from the building's roof provides a stunning vista of the port and city. In summer, the roof terrace becomes a popular sunning and leisure area.

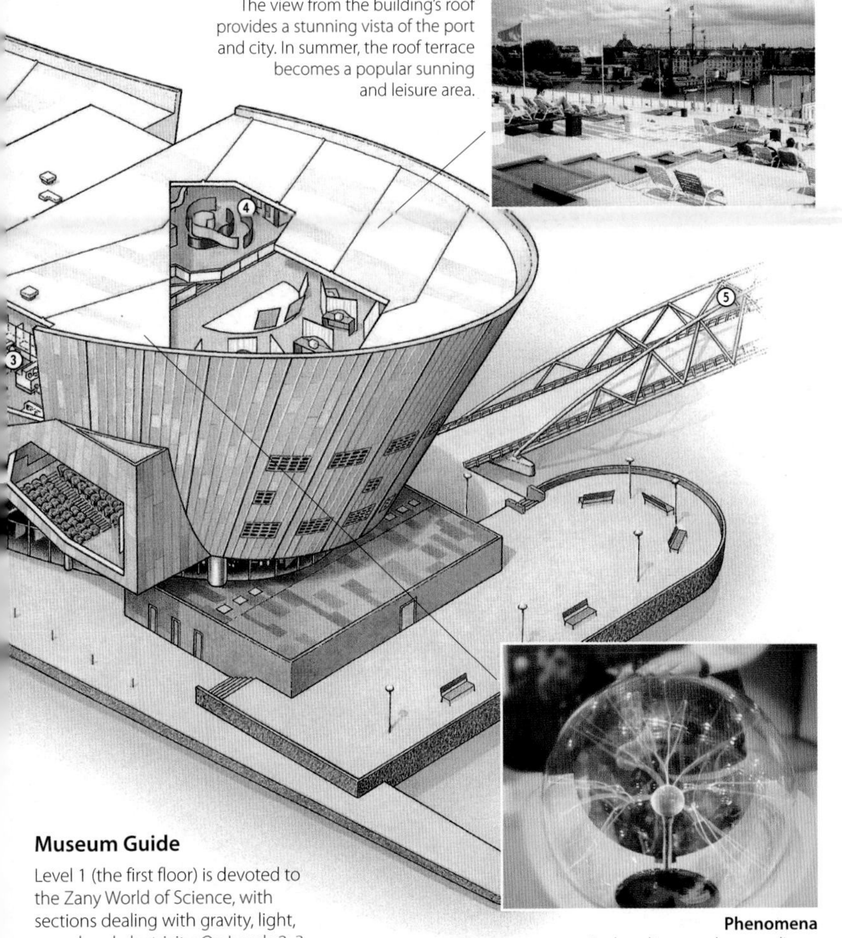

Phenomena
Both ordinary and extraordinary natural and scientific phenomena can be experienced in this interactive exhibition.

Museum Guide

Level 1 (the first floor) is devoted to the Zany World of Science, with sections dealing with gravity, light, sound and electricity. On Levels 2, 3 and 4 you will find areas such as The Search for Life, Machine Park, Water World and NEMO's Wonderlab.

⑩ Artis Royal Zoo

Amsterdam's royal zoo is in Plantage, an elegant Amsterdam neighbourhood of broad tree-lined streets with elegant painted sandstone houses. Some 750 different animal species live in Artis Zoo. Visitors can see the historic nature of the zoo as soon as they pass through the entrance gates, which have been decorated since 1854 with two "golden" eagles. The Artis complex includes a planetarium, where you can learn about the heavens and stars, and the fine Neo-Classical aquarium, containing a wide variety of marine life, from tropical fish and sharks to huge moray eels.

Tiger Python
The female specimen in Artis has borne young simply by cloning herself.

★ Planetarium
The planetarium explores the relationship between humans and the stars. The night sky is recreated on the dome, and interactive exhibitions show the positions of the planets. Model spacecraft are on display in the hall around the auditorium. The interesting slide show is specially designed for youngsters.

KEY

① **The playground,** situated next to the Two Cheetahs restaurant, is popular with children.

② **The northern side** of the zoo is currently used as a car park, but in the near future will be added to the Zoo, with parking underground.

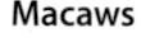

Macaws
These birds are a highly endangered species which Artis helps preserve. The zoo is renowned for its breeding programmes.

For hotels and restaurants in this region see pp396–397 and pp406–409

★ African Savannah
In the African Savannah, the animals roam in more natural surroundings. The zebras, gnus and gazelles feel at home here.

VISITORS' CHECKLIST

Practical Information
Plantage Kerklaan 38–40.
Tel 0900 2784796.
W artis.nl
Open summer: 9am–6pm daily (open until sunset on Sat); winter: 9am–5pm daily.

Transport
9, 10, 14.

Gorillas
Gorilla Binti's son Bwana was born as part of the zoo's breeding programme.

Sea Lions
Feeding time for the sea lions is a popular daily attraction at the zoo.

★ Aquarium
This fine Neo-Classical building from 1882 is home to thousands of marine animals but also contains fish from Amsterdam's canals.

⓫ Frankendael

Middenweg 72. **Map** 6 F5. 9.
41, 65, 101, 136, 152, 157.
Open dawn–dusk.

During the early part of the 18th century, many of Amsterdam's wealthier citizens built country retreats south of Plantage Middenlaan on reclaimed land called the Watergraafsmeer. The elegant Louis XIV-style Frankendael is the last survivor. The house is closed to the public; the best views of the ornamented façade are from Middenweg. This is also the best place to view the fountain made in 1714 by Ignatius van Logteren (1685–1732), a sculptor who, along with his son, played a central role in the development of Amsterdam's Louis XIV style.

The rear gardens have been restored and are open to the public. Behind the house is a small formal garden, and beyond lies a landscaped, English-style garden. There are also allotment gardens. The coach house is now home to café-restaurant Merkelbach.

The ornamental façade of Frankendael House

Ignatius van Logteren's fountain in the grounds of the Frankendael

⓬ Tropenmuseum

Linnaeusstraat 2. **Map** 6 E3.
Tropenmuseum: **Tel** 020-5688200.
Open 10am–5pm daily, 10am–3pm 5 Dec, 24 Dec, 31 Dec.
Closed 1 Jan, 27 Apr, 5 May, 25 Dec.
tropenmuseum.nl
Tropenmuseum Junior: **Tel** 020-5688233. **Open** for special programmes in Dutch language only *(phone or see website)*. **Closed** As Tropenmuseum. 9, 14.
kindermuseum.nl

Built to house the Dutch Colonial Institute, this vast complex was finished in 1926 by architects MA and J Nieuwkerken. The exterior is decorated with symbols of imperialism, such as stone friezes of peasants planting rice. Upon completion of the building's renovation in 1978, the Royal Tropical Institute opened a museum, with a huge central hall and three levels of galleries. The institute's aims are to study and to help improve the lives of the indigenous populations of the tropics. The displays focus on development issues regarding daily life, education and colonization. The impressive mask collection includes feathered fertility masks from Zaire and carved wooden masks from Central America. Gerrit Schouten's 1819 diorama made of papier-mâché and painted wood depicts life in Suriname.

Balinese tiger protector mask and model at the Tropenmuseum

⓭ Hermitage Amsterdam

Amstel 51. **Map** 8 E5. **Tel** 0900 437 648243. 4, 9, 14. Waterlooplein. Muziektheater. **Open** 10am–5pm daily (to 8pm Wed). free for under 16s. **Closed** 1 Jan, 27 Apr, 25 Dec.
hermitage.nl

In the early 1990s the State Hermitage Museum in St Petersburg, Russia, chose Amsterdam as the ideal city in which to open a satellite museum displaying temporary exhibitions drawn from the Hermitage's rich collection. It is housed in the former Amstelhof – a shelter for poor elderly women – and opened in 2004 with a spectacular exhibition of fine Greek gold jewellery from the 6th to the 2nd century BC. The museum, which has an auditorium and a children's wing, also has a fine restaurant, Neva, which is open to non-visitors.

For hotels and restaurants in this region see pp396–397 and pp406–409

⑭ Heineken Experience

Stadhouderskade 78. **Map** 4 F3. **Tel** 020-523 9222. 7, 10, 16, 24. **Open** 11am–5:30pm daily. **Closed** 1 Jan, 25 Dec. Under 18s with parents only.
heinekenexperience.com

This historic 1867 building once housed the Heineken brewery. Now it offers an exhibition of how beer is made, culminating in a tasting room where you can have a drink.

Interior of Amsterdam RAI with a trade fair in progress

⑮ Huizenblok De Dageraad

Pieter Lodewijk Takstraat. 4, 12, 25. **Closed** to the public.

One of the best examples of Amsterdam School architecture *(see pp146–7)*, De Dageraad (the Dawn) housing project was developed for poorer families following the Housing Act of 1901, by which the city council condemned slums and rethought housing policy. Architect HP Berlage drew up plans for the suburbs, aiming to integrate rich and poor by juxtaposing their housing. After Berlage's death, Piet Kramer and Michel de Klerk adopted his ideas. From 1918–23, they designed this complex for the De Dageraad housing association.

Imposing corner block of De Dageraad public housing

⑯ Verzetsmuseum

Plantage Kerklaan 61. **Map** 6 D2. **Tel** 020-6202535. 9, 14. **Open** 10am–5pm Tue–Fri, 11am–5pm Mon & Sat. **Closed** 1 Jan, 27 Apr, 25 Dec.
verzetsmuseum.org

Previously based in a former synagogue in Nieuw Zuid (New South), now at a site in the Plantage, the Resistance Museum holds a fascinating collection of memorabilia recording the activities of Dutch Resistance workers in World War II. It was set up by former members of the Resistance and focuses on the courage of the 25,000 people actively involved in the movement. False documents, weaponry, film clips, photographs and equipment are on display.

By 1945 there were 300,000 people in hiding in the Netherlands, including Jews and anti-Nazi Dutch. Subsequent events organized by the Resistance, like the February Strike against the deportation of the Jews, are brought to life by exhibits showing where the refugees hid and how food for them was smuggled in.

⑰ Amsterdam RAI

Europaplein. **Tel** 0900-2678373. 4. RAI. 62, 65. **Open** depending on exhibition. Enquiries: 8:30am–5:30pm Mon–Fri. with assistance. **rai.nl**

Amsterdam RAI is one of the largest exhibition and conference centres in the country. It hosts over 1,000 events annually, from cabaret to horse shows and trade fairs. The first Amsterdam trade fair was a bicycle exhibition in 1893. Subsequent shows included cars and became an annual event known as the "RAI" (Rijwiel Automobiel Industrie).

⑱ De Pijp/Albert Cuypmarkt

Albert Cuypstraat. **Map** 5 A5. 4, 16, 24. **Open** 9:30am–5pm Mon–Sat.

The Albert Cuypmarkt, part of the De Pijp area, began trading in 1904 and is still going strong, with over 325 stalls selling flowers, clothing, poultry, fish and other items. De Pijp, once a poor working class sector, has turned into one of the city's liveliest areas. The rest of the area has gentrified and now features designer bars, restaurants and trendy shops, while Sarphatipark is a haven of tranquility amidst the hustle and bustle.

The Amsterdam School

The industrial revolution at the end of the 19th century led to a boom in the growth of towns. New districts grew around Amsterdam to accommodate the growing number of factory workers. The architects of these districts, who sought new elements for decorating building façades, became known collectively as the Amsterdam School. Their designs were characterized by exotic rooflines, ornamental brickwork, cornices, window frames and corner formations which gave the façades "movement".

Curves and serpentines on façades are typical features of the Amsterdam School.

The Betondorp (Concrete Village), officially known as Tuindorp Watergraafsmeer, was the first place where experimental concrete-work was used. It also features many brick buildings in the Amsterdam School style.

The Scheepvaarthuis was erected on the spot where in 1595 Cornelis Houtman set off on his first voyage to the East Indies.

HP Berlage (1856–1934)

Berlage studied at the technical college of Zurich from 1875 to 1878, where he came into contact with architects such as Semper and Viollet-le-Duc. Inspired by their ideas, he developed his own style, which incorporated traditional Dutch materials. It later evolved into the Amsterdam School style of architecture. Berlage designed not only buildings but also interiors, furniture and graphics. In 1896, he was appointed to design the Beurs, the new stock exchange in Amsterdam *(see p95)*. Completed in 1903, it is an austere building whose structure is clearly visible. Berlage was also active as a town planner. His design of Amsterdam-Zuid ("Plan Zuid") consists of monumental residential blocks. At its centre stands JF Staal's *Wolkenkrabber* (skyscraper).

Detail of a set of windows on the Zaanstraat

Het Schip, built by Michel de Klerk, is a former post office which now provides a home for the Museum voor de Volkshuisvesting (museum of public housing).

An astonishing variety of decoration could be achieved with this kind of brickwork.

Interiors and exteriors are characterized by an excess of expressionist glass ornamentation and details.

Sculptures

Amsterdam School lettering

The Architecture of the Amsterdam School

From 1911 to 1923, the members of the Amsterdam School built a large number of office and residential complexes. One of the greatest examples of this is the Scheepvaarthuis (1913–16 and 1926–8), which is today the Grand Hotel Amrâth Amsterdam, which also organizes tours for non-residents.. It is the first building to be completed entirely in the Amsterdam School style. It was designed by the Van Gendt brothers and JM van der Meij. Michel de Klerk, who later designed Het Schip, was also involved in the project.

Michel de Klerk (1884–1923)

Street furniture was among the repertoire of the Amsterdam School architects. In the Spaarndammerbuurt in particular, many examples can still be seen, including fire alarms, cable boxes and post boxes.

SHOPPING IN AMSTERDAM

Amsterdam has a huge range of shops and markets. Most of the large clothing and department stores are to be found in the Nieuwe Zijde, especially along Kalverstraat, but there are many other shopping areas to discover. The narrow streets crossing the Canal Ring, such as Herenstraat and Hartenstraat, contain a diverse array of specialist shops selling everything from ethnic fabrics and beads to unusual games and handmade dolls. The best luxury fashion is to be found on PC Hooftstraat and Van Baerlestraat. However, if you are looking for a bargain, take time to etxplore the street markets and numerous second-hand shops.

The northern end of the Waterlooplein, home to the famous flea market

Opening Hours

Shops are usually open from 9am to 6pm Tuesday to Saturday, from 1pm to 6pm Mondays. Many are open Sundays. In the city centre most shops now close at 7pm (9pm on Thursdays) and are open on Sundays.

How to Pay

Cash is the most popular method of payment. If you intend to use a credit card, ask first if it is accepted. Cards are becoming more widely accepted, but department stores may require purchases to be paid for at a special till, and smaller shops may accept them only for non-sale items and goods costing more than 45 euros. Some tourist shops take foreign currency but usually offer a poor rate of exchange.

Vat Exemption

Most Dutch goods are subject to value added tax (BTW) of 21 per cent for clothes and other goods, and 6 per cent for books. Non-EU residents may be entitled to a refund. Shops that stock the relevant customs forms post a "Tax free for tourists" sign.

Sales

Sales occur mainly in January and July but smaller shops and boutiques may offer discounts at any time. *Uitverkoop* describes anything from a closing-down sale to a clearance sale; *korting* merely indicates that discounts are offered. Towards the end of a sale, further discounts are often calculated at the till. Beware of clothes rails marked, for example, *VA 40* or *Vanaf 40,* as this sign means "From 40", not exactly 40 euros.

Department Stores and Malls

Amsterdam's best-known department store is **De Bijenkorf**. It has a huge perfumery and stocks a wide range of clothing. **Maison de Bonneterie** is more exclusive. Among the less expensive stores, **Hema** is popular for household goods, children's clothes and underwear. Also popular for basic items **Vroom & Dreesmann**. The only shopping malls in central Amsterdam are the Kalvertoren (Kalverstraat, near Singel) and **Magna Plaza** *(see p91)*, containing upmarket boutiques and shops.

A shop in Amsterdam selling kitchen gadgets

Markets

Amsterdammers' love of street trading is best illustrated on Koningsdag *(see p36)*, when the city centre becomes the world's biggest flea

Trendy clothing for women and men in "De Negen Straatjes"

market as locals sell off their unwanted junk.

Each district in Amsterdam has its own market. The best-known is the Albert Cuypmarkt *(see p145)*. There are also many specialist markets. Visitors and residents alike are drawn to the array of seasonal flowers at the Bloemenmarkt. Another market popular with tourists is Waterlooplein flea market *(see p83)*, where bargains can be found among the bric-à-brac; new and second-hand clothes are also for sale.

Browsers will be fascinated by the dozens of stalls at the **Looier Kunst en Antiekcentrum** *(see p117)*, selling anything from antique dolls to egg cups. On Wednesdays and Saturdays on Nieuwezijds Voorburgwal there is a stamp and coin market. Gourmets should head for the **Noordermarkt** *(see p115)*, for the Saturday organic food market. The best prices, however, are to be found about 25 km (16 miles) northwest of Amsterdam at the weekend **Beverwijkse Bazaar**, one of Europe's largest indoor flea markets. Next door you will find Oriental merchandise.

Jenever of Amsterdam

Specialist Shops

Specialist shops are dotted throughout the city. The unusual **Condomerie Het Gulden Vlies**, located in a former squat, sells condoms from all over the world. **Christmas Palace** sells festive adornments year round, and **Party House** has a vast collection of paper decorations. **Capsicum Natuurstoffen** has a huge selection of silks and linens, while **Coppenhagen 1001 Kralen** offers over 1,000 types of beads. It is also worth exploring **Joe's Vliegerwinkel** for kites, **Simon Levelt** for tea and coffee and **De Kaaskamer** for cheese.

Books and Newspapers

English-language books are easily available, particularly at **The American Book Center**, **Waterstone's** and **The English Bookshop**. They can also be picked up cheaply at second-hand shops, such as **Polare**. Comics collectors should not miss **Lambiek**. *Het Financieel Dagblad* has a daily business update in English and a weekly English-language edition. For the latest news on events, parties and exhibitions, visit the city's official tourist website www.iamsterdam.com.

Organic foods for sale at the Saturday Noordermarkt

DIRECTORY

Department Stores and Malls

De Bijenkorf
Dam 1.
Map 2 D5.
Tel 0900-0919.

Hema
Kalvertoren, Kalverstraat.
Map 4 F1.
Tel 020-4228988.
Nieuwendijk 174–176.
Map 2 D4.
Tel 020-6234176.

Magna Plaza
Nieuwezijds Voorburgwal 182.
Map 2 D4.
Tel 020-6269199.

Maison de Bonneterie
Rokin 140–142.
Map 4 F1.
Tel 020-5313400.

Vroom & Dreesmann
Kalverstraat 201.
Map 4 F1.
Tel 0900-2358363.

Markets

Boerenmarkt
Open summer: 9am–4pm Sat; winter: 9am–3pm Sat.

De Beverwijkse Bazaar
Montageweg 35, Beverwijk.
Tel 0251-262666.

Looier Kunst en Antiekcentrum
Elandsgracht 109.
Map 4 D1.
7, 10, 17.
Open 11am–5pm Sat–Thu.

Noordermarkt
Noordermarkt.
Map 1 C3.
3, 10, 13, 14, 17.

Specialist Shops

Capsicum Natuurstoffen
Oude Hoogstraat 1.
Map 2 D5.
Tel 020-6231016.

Christmas Palace
Singel 508.
Map 4 F1.
Tel 020-4210155.

Condomerie Het Gulden Vlies
Warmoesstraat 141.
Map 2 D5.
Tel 020-6274174.

Coppenhagen 1001 Kralen
Rozengracht 54.
Map 1 B4.
Tel 020-6243681.

De Kaaskamer
Runstraat 7.
Map 4 E1.
Tel 020-6233483.

Joe's Vliegerwinkel
Nieuwe Hoogstraat 19.
Map 2 E5.
Tel 020-6250139.

Party House
Rozengracht 93a/b.
Map 1 B4.
Tel 020-6247851.

Simon Levelt
Prinsengracht 180.
Map 1 B4.
Tel 020-6240823.

Books and Newspapers

The American Book Center
Spui 12. **Map** 4 F1.
Tel 020-6255537.

The English Bookshop
Lauriergracht 71.
Map 1 B5.
Tel 020-6264230.

Lambiek
Kerkstraat 132.
Map 4 E1.
Tel 020-6267543.

Polare
Kalverstraat 48–52.
Map 2 D5.
Tel 020-6225933.

Waterstone's
Kalverstraat 152.
Map 4 F1.
Tel 020-6383821.

ENTERTAINMENT IN AMSTERDAM

Amsterdam offers a diverse array of world-class entertainment. A wide variety of performances are staged in hundreds of venues throughout the city, ranging from the century-old Concertgebouw (*see p124*) to the sleek modern Muziekgebouw on the IJ river. There is a huge choice of plays and films throughout the year, and plenty of free performances are given by a multitude of street performers and live bands in late-night bars and cafés. The city's hottest annual events include the Holland Festival and the Uitmarkt (*see pp37–8*). Club-goers are in their element in the canal city, which offers clubnights to meet most tastes in music and skilled DJs, such as Tiësto, who are renowned around the globe.

The colonnaded façade of the Concertgebouw theatre

Information

Amsterdam's various tourist offices are a good starting point for what's going on in the city. They can usually provide copies of free listings magazines, including the *AUB/Uitburo* and the monthly *Uitkrant*, the definitive source of entertainment information. The city's English website www.iamsterdam.com has up-to-date entertainment listings, and the Amsterdam daily newspaper *Het Parool* publishes a supplement on Saturday with a cultural calendar and performance reviews.

The **AUB/Uitburo** has a last-minute window (open noon–7:30pm daily) selling tickets for same-day shows.

Classical Music, Opera and Dance

Amsterdam is the country's touchstone for classical music and opera, and the principal venues host some of the world's finest events. The open-air theatre in the **Vondelpark** (*see pp124–5)* stages free concerts, and in summer, the Grachtenfestival features mainly classical music on floating canal stages.

The city's musical centrepiece is the **Concertgebouw** *(see p124)*, renowned for its acoustics and home to the celebrated Royal Concertgebouw Orchestra. International orchestras and soloists perform here regularly, and it hosts the Robeco Summer Concerts, a showcase of young talent. The **Beurs van Berlage** *(see p95)*, originally the city's stock exchange, is now a concert venue.

The Netherlands Opera stages performances in the 1,600-seat **Muziektheater** *(see p83)*, whose classical and modern repertoire is without parallel. The iconic **Muziekgebouw** is the place to go for anything from chamber music to the avant-garde.

The Netherlands is home to two world-class ballet companies. The Dutch National Ballet, based in the Muziektheater, puts on classical ballet but also daring works by contemporary Dutch choreographers, while the Nederlands Dans Theater (NDT) specializes in works by its Czech artistic director, Jiri Kylian. Modern companies to look out for include Introdans, which combines jazz with flamenco and other ethnic dance, and Conny Jansen Danst, which combines theatrical elements with strong physical power. **De Meervaart** is a venue that stages modern dance, concerts and theatre.

Jazz, Pop and World Music

The Dutch are avid jazz fans, and big names such as Wayne Shorter, Branford Marsalis and Nicholas Payton show up regularly on local stages. The foremost jazz club is the **Bimhuis**, housed in a purpose-built hall of the Muziekgebouw. The Concertgebouw also hosts regular jazz concerts. Keep an eye out for local talent such as

Bourbon Street, one of the city's jazz cafés

Disco in the Heineken Music Hall

saxophonists Hans and Candy Dulfer. Good jazz cafés can be found along Zeedijk and around Leidseplein, namely **Jazzcafé Alto** and **Bourbon Street**.

For most Amsterdammers, rock and pop are synonymous with two venues. **Paradiso**, which has hosted the Rolling Stones, is housed in a converted church just off Leidseplein, while **Melkweg** occupies a former dairy nearby. Both offer a varied and entertaining diet of rock, pop, dance, rap and world music.

Mega-concerts are booked into the 50,000-seat **Amsterdam ArenA**, and headline acts sometimes play at the more intimate **Heineken Music Hall**.

As a multi-cultural society, the Netherlands is a natural breeding ground for world music. Traditions from West Africa and the West Indies, Indonesia, Surinam and Turkey come together in this fascinating melting pot. **Akhnaton** is a cultural centre with a potent cocktail of Caribbean, African and Arabic music. **De Badcuyp**, in the lively Pijp district, plays with salsa, tango, African music and other dance options. In bars like **Café Nol** and **De Twee Zwaantjes** you can hear traditional Dutch folk music.

Theatre and Cabaret

The heart of the country's lively theatre scene is in Amsterdam. The premier venue is the **Stadsschouwburg** *(see p116)*, home to the Amsterdam Theatre Group and led by the imaginative director Ivo van Hove. The annual highlight for opera, theatre and dance is the Holland Festival, held from late May to June. It overlaps with the International Theatre School Festival, whose experi- mental drama pops up at **De Brakke Grond** and **Frascati**.

The chief musical theatre is the **Koninklijk Theater Carré** *(see p139)*. It stages box-office hits such as Les Misérables and Miss Saigon. **De Kleine Komedie**, a magnificent 17th-century building on the Amstel river, is a favourite venue for cabaret groups. Stand-up comedy has gained in popularity, led by the hilarious English-language routines of **Boom Chicago**.

Experimental theatre can be found at a range of venues including **Westergasfabriek**, a converted former gas works in a lovely park setting. The company De Dogtroep stages offbeat street theatre, while Theatergroup Hollandia has won great acclaim with its performances in large halls and aircraft hangars. The musical dramas of Orkater appear mainly at the Stadsschouwburg and the **Bellevue Theater**. Summer outdoor theater can be seen in the Vondelpark *(see pp124–5)* and the Amsterdamse Bos *(see p193)*, a sprawling woodland park on the edge of town.

The Art Deco Tuschinski Theatre, a luxurious cinema experience

Cinema

Film fanatics are well looked after, with more than 40 cinemas in town. Foreign- language films are shown in the original language with subtitles. The leading Dutch filmmaker is Amsterdam-born Paul Verhoeven (of *Basic Instinct* fame). He returned to his homel- and to shoot *Black Book*, the highest-grossing Dutch film ever.

Cinema programmes change every Thursday, so check www.filmladder.nl or the Wednesday newspapers for listings. *De Filmkrant* is a free monthly film magazine with complete listings. The most

Musicians providing entertainment in the Vondelpark

stunning cinema in town is the **Tuschinski**, an Art Deco masterpiece with a luxurious foyer and stained-glass windows *(see p119)*. Some cinemas such as the mainstream **Pathé de Munt**, **City Theater** and the arthouse **Kriterion** show children's films at weekends. The **Uitkijk** is a cosy, 158-seat venue dating from 1913 that shows mainly classics.

The bright lights of Amsterdam ArenA, a premier sporting venue

Clubs and Discos

Amsterdam's nightclubs are famous for their variety and high energy. The scene throbs hardest in and around Leidseplein, Rembrandtplein and Reguliersdwarsstraat. Most clubs open at 11pm and are at their busiest from around 1am; closing time is 4am during the week and 5am on Friday and Saturday.

Jimmy Woo is famous for its tough door policy. Inside, it's Hong-Kong hip, with lots of black leather and a great sound system. **Escape** draws a young, trendy crowd to its huge split-level complex on Rembrandtplein, and another large, popular venue is **AIR**. On the opposite side of the square, **Rain** spins Latin and World beats.

The leading non-house club in town is **Sugar Factory**, with its diverse menu of soul, funk and jazz-dance. The other discos around Leidseplein are basically extended bars with small dance floors, catering to tourists. At **Odeon** near Spui Square, you can party your way up from the basement restaurant to the dance palace on the third floor.

Dancers at one of Amsterdam's many clubs

Located in the former printing building of Dutch newspapers Trouw, Het Parool, NRC and De Volkskrant, **TrouwAmsterdam** is home to a restaurant and one of the city's leading nightclubs, which attracts creative hipsters and students. The college crowd also gravitates to the dancehall of **Hotel Arena**, located in a former orphanage.

Clubbing is also at the heart of Amsterdam's gay scene. Crowds are often mixed and most gay clubs will rarely turn away women or straight men. Reguliersdwarsstraat is home to a number of gay bars, such as **NYX**, a slick bar with three levels and a balcony for viewing the dance scene below. **Prik** is a hugely popular bar that turns into a small club at night. **De Engel van Amsterdam** attracts a mixed crowd and has a splendid terrace. Young women like **Vive La Vie**, while **Saarein II** is a friendly, relaxed bar tucked away in a small street in the Jordaan. Details of other venues are available from the Pink Point kiosk next to the Westerkerk (www.pinkpoint.org).

Spectator Sports

The Dutch are a sport-mad nation, and nothing makes their pulses race faster than football. Three teams enjoy international standing: Ajax Amsterdam, Feyenoord Rotterdam and PSV Eindhoven *(see p366)*. They sometimes face off at the spectacular Amsterdam ArenA.

Two footballers clashing at an Ajax game

For something completely different, try watching a game of korfball, which was invented by Amsterdam teacher Nico Boekhuysen over 100 years ago. It mixes elements of basketball, netball and volleyball, and is the only unisex sport played professionally. Each team has four men and four women. Top-level matches are played on the indoor courts of the Olympic Stadium, built for the Games held in 1928.

DIRECTORY

Entertainment Information

AUB Ticketshop
Leidseplein 26.
Map 4 E2.
Tel 020-7959950.
W **amsterdamsuitburo.nl**

Classic Music, Opera and Dance

Beurs van Berlage
Damrak 243.
Map 2 D4.
Tel 020-5304141.
W **beursvanberlage.nl**

Concertgebouw
Concertgebouwplein 2–6.
Map 4 D4.
Tel 0900 6718345.
W **concertgebouw.nl**

De Meervaart
Meer en Vaart 300.
Tel 020-4107700.
W **meervaart.nl**

Het Muziektheater
Amstel 3.
Map 5 B2.
Tel 020-6255455.
W **muziektheater.nl**

Muziekgebouw Aan 't IJ
Piet Heinkade 1.
Map 2 F3.
Tel 020-7882000.
W **muziekgebouw.nl**

Vondelpark
Stadhouderskade.
Map 4 E2.
Tel 020-7882000.
W **vondelpark.nl**

Jazz, Pop and World Music

Akhnaton
Nieuwezijds Kolk 25.
Map 2 D4. **Tel** 020-624 3396. **W** **akhnaton.nl**

Amsterdam ArenA
ArenA Boulevard 1, Zuidoost.
Tel 020-3111333.
W **amsterdamarena.nl**

Bimhuis
Muziekgebouw aan 't IJ
Piet Heinkade 3.
Map 2 F3.
Tel 020-7882188.
W **bimhuis.nl**

Bourbon Street
Leidsekruisstraat 6–8.
Map 4 E2.
Tel 020-6233440.
W **bourbonstreet.nl**

Café Nol
Westerstraat 109.
Map 1 B3.
Tel 020-6245380.

De Badcuyp
Sweelinckstraat 10.
Map 5 A5.
Tel 020-6759669.
W **badcuyp.nl**

De Twee Zwaantjes
Prinsengracht 114.
Map 1 C3.
Tel 020-6752729.

Heineken Music Hall
Arena Boulevard 590.
Tel 0900 687 4242 55.
W **heineken-music-hall.nl**

Jazzcafé Alto
Korte Leidsedwarsstraat 115.
Map 4 E2.
Tel 020-6263249.
W **jazz-cafe-alto.nl**

Melkweg
Lijnbaansgracht 234a.
Map 4 E2.
Tel 020-5318181.
W **melkweg.nl**

Paradiso
Weteringschans 6–8.
Map 4 E2.
Tel 020-6264521.
W **paradiso.nl**

Theatre and Cabaret

Bellevue Theater
Leidsekade 90.
Map 4 D2.
Tel 020-5305301.
W **theaterbellevue.nl**

Boom Chicago
Rozentheater
Rozengracht 117.
Tel 0900 BOOM CHICAGO.
Map 1 A5.
W **boomchicago.nl**

De Brakke Grond
Vlaams Cultureel Centrum, Nes 45.
Map 2 D5.
Tel 020-6266866.
W **brakkegrond.nl**

De Kleine Komedie
Amstel 56–58.
Map 5 B3.
Tel 020-6240534.
W **dekleinekomedie.nl**

Frascati
Nes 63.
Map 2 D5.
Tel 020-6266866.
W **frascati.nl**

Koninklijk Theater Carré
Amstel 115–125.
Map 5 B3.
Tel 0900 252 5255.
W **theatercarre.nl**

Westergasfabriek
Haarlemmerweg 8–10.
Map 1 A1.
Tel 020-5860710.
W **westergasfabriek.com**

Cinema

City Theater
Kleine Gartman plantsoen 15-19.
Map 5 C3.
Tel 0900 1458.

Kriterion
Roetersstraat 170.
Map 5 C3.
Tel 020-6231708.

Pathé de Munt
Vijzelstraat 15.
Map 4 F1.
Tel 0900 1458.

Tuschinski
Reguliersbreestraat 24–36. **Map** 5 A2.
Tel 0900 1458.

Uitkijk
Prinsengracht 452.
Map 4 E2.
Tel 020-6237460.

Clubs and Discos

AIR
Amstelstraat 16. **Map** 5 A2.
Tel 020-8200670.
W **air.nl**

Club Roque
Amstel 178. **Map** 5 A2.
W **clubroque.nl**

De Engel van Amsterdam
Zeedijk 21. **Map** 2 E4.
Tel 020-4276381.
W **engelamsterdam.nl**

Escape
Rembrandtplein 11.
Map 5 A2.
Tel 020-6221111.
W **escape.nl**

Hotel Arena
's-Gravesandestraat 51.
Map 6 D4.
Tel 020-850 2400.
W **hotelarena.nl**

Jimmy Woo
Korte Leidsedwarsstraat 18. **Map** 4 E2.
Tel 020-6263150.
W **jimmywoo.com**

NYX
Reguliersdwarsstraat 42.
Map 4 F1. **W** **clubnyx.nl**

Odeon
Singel 460. **Map** 4 F1.
Tel 020-5218555.
W **odeonamsterdam.nl**

Prik
Spuistraat 109. **Map** 1 C5.
Tel 020-3200002.
W **prikamsterdam.nl**

Rain
Rembrandtplein 44
Map 5 A2. **Tel** 020-6267078.
W **rain- amsterdam.com**

Saarein II
Elandstraat 119.
Map 1 B5.
Tel 020-6234901.
W **saarein.nl**

Sugar Factory
Lijnbaansgracht 238.
Map 4 E2.
Tel 020-6270008.
W **sugarfactory.nl**

TrouwAmsterdam
Wibautstraat 127.
Map 5 C4.
Tel 020-4637788.
W **trouwamsterdam.nl**

Vive La Vie
Amstelstraat 7. **Map** 5 A2.
Tel 020-6240114.
W **vivelavie.net**

Spectator Sports

Ajax Amsterdam Football team
W **english.ajax.nl**

Olympic Stadium
Oud Zuid.
Tel 020-3054400.
W **olympischstadion.nl**

STREET FINDER

The page grid superimposed on the *Area by Area* map below shows which parts of Amsterdam are covered in this *Street Finder*. Map references given for all sights, hotels, restaurants, shopping and entertainment venues described in this guide refer to the maps in this section (the *road map* is to be found on the book's inside back cover). An index of street names and places of interest marked on the maps is on pages 162–3. The key below indicates the maps' scale and other features marked on them, including transport terminals, emergency services and information centres. All major sights are clearly marked.

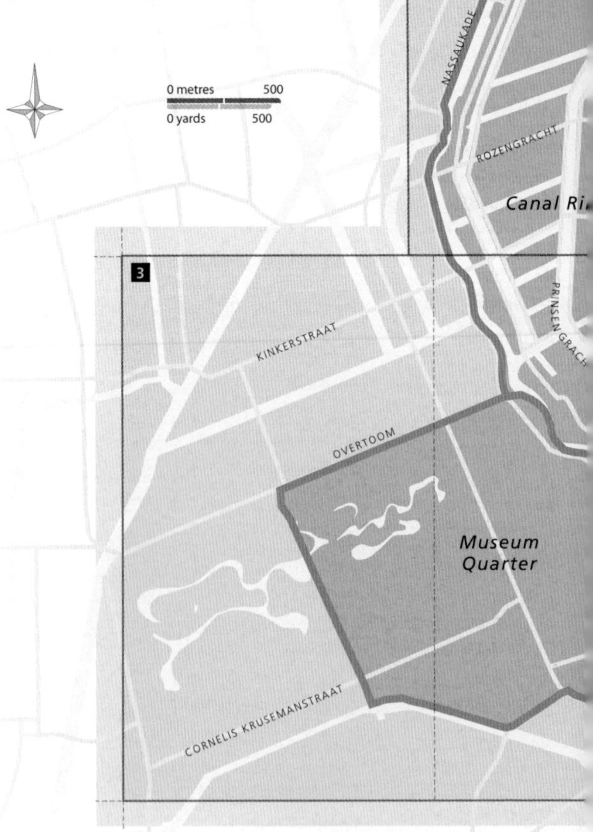

NASSAUKADE
ROZENGRACHT
Canal Ri
PRINSENGRACH
KINKERSTRAAT
OVERTOOM
Museum Quarter
CORNELIS KRUSEMANSTRAAT
1
3
0 metres 500
0 yards 500

Key to Street Finder

- Major sight
- Place of interest
- Other building
- Metro station
- Train station
- Coach station
- Tram stop
- Bus stop
- Tour boat boarding point
- Canalbus boarding point
- Museum boat boarding point
- Tourist information office
- Hospital with casualty unit
- Police station
- Church
- Synagogue
- Mosque
- Railway line
- Pedestrianized street

Scale of Map Pages 1-6

0 metres 250
0 yards 250
1:11,250

Fresh fruit for sale in the Noordermarkt *(see p115)*

House with an elevated neck gable *(see p101)* on the Geldersekade

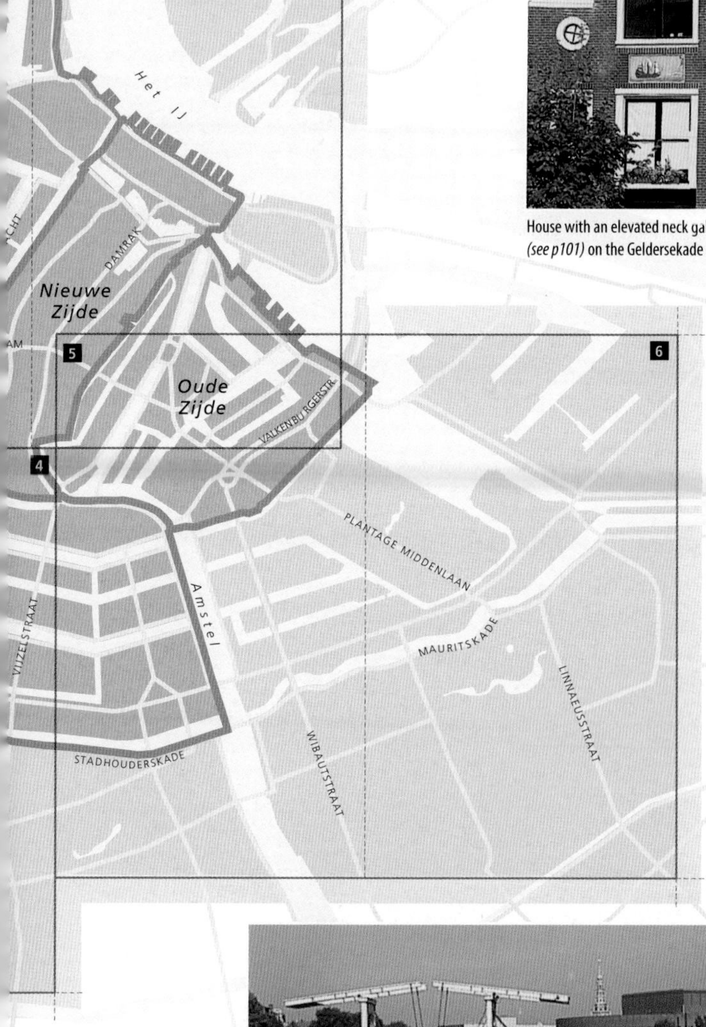

2

Het IJ

DAMRAK

Nieuwe Zijde

5

6

Oude Zijde

VALKENBURGERSTR

4

PLANTAGE MIDDENLAAN

MAURITSKADE

Amstel

VIJZELSTRAAT

LINNAEUSSTRAAT

WIBAUTSTRAAT

STADHOUDERSKADE

Magere Brug, the city's most famous bridge *(see p118)*

1
A
B
C
WESTERPARK
Haarlemmervaart
HAARLEMMERWEG
HOUTMANKADE
Westerkanaal
SPAARNDAMMERSTRAAT
ZOUTKEETSGRACHT
Zoutkeetsgracht
REALENGRACHT
Realengracht
PRINSENEILAND
BICKERSGRACHT
Bickersgracht
NASSAU PL
HAARLEMMERPL
Haarlemmerpoort
HAARLEMMERHOUTTUINEN
HAARLEMMERDIJK
BROUWERSGRACHT
NASSAUKADE
Singelgracht
MARNIXSTRAAT
LIJNBAANSGRACHT
PALMGRACHT
WILLEMSSTRAAT
GOUDSBLOEMSTRAAT
LINDENGRACHT
NOORDER MARKT
Noorderkerk
De Star Hofje
Zon's Hofje
Pianola en Piano Museum
JORDAAN
Claes Claesz-hofje
Huis met de Hoofden
EGELANTIERSGRACHT
Anne Frank Huis
WESTER MARKT
Westerkerk
Homomonument
Torensluis
RAADHUISSTRAAT
Magna Plaza
Koninklijk Paleis
ROZENGRACHT
PRINSENGRACHT
KEIZERSGRACHT
HERENGRACHT
SINGEL
SPUISTRAAT
Houseboat Museum
Felix Meritis Building
Amsterdam Museum
ELANDSGR
4

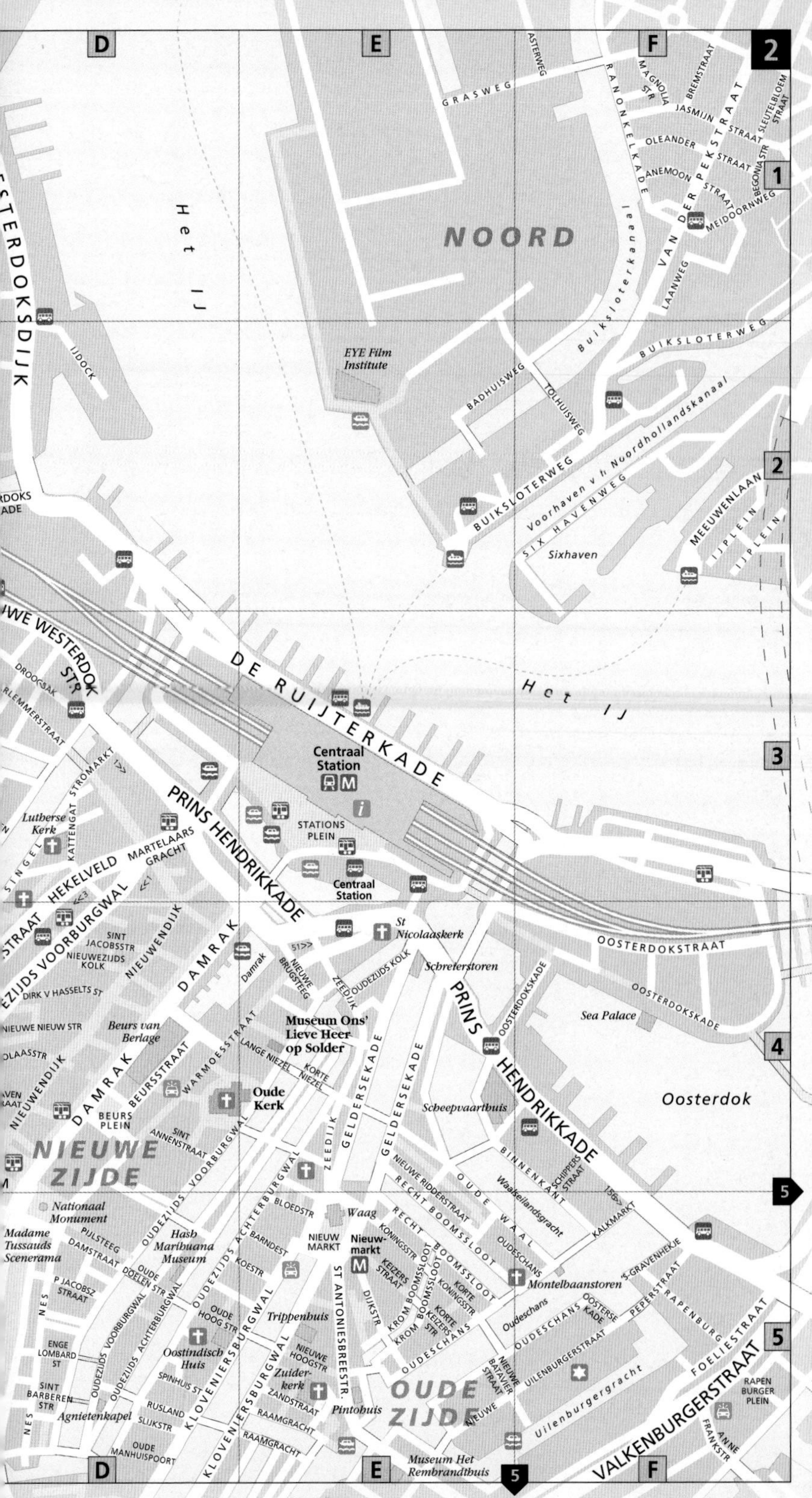
D
E
F
2
1
2
3
4
5
NOORD
Het IJ
EYE Film Institute
GRASWEG
ASTERWEG
RANONKELKADE
MAGNOLIA STR
BREMSTRAAT
JASMIJN STRAAT
SLEUTELBLOEM STRAAT
OLEANDER STRAAT
ANEMOON STRAAT
BEGONIASTR
MEIDOORNWEG
VAN DER PEKSTRAAT
LAANWEG
Buiksloterkanaal
BUIKSLOTERWEG
BADHUISWEG
TOLHUISWEG
Voorhaven v h Noordhollandskanaal
SIX HAVENWEG
Sixhaven
MEEUWENLAAN
IJPLEIN
IJDOCK
DE RUIJTERKADE
Centraal Station
STATIONS PLEIN
PRINS HENDRIKKADE
DROOGBAK
MARTELAARS GRACHT
HEKELVELD
KATTENGAT
STROMARKT
Lutherse Kerk
SINGEL
NIEUWEZIJDS VOORBURGWAL
SINT JACOBSSTR
NIEUWEZIJDS KOLK
NIEUWENDIJK
DAMRAK
DIRK V HASSELTS ST
NIEUWE NIEUW STR
Beurs van Berlage
BEURSSTRAAT
WARMOESSTRAAT
BEURS PLEIN
SINT ANNENSTRAAT
NIEUWE ZIJDE
Oude Kerk
Museum Ons' Lieve Heer op Solder
LANGE NIEZEL
KORTE NIEZEL
NIEUWE BRUGSTEEG
ZEEDIJK
OUDEZIJDS KOLK
St Nicolaaskerk
Schreierstoren
OOSTERDOKSKADE
OOSTERDOKSTRAAT
Sea Palace
Oosterdok
Scheepvaarthuis
GELDERSEKADE
BINNENKANT
SCHIPPERS STRAAT
Waalseilandsgracht
OUDE WAAL
NIEUWE RIDDERSTRAAT
RECHT BOOMSSLOOT
KALKMARKT
'S-GRAVENHEKJE
Montelbaanstoren
OUDESCHANS
Oudeschans
OOSTERSE KADE
PEPERSTRAAT
RAPENBURG
FOELIESTRAAT
RAPENBURGER PLEIN
VALKENBURGERSTRAAT
ANNE FRANKSTR
Uilenburgergracht
UILENBURGERSTRAAT
NIEUWE BATAVIER STRAAT
OUDE ZIJDE
Nationaal Monument
Madame Tussauds Scenerama
PIJLSTEEG
DAMSTRAAT
Hash Marihuana Museum
OUDEZIJDS VOORBURGWAL
OUDEZIJDS ACHTERBURGWAL
BLOEDSTR
BARNDEST
Waag
NIEUW MARKT
Nieuwmarkt
KONINGSSTR
KEIZERS STRAAT
KROM BOOMSSLOOT
KORTE KONINGSSTR
KORTE KEIZERS STR
DIJKSTR
ST ANTONIESBREESTR.
KOESTR
OUDE HOOG STR
Trippenhuis
Oostindisch Huis
NIEUWE HOOGSTR
Zuiderkerk
ZANDSTRAAT
Pintohuis
KLOVENIERSBURGWAL
SPINHUIS ST
RUSLAND
SLIJKSTR
RAAMGRACHT
P JACOBSZ STRAAT
OUDE DOELEN STR
NES
ENGE LOMBARD ST
SINT BARBEREN STR
Agnietenkapel
OUDE MANHUISPOORT
Museum Het Rembrandthuis
NIEUWE

3
OUD WEST
VONDELPARK
OUDZUID
OVERTOOM
Kostverlorenvaart
Jacob van Lennepkanaal
Amstelkanaal
Hollandse Manège
Vondelkerk
Sportpark Olympia Plein
De Lairessestraat
Cornelis Krusemanstr
Amstelveense Weg
Koningslaan
Oranje Nassaulaan
Prins Hendriklaan
Van Eeghenstraat
Willemsparkweg
Kinkerstraat
Bilderdijkstraat
Postjesweg
Apollolaan
Olympiaweg
Stadionweg

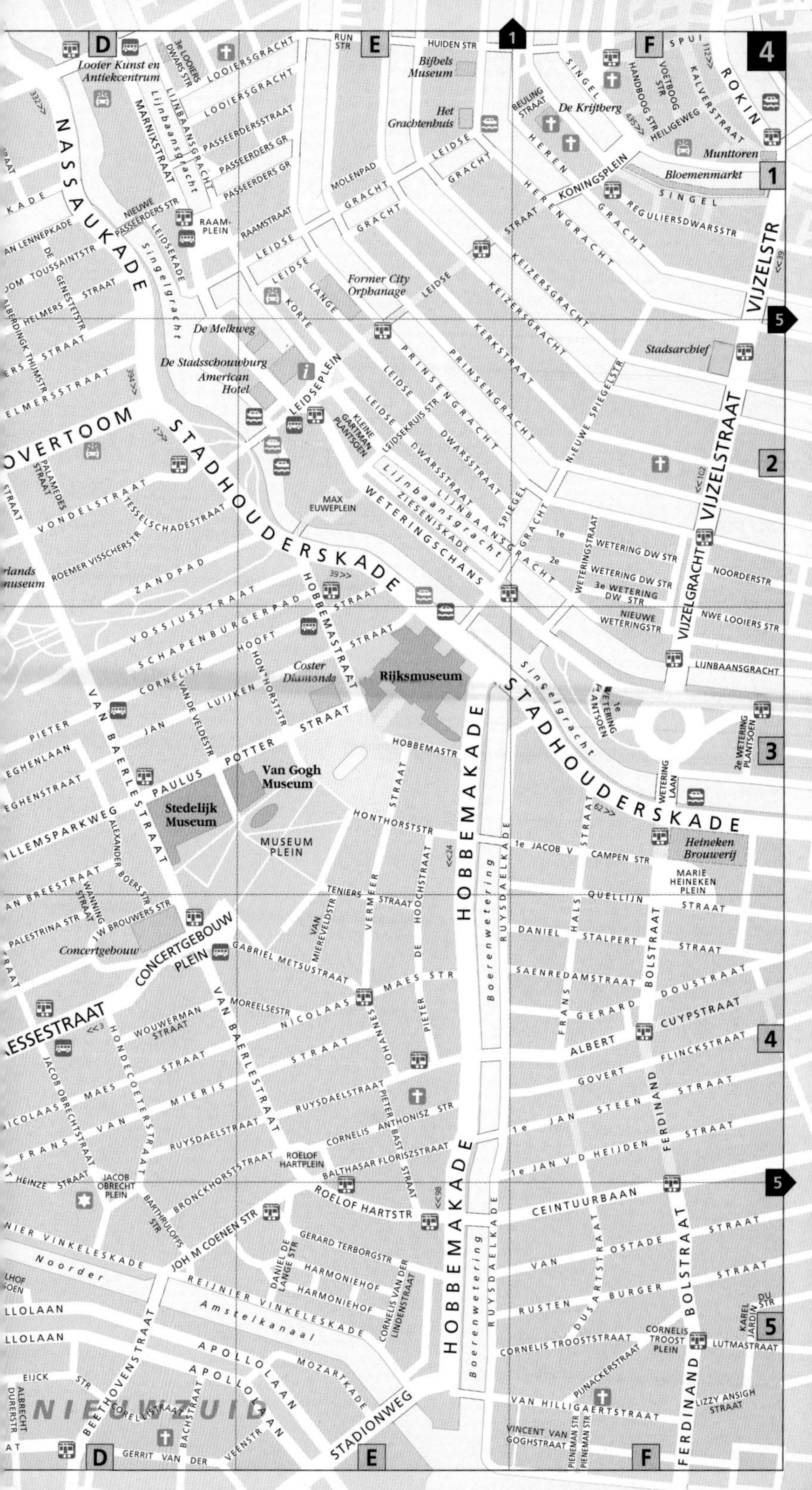

D
E
F
1
2
3
4
5
Looier Kunst en Antiekcentrum
Bijbels Museum
Het Grachtenhuis
De Krijtberg
Munttoren
Bloemenmarkt
Former City Orphanage
De Melkweg
De Stadsschouwburg
American Hotel
Stadsarchief
Max Euweplein
Coster Diamonds
Rijksmuseum
Van Gogh Museum
Stedelijk Museum
Museum Plein
Heineken Brouwerij
Marie Heineken Plein
Concertgebouw
Concertgebouwplein
Roelof Hartplein
Jacob Obrecht Plein
Cornelis Troost Plein
Nieuw Zuid
Nassaukade
Stadhouderskade
Overtoom
Leidseplein
Leidsegracht
Prinsengracht
Keizersgracht
Herengracht
Singel
Koningsplein
Vijzelstraat
Vijzelgracht
Weteringschans
Hobbemakade
Hobbemastraat
Van Baerlestraat
Paulus Potterstraat
Ferdinand Bolstraat
Albert Cuypstraat
Ceintuurbaan
Stadionweg
Apollolaan
Beethovenstraat
Rokin
Kalverstraat
Spui
Huidenstr
Runstr
Raamplein
Vondelstraat
Pieter Cornelisz Hooftstraat
Van Ostadestraat
Amstelkanaal
Boerenwetering
Ruysdaelkade

5
A
B
C
1
2
3
4
5
OUDE ZIJDE
DE PIJP
SARPHATIPARK
Hash Marihuana Museum
Waag
NIEUW MARKT
Nieuwmarkt
Montelbaanstoren
Oosterdok
PRINS HENDRIKKADE
Trippenhuis
Oostindisch Huis
Zuiderkerk
Pintohuis
Agnietenkapel
Museum Het Rembrandthuis
Mozes en Aäronkerk
Allard Pierson Museum
Stadhuis
Waterlooplein
Muziektheater
VALKENBURGERSTRAAT
WERTHEIM PARK
Portugese Synagoge
Hortus Botanicus Amsterdam
Hollandsche Schouwburg
Joods Historisch Museum
Blauwbrug
Tuschinski Theater
REMBRANDT PLEIN
Museum Willet-Holthuysen
Hermitage Amsterdam
FOAM Museum
Museum van Loon
Amstelkerk
Magere Brug
Amstelsluizen
Koninklijk Theater Carré
Weesperplein
WEESPERSTRAAT
MAURITSKADE
FREDERIKS PLEIN
STADHOUDERSKADE
AMSTELDIJK
WIBAUTSTRAAT
VAN WOUSTRAAT
Amstel

D
E
F
6
1
2
3
4
5
Het Scheepvaartmuseum
Oosterdok
KATTENBURGER STR
KATTENBURGERGRACHT
WITTENBURGERGRACHT
OOSTENBURGERGRACHT
Nieuwevaart
Kattenburgervaart
Wittenburgervaart
Oostenburgervaart
WINDROOSKADE
WINDROOS PLEIN
Werf 't Krombout Museum
Entrepotdok
ARTIS
PLANTAGE
PLANTAGE MIDDENLAAN
PLANTAGE DOKLAAN
Aquarium
Muiderpoort
SARPHATISTRAAT
ALEXANDER PLEIN
MAURITSKADE
Singelgracht
Muidergracht
Tropenmuseum
CRUQUIUSKADE
ZEEBURGERPAD
Lozingskanaal
De Gooyer Windmill
ZEEBURGER STR
ZEEBURGERDIJK
DAPPERSTRAAT
DAPPER PLEIN
LINNAEUSSTRAAT
Muiderpoort
OOST
OOSTERPARK
Onze Lieve Vrouwe Gasthuis
'S-GRAVESANDESTRAAT
'S-GRAVESANDE PLEIN
BEUKENWEG
BEUKEN PLEIN
MARITZSTR
STEVE BIKO PLEIN
TRANSVAALKADE
Ringvaart
RINGDIJK
MIDDENWEG
LINNAEUSKADE
HOGEWEG
POPULIERENWEG
VROLIKSTRAAT
POLDERWEG
BEIJERSWEG
ORANJE
OETEWALERSTRAAT
LINNAEUSPLANTSOEN
D
E
F

Street Finder Index

Each place name is followed by its arrondissement number and then by it's Street Finder reference

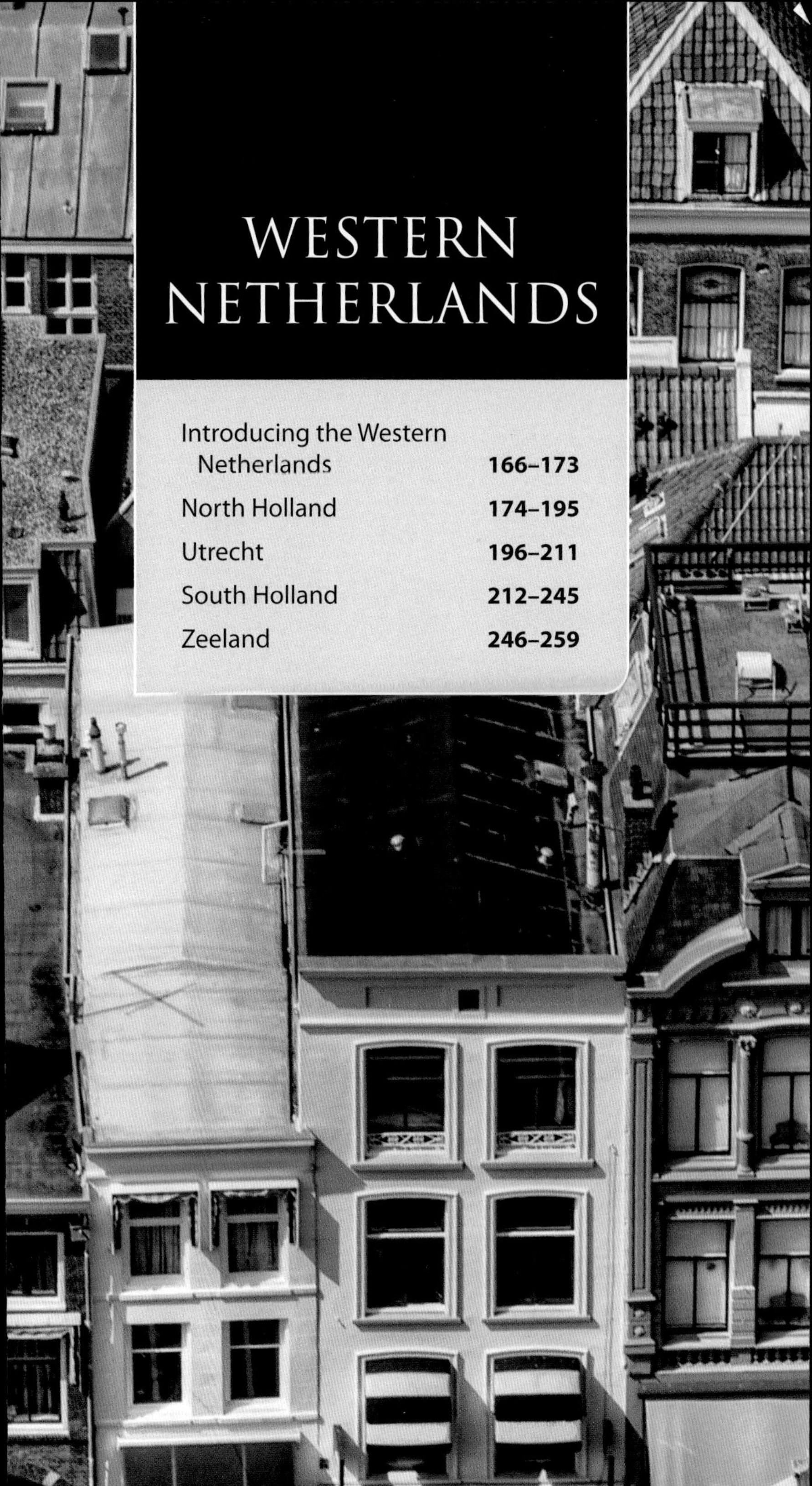

WESTERN NETHERLANDS

Western Netherlands at a Glance

The landscape of the Western Netherlands is strongly influenced by the old ports and commercial towns, which claim a prosperous past. During the 20th century, the most important ones have grown together to form the Randstad *(see pp170–71)*. But you can still find plenty of quiet outside the cities – in Europe's biggest coastal dune area, boasting its distinct flora and fauna; along the Vecht, with its pretty country houses; and along rivers such as the Vlist and the Linge. Main watersports areas are Zeeland, on the IJsselmeer and the lakes in the peat region.

The gothic Sint Bavo Church in Haarlem (*see p188*), known colloquially as the Grote Kerk, was built between 1400 and 1550. This gigantic building dominates the Grote Markt. Sint Bavo has one of the finest organs in Europe, built by Christiaan Müller.

The Mauritshuis at The Hague (*see pp226–7*) was built by Pieter Post in 1644 as instructed by Johan Maurits van Nassau, in the style of North Netherlands Neo-Classicism. Since 1821 it has been the home of the royal painting collection. This compact collection includes a number of first-rate works by old masters, including Rembrandt, Jan Steen and Johannes Vermeer.

Construction of the Oosterschelde Stormvloedkering (storm surge barrier) (*see pp250–51*) was prompted by the disastrous floods of 1953. To combat the water while preserving the unique mud-flat bed of the Oosterschelde, a half-open multiple buttress dam with 62 sliding gates was built.

◀ Colourful rooftops of Utrecht city, as seen from the Dom tower

The Zuiderzeemuseum in Enkhuizen *(see pp180–81)* is dedicated to the history of the fishing ports of the Zuiderzee. Access to the North Sea was closed off in 1932 by the Afsluitdijk (barrier dam). Enkhuizen is enjoying renewed prosperity with the opening of the museum and the conversion of the fishing port to a marina.

Gouda *(see p242)* is one of the many commercial towns in the Western Netherlands that also has its prime position on the waterways to thank for its period of prosperity. The spirit of liberalism prevalent in Gouda during the 16th and 17th centuries protected the magnificent St Janskerk from the Iconoclasm, meaning that the Gouda stained glass is still here to be enjoyed today.

The Rietveld Schröderhuis in Utrecht *(see pp208–9)* is a famous example of "nieuwe bouwen" (new building). It was Rietveld's first complete architectural work and reveals his background as a furniture maker. At the time it was considered to be radically modern. Visitors nowadays are struck by the modesty and human proportions of the house.

Reclaimed Land

The Netherlands is continually increasing in size. Various methods of reclaiming land have been employed as far back as the 11th century. One fairly simple method was to build a dyke around a marshy area. Later, deep lakes were drained with the help of windmills. The far-reaching IJsselmeer polders – fertile farmlands – were created after the Zuiderzee was closed off using ingenious reclamation methods. Even now, huge efforts are being made to extend areas of reclaimed land – hence the new Amsterdam residential area of IJburg, which has sprung up from the IJmeer.

To create a polder, a ditch was first dredged. The dredgings were used to build up the dyke.

Gradual Drainage

To overcome the height difference between the polder and the ring canal, which is sometimes large, the water is continually raised metre by metre by three windmills placed in a row, known as a *driegang* or row of three.

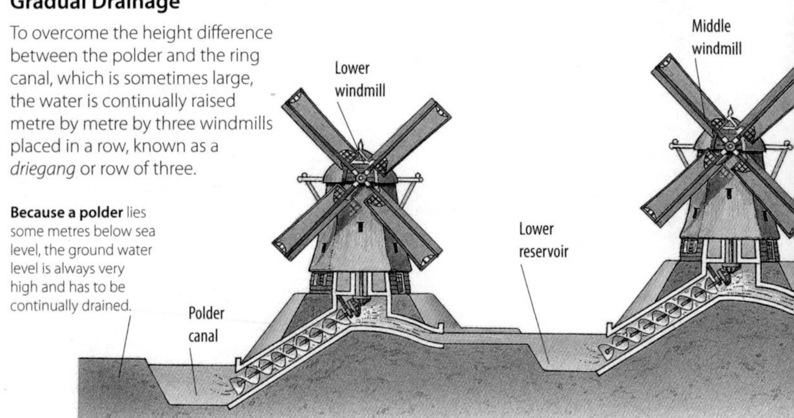

Because a polder lies some metres below sea level, the ground water level is always very high and has to be continually drained.

Land Reclamation

About 3,000 years ago, houses were built on mounds so that they would not be flooded when the water rose. As far back as the 4th to 8th centuries, dykes were built around the houses and land. Land reclamation was carried out on a large scale from the 11th century, when the population increased sharply. In the 17th and 18th centuries, deeper lakes were drained with the help of rows of windmills. The steam engine meant a new phase of land reclamation: it was now finally possible to control the Haarlemmermeer. It is thought that, in Leeghwater's time *(see p169)*, at least 160 windmills were necessary for this. In 1891, the engineer C Lely put forward a plan to close off the treacherous Zuiderzee. This only actually happened in 1932, when the Afsluitdijk (barrier dam) was completed. Construction of the IJsselmeer polders then got underway.

The old port of Schokland *(see p330)* now lies firmly on the mainland

Many dyke houses are facing a threat to their continued existence because of the raising of the river dykes.

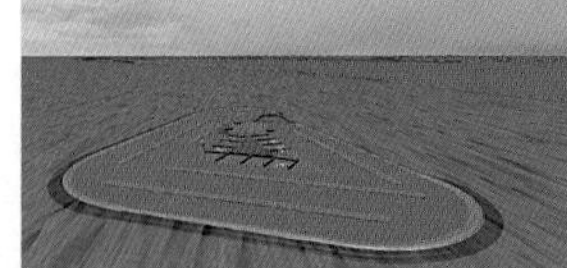

An artificial island in the North Sea is being considered for the site of a new airport, as Schiphol airport proves to be both inconvenient and with limited opportunities for expansion. Technical and financial problems, however, are delaying construction plans.

This view is of the oldest polder in North Holland (anonymous, c. 1600). The West Friesland Omringdijk, which runs around Het Grootslag, is 126 km (78 miles) long and was completed as far back as 1250. North Holland ceased to exist to the north of the dyke.

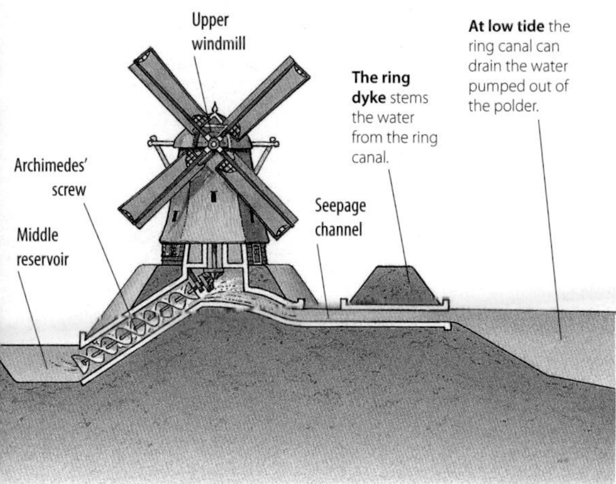

The ring dyke stems the water from the ring canal.

At low tide the ring canal can drain the water pumped out of the polder.

In the 16th century, Jan Adriaansz. Leeghwater invented a system that used windmills to drain a lake after a ring canal had been constructed around it. This meant that it became relatively easy to pump dry deeper and larger lakes, giving rise to the first pieces of reclaimed land.

Conquering the Sea

God created the earth – except Holland, for the Dutch did that. This statement by the French poet Voltaire comes close to the truth. This is because since the 14th century, the surface area of the Netherlands has increased by approximately 10 per cent, thanks to land reclamation. Land continues to be extended today, with the construction, for example, of IJburg, a new area of Amsterdam, which was built on an island in the IJmeer.

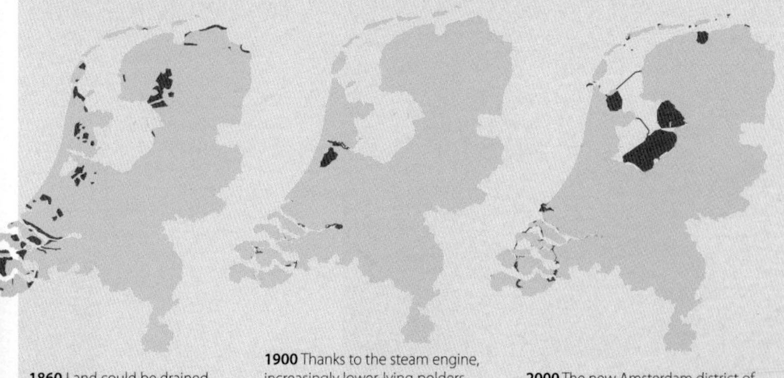

1860 Land could be drained only by using windmills. Limited areas were reclaimed.

1900 Thanks to the steam engine, increasingly lower-lying polders, such as the Zuidplaspolder, at -6.74 m (-22 ft), could be drained.

2000 The new Amsterdam district of IJburg is built in the IJmeer using the most modern methods available.

The Randstad

It appears that the term Randstad (literally, "rim city") was introduced by Albert Plesman, managing director of Dutch airline KLM, which was established in 1919. Apparently he pointed out to the passengers on one of his airplanes the horseshoe-shaped band of towns formed by Utrecht, Amsterdam, Haarlem, Leiden, The Hague, Rotterdam and Dordrecht. The relatively undeveloped area in the middle was quickly named the Groene Hart ("green heart").

By 2015, 500,000 new houses are to be built in the Randstad.

Groene Hart

The Groene Hart is a man-made landscape formed from an association with water that has lasted for centuries. It is characterized by elongated pieces of reclaimed land, peat lakes and river landscape with marshes and pools. The most important agrarian activity is dairy-cattle breeding; the cheese produced here is world-famous. Environmental organizations are dedicated to developing and protecting natural resources and historical landscapes. In de Venen, which surrounds the Nieuwkoopse and Vinkeveense lakes, a project is underway to combine extensive arable farming, natural development of the environment, and recreation facilities. It is hoped that this type of project will provide a balance to urbanization.

Hiking and cycling paths have been erected throughout the Groene Hart. They pass dairy farms, windmills and old villages. Visit the local VVV (tourist board) for more information on recreational paths.

Congestion is a major problem. During rush hour periods, the Randstad is clogged by traffic jams. The government is trying to reduce congestion on the roads by improving public transport and introducing other measures, such as road pricing. Up until now, this has not met with much success. The number of cars in the Randstad is constantly increasing. *Transferiums*, or park-and-rides, are meant to free up the town centres, which often still have old infrastructure and are not geared to a lot of traffic.

Car-pooling is another way of reducing the number of cars. Over 750,000 people have car-pooled in the last few years.

IJburg is a new district, built on the IJmeer to the east of Amsterdam. Another plan for municipal expansion into the water is Nieuw Holland, a long, narrow piece of land in front of the coast between Scheveningen and Hoek van Holland.

Schiphol was, in the last decade, the fastest-growing airport in Europe. It benefits from a central location – close to many of Holland's major cities – and good rail and road connections. Expansion of the airport was halted by the objections of residents and environmental groups, but after considering other locations, such as an artificial island in the North Sea, Schiphol will indeed expand into adjacent areas.

Growth of the Randstad

As far back as the end of the 15th century, the Western Netherlands was one of the most urbanized regions of Europe. It was only during the 20th century that the borders between the towns became blurred and what is now known as the Randstad emerged. At present 6.5 million people live here.

Randstad around 1900

Randstad around 1950

Randstad around 2000

In contrast, the Groene Hart has only 600,000 inhabitants. Earnings in the Randstad account for half of the gross national product. The main product is provision of services, with Amsterdam as the financial centre, The Hague as the administrative centre, Hilversum as the focus of the audio-visual media and Rotterdam-Rijnmond and Schiphol as an important port and airport respectively.

Dunes

The Dutch coast is famous for its dunes. These natural sea walls, with a vegetation of their own, were used in earlier times as common ground for cattle grazing (the *oerol*, *see p278*) in the absence of sufficient grassland. They now play an important role in the purification of water. The dunes are also a particularly popular recreational area – many of the protected dune areas are open to ramblers and cyclists.

A catamaran on the beach

Marram grass is a sturdy plant whose root system holds new dunes together. It plays an important role in the formation and protection of Holland's dunes.

The sea supplies the sand from which the dunes are built.

On the beach, the dry, white sand drifts and piles up.

A sea inlet is formed the sea breaks throug row of dunes.

Water collection is done by way of the dunes, which retain the fresh water that falls inside them in the form of precipitation. Drinking water has been collected since the 19th century from the dunes of North and South Holland (such as at Meyendel, near Wassenaar, pictured above), helping to eliminate diseases like cholera from densely populated cities.

Nature Reserves

The dunes are being used less and less as areas for water collection, meaning that the groundwater level is rising again and the damp dunes can once again be established. Protected against such environmentally damaging influences as industry and land development, they are becoming important nature reserves where there is a great deal for hikers and cyclists to enjoy. Vegetation includes gorse, spindle trees, creeping willow and hawthorn. Resident and migratory birds, such as curlews, tawny pipits and sometimes ospreys, inhabit the dunes. During World War II, anti-tank trenches with steep banks were built in the Midden- Heeren dunes (in Nationaal Park Zuid-Kennemerland). Today, even the rare kingfisher feels at home there.

The Dutch coast seriously damaged by storms

The first row of dunes, golden in colour because of the overgrowth, has higher summits.

The dune valleys have their own particular vegetation.

The sea inlet surface is home to many types of bird.

The dune overgrowth becomes richer as it moves inland, as limestone is replaced by humus.

The beachcomber gazes out to sea near the North Holland Camperduin, at the start of the Hondsbossche sea wall. The wall was constructed in the 19th century when the sea broke through the dunes. The lessons learned from this were used when building North Holland's Noorder- kwartier (north district).

Rabbits may look cute, but they have been known to seriously undermine the dunes with their intricate network of burrows.

Origins

Dunes are created by a process which can be seen time and time again during a stormy day on the country's long, flat beaches. The sand carried by the sea dries on the surface of the beach and is then dragged by the wind like a white shroud over the beach. Held back by any obstacles in its way, the sand starts to accumulate. If the obstacle is a plant, a dune begins to form. Plants involved in forming dunes are called pioneer plants. They must be able to tolerate being buried by the sand and also be able to grow back through the sand. Sand couch grass (*Elymus farctus*) is renowned for being one such plant. After the initial dune formation, marram grass often begins to stabilize the new dune with its enormous root system. Dunes along the coast of the Netherlands can become as high as 10 m (33 ft). The dunes here – new dunes – were formed after 1200. When the sea breaks through dunes which have collapsed or have been cut through, it creates a sea inlet, or channel, around which an entire vegetation system develops, attracting all types of birds.

Sea holly and bee

Common sea buckthorn

Bulb fields are evidence that the bulbs thrive in the sandy dune soil. The blooms' vivid colours are a pretty contrast to the yellowish-grey colour of the dunes.

NORTH HOLLAND

Although North Holland's landscape is mainly flat, it is by no means featureless. Low-lying polders, with windmills and grazing cows, give way to market gardens and colourful bulb fields. Around Amsterdam the land is more built-up, with lively towns and picturesque villages almost cheek by jowl.

North Holland has always been one of the most important areas of the Netherlands economically, due to its industry, fishing and commerce. The Zuiderzee ports played a major part in the voyages of the Dutch East India Company *(see p52)* and their merchants became wealthy from the trade in exotic imports. They built splendid houses and filled them with expensive furniture and fine art, much of which has found its way into the province's leading museums.

This part of the country has learned to live with and profit from water. The province has it on three sides, with the unpredictable North Sea to the west and the vast IJsselmeer (formerly the Zuiderzee) to the east. The flat land in between is bisected by two major canals; one connects Zaandam to Den Helder in the north, while the other, the important North Sea Canal, gives Amsterdam's busy port access to the North Sea at IJmuiden. Land reclamation, in which the Dutch excel, has been going on since the 14th century, and many historical island communities are now surrounded by dry land.

Tourism is a major industry in North Holland, with Schiphol, the country's major airport, at its heart. The North Sea coast has a string of delightful resorts and sea-front hotels among the dunes, while in the communities on the IJsselmeer such as Edam, famous for its cheese, and picturesque Volendam, you can still find villagers wearing traditional costume and the famous Dutch wooden clogs.

Enkhuizen, a fine historical fishing town on the IJsselmeer

◀ View of IJsselmeer Dam in the northern Netherlands

Exploring North Holland

The landscape of North Holland is varied and contains many old buildings and fine museums. The province can be easily explored on day trips from Amsterdam but areas such as West Friesland and Het Gooi, a woodland east of Amsterdam, are worth a longer visit. You can also alternate sightseeing with more relaxing activities such as walking in the beautiful nature reserve de Kennemerduinen (Kennemer dunes) near Zandfoort, sailing on the IJsselmeer or sunbathing on one of the many beaches. Round trips through towns or on rivers are also good ways of exploring the province.

The working windmills on the Zaanse Schans

Getting Around

During rush hour, roads around the large towns in the southern part of the province are fairly congested. Parking is also difficult to find in most of the larger towns and as bus and train connections in the area are good, it's often better to leave the car behind. The northern part of North Holland is also easily reached by public transport or by car on the A7 and A9 motorways. The natural landscape of North Holland lends itself to countless footpaths and cycle routes, each with different characteristics. Bicycles can be hired from most of the region's train stations.

Sights at a Glance

1. Marken
2. Monnickendam
3. Volendam
4. Edam
5. Jisp
6. Zaanse Schans
7. De Beemster
8. *Zuiderzee Museum pp180–81*
9. Enkhuizen
10. Hoorn
11. Broek-in-Waterland
12. Medemblik
13. Den Helder
15. Alkmaar
16. Haarlem
17. Egmond
18. Heemskerk
19. Velsen/IJmuiden
20. Zandvoort
21. Cruquius
22. Ouderkerk aan de Amste
23. Aalsmeer
24. Amstelveen
25. Muiden
26. Naarden
27. 's-Graveland
28. Hilversum
29. Naardermeer
30. Laren

Tour

14. West Friesland

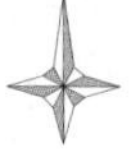

Julianad
Callantsoog
N9
Schoorl
ALKMAA
EGMOND 17
Heiloo
Uitgeest
HEEMSKERK 18
VELSEN/ 19
IJMUIDEN
Santpoort
Bloemendaal
HAARLEM 16
Zwanen
ZANDVOORT 20
CRUQUIUS 21
Hoofddorp
N208
A4
A44

For map symbols *see back flap*

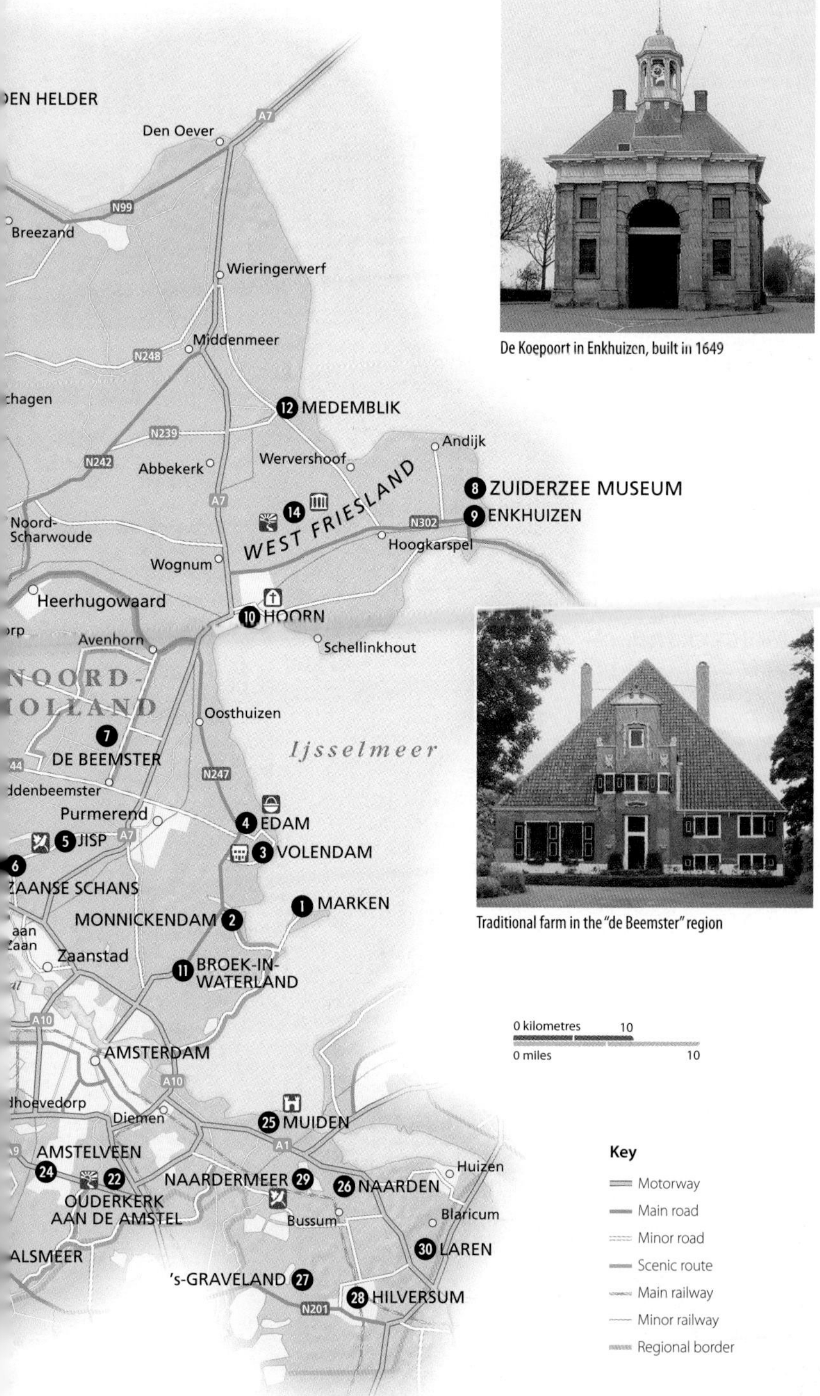

De Koepoort in Enkhuizen, built in 1649

Traditional farm in the "de Beemster" region

For hotels and restaurants in this region see p397 and pp409–410

❶ Marken

Road map C3. 2,000. from Volendam Apr–Oct. **vvv-waterland.nl**

For almost eight centuries, Marken was a fishing community that saw little change. The construction of a causeway link to the mainland in 1957 put an end to its isolation. The island, however, has kept its original atmosphere, retaining its wooden houses built on mounds and piles to guard against flooding. Het Paard Lighthouse is a famous landmark. **Marker Museum**, located in six historic houses, gives a flavour of past and present life in Marken. There is also a cheese factory and clog-making workshop.

Marker Museum
Kerkbuurt 44–47. **Tel** 0299–601904. **Open** Apr–Oct: daily.

Traditional dress, today worn as costume at Volendam's fishery

❷ Monnickendam

Road map C3. 10,000. Zuideinde 2 (0299 820046). Sat.

This old town on the Gouwzee, founded by monks, has many buildings dating back to the 17th and 18th centuries, including the Stadhuis, or town hall, and the Waag, or weigh house. The **Museum de Speeltoren** explains the town's history. It is located in the Stadhuis clock tower, with its ornate 15th-century cari- llon: every hour, clockwork horsemen parade outside.

Waterlandsmuseum de Speeltoren
Noordeinde 4. **Tel** 0299–652203. **Open** Apr–Oct: 11am–5pm Tue–Sat; Nov–Mar: 11am–5pm Sat & Sun. **despeeltoren.nl**

❸ Volendam

Road map C3. 21,000. Zeestraat 37 (0299–363747). Sat. **vvv-volendam.nl**

This old fishing village on the IJsselmeer is world-famous, attracting a huge number of tourists. The village is built along a dyke; at its small harbour, you can still buy all sorts of fish. Traditional costume is one of this town's biggest attractions: the women wear tight bodices, lace caps and brightly striped skirts; the men, loose trousers and jackets. You too can dress up and have your photo taken. On the other side of the dyke is a different Volendam: an ancient, atmospheric maze of narrow streets, wooden houses and little canals.

Distinctive 17th-century wooden houses at Marken

❹ Edam

Road map C3. 7,200. Damplein 1 (0299–315125). Wed; cheese market: Jul–mid-Aug: 10:30am–12:30pm Wed. **vvv-edam.nl**

Edam is known worldwide for the rounds of cheeses covered with red wax it exports. (Yellow wax is used if for local consumption.) Visit the **kaasmarkt** (cheese market) on Wednesday mornings in July and August to see how they are sold. Founded in the 12th century, the town has many historical buildings, including the brightly painted **Waag** (weigh house). The 17th-century stained-glass windows in the **Grote Kerk** are considered some of the finest in Holland.

The **Edams Museum** is located in a 16th-century merchant's house. Here you can see 17th-century portraits of famous Edammers, such as Trijntje Kever, who was supposedly 2.8 m (9 ft) tall.

Edams Museum
Damplein 8. **Tel** 0299–372644. **Open** Apr–Oct: Tue–Sun. **Closed** 27 Apr.

For hotels and restaurants in this region see p397 and pp409–410

Typical Dutch windmill on the Zaanse Schans

❺ Jisp

Road map B3. 760. 0299 472718. **laagholland.com**

The old whaling village of Jisp, on one of the many former Zuiderzee islands, has a 17th-century feel. The *stadhuis* (town hall) and *dorpskerk* (village church) are worth a visit. The village lies in the middle of the **Jisperveld**, a nature reserve which is home to many different birds, such as lapwings, black-tailed godwits, redshanks, ruffs and spoonbills. This is a lovely spot to cycle, row, fish or, in the summer, visit on an excursion. The tourist office, VVV, has information about the various excursions offered.

❻ Zaanse Schans

Schansend 7, Zaandam. **Road map** C3. 50. **Tel** 075–6810000. **Open** 9am-5pm daily, some buildings closed weekdays in winter. **zaanseschans.nl**

The Zaanse Schans is the tourist heart of the Zaan region. This open-air museum, created in 1960, has typical Zaan houses, windmills and buildings. When it's windy, you will be able to see the windmills working. The products (oil, paint, mustard) are for sale. All the houses are built from timber, as stone houses would sink at once into the soft peat earth. Also, at the time they were built, wood was readily available from local sawmills.

A visit to Zaanse Schans will also reveal **Albert Heijn's** first shop from 1887, a baking museum and cheese factory. The **Zaans Museum** showcases the history of the region. Pleasure boats offer trips on the Zaan.

Zaans Museum
Schansend 7, Zaandam. **Tel** 075–6810000. **Open** 10am–5pm daily. **Closed** 1 Jan, 25 Dec. **zaansmuseum.nl**

Environs

At the **Molenmuseum** (windmill museum) at Koog on the Zaan, you will learn everything you need to know about the windmills of the Zaan region. It is located in an 18th-century wooden house.

Haaldersbroek, opposite the Zaanse Schans, was once a boating village with narrow locks, brick paths and typical Zaan houses and farmhouses. Here, you'll feel as though you've gone back in time.

Molenmuseum
Museumlaan 18, Koog a/d Zaan. **Tel** 075–6288968. **Open** Tue–Sun. **Closed** 1 Jan, Easter Sun, Whitsun.

❼ De Beemster

Road map B3. VVV Middenbeemster (0299-621826). **beemsterinfo.nl**

The Beemster was once a lake that was drained in 1612 by **Jan Adriaans Leeghwater** *(see p167)*. This unusual region has hardly changed since the 17th century, and in 1999 it was named a World Heritage Site by UNESCO. You can see historic objects and period rooms in the **Museum Betje Wolff**.

Museum Betje Wolff
Middenweg 178, Middenbeemster. **Tel** 0299–681968. **Open** May–Sep: Tue–Fri 11am–5pm, Sat–Sun 2pm onwards; Oct–Apr: 2–5pm. **Closed** 1 Jan, 27 Apr, 25 Dec.

Czaar-peterhuisje (tsar Peter's House)

In 1697, the Russian Peter the Great visited the shipyards of Zaandam in order to learn how the local people built ships. He lodged with Gerrit Kist, a tradesman whom he had employed in St Petersburg. The tsar paid another visit to the town in 1717. The first mention of "Tsar Peter's house" in an official document was in 1780. This led to the tiny wooden house being supplied with a stone casing and foundations for protection. Every year, this humble house attracts great number of tourists. (Krimp 23, Zaandam, tel. 075-6810000. Open 10am–5pm Tue–Sun; closed 1 Jan, 25 Dec.)

Peter the Great, who stayed in Zaandam twice

❽ Zuiderzeemuseum

Enkhuizen was one of the towns whose economy was based on fishing and which was devastated when its access to the North Sea was blocked in 1932 by the construction of a barrier dam, the Afsluitdijk *(see p168)*. Enkhuizen is today enjoying renewed prosperity with the opening of the Zuiderzeemuseum complex and the restructuring of the fishing port into a marina. The museum consists of an open-air section in the form of a museum-park, and an indoor area with a large number of exhibition spaces for permanent displays and temporary presentations.

★ Houses from Urk
Houses from the former island of Urk *(see p330)* have been rebuilt here. Actors portray life at the beginning of the 20th century.

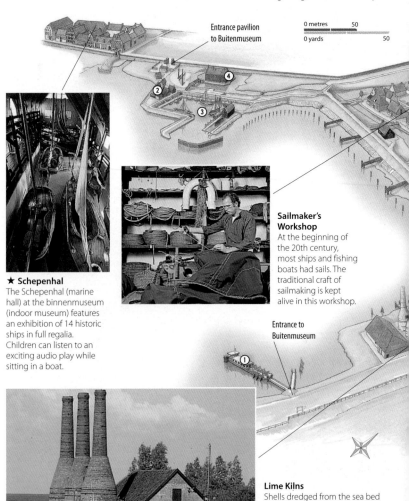

Entrance pavilion to Buitenmuseum

0 metres 50
0 yards 50

Sailmaker's Workshop
At the beginning of the 20th century, most ships and fishing boats had sails. The traditional craft of sailmaking is kept alive in this workshop.

★ Schepenhal
The Schepenhal (marine hall) at the binnenmuseum (indoor museum) features an exhibition of 14 historic ships in full regalia. Children can listen to an exciting audio play while sitting in a boat.

Entrance to Buitenmuseum

Lime Kilns
Shells dredged from the sea bed were burned in bottle-shaped lime kilns. The resulting quicklime was then used as an ingredient in mortar for brickwork. These ovens come from Akersloot in North Holland.

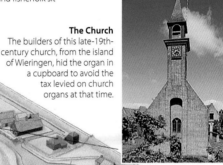

★ **Contemporary Delft Blue** Hugo Kaagman's paintings juxtapose traditional Delft motifs with present-day designs in refreshing combi-nations: windmills, tulips and fisherfolk sit beside portraits of popular singers.

VISITORS' CHECKLIST

Practical Information
Wierdijk 12–22, Enkhuizen.
Tel 0228–351111.
W **zuiderzeemuseum.nl**
Indoor and open-air museums
Open Apr–Oct: 10am–5pm daily; indoor museum also open Nov–Mar: 10am–5pm daily.
Closed 25 Dec. Enkhuizen. from the station.

The Church
The builders of this late-19th-century church, from the island of Wieringen, hid the organ in a cupboard to avoid the tax levied on church organs at that time.

Fish Smoking
The Zuiderzee fishing industry relied mainly on herrings and anchovies, which were often salted or smoked. Here, herrings are smoked above smouldering wood chips.

KEY

① **Ferries** take visitors from the station and entrance pavilion to the Buitenmuseum (open-air museum).

② **Monnickendam smoke-houses**

③ **Reconstruction of Marken harbour**

④ **VIS Museum for Children**

⑤ **Shipbuilding and repairs**

⑥ **A working windmill** shows how polder drainage works *(see pp168–9)*.

⑦ **The houses in this area** come from Zoutkamp, a fishing village on what was once the Lauwerszee.

⑧ **Houses from the Zuiderzee island of Urk**

Hoorn harbour

9 Enkhuizen

Road Map C2. 18,100.
Tussen twee havens 1 (0228-313164). Wed.
museumhoorn.nl

Enkhuizen is still a major port. Its many fine buildings are evidence of the wealth of the Golden Age. The most famous building is the **Drommedaris**, dating back to 1540, used to keep watch over the old port. The city walls also date back to the 16th century. Enkhuizen has two splendid churches, the **Westerkerk** and the **Zuiderkerk**. Summer boat trips to Medemblik, Stavoren and Urk are especially pleasant.

10 Hoorn

Road Map C3. 68,000.
Veemarkt 4 (0229-218343). Sat; Jun–Aug: Wed. **vvvhoorn.nl**

Hoorn's rich past, as the capital of the ancient province of West Friesland and one of the great seafaring towns of the Golden Age *(see pp54–5)*, has produced many beautiful buildings. The late gothic **Oosterkerk** has a marvellous Renaissance façade, just like the St Jans Gashuis. Hoorn's historic past is set out in the **Westfries Museum**. A glimpse of the more recent past and a nostalgic trip down memory lane can be experienced at the **Museum van de Twintigste Eeuw** (Museum of the 20th Century).

Westfries Museum
Rode Steen 1. **Tel** 0229-280028.
Open Tue–Fri 11am–5pm (Apr–Oct: also Mon), Sat & Sun 1–5pm.
Closed 1 Jan, 27 Apr, 3rd Mon in Aug, 25 Dec. **wfm.nl**

Museum van de Twintigste Eeuw
Krententuin 24. **Tel** 0229-214001.
Open Mon–Fri 10am–5pm, Sat–Sun & holidays from noon. **Closed** 1 Jan, 27 Apr, 25 Dec. **museumhoorn.nl**

11 Broek in Waterland

Road Map C3. 2350.
820046. **vvv-waterland.nl**

Broek in Waterland's status in the 17th century – as a retreat for sea captains of the East India Company – can still be seen everywhere in the village's crooked streets. The ornate clapboard villas are colour-coded: the captains lived in the pastel-tinted houses and non-seafarers in the ones painted grey. Along the **Havenrak**, the road winding along the lake, fine examples of *kralentuinen*, mosaics made from blue glass beads brought back by merchants from the East Indies, can be seen in several of the gardens. To explore the village and surroundings from a different perspective, canoes and electric motorboats can be rented from **Kano & Electroboot Waterland** (Drs. J. van Disweg 4, 020-4033209, www.fluisterbootvaren.nl).

Riverside setting of Broek in Waterland

12 Medemblik

Road Map C2. 8,000.
072-5114284. Mon.
vvvmedemblik.nl

Many pretty 17th-century houses can still be found in Medemblik. Also worth a look is **Kasteel Radboud**, built in 1288, and its museum. On the town's outskirts, an old pumping station is home to **Het Nederlands Stoommachinemuseum**, a hands-on collection of steam-driven industrial machinery.

Het Nederlands Stoommachinemuseum
Oosterdijk 4. **Tel** 0227-544732.
Open end Feb–early Nov: Tue–Sun.
stoommachinemuseum.nl

Kasteel Radboud in Medemblik

13 Den Helder

Road Map B2. 57,000.
Willemsoord 52A (0223-616100).
Jul & Aug: Tue. **vvvkopvannoordholland.nl**

This town, the base for the Dutch Royal Navy, has a **Marinemuseum** that displays marine history from 1488. At the North Sea Aquarium at Fort Kijkduin, a glass tunnel weaves among the fish.

Marinemuseum
Hoofdgracht 3. **Tel** 0223-657534.
Open May–Oct: daily; Nov–Apr: Tue–Sun. **Closed** 1 Jan, 25–26 Dec.
marinemuseum.nl

Windmills

Since the 13th century, windmills have been an inseparable part of the landscape of Holland. They have been used for a variety of purposes, including milling corn, extracting oil and sawing wood. One of their most important uses was to pump away excess water from the polders *(see pp168–9)*. Windmills consist of a fixed tower and a cap which carries the sails. The cap can be turned so that the sails face the wind. The sails can be very dangerous when they are turning – hence the Dutch saying, *"Een klap van de molenwiek hebben" ("To be struck by a windmill")*, that is, to have a screw loose. The Netherlands had thousands of windmills in earlier times, but since the arrival of modern machines, their number has dropped to just over 1,000. Many of these windmills are still working and are open for visits. See also *pp28–9*.

Watermill in the Schermer polder

Modern wind turbines are common in Holland. They supply electricity without the pollution caused by burning oil or coal.

Polder mills for draining became common during the 17th century. Standing in groups, they were each responsible for part of the pumping, through the use of an Archimedes' screw.

The cogs are turned by the sails. A rotating spindle makes a cog move, causing the water pump to start working.

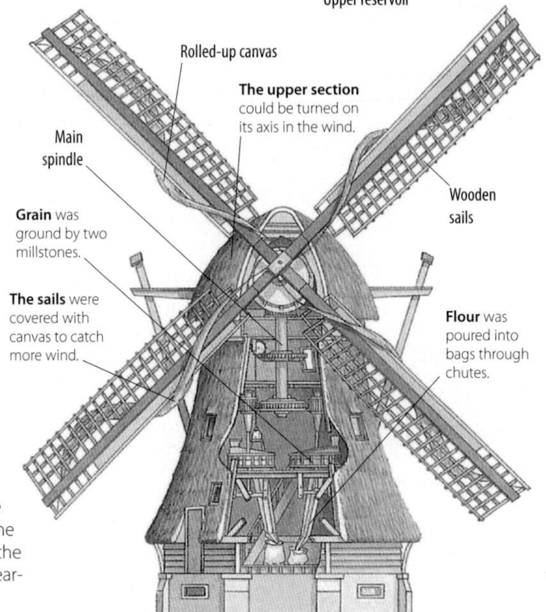

The upper section could be turned on its axis in the wind.

Grain was ground by two millstones.

The sails were covered with canvas to catch more wind.

Flour was poured into bags through chutes.

Flour Mills

Flour mills were covered with reeds and looked like enormous pepper mills. The millstones were linked to the sails by the spindle and gear-wheels and milled wheat, barley and oats.

⓮ West Friesland

During Holland's golden age, West Friesland played a major part in the Dutch economy as an important centre for trade and shipping. Nowadays the main inland activity is farming. Watersports bring in the most money on the IJsselmeer coast. If you take the route in spring, you will travel alongside blooming bulb fields and orchards. There is a pleasant bustle along the IJsselmeer in the summer, and part of the route is great for cycling.

Tips for Drivers

Length: 80 km (50 miles)
Places to stop: Cafés and restaurants in any of the villages and towns along the way.
Roads: The roads in West Friesland are good. Along the IJsselmeer you will travel over a narrow, winding dyke where you will certainly encounter many cyclists and walkers.

⑤ Twisk
This long village has pretty farmhouses, many of which can often be reached only by little bridges.

④ 't Regthuys, Abbekerk
This museum has collections of West Friesland clothing, curiosities and – most important for the children – toys.

③ Stoommachinemuseum (Steam Engine Museum)
The old steam pumping station "Vier Noorder Koggen" near Medemblik has a unique collection of steam-operated machinery.

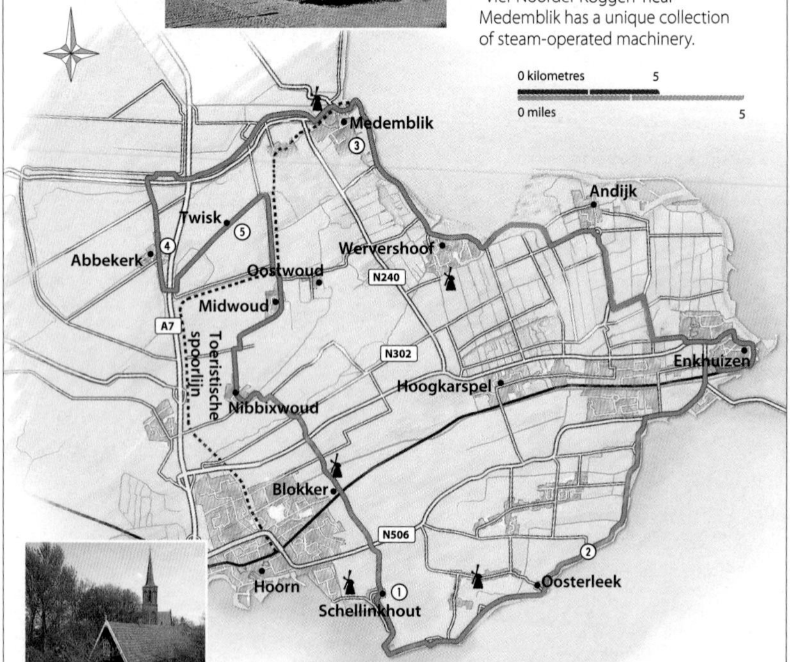

0 kilometres 5
0 miles 5

Medemblik
Andijk
Twisk
Abbekerk
Wervershoof
Oostwoud
N240
Midwoud
A7
Toeristische spoorlijn
N302
Enkhuizen
Hoogkarspel
Nibbixwoud
Blokker
N506
Hoorn
Schellinkhout
Oosterleek

① Schellinkhout
This attractive village just a stone's throw from Hoorn has been inhabited since prehistoric times. It once had an old sandy cove of the Zuiderzee.

Key

- Suggested route
- Other road
- Railway line
- Tourist railway
- Good viewing point
- Windmill

② West Friesland Omringdijk
In the 13th century, a ring dyke to protect against flooding was built around West Friesland. Through land reclamation, a large proportion of the dyke now lies inland. Two *wiels*, or pools, by the IJsselmeer are reminders of when water broke through the dyke.

Porters carrying cheese on sledges at Alkmaar's traditional cheese market

15 Alkmaar

Road map: B3. 94,000.
Waagplein 2 (072-5114284). Weekly market Sat; cheese market Fri morning, Apr–Sep.
vvvhartvannoordholland.nl

This old town has at least 400 monuments, and the street layout has barely changed over the centuries. Along the canals, old merchants' houses and small courtyards can still be seen. The **Stedelijk Museum** depicts the history of the town through paintings, videos and models. It also has a collection of paintings from the Bergen School of the 1920s and 1930s.

Alkmaar is famous for its traditional **kaasmarkt** (cheese market), which is held every Friday morning from early April to early September. The large yellow wheels of cheese arrive by barge. They are tossed from the barges by four groups of seven porters from the 400-year-old cheese porters' guild. The porters are dressed in white and divided into guild groups by the colour of their hats. The cheese is loaded onto sledges, which the porters run with to the **waaggebouw** (public weigh house), where the cheese is weighed. Once tasting has taken place, the cheese is auctioned off by a system called *handjeklap*, with sellers clapping each other on the hands. The **Kaasmuseum** (cheese museum) at the *waaggebouw* shows both modern and traditional methods of dairy farming. A little north of the cheese market is the **Nationaal Biermuseum De Boom**. Housed in an impressive 17th-century building, in what had formerly been the biggest brewery in the town, the museum explores a millennium of beer drinking in the Netherlands. The museum illustrates, for example, how in the middle ages Alkmaar lacked a supply of safe drinking water, so brewers would ship barrels of clean water from the surrounding dunes and streams, and then make it into beer. The collection of equipment shows the beer-making process over the last 100 years, from copper vats, kettles, barrels and bottles to examples of the modern laboratory technology that breweries now use. There is also a reconstruction of an old café interior. Under the same roof is a lovely waterside café and "tasting house" where 86 different beers, many of them Dutch, can be sampled.

The Biermuseum, where a variety of beers can be sampled

South of the *kaasmarkt*, on the corner where Mient meets Verdronkenoord, is the **vismarkt** or fish market, which dates back to the 1500s and was still in use until 1998. The low, colonnaded stalls are covered to protect traders and their wares from the elements, and contain brick and stone benches where catches of fish were displayed to customers. The current buildings date back to the mid-18th century. Further along Verdronkenoord is the Sint Laurenskerk or **Grote Kerk**. This 15th-century church has one of the most important organs in Europe, built from 1639–46, and is noteworthy for its painting on the ceiling depicting the *Last Judgment* by Jacob Cornelisz. van Oostzanen. The scene was painted on nine wooden panels in 1518–1519. In 1885, due to water damage, the panels were taken to the Rijksmuseum, only to return during the German occupation. An extensive restoration ended in 2011, and the work can now be seen here again.

The Renaissance façade of the weigh house

Stedelijk Museum
Canadaplein 1. **Tel** 072-5489789.
Open 10am–5pm Tue-Sun.
Closed 1 Jan, 27 Apr, 25 Dec.
stedelijkmuseumalkmaar.nl

Waaggebouw and Kaasmuseum
Waagplein 2. **Tel** 072-5114284.
Open Easter–Oct: Mon–Sat, Oct–Easter: Sat.

Nationaal Biermuseum De Boom
Houttil 1. **Tel** 072-5113801.
Open Mon–Sat. **Closed** public hols.
biermuseum.nl

Grote Kerk
Koorstraat 2. **Tel** 072-5140707. **Open** Apr–Jun: Thu–Sat 10am–4pm, Jul–Aug: Tue–Sun 10am–4pm; during exhibitions. **grotekerk-alkmaar.nl**

For hotels and restaurants in this region see p397 and pp409–410

⓰ Street-by-Street: Haarlem

Haarlem is the commercial capital of North Holland province and the eighth largest city in the Netherlands. It is the centre of the Dutch printing, pharmaceutical and bulb-growing industries, but there is little sign of this in the delightful pedestrianized streets of the historic heart of the city. Most of the sights of interest are within easy walking distance of the Grote Markt, a lively square packed with ancient buildings, cafés and restaurants. Old bookshops, antique dealers and traditional food shops are all to be discovered in nearby streets.

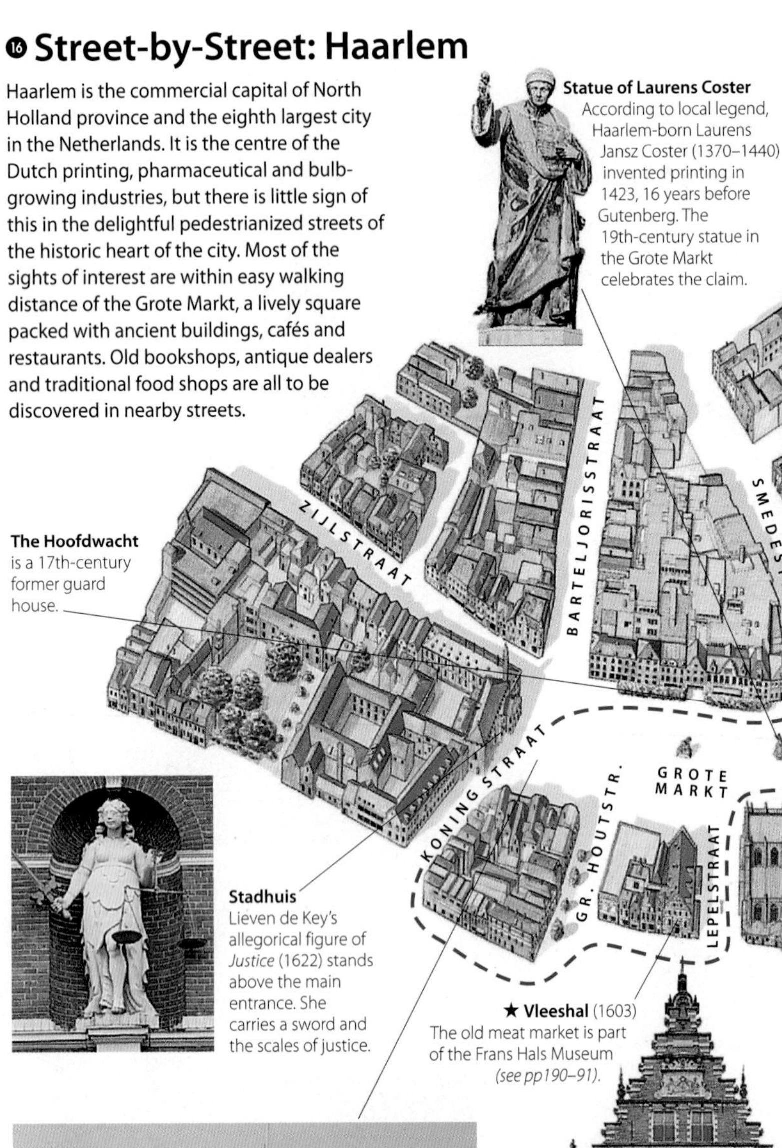

Statue of Laurens Coster According to local legend, Haarlem-born Laurens Jansz Coster (1370–1440) invented printing in 1423, 16 years before Gutenberg. The 19th-century statue in the Grote Markt celebrates the claim.

The Hoofdwacht is a 17th-century former guard house.

Stadhuis Lieven de Key's allegorical figure of *Justice* (1622) stands above the main entrance. She carries a sword and the scales of justice.

★ Vleeshal (1603) The old meat market is part of the Frans Hals Museum *(see pp190–91).*

Grote Markt The tree-lined market square is bordered with busy pavement restaurants and cafés. It has been the meeting point for the townspeople for centuries.

VISITORS' CHECKLIST

Practical Information
Road Map B3. 151,000.
haarlem.nl
Verwulft 11 (0900-6161600).
Mon & Sat. Haarlem Jazz Festival: end Aug; Bloemen Corso: end of Apr.

Transport
Stationsplein.

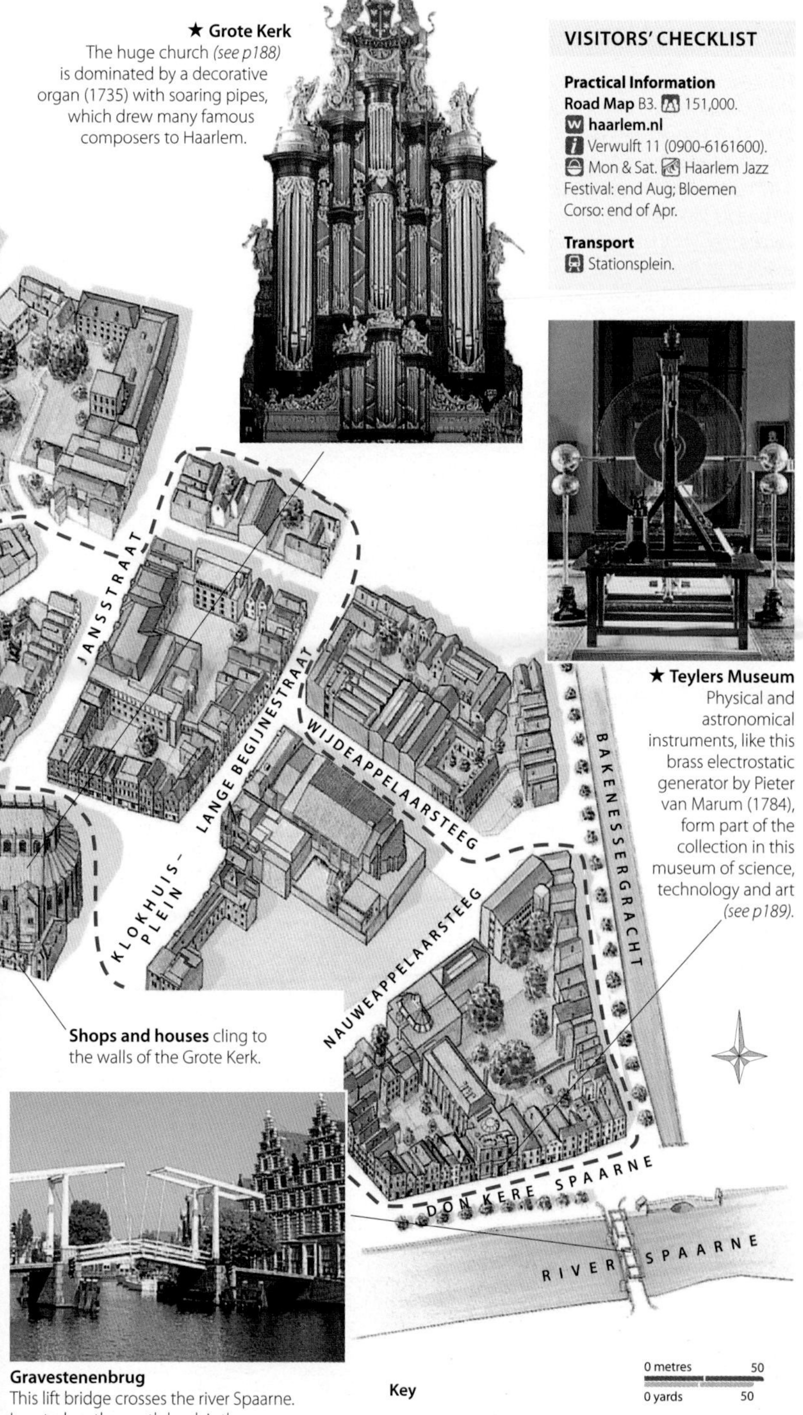

★ Grote Kerk
The huge church *(see p188)* is dominated by a decorative organ (1735) with soaring pipes, which drew many famous composers to Haarlem.

★ Teylers Museum
Physical and astronomical instruments, like this brass electrostatic generator by Pieter van Marum (1784), form part of the collection in this museum of science, technology and art *(see p189)*.

Shops and houses cling to the walls of the Grote Kerk.

Gravestenenbrug
This lift bridge crosses the river Spaarne. Located on the south bank is the embarkation point for boat trips along the river and canals.

Key

— Recommended route

Exploring Haarlem

Haarlem became a city in 1245, and had grown into a thriving clothmaking centre by the 15th century. But in the Spanish siege of 1572–3, the city was sacked, and a series of fires wreaked further destruction in 1576. The town's fortunes changed in the 17th century, when industrial expansion ushered in a period of prosperity lasting throughout the Golden Age. The centre was largely rebuilt by Lieven de Key (1560–1627) and still retains much of its character. The Grote Kerk continues to overlook the city's *hofjes* (almshouses), and the brick-paved lanes around the Grote Markt are little changed.

Grote Markt, Haarlem (c.1668) by Berckheijde, showing the Grote Kerk

Frans Hals Museum

See pp186–7.

Grote Kerk

Grote Markt 22. **Tel** 023-5532040. **Open** Mon–Sat 10am–4pm (Apr–Oct till 5pm). **Closed** Easter, Whitsun, 27 Apr, 5 May, 25 Dec–2 Jan. **bavo.nl**

The enormous Gothic edifice of Sint Bavo's great church, or Grote Kerk, was a favourite subject of the 17th-century Haarlem School artists Pieter Saenredam (1597–1665) and Gerrit Berckheijde (1639–98). Built between 1400 and 1550, the church and its ornate bell tower dominate the market square. Clinging on to the exterior of the south wall is a jumble of 17th-century shops and houses. The rents raised from these ramshackle, untidy buildings contributed to the maintenance of the church.

Today, the entrance to the Grote Kerk is through one of the surviving shops, a tiny antechamber that leads straight into the enormous nave. The church has a high, delicately patterned, vaulted cedarwood ceiling, white upper walls and 28 supporting columns painted in greens, reds and golds. The intricate choir screen, like the magnificent brass lectern in the shape of a preening eagle, was made by master metal worker Jan Fyerens in about 1510. The choirstalls (1575) are painted with coats of arms, and the armrests and misericords are carved with caricatures of animals and human heads. Not far away is the simple stone slab covering the grave of Haarlem's most famous artist, Frans Hals.

The Grote Kerk boasts one of Europe's finest and most flamboyant organs, built in 1735 by Christiaan Müller. In 1738 Handel tried the organ and pronounced it excellent. It also found favour with the infant prodigy Mozart, who shouted for joy when he gave a recital on it in 1766. The organ is still often used for concerts, recordings and teaching.

Stadhuis

Grote Markt 2. **Tel** 023-5115115. **Open** by appt only.

Haarlem's Stadhuis (town hall) has grown rather haphazardly since 1250 and is an odd mixture of architectural styles. The oldest part of the building is the beamed medieval banqueting hall of the counts of Holland, originally known as the Gravenzaal. Much of this was destroyed in two great fires in 1347 and 1351, but the 15th-century panel portraits of the counts of Holland can still be seen.

The wing of the town hall bordering the Grote Markt was designed by Lieven de Key in 1622. It is typical of Dutch Renaissance architecture, combining elaborate gables, ornate painted detail and Classical features, such as pediments over the windows.

In a niche above the main entrance is a plump allegorical figure of Justice, bearing a sword in one hand and scales in the other as she smiles benignly upon the pavement cafés in the market below. To the left, in Koningstraat, an archway leads to the university buildings behind the Stadhuis, where there is a 13th-century cloister and library.

De Hallen

Grote Markt 16. **Tel** 023-5115775. **Open** daily. **Closed** 1 Jan, 25 Dec. **dehallen.nl**

The Verweyhal (museum for modern art) and the Vleeshal (exhibition space), both in the Grote Marskt, are part of the Frans Hals Museum *(see pp190–91)*. The Verweyhal accommodates exhibitions of Dutch Expressionism, the Cobra School *(see p193)*, Impressionism and contemporary works. It is named after the painter Kees Verwey, whose Impressionist still lifes are an important feature of the collection. The heavily ornamented Vleeshal (meat market), just to the west of the church, houses temporary exhibitions of modern

Detail on Vleeshal façade by Lieven de Key

The west gate of the Amsterdamse Poort (1355)

art. It was built in 1602 by the city surveyor, Lieven de Key, and has a steep step gable which disguises the roof line. The extravagantly over-decorated miniature gables above each dormer window bristle with pinnacles. A giant painted ox's head on the façade signifies an earlier function of the building.

Amsterdamse Poort

Amsterdamsevaart. **Closed** to public.

The imposing medieval gateway that once helped protect Haarlem lies close to the west bank of the river Spaarne. The Amsterdamse Poort was one of a complex of 12 gates guarding strategic transport routes in and out of Haarlem. The gate was built in 1355, though much of the elaborate brickwork and tiled gables date from the late 15th century.

The city defences were severely tested in 1573, when the Spanish, led by Frederick of Toledo, besieged Haarlem for seven months during the Dutch Revolt. The city fathers agreed to surrender the town on terms that included a general amnesty for all its citizens. The Spanish appeared to accept the terms, but once the city gates were opened, they marched in and treacherously slaughtered nearly 2,000 people – almost the entire population of the city.

Teylers Museum

Spaarne 16. **Tel** 023-5160960. **Open** Tue–Sat 10am–5pm, Sun & holidays noon–5pm. **Closed** 1 Jan, 25 Dec. **teylersmuseum.nl**

This was the first major public museum to be founded in the Netherlands. It was established in 1778 by the silk merchant Pieter Teyler van der Hulst to encourage the study of science and art. The museum's eccentric collection of fossils, drawings and scientific paraphernalia is displayed in Neo-Classical splendour in a series of18th-century rooms. The two-storey Oval Hall was added in 1779 and contains bizarre glass cabinets full of minerals and cases of intimidating medical instruments. A significant collection of sketches by Dutch and Italian masters, including Rembrandt and Michelangelo, is shown a few at a time.

Tiles in Haarlem Station

Historisch Museum Haarlem

Groot Heiligland 47. **Tel** 023-5422427. **Open** Tue–Sun. **Closed** 1 Jan, Easter, Whitsun, 25 Dec.
historischmuseumhaarlem.nl

Haarlem is well known for its *hofjes* (almshouses), set up to minister to the poor and sick *(see p115)*. They first appeared in the 16th century and were run by rich guild members, who took over the role traditionally filled by the monasteries until the 1578 Alteration.

St Elisabeth's Gasthuis was built in 1610 around a courtyard opposite what is now the Frans Hals Museum. A 1612 plaque above the main doorway depicts an invalid being carried off to hospital. After restoration, the almshouse was opened in 1995 as Haarlem's principal historical museum.

Haarlem Station

Stationsplein.

The first railway line in the Netherlands opened in 1839 and ran between Haarlem and Amsterdam. The original station, built in 1842, was refurbished in Art Nouveau style between 1905 and 1908. It is a grandiose brick building with an arched façade and rectangular towers. The interior is decorated with brightly coloured tiles depicting various modes of transport. Other highlights are the woodwork of the ticket offices and the highly decorative wrought ironwork, particularly on the staircases.

17th- and 18th-century gabled houses along the river Spaarne in Haarlem

Frans Hals Museum

Celebrated as the first "modern" artist, Frans Hals (c.1582–1666) introduced a new realism into painting. Although his contemporaries strove for perfect likenesses, Hals knew how to capture his models' characters by using an impressionistic technique. Even at the age of 80, he still painted impressive portraits, such as *De regentessen van het Oude Mannenhuis in Haarlem* (Regentesses of the Old Men's Home in Haarlem) (1664). The Oude Mannenhuis (old men's home) became the Frans Hals Museum in 1913. It also has on show many paintings by other artists from the Dutch Golden Age.

★ Banket van de Officieren van de St-Jorisdoelen (Banquet of the Officers of the Civic Guard of St George)
(1616) The features of each of the archers and the luxury of their banquet room are beautifully portrayed in this group portrait by Frans Hals.

Key to Floorplan

- Works by Frans Hals
- Renaissance Gallery
- Old Masters
- History of 17th-century Haarlem
- New exhibition room
- Non-exhibition space

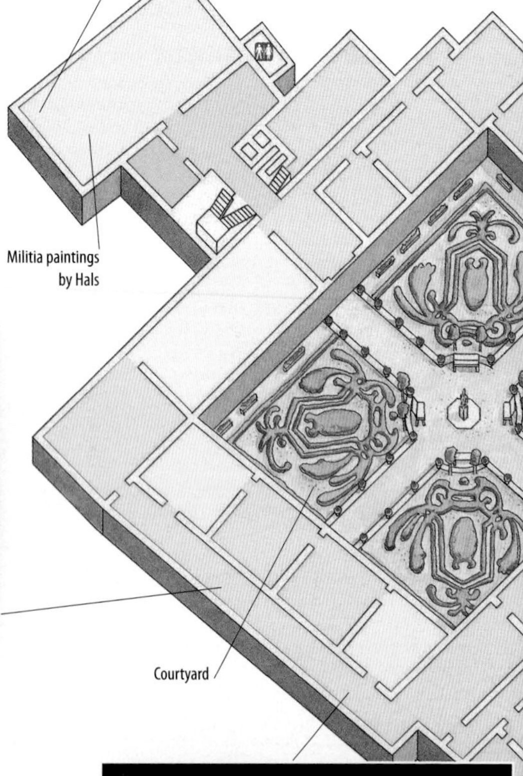

Moeder en Kind (Mother and Child)
After the Reformation *(see pp56–7)*, artists such as Pieter de Grebber (1600–53) painted secular versions of religious themes. This work of a mother feeding her child (1622) is reminiscent of Mary with Jesus.

★ Stilleven (Still Life) (1613)
Floris Claeszoon van Dyck (1574–1651) was famous for his minute attention to detail and texture.

★ **Mercurius** (1611) Hendrick Goltzius (1558–1617) is particularly well known for his studies of classical nudes. One of a three-part set, this canvas was donated to the museum by a rich Haarlem mayor.

VISITORS' CHECKLIST

Practical Information
Groot Heiligland 62, Haarlem
Tel 023-5115775.
W franshalsmuseum.nl
Open 11am–5pm Tue–Sat, noon–5pm Sun & public hols.
Closed 1 Jan, 25 Dec. 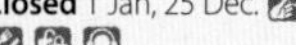

St Luke Painting the Virgin and Child (1532), Maerten Jacobsz van Heemskerck. St Luke was the patron saint of artists' professional associations, the Guilds of St Luke. This was painted for the Haarlem Guild.

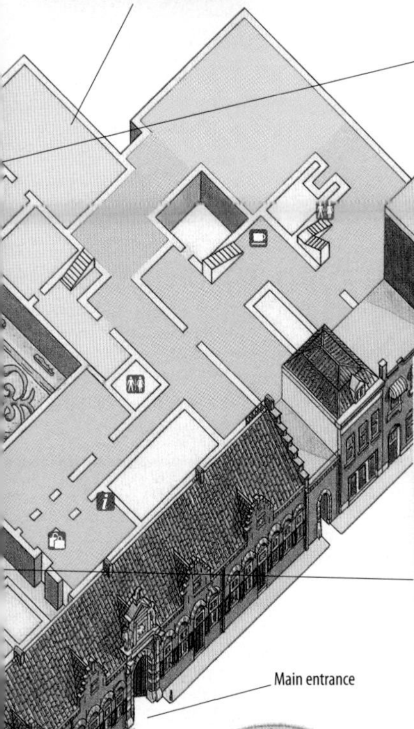

The Grote Markt in Haarlem, (1696), Gerrit Adriaensz Berckheijde. The Grote Kerk or St Bavokerk, seen here from the west, is built in the Gothic style and is Haarlem's largest church.

Main entrance

Delft Plate (1662) The Grote Markt and Grote Kerk in Haarlem *(see p186)* are depicted on this earthenware plate by M Eems.

Museum Guide

The best direction to take through the museum is counter-clockwise, as exhibitions of the works of Frans Hals, other portraits, still lifes and pieces of genre paintings are displayed in roughly chronological order. In the Verweyhal and the Vleeshal *(see p188)* *temporary exhibitions are held of modern and contemporary art.*

Egmond lighthouse, a welcoming beacon for ships at sea

⓱ Egmond

Road Map B3. 11,600. Voorstraat 82a, Egmond aan Zee (072-5070571). Thu. **vvvegmond.nl**

Egmond is divided into three parts: Egmond aan de Hoef, Egmond-Binnen and the seaside resort of Egmond aan Zee. The counts of Egmond once lived in Egmond aan de Hoef. Only the foundations remain of the **kasteel** (castle), which is open to visitors.

Egmond abbey, in Egmond-Binnen, is the oldest abbey in Holland and Zeeland. This 10th-century structure was destroyed, however, by Sonoy, chief of the Beggars of the Sea *(see p245)*. It was not until 1934 that a new abbey was built; Benedictine monks still live here today. The small **Abdijmuseum** (abbey museum) and **candle factory** can be visited (tel. 072-5061415, www.abdijvanegmond.nl).

⓲ Heemskerk

Road Map B3. 36,200. **Tel** 020-7026000. Fri. **vvvijmuidenaanzee.nl**

An obelisk honouring Dutch artist Maarten van Heemskerck stands in the cemetery of the 17th-century **Hervormde Kerk** (Reformed church). **Slot Assumburg** (Assumburg castle), dating from the 15th century, was built on the site of a 13th-century fortified house. **Slot Marquette** is just as old but acquired its present form only two centuries ago. **Fort Veldhuis** is part of the **Stelling van Amsterdam**, a 135-km (84-mile) defensive line that encircles Amsterdam. It is now a small war museum, dedicated to the sacrifices made by pilots during World War II.

Fort Veldhuis
Genieweg 1. **Tel** 0251-230670. **Open** May–Oct: Sun.

⓳ Velsen/IJmuiden

Road Map B3. 67,600. Dudokplein 16, IJmuiden (020-7026000). Thu.

Holland's largest fishing port is IJmuiden. This can easily be guessed from the penetrating smell of fish and the many wonderful restaurants in the port. The **Noordersluis** (north lock), which forms part of the North Sea canal lock system, is one of the biggest locks in the world. As you come across you will pass by the Hoogovens (blast-furnaces), where you can take a round trip on a steam train.

The area around Velsen was already inhabited in Roman times; archaeological findings are exhibited in the **Ruïne van Brederode**, a 13th-century fortress. You will also feel you are going back in time in the Romanesque **Engelmunduskerk. Slot Beeckestijn** is one of the many houses built on the coast in the 17th and 18th centuries by rich Amsterdammers. Its gardens as well as the period rooms on the ground floor are open to public.

Ruïne van Brederode
Velserenderlaan 2, Santpoort. **Tel** 023-5378763. **heerlijkheid brederode.nl**

Slot Beeckestijn
Rijksweg 136. **Tel** 0255-522877.

⓴ Zandvoort

Road Map B3. 15,500. Bakkerstraat 2b (023-5717947). Wed. **vvvzandvoort.nl**

Once a fishing village, Zandvoort is now a modern seaside resort where in the summer half the population of Amsterdam relaxes on the beach or saunters down the busy main street. The village centre still has old fishermen's houses. Zandvoort is famous for its motor racing circuit, where Formula 1 races were once held. It has since been restored and is now attempting to achieve its former status. To escape the crowds, ramble through the **Amsterdamse Waterleidingduinen**.

Circuit Park Zandvoort
Burg. van Alphenstraat 108. **Tel** 023-5740740. **Open** daily. during meets. **cpz.nl**

㉑ Stoomgemaal De Cruquius

Road Map B3. Cruquiusdijk 27. **Tel** 023-5285704. **Open** Mar–Oct: daily; Nov–Feb: Sat & Sun. **museumdecruquius.nl**

The Stoomgemaal (steam-driven pumping station) at De Cruquius is one of the three steam-driven pumping stations used to drain the

Slot Assumburg in Heemskerk, a youth hostel since 1933

For hotels and restaurants in this region see p397 and pp409–410

The Cruquius steam pump

Haarlemmermeer. It has not been in use since 1933 and is now a museum. The original steam engine is in the machine hall, which has eight pumps moved by beams. An exhibition gives a comprehensive overview of water management in the Netherlands.

22 Ouderkerk aan de Amstel

Road Map B3. 8,200. Amstelveen.

This pretty village at the junction of the Amstel and the Bullewijk rivers has been a favourite with Amsterdammers since the Middle Ages. They had no church of their own until 1330, and worshippers had to travel to the 11th-century Ouderkerk that gave the village its name. The Old Church was destroyed in a tremendous storm in 1674, and a fine 18th-century church now stands on its site. Today Ouderkerk aan de Amstel is popular with cyclists who come to enjoy its waterfront cafés and restaurants.

23 Aalsmeer

Road Map B3. 22,900. Tue.

Aalsmeer is famous as the centre for floriculture in the Netherlands *(see pp34–5)*. It also holds the biggest **bloemenveiling** (flower auction) in the world; you can take part in the auction from a special gallery.

Many greenhouses are to be seen around Aalsmeer. One important activity here is the development of new varieties and colours of flower. Many modern heroes have a "new" flower named after them.

Electric tram

Bloemenveiling Flora Holland
Legmeerdijk 313. **Tel** 0297-397000.
Open 7–11am Wed & Fri, until 9am Thu. **floraholland.nl**

24 Amstelveen

Road Map B3. 78,800. Fri.

Amstelveen is home to many interesting modern art museums, such as **Museum van der Togt**, with its unique collection of glass objects. The **Electrische Museumtramlijn** (electric museum tramline) (tel. 020-6737538) keeps the past alive. On Sundays from April to October (and Wednesdays from July to August) you can take a return trip from Amsterdam to Amstelveen on a historic tram. The **Amsterdamse Bos** (Amsterdam forest) is lovely for rambling, picnicking or playing sport. The **Bosmuseum** is dedicated to the origins of the forest.

The **Cobra Museum voor Moderne Kunst** (Cobra museum of modern art) concentrates on the work of the Cobra group, established in 1948 by Danish, Belgian and Dutch artists. During its brief existence, Cobra abandoned dreary postwar art and introduced modern art definitively to the Netherlands.

Museum Van der Togt
Dorpsstraat 50. **Tel** 020-6415754.
Open Wed–Sun. **Closed** 1 Jan, 27 Apr, 25 Dec. **jvdtogt.nl**

Cobra Museum voor Moderne Kunst
Sandbergplein 1–3. **Tel** 020-5475050.
Open Tue–Sun. **Closed** 1 Jan, 27 Apr, 25 Dec. **cobra-museum.nl**

Women, Children, Animals (1951) by Karel Appel in the Cobra Museum

The Muiderslot, built in 1280, a site of many legends

25 Muiden

Road Map C3. 6,700.

In the Middle Ages, the pretty town of Muiden was an outport for Utrecht but later became part of the defence system of the **Stelling van Amsterdam** *(see p192)*, together with **forteiland Pampus**. The town is mainly known for its castle, the **Muiderslot**, which is more than 700 years old and was built by Floris V. After his death it was demolished and rebuilt. The most famous inhabitant was the 17th-century poet PC Hooft, who formed the *Muiderkring* (Muiden circle), a circle of friends occupied with literature and music. Most of the castle rooms are furnished in 17th- and 18th-century style. The garden and orchard also retain their former glory. Boats once left from the castle jetty for the fortified island of Pampus.

Knight in armour

Muiderslot
Herengracht 1. **Tel** 0294-256262.
Open Apr–Oct: daily; Nov–Mar: Sat & Sun. **muiderslot.nl**

26 Naarden

Road Map C3. 17,000.
Sat.

The fortified town of Naarden lies behind a double ring of canals and walls. The original town is thought to have been founded in the 10th century, then later destroyed and rebuilt around 1350. In the 15th and 16th centuries, it was occupied in turn by the Spanish and the French. The first thing you notice on arrival is the tower of the 14th-century **Grote Kerk**. The church's wooden vaulted ceiling has been beautifully decorated with pictures from the Old and New Testament. Around 400 years ago, Czech priest Comenius fled to the Netherlands, and now lies buried in the 15th-century **Waalse kapel** (Walloon chapel). The Spaanse Huis (Spanish house), which was converted into the Waag (weigh house), is now home to the **Comeniusmuseum**, which explores the life and ideas of the Czech scholar Jan Amos Comenius (1592–1670), who is buried here. The **Nederlands Vestingmuseum** (fortress museum) is in one of the six bastions of the fortress and has an exhibition of the Hollandse Waterlinie, a strip of land flooded as a defence line in Holland, and of Naarden's eventful past. Costumed gunners regularly demonstrate the ancient artillery. There is a nice walk around the town along the footpaths on the walls.

Aerial view of the fortress of Naarden's star formation

Comeniusmuseum
Kloosterstraat 33. **Tel** 035- 6943045.
Open Tue–Sun. **Closed** 1 Jan, 27 Apr, 25 Dec, 31 Dec.
comeniusmuseum.nl

Nederlands Vestingmuseum
Westwalstraat 6. **Tel** 035-6945459.
Open 10.30am–5pm Tue–Fri, from noon Sat & Sun. **Closed** 1 Jan, 27 Apr, 25 Dec.
vestingmuseum.nl

27 's-Graveland

Road Map C3. 9,200.

's-Graveland is a special place in Het Gooi *(see p176)*. In the 17th century, nine country estates were built here for rich Amsterdammers. Just across from these lie the modest houses that belonged to the labourers. Businesses now use the country houses, as the upkeep is too expensive for individuals. Five parks are owned by the Vereniging Natuurmonumenten and are open to visitors. You can learn more at the **Bezoekers-centrum** (visitors' centre).

Bezoekerscentrum Gooi-en Vechtstreek
Noordereinde 54b. **Tel** 035-6563080.
Open Apr–Nov: Tue–Sun, Dec–Mar: Wed–Sun.
natuurmonumenten.nl

Hilversum town hall, finished in yellow brick

28 Hilversum

VVV Kerkbrink6. **Tel** 035 5446971.
Road Map C3. 84,500. Wed & Sat. vvvhilversum.nl

This dynamic centre in Het Gooi is known as the media centre of the Netherlands, because of the large number of broadcasting companies that have been established here.

Hilversum boasts a busy shopping centre and attractive residential areas with a lot of greenery. Here and there you will see houses and buildings designed by architect Willem Dudok (1884–1974), a representative of the Nieuwe Bouwen. One of his most famous creations is the 1931 **Raadhuis** (town hall), with its towers and beautiful interior (tours are given on Sundays). Its basement holds an exhibition on Dudok and temporary architectural exhibitions. The **Museum Hilversum** combines the Goois Museum and the Dudok Centrum, illuminates the past of Het Gooi and features an archaeological collection. The Neo-Gothic **Sint-Vituskerk**, designed by PJH Cuypers *(see p94)*, with its 98-m (322-ft) tower, dates from 1892 and is worth a visit.

The Erfgooiers

During the Middle Ages, the farmers of Het Gooi *(see p176)* joined together in a group to regulate the use of the heathland and meadows. Since 1404, their rights were held in plough share notes. Members of the group were known as *erfgooiers*, men living in Het Gooi who were descendants of these medieval farmers. The right of use was later converted into common property. The *erfgooiers* had to constantly fight for their rights. From the 19th century onwards, the government strived to disband the group. In 1932, the heathland was sold, as were the meadows after 1965. The Association of *Erfgooiers* was disbanded in 1971.

De Erfgooiers (1907) by F Hart Nibbrig

Museum Hilversum
Kerkbrink 6. **Tel** 035-5339601.
Open Tue–Sun. **Closed** 1 Jan, 27 Apr, 25 Dec. museumhilversum.nl

29 Naardermeer

Road Map C3. Meerkade 2 Naarden (035-6990000). natuurmonumenten.nl

The Naardermeer is an area of lakes and marshland renowned for its breeding colonies of cormorants and purple herons. Several other birds, such as the marsh harrier, the bittern, the reed warbler and the spoonbill, can also be observed here. Unusual orchids, rare mosses and fungi grow here. The Naardermeer is the oldest protected nature reserve in the Netherlands. Its creation was the start of the Vereniging Natuurmonumenten (nature reserve association). The association has set out several walking tours around the area, which are accessible to everyone. From April to November there are guided boat tours on the lakes. Book on 035-6559955. No dogs.

30 Laren

Road Map C3. 11,100. Fri.

Alongside pretty villas and country houses, Laren has many converted old farmhouses, a reminder of the time when it was a farming village. In the 19th and early 20th century, Laren and its surroundings was the inspiration for many landscape and interior painters, such as Mauve, Israëls and the American W Singer. The **Singer Museum** has been set up in his old house. Here you can see his work and that of other 19th- and 20th-century artists. There is also a sculpture garden. **Sint-Jansbasiliek** (1925) towers above the Brink and its charming restaurants.

Singer Museum
Oude Drift 1. **Tel** 035-5393956.
Open Tue–Sun. **Closed** 1 Jan, 25 Dec. singerlaren.nl

73-HT-HK

UTRECHT

The province of Utrecht, with the lively university city of the same name at its heart, has a vast range of attractions for visitors, including farmhouses, mansions, museums and castles, all set in a varied and attractive wooded landscape, and with a fascinating history dating back to Roman times.

The city of Utrecht has its origins in AD 47, when the Romans built a camp by a ford *(trecht)* at the river Rhine, which followed a different course in those days. In 695, Bishop Willibrord established himself here to promote the spread of Christianity. From the 11th century, the church authorities enjoyed not only spiritual but also secular power in this region, which has seen much conflict: over the centuries the counts of Holland, the dukes of Burgundy, the Spaniards, the French and the Germans have all tried to make their mark here.

The region's proximity to Amsterdam has meant that it has been able to share in the capital's prosperity as wealthy merchants and landowners built their mansions and estates along the river Vecht *(see p202)*. In more recent times, the University of Utrecht has been a great source of economic and artistic development, and the city is home to a modern manufacturing industry and major Dutch corporations.

Visitors will enjoy the pretty countryside – ideal for car or cycle touring – the country houses and historic buildings, the street markets and a great variety of attractions ranging from eclectic furniture and old steam locomotives to barrel-organs and Australian Aboriginal art. But in this eco-conscious country, with its awareness of the need for conservation, it may be the outdoors, with its sparkling lakes and possibilities for leisurely country walks, that will appeal the most.

De Haar castle in Haarzuilens, a Neo-Gothic construction (1892) built by Pierre Cuypers

◀ Koppelpoort, one of Amersfoort's 15th-century gates

Exploring Utrecht

The city of Utrecht is the central point of the province and is therefore the ideal base for sightseeing in the surrounding area. The Vinkeveense Plassen (Vinkeveense Lakes) are popular for watersports, and nature lovers will appreciate the woodland area of the Utrecht Heuvelrug. There are castles in Amerongen and Wijk bij Duurstede and numerous imposing country houses along the Vecht. Windmills and working farms can be spotted here and there in the countryside. Many defence points, such as in Woerden, serve as reminders of the turbulent past of this province, which has been at stake during fierce battles more than once.

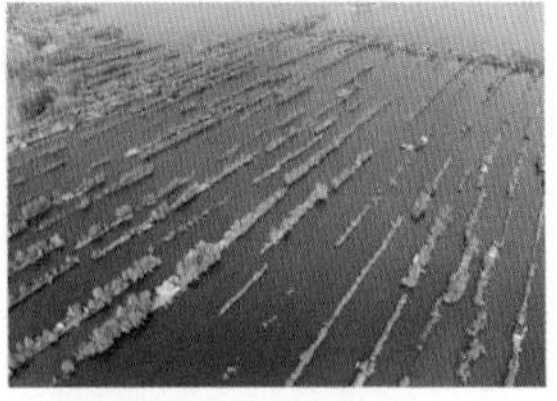

The Vinkeveense Plassen, formed by excavations

The *heksenwaag* (witches' scales) in Oudewater

Getting There

Larger towns have railway stations; smaller ones can be reached easily by bus. Utrecht, the capital of the province, is the biggest railway junction in the Netherlands and so train connections from this town are excellent. There is also a regional bus station. Utrecht has a highly developed road network and is served by important main roads such as the A2 (north-south) and the A12 (east-west), but there is also a large number of minor roads, tourist routes and cycle paths in the area.

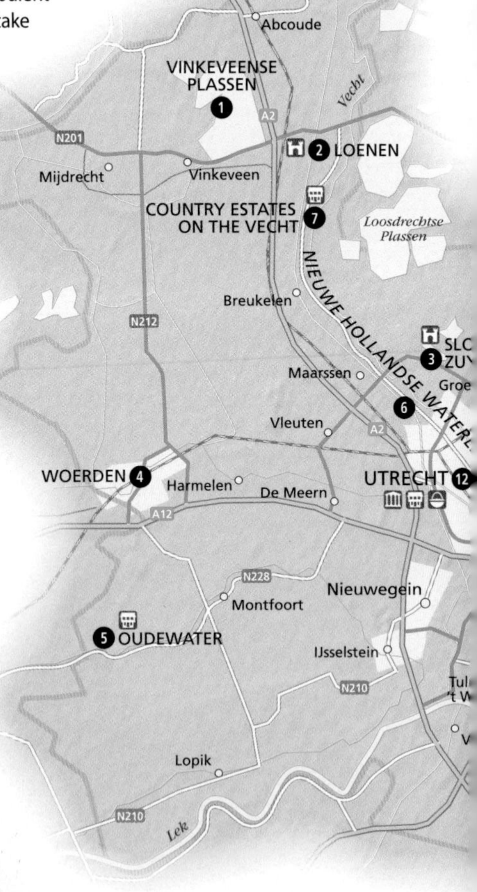

View of Rhenen, with its characteristic Cuneratoren

Key

- Motorway
- Main road
- Minor road
- Scenic route
- Main railway
- Minor railway
- National border

For map symbols *see back flap*

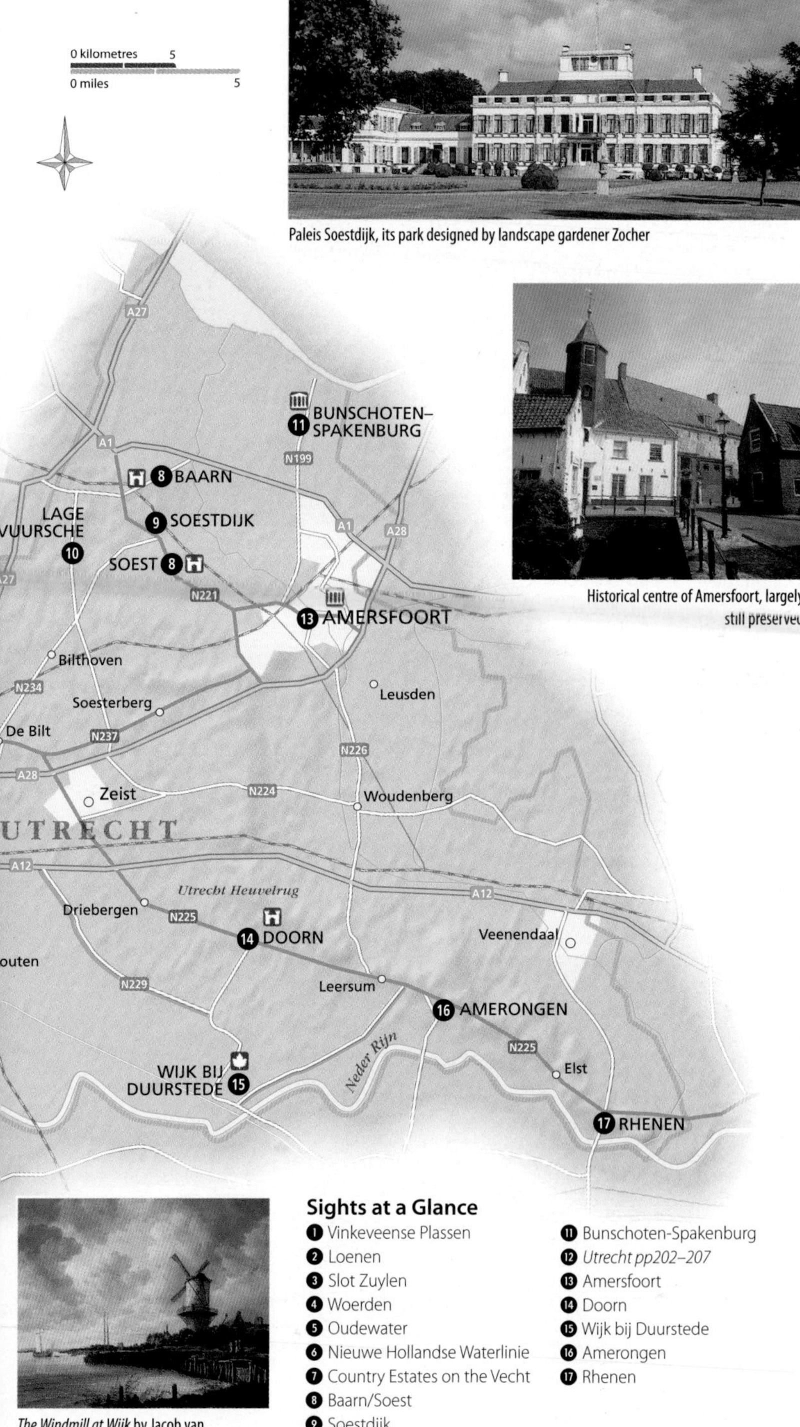

Paleis Soestdijk, its park designed by landscape gardener Zocher

Historical centre of Amersfoort, largely still preserved

The Windmill at Wijk by Jacob van Ruisdael *(see p128)*

Sights at a Glance

1. Vinkeveense Plassen
2. Loenen
3. Slot Zuylen
4. Woerden
5. Oudewater
6. Nieuwe Hollandse Waterlinie
7. Country Estates on the Vecht
8. Baarn/Soest
9. Soestdijk
10. Lage Vuursche
11. Bunschoten-Spakenburg
12. *Utrecht pp202–207*
13. Amersfoort
14. Doorn
15. Wijk bij Duurstede
16. Amerongen
17. Rhenen

For hotels and restaurants in this region see p397 and p410

❶ Vinkeveense Plassen

Road Map C3.

De Vinkeveense Plassen (Vinkeveense Lakes) came about through human intervention – this site was once marsh. The thick peat layers have been excavated over the centuries. The large towns in the surrounding area needed peat; sales of this fuel meant that the people here started to earn a decent living. The peat was therefore dug up more and more extensively, eventually leading to a large area of lakes.

Today, the Vinkeveense Lakes attract many watersports lovers, as well as cyclists and walkers. When it's not the breeding season, you can take a rowing boat through the nature reserve of **Botshol**, which is home to marsh and grassland birds.

Stately Slot Zuylen, where Belle van Zuylen lived in the 18th century

❷ Loenen

Road Map C3. 8,350. Tue am.

In the 10th century, this place was called Lona, meaning "water" or "mud". Loenen fell under two different jurisdictions and has, therefore, two courts dating from the beginning of the 18th century. Loenen on the Vecht is famous for its rural atmosphere as well as for its castles and country estates complete with coach houses, summerhouses and boathouses, built over the centuries by wealthy citizens. It is now a protected village.

Kasteel Loenersloot, built on the bank of the Angstel, is one of the oldest country estates. The building dates back to the 13th century, though only the round defence tower remains; the rest dates from the 17th and 18th centuries. The castle is not open to the public.

Loenen on the Vecht still has an aristocratic appearance

❸ Slot Zuylen

Road Map C3. 36,120. Castle: Tournooiveld 1, Oud-Zuilen. **Tel** 030-2440255. **Open** 15 Mar–15 May & 15 Sep–15 Nov: Sat & Sun; groups by appointment; 15 May–15 Sep: Tue–Thu, Sat & Sun. **Closed** 15 Nov–15 Mar. **slotzuylen.nl**

The original U-shaped castle was built around 1520 on the remains of a medieval residential tower. At the beginning of the 16th century, a new castle was built on the foundations of the old house and the gateway was added. Up to the 18th century, extensive rebuilding brought the castle into line with contemporary architectural style.

The author Belle van Zuylen (1740–1805) was one of the castle's most famous inhabitants. She was famous for her correspondence at home and abroad, which she cleverly used to show her modern attitude. Several rooms are furnished as they were when she resided here.

The serpentine wall that runs alongside the castle is interesting because its unique shape provides so much protection that even in this cool sea climate, subtropical fruits such as peaches and grapes can flourish here.

❹ Woerden

Road Map C4. 34,800. Sat am.

Woerden came into being on the dykes along the Rhine and Lange Linschoten. Granted its town charter in 1372, it has been besieged many times but always managed to hold out. Between 1575 and 1576, during the 30 Years War, the Spaniards tried to conquer Woerden, as did the French in 1672, but neither invader succeeded in capturing the town. Impenetrable **kasteel van Woerden** (Woerden castle), built between 1405 and 1415, was extensively restored around 1990.

In the 18th century, the **Oude Hollandse Waterlinie** (old Holland waterline) – a strip of land flooded as a defence line – was extended, thereby strengthening Woerden.

❺ Oudewater

Road Map C4. 10,000. Leeuweringerstraat 10 (0348-561628). Wed. **visit-oudewater.nl**

This little town, thanks to its favourable position on the IJssel and the Linschoten, became a prosperous town early on and, by 1265, had been granted its city charter. The counts of Holland

Nesting storks in Oudewater

and the bishops of Utrecht fought fiercely for Oudewater, which was converted into a border stronghold by Floris V. In 1349, Oudewater was captured by Jan van Arkel, the Bishop of Utrecht. In 1572, Oudewater sided with the Prince of Orange and, as a result, the town was seized in 1575 by the Spanish. They exacted a bloody revenge by burning the town to the gro-und. Oudewater flourished again during Holland's Golden Age.

The town's most famous attraction is the scales, dating from the 16th century, better known as the ***heksenwaag*** (witches' scales). Women who were suspected of witchcraft came here to be weighed. If their weight and their outward appearance tallied, they were given a certificate as proof of their innocence. Oudewater was the only place where "witches" could be legally weighed in public.

Heksenwaag
Leeuweringerstraat 2. **Tel** 0348-563400. **Open** Apr–Oct: 11am–5pm Tue–Sun, Nov–Mar: 11am–5pm Sat & Sun. ground floor. **heksenwaag.nl**

❻ Nieuwe Hollandse Waterlinie

Road Map C3–C4. **hollandsewaterlinie.nl**

The Nieuwe Hollandse Waterlinie (New Dutch Inundation Line), laid out from 1815 to 1940, is comprised of 68 forts and public works, from Muiden and Naarden in North Holland to Werkendam in North Brabant. Utrecht has 27 installations, more than any other province. The Waterlinie was intended as a defence against invading armies; a wide strip of land would simply be flooded. Utrecht's installations are now being protected, and have been put forward for UNESCO's World Heritage Site register. The original reconnaissance positions and unimpeded lines of fire will hopefully be preserved. The best installations are at Rijnauwen, Groenekan en Tull and 't Waal.

"Bombproof" barracks of the Nieuwe Hollandse Waterlinie (Fort Rijnauwen, Bunnik)

7 Country Estates along the Vecht

Country estate houses, with their summerhouses, magnificent railings and extensive gardens, can be seen threaded along the Vecht, especially between Maarssen and Loenen. They were built in the 17th and 18th centuries by wealthy Amsterdam inhabitants who wanted to escape the noise and stench of the city in the summer. The estates were status symbols, places where city-dwellers could devote themselves to hobbies such as tree cultivation, hunting and still-life painting.

VISITORS' CHECKLIST

Practical Information
Road Map C4. Vechtstreek-museum: Diependaalsedijk 19, Maarssen. **Tel** 0346-554440. **Open** 2–5pm Wed, Sat & Sun. ground floor.

Goudestein in Maarssen

One of the first country estates in the Vecht, Goudestein was built in 1628 by Joan Huijdecoper. The present building, which dates from 1775, is now used as government offices. The coach house is now a fascinating pharmacy museum.

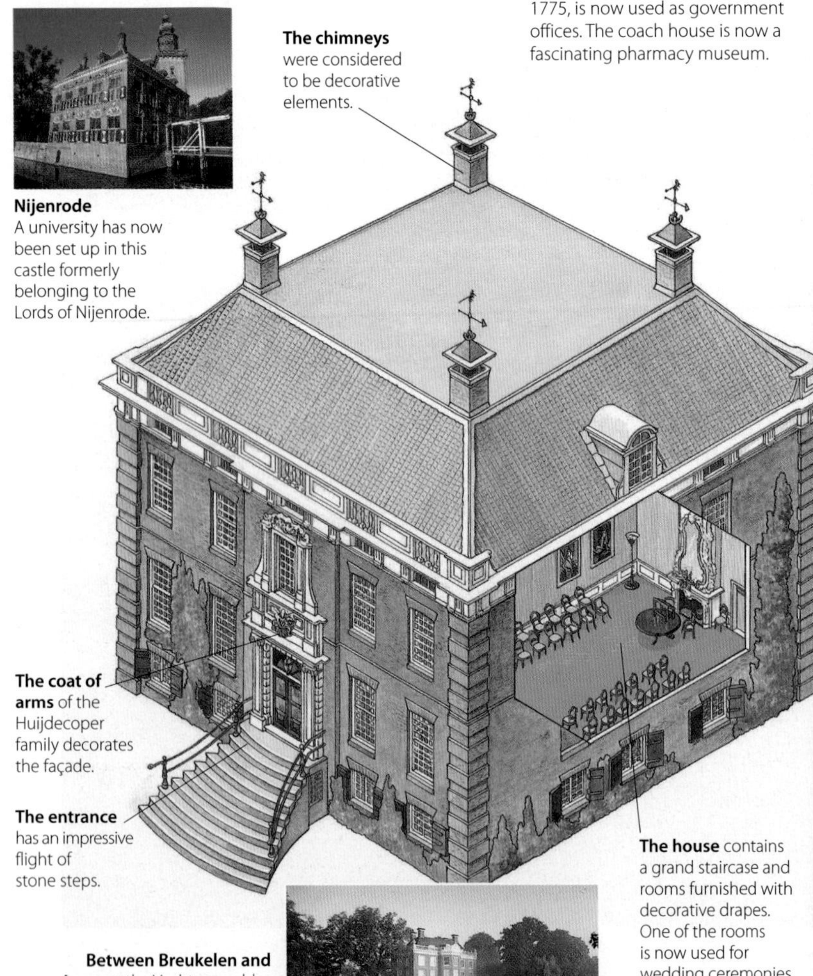

Nijenrode
A university has now been set up in this castle formerly belonging to the Lords of Nijenrode.

The chimneys were considered to be decorative elements.

The coat of arms of the Huijdecoper family decorates the façade.

The entrance has an impressive flight of stone steps.

The house contains a grand staircase and rooms furnished with decorative drapes. One of the rooms is now used for wedding ceremonies.

Between Breukelen and Loenen the Vecht resembles an architectural museum. The country estates (Vechtvliet is shown here) are surrounded by established parks and ornamental outbuildings.

For hotels and restaurants in this region see p397 and p410

❽ Baarn/Soest

Roadmap C4. 70,000. Brinkstraat 12, Baarn (035-5413226). Baarn Tue, Soest Thu.

During the Netherlands' Golden Age, regents and wealthy merchants had splendid summer residences built in Baarn and its environs. This place has retained its leafy, elegant appearance. The **Kasteel Groeneveld** (1710) lies in the middle of a magnificent park. Soest's past is pre-9th century, and the old centre remains largely in its original state. The church dates from 1400. The surrounding area is beautiful and offers a wealth of leisure activities.

Kasteel Groeneveld
Groeneveld 2. **Tel** 035–5420446.

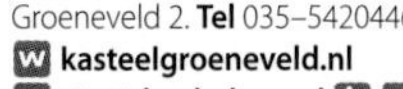

kasteelgroeneveld.nl
staatsbosbeheer.nl

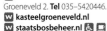

❾ Soestdijk

Road Map C3. Steenhoffstraat 9b (035-6012075). Paleis Soestdijk: Amsterdamsestraatweg 1Baarn, 035-5412841

Just outside Baarn lies **Paleis Soestdijk**. It was built in 1674 as a place for Viceroy William III to hunt. In 1815, it came into the hands of the crown prince, who later became King William II. The two wings of the palace were added in 1816 and the park was designed by landscape gardener Zocher. The **Naald van Waterloo** (Waterloo needle) stands opposite, erected in honour of William Frederick, Prince of Orange, for his services during the Battle of Waterloo. The estate closes for renovation in 2015.

❿ Lage Vuursche

Road Map C3. 250. Brinkstraat 12, Baarn (035-5413226).

The name "Furs" for Lage Vuursche has been around since 1200, though the village itself has existed only since the 17th century. The village, surrounded by woodland, is very popular with ramblers. The small octagonal castle **Drakenstein**, which dates back to 1640–43, is the residence of Princess Beatrix, former Queen of the Netherlands.

Bunschoten-Spakenburg, once home to an important fishing industry

⓫ Bunschoten-Spakenburg

Road Map C3. 19,500. Oude Schans 90 (033-2982156). Sat.

Over the years, the towns of Bunschoten and Spakenburg have merged into one another. Livestock farming was the traditional livelihood in Bunschoten, and there are still some pretty farms to see here. Bunschoten, granted its town charter in 1383, is older than Spakenburg, which came into being in the 15th century. It was once an important fishing town; its smoke-houses, fishermen's houses and shipbuilding yard are reminders of this time. When the Zuiderzee was closed in 1932 because of partial land reclamation, the inhabitants had to look for other work. Some of the women in the town still wear traditional dress. Museum Spakenburg brings the fishing activities of the past back to life.

Museum Spakenburg
Oude Schans 47–63. **Tel** 033-2983319. **Open** Apr–Oct: 1:30–5pm Mon, 10am–5pm Tue–Sat; Nov–Mar: 1–4pm Wed–Sat.
museumspakenburg.nl

Outdoor cafés in Lage Vuursche offering respite after a walk in the woods

⓬ Street-by-Street: Utrecht

The area to the south of the centre gives one a good idea of how people once lived in Utrecht. Rich citizens lived in the stately houses on the Nieuwegracht, with its typical Utrecht wharves, and built almshouses for their less fortunate neighbours. No doubt because of the great number of museums in this area, it came to be called Museumkwartier (museum district). The old city walls gave way to a magnificent park which was designed by landscape gardener Zocher.

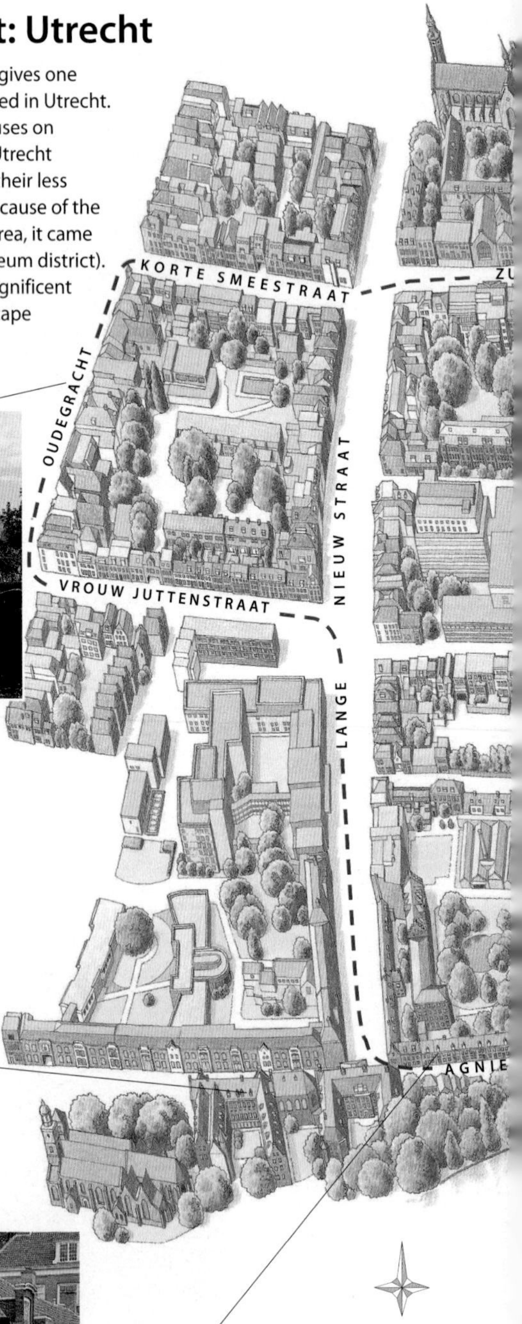

KORTE SMEESTRAAT

OUDEGRACHT

NIEUW STRAAT

VROUW JUTTENSTRAAT

LANGE

AGNIE

★ Oudegracht
The Oudegracht represented a vital transport route for the economy of Utrecht in the 13th century. When the water level fell, cellars were built along the wharves. These were used as warehouses or workshops. Today, some of them house cafés and restaurants.

Centraal Museum
The rich and varied contents include works by the 16th-century artist Jan van Scorel, as well as the largest collection of Rietveld furniture in the world.

0 metres 100
0 yards 100

Almshouses
The Pallaeskameren (Pallaes rooms) are 12 little almshouses built on the instructions of Maria van Pallaes in 1651.The inhabitants had free accommodation and a certain amount of food and drink annually.

Cathedral

BRIGITTENSTRAAT

NIEUWE GRACHT

BRUNTENHOF

SERVAASBOLWERK

NIEUWEGRACHT

VISITORS' CHECKLIST

Practical Information
Road Map C4.
visit-utrecht.com
234,000. Domplein 9–10 (030-236000). Wed, Fri & Sat. Liberation festival: 5 May; Festival Oude Muziek: end Aug; Netherlands Film Festival: end Sep.

Transport
Stationsplein.
Stationsplein .

★ Catharijneconvent
Museum Catharijneconvent (Lange Nieuwstraat 38) is devoted to religious art. It is located in the former St Catherine's convent, dating back to 1468. Part of the convent church dates from 1529.

Nederlands Spoorwegmuseum
(Dutch railway museum) Old carriages and steam locomotives can be seen in the former Maliebaan Station, dating back to the 19th century. The exhibition room features the history of the Dutch railways.

Key

▬ Recommended route

Sonnenborgh
The 19th-century observatory, now home to an astronomy museum,, was established on one of the four bulwarks along the Singel.

Exploring Utrecht

Utrecht, founded by the Romans in AD 47, has been a bishopric and university town for centuries. It has grown into a lively city, thanks to its central position. Utrecht was very prosperous during the 16th and 17th centuries, when many of the magnificent canalside houses were built. These houses are a characteristic feature of the town centre, as are the medieval churches and monasteries. The city centre is compact so is very suitable for exploring on foot.

The 112-m (367-ft) Domtoren rises above the town

Domtoren

Domplein. **Tel** 030-2360010. **Open** obligatory. Apr–Sep: hourly 11am–4pm Tue–Sat, noon–4pm Sun & Mon; Oct–Mar: 2pm & 4pm Sun–Fri, hourly 11am–4pm Sat. **Closed** 1 Jan, 27 Apr, 25 & 26 Dec.

The first thing you will see from the distance is the Domtoren (cathedral tower) rising above the town. The Dom (cathedral) has become the symbol of the town. Utrecht came into being on the Domplein (cathedral square), where the Romans had a settlement in the 1st century AD. In 695, Bishop Willibrord established himself here. In 1040, Bishop Bernold ordered a "cross of churches" to be built, which meant four churches with the later Domkerk in the centre. Work began on building the Domkerk in 1254 and in 1321 on the tower. The Gothic tower was finally finished in 1382.

Collegiate churches usually have two towers, but the Domkerk has only one. The nave of the church was connected to the tower by an arch, allowing the bishop to move safely to and from the church. In 1674, the nave was destroyed by a hurricane. The tower has stood on its own since then. The interior of the church, with its stained-glass windows, Neo-Gothic organ (1831) and magnificent chancel, is worth a visit.

Aboriginal Art Museum

Oudegracht 176. **Tel** 030-2380100. **Open** 10am–5pm Tue–Fri, 11am–5pm Sat & Sun. **Closed** 1 Jan, 27 Apr, 25 Dec. **aamu.nl**

This museum, the only one of its kind in Europe, is devoted to the many different styles of Aboriginal art, including painting and sculpture. The focus is on traditional art produced in Australian co-operatives.

Museum Catharijneconvent

Lange Nieuwstraat 38. **Tel** 030-2313835. **Open** 10am–5pm Tue–Fri, 11am–5pm Sat, Sun & hols. **Closed** 1 Jan, 27 Apr, 31 Dec. **catharijneconvent.nl**

The museum is split between a canalside house and a 15th-century former convent. Its fascinating collection provides a good overview of the troubled history of Christianity in the Netherlands. It includes paintings by, among others, Rembrandt van Rijn, ancient manuscripts and richly decorated books. The museum also houses numerous visiting exhibitions. From the museum you can enter into the Catharijnekerk (1529).

Centraal Museum

Nicolaaskerkhof 10. **Tel** 030-2362362. **Open** 11am–5pm Tue–Sun. **Closed** 1 Jan, 27 Apr, 25 Dec. **centraalmuseum.nl**

Centraal Museum, the oldest municipal museum in the Netherlands, has a large and extremely varied collection, the oldest pieces of which date from the Middle Ages. Extensive rebuilding and renovations were carried out in 1999, giving rise to an interesting combination of old and new. The museum has the largest collection of Gerrit Rietveld furniture in the world. Works by Utrecht artists such as Van Scorel and Bloemaert, as well as 20th-century artists such as Pyke Koch and Dick Bruna – creator of the children's character Nijntje (Miffy) – are also showcased. Bruna's works are shown in the Brunahuis across the road. The varied exhibitions range from traditional art to fashion and historical costumes, to modern art and applied art and design, to the local history of Utrecht.

The Matchmaker by Gerard van Honthorst in the Centraal Museum

For hotels and restaurants in this region see p397 and p410

Garden of the beautiful inner Domkerk quadrangle

Nederlands Spoorwegmuseum

Maliebaanstation. **Tel** 030-2306206. **Open** 10am–5pm Tue–Sun & public hols (also Mon in school hols). **Closed** 1 Jan, 27 Apr. **spoorwegmuseum.nl**

The superb Dutch railway museum is very appropriately situated in a former railway station dating from 1874 which was used as such until 1939. Magnificent old locomotives, carriages and trains line the platforms. Children can ride over the museum grounds on a miniature railway. Adults and children alike will enjoy the exhibition inside, which includes old advertising posters and model trains.

Nationaal Museum van Speelklok tot Pierement

Steenweg 6. **Tel** 030-2312789. **Open** 10am–5pm Tue–Sun & hols. **Closed** 1 Jan, 27 Apr, 25 Dec. **museumspeelklok.nl**

This museum is inside the 13th-century Buurkerk – Utrecht's oldest church. The museum's collection displays the history of mechanical musical instruments. The showpiece is a rare 15th- century musical clock. You will also see – and hear – *pierementen*, the large organs pushed by organ grinders, music boxes, fairground organs and chiming clocks, as well as many smaller instruments with chiming mechanisms. Many of the instruments are demonstrated on the guided tour.

Universiteitsmuseum

Lange Nieuwstraat 106. **Tel** 030-2538008. **Open** 11am–5pm daily. **Closed** 1 Jan, 27 Apr, 25 Dec. **museum.uu.nl**

The Universiteitsmuseum is in a purpose-built building close to the Centraal Museum. The collection here covers education since the university was established in 1636 and includes weighing and measuring instruments and a "collection of curiosities". Behind the museum is the University of Utrecht's lovely Old Botanical Garden (1723), which is open to the public.

Markets

The Vredenburg holds a general market on Wednesdays and Saturdays. On Fridays it holds a market for ecologically genuine agricultural produce. On Saturdays, the Janskerkhof hosts a large flower and plant market. On the same day, magnificent bouquets are sold along the Oudegracht, the old canal. The Breedstraat market, also held on Saturdays, is the venue of the cloth market.

Utrecht City Centre

① Nationaal Museum van Speelklok tot Pierement
② Domtoren and Domkerk
③ Aboriginal Art Museum
④ Museum Catharijne-convent

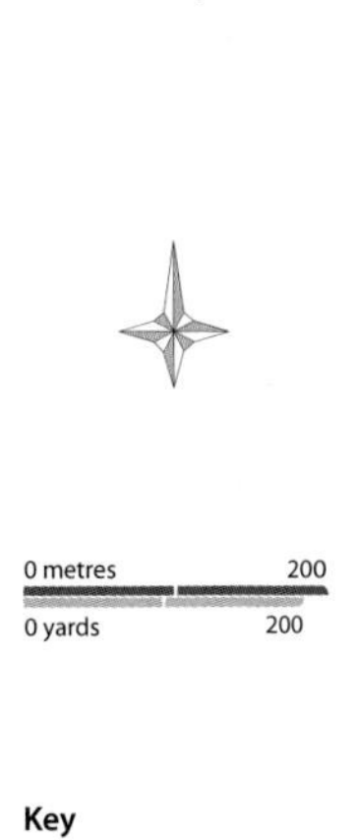

Key

Street-by-street map *(pp204–5)*

Rietveld Schröderhuis

When designing this house, architect Gerrit Rietveld worked closely with his client, Mrs Schröder, who lived here from 1924 until her death in 1985. The house was to epitomize all that was "modern" and broke with many of the architectural standards of the time. This can be seen in the design of the top floor, which may be divided in different ways by sliding partitions, according to the requirements of the inhabitants. The house was declared a World Heritage Site by UNESCO in 2001.

The Hanging Lamp
Rietveld designed this unusual lamp in around 1922.

★ Sliding Partitions
Using sliding partitions, the top floor could be divided into separate rooms for Mrs Schröder's children.

Telephone Seat
The house was to reflect the modern times in which it was designed, and so functional items like the telephone and fuse box were given a prominent location.

De Stijl

This Dutch artistic movement, founded in 1917, aimed to integrate art further into everyday life. Proponents wanted to bring painting and architecture closer together in a new way. The use of colour in the Rietveld Schröder-huis is one expression of this idea. Rietveld was a member of De Stijl from 1919, though he disagreed with certain ideas held by others in the group *(see p132)*.

De Stijl member Theo van Doesburg was mainly interested in straight lines and primary colours. The geometric surfaces of this painting do not depict reality but offer a glimpse of universality.

BOODSCHAPPEN
EERST BELLEN BIJ GEEN GEHOOR SPREEKBUIS

Intercom
The Schröder's intercom sign instructed visitors to "First ring. If no answer use mouthpiece".

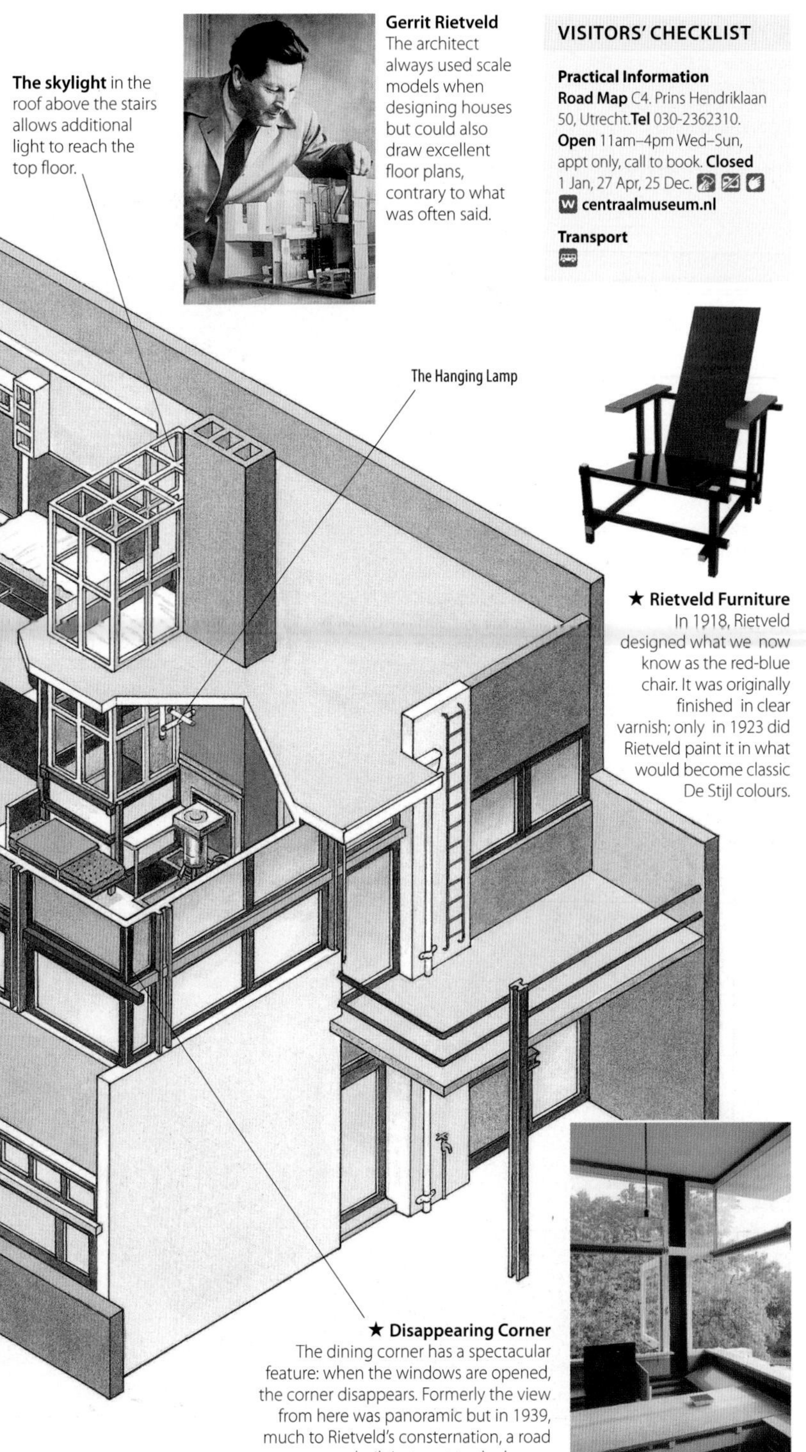

The skylight in the roof above the stairs allows additional light to reach the top floor.

Gerrit Rietveld
The architect always used scale models when designing houses but could also draw excellent floor plans, contrary to what was often said.

VISITORS' CHECKLIST

Practical Information
Road Map C4. Prins Hendriklaan 50, Utrecht. **Tel** 030-2362310.
Open 11am–4pm Wed–Sun, appt only, call to book. **Closed** 1 Jan, 27 Apr, 25 Dec.
centraalmuseum.nl

Transport

★ Rietveld Furniture
In 1918, Rietveld designed what we now know as the red-blue chair. It was originally finished in clear varnish; only in 1923 did Rietveld paint it in what would become classic De Stijl colours.

★ Disappearing Corner
The dining corner has a spectacular feature: when the windows are opened, the corner disappears. Formerly the view from here was panoramic but in 1939, much to Rietveld's consternation, a road was built just next to the house.

⓭ Amersfoort

Road Map C4. 149,700. Breestraat 1 (0900-1122364). Thu, Fri & Sat. **vvvamersfoort.nl**

The old town centre of Amersfoort contrasts sharply with the districts that surround it, which reflect a contemporary architectural style. The centre is defined by small streets with old houses and gardens. The **Muurhuizen** (wall houses) were built on the site of the old defence ring. The **Onze Lieve Vrouwetoren** (Tower of Our Lady) is difficult to miss. The contours of this old chapel can still be seen in the stones of the pavement. In 1787, the chapel, which was used to store gunpowder, was blown up.

The **Amersfoortse kei** boulder appeared in the town in 1661, when a nobleman bet he could drag the stone from the Leusderheide. Ever since, Amersfoort has held the annual Keistadfeest (Keistad festival) in celebration of the event.

The **Museum Flehite** gives an overview of the history of Amersfoort from the Middle Ages. The town was the birthplace of the abstract painter Mondriaan, the leading light of the De Stijl and Neo-Plasticist movements. The house where he was born is now home to the **Mon-driaan voor Constructieve en Concrete Kunst**, a study centre and archive of the artist's life and work, including several of his paintings. On the edge of town, housed in an eye-catching building named Eemhuis, is **Kunsthal KAdE**. This artspace does not have its own collection but curates exhibitions on contemporary art and culture, architecture and design. Attached to it is an art school and a shop that sells books on art and other memorabilia. The library, the Amersfoot Archives, is a must visit.

Onze Lieve Vrouwetoren, a church tower in Amersfoort

The 15th-century Koppelpoort, one of Amersfoort's three surviving gates

Environs

Some 4 km (2 miles) away, in the village of Leusden, **Kamp Amersfoort** is a grim reminder of the area's history. A Dutch army barracks was transformed in 1941 into a work camp for more than 35,000 people, including Jewish prisoners and Jehovah's Witnesses. Many were later transported to concentration camps. The camp also held American and Russian prisoners of war. The site is now a national monument. Several commemorative ceremonies are held each year.

Museum Flehite
Westsingel 50. **Tel** 033-2471100. **Open** 11am–5pm Tue–Fri, noon–5pm Sat & Sun. **Closed** Mon & public hols. **museumflehite.nl**

Mondriaanhuis voor Constructieve en Concrete Kunst
Kortegracht 11. **Tel** 033-4600170. **Open** Tue–Fri 11am–5pm, Sat–Sun noon–5pm. **mondriaanhuis.nl** .

Kunsthal KAdE
Eemplein 77,. **Tel** 033-4225030. **Open** 11am–5pm Tue–Fri, noon–5pm Sat–Sun.

Kamp Amersfoort
Loes van Overeemlaan 13, Leusden. **Tel** 033-4613129. **Open** Tue–Sun. **kampamersfoort.nl**

⓮ Doorn

Road Map C4. 10,000. Amersfoortseweg 27a (0343-412015). Thu am. **vvvheuvelrug.nl**

Doorn, originally called Thorheim (home of Thor, god of thunder), is a pretty village in wooded surroundings. The greatest tourist attraction here is **Huis Doorn**, where between 1920 and 1941 the German Kaiser, Wilhelm II, lived with his retinue. (He fled his cou-ntry after World War I.) The kaiser lies buried in a mausoleum in the castle gardens. Deer and birds of prey live in the **Kaapse Bossen**, woods situated east of Doorn.

The **Von Gimborn Arboretum** is a 27-hectare botanical garden begun in 1924. Part of the University of Utrecht, it was originally the private garden of Max von Gimborn, an ink manufacturer who was a tree expert and plant collector in his

Von Gimborn Arboretum, one of the Netherlands' largest gardens

For hotels and restaurants in this region see p397 and p410

spare time. One of the country's largest gardens, it is home to ten huge sequoia trees and a collection of rhododendrons. Although best visited in spring and summer to see (and smell) the flowers in bloom, the gardens contain plants for all seasons.

Huis Doorn
Langbroekerweg 10. **Tel** 0343-421020. **Open** timings vary, check website for details.. mandatory.
huisdoorn.nl

Von Gimborn Arboretum
Velperengh 13. **Tel** 0343-412144 **Open** daily.
gimbornarboretum.nl

⓯ Wijk bij Duurstede

Road Map C4. 23,000.
Markt 24 (0343-575995). Wed.

Dorestad was an important trade centre in Carolingian times. Plundering Vikings and a shift in the river basin of the Rhine led to its decline. Then soon after, in the 13th century, Wijk (near Dorestad) emerged and became the home of the Utrecht bishops around 1450. They brought prosperity and influence to the town until, in 1528, the bishop lost his secular power. The impressive **Kasteel Duurstede** dates from the 13th century, when it was originally built as a donjon, the castle's fortified inner tower. This was extended in 1500, and bishops lived here until 1580. The castle's park was laid out in 1850 by Jan David Zocher.

Kasteelpark Duurstede
Langs de Wal 7. **Tel** 088-0001510. **Open** park: daily, (castle by appt).

⓰ Amerongen

Road Map C4. 7,000.
0343-412015

Situated on the bank of the lower Rhine, which can be crossed by ferry, Amerongen lies in the ridge of hills known as the Utrechtse Heuvelrug, a national park. The Amerongense Berg marks the highest point in the ridge and has earned the name "mountain", despite being just 69 m (225 ft) high. The town lay originally on the Via Regia, the "royal route" from Utrecht to Cologne. From the 17th to 19th centuries, tobacco was grown in this area, as is evident by the drying sheds which are still standing. You can have a proper look at an old drying shed in the **Tabakteelt Museum**. In 1672, the town's castle, **Kasteel Amerongen**, was destroyed by the French. It was rebuilt in the Dutch Classical style.

Medieval castle tower in Wijk bij Duurstede

Tabakteelt Museum
Burg. Jhr van den Boschstraat 46. **Tel** 0343-456500. **Open** Tue–Sun pm.

Kasteel Amerongen
Drostestraat 20. **Tel** 0343-563766. **Open** check website.
mandatory.
kasteelamerongen.nl

⓱ Rhenen

Road Map C4. 19,000.
Markt 20 (0317-612333). Thu.

Rhenen lies on the north bank of the Rhine, at the border between the flat Betuwe and the Utrecht Heuvelrug. This area was inhabited as far back as the Iron Age. Many of the town's historic buildings were destroyed during World War II, but the Late Gothic **Cuneratoren** (Cunera tower), built between 1492 and 1531, escaped the bombs. The **Raadhuis** (town hall) dates from the Middle Ages. May 1940 saw a fierce battle on the 53-m (174-ft) **Grebbeberg**, a long-time strategic point in the surrounding area. The victims lie buried in the military cemetery.

East of the town, on the road to Wageningen, is the **Ouwehands Dierenpark**. This zoo contains all the favourites, like tigers, monkeys and elephants. There is also a large "bear wood", the *berenbos*, 20,000 sq m (66,000 sq ft) of forest-like landscape, where brown bears and wolves wander free. Other attractions include a tropical aquarium and plenty of children's activities, from a huge, jungle-themed adventure playground called RavotAapia, to special weekends dedicated to particular animals, and educational programmes.

Ouwehands Dierenpark
Grebbeweg 111. **Tel** 0317-650200. **Open** daily. **ouwehand.nl**

A country house set in one of the large parks surrounding Wijk bij Duurstede

SOUTH HOLLAND

For tourists, South Holland is pure delight. Although densely populated, the province still has plenty of open space and offers a remarkable range of attractions for visitors of all kinds. The landscape is typically Dutch, with large areas of reclaimed land dotted with windmills and grazing cattle.

From Roman times on, South Holland was principally a low lying swampy delta as the various courses of the river Rhine reached the sea. The influence of the counts of Holland (9th–13th centuries), who took up residence in The Hague, attracted trade with Flanders, Germany and England, and settlements became towns. Leiden's university, the oldest in the country, was founded as long ago as 1565. Peat extraction for fuel created lakes, reclaimed land *(see pp26–7)* was turned into productive farmland, and the Dutch dairy industry flourished. Other products in international demand included beer and textiles and, in more recent times, year-round flowers and the famous Dutch bulbs. Overseeing all this activity is the port of Rotterdam, one of the largest in the world, and The Hague, home of the Dutch government, the royal family, and the International Court of Justice. Delft is famous for its exquisite hand-painted porcelain and china, while Gouda is renowned for its cheese. The North Sea coast has charming resorts, from busy Scheveningen, with its attractive pier, to the smaller seaside towns of Katwijk and Noordwijk, with long sandy beaches. It is an ideal region for family holidays and for children of all ages.

Visitors in spring are in for a treat when they tour the north of the province. Bulb fields erupt in a riot of colour, and the Keukenhof's flower gardens are simply unforgettable.

Servants waiting for the queen next to her Golden Coach on the third Tuesday of September (Prinsjesdag)

◀ Sunrise over the windmills at Kinderdijk

Exploring South Holland

In the north of the province of South Holland are the colourful bulb fields and the Keukenhof, while to the south in a semi-circle lie the old university town of Leiden, bustling The Hague, cosy Delft and the modern port city of Rotterdam. The islands of South Holland bear witness to the country's military history in Hellevoetsluis and Brielle. Ramblers will find all they wish for in the dunes by Wassenaar or in the river countryside at Leerdam, which is best known for its glass-blowing industry. From Gorinchem you can take a passenger ferry to the 14th-century castle of Slot Loevestein, which played a key role in the history of Holland.

The 14th-century Huis Dever by Lisse

The Panorama Mesdag in The Hague

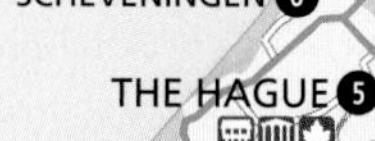

Greenhouses in the Westland

Getting Around

South Holland has a comprehensive system of roads, and both big cities and small towns can be reached equally quickly. However, during the morning and afternoon rush hours you should watch out for traffic jams. In the centres of the big cities it is best to leave your car in a car park, as finding an on-street parking space can often be a problem. Trains are a fast way of getting from A to B. As a rule you will find a train for your particular destination departing every quarter or half hour. Lisse and the bulbfields, Nieuwpoort and the towns on South Holland's islands can be reached only by local bus. VVV and ANWB tourist information offices provide information on cycling routes.

Knotwilgen in the Groene Hart

For map symbols *see back flap*

Sights at a Glance

2 Lisse
3 Keukenhof
4 *Leiden pp218–19*
5 *The Hague pp222–29*
6 Scheveningen
7 *Delft pp230–33*
8 Maassluis
9 Schiedam
10 *Rotterdam pp234–41*
11 *Gouda pp242–3*
12 Reeuwijkse Plassen
13 Nieuwpoort
14 Gorinchem
15 Leerdam
16 Dordrecht
17 Kinderdijk
18 Brielle
19 Hellevoetsluis
20 Middelharnis
21 Goedereede

Tour

1 *Bulb Fields pp216–17*

Key

Motorway
Main road
Minor road
Scenic route
Main railway
Minor railway
Regional border

The Flemish Gothic Stadhuis in Gouda

For hotels and restaurants in this region see p398 and pp410–411

❶ Bulb Fields

The Bollenstreek, a 30-km (19-mile) stretch between Haarlem and Leiden, is Holland's primary bulb-growing area. From March, the polders are aglow with glorious colours – the crocuses are the first to flower and the season culminates around mid-April with the majestic tulips. The lilies then follow at the end of May. Visitors without cars can obtain information about cycle routes from the tourist information office, the VVV, at Lisse *(see p217)*. Bikes can be hired at railway stations in Haarlem and Heemstede-Aerdenhout.

Tips for Drivers

Starting point: Haarlem.
Distance: Approximately 30 km (19 miles).
Stopping-off points: Along with the places discussed below, where various cafés and restaurants are to be found, Noordwijk aan Zee is worth a short detour. This lively coastal town, with its wonderful beach and dunes, makes an ideal place for a stopover.

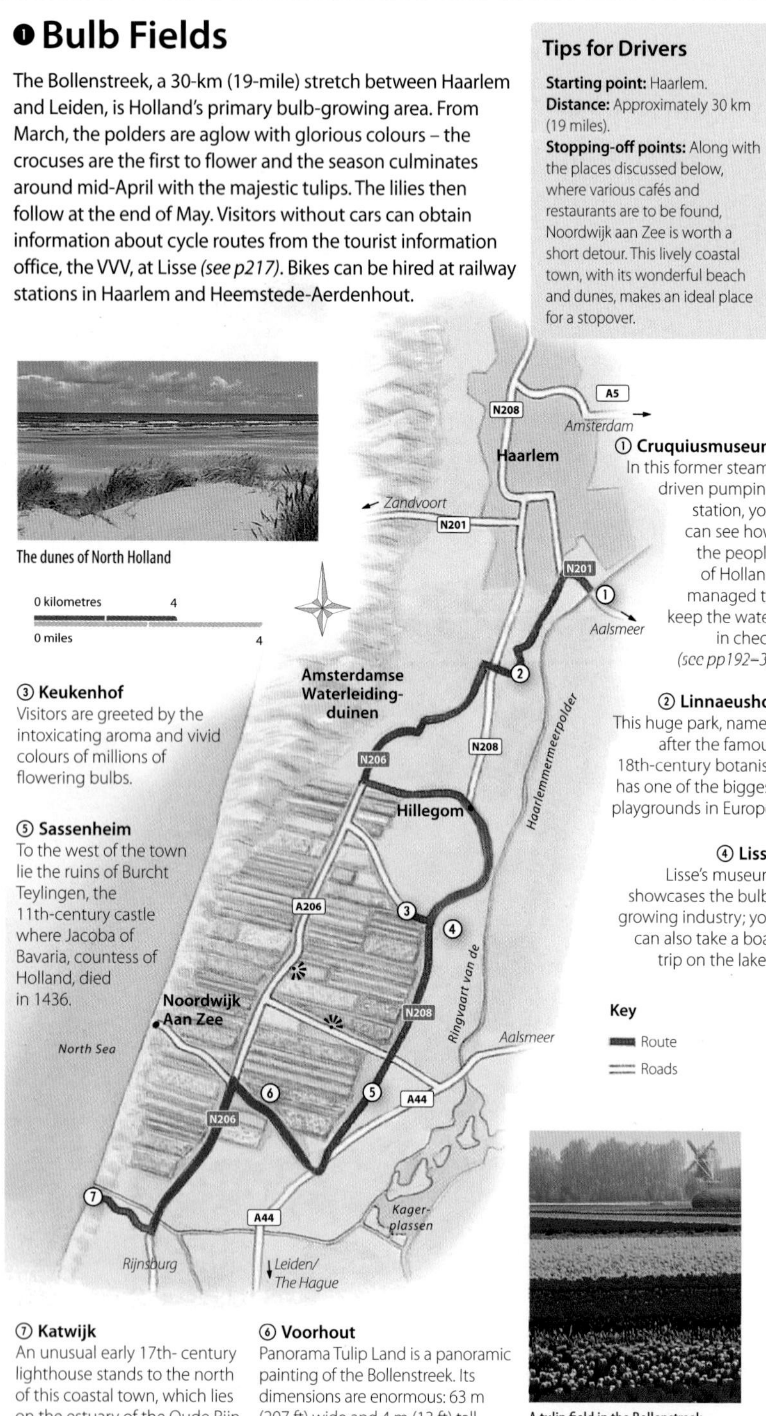

The dunes of North Holland

① Cruquiusmuseum
In this former steam-driven pumping station, you can see how the people of Holland managed to keep the water in check *(see pp192–3)*.

② Linnaeushof
This huge park, named after the famous 18th-century botanist, has one of the biggest playgrounds in Europe.

③ Keukenhof
Visitors are greeted by the intoxicating aroma and vivid colours of millions of flowering bulbs.

④ Lisse
Lisse's museum showcases the bulb-growing industry; you can also take a boat trip on the lakes.

⑤ Sassenheim
To the west of the town lie the ruins of Burcht Teylingen, the 11th-century castle where Jacoba of Bavaria, countess of Holland, died in 1436.

⑥ Voorhout
Panorama Tulip Land is a panoramic painting of the Bollenstreek. Its dimensions are enormous: 63 m (207 ft) wide and 4 m (13 ft) tall.

⑦ Katwijk
An unusual early 17th- century lighthouse stands to the north of this coastal town, which lies on the estuary of the Oude Rijn.

A tulip field in the Bollenstreek

Flowering Bulbs

Flowers such as gladioli, lilies, narcissi, hyacinths, irises, crocuses and dahlias are mainly grown in the Bollenstreek. By far the most important, though, is the tulip, which originally came from Turkey and was cultivated by Carolus Clusius in 1593 for the first time in the Netherlands.

"Aladdin" tulips

"China Pink" tulips

"Tahiti" narcissi

"Minnow" narcissi

"Blue Jacket" hyacinths

Colourful flowering bulbs in the shady Keukenhof

❷ Lisse

Map B3. 20,000. 50 & 51 (from Leiden & Haarlem) & 59 (from Noordwijk). Grachtweg 53 (0252-414262). **vvvlisse.nl**

The best time to see Lisse is at the end of April, when the colourful **Bloemen Corso** (flower parade) takes place *(see p36)*. A vibrant procession of floats passes from Noordwijk to Haarlem, where they are brightly illuminated at night and can still be seen the next day. On the two days before the parade, you can see close-up how the floats are decorated in the *Hobaho* halls in Lisse.

The **Museum De Zwarte Tulp** (black tulip museum) covers the history of bulb growing and illustrates the life cycle of bulbs. It also touches upon the "tulipomania" from 1620–37 *(see pp34–5)*, when investors pushed up the demand for rare tulip bulbs to such an extent that they were worth their weight in gold.

Bloemen Corso
bloemencorsobollenstreek.nl

Museum De Zwarte Tulp
Grachtweg 2a. **Tel** 0252-417900.
Open 1–5pm Tue–Sun.
Closed public hols.
museumdezwartetulp.nl

Environs

Just outside Lisse is **Huys Dever**, a fortified residential tower which dates from the second half of the 14th century. The permanent exhibition at the tower illustrates the lives of the families who lived here.

Huys Dever
Heereweg 349a. **Tel** 0252-411430.
Open 2–5pm Tue–Sun.
Closed public hols. by arrangement. **kasteeldever.nl**

❸ Keukenhof

Map B3. 854 (from Leiden Centraal Station), 858 (from Schiphol airport). **Tel** 0252-465555. **Open** daily late Mar–mid-May, 8am–6pm (ticket office). **keukenhof.nl**

Lying in a wooded park of 32 ha (79 acres) close to Lisse, the Keukenhof is one of the most spectacular public gardens in the world. It was set up in 1949 as a showcase for bulb-growers and currently has around 6 million bulbs planted in it. Fields are full of dazzling narcissi, hyacinths and tulips in bloom from the end of March to the end of May. You can also see the white blossom of the Japanese cherry tree in the park early in the season and, later, the bright flowers of the azaleas and rhododendrons.

❹ Street-by-Street: Leiden

Leiden is a thriving university town which dates from Roman times. The town developed because of its position on a branch of the Rhine and is still an important trade centre. Some excellent museums chart Leiden's eventful past, including the Golden Age, when the town was a centre for world trade *(see pp52–3)*. Rembrandt van Rijn *(see pp30–31)* was born here in June 1606 – a plaque on the façade of a Weddesteeg house marks his birthplace. During term time, the streets of Leiden are busy with students cycling between lectures or frequenting the cafés and bookshops.

★ Rijksmuseum van Oudheden
This squat statue of a kneeling treasury scribe is just one of the many impressive Egyptian artefacts on display in this fascinating museum of antiquities.

★ Hortus Botanicus
The botanical gardens belonging to the University of Leiden *(see p216)* were started in 1590 "for the teaching of every body who studies in the medicinal sciences".

Façades
Aristocrats, professors and textile families all contributed to the face of the Leiden canals.

Dutch Classicism can be seen in the university buildings on Rapenburg.

Het Gravensteen
Part of the law faculty is now accommodated in this former count's prison, built between the 13th and 17th centuries.

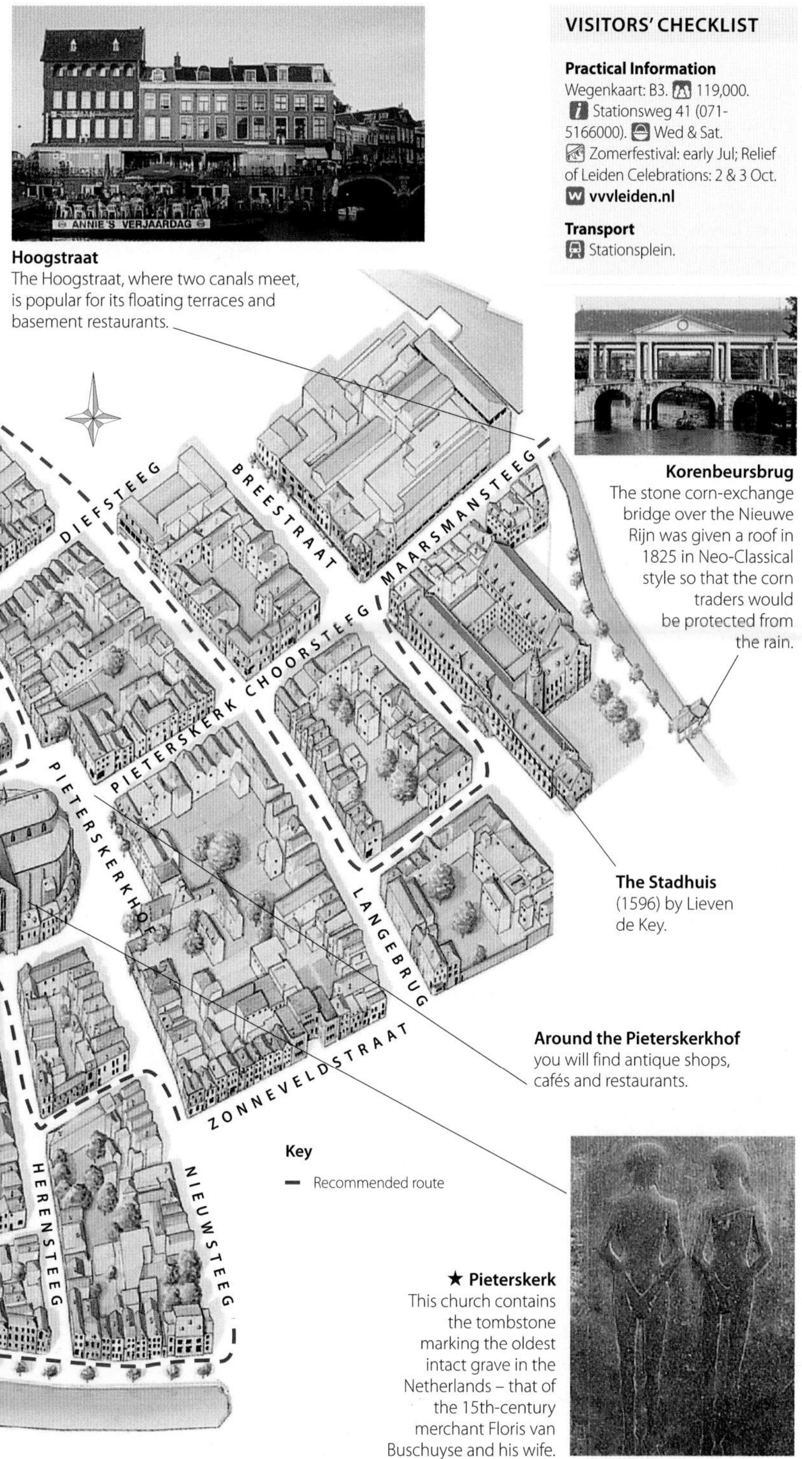

VISITORS' CHECKLIST

Practical Information
Wegenkaart: B3. 119,000.
Stationsweg 41 (071-5166000). Wed & Sat.
Zomerfestival: early Jul; Relief of Leiden Celebrations: 2 & 3 Oct.
vvvleiden.nl

Transport
Stationsplein.

Hoogstraat
The Hoogstraat, where two canals meet, is popular for its floating terraces and basement restaurants.

Korenbeursbrug
The stone corn-exchange bridge over the Nieuwe Rijn was given a roof in 1825 in Neo-Classical style so that the corn traders would be protected from the rain.

The Stadhuis
(1596) by Lieven de Key.

Around the Pieterskerkhof
you will find antique shops, cafés and restaurants.

Key
— Recommended route

★ Pieterskerk
This church contains the tombstone marking the oldest intact grave in the Netherlands – that of the 15th-century merchant Floris van Buschuyse and his wife.

Exploring Leiden

Leiden is famous for its university, which is the oldest in the country. It was founded in 1575, one year after the Beggars of the Sea *(see p245)* freed the town from a protracted siege by the Spanish *(see p53)*. As a reward for their endurance, William of Orange offered the people of Leiden the choice between a university and the abolition of taxes. The people made a shrewd choice and the town went on to become a centre of intellectual progress and religious freedom. English Puritan dissidents, victims of persecution in their homeland, were able to settle here in the 17th century before undertaking their journey to the New World.

One of the 35 almshouses in Leiden

Museum de Lakenhal

Oude Singel 28–32. **Tel** 071-5165360. **Open** Ongoing renovations, check website for timings . **Closed** 1 Jan, 25 Dec. **lakenhal.nl**

In the 17th century, the *lakenhal* (cloth merchants' hall) was the centre of the Leiden textile industry. Arent van 's Gravesande designed the building in 1640 in Dutch Classical style. The municipal museum has been here since 1874. The showpiece of the collection, which was rescued from the Pieterskerk (St Peter's Church) during the religious disputes of 1566 *(see pp56–7)* is *The Last Judgment* (1526–7), a triptych in Renaissance style by Lucas van Leyden. Other Leiden artists, from Rembrandt to Theo van Doesburg, are also featured. The museum has displays of silver, glass, tin and tiles and explores the history of Leiden. Not to be missed is the large bronze cooking pot said to have been left by the Spaniards during the relief of Leiden in 1574. The spicy casserole it contained is recreated as a stew cooked every year on 3 October to commemorate Dutch victory over the Spanish.

Hortus Botanicus Leiden

Rapenburg 73. **Tel** 071-5277249. **Open** summer: 10am–6pm daily; winter: 10am–4pm Tue–Sun. **Closed** 3 Oct, 24 Dec–1 Jan. (partial). **hortusleiden.nl**

The botanical garden of Leiden was founded in 1590 as part of the university. A number of its trees and shrubs are particularly old, such as a laburnum dating from 1601. In 1593, Carolus Clusius, who introduced the tulip to Holland *(see pp34–5)*, became the first professor of botany at the University of Leiden. The Hortus Botanicus features a reconstruction of his walled garden. Also worth a look are the tropical greenhouses, the rose garden and the Von Siebold Japanese memorial garden.

Museum Boerhaave

Lange St Agnietenstraat 10. **Tel** 071-5214224. **Open** 10am–5pm Tue–Sun (Mon on school hols) & public hols. **Closed** 1 Jan, 27 Apr, 3 Oct, 25 Dec.. **museumboerhaave.nl**

Located in the former Caecilia Hospital in the centre of Leiden, this is the Netherlands' National Museum of the History of Science and Medicine. It is named after the

Lucas van Leyden's triptych of *The Last Judgment*, in the Stedelijk Museum de Lakenhal

great Dutch professor of medicine Herman Boerhaave (1668–1738). The collection reflects the development of mathematics, astronomy, physics, chemistry and medicine. Exhibits range from a magnificent 15th-century astrolabe and pendulum clocks by Christiaan Huygens (1629–95) to surgeons' equipment of yesteryear and early electron microscopes.

Museum Volkenkunde

Steenstraat 1. **Tel** 071-5168800. **Open** 10am–5pm Tue–Sun & public hols. **Closed** 1 Jan, 27 Apr, 3 Oct, 25 Dec.
volkenkunde.nl

This excellent ethnological museum, founded in 1837, has collections which feature non-Western cultures, such as ethnographic items brought by the German explorer Philipp von Siebold from Japan in the 19th century. The vast collection focuses on the interaction between various cultures and their links with the Netherlands; hence Indonesia has a considerable amount of floor space. The museum covers practically the whole world, from the Arctic to Oceania.

Heraldic lion at De Burcht

Naturalis Biodiversity Center

Darwinweg 2. **Tel** 071-5687600. **Open** 10am–5pm daily. **Closed** 1 Jan, 27 Apr, 4 Oct, 25 Dec.
naturalis.nl

As soon as it opened in 1998, the national natural history museum attracted a record number of visitors. It provides a truly fascinating insight into the evolution of the earth and its inhabitants with displays of fossils more than a million years old, and lifelike replicas of animals, stones and minerals. Special exhibitions for children are also held.

Pieterskerk

Pieterskerkhof 1a. **Tel** 071-5124319. **Open** check website. **Closed** 3 Oct & when church is hired out.
pieterskerk.com

This impressive Gothic cruciform church, built mainly in the 15th century, stands in the middle of a shady square that seems to be from a different age. It is worth a visit for its austere interior and the carefully restored Van Hagerbeer organ (1639–43), one of the few meantone-tuned organs. The floor of the nave is covered with worn stones which mark the graves of famous 17th-century intellectuals such as Puritan leader John Robinson, physician Hermanus Boerhaave and Golden Age artist Jan Steen.

The Pilgrim Fathers

In the 17th century, the Netherlands was a refuge for English Puritans. Minister John Robinson (1575–1625) founded a church in Leiden in 1609, where he inspired his congregation with his dream of the New World. The Pilgrim Fathers set out in 1620 from Delfshaven aboard the *Speedwell*, but the ship proved to be unseaworthy. They then crossed the Atlantic from Plymouth, England, on the *Mayflower*, but Robinson stayed behind, too ill to travel. He died in Leiden in 1625.

The *Mayflower* crossing the Atlantic Ocean

De Burcht

Burgsteeg. **Open** daily.

The Burcht is a 12th-century fortress which features a still-intact circular wall and crenellated battlements. At the foot of the 12-m (39-ft) artificial mound is a wrought-iron gate covered in heraldic symbols. There is a marvellous view of Leiden's historic centre from the gallery.

Rijksmuseum van Oudheden

Rapenburg 28. **Tel** 0900-6600600. **Open** 10am–5pm Tue–Sun & public hols. **Closed** 1 Jan, 27 Apr, 3 Oct, 25 Dec. **rmo.nl**

This museum has one of the top seven Egyptian collections in the world, the centrepiece of which is the 2,000-year-old Taffeh Temple. Other civilizations from the Near East and from Classical Antiquity are also represented. The section on archaeology of the Netherlands gives visitors an idea of what the Low Countries were like from prehistoric times to the Middle Ages. Mummies, textiles and shoes, musical instruments and fragments of Roman mosaics and frescoes form just part of the museum's impressive holdings.

A drawbridge across the Oude Rijn in Leiden

❺ Street-by-Street: The Hague

The village of Die Haghe ("the hedge") grew around the Binnenhof (inner courtyard), which has been an important political centre since the 13th century. The princes of Orange, the upper classes and an extensive diplomatic corps gave instructions for palaces and mansion houses to be built, and a stroll across the Voorhout or along the Hofvijver will still evoke its aristocratic charm.The Hague today is represented by the new Spuikwartier (Spui district), with the city hall by Richard Meier and the Lucent Danstheater by Rem Koolhaas. To the west, the dunes and many parks and woods are still reminiscent of the country estate it once was.

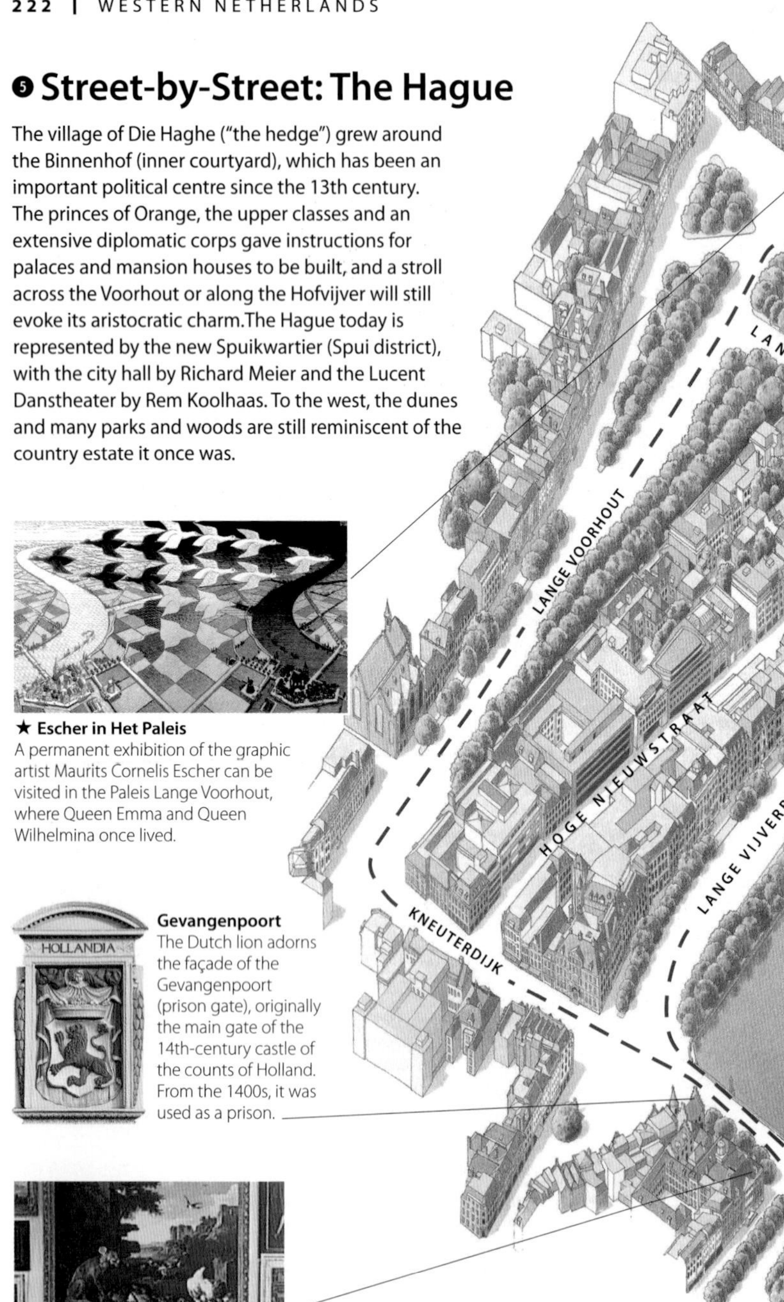

★ Escher in Het Paleis
A permanent exhibition of the graphic artist Maurits Cornelis Escher can be visited in the Paleis Lange Voorhout, where Queen Emma and Queen Wilhelmina once lived.

Gevangenpoort
The Dutch lion adorns the façade of the Gevangenpoort (prison gate), originally the main gate of the 14th-century castle of the counts of Holland. From the 1400s, it was used as a prison.

Key

— Recommended route

0 metres 50
0 yards 50

Prince William V's Picture Gallery
This was the first public art gallery in the Netherlands.

For hotels and restaurants in this region see p398 and pp410–411

Jantje, famous from a Dutch nursery rhyme, points to the Binnenhof.

Haags Historisch Museum
Featured is the history of The Hague, from the Middle Ages to the present day.

VISITORS' CHECKLIST

Practical Information
Road Map B4. 497,000.
denhaag.com
Spui 68 (0900-3403505).
Mon–Fri. Scheveningen Sand Sculpture Festival: May; Scheveningen Vlaggetjesdag: end of May/beg of Jun; Parkpop: end of Jun; Pasar Malam Besar: mid-May; Prinsjesdag: 3rd Tue in Sep; Crossing Borders Festival: mid–Nov

Transport
Centraal Station (CS); Koningin Julianaplein 10; Hollands Spoor (HS); Stationsplein 25.

★ Mauritshuis
On display here in an exquisite collection are 17th-century old masters, including works by Rembrandt and Vermeer.

The Tweede Kamer
The accommodation for the Tweede Kamer, the Dutch Lower House, was designed by Pi de Bruijn and has been in use since 1992. The building blends tastefully with the older buildings surrounding it. Plenary sessions are held in the Grote Vergaderzaal (great assembly hall) behind the circular extension.

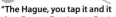

"The Hague, you tap it and it sings" wrote Dutch poet Gerrit Achterberg in "Passage". The elegant covered arcade of shops in Neo-Renaissance style on the Hofweg is a famous feature of the town centre.

★ Binnenhof
This ancient structure comprises the parliament and government buildings and was originally the 13th-century hunting lodge of the counts of Holland.

Exploring The Hague

The Hague has numerous attractions and museums, of which the Mauritshuis *(see pp226–7)* and the Gemeentemuseum (municipal museum) *(see p228)* are the most famous. There are many bookshops, antique shops and cafés on and around the Denneweg, which comes out onto the Lange Voorhout, as well as luxury boutiques on the promenade beginning at Paleis Noordeinde *(see p225)*. Behind the Mauritskade lies the stately late 19th-century Willemspark, which is still almost completely intact, with the Panorama Mesdag *(see p228)*. You can admire the peaceful Japanese garden in Park Clingendael *(see p228)*. The old fishing village of Scheveningen has expanded to become a lively seaside resort but the dunes all around still offer peace and quiet.

Binnenhof met Ridderzaal

Binnenhof. **Tel** 070-7570200. **Open** for guided tours only. **Closed** Sun, public hols, 3rd Tue in Sep. Booking obligatory (via website). **prodemos.nl**

The historic Binnenhof is a series of buildings erected around the hunting lodge of the counts of Holland. In 1247, William II was proclaimed Holy Roman Emperor; he later had the gothic Ridderzaal (Hall of the Knights) built as a banqueting hall. The Binnenhof has since then been the residence of stadholders, princes and governments. The court of Holland has administered justice since 1511 in the Rolzaal (roll court). The northern provinces of the Netherlands broke free from Spanish rule in 1581 with the *Plakkaat van Verlatinge* ("Decree of Abandonment"); they held a huge feast for William of Orange in the Ridderzaal. The Binnenhof was one of the most important European centres of diplomacy in the Golden Age. The magnificently ornate meeting hall dates from this period and is where the Upper House curre-ntly sits. The Lower House met in William V's old ballroom until 1992, when it was moved to a new location. Tours of the building begin in the medieval cellars and pass through the Ridderzaal and debating chambers of the Upper or Lower House.

Porcelain from the Museum Bredius collection

Landscape by Fading Light by Albert Cuyp (Museum Bredius)

Museum De Gevangenpoort

Buitenhof 33. **Tel** 070-3460861. **Open** check website. **Closed** 1 Jan, 25 Dec. obligatory; last guided tour 3:45pm. **gevangenpoort.nl**

The prison gate museum, in a 14th-century gatehouse, contains an old prison still largely in its original state. Cornelis de Witt was kept here on suspicion of conspiracy against Prince Maurice. In 1672, as he and his brother Johan left the prison, they were murdered by a provoked mob. The museum has a unique collection of horrific torture instruments. It shares an entrance with Galerij Prins Willem V.

Galerij Prins Willem V

Buitenhof 33. **Tel** 070-3023456. **Open** noon–5pm Tue–Sun. **galerijprinswillemv.nl**

Prince William V was an enthusiastic collector of 17th-century art. In 1774, his private collection was put on show for the public in this former inn, which the prince had converted into his office. The treasures in this gallery include paintings by Rembrandt, Jan Steen and Paulus Potter (1625–54).

Museum Bredius

Lange Vijverberg 14. **Tel** 070-362 0729. **Open** 11am–5pm Tue–Sun. **Closed** 1 Jan, 25 Dec. **museumbredius.nl**

Art historian and art collector Abraham Bredius was also director of the Mauritshuis *(see pp226–7)* from 1895 to 1922. On his death in 1946 he bequeathed his collection of 17th- and 18th-century art, including paintings by Rembrandt and Jan Steen, to the city of The Hague. The elegant 18th-century mansion on the north side of the Hofvijver which houses the museum also has fine antique furniture and porcelain and beautifully engraved silver.

The Classical-style Paleis Noordeinde, where Queen Beatrix has her offices

Escher in Het Paleis

Lange Voorhout 74. **Tel** 070- 427 7730. **Open** 11am–5pm Tue–Sun. **Closed** 1 Jan, 3rd Tue in Sep, 25 Dec. **escherinhetpaleis.nl**

A large proportion of MC Escher's (1898–1972) work is displayed in the Paleis Lange Voorhout, including well-known works such as *Day and Night*, *Rising and Falling* and *Belvédère*. In addition to graphic works, there are sketches, personal documents and photographs. The museum also features the Escher Experience, a virtual journey through his world.

Paleis Noordeinde

Noordeinde. **Open** only the Paleistuin *(palace garden)* is open to the public.

In 1640, Stadholder Frederik Hendrik had his mother's house converted into a palace in the classical style. The property of the Princes of Orange since William V (1748–1806), this is where King Willem Alexander has his offices and also where he leaves from for the state opening of parliament.

Vredespaleis

Carnegieplein 2. 22 and 24. 17. **Tel** 070-3024137. **Open** Tue–Sun (Visitor's Centre). Sat–Sun. **Closed** public hols and when court is in session. **vredespaleis.nl**

In 1899, The Hague hosted the first international peace conference. Contributions from the court's members decorate the interior of the mock-Gothic Vredespaleis (peace palace), designed by the French architect Louis Cordonnier and completed in 1913. The International Court of the United Nations, formed in 1946, is based here.

Passage

Between the Spuistraat, Hofweg and Buitenhof.

A visit to The Hague would not be complete without a stroll along the elegant Passage, the only covered arcade remaining from the 19th century in the Netherlands. Unusual specialist shops can be found here, such as the umbrella and fountain pen shop. The arcade wing that leads to the Hofweg was added in 1928–9.

Den Haag City Centre

1. Het Paleis
2. Museum De Gevangenpoort
3. Galerij Prins Willem V
4. Museum Bredius
5. Ridderzaal
6. Passage
7. Mauritshuis

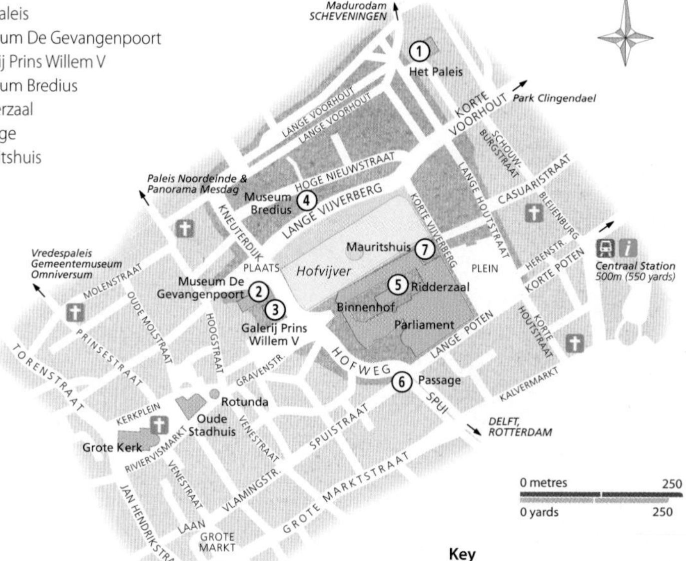

Key

Street-by-street map *(pp222–3)*

Mauritshuis

After he was recalled as captain general of Brazil, Johan Maurits of Nassau commissioned this house. It was completed in 1644 by Pieter Post in the North Dutch Classical style with influences from the Italian Renaissance and has a marvellous view of the Hofvijver. After the death of Maurits in 1679, the house passed into state hands and, in 1822, became the home of the royal painting collection. Though the collection is not large, it contains almost exclusively superior works by old masters. The Mauritshuis is closed until mid-2014 for renovation, during which time the highlights from the collection will be housed in the Gemeentemuseum *(see p228)*. Check website for details.

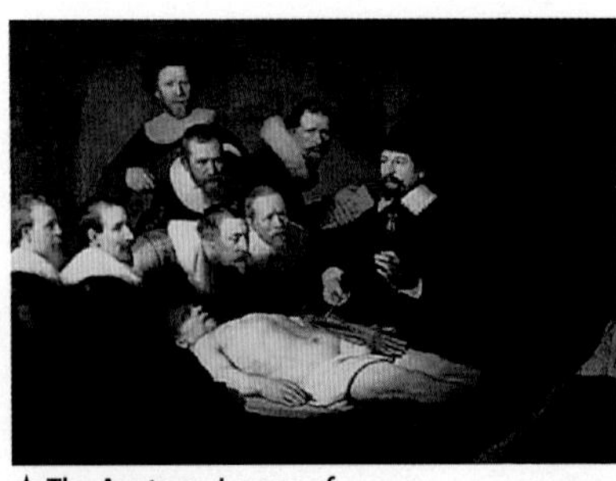

★ The Anatomy Lesson of Dr Nicolaes Tulp (1632)
Rembrandt's painting of doctors examining a corpse reflects the burgeoning contemporary interest in anatomy and science.

Museum Guide

The three floors of this little museum are hung with paintings from top to bottom. To feature all aspects of the collection, the exhibited artwork is constantly changing. The masterpieces are always on view, although not always hanging in the same location. Presentation is pleasantly haphazard, but all the paintings are labelled with the artist, title and year. If you have any questions, you can ask for help at the information desk located in the museum's golden room.

Bordello Scene
(1658) This typical 17th-century genre painting of a brothel scene by Frans van Mieris de Oude (1635–81) has an unmistakable erotic undertone.

Vase with Flowers (1618)
Ambrosius Bosschaert captured the beauty of summer flowers but added the flies to remind us of our mortality.

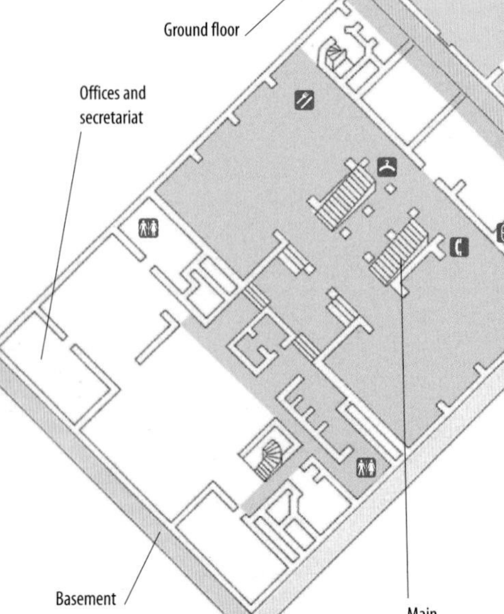

The Goldfinch (1654)
This small, elegant painting is by Carel Fabritius (1622–54), a pupil of Rembrandt.

VISITORS' CHECKLIST

Practical Information
Korte Vijverberg 8, The Hague.
Tel 070-3023456.
mauritshuis.nl
Open check website for details.
Closed 1 Jan, 25 Dec.

Transport
22, 24. 2, 3, 4, 6.

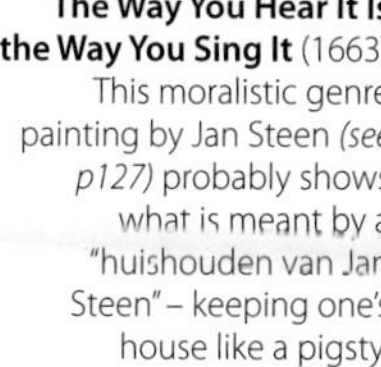

The Way You Hear It Is the Way You Sing It (1663)
This moralistic genre painting by Jan Steen *(see p127)* probably shows what is meant by a "huishouden van Jan Steen" – keeping one's house like a pigsty.

★ **The Louse Hunt** (1653)
Gerard ter Borch's painting depicts a domestic tableau and reflects the Dutch preoccupation with order and cleanliness during the 17th century.

★ **Girl with a Pearl Earring** (1665)
At the mid-point of his career, Johannes Vermeer painted this haunting portrait of a girl wearing a pearl earring. Stories about the true origins of the girl abound.

Key to Floorplan

- Portrait gallery
- 15th- and early 16th-century works
- Late 16th- and 17th-century works
- Golden room
- 17th-century art
- 17th-century Flemish artists
- Early 17th-century collection
- Non-exhibition space

The Hague's municipal museum, one of HP Berlage's most handsome designs

Panorama Mesdag

Zeestraat 65. 22, 24. 17.
Tel 070-3644544. **Open** 10am–5pm Mon–Sat, noon–5pm Sun & public hols. **Closed** 1 Jan, 25 Dec.
By request.
panorama-mesdag.com

Panorama Mesdag is one of the best remaining panoramic paintings of the 19th century. The circular canvas, with an impressive circumference of 120 m (395 ft), depicts the old fishing village of Scheveningen. It is a breathtaking moment when, after climbing the creaking stairs leading up to the panorama, you suddenly emerge into daylight, to be surrounded by the dunes and the sea. The illusion is strengthened by genuine sand and pieces of wreckage laid at the foot of the painting. The painting was done in 1881 by members of the Haag School, led by HW Mesdag (1831–1915) and his wife Sientje (1834–1909). George Hendrik Breitner (1857–1923) painted the cavalrymen on the sand.

Gemeentemuseum Den Haag en Fotomuseum

Stadhouderslaan 41. 24.
Tel 070-3381111. **Open** 11am–5pm Tue–Sun. **Closed** 1 Jan, 25 Dec.
gemeentemuseum.nl

The Gemeentemuseum (municipal museum) was the last piece of work to be carried out by HP Berlage, founder of the Amsterdam School. The museum was completed in 1935, one year after his death, and now contains the largest collection of paintings by Mondriaan in the world, with works from all his various periods. One of the high points of the collection is *Victory Boogie Woogie* (1943). Other works exhibited here include paintings by JH Weissenbruch and brothers Maris and Josef Israëls, all of whom were representatives of the Haag School, which was profoundly inspired by the coastal landscape. The main feature of the applied art section is the antique Delftware and oriental porcelain. The 'Wonder *kamers*' or 'Wonder Rooms' are housed in the basement which is a labyrinthe of quirky displays, with teenagers as the target audience. Part of the Gemeentemuseum, with its entrance next door, is the **Fotomuseum**, (www.fotomuseumdenhaag.nl) which stages temporary exhibitions of Dutch and international photography.

Victory Boogie Woogie

Omniversum

President Kennedylaan 5. 24.
17. **Tel** 0900-6664837.
Open hours depends on programme, phone or check website.
omniversum.nl

The Omniversum (next to the Gemeentemuseum) is a cross between a planetarium and a high tech cinema. It puts on a great programme of exciting films of space flights, volcanic eruptions and ocean life.

Park Clingendael

Entrance from Alkemadelaan or the Ruychrocklaan. 18.
Japanese Gardens: Park Clingendael. **Open** end of Apr–mid-Jun: from sunrise to sunset daily.

This country estate already existed in the 16th century, when it had a large, formal French-style garden. In 1830 it was converted into a pretty landscaped park. It contains a Dutch garden, a rose garden, grazing land for animals, rhododendron woods and an ancient beech tree.

Overgrown bunkers in the wood are a sombre reminder of World War II, when the Netherlands was occupied and

The picturesque Japanese garden in Park Clingendael

For hotels and restaurants in this region see p398 and pp410–411

the most senior German authorities took up quarters in Huis Clingendael. At the centre of the park lies the famous Japanese garden, which was laid out in 1903 on the instructions of Baroness Marguérite Mary after a trip to Japan. The tea house and all the stones and ornaments in the garden were brought over from Japan by boat at the time.

Madurodam

George Maduroplein 1. 22. 9. **Tel** 070-4162400. **Open** Sep–Oct & Mar: 9am–7pm; Nov–Dec: 9am–5pm; Jan–Feb: 9am–6pm; Apr–Jun: 9am–8pm; Jul–Aug: 9am–9pm. **madurodam.nl**

Madurodam depicts the Netherlands in miniature – it consists of replicas of historical buildings like the Binnenhof in The Hague *(see p224)*, canalside houses in Amsterdam and the Euromast tower in Rotterdam *(see p236)*, built to a scale of 1:25. Other models here include Schiphol Airport, windmills, polders, bulb fields and some examples of the country's modern architecture. At night time the streets and buildings are illuminated by 50,000 tiny lamps.

Madurodam was opened in 1952 by Queen Juliana. JML Maduro designed the town in memory of his son George, who died at Dachau concentration camp in 1945. Profits go to children's charities.

The model city of Madurodam

6 Scheveningen

Road Map B4. 52,000. 22. 1. Keizerstraat 50 (0900-3403505). Thu.

This pleasant seaside resort is just 15 minutes by tram from the centre of The Hague. Like so many of the North Sea beach resorts, Scheveningen had its heyday in the 19th century. Nowadays it is a mixture of faded charm and modern garishness, though it remains a popular holiday resort because of its long sandy beach and the once famous **Pier,** which is now in disrepair. There are many places to eat, including good seafood restaurants.

The impressive **Kurhaus**, designed in the Empire style and now a luxurious hotel, was built in 1885, when Scheveningen was still a major spa town. Not far from the Kurhaus is **Sea Life Scheveningen**, where you can look through transparent tunnels at stingrays, sharks and many other fascinating sea creatures. **Muzee Scheveningen** is devoted to the history of the fishing village and the spa. Tours of Scheveningen lighthouse can also be booked.

Designed by Wim Quist, **Museum Beelden aan Zee** (seaside sculpture museum) can be found on the boulevard, half-hidden by a sand dune. Contemporary sculptures on the theme of the human figure are shown in the light, airy rooms, on the terraces and in the garden.

Although the seaside resort has all but swallowed up the original fishing village, there is still a harbour and a large fish market. Fishing boat trips can be booked on the southern side of the harbour – a fun outing for the afternoon.

Sea Life Scheveningen

Strandweg 13. **Tel** 070-3542100. **Open** 10am–6pm Sep–Jun. **Closed** 25 Dec. **sealife.nl**

Muzee Scheveningen

Neptunusstraat 92. **Tel** 070-3500830. **Open** 10am–5pm Tue–Sat, noon–5pm Sun. **Closed** 1 Jan, 25 Dec. **muzee.nl**

Museum Beelden aan Zee

Harteveltstraat 1. **Tel** 070-3585857. **Open** 10am–5pm Tue–Sun. **beeldenaanzee.nl**

Thsuki-no-hikari (Light of the Moon) by Igor Mitoraj in the dunes of the Museum Beelden aan Zee

❼ Street-by-Street: Delft

Delft dates back to 1075, its prosperity based on the weaving and brewing industries. In October 1654, however, an enormous explosion at the national arsenal destroyed much of the medieval town. The centre was rebuilt at the end of the 17th century and has remained relatively unchanged since then – houses in Gothic and Renaissance styles still stand along the tree-lined canals. Town life is concentrated on the Markt, which has the town hall at one end and the Nieuwe Kerk at the other. Visitors can dip into the scores of shops selling expensive, hand-painted Delftware or take a tour of local factories, the shops of which are often reasonably priced.

★ Stedelijk Museum Het Prinsenhof
William of Orange was killed on this staircase in 1584, the bullet holes still visible.

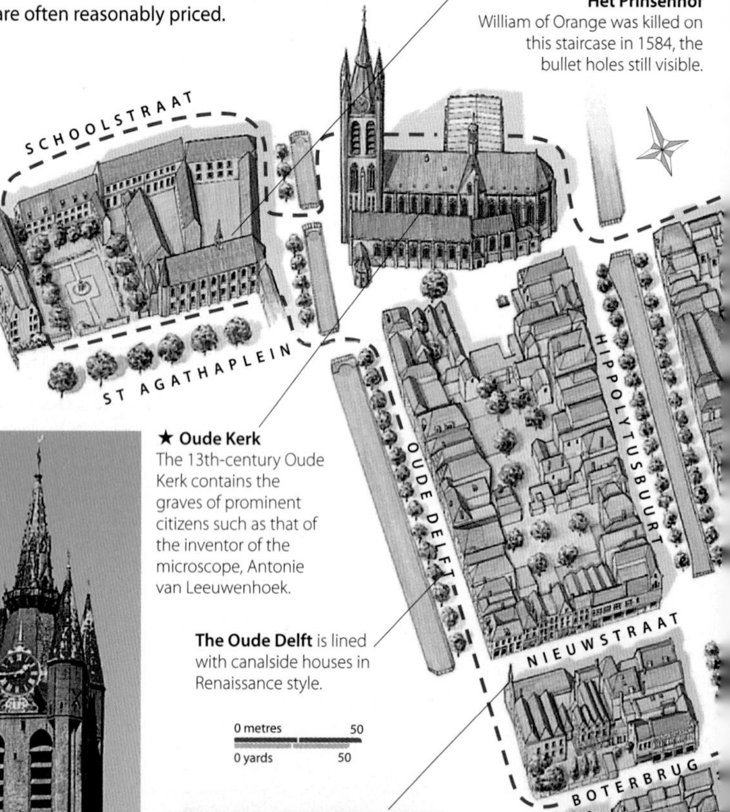

SCHOOLSTRAAT
ST AGATHAPLEIN
HIPPOLYTUSBUURT
OUDE DELFT
NIEUWSTRAAT
BOTERBRUG
OUDE DELFT
PEPERSTR

★ Oude Kerk
The 13th-century Oude Kerk contains the graves of prominent citizens such as that of the inventor of the microscope, Antonie van Leeuwenhoek.

The Oude Delft is lined with canalside houses in Renaissance style.

0 metres 50
0 yards 50

Sint-Hippolytuskapel
This austere red-brick chapel (1396) was used as an arsenal during the Reformation *(see pp56–7)*.

Key

— Recommended route

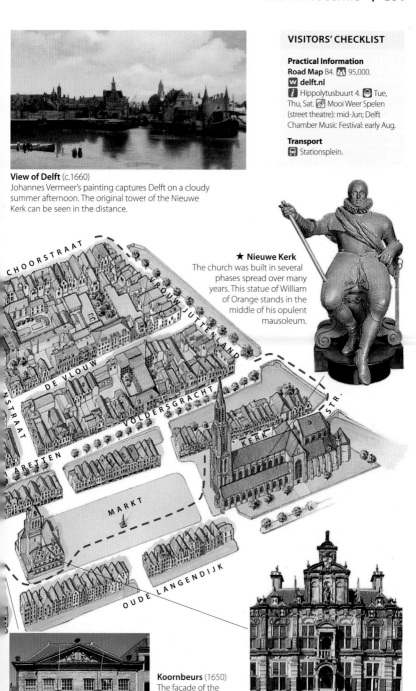

View of Delft (c.1660)
Johannes Vermeer's painting captures Delft on a cloudy summer afternoon. The original tower of the Nieuwe Kerk can be seen in the distance.

VISITORS' CHECKLIST

Practical Information
Road Map B4. 95,000.
delft.nl
Hippolytusbuurt 4. Tue, Thu, Sat. Mooi Weer Spelen (street theatre): mid-Jun; Delft Chamber Music Festival: early Aug.

Transport
Stationsplein.

★ Nieuwe Kerk
The church was built in several phases spread over many years. This statue of William of Orange stands in the middle of his opulent mausoleum.

Koornbeurs (1650)
The façade of the old meat hall is decorated with animal heads. After 1871, the building was used as a corn exchange.

Stadhuis (1618)
The Renaissance-style town hall was designed by Hendrick de Keyser. The building is erected around a 13th-century Gothic tower.

Exploring Delft

Attractive Delft is world-famous for its blue-and-white pottery and is renowned in Holland as being the resting place of William of Orange (1533–84), the "father of the Netherlands". William led the resistance against Spanish rule in the 80 Years War *(see p53)* from his Delft headquarters; his victory meant religious freedom and independence for the Dutch. Delft was the Republic's main arsenal in the 17th century; an explosion of gunpowder destroyed a large part of the town in 1654. Artist Johannes Vermeer (1632–75) was born and lived in Delft.

Oude Kerk

Heilige Geestkerkhof 25. **Tel** 015-2123015. **Open** Apr–Oct: 9am–6pm Mon–Sat; Nov–Jan: 11am–4pm Mon–Fri, 10am–5pm Sat; Feb & Mar: 10am–5pm Mon–Fri.
oudekerk-delft.nl

The original 13th-century church on this site has been extended many times. The beautifully carved clock tower, with its eye-catching steeple, dates from the 14th century. The Gothic north transept was added in the early 16th century by architect Anthonis Keldermans. Inside, the most striking feature is the wooden pulpit with canopy. The floor is studded with 17th-century gravestones, many beautifully decorated, including those for Johannes Vermeer and admiral Piet Hein (1577–1629).

The Nieuwe Kerk overlooking Delft market

The impressive Renaissance-style pulpit (1548) in the Oude Kerk

Nieuwe Kerk

Markt 80. **Tel** 015-2123025. **Open** Apr–Oct: 9am–6pm Mon–Sat; Nov–Jan: 11am–4pm Mon–Fri, 10am–5pm Sat; Feb & Mar: 10am–5pm Mon–Fri.
nieuwekerk-delft.nl

The Nieuwe Kerk was built between 1383 and 1510 but needed large-scale restoration after the fire of 1536 and the massive explosion of 1654 in the arsenal. In 1872, PJH Cuypers *(see p375)* added the 100-m (328-ft) tower to the Gothic façade. Inside, the most noticeable feature is William of Orange's imposing mausoleum, designed in 1614 by Hendrick de Keyser. In the middle stands a statue of William, impressive in his battledress. Not far from him is the lonely figure of his dog, which died a few days after his master. The tombs of the royal family lie in the crypt.

Stedelijk Museum Het Prinsenhof

St-Agathaplein 1. **Tel** 015-2602358. **Open** 11am–5pm Tue–Sun & hols. **Closed** 1 Jan, 30 Apr, 25 Dec.
prinsenhof-delft.nl

This peaceful former convent was the scene of William of Orange's assassination. It now houses Delft's history museum, with pottery, tapestries and portraits of royalty. In 1572, during the uprising against the Spanish, William commandeered the convent as his headquarters. In 1584, a fanatical Catholic, Balthasar Geraerts, shot and killed him on the instructions of Philip II of Spain.

Delftware

Delftware *(see pp32–3)* stems from majolica, introduced to the Netherlands in the 16th century by Italian immigrants who had settled around Delft and Haarlem and begun producing wall tiles with Dutch designs, such as birds and flowers. By the next century, however, Dutch traders had started to deal in delicate Chinese porcelain; this eventually led to the collapse of the market for the less refined Dutch earthenware. Towards 1650, though, the Chinese example was adopted in the Netherlands and craftsmen designed plates, vases and bowls with pictures of Dutch landscapes, biblical tableaux and scenes from everyday life. De Porceleyne Fles factory, which dates from 1652, is one of the several Delftware potteries open to the public for tours.

17th-century hand-painted Delft tiles

Vermeer Centrum Delft

Voldersgracht 21. **Tel** 015-2138588. **Open** 10am–5pm daily. **Closed** 1 Jan, 25 Dec. Fri & Sun (Dutch) **vermeerdelft.nl**

The Vermeer Centrum celebrates the work of one of Delft's most enigmatic artists, Johannes Vermeer (1632–75). The space, dedicated entirely to the life of the artist, has a series of beautifully designed displays including a life-size copy of his famous masterpiece, *The Girl with a Pearl Earring (1665–67)*. On the upper floor, visitors can learn about his painting techniques, particularly his use of perspective, colour and light.

8 Maassluis

Road Map: B4. 31,600. Heldringstraat (010-5911440). Tue, Fri. **vvvmaassluis.nl**

The settlement of Maassluis grew up around the locks, which date from 1367; the herring trade brought prosperity to the town. The historic town centre is adorned with 17th-century buildings, such as the **Grote Kerk**, with its famous organ, and the **Stadhuis**, from 1650. The town's fine steam tug still goes out to sea. Many of Maarten 't Hart's novels are set in the Maassluis of his youth.

Genever and corn brandy, products of the Genever capital of Schiedam

9 Schiedam

Road Map: B4. 75,000. Buitenhavenweg 9 (010-4733000). Tue am, Fri. **ontdekschiedam.nu**

Schiedam was granted its city charter in 1275 and soon afterwards expanded into a centre for trade and fishing. It became the centre of the genever (Dutch gin) industry. The production of genever is still important to the town, as evidenced by the **five tallest windmills in the world** and the old warehouses and distilleries. In the bar of the **Jenever Museum** (national genever museum), you can familiarize yourself with the enormous range of Dutch genevers and liqueurs.

The **Stedelijk Museum** (municipal museum), with exhibits of contemporary art and on modern history, is in the former St-Jacobs Gasthuis. Its main attraction is the collection of artwork by the group known as COBRA (consisting of painters from COpenhagen, BRussels and Amsterdam).

Jenever Museum

Lange Haven 74. **Tel** 010-2469676. **Open** noon–5pm Tue–Fri, 11am–6pm Sat, Sun & public hols. **Closed** 1 Jan, Easter Mon, 27 Apr, Pentecost, 25 Dec. **jenevermuseum.nl**

Stedelijk Museum

Hoogstraat 112. **Tel** 010-2463666. **Open** 10am–5pm Tue–Sun. **Closed** 1 Jan, 25 Dec. **stedelijkmuseumschiedam.nl**

⑩ Street-by-Street: Rotterdam

This route takes you through the area to the south of the town centre, which was devastated by heavy bombing in May 1940. On your way you will see the Witte Huis (white house), one of the few buildings spared by the bombs. Further on you will pass by some unusual modern architecture, such as the cube-shaped apartments, "Het Potlood" ("the pencil"), and the maritime museum, devoted to the history of shipping. In front of this museum is a monument by Ossip Zadkine, which is one of the symbols of Rotterdam. The undeveloped area around Station Blaak was completely built up before the bombing.

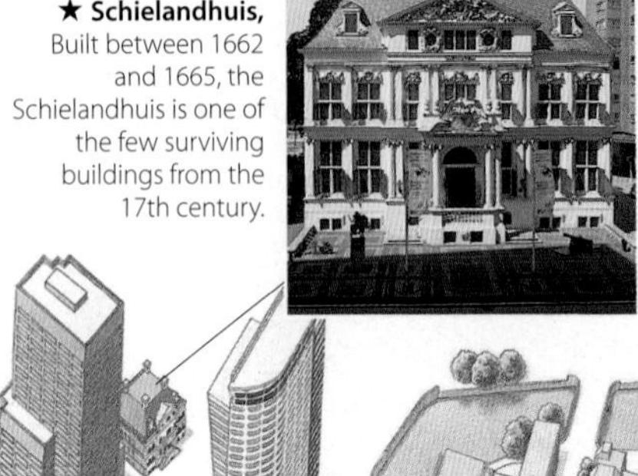

★ Schielandhuis,
Built between 1662 and 1665, the Schielandhuis is one of the few surviving buildings from the 17th century.

★ De Verwoeste Stad
The statue *De Verwoeste Stad* (The Devastated City) by Ossip Zadkine, located in front of the maritime museum, commemorates the bombing of May 1940. It is considered one of the most famous statues in the country.

De Buffel
The old armoured vessel *De Buffel*, now open for visitors, was for many years a training ship.

Key

— Recommended route

Erasmusbrug (Erasmus Bridge) The glittering Erasmusbrug is now one of the symbols of Rotterdam.

VISITORS' CHECKLIST

Practical Information
Road Map B4. 598,500.
rotterdam.info
Coolsingel 195–7 (010-7900 185). Tue–Sun. Film festival: Jan; ROBIN Rotterdam Unlimited *(carnival)*: Apr; Metropolis *(pop concerts)*: Jul; Zomercarnaval: Jul; Wereldhavendagen: Sep.

Transport
Stationsplein.
Stationsplein.

0 metres 150
0 yards 150

Station Blaak is an unusual metro and railway station,designed by architect HCH Reijnders.

Het Potlood (the pencil), an unusually shaped apartment block near Station Blaak, was designed by P Blom.

★ Kubus-Paalwoningen
A bizarre creation (1978–84) by architect P Blom, the cube-shaped apartments are among the most striking buildings of modern Rotterdam.

VERLENGDE WILLEMSBRUG

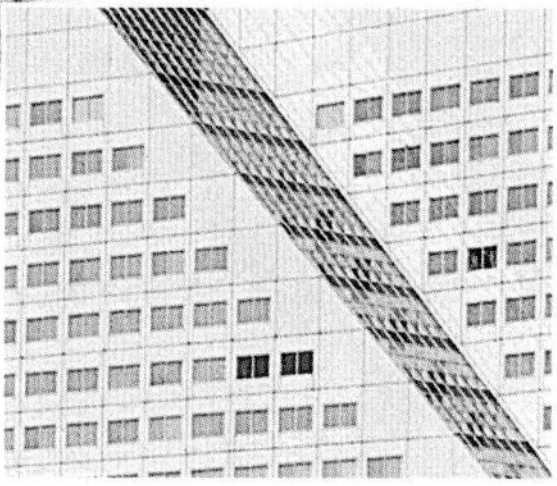

Willemswerf
Willemswerf is one of Rotterdam's highest and most impressive office blocks. The building, which is completely white, was completed in 1989 and is a design by architect WG Quist.

Witte Huis (White House)
This is one of the few buildings to survive the World War II bombing raids. For a long time, the 45-m (148-ft) building was one of the tallest office blocks in Europe.

Exploring Rotterdam

Rotterdam is not only a symbol of post-war economic recovery – it has more to offer than endless stretches of thriving docklands and industrial areas. Rotterdam has increasingly become one of the most important cultural centres of the Netherlands. Although the city was a wasteland immediately after World War II, it quickly recovered and now boasts one of the country's largest universities, a park containing a number of interesting museums and a large zoo.

Canalside houses in a peaceful corner of Delfshaven

Gorilla and her young at Blijdorp

Blijdorp

Blijdorplaan 8. 33, 40, 44. **Tel** 010-4431495. **Open** Nov–Mar: 9am–5pm daily; Apr–Oct: 9am–6pm daily.
W rotterdamzoo.nl

Rotterdam Zoo, often called *Diergaarde Blijdorp,* is in many ways a unique zoo. Its predecessor, De Rotterdamsche Diergaarde (Rotterdam zoo), was built in 1857 in the town centre. In 1937, the zoo was moved to Blijdorp polder, outside the centre. The architect Van Ravesteyn designed the new zoo and Blijdorp became one of the first zoos to be designed by one architect.

Blijdorp is also one of the few European zoos to have its own research department. It plays an important part in breeding programmes for rare and endangered species, such as the black-footed penguin.

For the last few years, attempts have been made to convert Blijdorp to the type of zoo which tries to present the animals in the most natural habitat possible. Another addition at the zoo is the gorilla island. The huge, extremely popular, Oceanium is a theme park showcasing sea creatures, including sharks.

Delfshaven

Informatiecentrum Historisch Delfshaven, Voorhaven 3. M

Delfshaven, which is outside the town centre and is mainly famous for being the birthplace of naval hero Piet Hein, looks very different from the rest of Rotterdam. This oasis of both history and culture within the modern city consists of a few streets with historic buildings and a harbour with old sailing boats. The former warehouses are now shops selling antiques, paintings and antiquarian books. There are also museums and restaurants.

It was from Delfshaven that the Dutch Pilgrim Fathers left for America in 1620.

Euromast

Parkhaven 20. M Dijkzicht. **Tel** 010-4364811. **Open** Apr–Sep: 9:30am–11pm daily; Oct–Mar: 10am–11pm daily.
W euromast.nl

One of the most famous symbols of Rotterdam, Euromast is the tallest building in the town. Before its construction began, in 1960, the mayor at the time, Van Walsum, complained that there was only enough money to build a 50 m (165 ft) tower. This caused an uproar, because the mast was meant to be higher than the Utrecht Domtoren (cathedral tower), which was, at 112 m (367 ft), the highest building in the country. That same evening, the mayor was called by rich Rotterdam port barons wanting to contribute money to the construction of the building. These donations in part enabled the tower to reach 110 m (361 ft). A space tower was later added to the top of the building for the Communicatie-'70 show in 1970, bringing the tower to a total height of 185 m (607 ft).

The Rotterdam Beurstraverse, or "Koopgoot", a bustling shopping mall

For hotels and restaurants in this region see p398 and pp410–411

Peter Struycken's masterpiece of light effects under the NAI

Kunsthal

Westzeedijk 341, Museumpark. 8, 20. **Tel** 010-4400301. **Open** Tue–Sun. **Closed** Mon, 27 Jan, 30 Apr, 25 Dec. P W **kunsthal.nl**

The Kunsthal, with its very austere style, is used for temporary exhibitions. It offers museums the opportunity to show those parts of their collections which would normally be in storage due to lack of exhibition space. This gives refreshing insight into the possessions of Dutch museums and gives the Kunsthal a unique and respected position in the art-life of the country.

Designed by the avant-garde architects OMA, the building has ramps instead of stairs.

Kinderkunsthal Villa Zebra

Stieltjesstraat 21. **Tel** 010-2411717. 20, 23, 25. 48. M D. **Open** noon–5pm Wed, Fri–Sun; Tue–Sun summer hols. **Closed** 1 Jan, 27 Apr, 25 Dec. P W **villazebra.nl**

This is an arts centre specifically for children, where they can become familiar with art and express themselves via poetry, theatre and visual arts.

NAI

Museumpark 25. **Tel** 010-4401200. 4, 5. 32. M Eendrachtsplein. **Open** 10am–5pm Tue–Sat, 11am–5pm Sun & public hols. **Closed** 1 Jan, 27 Apr, 25 Dec. W **nai.nl**

After being bombed in 1940 and then ravaged by fire, the old city centre was a wasteland. Because of large-scale rebuilding after the war, Rotterdam now has more modern architecture than any other town in the Netherlands. This includes famous structures such as the *paalwoningen* (cube-shaped apartments). It is appropriate that Nederlands Architectuur Instituut (the Netherlands Architectural Institute), housing the country's architectural archives, should be in Rotterdam, in a building that is itself an architectural phenomenon. Temporary exhibits are held here.

Rotterdam City Centre

1. Kunsthal
2. Euromast
3. Nederlands Architectuur Instituut
4. Museum Boijmans Van Beuningen *(see pp238–9)*

0 metres 250
0 yards 250

Key

Street-by-street map *(pp234–5)*

For map symbols *see back flap*

Museum Boijmans Van Beuningen

The museum is named after two art experts, FJO Boijmans and DG van Beuningen, who presented their own private collections to the town. The museum thus ended up with one of the finest collections in the Netherlands. Although it is particularly renowned for its unique collection of old masters, the museum also represents all aspects of art and design, from medieval works by Jan van Eyck to imaginative exhibitions of contemporary artists' work. The museum's layout is currently being re-worked.

Three Marys at the Open Sepulchre
(1430) Brothers Jan and Hubert Van Eyck collaborated on this colourful work depicting the tomb of the resurrected Christ.

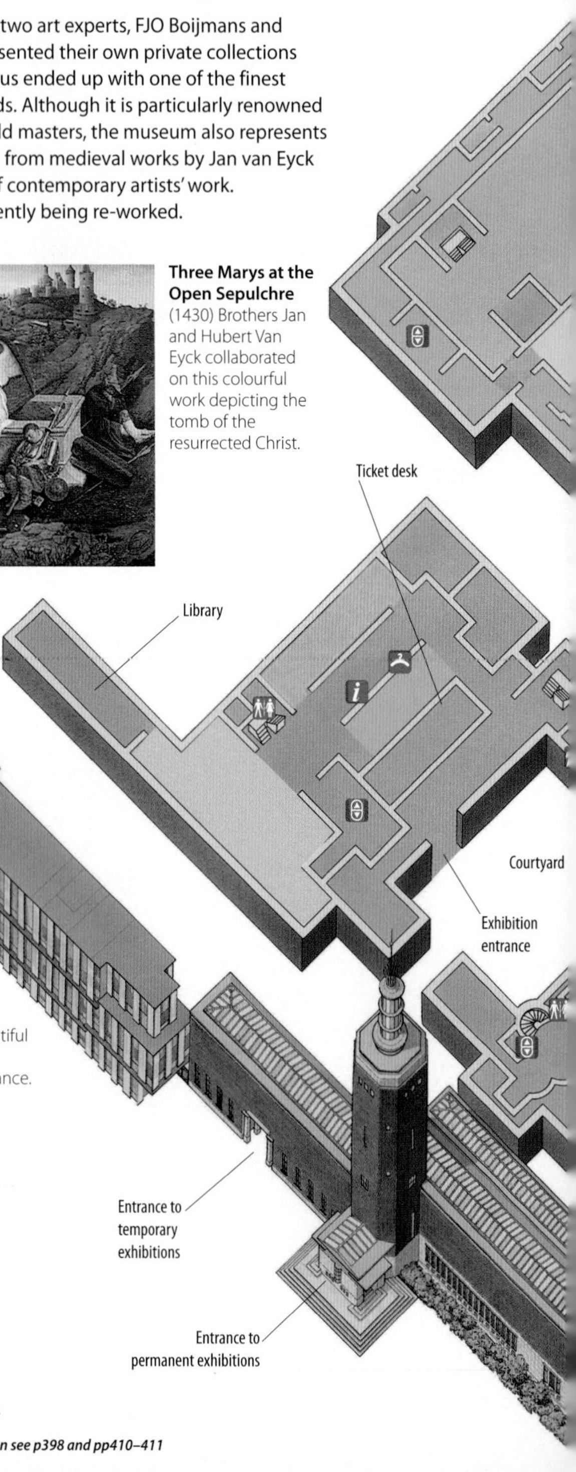

Ticket desk

Library

Ground floor

Courtyard

Exhibition entrance

Nautilus Cup
(1590) The god Neptune sits on top of this beautiful piece from the Dutch Renaissance.

Entrance to temporary exhibitions

Entrance to permanent exhibitions

Key to Floorplan

- Old Masters
- Surrealists
- Modern art
- Print collection
- Applied art and design
- Temporary exhibitions
- Non-exhibition space
- Art 1750-1945 and Surrealists
- Contemporary art installations

For hotels and restaurants in this region see p398 and pp410–411

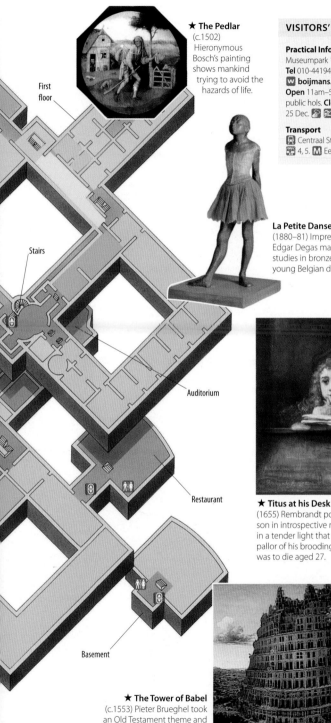

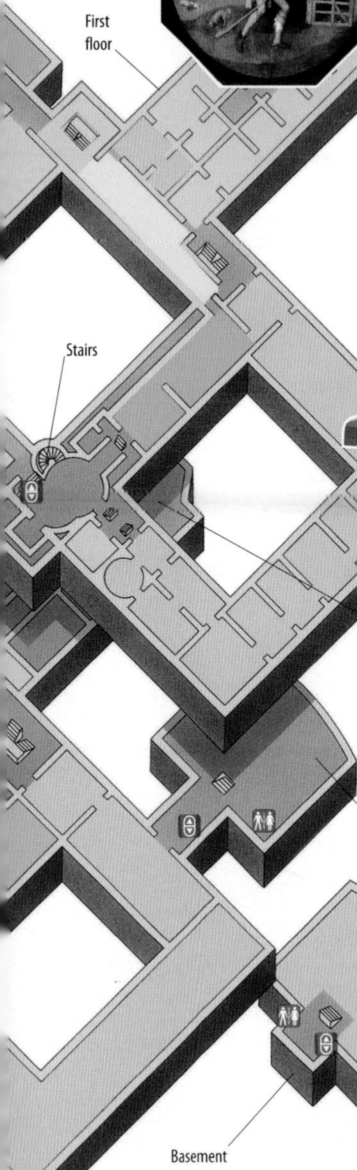

★ The Pedlar
(c.1502) Hieronymous Bosch's painting shows mankind trying to avoid the hazards of life.

First floor

Stairs

Auditorium

Restaurant

Basement

VISITORS' CHECKLIST

Practical Information
Museumpark 18–20, Rotterdam.
Tel 010-4419400.
boijmans.nl
Open 11am–5pm Tue–Sun & public hols. **Closed** 1 Jan, 27 Apr, 25 Dec.

Transport
Centraal Station. 32.
4, 5. Eendrachtsplein.

La Petite Danseuse
(1880–81) Impressionist Edgar Degas made several studies in bronze of this young Belgian dancer.

★ Titus at his Desk
(1655) Rembrandt portrayed his sickly son in introspective mood, bathed in a tender light that heightens the pallor of his brooding features. Titus was to die aged 27.

★ The Tower of Babel
(c.1553) Pieter Brueghel took an Old Testament theme and painted a 10-storey structure swarming with people.

Rotterdam, City of Water

One of Rotterdam's biggest and busiest attractions is its port, one of the largest ports in the world. Various operators organize daily tours around the port area, where you will see container ports, shipyards and dry docks. The sheer scale of the port and related industrial areas, which have a turnover of billions of euros, is quite staggering. Europe's largest container port, the Europoort alone stretches for 40 km (25 miles) along the river banks.

Rotterdam
The port sees approximately 30,000 vessels docking each year. Germany's Ruhr district is the main destination for the transported goods.

The Port of Rotterdam

The port of Rotterdam, of which only a fraction is shown by this map, stretches from the town centre to the North Sea coast and is divided into nine areas. These are, from east to west, the Stadhavens, the Vierhavens, Merwehaven, Waalhaven, Eemhaven, Vondelingenplat, Botlek, Europoort and the Maasvlakte. The port is still expanding and will soon run out of available space. Land reclamation from the North Sea is considered the most appropriate solution.

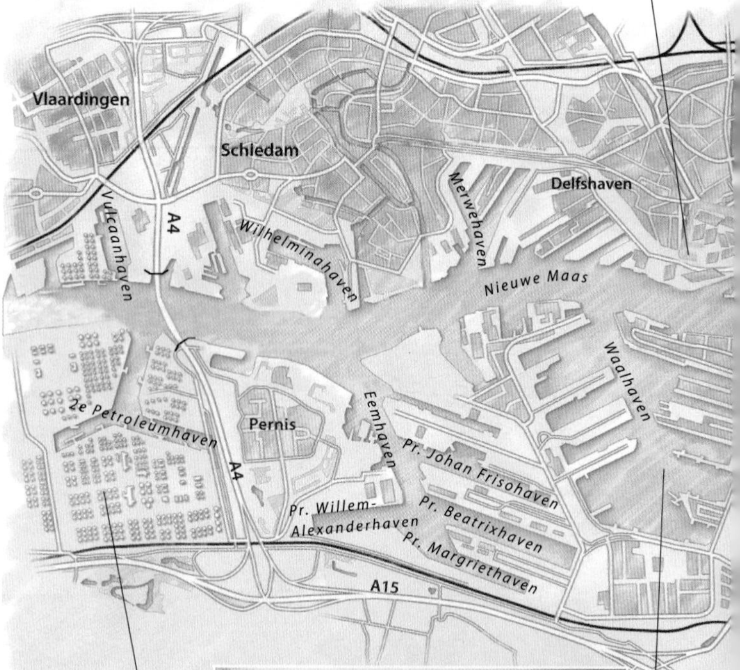

Old Delfshaven

Vlaardingen
Schiedam
Delfshaven
Vulcaanhaven
A4
Wilhelminahaven
Merwehaven
Nieuwe Maas
Waalhaven
2e Petroleumhaven
Pernis
Eemhaven
Pr. Johan Frisohaven
Pr. Willem-Alexanderhaven
Pr. Beatrixhaven
Pr. Margriethaven
A15

Pernis
The biggest refinery in the world, Pernis operates day and night refining crude oil, which is used to make hundreds of products. Lit up at night, it looks like something out of science fiction.

Dry docks

Spido Tour
Various tours around the port of Rotterdam are available. Those lasting an hour and a half visit the town centre ports *(see map below)*, whereas the day-long tours travel as far as the Maasvlakte.

World Port Days
There are many types of ships to be admired on the World Port Days, which are held in early September and attract thousands of visitors.

Hotel New York
This hotel has been set up in the early 20th-century head office of the former Holland-America Line. The nearby arrival halls are also of architectural significance.

0 Kilometres 3

0 miles 3

Key

Road

Railway

Europoort

A total of 33,252 ocean-going vessels and 110,000 inland vessels put in at Rotterdam Port during 2008. This makes it the busiest port in Europe. The name "Europoort" says it all – Rotterdam is Europe's port. Rotterdam Port is one of the major employers of the Netherlands, with more than 300,000 people working for it either directly or indirectly. Total added value of the port is more than €28 billion, approximately 10 per cent of the country's gross domestic product.

Bustling Rotterdam port, loading and unloading many millions of containers every year

St Janskerk, Gouda

This former Catholic church dating from 1485 was rebuilt in the Gothic style after it was struck by fire in 1552. The church received a number of unusual stained-glass windows from rich Catholic benefactors, such as Philip II of Spain, between 1555 and 1571. After the Reformation *(see pp56–7)*, the church became Protestant, but even the fanatical Iconoclasts did not have the heart to destroy the windows. Prominent Protestants, including Rotterdam aldermen, donated stained-glass windows to the church up to 1604. The stained-glass windows are heavily symbolic of the politics of the time – Bible stories had to be covered after the conflict between the Catholics and Protestants, which led to the 30 Years War between Spain and the Netherlands.

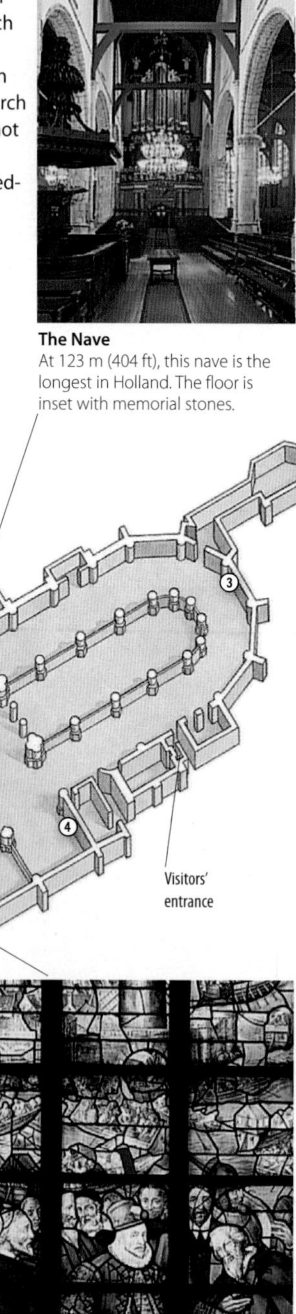

The Nave
At 123 m (404 ft), this nave is the longest in Holland. The floor is inset with memorial stones.

Judith Beheading Holofernes
This is a detail from a window which depicts Judith beheading Holofernes. Dirck Crabeth, who made the window, shows John the Baptist holding a lamb. Next to him kneels Jan de Ligne, the count of Arenberg, who commissioned the window.

Visitors' entrance

The Relief of Leiden (1603)
William of Orange as leader of the resistance of the people of Leiden against the Spanish siege of 1574.

KEY

① **The Adulteress** (1601) Dressed as a Franciscan monk, Jesus appeals to the people in the temple to forgive the adulteress, who is being guarded by Spanish soldiers.

② **North aisle**

③ **Baptism of Jesus**

④ **The Purification of the Temple**

⑤ **South aisle**

VISITORS' CHECKLIST

Practical Information
Achter de Kerk.
Tel 0182-514119.
Open Mar–Oct: 9am–5pm Mon–Sat; Nov–Feb: 10am–4pm Mon–Sat, 11am–5pm public hols.
Closed 1 Jan, 25 & 26 Dec.

The Purification of the Temple William of Orange donated this window, symbolizing the Netherlands' longing to drive out the Spaniards, in 1567. Traders watch angrily as Jesus drives moneylenders from the temple.

Baptism of Jesus (1555) John the Baptist baptizes Jesus in the Jordan River. The window was a gift from the Bishop of Utrecht.

Nieuwpoort town hall, built over the canal in 1696

⓫ Gouda

Road Map B4. 72,000. Market 35 (0182-589110). Thu am & Sat; phone tourist office for information on cheese markets. **welcometogouda.com**

In 1272, Floris V granted Gouda its city charter. Thanks to its strategic position on the Hollandse IJssel and the Gouwe, the town developed into a flourishing centre for beer brewing and the textile industry in the 15th century. However, Gouda became economically and politically isolated during the 30 Years War. The town recovered in the 17th and beginning of the 18th century due to its trade in cheese, candles and pipes.

Gouda is still famous today for its **cheese** and **cheese markets**. The markets are held on an enormous three-sided square around the **Stadhuis**, which dates from 1450 and is one of the oldest in the Netherlands. With its many pinnacles and turrets, the building gives the impression of being in the Flemish Gothic style.

The **Museum Gouda** (municipal museum) is in the former **Catharina Gasthuis** (St Catherine's hospital), which dates from the 14th century and later. The museum features paintings from the Hague School and unusual 16th-century altar pieces.

Stadhuis
Markt 1. **Tel** 0182-589110. **Open** timings vary, call to check. **Closed** public hols. by appt.

Museum Gouda
Achter de Kerk 14. **Tel** 0182-331000. **Open** 10am–5pm Tue–Fri, noon–5pm Sat & Sun. **Closed** 1 Jan, 27 Apr 25 Dec. over 18s. **museumgouda.nl**

⓬ Reeuwijkse Plassen

Road Map B4 VVV by Gouda.

The Reeuwijk lake district was formed through peat excavation. Narrow roads pass through the rectangular lakes, which owe their shape to former parcels of land. The small village of **Sluipwijk** seems almost to fade away into the water. The best way to explore this area is by bicycle or on foot. In the summer months you can also take a boat trip through this typically Dutch lakeland scenery.

⓭ Nieuwpoort

Road Map C4. 1,600. 90 from Utrecht.

The whole of this magnificent fortified town, which obtained its city charter in 1283, has been declared a listed area. The 17th-century street layout is practically intact. The city walls, which are also intact, were originally built to ward off attacks from the French but served mainly to protect the town against flooding. The town hall, built over the inundation lock, dates from 1696, while the arsenal dates from 1781. Restoration work was carried out in 1998.

⓮ Gorinchem

Road Map C4. 35,000. Grote Markt 17 (0183-631525). Mon am. **vvvgorinchem.nl**

Gorinchem, situated on the Linge and the Waal, was the property of the Lords van Arkel in the 13th century. They were driven out by Count William VI and the town was then absorbed into Holland. Fortifications built at the end of the 16th century are still partially intact and offer marvellous views over the water meadows and the Waal. Of the four town gateways, only the **Dalempoort** remains. The Linge harbour, in the heart of the town, is still mostly authentic, especially the narrow part.

Environs

On the other side of the Waal is the 14th-century **Slot Loevestein**. It has a very eventful history as a toll castle, a defence point along the Hollandse Waterlinie (a strip of land flooded as a defence line) and a state prison in the 17th century. A ferry for foot passengers runs between Gorinchem and the castle between May and September.

Slot Loevestein

Poederoijen. **Tel** 0183-447171. **Open** May–Sep: 11am–5pm Tue–Fri, 1–5pm Sat & Sun; Oct–Apr: 1–5pm Sat & Sun. **Closed** 1 Jan, 25, 26, 31 Dec. **slotloevestein.nl**

Glass blower in Leerdam

⓯ Leerdam

Road Map C4. 20,000. Dr Reilinghplein 3 (0345-613057). Thu am, Sat pm. **vvvleerdam.nl**

Leerdam is renowned for its glass industry. Royal Dutch Glass Factory designs by Berlage, Copier and other artists can be admired in the **Nationaal Glasmuseum** (national glass museum), and traditional crystal production can be observed at Royal Leerdam Kristal. **Fort Asperen**, on the Linge, is one of the best- preserved defence points remaining along the Nieuwe Hollandse Waterlinie.

Nationaal Glasmuseum

Lingedijk 28. **Tel** 0345-614960. **Open** 10am–5pm Tue–Sat, noon–5pm Sun. **nationaalglasmuseum.nl**

⓰ Dordrecht

Road Map B4. 118,600. Spuiboulevard 99 (0900-4636888). Tue am, Fri & Sat. **vvvdordrecht.nl**

The oldest town in Holland, Dordrecht received its city charter in 1220 and was the most important harbour and commercial town of the region until the 1500s. Even after being outstripped by Rotterdam, Dordrecht remained an important inland port. In the old port area, mansions, warehouses and almshouses are reminders of the past. The **Grote Kerk** (13th to 17th century), in the Brabant Gothic style, has an ornate interior. **Museum Simon van Gijn**, in the period rooms of an 18th-century house, has a collection of old prints, clothes and toys. The shady **Hof** (court of justice) (1512) contains the **Statenzaal** (state room), where the States of Holland met. The Hof complex will be closed until Spring 2015 for restoration.

Grote Kerk

Lange Geldersekade 2. **Tel** 078-614 4660. **Open** Apr–Oct:10:30am–4:30pm Tue–Sat, noon–4pm Sun; Nov & Dec: 2–4pm Tue, Thu & Sat. Apr–Oct: 2:15pm Thu & Sat. **grotekerk-dordrecht.nl**

Hof and Statenzaal

Hof 6. **Tel** 078-7708710. **Open** timings vary, check website. **hethofdordrecht.nl**

A group of windmills at Kinderdijk, for centuries draining water from the Alblasserwaard

For hotels and restaurants in this region see p398 and pp410–411

⑰ Kinderdijk

Road Map B4. 🚌 90, 190 from Rotterdam Lombardijen station; 19 from Dordrecht Centraal Station.

The famous **19 windmills** which were used to drain the Alblasserwaard in the past are situated where the Noord and the Lek converge. New *boezems* (drainage pools) and windmills, however, were needed time and time again in order to span the height differences as the land settled. The group of windmills is a UNESCO World Heritage Site.

⑱ Brielle

Road Map B4. 16,000. 🚌 metro Rotterdam CS to Spijkenisse, then 103. Turfkade 18 (0181-472662). Mon; Jul & Aug: Wed. **zuid-hollandse-eilanden.nl**

The magnificent port of Brielle is a protected town. The 18th-century fortifications are still mostly intact. The town, birthplace of Admiral van Tromp, held a strategic position until the 1872 opening of the *Nieuwe Waterweg* (new waterway). The **Historisch Museum Den Briel** (historic museum of Brielle) depicts this and the famous Beggars of the Sea invasion in 1572 *(see box)*. The 15th-century **St.-Catharijnekerk**, in Brabant Gothic style, rises from the surrounding monuments.

Historisch Museum Den Briel
Markt 1. **Tel** 0181-475477. **Open** 10am–5pm Tue–Sat, 1–5pm Sun. **Closed** Mon, public hols. **historischmuseumdenbriel.nl**

⑲ Hellevoetsluis

Road Map B4. 40,000. 🚌 metro Rotterdam CS to Spijkenisse, then 101. Oostzanddijk 3 (0181-312318). Sat.

At the end of the 16th century, this was the naval port for the States of Holland. Fleets led by van Tromp, de Ruyter and Piet Hein left from Hellevoetsluis for their naval battles in the 1600s. Within the old fortifications, visitors are reminded of the town's naval past by the **Prinsehuis**, the 17th-century lodgings of the Admiralty of the Maze, the dry dock and **Fort Haerlem** from the 19th century.

You can learn all about fire and fire-fighting in the local **National Brandweermuseum** (fire service museum).

Nationaal Brandweermuseum
Industriehaven 8. **Tel** 0181-314479. **Open** Apr–Oct: 10am–4pm (from noon Sun). **nationaalbrandweermuseum.nl**

Middelharnis Lane (c.1689) by Meindert Hobbema

⑳ Middelharnis

Road Map B4. 17,900. 🚌 136, 396 from Rotterdam Zuidplein. Vingerling 3 (0187-484870). Wed.

During the 16th century, Middelharnis became the regional port, outstripping Goedereede. Until the end of the 19th century, fishing remained the most important source of income.

The Late Gothic cruciform church (15th century) stands at the heart of the village. Outside the town hall (1639) hang the wooden blocks that women branded as gossips had to carry through the town.

㉑ Goedereede

Road Map A4. 1,900. 🚌 metro R'dam CS to Spijkenisse, then 111 to Hellevoetsluis, then 104 or 139 from Rotterdam Zuidplein. Bosweg 2, Ouddorp (0187-681789). Tue.

Goedereede was an important port in the 14th and 15th centuries. This town, where Pope Adrianus VI was born, began to decline when it began to silt up. The early harbour houses are reminiscent of the livelier days of old.

The Beggars of the Sea

The Beggars of the Sea were a pirate fleet which consisted of minor Dutch and Flemish nobles who had fled at the beginning of the Inquisition and sailed across the North Sea. They plundered other ships and caused trouble in English and German ports. They were forced to leave England, where some of their ships were berthed, in spring 1572. Without any clear plan, they entered Den Briel on 1 April under the command of van Lumey, which they then held "for the Prince". Other towns joined the Beggars of the Sea or were forcibly occupied by them. Their pursuits represented the first steps towards Dutch independence from Spain and the creation of Dutch sea power.

Van Lumey

ZEELAND

The tiny province of Zeeland, as its name implies, is inextricably linked with water and the sea. From earliest times, the power of the North Sea and the flooding deltas of the Maas and Schelde rivers have shaped the landscape, encouraging resilience in the inhabitants and the desire to control the elements.

From earliest times, storms and floods have taken their toll here. In the last century, the devastation of two world wars was followed by the disastrous floods and storm surges of 1953. Although there are a number of fine churches and public buildings dating as far back as the 14th century, in places near the coast there are very few houses more than 50 years old. As a result, determination to keep the waters at bay has spawned massive construction and canal building, with giant dams and land reclamation schemes offering a level of security that has changed the landscape forever.

The storms were not all bad news. Traces of Roman settlements were uncovered, and lakes and inland waterways have become a haven for wildlife and a playground for lovers of watersports. Towns such as Middelburg, Zierikzee and Veere and villages such as Nisse, St Anna-ter-Muiden and Dreischor have lots of old buildings, some of which have been restored to their 17th-century grandeur, with attractive features such as bell towers and frescoes.

The close relationship with water and the sea is well documented in a variety of small museums. The tangible benefits are perhaps twofold: an abundance of seafood for the province's restaurants, and marvellous opportunities for water-sports. Few regions in Europe offer as much scope for sailing, windsurfing, water skiing and diving as does little Zeeland.

The 15th-century Stadhuis (town hall) dominating the historic town of Veere

◀ Aerial view of the beach at low tide, Domburg

Exploring Zeeland

Touring around Zeeland, you cannot ignore the sea. The journey becomes a small adventure as you encounter bridges, dams and ferry docks. Sometimes you will travel along a straight ribbon of a road, sometimes a windy lane. The ever-present and often turbulent water is never the same colour for long: it can quickly change from a grey green reflecting the vivid blue sky to the white of wave crests beneath leaden skies. Passing over one of the many dams, you will reach the next island, with its own special character. Tholen, for example, is quiet – almost morose – whereas Walcheren is full of surprises and has a wonderful atmosphere. Travelling through Zeeland is a journey of discovery.

Getting Around

The best way to visit all the islands of Zeeland is by car. The roads here are excellent – the A58 or the N57 will quickly bring you to the centre of the province, where you can choose one of the smaller roads to take you to your destination. The through train will take you from Amsterdam to Middelburg and Vlissingen in just two and a half hours. If you want to explore other islands, you will need to continue on a regional bus – though this can be quite time-consuming. There are many cycle paths and it is great fun cycling over the dykes.

Sights at a Glance

1 *Oosterschelde Stormvloedkering pp250–51*
2 *Middelburg pp252–3*
3 Veere
4 Domburg
5 Vlissingen
6 Westkapelle
7 Zierikzee
8 Haamstede
9 Brouwershaven
10 Bruinisse
11 St Annaland
12 St Maartensdijk
13 Tholen
14 Goes
15 Yerseke
16 Nisse
17 Hulst
18 Terneuzen
19 Sluis
20 Cadzand

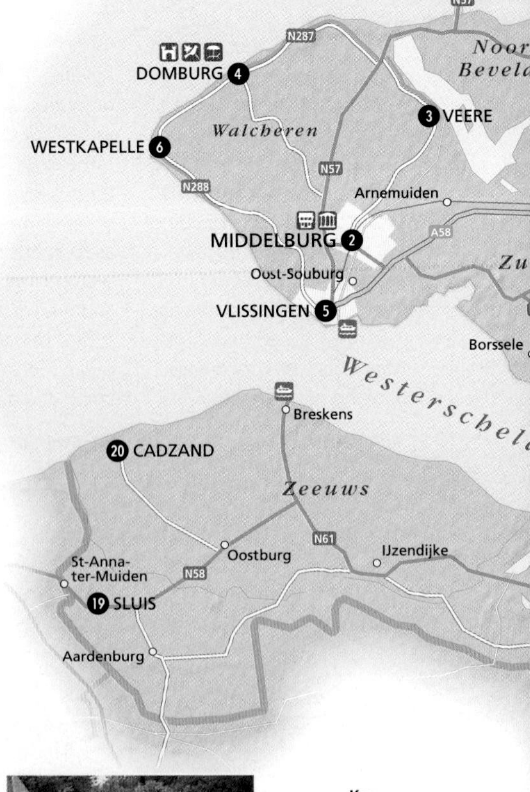

Tilting at the ring – a Zeeland sport

Key

- Motorway
- Main road
- Minor road
- Scenic route
- Minor railway
- National border
- Regional border

For map symbols *see back flap*

Divers at Zeeland's inland lakes

Fishing nets drying at Yerseke

The fertile black clay soil of Zeeland

For hotels and restaurants in this region see p398 and pp411–412

❶ Oosterschelde Stormvloedkering

Throughout the centuries, the history of the Netherlands has been dominated by its people's struggle against the sea. After the disastrous floods of 1953, which hit Zeeland heavily, the battle to remove the danger of the sea once and for all was undertaken in earnest. Now the Dutch seem to have minimized the threat of flooding by building dykes and dams and closing off tidal inlets, all of which has had a major impact on the landscape.

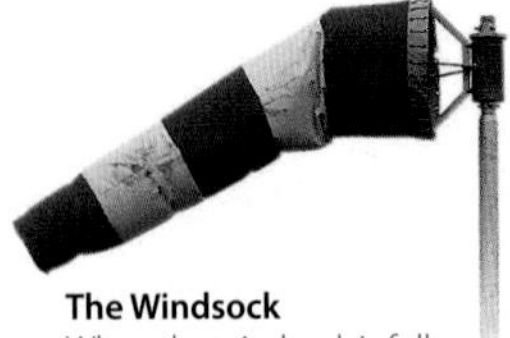

The Windsock
When the windsock is full, a warning is sounded, and people are advised to avoid driving over the dams and bridges between the islands. Vigilance saves lives.

Storms
Storms are a part of everyday life in Zeeland: storms on the beach or over the flat polders, storms which blow the cobwebs away and storms which make you fear for your life.

The Fateful Night of 1953
On the night of 31 January 1953, an event considered impossible in modern times occurred. A combination of spring tides and storms breached the dykes and washed them away as loose sand. A total of 1,835 people lost their lives.

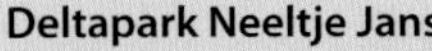

Deltapark Neeltje Jans

This attraction has been built on an artificial island, Neeltje Jans, on which the piers for the Oosterschelde Stormvloedkering (storm surge barrier) were assembled, then taken by special barges to their positions. Now that task is finished, the island is being used mainly for recreational and informative purposes. At the Deltapark you can find out about the Delta projects and about how the barrier works. You can see the barrier from the inside, and then take a boat trip to view it from the outside. There is an aquarium here, as well as a seal show; you can also experience a simulated hurricane in the "hurricane machine".

Neeltje Jans, educating about the sea

Luctor et Emergo
This Latin motto meaning "I struggle and emerge victorious" is on Zeeland's coat of arms, which depicts the Netherlands lion half in the water. This was wholly appropriate for 1953.

For hotels and restaurants in this region see p398 and pp411–412

Concrete Piers
The piers were made on the artificial island of Neeltje Jans and then transported by special barges to their destination. This mighty task attracted a great deal of attention.

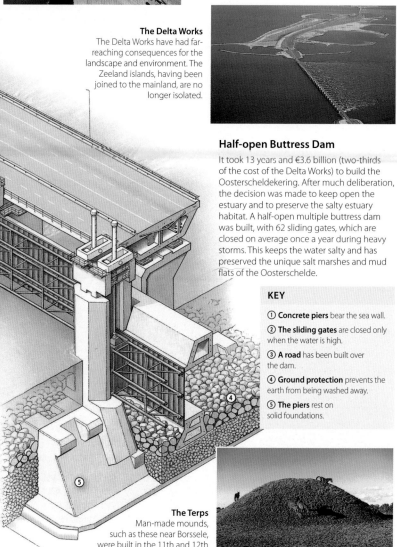

VISITORS' CHECKLIST

Practical Information
Road Map A4–5. Deltapark Neeltje Jans, Faelweg 5, Vrouwenpolder.
Open Apr–Oct: 10am–5:30pm daily; Nov–Mar: 10am–5pm Wed, Sat & Sun.

Transport
133.

The Delta Works
The Delta Works have had far-reaching consequences for the landscape and environment. The Zeeland islands, having been joined to the mainland, are no longer isolated.

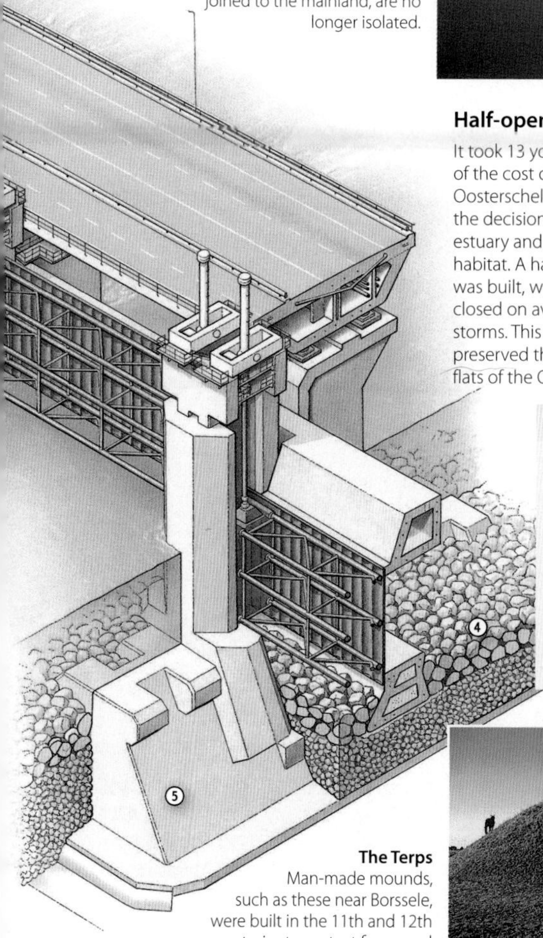

Half-open Buttress Dam

It took 13 years and €3.6 billion (two-thirds of the cost of the Delta Works) to build the Oosterscheldekering. After much deliberation, the decision was made to keep open the estuary and to preserve the salty estuary habitat. A half-open multiple buttress dam was built, with 62 sliding gates, which are closed on average once a year during heavy storms. This keeps the water salty and has preserved the unique salt marshes and mud flats of the Oosterschelde.

KEY

① **Concrete piers** bear the sea wall.

② **The sliding gates** are closed only when the water is high.

③ **A road** has been built over the dam.

④ **Ground protection** prevents the earth from being washed away.

⑤ **The piers** rest on solid foundations.

The Terps
Man-made mounds, such as these near Borssele, were built in the 11th and 12th centuries to protect farms and villages from the water.

Street-by-Street: Middelburg

Middelburg suffered heavy Nazi bombing in 1940. A lot of what is to be seen in the town today has been rebuilt, including the Stadhuis (town hall) and the abbey. The town is still redolent with the atmosphere of the Golden Age, an era during which the Dutch East India Company thrived in the port area along the quay. Middelburg is a pretty town and there is plenty to be seen on a walk around the centre. Children will be kept busy by Miniatuur-Walcheren.

★ St-Jorisdoelen
This *doelen*, the guardsmen's guild building, was built in 1582 and destroyed in 1940; the façade was rebuilt in 1969.

Zeeuws Archief, the archives of the province, are now housed in a historic monument, the van de Perre House on the Hofplen, which has been given a spectacular new wing.

Key

▬ Recommended route

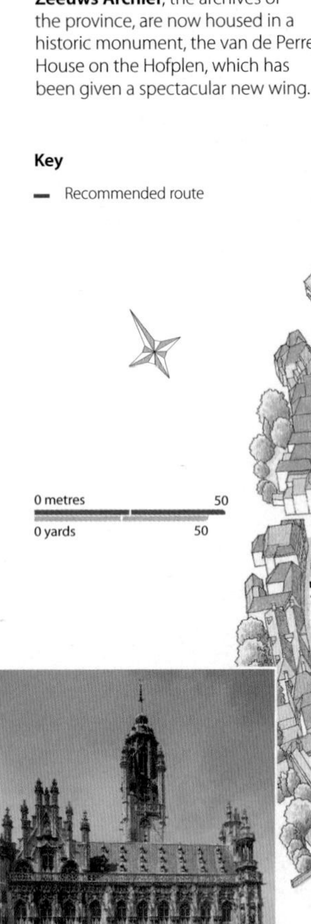

★ Stadhuis
The 15th-century town hall was completely destroyed by fire in 1940 and has been partially rebuilt. A 20th-century extension can be seen on the northern side.

The fish market already existed in 1559. The passageway, with its Tuscan pillars, dates from 1830.

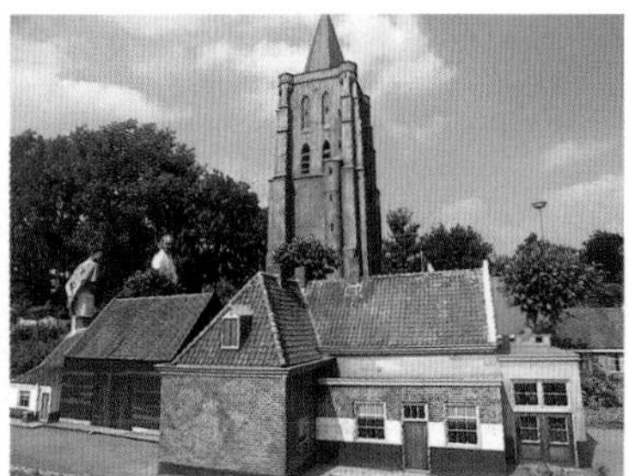

Mini Mundi
This miniature town started in 1954 now contains more than 350 buildings, and forms part of the Mini Mundi amusement park.

VISITORS' CHECKLIST

Practical Information
Road Map A5. Markt 51.
47,500.
Open check website.
Tel 0118–674300.
minimundi.nl
uitinmiddelburg.nl
Thu, Sat. Stadhuis: Markt.
Abbey: *(see p254)*.

Transport

★ Abbey
Many years of restoration work on the abbey have finally paid off.

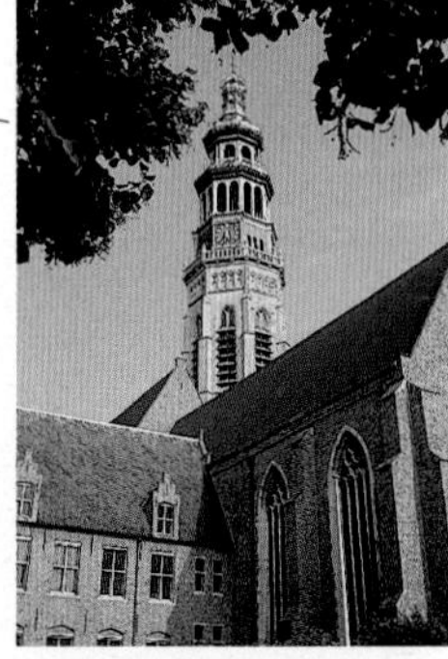

Lange Jan
The 91-m (300-ft) tower called the tall Jan belongs to the Nieuwe Kerk in the abbey complex. It has an octagonal plan and dates from the 14th century.

London Quay
The names of the quays reflect the goods that were being exported from and imported to the Netherlands during the Golden Age *(see pp54–5)*.

Zeeuws Museum

Middelburg Abbey dates back to 1100, when it was inhabited by Norbertine monks from the monastery of St Michiel of Antwerp. These very powerful monks were driven away in 1574 by William of Orange, after which the abbey was secularized. The renovated Zeeuws Museum is situated in the wing of the building that was once the monks' quarters. The completely redesigned interior presents the museum's fine collections of china, silver, paintings and its famous tapestries in a completely new light.

VISITORS' CHECKLIST

Practical Information
Zeeuws Museum.
Road Map A5. **Tel** 0118-653000.
Open 11am–5pm Tue–Sun.
Closed 1 Jan, 27 Apr, 25 Dec.
zeeuwsmuseum.nl

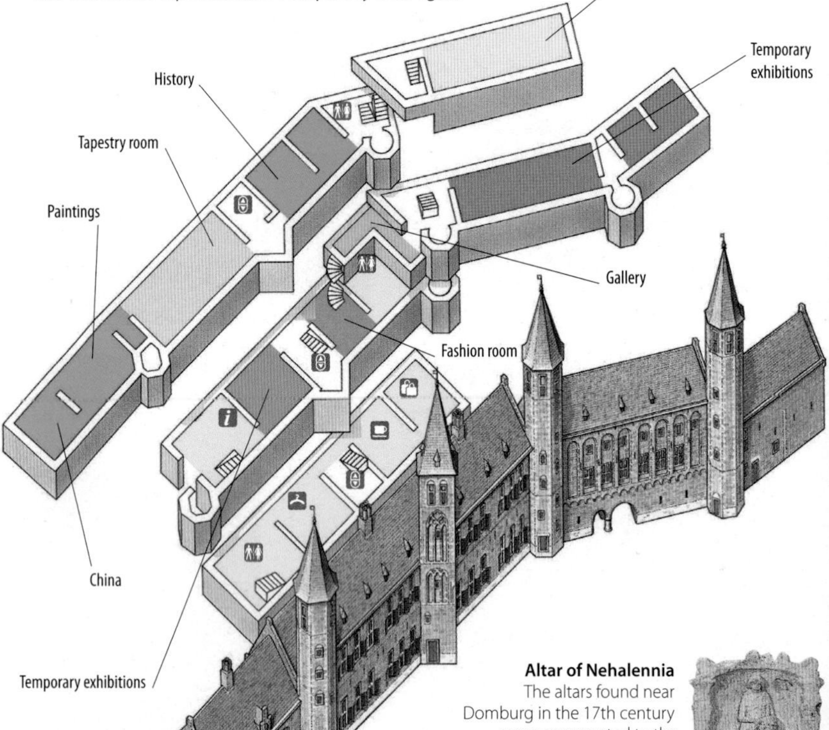

Wonders

Temporary exhibitions

History

Tapestry room

Paintings

Gallery

Fashion room

China

Temporary exhibitions

Altar of Nehalennia
The altars found near Domburg in the 17th century were consecrated to the indigenous goddess Nehalennia,who was worshipped by the Romans.

Costume Collection
The museum has a collection of jewellery, accessories and costumes, here displayed with video made for the museum by contemporary artists.

Museum Guide

The Zeeuws Museum is accommodated in one of the oldest wings of the abbey. It is a provincial museum with various different sections, including History, Fashion, Wonders and the famous Tapestry Room. There are also temporary exhibitions that cover a wide variety of subjects.

❸ Veere

Road Map A5. 1,500.
Oudestraat 28 (0118-506110).
vvvzeeland.nl

Past and present merge in Veere. Modern pleasure boats moor along the quay opposite the Gothic façades of **Het Lammetje** (the lamb) (1539) and **De Struijs** (the ostrich) (1561). These **Schotse Huizen** (Scottish houses) serve as a reminder of the time that the port was important for its trade in precious Scottish wool. Other monuments to Veere's illustrious past are the **stadhuis** (1474), the **Camp- veerse Toren,** a tower dating to around 1500, and the **OL-Vrouwekerk** (Church of Our Lady), dating from the 15th–16th centuries. This enormous church, once almost demolished, is now used as a venue for contemporary music concerts.

❹ Domburg

Road Map A5. 1,600.
Schuitvlotstraat 32 (0118-581342).

Domburg was one of the first seaside resorts in the Netherlands. In the 19th century, this little town on Walcheren was popular among prominent Europeans, who came here to relax and recuperate in the chic seaside hotels on the dunes. It has now given way to mass tourism.

Environs

An inland lake lies hidden between dunes, woods and the Oost-kapelle polder. The pretty nature reserve **De Manteling** is worth visiting, as is **Westhove** castle, which was the Abbot of Middelburg's country house until the 16th century. **Terra Maris**, Zeeland's natural scenery museum, is in the castle's former orangery.

Terra Maris
Duinvlietweg 6. **Tel** 0118-582620.
Open May–Oct: 10am–5pm daily; Nov–Apr: noon–5pm Wed–Fri, noon–4pm Sat & Sun.
terramaris.nl

Pleasure boats moored at the marina in Vlissingen

❺ Vlissingen

Road Map A5. 43,200.
Spuistraat 46 (0118-715320). Fri.

Vlissingen is a bustling town.The main thrust behind the economy of this, the largest town in Zeeland, are the ports in Vlissingen itself, as well as those of the industrial area Vlissingen-Oost and the famous **scheepswerf De Schelde** (De Schelde shipyard).

Vlissingen has always been of great military significance. The wartime activity this attracted meant that the town could not escape the consequences. One of the few remaining buildings from the time of Michiel de Ruyter to have withstood the ravages of time is the **Arsenaal**, dating from 1649. A second arsenal dating from 1823 is now the **Amusement Park Het Arsenaal** *(see p426)*, which is especially interesting for children.

Mi chiel de Ruyter

Exterior façade of the chic Badhôtel in Domburg

The reptiles and insects showcased at **Reptielenzoo Iguana**, which is housed in two adjoining 18th-century mansions, offer a completely different type of attraction.

Amusement Park Het Arsenaal
Arsenaalplein 7. **Tel** 0118-415400.
Open check website for opening times. **Closed** 1 Jan, 25 Dec, 31 Dec.
arsenaal.com

Reptielenzoo Iguana
Bellamypark 35. **Tel** 0118-417219.
Open Jun–Sep: 10am–5:30pm Tue–Sat, 1–5:30pm Sun & Mon; Oct–May:1–5:30pm daily. **Closed** 1 Jan, 25 Dec.
iguana.nl

❻ Westkapelle

Road Map A5. 2,800.
Zuidstraat 134 (0118-581342). Fri.

The most impressive sight in Westkapelle is its sea wall, the history of which is fascinating. In former times, this town lay securely behind the dunes, but these were washed away in the 15th century. This meant that the access route to the island shifted. A dyke was built, which was completed in 1458. The lighthouse also dates from this time; it was once a church tower, until the demolition of the church in 1831. In 1944, the dyke was bombed by the Allies in order to flood Walcheren so it could be liberated. In 1987 the dyke was built to the height of the delta.

The medieval Zuidhavenpoort in Zierikzee

❼ Zierikzee

Road Map A4. 9,900. Nieuw Haven 7 (0111-450524). Thu.

With 558 listed houses, Zierikzee ranks eighth in the list of Dutch historic towns. The impressive city gateways can be seen from afar. The many terraces on the Havenplein offer a marvellous view of the two harbour entrances and ornate mansion houses on Oude Haven (old harbour), and the trickle of the **Gouwe**, the creek that brought trading prosperity to Zierikzee. The Gothic **Gravensteen** (1524–6), once the home of the Count of Holland, now houses a fair-trade shop.

The Zierikzee skyline shows the still unfinished **Dikke Toren** (great tower), construction of which began in 1454. At 130 m (425 ft), it must have been the highest point of the colossal 12th-century **St-Lievenskerk**, which burnt to the ground in 1832.

Strolling through the narrow streets along the new and old harbours, you will chance upon passageways that offer glimpses of old façades, such as of the 14th-century De Haene house, or the former Stadhuis (1550–54), now the **Stadhuismuseum**.

One of the most famous historic events in Holland, the revolt of Zierikzee in 1472 against Charles the Stout, is re-enacted each summer.

Stadhuismuseum
Meelstraat 6. **Tel** 0111-454464. **Open** 11am-5pm Tue-Sat, 1-5pm Sun. **Closed** 1 Jan, 25 Dec. **www.schouwen-duiveland.nl/museum**

Environs
A museum in Ouwerkerk is devoted to the floods of 1953.

Museum Watersnood 1953
Weg van de buitenlandse pers 5. **Tel** 0111-644382. **Open** Apr–Oct: 10am–5pm daily; Nov–Mar: noon–4pm Tue–Sun. **watersnoodmuseum.nl**

❽ Haamstede

Road Map A4. 3,800. Noordstraat 45a (0111-450524). Thu.

Haamstede is a peaceful town built around a church. The nearby **Slot Haamstede**, a castle dating from the 13th century, is surrounded by a park with pleasant walks.

Slot Haamstede, painstakingly restored in the 1960s

Slot Haamstede
Haamstede, near church.
Open grounds only; castle closed to public.

Environs
Westerschouwen, 5 km (3 miles) southwest of Haamstede, has an impressive landscape and illustrious past. The dunes lie on the western edge, sometimes barren with a scattering of gorse, sometimes covered with coniferous forest.

You can climb to the top of **Plompetoren**, the tower of the now-submerged Koudekerke, which rises from the salt marshes. On the edge of the dunes is **Slot Moermond**.

Plompe Toren
Corner of Plompetorenweg & Koudekerkseweg. **Open** 10am–4:30pm daily.

Isolated Plompe Toren of the now-submerged Koudekerke

❾ Brouwershaven

Road Map A4. 1,400. Mon.

Quiet Brouwershaven combines a historic centre with a modern port. The Havenkanaal to the marina and the Stadhuis date from 1599. The 14th-century **St-Nicolaaskerk** (Church of St Nicholas) is a monument to past glory. The town prospered again as an outport to Rotterdam until the Nieuwe Waterweg (new waterway) was built in 1870.

Brouws Museum
Haven Zuidzijde 14–15. **Tel** 0111-691342. **Open** 9am–5pm Mon–Fri. **brouwsmuseum.nl**

Brouwershaven, now a focus for water recreation

⑩ Bruinisse

Road Map B4. 3,000. VVV Zierikzee (0111-450524). Wed.

Bruinisse is now mainly a centre for watersports. The modern bungalow park **Aqua Delta** is situated outside the old village next to the marina.

Environs

To get an idea of what this countryside looked like in earlier times, visit the *ringdorp* (circle-shaped village) **Dreischor**, 10 km (6 miles) west of Bruinisse. It has a typical village church and town hall. On the edge of the village is **Goemanszorg**, an agricultural museum devoted to farming past and present.

Goemanszorg

Molenweg 3, Dreischor. **Tel** 0111-402303. **Open**Easter–Oct: 11am–5pm Mon–Fri, 1–5pm Sat–Sun & public hols. **goemanszorg.nl**

⑪ St. Annaland

Road Map B5. 3,000. see St Maartensdijk.

Tholen is the least well- known island of Zeeland. Here there is a constantly changing scenery of poplars and pollard willows, fields and quiet towns, such as St Annaland, with its picturesque harbour on the Krabbenkreek. **Streekmuseum De Meestoof** (regional madder museum) is an interesting reminder of Zeeland's industrial past. The cultivation of the madder plant and processing of its root into a red dye was, until the 19th century, one of the main livelihoods of the region. It was brought to an end in 1868 by the invention of artificial dyes.

Streekmuseum De Meestoof

Bierensstraat 6–8. **Tel** 0166-652901. **Open** Apr–Oct: 2–5pm Tue–Sat. **demeestoof.nl**

⑫ St Maartensdijk

Road Map B5. 3,300. Haven 10 (0166-663771).

St Maartensdijk has been the "capital" of Tholen since 1971. This town has much to remind us of its patrons, the powerful Lords van Borssele. The remains of the tomb of Floris van Borssele (who died in 1422) and his wife are still to be seen in a burial chapel of the slender 14th- to 15th-century church. Much of the original carving and fragments of the old painting have been preserved. The foundations and moat of the van Borssele castle, which was demolished in 1820, can still be found outside the town.

The most impressive part of the town itself is the Markt, with its 16th-century houses and elegant Stadhuis.

⑬ Tholen

Road Map B5. 6,100. see St Maartensdijk.

Tholen is a Zeeland town with a Brabant flavour. Two buildings dominate the town – the marvellous Stadhuis (1452) with its robust battlements and the ornate **OL-Vrouwekerk** (Church of Our Lady), dating from the 14th to 16th centuries. The **kapel van het St-Laurensgasthuis** (St Laurensgasthuis chapel), which has been rebuilt into a residential home, stands opposite the church. Even though Tholen became a fortified town in the 16th century, it has retained its old character. Gothic façades are everywhere to remind us of its former prosperity.

Pumping station in a rural setting in the neighbourhood of Tholen

⓮ Goes

Road Map A5. 24,000. Singelstraat 13 (0113-235990). Tue, Sat.

Some of the historical towns of Zeeland are charming but sleepy, but Goes is wide-awake. Every Tuesday there is an old-fashioned market featuring fabrics and groceries which takes place on a square full of Brabant atmosphere, the Grote Markt. The Raadhuis (town hall), dating from 1463 (rebuilt between 1771 and 1775), stands at the front of the square, representing the magistrates' power with all its bulk and loftiness. The rococo interior with its grisailles and stucco ceiling is particularly attractive. The majestic St-Maria-Magdalenakerk (Church of Mary Magdalen) (15th to 16th century) rises up behind the town hall. The cruciform basilica has been restored.

Imposing heraldic ornament on Goes Raadhuis

⓯ Yerseke

Road Map A5. 6,100. Kerkplein 1 (0113-571864). Fri.

As they say in Zuid-Beveland, *"De een zijn dood de ander zijn brood"* ("One man's meat is another man's poison"). Yerseke came to be situated on the Oosterschelde following the St-Felixstormvloed (St Felix storm flood) of 1530. So began a tradition of oyster farming and mussel fishing that has continued until the present day.

The nature reserve Yerseke Moer to the west of the village shows how the island used to look: a desolate patchwork of inlets, hamlets, rough pasture lands, coves, castles, peat moors and water holes. To the east of Yerseke lies the submerged land of Zuid-Beveland, lost in 1530 along with Reimerswaal, at the time the third largest Zeeland town.

A fishing boat in Yerseke bringing home the catch

Oyster Farming

Oysters apparently have all sorts of beneficial side effects, improved virility being the most well known. Whether this is true or not, this slippery delicacy makes any meal seem festive. Oyster farming began in 1870 when suitable parts of the river bed were no longer available for free fishing and were transferred to private use. Oyster farming flourished along the Oosterschelde, particularly in Yerseke, but the oysters were vulnerable to disease and harsh winters. Concern that oyster farming would be impossible when the Grevelingen was changed from an open estuary to a lake after the completion of the Delta Works *(see pp250–51)* has so far proved unfounded – the oysters already are less prone to disease.

Oysters, a tasty delicacy

⓰ Nisse

Road Map A5. 580. see Goes.

Nisse is a typical Beveland village with square, ford and church. The church is worth a visit; though it does not look like much from the outside, inside you will be surprised by unique, 15th-century frescoes depicting the saints, scenes from the life of Mary and the coats of arms of the Lords van Borssele. Carvings on the choir vault and stalls are also from the 15th century.

Hervormde kerk
Key available from church secretary (0113-649650/649780).

Environs
The **Zak van Zuid-Beveland**, south of the railway line to Middelburg, is characteristic for its balance between nature and culture. The landscape is a succession of polders, divided by dykes covered with flowers or sheep grazing.

⓱ Hulst

Road Map B5. 10,800. Steenstraat 37 (0114-315221). Mon.

Cross over the Westerschelde and you are at the same time in Flanders and in the Netherlands. **St-Willibrordus-basiliek** (St Willibrordus basilica) towers above the town from the distance. Generations of Keldermans, a Mechelen building family, have worked on this church. One unusual feature in Hulst is the trio of hostels, once safe houses for the monks from the Flemish abbeys Ten Duinen, Baudelo and Cambron.

Nearby is the former village of Hulsterloo, famous from the medieval epic Reynard the fox.

⓲ Terneuzen

Road Map A5. 24,500. Markt 11–13 (0115-760122). Wed, Fri.

Terneuzen has an important port. The mighty sea locks in the **Kanaal van Gent naar Terneuzen** (Gent-Terneuzen canal), built between 1825 and 1827, are also impressive. The town has industrial areas to the north and nature reserves to the west (de Braakman) and the east (Otheense Kreek).

⓳ Sluis

Road Map A5. 2,100. Groote Markt 1 (0117-461700). Fri.

The Zeeland-Flanders landscape is scarred by the effects of floods and the dykes built to deal with them. Both polders and inner dykes bear witness to the constant struggle with the sea. The liberation of Zeeland-Flanders in 1944 was also hard-fought, devastating towns and villages such as Sluis. The 14th-century **Stadhuis**, with its belfry, the only one existing in the Netherlands, was restored in its former style after 1945, including the bell tower with the statue which has the nickname Jantje van Sluis.

Environs

St-Anna-ter-Muiden, 2 km (1.5 miles) to the west of Sluis is a village beloved by artists. Once prosperous, the town now has just a few houses around the square, with a village pump and the stump of a tower. To the south is the oldest town in Zeeland: **Aardenburg**. The Romans built a fort here in the 2nd century to ward off Saxon pirates. Aardenburg later became one of the most powerful towns in Flanders. This can still be seen from **St-Baafskerk**, a flawless 13th-century example of the Scheldt Gothic style famous for its painted sarcophagi. The **Gemeentelijk Archeologisch Museum Aardenburg** (Aardenburg municipal archaeological museum) deals solely with the Romans.

Gentse Poort, the gateway to the Flemish-tinged town of Hulst

Gemeentelijk Archeologisch Museum Aardenburg
Marktstraat 18. **Tel** 0117-492888. **Open** Apr–Sep Tue–Fri 10am–5pm, Sat–Sun 1–5pm. **Closed** Oct–Mar. **museumaardenburg.nl**

⓴ Cadzand

Road Map: A5. 800. Boulevard de Wielingen 44d (0117-391298). Jul & Aug: Mon pm.

Modern seaside resort Cadzand is particularly popular for its wide stretch of sand. A popular pursuit here is to search for fossilized sharks' teeth. Along the dunes are dignified seaside hotels reminiscent of those of Domburg. A little way past Cadzand is the nature reserve the Zwin, which extends as far as Knokke in Belgium. The resort Nieuwvliet lies to the east of Cadzand.

The broad sandy beaches of Cadzand, always popular in summer

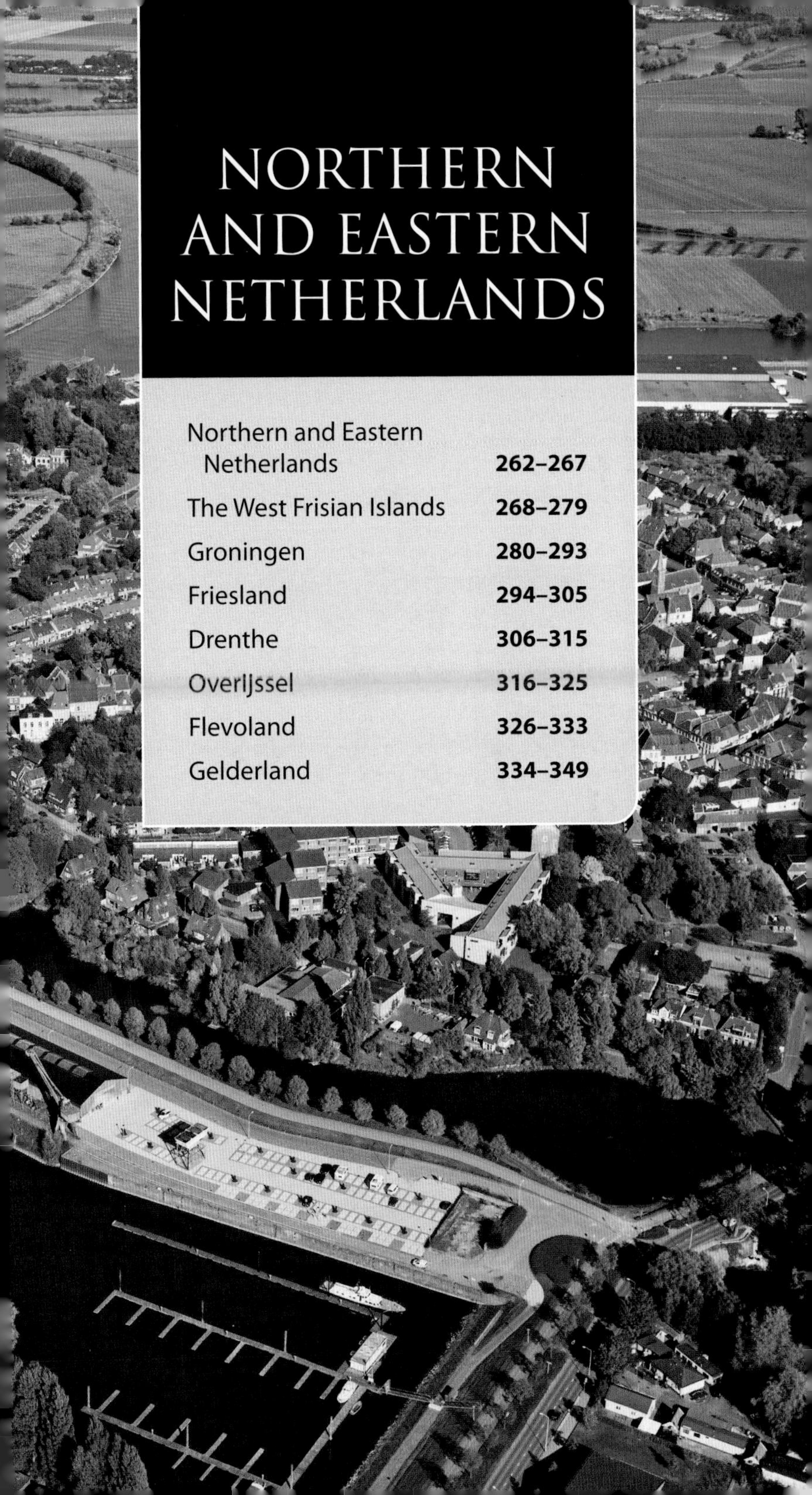

NORTHERN AND EASTERN NETHERLANDS

Northern and Eastern Netherlands at a Glance

The Northern and Eastern Netherlands are comparatively sparsely populated. They encompass the West Frisian Islands (Waddeneilanden) and the provinces of Groningen, Friesland, Drenthe, Overijssel, Flevoland and Gelderland. Agriculture has always played a predominant role here. This part of Holland has many natural and recreation areas, such as the Waddenzee mud flats, Frisian coast, coastal Lauwersmeergebied, Hondsrug, Nationaal Park De Hoge Veluwe, Sallandse Heuvelrug and the Oostvaardersplassen.

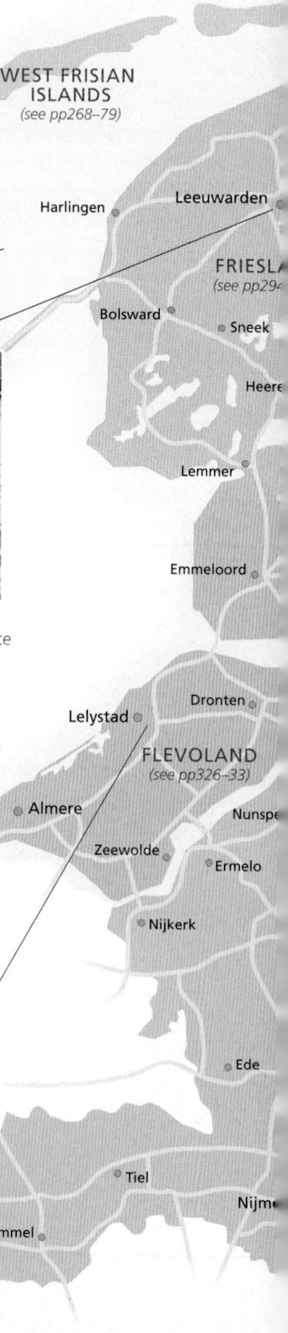

WEST FRISIAN ISLANDS
(see pp268–79)

Den Burg
Harlingen
Leeuwarden
FRIESL
(see pp29
Bolsward
Sneek
Heere
Lemmer
Emmeloord

The waddengebied (*see pp272–3*) provides a habitat for many species of birds. It is an important area for annual and migrating birds. The worms, molluscs and crustaceans are an ideal source of food for ducks, seagulls and wading birds.

De Elfstedentocht (*see pp298–9*), a long-distance ice-skating race, has been held 15 times during the last century. Over 16,000 skaters have skated the Tocht der Tochten, a 200-km (124-mile) stretch.

Lelystad
Dronten
FLEVOLAND
(see pp326–33)
Almere
Nunsp
Zeewolde
Ermelo
Nijkerk
Ede
Tiel
Nijm
Zaltbommel

0 metres 20
0 yards 20

The Batavia (*see p331*) was owned by theDutch East India Company. This three-master was 45 m (148 ft) long and had room for 350 men. A replica of the Batavia was built between 1985 and 1995 at the Batavia-Werf (Batavia wharf) in Lelystad, which is now working on a replica of Michiel de Ruyter's 17th-century flagship, De Zeven Provinciën.

◀ A view of the fortified city of Doesburg in Gelderland

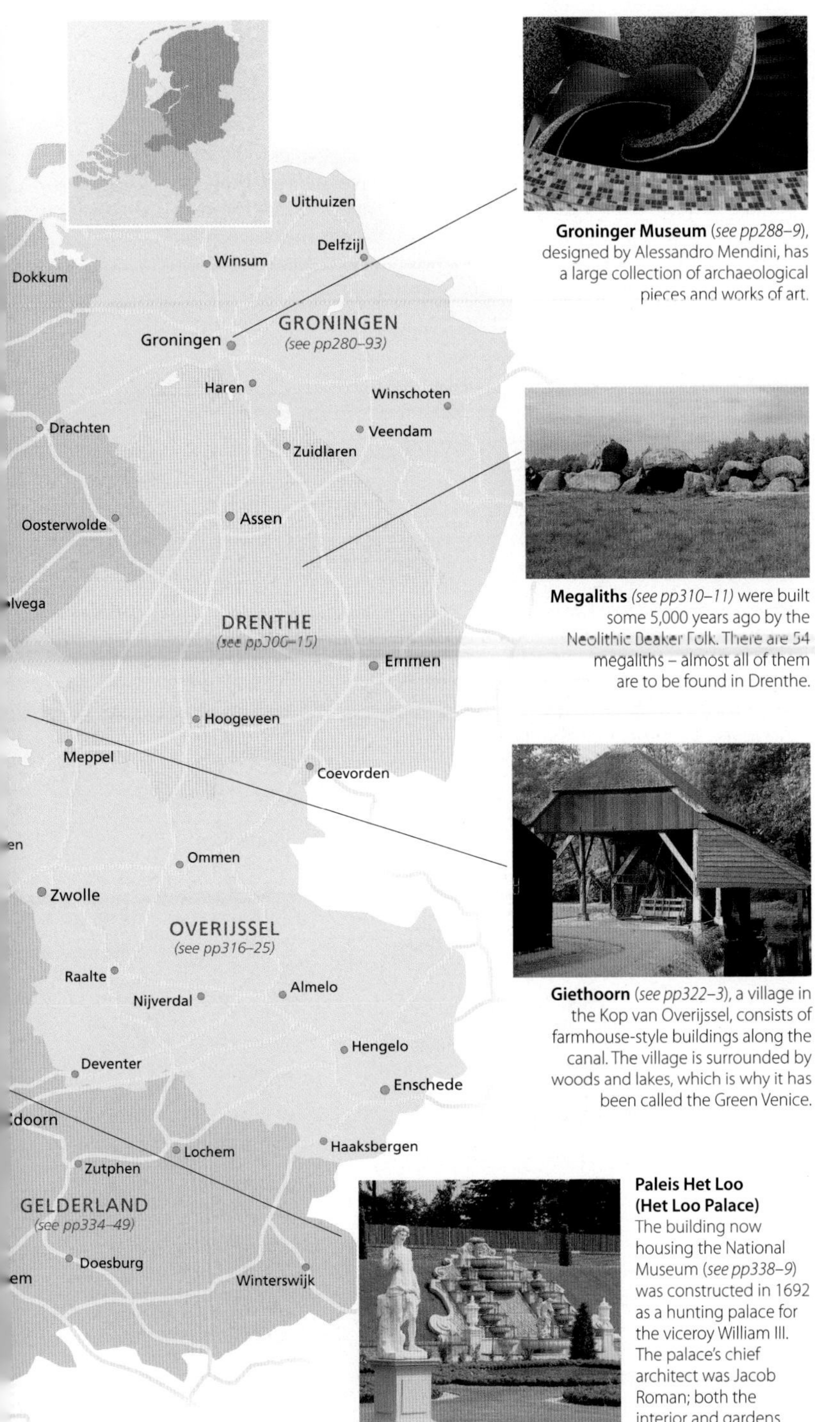

Groninger Museum (*see pp288–9*), designed by Alessandro Mendini, has a large collection of archaeological pieces and works of art.

Megaliths (*see pp310–11*) were built some 5,000 years ago by the Neolithic Beaker Folk. There are 54 megaliths – almost all of them are to be found in Drenthe.

Giethoorn (*see pp322–3*), a village in the Kop van Overijssel, consists of farmhouse-style buildings along the canal. The village is surrounded by woods and lakes, which is why it has been called the Green Venice.

Paleis Het Loo (Het Loo Palace)
The building now housing the National Museum (*see pp338–9*) was constructed in 1692 as a hunting palace for the viceroy William III. The palace's chief architect was Jacob Roman; both the interior and gardens were designed by Daniël Marot.

Environmental Policy

In the 1990s, the Dutch government drew up the Natuurbeleidsplan, a programme designed to make nature reserves accessible to the public. This is of great importance to the northern and eastern Netherlands, with their many lakes, woods and polders. The region's ecosystem has been divided into core areas, development areas and connecting zones in an attempt to give permanence to the natural environment. The connecting zones join the areas together. When the policy is fully implemented, it will aid in the survival of many plant and animal species.

Key

Core area
Natural development area
Existing or planned connecting zone
Existing or planned connecting zone to cross-border nature reserve

0 kilometres 10
0 miles 10

WEST FRISIAN ISLANDS
VLIELAND
TEXEL
NORTH HOLLAND
AMSTERDAM
Haarlem
The Hague
SOUTH HOLLAND
Rotterdam
UTRECHT
ZEELAND
Middelburg
's-Hertogenbosch
Antwerp
BELGIUM

The Waterleidingduinen (water supply dunes) are only partly open to the public.

The osprey was a rare sight in Holland for many years. Thanks to the Natuurbeleidsplan, sightings of this bird of prey have become more frequent in recent years.

Special road signs have been designed to warn motorists of migrating toads during that animal's mating season. Usually shy, toads come out en masse when mating.

Read the Signs!

Most natural areas (or parts of them) in the northern and eastern Netherlands are freely accessible. However, some parts are open only from sunrise *(zonsopkomst)* to sunset *(zonsondergang)*, and it is therefore important to read the signs. It goes without saying that you should not make excessive noise, cause damage or leave litter in the area. Further information is available at VVV offices, the ANWB and the Vereniging Natuurmonumenten (tel. 035-6559933).

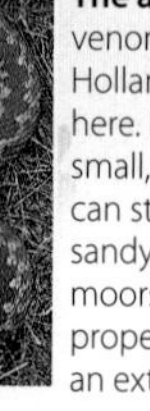

The adder is the only venomous snake in Holland and is very rare here. However, this small, distinctive snake can still be found in sandy regions and peat moors. In order to feed properly, adders require an extensive habitat.

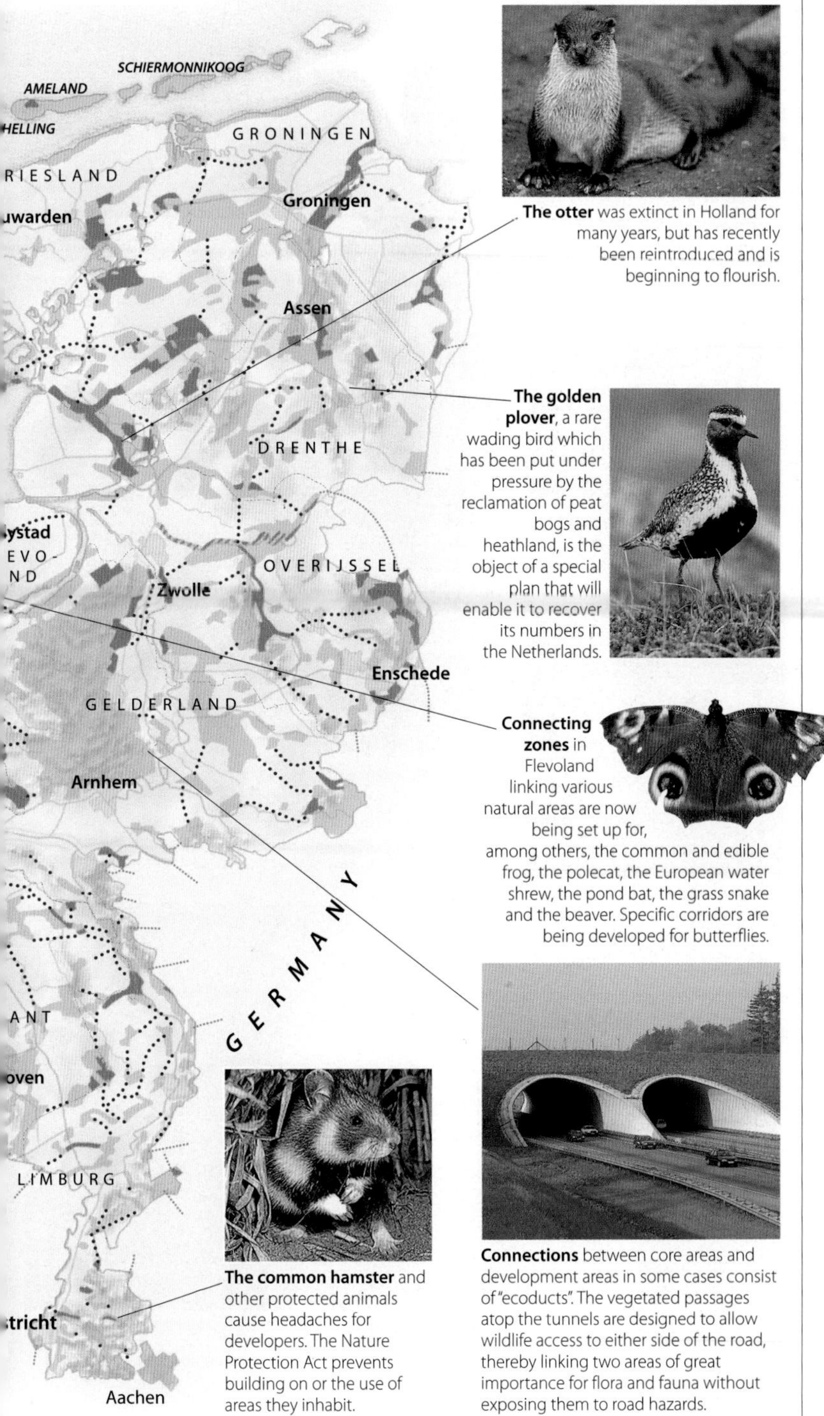

The otter was extinct in Holland for many years, but has recently been reintroduced and is beginning to flourish.

The golden plover, a rare wading bird which has been put under pressure by the reclamation of peat bogs and heathland, is the object of a special plan that will enable it to recover its numbers in the Netherlands.

Connecting zones in Flevoland linking various natural areas are now being set up for, among others, the common and edible frog, the polecat, the European water shrew, the pond bat, the grass snake and the beaver. Specific corridors are being developed for butterflies.

The common hamster and other protected animals cause headaches for developers. The Nature Protection Act prevents building on or the use of areas they inhabit.

Connections between core areas and development areas in some cases consist of "ecoducts". The vegetated passages atop the tunnels are designed to allow wildlife access to either side of the road, thereby linking two areas of great importance for flora and fauna without exposing them to road hazards.

Distinctive Landscapes

The northeast of the Netherlands has a number of distinctive landscape types, such as the unique mud flats, or Waddenzee, where the sand and clay is exposed at low tide; the peat moors in southeast Groningen; the enchanting heathland of Drenthe; the endless polder landscape of Flevoland; the splendid forests of Gelderland (Hoge Veluwe and Posbank) and the magnificent riverscapes and seascapes in the northeast of Overijssel.

The Oostvaardersplassen (lakes), between Lelystad and Almere, make up a unique natural landscape. It is a breeding ground and feeding area for hundreds of species of birds.

Glasswort is a wild plant which grows in mud flats and on silt deposits. It is a prized culinary delicacy.

West Frisian Islands

The Waddenzee *(see pp274–5)* is an area of mud flats which is largely dry at low tide. It attracts many species of birds that come here to forage and to feed. The island of Texel features the peat walls of the Hoge Berg.

Water crowfoot occurs in both flowing and standing water.

Rapeseed plantations are used for land improvements in new polders. The yellow fields seem to stretch endlessly to the horizon.

Bulrushes were once common in the region. The "cigars" grow only by fresh water and are now protected.

Polder Landscape

Forests (het Knarbos), lakes (the Oostvaardersplassen) and coastal lakes (the Veluwemeer) punctuate the flat polder landscape of the "new" province of Flevoland *(see pp326–33).*

Boletus edulis is a delicious edible mushroom. Picking it, however, is no longer allowed.

Bracken fern grows in sparse woodland on lime and nutrient-poor sand and loamy ground, and on dried peat moors.

Common polypody occurs in juniper brush and in woodlands on poor sandy soil.

Mosses thrive in humid environments such as forest floors. Shady areas with acidic soil are ideal for sphagnum moss.

Forests

One of the best-known and largest forest areas in the Netherlands is at Hoge Veluwe in the province of Gelderland *(see pp334–49)*, where a variety of animals, such as wild boar and red deer, are to be found.

The cranberry grows in sphagnum moss on peat moors and in fens.

Common sundew, an insect-eating plant, grows on heathland and in the fenland of Groningen and Drenthe.

Cross-leaved heath thrives on nutrient-poor, dry, sandy soil and in the troughs of dunes.

Heathland

The northeastern Netherlands abounds with delightful heathland. Some of the most picturesque heathland can be found at Drenthe *(see pp306–15)*; herds of sheep still graze in the region of Ellertsveld.

Heather occurs mainly in sand and peat bogs, typically poor in nutrients.

THE WEST FRISIAN ISLANDS

Perhaps the least known part of the Netherlands despite their natural beauty, the West Frisian Islands form a barrier protecting the north of the country from the turbulent waters of the North Sea. Comprising five main islands and a few sandbanks, they are among Europe's last areas of wilderness.

The West Frisian Islands are the remaining fragments of an ancient sandbank that once stretched from Cap Gris Nez in France to Esbjerg in Denmark, a remnant of the last Ice Age. Since Roman times the sea has been eroding this sandbank, creating the shallow Waddenzee behind and washing away much of the peat soil that lay beyond the dunes. The islands of Griend and Rottumeroog were threatened to such an extent that they were abandoned. Rottumerplatt, too, is uninhabited.

Monks established the first settlements as far back as the 8th century; islanders made a living from farming, fishing and collecting shellfish. On Texel and Terschelling, the two largest islands, churches dating from the 15th century still stand. Later, the islands prospered from links with the Dutch East India Company and, in the 19th century, from whaling. Vlieland and Ameland are quieter islands, good for bird-watching. Schiermonnikoog is the most isolated, with rare plant life.

Nowadays the islands, reached by ferries from the mainland, have much to offer the visitor in search of peace and quiet, with nature rambles over dunes and salt marsh, and seal- and bird-watching, especially in summer. The islands' quaint museums are strong on ecology and conservation. The best way to get around is by bicycle and visitors will find a wide range of hotels and guesthouses, excellent seafood restaurants, and some of the best sunsets anywhere.

Former captain's house *(commandeurhuisje)* on Ameland

◀ Traditional cargo ships sail down the Wadden Sea at dusk

Exploring the West Frisian Islands

The history of the West Frisian Islands (Waddeneilanden) has been shaped by the wind and the sea. It was not until the 17th century that the larger islands were stabilized by dykes. Den Burg on Texel, the largest village on the islands, is a historic fortification with a pleasant old centre. Nearby is Hoge Berg, with its characteristic peat walls; in the west, the distinctive tower of Den Hoorn can be seen. To the north is the unique natural area of De Slufter. The crown of the Frisian Islands, Vlieland, has the prettiest village of the islands. Terschelling, Ameland and Schiermonnikoog are typical Frisian islands, with wide beaches, partly forested dunes, villages and polders or mud flats on the Waddenzee side.

Shrimp fishermen sorting their catch

Bird-watching in the Mookbai, Texel

Sights at a Glance

1. Noorderhaaks
2. Den Burg
3. De Koog
4. De Slufter
5. Den Hoorn
6. Vlieland
7. Griend
8. Terschelling
9. Ameland
10. Schiermonnikoog
11. Rottumerplaat
12. Rottumeroog

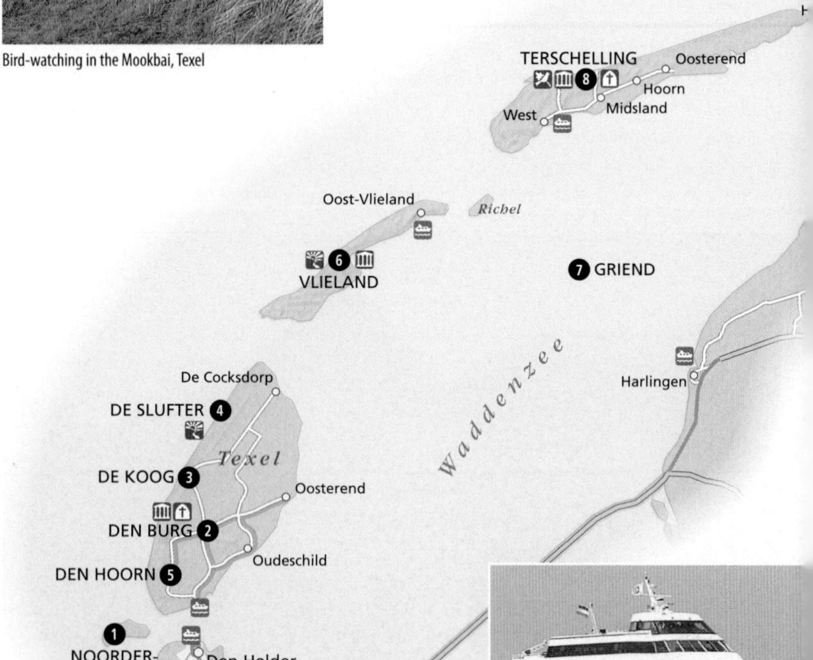

TERSCHELLING 8
Oosterend
Hoorn
Midsland
West
Oost-Vlieland
Richel
6 VLIELAND
7 GRIEND
Waddenzee
Harlingen
De Cocksdorp
DE SLUFTER 4
Texel
DE KOOG 3
Oosterend
DEN BURG 2
Oudeschild
DEN HOORN 5
1 NOORDER-HAAKS
Den Helder

The Koegelwieck seacat (West Terschelling)

For map symbols *see back flap*

De Wadden – the mud flats are ideal for beach walks

Getting Around

The West Frisian Islands are reached by ferries from the mainland. **Texel** is served by TESO (tel. 0222-369600). Foot passengers can take a bus to De Koog or De Cocksdorp via Den Burg, or order a taxi-bus when buying their ticket. **Vlieland** is served by Rederij Doeksen (tel. 0900-3635736); cars not permitted. On arrival, a bus takes passengers to Posthuis, where there are taxis. **Terschelling** is served by Rederij Doeksen (0900-3635736); reservations recommended for cars. There is a bus service on the island, and taxis are available on arrival. **Ameland** is served by Rederij Wagenborg (tel. 0519-546111); reservations recommended. There are bus services to all villages. **Schiermonnikoog** is served by Rederij Wagenborg (tel. 085-4011008); foot passengers only. Bus service and taxi-buses connect the dock and village. Bicycles can be hired easily.

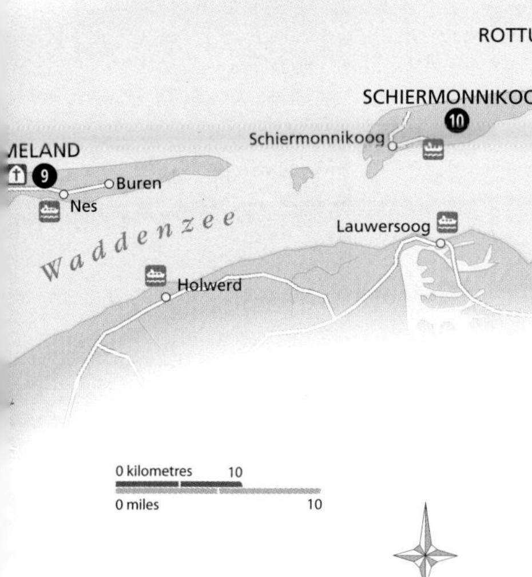

Rescued seals being returned to the wild by members of EcoMare, Texel *(see p427)*

Key

- Motorway
- Main road
- Minor road
- Scenic route
- Minor railway

The splendid coastline of Vlieland

Birds of the Waddenzee

The extensive wetlands of the Waddenzee are an important area for breeding and migratory birds. The North Sea coasts of the islands are sandy, with little animal life; the Waddenzee coasts of the islands, however, consist of fine sand and clay which are rich in minerals and nutrients. The innumerable worms, molluscs and crustaceans that live here are an ideal source of food for a huge variety of ducks, seagulls and wading birds. At the peak of the migratory season (August), the number of birds here runs into millions.

Curlew
This is the largest European wading bird and is easily recognizable by its long, curved beak.

Bird-watching Hide
There are many hides for bird-watchers on the mud flats of the Waddenzee, allowing the birds to be observed without being disturbed.

Bird Catchers

Bird catchers, whose interests in The Netherlands have gone far beyond mere hunting, have become an important pressure group for the protection of birds and the natural environment. Their organization is Vogelbescherming Nederland, based in Zeist.

Beak Shapes

People are often surprised at the many varieties of birds that feed on the mud flats. The different species, however, have managed to avoid competing with one another. The various shapes and lengths of their beaks are suitable for the assorted types of food that can be found in the water and in the sand. Ducks get their food from the surface or dive for it, whereas wading birds get their food from underground – what prey at which depth underground depends on the shape of the beak. Other birds catch fish (spoonbills, cormorants or terns), shellfish (eider ducks) or even other seabirds (the white-tailed eagle), or steal their food from other birds.

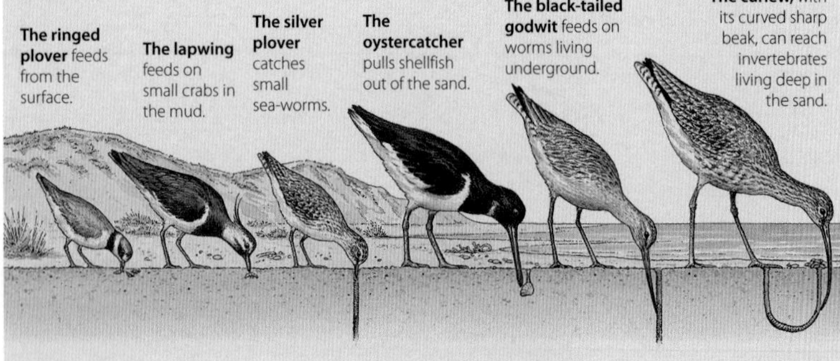

The ringed plover feeds from the surface.

The lapwing feeds on small crabs in the mud.

The silver plover catches small sea-worms.

The oystercatcher pulls shellfish out of the sand.

The black-tailed godwit feeds on worms living underground.

The curlew, with its curved sharp beak, can reach invertebrates living deep in the sand.

Arctic Tern
This extremely rare bird, which breeds in the West Frisian Islands, spends the winter in the Antarctic. This gives it the longest migratory path of all birds.

Sandwich Tern
This bird has its largest breeding colony in Holland on Griend. Its dwindling numbers mean it requires careful protection.

Oystercatcher
The oystercatcher is characteristic of the Waddenzee. It forages for cockles and mussels.

Large numbers of oystercatchers can be seen both in winter and in summer.

Bird Species

The wealth of bird species – including diving birds, petrels, cormorants, spoonbills, ducks, birds of prey, waders, scavengers, seagulls, terns, razorbills and songbirds – that occur in the Waddenzee is a good reason to ensure that the area is carefully protected. For many of the birds, these are the only breeding grounds in the Netherlands, as they are the only wetlands remaining in the Netherlands. Various parts are closed to visitors, and it is important to observe the regulations in order to help preserve the bird population.

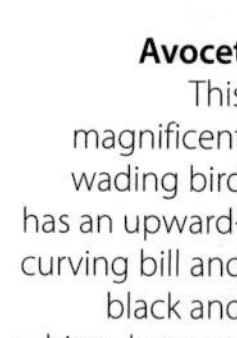

Avocet
This magnificent wading bird has an upward-curving bill and black and white plumage.

Black-Tailed Godwit
This wading bird, with fiery red-brown plumage, is a bird of passage but spends the winters and summers in the Waddenzee.

Ringed Plover
This is an active bird that rarely breeds here but passes through in large numbers.

Eider Duck
The eider duck has breeding colonies on Texel, Vlieland and Terschelling. The male is far more impressive in appearance than the brown-coloured female.

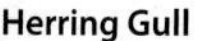

Herring Gull
The herring gull is just one of the many varieties of gull that occur here. At more than half a metre (1.5 ft) long, it is an impressive bird.

Red Knot
This bird of passage stops over sometimes in summer and sometimes in winter. It is a robust bird, one that is always on the move.

The Waddenzee

The Waddenzee is a tidal area whose sand or mud flats *(wadden)* are mainly exposed at low tide and disappear at high tide. Together with the West Frisian Islands, the Waddenzee forms the last extensive wild part of Holland. The entire area has an extremely rich ecosystem because of the large sources of nourishment. It is a feeding and breeding ground for many species of birds. Two species of seal, 30 species of fish, shrimps and crabs live in the Waddenzee or come here to breed.

Cockles *(Cardium edule)*, which form the diet for many bird species, are intensively harvested using mechanical methods. The catch is exported.

The VVVs (tourist offices) on the West Frisian Islands offer all kinds of sailing trips around the islands, including romantic luxury cruises on a three- master. Rederij Vooruit (tel. 0515-531485) arranges sailing trips on local boats.

Sea Lavender *(Limonium vulgare)*, along with sea purslane and sea aster, grows in the higher parts of the salt marshes. Fields of blue-violet sea lavender flowers make a very pretty sight.

Exposed Sections of the Mud Flats

Much of the Waddenzee mud flats is exposed during low tide. This leaves places like the marina pictured below high and dry. Mooring places that are inaccessible at low tide are increasingly being dredged as marinas.

Low tide

High tide

Flora in the Waddenzee

Because of the diversity of the Waddenzee landscape, with its changing environment (salt water and fresh water, lime-rich soil and lime-poor soil, wet land and dry land, clay ground and sandy ground), almost 900 plant species grow here. Many of them grow on the island-side of the old dunes in the dune valleys. Amongst the flowers to be found here are autumn gentian and creeping willow, as well as grasses and weeds such as black bog-rush, fragrant orchid and grass of Parnassus. Lavender is among the plants which grow on the higher ground.

Lavender *(Salicornia europaea)* is one of the first plants to colonize the mud flats and the low-lying parts of the salt marshes. When the land has silted up completely, the salt marsh grass establishes itself.

Cracks in the dried silt provide a good foothold for lavender, as well as for other plants.

Wadlopen (walking the Mud Flats)

A walk on the Waddenzee takes you through salt marshes and past the *wantij*, a place below an island where two tidal flows meet. Since the mid-1970s, walking on the mud flats has been a popular hobby. There are now six major mud-flat walking societies: Dijkstra's Wadlooptochten (Pieterburen, tel. 0595-528345); Lammert Kwant (Ezinge, tel. 0594-622029); Stichting Uithuizer Wad (only for Rottumeroog; tel. 0511-522271), Stichting Wadloopcentrum Friesland (Holwerd, tel. 0519-542100) and Stichting Wadloopcentrum Pieterburen (tel. 0595-528300).

Threats to the Waddenzee

According to the Dutch oil company NAM, there are between 70 and 170 billion cubic metres (2,500 and 6,000 billion cubic feet) of natural gas beneath the Waddenzee. The value of this gas runs into many billions of euros. The Waddenzee Society is completely opposed to any gas drilling in the Waddenzee on several grounds: first, because there is no social need for it and second, because the environmental effects of drilling – in particular, the consequences the falling ground level would have on life in the Waddenzee – have not been properly investigated. For the time being, therefore, drilling on the Waddenzee is banned, pending further environmental impact studies. But the Waddenzee is also threatened by the harvesting of mussels and cockles. Since 1992, the Dutch government has scaled this back, and is considering closing the area to the shellfish industry.

Cockle harvesting

Noorderhaaks, above sea level at high tide for some decades now

❶ Noorderhaaks

Road Map B2. 👥 none. ℹ district Den Helder (0223-671333).

Noorderhaaks, also known as Razende Bol (raging ball), is a fairly bleak sandbank west of Den Helder, 2.5 km (1.5 miles) offshore. The sea currents cause the island to shift eastwards towards Texel, after which another "raging ball" appears at the same point off Den Helder. The Dutch air force occasionally uses the island for target practice, but it is not off-limits for visitors. Rowing and swimming here are risky because of the powerful currents. Adventure-seekers regularly visit Noorderhaaks by boat or by helicopter, unable to resist this piece of total wilderness, where mirages are common.

❷ Den Burg

Road Map B2. 👥 6,000. 🚢 🚌 ℹ Emmalaan 66 (0222-314741). Mon am.

Den Burg is the main town of Texel and situated right in its centre. Around 1300, the village was fortified by a circular rampart with a moat, which are now marked by the Burgwal and Parkstraat Streets. A sheep market was once held in April and May at the Groeneplats, Den Burg's main square with the present-day town hall. Today, a sheep day is held on the first Monday of September. Further on, by the Binnenburg, or inner castle, stands the 15th-century Late Gothic **Hervormde kerk** (Protestant church). The Kogerstraat runs the length of the Binnenburg. Located here is the **Oudheidkamer**, an antiquities museum set up in a picturesque 16th-century building, which used to be a doss-house. Today it contains period rooms, a display of artefacts and works of art in the attic, and a herb garden.

Along and around the town wall are several interesting shopping streets, such as the Weverstraat. A number of excellent restaurants are to be found on the Warmoesstraat.

Environs

South of Den Burg is a sloping landscape with the 15 m (50 ft) **Hoge Berg** (high mountain), which offers a great view of the island. For a good walk, follow the Skillepaadje from the tomb of the Georgiers (resistance fighters who died fighting the Germans in 1945) to the fishing village of Oudeschild, past the peat walls and sheep pens.

Oudheidkamer

Kogerstraat 1, Den Burg.
Tel 0222-313135. **Open** 2 Apr–31 Oct: 11am–5pm Mon–Fri, 2–4pm Sat & Sun. **Closed** 1 Jan, Easter, Whitsun, 25, 26 & 31 Dec.

Beachcomber on Texel, the most populated of the Frisian Islands

❸ De Koog

Road Map B2. 👥 825. 🚢 🚌 ℹ Emmalaan 66, Den Burg (0222–314741). Tue.

In 1900, the former fishing settlement of De Koog consisted of a church (built in 1415) and a few houses and farms. The first tourist facility was the Badhotel, later the Hotel Prinses Juliana, with a garden overlooking the sea. Today, Den Koog has accommodation for 20,000 visitors in hotels, pensions and camp sites. The centre of De Koog is the Dorpsstraat, which has cafés, snack bars and discos. De Koog's attractions for visitors are the Calluna waterpark and Eco Mare, an information centre for the Waddenzee and the North Sea *(see p441)*.

The Nederlands-Hervormde church in Den Burg (1481)

For hotels and restaurants in this region see pp398–399 and p412

❹ De Slufter

Road Map B2. none. **Open** all year, northern part closed 1 Mar–1 Sep. Emmalaan 66, Den Burg (0222-314741).

The unique natural area of De Slufter, consisting of salt marshes covering 450 ha (1,100 acres), is covered with salt-loving plants such as sea thrift and sea lavender, and is an important breeding and feeding ground for many different bird species. De Slufter, and the neighbouring **De Muy**, where spoonbills breed, are magnificent rambling areas.

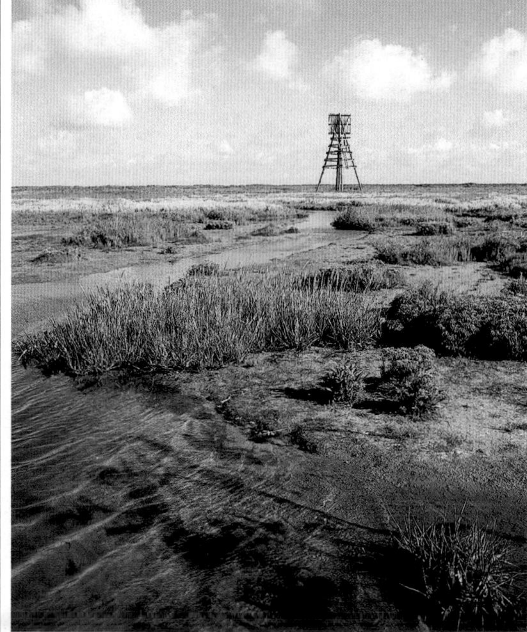

Salt-loving plants thriving at the water's edge, De Slufter

❺ Den Hoorn

Road Map B2. 450. Emmalaan 66, Den Burg (0222-314741). Thu.

Like Den Burg, Den Hoorn stands on boulder clay. It has a distinctive **Hervormde kerk** (Protestant church) with a pointed steeple and churchyard dating from 1425. This exquisitely restored village has been given protected status.

❻ Vlieland

Road Map C1. 1,150. Havenweg 10 (0562-451111).

Vlieland is the smallest of the Waddenzee Islands. In some places, less than one kilometre (half a mile) separates the Waddenzee and the North Sea. Unlike the other islands, Vlieland consists only of dunes, covered with a purple haze of heather, marram grass and sea buckthorn. In the east, the woods planted just after 1900 provide a bit of variety in the landscape.

In the south is the only village, **Oost-Vlieland**, where the boat from Harlingen docks. Many old buildings line the main street. One of them, the **Tromp's Huys** (1576), used to belong to the Amsterdam Admiralty. Today it houses a museum with 19th-century paintings. The houses are separated by alleys known as "gloppen". There is no room for cars here, not even for those of the islanders.

The best way to explore Vlieland is by bicycle; the island can be covered in one day. From Oost-Vlieland, you can cycle westwards along tracks through the dunes or along the Waddenzee shoreline to the **Posthuys** (post house), where in the 17th century the overseas mail was brought from Amsterdam to be loaded onto ships waiting to sail. Further westwards is **de Vliehors**, an area of natural interest which can be explored if no military exercises are taking place here. Beware, though: you run the risk of getting stuck in the soft drifting sand. This is also where the wealthy village of **West-Vlieland** once stood. It was consumed by the waves after it was abandoned in 1736.

The village hall in Oost-Vlieland

Tromp's Huys

Dorpsstraat 99, Vlieland. **Tel** 0562-451600. **Open** 10am–5pm Tue–Sat, 2–4pm Sat (school holidays); 2–5pm Tue–Thu, 10am–1pm Fri, 2–5pm Sat. **Closed** 1 Jan, Easter, Pentecost.

The Oerol Festival on Terschelling

7 Griend

Road Map C1. none. very limited. Vereniging Natuurmonumenten (035-6559933).

Half-way through the boat trip from Harlingen to Terschelling or Vlieland, one will come across Griend. The island was abandoned by its inhabitants after the St Lucia's of 1287. For centuries it seemed about to disappear beneath the waves. In 1988, the Natuurmonumenten trust, which has leased Griend since 1916, had a dam built to prevent further erosion. At high tide, the highest part of the island is just 1 m (3 ft) above the water. Access to Griend is forbidden, save for a handful of bird wardens and biology students. This is Holland's largest breeding ground for great tern.

8 Terschelling

Road Map C1. 5,000. Willem Barentszkade 19a, West-Terschelling (0562-443000).

Terschelling is the second largest of the West Frisian Islands. The north of the island consists of dunes, where in the olden days cattle were let out to graze everywhere ("oerol"). This is where the Oerol Festival, held each year in June, gets its name.

In Formerum, West, and Hoorn, the dunes have been planted with coniferous and deciduous woods. In the south are polders, and beyond the dykes are the salt marshes. There is a nature reserve at either end of the island: the Noordvaarder in the west, and the Boschplaat in the east. If you happen to be sailing over from Harlingen at low tide on a sunny day, you may see seals basking in the sun on the de Richel and Jacobs Ruggen sandbanks.

West is a real mud-flat village, with old houses and a famous lighthouse, the **Brandaris**, dating from 1594. It is closed to visitors, but the same view can be enjoyed from the high dune known as the Seinpaalduin behind the village. **Het Behouden Huys** is a local history museum dedicated to famous islanders such as Willem Barentsz; there is also the educational **Centrum voor Natuur en Landschap**, where you can learn about the ecology of the mud flats.

Tombstone from Striep

The two largest villages in the west are Midsland and Hoorn. Midsland is surrounded by small hamlets with intriguing names such as Hee, Horp and Kaart, which date back to when the Frisians settled on the islands. The hamlet with the **kerkhof van Striep** cemetery is where the first church on the island was built, in the 10th century. Its outline is still visible. Further eastwards is Hoorn, with 13th-century Gothic-Romanesque St Janskerk standing on the site of the original church.

Museum 't Behouden Huys
Commandeurstraat 32, West-Terschelling. **Tel** 0562-442389.
Open 10am–5pm Tues-Fri, 1–5pm Sat & Sun; July–Aug: also Mon 1–5pm.
Closed Nov–Mar (except for school holidays).

Centrum voor Natuur en Landschap
Burg. Reedekerstraat 11, West-Terschelling. **Tel** 0562-442390.
Open Apr–Oct: 9am–5pm Mon–Fri, 2–5pm Sat & Sun.

9 Ameland

Road Map C/D1. 3,200. Bureweg 2, Nes (0519-546546). **vvvameland.nl**

The dunes in the north of this island are dry, with the exception of **Het Oerd**, a wet valley in the east which is a bird reserve. The region is best explored by bicycle; there is a cycle track to a scenic spot on a 24-m (79-ft) dune. In the mud flats in the south there are four villages. The largest of these is **Nes**, where the boat from Holwerd calls. **Commandeurshuizen** (commodores' houses)

Het Oerd – the edge of the mud flats on Ameland

A horse-drawn lifeboat, the pride of Ameland

in the old centre recall the days when many islanders made their living from whaling.

If you want to see the real Ameland, you must visit Hollum. The Zuiderlaan and Oosterlaan are steeped in the atmosphere of past times. At the southern end of the village is the church, surrounded by an oval cemetery with tombstones where the deeply pious inscriptions are overgrown with lichen.

Beyond Hollum lies the **Reddingsmuseum Abraham Fock**, a museum dedicated to life-saving, where the pride of Ameland, a lifeboat launched by horses, is kept operational.

Reddingsmuseum Abraham Fock
Oranjeweg 18, Hollum. **Tel** 0519 542737. **Open** Apr–Nov: 10am–noon & 1:30–5pm daily.

⑩ Schiermonnikoog

Road Map D1. 1,000.
Reeweg 5, Schiermonnikoog (0519-531233/531900).

Schiermonnikoog, or Lytje Pole (small land), was a farm belonging to Cistercian monks during the Middle Ages. The village of Schiermonnikoog, which is named after them, has many exquisitely restored houses. The island as a whole is a national park and under the protection of Natuurmonumenten. The beach of Schier is one of the widest in Europe. The eastern side of the island (Het Balg, Kobbeduinen and the salt marshes) in particular make for wonderful walking areas, with their varied flora (including many orchids) and bird life. No cars at all are allowed on the island.

⑪ Rottumerplaat

Road Map D1. none.
Staatsbosbeheer (050-5207247).

Nature has been left to her own devices with the 900 ha (2,225 acre) uninhabited island of Rottumerplaat. This protected nature reserve is jointly managed by the Ministry of Agriculture, Waterways and Planning, and the Friends of Rottumeroog and Rottumerplaat Society (SVRR). Outsiders are rarely admitted to the island. This has had a good effect on Rottumeroog as well as on Rottumerplaat, which has been expanding quickly. Dunes many metres in height and an impressive salt marsh are its characteristic features. The island also belongs to the seals and birds.

⑫ Rottumeroog

Road Map D1. none. very limited. Staatsbosbeheer (050-5207247).

This most eastern of the West Frisian Islands is due to disappear into the mouth of the Ems soon. Since 1991 it has been left in the hands of nature. Attempts over many years to prevent it from drifting eastwards were unsuccessful. In 1998, the northern dunes collapsed, after which the last traces of human settlement were removed by the state forestry commission. The island is now less than 300 ha (740 acres) in size and shrinks with each storm. Walkers are prohibited in the area.

The uninhabited island of Rottumerplaat, with its high dunes

CARS

GRONINGEN

The Netherland's northernmost province is distinguished by its rich cultural history and unusual landscape, where you often see terps or small areas of elevated land. To the north and west it is bounded by the shallow Waddenzee and to the east by the Ems river estuary and the border with Germany.

The *terps* originated centuries ago, when the inhabitants of this region needed to protect themselves from high water levels. The elevated land is sometimes crowned by a solitary Romanesque church, visible for miles across the fens. Elsewhere in the province you will see straight roads and canals, often evidence of reclaimed land. The region grew rich during the Middle Ages from agriculture and peat extraction, and the medieval port of Appingedam, nowadays a little town inland from the port of Delfzijl, was once a member of the powerful Hanseatic League.

Groningen province is also noted for its windmills, castles and moated manor houses and, in the east, for its restored fortified towns, such as picturesque Bourtange, which is right on the border with Germany. Conservation areas abound. Close to Lauwersoog, where you can catch a ferry to Schiermonnikoog, one of the West Frisian Islands *(see p279)*, a vast nature reserve has been established. Nearby Pieterburen has a seal sanctuary.

Groningen, the provincial capital, is proud of its glorious past and boasts a wealth of world-class museums, historic buildings and other attractions. A number of Dutch corporations have their headquarters in this thriving university city, and a further boost to the economy arrived in the 1960s after the discovery in nearby Slochteren of some of the world's largest natural gas deposits.

Hay bales in Westerwolde near the old fortified town of Bourtange

◀ Fair by the Martinitoren in Groningen, Netherlands

Exploring Groningen

Some of the most attractive and historically interesting castles, or *borgs*, are in the Groningen region: the medieval Fraeylemaborg in Slochteren, Menkemaborg in Uithuizen and the charming Verhildersum in Leens. The natural area around the Lauwersmeer is particularly suitable for rambling. Not far from here, in Pieterburen, is a famous refuge for seals. Ter Apel, which is on the province's eastern boundary, is a magnificent medieval monastery. Groningen itself *(see pp284–9)* has much to offer, including the peaceful Prinsenhof, with its beautiful gardens, and the ultra-modern Groninger Museum *(see pp288–9)*, which houses collections that range from archaeology to oriental porcelain to modern art.

Wensum, one of the prettiest villages in Groningen

The Lauwersmeer nature reserve, created through the draining of the Lauwerszee

Getting Around

Groningen can be reached from the south along the A28 motorway; the A7 crosses the province from Friesland in the west to Germany in the east. The best way to see the town of Groningen is on foot. From Groningen there are rail links to Roodeschool in the north, Delfzijl in the northeast and to Nieuweschans in the east. Most of the countryside is accessible by regional *(interlokal)* or local *(buurt)* buses. The Groningen region is well suited for cycling and rambling, especially the area around the Lauwersmeer, the mud-flat region *(waddengebied)* and Westerwolde, in the south.

Sights at a Glance

1. *Groningen pp284–9*
2. Grootegast
3. Leek
4. Zoutkamp
5. Lauwersoog
6. Pieterburen
7. Uithuizen
8. Appingedam
9. Slochteren
10. Fraeylemaborg
11. Winschoten
12. Veendam
13. Bourtange
14. Oude and Nieuwe Pekela
15. Ter Apel

Recreation possibilities on the Paterswoldse Meer, south of Groningen

For map symbols *see back flap*

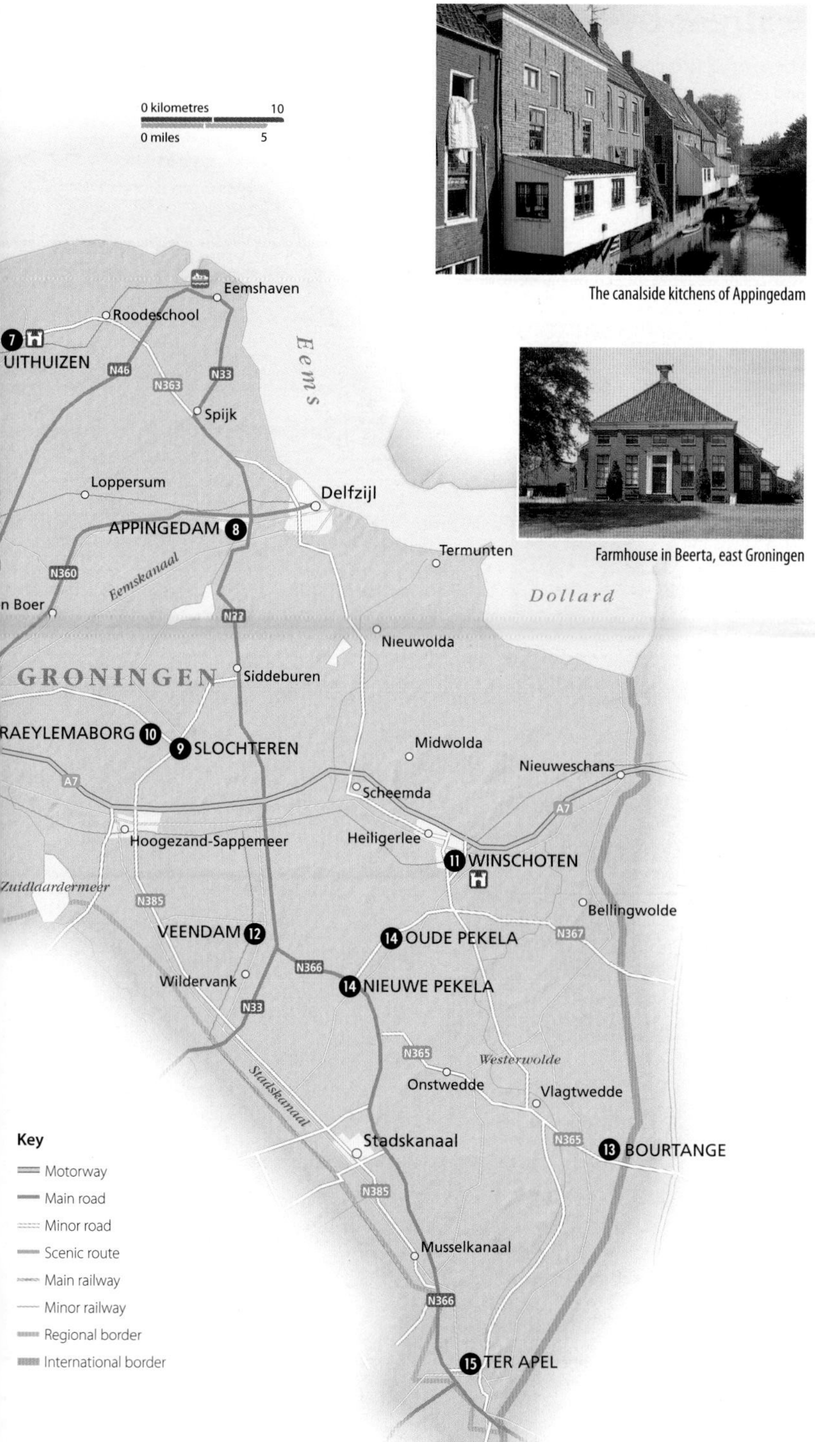

The canalside kitchens of Appingedam

Farmhouse in Beerta, east Groningen

For hotels and restaurants in this region see p399 and pp412–413

❶ Street-by-Street: Groningen

The town of Groningen has for centuries been the cultural and historical capital of the province. Its glory was at its height in the 15th century, when the town was freed from the jurisdiction of the Bishop of Utrecht and was able to extend its influence into the present-day province of Friesland. In 1614, the Groninger Academie was founded, which was the precursor of the Rijksuniversiteit. Thus, in addition to being a centre of trade and government, the town also became an academic centre.

★ Prinsenhof
In the gardens of the Prinsenhof, where in 1568 the first Bishop of Groningen, and later the stadholder, resided, stands a magnificent sundial from 1730. The garden is laid out as it was in the 18th century.

★ Martinitoren
The 97-m (318-ft) Martinitoren (St Martin tower) dating from 1496 is called The Old Grey by the locals because of the colour of the Bentheim sandstone.

The Martinikerk (St Martin's Church) dates back to the 13th century, though only parts of the original basilica are preserved. The Romanesque church was extensively remodelled in Gothic style in the 1400s.

Stadhuis
The Stadhuis on the Grote Markt is a monumental Neo-Classical building, completed in 1810.

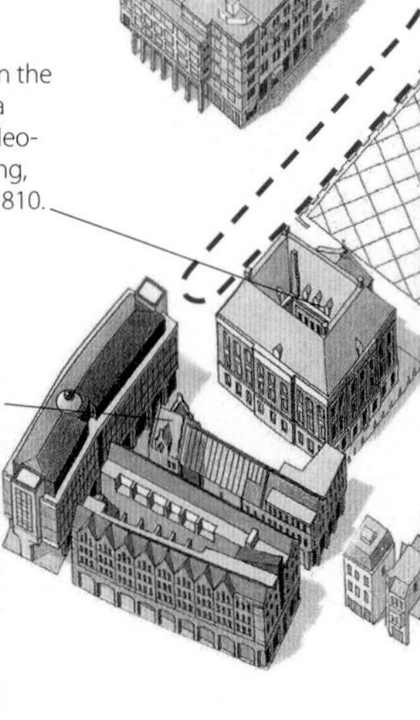

Goudkantoor
This 1635 Renaissance building on the Waagplein was known as the "Goudkantoor" (gold depository) in the 19th century, when it functioned as a treasury. It now houses an inn.

VISITORS' CHECKLIST

Practical Information
Road Map D1. 177,000.
Grote Markt 25 (050-3139741). Tue–Sat. Good Friday: flower fair; 5 May: Bevrijdingsfestival (Liberation festival); May: funfairs; 28 Aug: Groningen holiday.

Transport
Stationsplein.
Stationsplein.

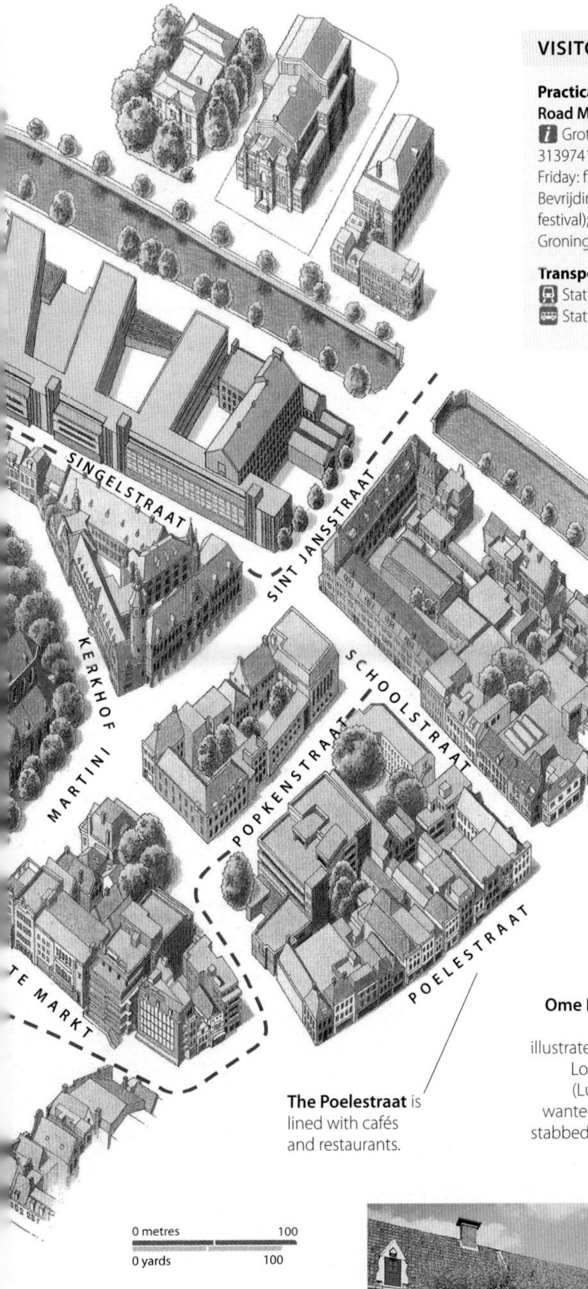

Key

— Recommended route

Ome Loeks' horse, a statue by Jan de Baat in front of the train station, illustrates a famous local folksong, "Ome Loeks' horse is dead". Pikeur "Loeks" (Lucas) van Hemmen (1876–1955) wanted to shoo away his horse and so stabbed it with his pitchfork. The animal got an infection and later died.

The Poelestraat is lined with cafés and restaurants.

0 metres 100
0 yards 100

★ St Geertruidshofje
This inn on Peperstraat, founded in 1405 as a hostel for poor pilgrims, has two courtyards. The first is bounded by the convent church, refectory and warden's chambers; guest rooms surround the second.

Exploring Groningen

The city of Groningen has a number of interesting buildings and museums, among them the Noordelijk Scheepvaartmuseum (northern maritime museum) which illustrates the history of navigation. The Groninger Museum *(see pp288–9)* possesses an art collection of international stature. A visit to one of the gardens of Groningen will provide peace in the middle of the bustling university city.

The distinctive Gasunie building, known locally as the "monkey cliff"

Martinikerk and Martinitoren

Martinikerkhof 3. **Tel** 050-3111277. **Open** Easter–11 Nov: noon–5pm Sat; Jun–Aug & two Sats in Sep: noon–5pm Tue–Sat. 1:30pm. Martinitoren Grote Markt. **Tel** 050-3135713. **Open** 1 Apr–31 Oct: 11am–5pm Mon–Sat; 1 Nov–31 Mar: noon–4pm Mon–Sat; Jul & Aug: 11am–4pm Sun. **Closed** 1 Jan, 25 Dec.

The Grote Markt is the old city centre. Many of the buildings standing on the square were badly damaged by air raids near the end of World War II. When it was rebuilt, the market was enlarged on the northern and eastern sides, and new buildings of a modern character were added.

The famous Martinitoren (St Martin tower) was also damaged but still standing, and it was possible to rebuild it. The carillon of d'Olle Grieze ("The Old Grey"), whose bells were cast by the Hemony brothers, has since been enlarged and now has four octaves and 49 bells. The Martinikerk (St Martin's Church), dating from the 13th century, still retains traces of the original building: both the northern and southern façades of the transept and the ornamental brickwork of the windows and window niches of the northern side are recognizably 13th century. During the 15th century, when the city was at the height of its development, the church was extended in Gothic style. The choir, which features sumptuous murals from 1530 illustrating the life of Christ, had been completed before 1425. The central part of the church became a hall-type church. East of the Grote Markt is the Poelestraat, which on fine days comes to life with outdoor cafés and restaurants.

Gebouw van de Gasunie

Concourslaan 17. **Tel** 050-5219111. **Closed** to the public.

The main office of the Dutch Gasunie (gas board) was designed by the Alberts and Van Huur architects on the principles of "organic" architecture, the inspiration of which lies with natural forms. The "organic" nature of the building can be seen at every turn, even in the specially designed furniture. The locals' nickname for the building is the "apenrots" (monkey cliff).

St Geertruidshofje

Peperstraat 22. **Tel** 050-3124082.

Groningen has a number of pretty *hofjes*, or courtyards surrounded by almshouses, often belonging to inns. They were once charitable institutions whose aim was to help the poor. The finest of these is the complex of the 13th-century Heilige Geestgasthuis, or Pelstergasthuis (in the Pelsterstraat), and St Geertruidshofje *(see p285)*, whose Pepergasthuis inn was established in 1405. It later became a senior citizens' home. The pump in the courtyard dates from 1829.

The Poelestraat: a favourite haunt for the students of Groningen

Noordelijk Scheepvaartmuseum

Brugstraat 24–26. **Tel** 050-3122202. **Open** 10am–5pm Tue–Sat, 1–5pm Sun & hols. **Closed** public holidays.

This maritime museum, arranged over two restored medieval houses, deals with the history of navigation in the northern provinces from 1650 to the present. Exhibits are arranged in chronological order, from the Utrecht ships, Hanseatic cogs, West Indies merchantmen, peat barges and Baltic merchant ships to Groningen coasters from the 20th century. A number of historical workshops, such as a carpenter's shop and a smithy, are held in the attic of the museum. The museum also has an excellent programme of temporary exhibitions, featuring all things marine.

Decorative element from the Provinciehuis of Groningen

Prinsenhof and Prinsenhoftuin

Martinikerkhof 23. **Tel** 050-3176555. **Open** daily 9am–noon.

The Prinsenhof originally housed the monastic order of the Broeders des Gemenen Levens. It later became the seat of the first Bishop of Groningen, Johann Knijff, who had the entire complex converted into a magnificent bishop's palace. Until late into the 18th century, the building served as the residence of the stadholder. The Prinsenhoftuin (Prinsenhof Gardens) is truly an oasis in the midst of the busy city. Its high-lights include a herb garden and a rose garden. There is also a flowerbed that is arranged into two coats of arms, one with the letter W (for William Frederick, the stadholder of Friesland), the other with a letter A (for Albertine Agnes, William's wife). At the side of the entrance is a fine sundial *(see p284)* which dates back to 1730. The course of the old city walls of Groningen is still clearly discernible in the Prinsenhoftuin.

The magnificent Prinsenhof, formerly the stadholder's residence

Hortus Haren

Kerklaan 34, Haren. **Tel** 050-5370053. **Open** 9:30am–5pm daily. **Closed** 1 Jan, 25 Dec.

Immediately south of the city is the fashionable town of Haren, where an extensive park, Hortus Haren, is situated. The park was set up in 1642 by Henricus Munting. Its 20 ha (50 acres) include a large hothouse complex comprising several different greenhouses dedicated to a wide array of climatic zones. There is a tropical rainforest with a great variety of exotic flowers. A sub-tropical hothouse numbers orange trees among its plants. The various climatic areas continue with a desert section. Here, gigantic cacti are show-cased. Another greenhouse featuring a monsoon climate contains unusual carnivorous plants. In the tropical culture greenhouse, you can admire a traditional Indonesian *sawah* (ricefield).

The Chinese garden ("Het verborgen rijk van Ming", or "The hidden Ming Empire") is well worth a visit. It is a faithful reconstruction of a real garden owned by a 16th-century high Chinese official of the Ming Dynasty (1368–1644). It features original Chinese pagodas, which have been painstakingly restored by Chinese craftsmen into fine pavilions and then beautifully decorated with carvings of lions and dragons. Het verborgen rijk van Ming also has a waterfall and a tea house where visitors can enjoy Chinese refreshments.

Another interesting theme garden is the Ogham Gardens, a Celtic garden whose main attractions is the Horoscope of Trees, consisting of an earth-and-stone circular wall, which is a replica of the enclosures the ancient Celts built to live within. Inside the circle is a labyrinth representing life; at its centre is a small garden and the Well of Wisdom.

In summer, a variety of exhibitions and events are held on the grounds, attracting locals and tourists alike.

The fascinating Hortus Haren, with its innumerable attractions

Groninger Museum

Between the central station and the inner city lies the Groninger Museum, standing on an island in the 19th-century Verbindingskanaal. Designed by internationally renowned Italian architect Alessandro Mendini and opened in 1994, the museum showcases archaeology and history, applied arts (including a remarkable collection of Chinese and Japanese porcelain), early art and cutting-edge modern art.

★ Spiral Staircase
The spiral staircase which visitors have to descend to see the exhibits is the museum's main meeting point and a work of art in itself.

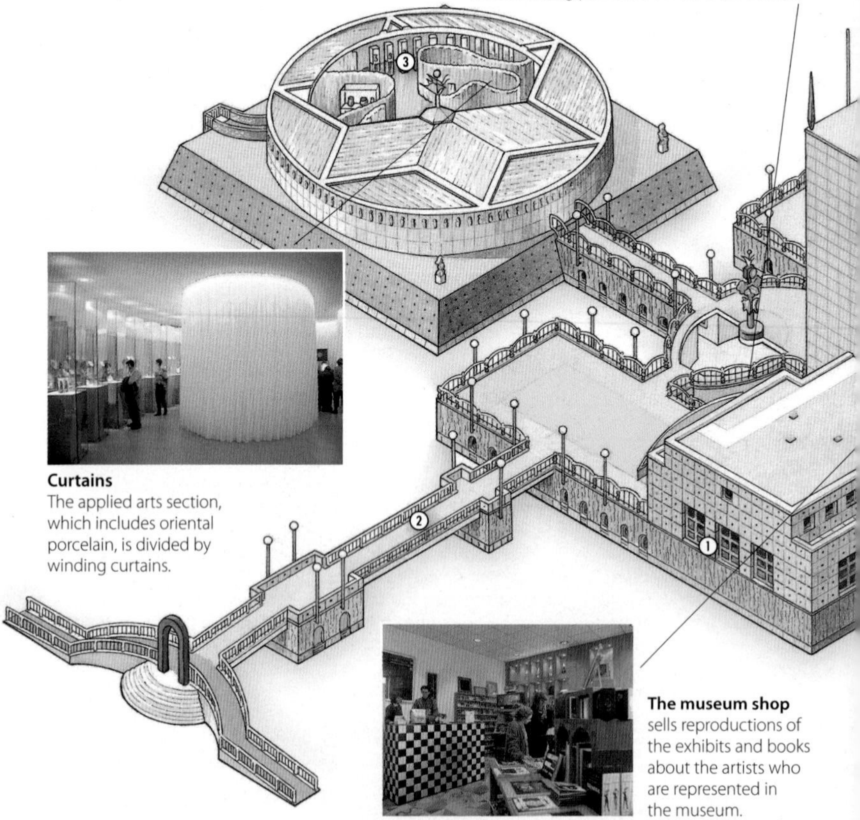

Curtains
The applied arts section, which includes oriental porcelain, is divided by winding curtains.

The museum shop sells reproductions of the exhibits and books about the artists who are represented in the museum.

KEY

① **The museum café** features furniture by various designers and was set up as an addition to the museum collection.

② **A cycle and pedestrian bridge** connects the museum with the station square. There is also a direct connection with the station and the town centre.

③ **Temporary exhibitions**

④ **The Mendini Pavilion** is easily distinguished by its apparent haphazardness and chaos, and is a good example of deconstructivism.

⑤ **This wing** of the museum was designed by Wolfgang Prix and Helmut Swiczinsky.

⑥ **A large concrete staircase** in the spectacular Mendini Pavilion leads to the upper pavilion, where some of the collection of art is on display.

Rembrandt
This ink drawing of *Saskia in Bed* by Rembrandt can sometimes be seen in the Mendini Pavilion.

VISITORS' CHECKLIST

Practical Information
Museumeiland 1.
Tel 050-3666555.
Open 10am–5pm Tue–Sun (also Jul &Aug: 1–5pm Mon).
Closed Mon, 1 Jan, 5 May, 25 Dec.
Open 9.30am– 4.30pm Tue–Sun. **Closed** same as above.

★ De Ploeg
The Groningen art collective De Ploeg has its own pavilion. In addition to works by the group, the section also displays works by other expressionists from northern Europe. The picture *Rotating Door of the Post Office* is by De Ploeg painter HN Werkman.

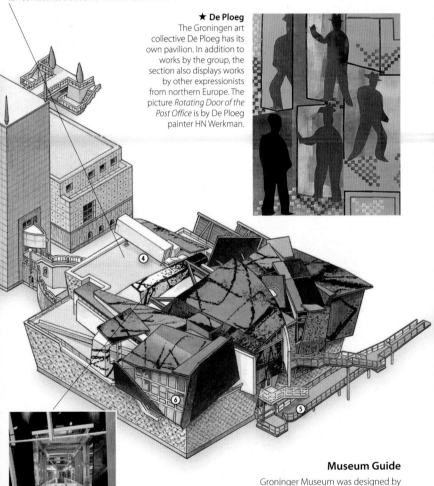

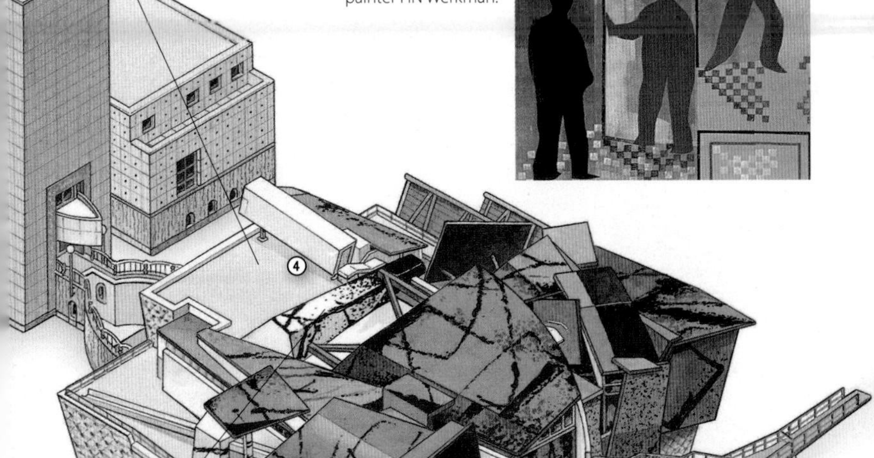

Bridge in the Coop Himmelb(l)au Pavilion

Museum Guide
Groninger Museum was designed by Alessandro Mendini (born 1931). He based the design around the collections of the museum, which consisted of archaeology, applied arts and early and modern pictorial arts. The focus of the building is the 30-m (98-ft) tower in the middle.

❷ Grootegast

Road Map D1. 11,500. 33, 38, 39, 98, 101, 133. Nienoord 20, Leek (0594-512100). Fri.

The little town of Lutjegast, close to Grootegast, is the birthplace of the 17th-century explorer Abel Tasman *(see box)*. The **Abel Tasmankabinet** houses an interesting exhibition about his life. The collection includes old sea charts and books.

Abel Tasmankabinet
Kompasstraat 1. **Tel** 0594-613576.
Open 1:30–4:30pm Tue–Sat.

❸ Leek

Road Map D2. 18,000. 81, 85, 88, 98, 306, 316. Nienoord 20 (0594-512100). Thu.

In the small town of Leek stands the castle of Nienoord, built in approximately 1524 by Wigbold van Ewsum. During the 19th century, things at the castle seemed to be taking a turn for the worse.

Landgoed Nienoord

The harbour of the delightful fishing village of Zoutkamp

In 1846, the then owner, Ferdinand Folef Kniphausen, nicknamed "the mad squire", burned all the family portraits in a drunken fit. Later, the orangery and part of the upper floor were destroyed by fire. In 1950, the municipality bought the castle. Eight years later, the **Nationaal Rijtuigmuseum**, featuring horse-drawn vehicles, was established here. It contains a unique collection of royal coaches, gigs, mail coaches and hackney carriages.

Nationaal Rijtuigmuseum
Nienoord 1. **Tel** 0594-512260.
Open Apr–Oct: 11am–5pm, Tue–Sun. **Closed** Mon.

❹ Zoutkamp

Road Map: D1. 1,200. 63, 65, 69, 136, 163, 165. Reitdiepskade 11 (0595-401957).

The small fishing village of Zoutkamp changed its character dramatically after the damming of the Lauwerszee in 1969. By the waterside (Reitdiepskade) there are still a number of fisherman's cottages retaining the erstwhile charm of the village.

❺ Lauwersoog

Road Map D1. 350. 50, 63, 163. Reitdiepskade 11, Zoutkamp (0595-401957).

At Lauwersoog, from where the ferry leaves for Schiermonnikoog *(see p279)*, is the Lauwersmeer, a 2,000-ha (4,940-acre) nature reserve. When the Lauwerszee was drained, the land was designated for four purposes: agriculture, recreation, a nature reserve and an army training area.

Environs

Lauwersoog is a good base from which to explore the tuff churches that, in the middle ages, were built in villages such as Doezum, Bedum and Zuidwolde. They can be recognized by their grey or green porous stone.

Abel Tasman (1603–59)

Abel Janszoon Tasman was born in Lutjegast in 1603 but lived in Amsterdam from an early age. In 1633, as a navigating officer for the Dutch East India Company *(see pp52–3)*, he travelled to Asia. In 1642, he sailed on the yacht *De Heemskerck* and then with the cargo ship *Zeehaen* in search of the legendary southern continent. Tasman charted some of the coast and later reached New Zealand's South Island. On 13 June 1643, he arrived in Batavia (now Jakarta), which he called home until his death 16 years later. From 1644 to 1648, he sat on the Batavian council of justice; during this time he also joined trading missions to Sumatra (1646) and Siam (1647). Tasman died on 10 October 1659, having bequeathed his money to the poor of Lutjegast.

❻ Pieterburen

Road Map D1. 500. 65, 67, 68. Waddencentrum, Hoofdstraat 83 (0595-528522).

One of the best-known places in Groningen is Pieterburen, home to the **Zeehondencrèche**. This seal nursery was founded by Lenie 't Hart and others as a reception centre for sick and disabled seals from the nearby Waddenzee, where some 1,750 seals live. Half of these owe their lives to care they received here.

The **Waddencentrum**, also located here, is an exhibition centre dedicated to the mud flats of the Waddenzee. It also provides useful information for people wishing to walk there.

Zeehondencrèche Pieterburen
Hoofdstraat 94a. **Tel** 0595-526526.
Open 10am–5pm daily.

Het Waddencentrum
Hoofdstraat 83. **Tel** 0595-528522.
Open 9am–6pm daily.

Environs
In Leens, 10 km (6 miles) to the southwest of Pieterburen is the stunning 14th-century *borg* (moated manor house) Verhildersum, which contains 19th-century furnishings. The castle is surrounded by a wide moat. Its gardens include an arbour and sculptures. The castle's coach house is regularly used as a venue for exhibitions, while the Schathuis (treasury) is now a lively café and restaurant.

Recovering seal in one of the ponds at Pieterburen

Borg Verhildersum
Wierde 40, Leens. **Tel** 0595-571430.
Open Apr–Oct: 10:30am–5pm Tue–Sun.

❼ Uithuizen

Road Map E1. 5,300. 41, 61, 62, 641, 662. Mennonietenkerk-straat 13 (0595-434051). Sat.

The exceptionally pretty castle of Menkemaborg in Uithuizen dates back to the 14th century. It acquired its present-day form around 1700. The bedroom features a ceremonial bedstead dating from the early 18th century, when King William III stayed here. The kitchen in the cellar has all the old fittings. The gardens were laid out during restoration work in the 18th century. The Schathuis (treasury), formerly used to store the food brought by the townspeople to the castle, currently houses a café and restaurant.

Menkemaborg
Menkemaweg 2. 61. **Tel** 0595-431970. **Open** Mar–Jun & Sep: Tue–Sun 10am–5pm, Jul–Aug: 10am–5pm daily, Oct–Dec: Tue–Sun 10am–4pm. **Closed** Jan–Easter.

Wedding in traditional dress in the gardens of the 14th-century Menkemaborg in Uithuizen

❽ Appingedam

Road Map E1. 12,400. 40, 45, 78, 140, 178. Oude Kerkstraat 1 (0596-620300). Sat.

This town, a member of the Hanseatic League in the Middle Ages, was granted its charter in 1327. Standing at a junction of waterways as it once did and with a seaport, it quickly grew into a major international trading city. The medieval layout of the city has remained largely unchanged. The **hanging kitchens**, visible from the Vlinterbrug bridge, were built this way to create more space in the houses. Directly over the water are doors from which people drew water for their household needs.

In the 18th century, the town again prospered, as the **Ebenhaëzerhuis** well illustrates. Appingendam, with over 65 listed buildings, has a preservation order as a town of historical interest.

Steam pumping station (1878) at the Winschoten polder, now a museum

❾ Slochteren

Road Map E1. 2,600. 78, 178. Noorderweg 1 (0598-422970). Thu.

When a natural gas field was discovered here in 1959, Slochteren gained overnight national renown. The "Slochteren Dome" appeared to be the largest in the world when it was first discovered, and the revenue it brought in made Holland rich.

The past of this historic town is closely associated with the lords of the Fraeylemaborg. The Reformed Church in Slochteren consists of the remnants of a 13th-century Romanesque-Gothic cross-naved church. The environs are excellent for walking or cycling, particularly around places like nearby Schildmeer.

The historical castle of Fraeylemaborg at Slochteren

❿ Fraeylemaborg

Road Map E1. Noorderweg 1, Slochteren (0598-422970).

Fraeylemaborg is one of the most imposing castles of Groningen. It dates back to the Middle Ages. Three embrasures in the kitchen and the hall above it bear silent witness to the defensive functions the castle once had. In the 17th century, two side wings were added, and in the 18th century it was given its present form with the addition of the monumental main wing. The castle is surrounded by a double moat.

The extensive wooded park just beyond the castle is an interesting combination of the 18th-century Baroque garden style and the 19th-century English landscape gardens.

Fraeylemaborg
Hoofdweg 30–32, Slochteren. **Tel** 0598-421568. **Open** 2 Jan–31 Dec: 10am–5pm Tue–Fri, 1–5pm Sat, Sun & public hols.

⓫ Winschoten

Road Map E2. 18,500. 10, 12, 13, 14, 17, 29. Torenstraat 10 (0597-430022). Sat.

This little town in Oost-Groningen is known primarily for its three mills: Berg, a corn and hulling mill from 1854; Dijkstra, which is 25 m (82 ft) in height and dates from 1862; and Edens, a corn and hulling mill from 1761. The interesting **Museum Stoomgemaal** contains a steam-powered pump from 1878 which was used to drain the flooded polderland.

Museum Stoomgemaal
Oostereinde 4. **Tel** 0597-425070. **Open** call for timings.

Environs

In Heiligerlee stands a monument to the Battle of Heiligerlee in 1568. This battle is famous for being over in just two hours and for the death of Count Adolf of Nassau. The **Museum "Slag bij Heiligerlee"** has an exhibition dedicated to the bloody battle.

Museum "Slag bij Heiligerlee"
Provincialeweg 55. **Tel** 0597-418199. **Open** Apr & Oct: Tue–Sun 1–5pm, May–Sep: Tue–Sat 10am–5pm, Sun 1pm–5pm. **Closed** public hols.

⓬ Veendam

Road Map E2. 28,500. 71, 73. Museumplein 5b (0598-364224). Mon am, Thu pm.

Parkstad Veendam (Veendam Garden City) is so called for the lush greenery in the town, which for centuries was the industrial heart of the peat colonies. However, at the end of the 19th century, peat-cutting fell into decline. Although shipping grew in importance – Veendam even had its own maritime school – the town retained its character as a peat-cutting centre.

The **Veenkoloniaal Museum** (peat colony museum) offers a permanent exhibition illustrating the history of peat-cutting, navigation, agriculture and industry in the Groningen peatlands.

The most renowned inhabitant of Veendam was Anthony Winkler Prins (1817–1908), who wrote the famous encyclopaedia which is still associated with his name.

Veenkoloniaal Museum
Museumplein 5. **Tel** 0598-364224. **Open** 11am–5pm Tue–Thu, 1–5pm Fri–Mon. **Closed** public hols.

⓭ Bourtange

Road Map E2. 600. 70, 72. Willem Lodewijkstraat 33 (0599-354600). **bourtange.nl**

Right at the German border is the magnificent fortified town of Bourtange, whose history dates back to 1580, when William of Orange ordered that a fortress with five bastions be built here on what had once been swampland. The defence works were continuously upgraded, until the fort gradually lost its defensive functions. It has now been painstakingly restored to its 18th-century appearance. **Museum "De Baracquen"** exhibits artifacts excavated in the fort.

The charming town itself lies within a star-shaped labyrinth of moats.

Aerial view of the impressive fortress of Bourtange

Museum "De Baracquen"
Willem Lodewijkstraat 33. **Tel** 0599-354600. **Open** Mid-Mar–Oct: 10am–5pm daily; Nov–mid-Mar: noon–5pm Sat & Sun. **Closed** 25 & 26 Dec.

⓮ Oude en Nieuwe Pekela

Road Map E2. 13,500. 75. Restaurant Het Turfschip/Flessings-terrein 3, Oude Pekela (0597-618833). Wed pm, Thu pm.

The "old" and "new" villages of Pekela are typical ribbon developments with a marked rural, peatland character. In the 18th century, potato flour and straw-board manufacture grew in importance in the region. There are pleasant footpaths along the main canal.

⓯ Ter Apel

Road Map E2. 7,800. 26, 70, 73. Hoofdstraat 49a (0599-581277). Thu.

In Ter Apel, situated in the Westerwolde region between Drenthe and Germany, is a 1465 **monastery** of the same name. In 1933, the monastery was thoroughly restored and now functions as a museum devoted to ecclesiastic art and religious history. The fragrant herb garden located in the cloisters contains a collection of nutrient-rich herbs such as birthwort and common rue.

Museum-klooster Ter Apel
Boslaan 3. **Tel** 0599-581370. **Open** 10am–5pm Tue–Sat, 1–5pm Sun & public hols. **Closed** 1 Jan, Mon (Nov–Mar).

The beautifully restored cloisters at the Ter Apel monastery

DE MAAN KOOMT OP
ZONS OP GANG

FRIESLAND

Friesland, or Fryslân as it is officially called, is a remarkable province perhaps best known outside the Netherlands for its distinctive Frisian cows. Parts of it are below sea level, and its size has increased since historic times as a result of land reclamation schemes on the former Zuiderzee.

Much of the province is fenland, whose myriad canals and channels no doubt helped the freedom-loving Frisians fight off invaders. The 1345 battle of Warns, when the Frisians beat the Dutch army, is still commemorated every year. In the 7th century, the Frisians under their king Radboud inhabited an independent territory that stretched all the way to Flanders and Cologne *(see pp48–9)*, and they have preserved their distinctive language to this day. Other features peculiar to this province are unique sports and recreations like sailing and racing in *skûtjes* (traditional Frisian boats), hunting for plovers' eggs, *fierljeppen* (pole-vaulting), *keatsen* (a ball game), and the famous *Elfstedentocht*, a winter ice-skating marathon around 11 Frisian towns.

The provincial capital of Leeuwarden has some interesting and unique museums, while elsewhere in the province visitors can enjoy collections consisting of items as diverse as historic costumes and hats, ceramics, letters, ice skates and sledges, vernacular paintings, bells, model boats and human mummies. Outside the towns, the landscape is interesting too, from the mud flats on the Waddenzee to the forests and heathland of the Drents-Friese Woud National Park, away to the east. Tourism is becoming increasingly important in Friesland nowadays and its inhabitants less insular. Visitors are greeted with open arms and *Jo binne tige welcom* – "You are heartily welcome."

Bartlehiem, the junction of the *Elfsteden* (11 towns) – a favourite summer destination for day-trippers

◀ Display showing the position of planets in the solar system, Eise Eisinga Planetarium in Friesland

Exploring Friesland

Friesland is famous for its vast meadows and its distinctive farmhouses of the *kop-hals-romp* and *stelp* types. It also boasts a varied landscape. In the southwest are the popular *Friese meren* (Frisian lakes), while the north is typified by undulating dykes, *terp* villages and church steeples with pitched roofs. Gaasterland in the south has rolling woodlands and cliffs, whereas the *Friese wouden* (Frisian woods) in the province's southeastern corner, with their forests, heathland and drifting sands, are more reminiscent of Drenthe.

The sea dyke at Wierum

Sights at a Glance

1. Leeuwarden
2. Dokkum
3. Franeker
4. Harlingen
5. Bolsward
6. Workum
7. Hindeloopen
8. Gaasterland
9. Sloten
10. Sneek
11. Thialfstadion
12. Oude Venen
13. Beetsterzwaag
14. Appelscha

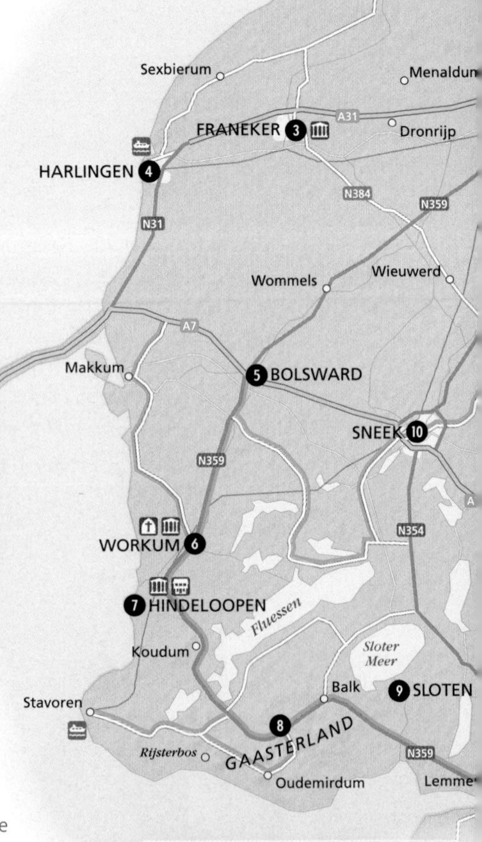

The Noorderhaven in Harlingen

Getting Around

Friesland is convenient and easy to get to. It is crossed by the A7 (east-west) and the A32 (north-south) motorways. Rail and bus links are unproblematic. Most of the larger villages and towns have a railway station; those which don't can be reached by bus. From Harlingen, Holwerd or Lauwersoog, the islands are only a short boat ride away. The province also has a good network of minor roads, walking routes and cycle tracks.

Gabled houses along Het Diep in Sloten

For map symbols *see back flap*

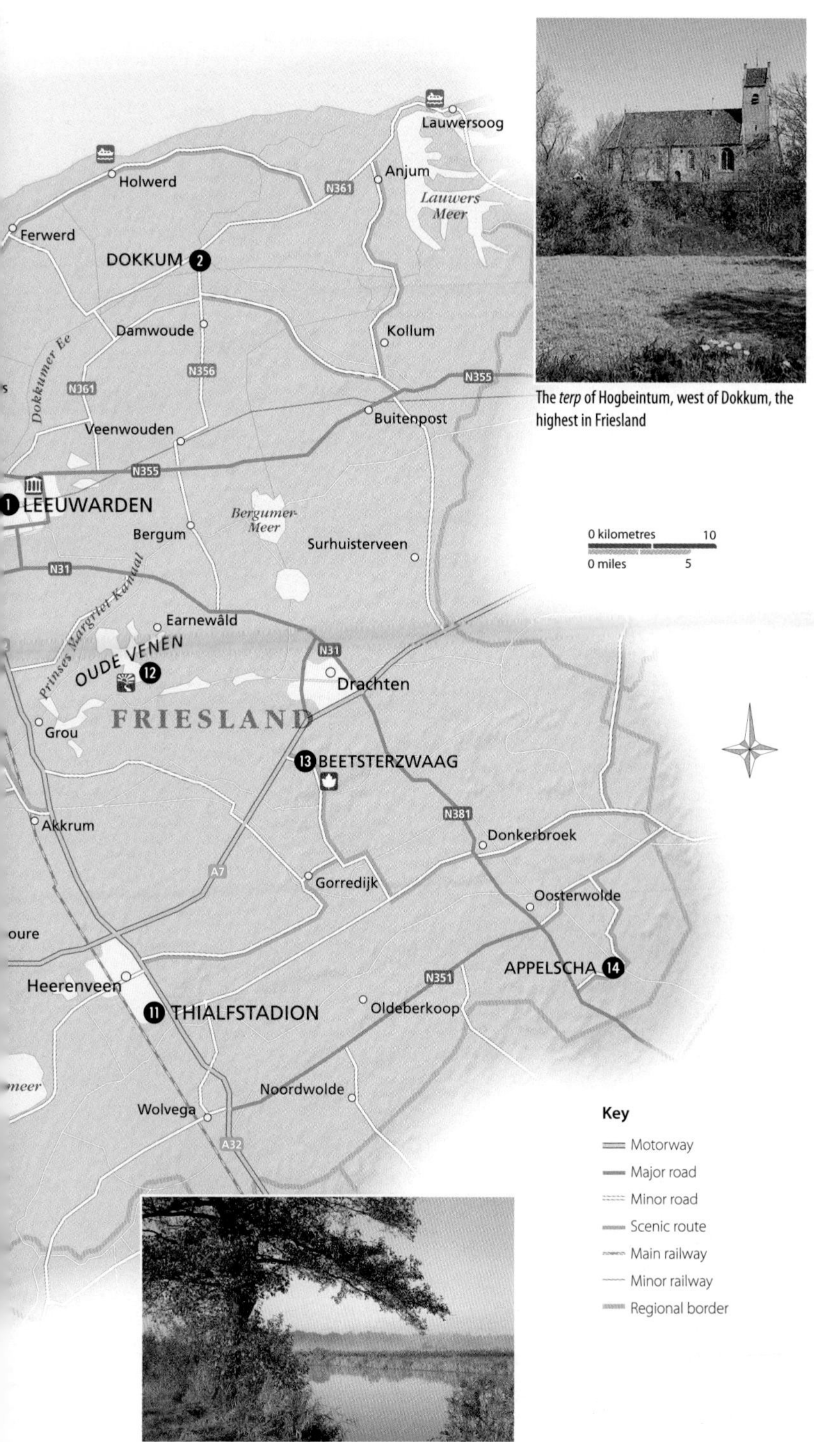

The *terp* of Hogbeintum, west of Dokkum, the highest in Friesland

Picturesque Lindevallei at Wolvega, near Thialfstadion

The Elfstedentocht

The Elfstedentocht, or 11-town race, is a 200-km (124-mile) ice-skating marathon which passes through Leeuwarden, Skeen, IJlst, Sloten, Stavoren, Hindeloopen, Workum, Bolsward, Harlingen, Franeker, Dokkum and back to Leeuwarden. Participants are awarded the famous Elfstedenkruisje only when they have collected all the stamps on their starter's card and provided they get back to Leeuwarden before midnight. The winner of the race is guaranteed local fame.

The "Elfstedenkruisje" (Elfsteden cross) is in the shape of a Maltese cross. In the middle is an enamel coat of arms of Friesland and the inscription "De Friesche Elf Steden" –"The 11 Frisian towns".

The Tocht Der Tochten

The Tocht der Tochten (literally, "Race of Races"), as the Elfstedentocht is known, is a combination of race and touring marathon and has acquired almost mythical status in the Netherlands. The race is a real media event, keeping millions glued to their television screens. Although the marathon has been held only 15 times in the last century, the entire country falls under the spell of the event as soon as the mercury falls even slightly below zero. If there is a lasting frost, the area supervisors measure daily the thickness of the ice, as it has to be at least 15 cm (6 in) thick for the race to be held. When the magic words *It sil heve* (It shall happen) are uttered by the supervisors, Friesland is transformed, overflowing with excited crowds. Trains are packed, the roads are jammed with cars and entire villages are mobilized to provide hot tea and oranges for the skaters. Wandering musicians whip the crowd into a frenzy of enthusiasm. The Dutch language has been enriched with the Frisian word *klúnen*, which means to walk overland on skates past places where the ice is impassable.

Franeker in a festive mood

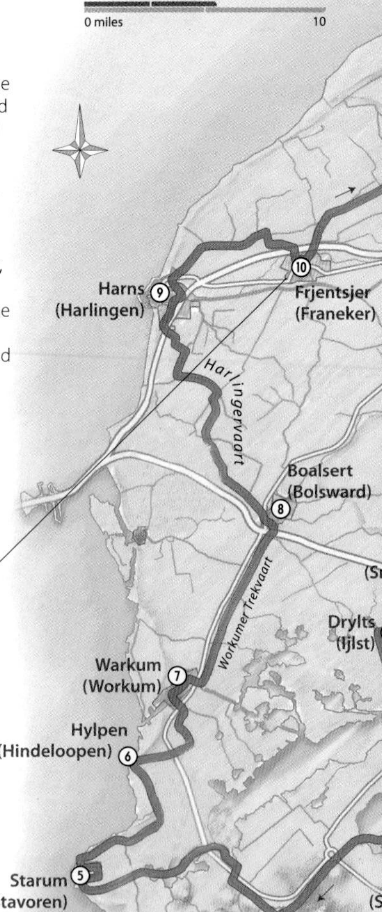

Dropping out is a common occurrence during the race. Despite being affected by snow blindness and symptoms of frostbite, many participants in the race attempt to complete the course. Some break down in tears when they realize that they will be unable to collect the much-coveted Elfstedenkruisje (Elfsteden cross).

The hamlet of Bartlehiem is famous for its footbridge over the Finkumervaart. Bartlehiem is the best-known skating area in all of Holland and is a psychological milestone for the skaters. Those who still must get to Dokkum may pass skaters travelling in the opposite direction, having already won their stamp from the northernmost point on the route. Many skaters have to take the Bartlehiem-Dokkum section in the dark. The Northern Lights seen at this time of year also attract thousands of spectators.

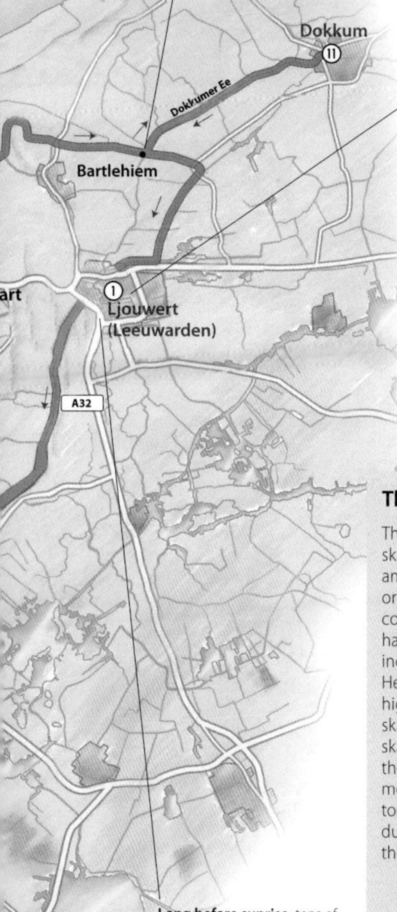

Two-time winner Evert van Benthem

All winners of the Elfstedentocht are national heroes, but Evert van Benthem even more so. A farmer from Sint- Jansklooster, he managed to cross the finishing line at the Bonkevaart in Leeuwarden in first place twice in a row (1985 and 1986). Van Benthem's double victory gave him a legendary status throughout the Netherlands. The prize itself is a laurel wreath, both for men and for women. The names of the winners are engraved on the Elfstedenrijder monument in Leeuwarden.

Long before sunrise, tens of thousands of skaters start off from the FEC (Frisian Exhibition Centre) in Leeuwarden.

The Eerste Friese Schaatsmuseum

The Eerste Friese Schaatsmuseum (first Frisian skating museum) in Hindeloopen *(see p302)* has among its exhibits such items as antique skates, original workshops, sleds and historical documents covering the 90 or so years that the Elfstedentocht has been held. Displays on innumerable winners, including Reinier Paping, Jeen van den Berg and Henk Angenet, are also featured here. Among the highlights of the museum's collection are the skating packs of various heroes of the event, the skates of two-time winner Evert van Benthem and the starter's card of WA van Buren. One of the most moving exhibits in the collection is the right big toe of Tinus Udding, which he lost to frostbite during the harsh race in the cold winter of 1963.

Willem-Alexander, alias WA van Buren, in the arms of his mother, Queen Beatrix, after the 1985 race

❶ Leeuwarden

Road Map D1. 89,000. Achmeatoren, Sophialaan 4 (0900-2024060). Fri & Sat.

Frisian capital and home to Mata Hari, Peter Jelles Troelstra and Jan Jacob Slauerhoff, Leeuwarden was also the residence of the Frisian Nassaus (1584–1747). The town park and gardens of the Prinsentuin and Stadhouderlijk Hof date back to this period.

Characteristic of Leeuwarden is the statue of **Us Mem** (our mother), honouring the famous Frisian cattle. The **Fries Museum**, situated in an 18th-century patrician house, has a large collection of items excavated from *terps*, as well as collections of clothes, art and applied arts. The same building also houses the **Verzetsmuseum Friesland**, a collection and educational facility dedicated to the Friesland resistance movement of World War II, in which more than 600 Jewish people were killed, and nearly 300 members of the resistance also lost their lives. There is a chronological exhibition on the Second World War and its aftermath, explorations of contemporary wars and racism, and documents and artifacts from the time.

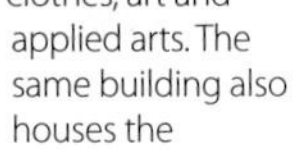

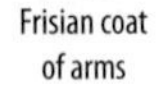

Frisian coat of arms

On Oldehoofsterkerkhof, the leaning tower of the **Oldehove** dominates the skyline. When building began in 1529, the church tower was going to be the tallest in the Netherlands. Unfortunately, the foundations began to sink, and so the work stopped just three years later. The tower has remained incomplete ever since. The top of the tower offers an excellent view over Leeuwarden and its environs, reaching as far as the coast.

The museum **Het Princessehof**, housed in a palace which was formerly the residence of Maria Louise van Hessen-Kassel (also known as Marijke Meu), contains a unique collection of ceramics of international importance. The artefacts include Asian, European and contemporary ceramics and tiles.

The old municipal orphanage is now home to the **Natuurmuseum Fryslân** (natural history museum), whose exhibition of "Friesland underwater" is well worth a visit.

Atmospheric Dokkum, a major port in the 8th century

Fries Museum
Wilhelminaplein 92. **Tel** 058-2555500.
Open 11am–5pm Tue–Sun.

Verzetsmuseum Friesland
Turfmarkt 1. **Tel** 058-2120111.
Open 11am–5pm Tue–Sun. **Closed** 1 Jan, 25 Dec.

Het Princessehof
Grote Kerkstraat 11. **Tel** 058-2948958.
Open 11am–5pm Tue–Sun. **Closed** 1 Jan, 30 Apr, 25 Dec.

Natuurmuseum Fryslân
Schoenmakersperk 2. **Tel** 058-2332244.
Open 11am–5pm Tue–Sun.

The leaning tower of the Oldehove (1529), still incomplete

❷ Dokkum

Road Map D1. 13,000. Op de Fetze 13 (0519-293800). Wed.

The trading and garrison town of Dokkum was the headquarters of the Frisian Admiralty between 1596 and 1645, though it owes its fame above all to the killing here of St Boniface by pagan Frisians in AD 754 *(see pp48–9)*. The local history museum, the **Admiraliteitshuis**, has an exhibition on the life of the saint. Other exhibits include artifacts excavated from *terps*, costumes, silverware, handicrafts and folk art. In addition to the **Bonifatiuskerk**, Dokkum has a park for religious processions with the stations of the cross and a chapel. Water drawn from the well of **Bonifatiusbron** is believed to have therapeutic qualities. Near the well is a statue of the saint after whom it is named. Saint Boniface was actually an Englishman, born in 675, who came to the region on a mission to convert the Frisians. Heathens attacked Boniface and his companions. Despite holding a bible in front of his face, Boniface was killed by a sword.

In the centre, **Natuurmuseum Dokkum** explores all aspects of the natural world in Friesland, both living and inanimate. There are cabinets of rocks, stones, shells and insects, and there is a "sound cabinet" that plays the songs of various birds from the area.

On the former **town walls**, now a park, are two

19th-century **stellingmolen**-type mills known as *De Hoop* and *Zeldenrust* *(see p29)*.

Admiraliteitshuis
Diepswal 27. **Tel** 0519-293134. **Open** Apr–Oct: 1–5pm Tue–Sat.
museumdokkum.nl

Natuurmuseum Dokkum
Kleine Oosterstraat 12. **Tel** 0519-297318. **Open** Oct–May: Sat & Suni; Jun–Sep: Mon–Sat. **Closed** public hols.

3 Franeker

Road Map C1. 13,000. Voorstraat 35 (058-2572590). Wed & Sat.

Franeker was a university town from 1585 to 1811. Today, it is the centre of skating in Friesland. In and around the Voorstraat are several monumental buildings, including the 15th-century Martenahuis. The Camminqahuis, which dates from the 14th century, now houses the **Kaats-museum** (skating museum). The **Museum Martena**, in a fine 18th-century building, has a collection about the former university. The Renaissance **Stad-huis** (town hall) has an ornate façade. Opposite is the **Planetarium Friesland** (1781), built by wool industrialist Eise Eisinga. For two centuries, the planets have rotated around its ceiling. Beside the Sjûkelân, a sacred place for Frisian skating, is the Bogt fen Guné (16th century), Holland's oldest student residence.

Eise Eisinga Planetarium

Kaatsmuseum
Voorstraat 2. **Tel** 0517-393910. **Open** 15 May–Sep: 1–5pm Tue–Sat.

Museum Martena
Voorstraat 35. **Tel** 0517-392192. **Open** 10am–5pm Tue–Fri, 1–5pm Sat & Sun.

Planetarium Friesland
Eise Eisingastraat 3. **Tel** 0517-393070. **Open** 10am–5pm Tue–Sat, 1–5pm Sun; also Apr–Oct: 1–5pm Mon.

4 Harlingen

Road Map C2. 14,500. Grote Bredeplaats 17b (0517-430207). Wed am, Sat.

The port town of Harlingen retains much of its old charm. The **Zoutsloot** and **Noorderhaven** have been painstakingly restored. A statue of **Hans Brinker** *(see p27)* stands at the ferry port. South of Harlingen is **Pingjum**. Menno Simons (1496–1561), the evangelical preacher after whom many of the Dutch Anabaptists named themselves, started his religious life here. Mennonites from all over the world now visit.

5 Bolsward

Road Map C2. 10,000. Wipstraat 6 (0515-577701). Thu.

Modest Bolsward first arose in the 11th century as a trading post, enjoying the height of its development in the 15th century. **Martinikerk**, a pseudo-basilica whose tower features a saddleback roof, was built during this period. The **Stadhuis** (town hall), with its local history museum, the **Oudheidkamer**, is the town's centrepiece.

Bolsward town hall

Local brews can be sampled at the **Us Heit Bierbrouwerij**, the smallest brewery in the country. A museum has displays of beer-making equipment while a guided tour shows how the beer is made. Attached to the brewery is a bar selling the house ales, with plenty available by the bottle to take away as souvenirs.

Oudheidkamer
Jongemastraat 2. **Tel** 0515-578787. **Open**Apr–Oct: 9am–noon & 2–4pm Mon–Thu.

Us Heit Bierbrouwerij
Snekerstraat 43. **Tel** 0515-577449. **Open** Mon, Tue, Thu–Sat (call ahead).

Mata Hari

Margaretha Geertruida Zelle (1876–1917), who became known to all the world as Mata Hari (Malaysian for "eye of the day"), grew up in Leeuwarden. Her life came to a tragic end in Vincennes outside Paris, where she was executed by a firing squad after a French tribunal found her guilty of spying for the Germans. The Fries Museum tells you more about this legendary woman, who has gained international notoriety through films and books about her life. The house where she lived with her parents from 1883 to 1890 on Grote Kerkstraat 212 now houses the Frysk Letterkundig Museum (Frisian museum of letters).

❻ Workum

Road Map C2. 4,000.
Merk 4 (0515-541045).

The elongated Zuiderzee town of Workum flourished around 1300. Workum is known for the fine façades of its houses and its unfinished 16th-century church, the **Grote of Gertrudiskerk**. Beside the lock is the centuries-old wharf of **de Hoop**, where traditional boats are still built. The most popular attraction in Workum is **Jopie Huisman Museum**, which is the most-visited museum in Friesland. It features the autodidactic art of painter and scrap metal merchant Jopie Huisman (1922–2000). His drawings and paintings tell the stories of the daily grind and poverty, the drudgery and toil of the tradesman, the housewife and the ordinary person.

The picturesque 17th-century weigh house contains the **Museum Warkums Erfskip**. This museum delves into the history of Workum, and, principally, that of its shipping and pottery industries.

Jopie Huisman Museum
Noard 6. **Tel** 0515-543131. **Open** Apr–Oct: 10am–5pm Mon–Sat, 1–5pm Sun; Mar & Nov: 1–5pm daily.

Museum Warkums Erfskip
Merk 4. **Tel** 0515-543155. **Open** Apr–Oct: 10am–5pm Mon–Sat, 1:30–5pm Sun; Nov–Dec & Mid-Feb–Mar: 1–5pm daily.

The Football Boots of Abe Lenstra by Jopie Huisman

A sea rescue centre with its inviting bench, in Hindeloopen

❼ Hindeloopen

Road Map C2. 850.
Nieuwstad 26 (0514-851223).

Hindeloopen plays a special role in Friesland. This picturesque old town of seafarers and fishermen has its own dialect, its own costume and its own style of painting. The town is full of little canals with wooden bridges and a variety of pretty captains' houses, with their characteristic façades. One of the most distinctive spots is the picturesque 17th-century lock-keeper's house by the port, with its wooden bell-tower.

In the **Museum Hidde Nijland Stichting** (museum of the Hidde Nijland foundation), the life of the wealthier citizens of Hindeloopen during the 18th century is showcased. Well-appointed period rooms show the colourful clothes and the now-famous painted furniture of the time. A substantial exhibition of paintings vividly illustrates the development of painting in Hindeloopen.

The **Eerste Friese Schaatsmuseum** (first Frisian skating museum) *(see p299)* offers a unique collection of old skates. It also has a fine exhibition dedicated to the Elfstedentocht and various traditional workshops (such as a smithy and a carpenter's), as well as a comprehensive collection of sledges and historical material such as old tiles and prints.

Museum Hidde Nijland Stichting
Dijkweg 1. **Tel** 0514-521420. **Open** Mar–Oct: 11am–5pm Mon–Fri, 1:30–5pm Sat, Sun & public hols.

Eerste Friese Schaatsmuseum
Kleine Weide 1–3. **Tel** 0514-521683. **Open** 10am–6pm Mon–Sat, 1–5pm Sun.

❽ Gaasterland

Road Map C2. De Brink 4, Oudemirdum (0514-571777).

This area of fine, rolling woodlands in the southwestern corner of Friesland offers many opportunities for walking and cycling. The region's name comes from the word "gaast", which refers to the sandy heights formed during the last two Ice Ages.

At the edge of Gaasterland are a number of steep cliffs, such as the **Rode Klif** and the **Oudemirdumerklif**, formed when the Zuiderzee eroded the coastline. On the Rode Klif at Laaxum is an enormous boulder bearing the inscription *Leaver dea as slaef*, or, *Rather dead than a slave*, a memento of the 1345 Frisian victory over the Dutch. The **Rijsterbos** wood, with its abundant bracken, dates from

A cyclist in Gaasterland

the 17th century and once consisted mainly of oak. The little river of Luts, which is now known because of the Elfstedentocht, was used for the transport of oak logs and oak bark for tanneries. In the village of **Oudemirdum** is a hostel, shops and an old pump. **Informatiecentrum Mar en Klif** (Sea and Cliff Information Centre) has information about how the landscape was formed and about local flora and fauna. Special attention is paid to badgers, and in the wild garden, a bat tower has been built.

The Luts river in **Balk**, flanked by linden trees, inspired the poem *Mei* by Herman Gorter (1864–1927).

Informatiecentrum Mar en Klif
De Brink 4, Oudemirdum. **Tel** 0514-571777. **Open** Apr–Oct: 10am–5pm Mon–Sat, 11am–5pm Sun.

9 Sloten

Road Map C2. 650.
Museum Stedhûs Sleat, Heerenwal 48 (0514-531541).

The smallest town in Friesland, replete with pretty canals, embankments and water-gates, was designed by famous Frisian military engineer Menno van Coehoorn. Built at a junction of roads and waterways, it was at the height of its development in the 17th and 18th centuries. On either side of the town are old cannons. The old fortress mill at the Lemsterpoort is an octagonal *bovenkruier*-type mill from 1755. The **Museum Stedhûs Sleat** houses the **Laterna Magica**, a museum of magic lanterns, an antique museum and a collection of costumes, hats, fans and bells.

Museum Stedhûs Sleat
Heerenwal 48. **Tel** 0514-531541. **Open** Apr–Oct 11am–5pm Tue–Fri, 1–5pm Sat & Sun.

10 Sneek

Road Map C2. 31,600.
Marktstraat 20 (0515-750678).
Tue am, Sat.

Sneek's centrepiece is the Waterpoort (water-gate) dating from 1613. Sneekweek is the name of a popular sailing event that in early August brings together amateur sailors and partygoers from all over the country. **Fries Scheepvaart Museum** focuses on the history of navigation and shipbuilding. Its exhibits include a *skûtje* deckhouse, the cabin of a *boeier* yacht and approximately 200 model ships. The *zilverzaal* (silver room) houses one of the richest collections of Frisian silver.

Typical stepped gables in Sloten, the smallest town in Friesland

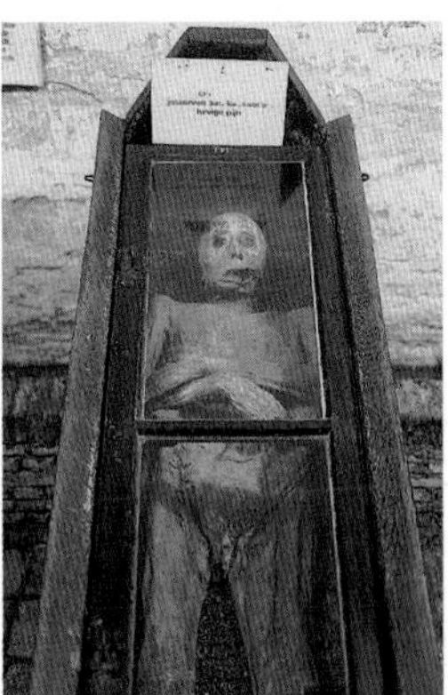
Mummy in Wieuwerd, a small village in Littenseradiel

Fries Scheepvaart Museum
Kleinzand 14. **Tel** 0515-414057. **Open** 10am–5pm Mon–Sat, noon–5pm Sun. **Closed** public hols. partly.

Environs

The village of **Wieuwerd**, north of Sneek, is known for the human mummies in its 13th-century St Nicholas church (open in summer). They were discovered by chance in 1765 and the reason for their mummification is not known.

Schuitje Sailing

Schuitje sailing, *or skûtsjesilen,* is a sport which has gained great popularity in the lakes of Friesland, *skûtje* being the name of the typical local spritsail barges. Originally used for the carriage of goods and as ferries, these boats are raced by representatives of various towns and villages. The result is a series of spectacular events held in July and August in various places, each time on a different lake and from a different base. Every day certain prizes are won, and on the last day, in Sneek, the champion of the year is announced and fêted. The races are held over the course of 11 racing days and three rest days.

⓫ The Thialfstadion

The Thialfstadion in Heerenveen, completely renovated in 2001, is regarded as the temple of Dutch ice-skating and has international renown. The exuberant crowds that converge on the stadium for international events create a unique atmosphere. Skating heroes such as Marianne Timmer, Gunda Niemann and Rintje Ritsma have all experienced emotional highlights in their sporting careers here.

VISITORS' CHECKLIST

Practical Information
Pim Mulierlaan 1, Heerenveen.
Tel 0513-637700/0900-2020026.
Open variable opening hours so visitors should phone ahead or check website for exact opening hours. **Closed** Apr–Sep.
thialf.nl

Transport
Heerenveen.

The Art of Ice-making

Making a good ice surface is an art. The Thialf ice-makers strive to strike a balance between deformation – the extent to which the ice breaks down under the pressure of the skate – and the smoothness of the ice.

Thialf Spectators
The fans here are famous for their colourful garb and their imaginative banners.

Underneath the ice are 70 km (43 miles) of cooling elements.

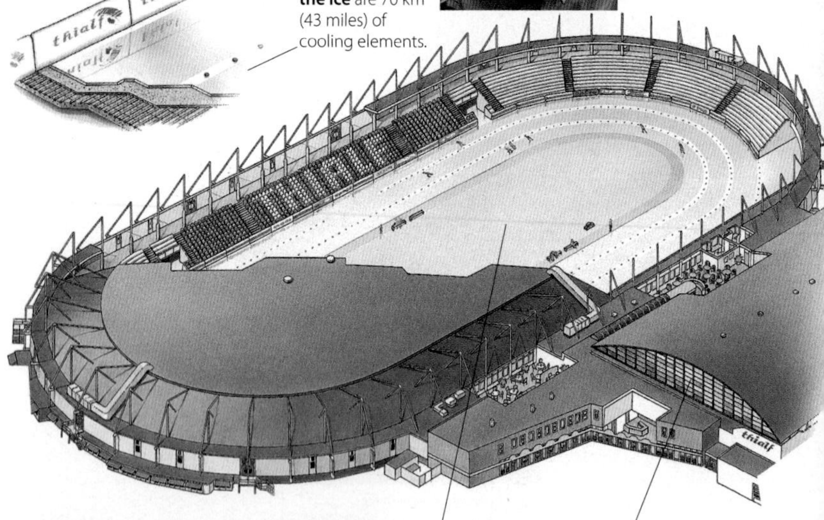

The great hall covers an area of 15,000 m^2 (17,950 sq yd) and can accommodate 13,000 spectators.

The ice hockey hall is 1,800 m^2 (2,150 sq yd) and has room for 4,000 spectators.

Triumph
The climax of every major skating event in the Thialfstadion is the procession of winners through the stadium on a special sleigh drawn by a Frisian horse.

Hinged Skates
Skates which have a hinge between the shoe and the blade give significantly better results. All new world records have been achieved with the help of *klapschaatsen* (hinged skates).

Stately Lauswolt, now a luxury hotel with a restaurant

⓬ Oude Venen

Road Map D2. 🚌 ℹ P Miedema-weg 9, Earnewâld (0511-539500).

This region, whose name literally means "the old fens", is a fine area of peat- marshes with reedlands, swampy woodlands and sunken polders between Earnewâld and Grou. The lakes

The swampy marshes of Oude Venen

were formed in the 17th and 18th centuries by peat-cutting and now offer a home to over 100 species of birds and approximately 400 plant species. There is a large colony of great cormorants and various rare birds such as the spotted crake, the purple heron, the white-fronted goose, the barnacle goose, the Eurasian wigeon and the ruff, all of which are best watched in spring.

In and around the water are water lilies, yellow water lily, marsh lousewort and cotton-grass. The area's hayfields are yellow with marsh marigold in spring.

Reidplûm visitors' centre of *It Fryske Gea* at Earnewâld provides information on the surrounding area and is a good starting point for hiking and sailing expeditions. Beside the centre is the Eibertshiem, a breeding centre for storks.

A great deal of attention has been paid to water cleanliness in the region, and now otters have returned to breed. In winter, the area hosts many skating tours.

Bezoekerscentrum De Reidplûm
Ds v.d. Veenweg 7, Earnewald.
Tel 0511-539410.
Open mid-Apr–Sep: 1–5pm daily.

⓭ Beetsterzwaag

Road Map D2. 3,700. 🚌
ℹ Hoofdstraat 67 (0512-381955).

This village was once one of the seats of the Frisian landed gentry and so has a number of stately homes and gardens. Fine examples of these are **Lauswolt,** the **Lycklamahuis** and the **Harinxmastate**. Beetsterzwaag is surrounded by a varied countryside, with coniferous and deciduous forests, heath and fens offering ample opportunities for a leisurely afternoon of rambling and cycling.

⓮ Appelscha

Road Map D2. 4,500. 🚌
ℹ Boerestreek 23 (0516-431760).

The vast coniferous forests, drifting sands and colourful heath and fen areas around Appelscha form stunning surroundings. The village was created in the 19th century when the main industry was peat-cutting and is now on the edge of the **Nationaal Park Drents-Friese Woud**.

A favourite place with visitors is the **Kale Duinen** area of drifting sands. On the Bosberg – at 26 m (85 ft) above sea level, the highest spot in the area – is a viewing tower and information centre.

A distinctive phenomenon in southeast Friesland is the **Klokkenstoel** (bell stool). This "poor men's church tower" was a provisional church tower built when funds were low; it was usually situated in the churchyard. In Appelscha you will find a *klokkenstoel* dating from 1453. Langedijke is home to what is presumed to be the oldest bell in the Netherlands, dating from 1300.

Environs
At Ravenswoud, 5 km (3 miles) northeast of Appelsche, an 18-m (59-ft) observation tower provides outstanding views.

Drifting sand dune near the small town of Appelscha

For hotels and restaurants in this region see p399 and p413

DRENTHE

Drenthe was once a free republic of farmers, and its inhabitants have always lived close to the land. Although the region has no cities and few towns, the rural poverty that once prevailed is no more, and tourists, especially those interested in archaeology and nature, are arriving in increasing numbers.

Drenthe, whose landscape is a product of the last Ice Age, has managed to keep time at bay by holding on to its character, reputed by the rest of the country to have been born of peat, gin and suspicion. Moraines and megaliths dot the countryside. The extensive woodland, heathland and peat bogs have a primeval atmosphere, although this does not mean that there has been no human intervention. The top level of peat has been largely removed, while the traditional *esdorps,* the local hamlets, have modern outskirts. However, peat moors and forests, ancient burial mounds, canals, flocks of sheep and green fields are the principal features here.

There are more than 50 megaliths in Drenthe, the remains of tombs dating from the Neolithic era; information about this period, with archaeological finds, is displayed in the museum at Borger. Other museums in the region feature glass blowing, artworks, natural history and paper-cutting. Orvelte boasts a fine open-air museum with Saxon farmhouses and traditional crafts, while Dwingeloo looks to the future at the Planetron observatory and planetarium.

Visitors come to Drenthe for peace and quiet after the rigours of city life. But this does not mean there are no facilities – local centres such as Assen, Emmen and Hoogeveen are urbanized areas that grew out of villages, and there is a variety of hotels, guesthouses and restaurants throughout the region.

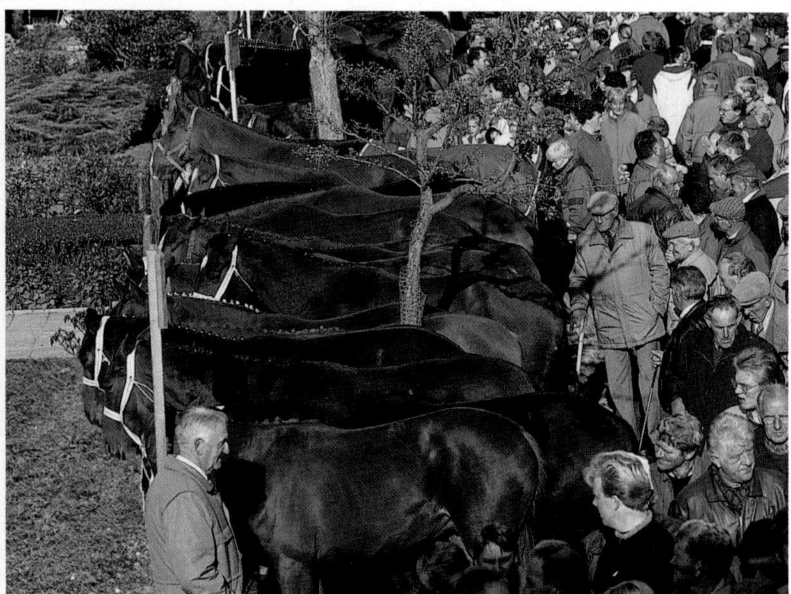

The largest horse market in western Europe, at Zuidlaren

◀ Papeloze Kerk, a megalith near Schoonoord in Drenthe

Exploring Drenthe

The finest natural areas of Drenthe are the Hondsrug ridge, between Zuidlaren and Emmen, and the Ellertsveld region between Assen and Emmen. The areas around Diever, Dwingeloo and Norg are a resplendent green (or purple, when the heather is in bloom). The eastern part of the region, with its endless excavated peatlands and the wilderness of the Amsterdamsche Veld, is relatively unknown. The provincial capital of Assen is also a regional centre, as is Emmen, where Noorder Dierenpark Zoo, in the middle of the town, has become one of the most-visited attractions in Holland. The megaliths are concentrated around Emmen, along the Hondsrug and at Havelte.

Sights at a Glance

2 Assen
3 Norg
4 Eelde-Paterswolde
5 Zuidlaren
6 Hondsrug
7 Rolde
8 Borger
9 Orvelte
10 Westerbork
11 Dwingeloo
12 Diever
13 Coevorden
14 Emmen

Tour

1 *The Megalith Route pp310–11*

The 14th-century Siepelkerk at Dwingeloo

The broad and silent heath

Thatcher at work in Havelte

Key

- Motorway
- Major road
- Minor road
- Scenic route
- Major railway
- Minor railway
- Regional border
- International border

For map symbols *see back flap*

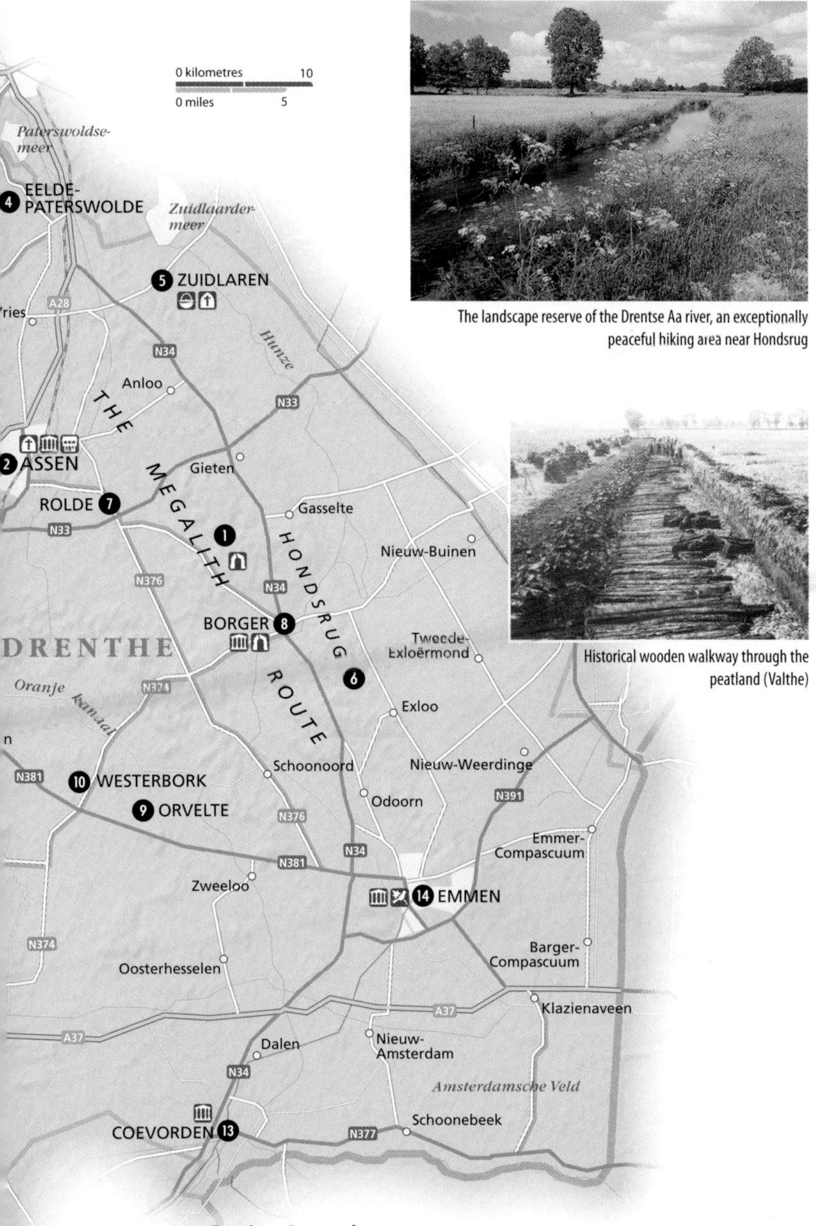

The landscape reserve of the Drentse Aa river, an exceptionally peaceful hiking area near Hondsrug

Historical wooden walkway through the peatland (Valthe)

Getting Around

Every year in July, Drenthe is the venue of the *Rijwielvierdaagse*, a four-day cycle tour that attracts more than 25,000 participants. There are 500 km (310 miles) of marked cycle routes in the region. The A28 motorway crosses the province through Meppel, Hoogeveen and Assen, and the railway follows the same route. Other motorways include the N371 from Meppel to Assen along the Drentse Hoofdvaart, the N37 Hoogeveen-Emmen and the N34 Emmen-Zuidlaren. Emmen is also the last stop on the railway to Zwolle via Coevorden. Bus service is limited, particularly in the evenings and on weekends.

❶ The Megalith Route

Of the 54 Megaliths in Holland, 52 are in Drenthe and the remaining two are in Groningen. These megaliths, or *hunebedden,* are the remains of ancient tombs built of boulders some 5,000 years ago by the Neolithic Beaker People. What can be seen today are only the frameworks of the tombs, which were all hidden underneath sandhills. It is still not known whether these were common graves or the tombs of prominent individuals.

At Diever and Havelte are three megaliths which are not on the route described here. The largest consists of 23 upright stones, 9 top stones, 2 keystones and a gate of 4 uprights and 2 top stones. At least 665 ancient pots have been found here. In World War II, the megalith was demolished to make way for an airfield. It was reconstructed in 1950.

⑨ **Megalith at Loon**
One of the best- preserved megaliths in Holland is at Loon, northeast of Assen. Before 1870 it was in even better condition, when the original top stone was still in place.

① **Witte Wieven** are ghosts that inhabit the tumuli, such as the Negen Bergen at Norg. They come out at midnight – particularly when it is misty – to dance.

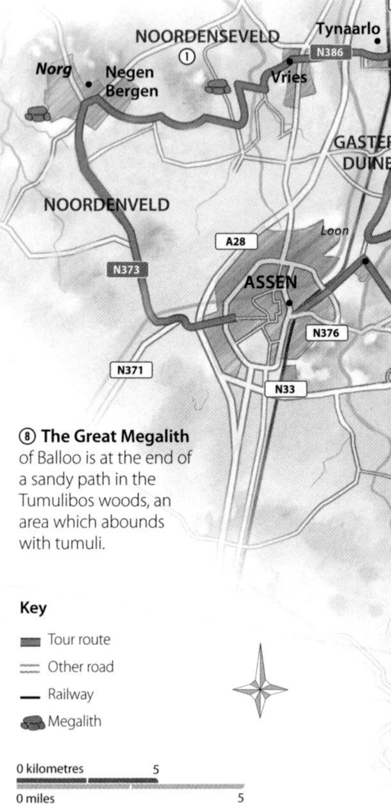

⑧ **The Great Megalith** of Balloo is at the end of a sandy path in the Tumulibos woods, an area which abounds with tumuli.

⑦ **De Zeven Marken,** the open-air museum of Schoonoord, tells you about such things as the legend of the giants Ellert and Brammert.

Building the Megaliths

Until the 19th century, it was believed that the megaliths were built by the *huynen,* giants of great strength and after whom the *hunebedden* are named. Modern historians believe that the boulders were placed with their flat edges on rollers, which thus allowed them to be moved to the site of the tomb. The upright stones were placed in pits dug beforehand. A gentle slope of earth was then made to allow the top stones to be dragged up. There is, however, no explanation of how the people of the Stone Age managed to organize such large-scale projects.

17th-century depiction of megalith builders

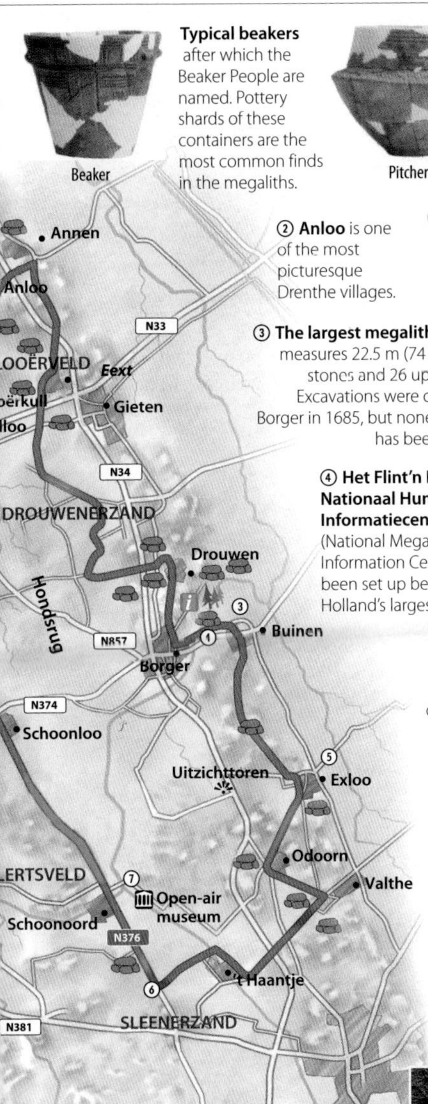

Typical beakers after which the Beaker People are named. Pottery shards of these containers are the most common finds in the megaliths.

② **Anloo** is one of the most picturesque Drenthe villages.

Tips for Drivers

Length: 95 km (60 miles)
Stopping-off places: All villages on the route offer refreshments and meals. To see most megaliths you will need to leave your car and walk, as only a few are by the roadside. They are almost invariably well sign-posted and make excellent picnic spots.

③ **The largest megalith in Holland** measures 22.5 m (74 ft), has 9 top stones and 26 upright stones. Excavations were carried out in Borger in 1685, but none of the finds has been preserved.

④ **Het Flint'n Hoes, the Nationaal Hunebedden Informatiecentrum**, (National Megalith Information Centre), has been set up beside Holland's largest megalith.

⑤ **The Exloo Necklace** was found in the peat in 1881. It is made of beads of tin, faience, bronze and amber, which is evidence of trading links between prehistoric Drenthe and the Baltic countries, Cornwall and even Egypt.

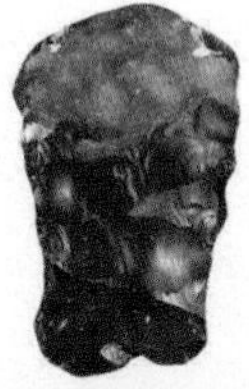

Flint was the main material used by the hunter-gatherers of prehistoric Drenthe to make such items as knives, axes, scrapers and arrowheads.

Megaliths (hunebedden)

There are no longer any complete megaliths. Until 1734, when trading in boulders was forbidden, thousands of megaliths were hacked up to be used as building material. There are definite traces of 88 megaliths, 82 of them in Drenthe. The 54 surviving megaliths are all restorations. The most common finds from excavations are pottery shards. Scrapers, axes, arrowheads, and amber and copper jewellery – all extremely valuable trading goods in Drenthe in 3000 BC – are much rarer finds.

⑥ **De Papeloze Kerk** (the Popeless Church)
This megalith is so called because of the Calvinist sermons that were held here in the early 16th century against the "popish" (Catholic) faith. In 1959, the megalith was restored to its original state, to the extent of covering half of the tomb with sand.

❷ Assen

Road Map D2. 61,500.
Marktstraat 8 (0592 243788).
Wed, Sat.

Assen is the capital of Drenthe, although it was only upgraded from a village to a town in 1809. The **cloister** of the abbey church of Maria in Campis (1258–1600) now forms part of the Rijksarchief (national archive) on the Brink. Also on the Brink is the **Drents Museum** of local history, which is housed in the abbey church, the Ontvangershuis (1698), the Drostenhuis (1778) and Provinciehuis (1885). The museum contains a wealth of exhibits on prehistoric times and the town's history as well as collections of local art and a "discovery room" for children. There are also collections of local art, including works by Bernard Von Dülmen-Krumpelmann (1897–1987).

The controversial finds of Tjerk Vermaning (1929–87), who in the 1960s extended the history of human habitation in Holland by tens of thousands of years, are in a separate display case: disputes on the authenticity of the flint tools he found have not yet been resolved.

Bartje

Outside the formal gardens of the Drostenhuis is the town's trademark **Bartje**, a statue of the little peasant boy from Dutch author Anne de Vries' book (1935) who did not want to pray before his daily meals of brown beans. The Vaart and the Markt have the characteristic stately white houses of Assen, which were built in the late 18th to the early 19th century.

Between Markt and Brink is the commer-cial centre with its pedestrian precinct and excellent facilities. Modern-day Assen comes to life when the **circuit van Assen** TT motorcycle racing event is held here each year on the last Saturday in June. Around 100,000 spectators descend on the town, which is home to the only remaining circuit from the championship's inaugural season in 1949. Younger children who have gained a taste for speed and bikes at the TT circuit will enjoy a visit to **Verkeerspark Assen** *(see p435)*. This is a "traffic park" for children, where they can learn the rules of the road while driving miniature cars and scooters around an artificial town, complete with traffic lights, road signs and traffic police. Older children can use quad bikes and go-karts. Other attractions include a boating lake, mini-golf and a climbing tower.

The 13th-century Romanesque church on the Brink of Norg

Drents Museum
Brink 1–5. **Tel** 0592-37773.
Open 11 am–5pm Tue–Sun (Mon on public hols). **Closed** 1 Jan, 25 Dec.

Verkeerspark Assen
De Haar 1–1a. **Tel** 0592-350005.
Open Apr: days vary; May–Aug: daily; Sep & Oct: days vary. **Closed** 29 Nov–Mar. **verkeersparkassen.nl**

Children Bathing in a Stream (c.1935) by Von Dülmen-Krumpelmann

❸ Norg

Road Map D2. 3,500. Brink 1 (0592-613128). Wed.

The Romanesque church on the Brink dates from the 13th century. The unique frescoes in the choir have barely survived through the centuries and are in very poor condition.

Environs

The area around Norg is steeped in prehistory. Three megalithic tombs are to be found there, while in the Noorderveld are Bronze Age tumuli (the **Negen Bergen**). Norgerholt is the name given to the oak woods where the local people used to assemble during the Middle Ages.

❹ Eelde-Paterswolde

Road Map D2. 10,500. 52. B Boermalaan 4 (050-3092136). Wed.

Two villages merge together at Eelde-Paterswolde and are squeezed between the **Paterswoldse Meer** lake and **Groningen Airport**, which despite its name is in Drenthe not Groningen. The lake is popular among water sports enthusiasts. The airport serves mainly domestic flights (it is a half-hour flight to Schiphol) and flying enthusiasts.

The distinctive modern brick building housing the **Museum De Buitenplaats** (De Buitenplaats museum of figurative art) was designed by the architects Alberts and Van Huut. It is a fine example of their organic architecture. In addition to hosting changing exhibitions, the museum is used as a concert hall. There are also formal and landscape gardens, the former fronting the 17th-century curator's residence, the **Nijsinghuis**. Since 1983 the house has been painted by figurative artists and is periodically opened to visitors by arrangement.

The Eelde part of town is home to the **Internationaal Klompenmuseum (Gebroeders, Wietzes)**. Named in honour of the last two clog-makers to live in the village, the museum gives an overview of the development of the clog. It displays examples of clogs from around the world. Most visitors, however, come to see the world's largest clog, which is 6.5 m (21 ft) long.

Dense woodland in the Hondsrug area

Museum De Buitenplaats
Hoofdweg 76. **Tel** 050-3095818.
Open 11am–5pm Tue–Sun, Easter Sun & Easter Mon. **Closed** 1 Jan, 25 Dec.

Klompenmuseum Gebroeders Wietzes
Wolfhorn 1a. **Tel** 050-3091181.
Open 1 Apr–1 Oct: Tue–Sun 2–5pm.

❺ Zuidlaren

Road Map E2. 10,000. Stationsweg 69 (050-4092333). Fri.

The colourful Zuidlaren **horse market**, now the largest in Western Europe, predates even the 13th-century church which stands on the Brink. The market is held in April and October. The 17th-century **Havezathe Laarwoud** was built on the remnants of the fortified residence of the counts of Heiden, who ruled the region in the 14th century. Today it is the town hall. The **Zuidlaardermeer** lake offers everything that watersports enthusiasts may require. Children will especially enjoy the subtropical swimming complex of Aqualaren as well as De Sprookjeshof recreation centre with playpark; they can be combined on a round tour.

Colourfully decorated Klompenmuseum Gebroeders Wietzes

❻ Hondsrug

Road Map E2. VVVs in Zuidlaren (050-4092333), Rolde, Gieten, Exloo (0591-549515), Borger, SchoonoOrd (0591-381242) or Emmen.

Between the Drentse sand plateau in the west and the Drents-Groningen peat moors in the east lies the Hondsrug ridge. Prehistoric people found it a safe place to settle, and it is the area where the megaliths now stand *(see pp306–7)*.

The Drentse Aa river basin, the old villages of Gieten, Gasselte, Exloo and Odoorn, the drifting sand areas of the Drouwenerzand and the heathland of Ellertsveld are particularly attractive hiking areas, with plenty of streams in which to cool off.

In the centre of Eexloo, the **Bebinghehoes** is a cultural museum in a beautiful 18th-century, thatched farmhouse. The house itself gives an impression of farming life 200 years ago, while the coach house presents a display of carriages from the age of horse-drawn transport. There is also a children's farm, with goats, sheep, chickens and ducks, and a petting area.

Bebinghehoes
Zuiderhoofdstraat 6. **Tel** 0591-549242.
Open 1 Apr–1 May: Wed–Sat; May, Jun & Sep: Tue–Sat; Jul & Aug: daily.

7 Rolde

Road Map E2. 6,200.
Onder de Molen, Grote Brink 22 (0592-241502).

Rolde was important for a considerable time. There are prehistoric tumuli (in the **Tumulibos** woods), and three megaliths, two of which are on the mound directly behind the church. During the Middle Ages, people were tried at the **Ballooërkuil**; if guilty they were held prisoner in the 15th-century church, a magnificent Gothic edifice. Forests, peatland and drifting sands surround the village. Sheep graze on the Ballooërveld.

8 Borger

Road Map E2. 4,700. 59.
Grote Brink 2a (0599-234855). Tue.

Borger is the capital of the *hunebeddengebeid,* or megalith region. There are eight megaliths in and around the town, including the largest in Holland. Nearby is the **Nationaal Hunebedden Informatiecentrum** ('t Flint'n Hoes), with a fine exhibition about the Beaker People and a stone casket from the most recently excavated megalith, which was discovered in 1982 in Groningen.

Nationaal Hunebedden Informatiecentrum
Bronnegerstraat 12. **Tel** 0599-236374.
Open daily. **Closed** 1 Jan, 25 Dec.

Environs
Drents Boomkroonpad (tree-top walk), 2 km (1 mile) down the "Staatsbossen" turn-off on the Rolde-Borger road, is an

Boomkroonpad's tree-top walkway, a well-known tourist attraction

interesting attraction. The walk starts at the roots, with a 23-m (75-ft) tunnel. This leads into a 125-m (410-ft) ascent to a height of 22.5 m (74 ft), affording a fascinating view of the forest.

Drents Boomkroonpad
Bezoekerscentrum, Drents Boomkroonpad, Steenhopenweg 4, Drouwen. **Tel** 0592-377305.
Open daily. **Closed** 1 Jan.

9 Orvelte

Road Map E2. 90. 22, 23.
Dorpsstraat 1a (0593-322335).

The whole of Orvelte is in effect an open-air museum. In the restored Saxon farmhouses from the early 19th century, there are exhibits on agriculture and displays of traditional crafts. Cars are banned from the area, but tours in horse-drawn trams or covered waggons are offered. The more interesting attractions of the town include a tinsmith's shop.

Bezoekerscentrum
Dorpsstraat 3. **Tel** 0593-322335.
Open Apr–Oct daily. 

Farmers at work in the Orvelte open-air museum

10 Westerbork

Road Map E2. 8,000. 22.
BG van Wezelplein 10 (0593-331381).

The Hoofdstraat (main street) features a Late Gothic 14th-century church, which now houses the **Museum voor Papierknipkunst** (paper-cutting museum) and Saxon farmhouses which bear witness to a prosperous past. However, Westerbork is visited primarily for its more recent history. In World War II, the Westerbork Transit Camp stood here. It was from this camp that 107,000 Jews, Gypsies and resistance fighters were held before deportation to the Nazi concentration camps. Anne Frank *(see pp112–13)* was one of its inmates.

Herinneringscentrum Kamp Westerbork
Oosthalen 8, Hooghalen.
Tel 0593-592600. **Open** daily.

11 Dwingeloo

Road Map: D2. 1,800. 20.
Brink 4b (0521 - 591000). Tue.

The first thing that strikes visitors about Dwingeloo is the onion dome of the 14th-century church tower (the **Siepelkerk**). You can read about the legend behind this oddity on the information board located nearby.

There is some impressive countryside around the town. The **Dwingelderveld** is a national park and the **krentenbossen** (currant plantations) which flower in April and May – the fruit ripening in July or August – are delightful in every respect: they are pleasant to the eye and to the taste buds. At the edge of the Dwingelose Heide heath is a radio-telescope.

The interesting and child-friendly **Planetron** nearby is an observatory where there is a planetarium as well as an electronic games area.

Planetron
Drift 11b. **Tel** 0521-593535. **Open** daily during school hols. **Closed** 1 Jan, Mon outside school hols.

⓬ Diever

Road Map D2. 3,700. 20.
Bosweg 2a (0521-591748).

Diever was an important centre from prehistoric times to the Middle Ages. Tumuli, megaliths and remains of the 9th-century wooden foundations of the village church lend it historical importance. The church features a 12th-century Romanesque tower of tufa stone. Diever is in the middle of the **Nationaal Park Het Drents-Friese Woud**: the town is now synonymous with cycling and rambling.

In summer, the **Shakespeare-markten** (Shakespeare fair) is held during performances of the playwright's works in the open-air theatre.

Environs

In **Vledder**, 10 km (6 miles) west of Diever, is a **museum** of graphic art and glass-blowing and art forgery.

Museum voor Valse Kunst/ Museum voor Hedendaagse Grafiek/ Museum voor Glaskunst
Brink 1, Vledder. **Tel** 0521-383352. **Open** Apr–Oct: 11am–4pm Wed–Sun, Nov–Dec 11am–4pm Sat & Sun.

Lime kilns at in the village of Diever

⓭ Coevorden

Road Map E3. 34,000.
Kerkstraat 2 (0524-525150).
Mon.

The castle here dates from around 1200. The star-shaped moat and surviving bastions and town walls define the look of the town, while the façades of the Friesestraat and Weeshuisstraat are telling of past centuries. **Stedelijk Museum Drenthe's Veste** highlights the town's history.

Stedelijk Museum Drenthe's Veste
Haven 6. **Tel** 0524-516225.
Open 9:30–5pm Tue–Sat, noon–5pm Sun.

Brown bears in the popular Noorder Dierenpark in Emmen

⓮ Emmen

Road Map E2. 105,000.
Hoofdstraat 22 (0591 649712).
Fri am.

A modern town, Emmen is the result of the amalgamation of several former villages. Eleven megaliths, including **Langgraf op de Schimmer Es** or long barrow on the Schimmer Es, the urn-fields *(see p43)* and prehistoric farmland (the **Celtic Fields**) in the vicinity and the 12th-century tower on the Hoofdstraat reflect the district's history. At **Noorder Dierenpark**, animals roam freely. The Biochron museum and Vlindertuin butterfly gardens are also here.

Noorder Dierenpark
Hoofdstraat 18. **Tel** 0591-850855.
Open daily.
dierenparkemmen.nl

Environs

Roughly 10 km (6 miles) east of Emmen are the **Amsterdamsche Veld** upland peat marshes, perhaps the loneliest place in Holland. In Barger-Compascuum, **Veenpark** re-creates the times when the people of Drenthe lived in poverty, cutting peat. In 1883, Vincent van Gogh stayed at the Scholte ferry-house in Veenoord (Nieuw-Amsterdam). At the **Van Gogh House**, his room on the first floor has been restored to the way it was in 1883, as has the café-restaurant below.

Veenpark
Berkenrode 4, Barger-Compascuum.
Tel 0591-324444. **Open** Apr–Nov: 10am–5pm daily.

Van Gogh Huis
Van Goghstraat 1, Nieuw-Amsterdam.
Tel 0591-555600. **Open** 1–5pm Tue–Sun.

Van Gogh's *Peat Boat with Two Figures* (1883) in Drents Museum, Assen

12
15
30
30
4

OVERIJSSEL

Overijssel, a province in the east of Holland, has many areas of natural beauty and lovely old towns. In a sense it is a province of two halves, divided by the heathland and woods of the Sallandse Heuvelrug near Nijverdal, which separate the eastern district of Twente from the rest of the province.

This division is noticeable in many ways. The two halves differ in their spoken dialect, and they each have their own cultural traditions. There are also religious differences, with Twente being mainly Catholic while the rest of the province is strictly Protestant. Twente, with its larger towns, has a more modern appearance, and Enschede, for example, is livelier than western towns like Zwolle and Deventer.

Zwolle, however, is the capital of the province, a charming town dating back to the 13th century, when its port at a busy river junction led it to join the powerful Hanseatic League, growing rich from trade with England and the Baltic. Kampen and Deventer, on the IJssel river, were later members of the same league.

Overijssel's numerous unique museums and attractions highlight local history and printing, tobacco, salt and farmhouses, as well as traditional costumes, tin soldiers, Dutch painting and modern art. For children, the Hellendoorn adventure park *(see p426)*, the Los Hoes open-air museum and Ecodrome Park are always popular.

Apart from these activities, however, the principal attraction in Overijssel is the countryside, which is ideal for walking, hiking and touring by bicycle. In places like Giethoorn you can tour the rivers, lakes and canals by boat, while the Weerribben wetlands in the northwest offer opportunities for nature rambles and watersports.

Open-air dining at a restaurant in the historic town of Zwolle in Overijssel

◀ Blue boats line a canal in the village of Giethoorn, Overijssel

Exploring Overijssel

The impressive historical monuments of Deventer and Kampen recall their prosperous pasts as Hanseatic cities. However, Overijssel has plenty to offer those who are interested in more than splendid old buildings. Those who enjoy peace and natural surroundings will find some of the finest spots in Holland. The peaceful countryside of the Sallandse Heuvelrug is ideal for rambling, while De Weerribben is suitable for yachting. There are many picturesque spots, such as Ootmarsum, Delden and Giethoorn, and children will love the amusement part at Hellendoorn *(see p426)*. In addition to this, Overijssel also has many interesting museums, such as the national tin figure museum in Ommen.

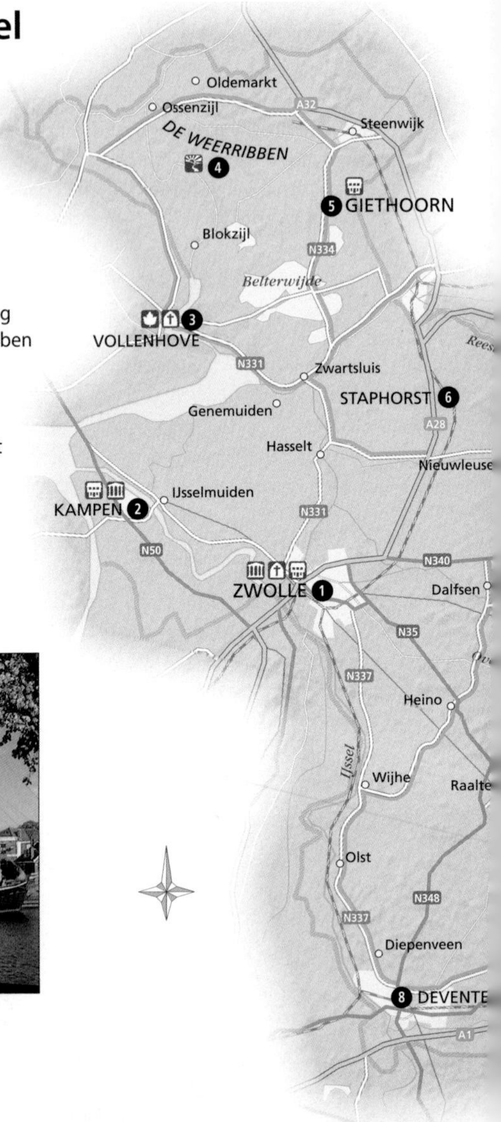

The quiet port of Blokzijl near Vollenhove

Overijssel at a Glance

1. Zwolle
2. Kampen
3. Vollenhove
4. De Weerribben
5. *Giethoorn pp322–3*
6. Staphorst
7. Ommen
8. Deventer
9. Nijverdal
10. Delden
11. Enschede
12. Ootmarsum

The IJssel north of the old Hanseatic city of Deventer

For map symbols *see back flap*

Getting Around

Overijssel can be explored easily by car, bicycle or on foot. Large parts of the region are also well connected by public transport. Note, however, that bus timetables are sketchier on weekends than on weekdays. Areas of natural beauty such as De Weerribben, for example, are not easy to reach by public transport on weekends. In some places, too, buses operate only during the daytime.

Key

- Motorway
- Major road
- Minor road
- Scenic route
- Major railway
- Minor railway
- Regional border
- International border

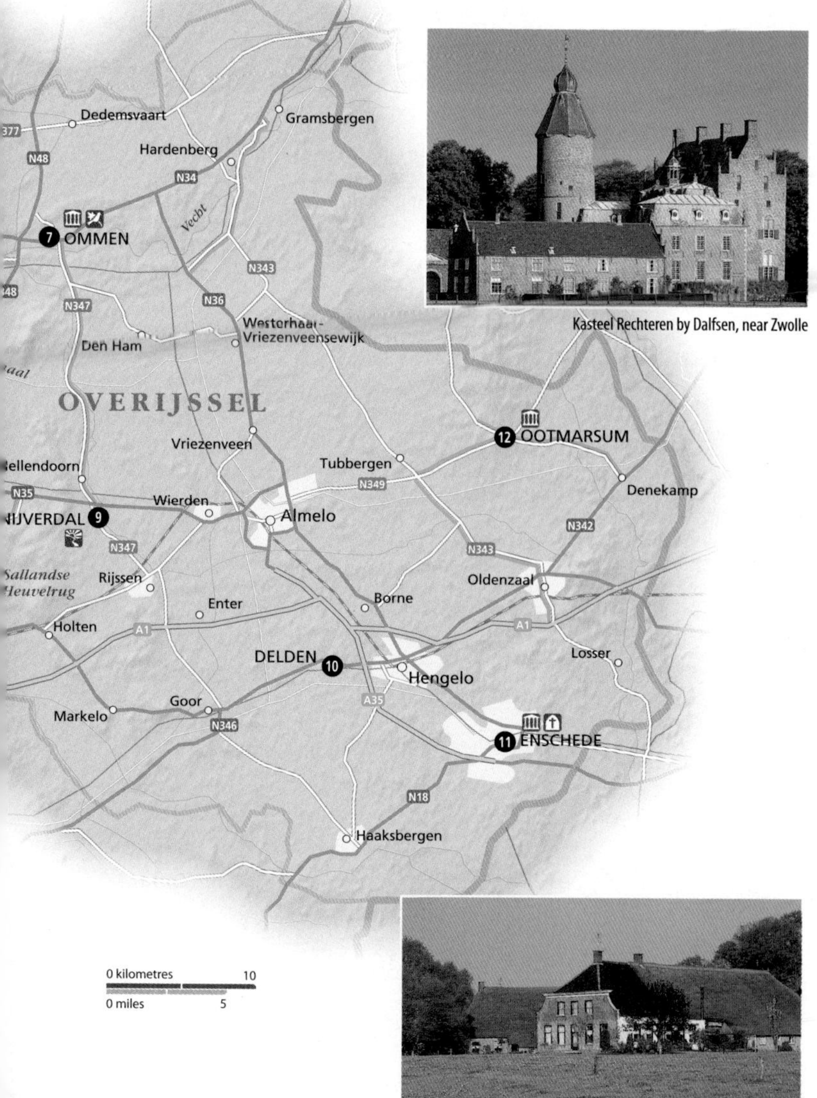

Kasteel Rechteren by Dalfsen, near Zwolle

Farmhouse by the river Reest, separating Drenthe from Overijssel

❶ Zwolle

Road Map D3. 107,000. Grote Kerkplein 15 (0900-1122375). Fri (cattle market), Sat.

View of Zwolle during the Hanseatic Period (anonymous, c.14th century)

In the middle ages, Zwolle, capital of the province of Overijssel, was, along with towns such as Deventer, Kampen and Zutphen, a city of the Hanseatic League, a network of trading cities. Its past is evident in the relatively large historical centre. The finest buildings in Zwolle, which was granted its city charter in 1230, are largely to be found in the area that used to fall within the city fortifications, which can still be seen in the form of a moat. However, only a few dozen metres of these ancient fortifications are left standing, along with the fine Sassenpoort gate, dating from 1406, and the Late Gothic 15th-century Pelsertoren tower.

On one side of the Grote Kerkplein is a sculpture by Rodin entitled *Adam*, while on the Grote Markt stands the magnificent building of the Hoofdwacht (guard house), which dates from 1614.

The **Grote Kerk**, also known as **St Michaelskerk**, is worth a visit as well. The original Romanesque church, built in 1040, was enlarged in 1370 and again in 1452 to become the present-day three-naved Gothic church.

The most recent addition to Zwolle's cultural landscape is the **Paleis aan de Blijmarkt**, a contemporary art museum that opened in 2005. Housed in a grand Neo-Classical building dating from 1838, the renovated light-filled galleries hold works by the likes of Van Gogh, Picasso and Mondrian.

The **Stedelijk Museum Zwolle** (Zwolle local history museum) features, among its other interesting exhibits on local history, an 18th-century kitchen and a Renaissance room from Blokzijl. The fine façade of the old part of the building, which dates from 1741, is impressive.

The town is also home to the **Ecodrome Park**, which is dedicated to the natural environment in the past, present and future.

Stedelijk Museum Zwolle
Melkmarkt 41. **Tel** 038-4214650. **Open** 11am–5pm Tue–Sun. **Closed** public hols.

Ecodrome Park
Willemsvaart 19. **Tel** 038-4237030. **Open** Nov–Mar: 10am–5pm Wed, Sat & Sun; Apr–Oct: 10am–5pm daily.

Paleis aan de Blijmarkt
Blijmarkt 20. **Tel** 0572-388188. **Open** 11am–5pm Tue–Sun.

Environs

The Kunstwegen (Art Paths) are outdoor sculpture installations on the country estate of **Landgoed Anningahof**. The five-hectare open-air sculpture park was the brainchild of art collector Hib Anninga and contains dozens of works, from bright blue ceramic dogs to giant iron hoops, by around 80 contemporary Dutch sculptors. The work is spread throughout meadows and landscaped gardens, and exploring them makes for a pleasant afternoon's stroll.

Landgoed Anningahof
Hessenweg 9. **Tel** 038-4534412. **Open** May–Oct: Wed–Sun.

The grand Neo-Classical façade of the Paleis aan de Blijmarkt

❷ Kampen

Road Map D3. 48,000. Oudestraat 41 (038-3313500). Mon am.

Kampen, known for its theological university where Protestant theologians are educated, is a pleasant and lively town containing 500 historic buildings. The beauty of this former Hanseatic city is immediately apparent from the IJssel riverfront. The fact that the town used to be well fortified is evident from the three remaining town gates: the Koornmanspoort, the Broederpoort and the Cellebroederspoort. The area inside the old fortifications

For hotels and restaurants in this region see p400 and pp413–414

The waterfront of the magnificent, well-preserved Hanseatic city of Kampen on the river IJssel

features the magnificent Dutch Reformed church St Nicolaaskerk, and the Gotische Huis, which now houses the **Stedelijk Museum Kampen**, the town's local history museum. Particularly noteworthy is the old town hall, or Oude Raadhuis, with a façade decorated with fine sculptures.

Kampen, which is first mentioned in documents in 1227, is also famed for its cigars, which explains why the **Kamper Tabaksmuseum** (Kampen tobacco museum) is located here. A rather more surprising find is the **Ikonenmuseum**, a collection of religious icons and the only museum of its kind in the Netherlands. The museum is housed in a former cloister, and is home to 150 mainly Russian and Greek Orthodox painted icons, spanning the 16th to 19th centuries. It also hosts temporary exhibitions.

Kampen was at the height of its development between 1330 and 1450. It revived its fortunes only when the Flevoland and Noordoostpolder regions were reclaimed and it acquired the function of regional centre. However, Kampen was never a mighty city because it did not have any powerful ruler. Kampen did not apply to join the Hanseatic League until relatively late – 1440. At that time, the Netherlands was involved in a war with the Hanseatic League, and Kampen joined the powerful league for the sake of security.

Stedelijk Museum Kampen
Oude Straat 133. **Tel** 038-3317361. **Open** 11am–5pm Tue–Sat.

Kamper Tabaksmuseum
Botermarkt 3. **Tel** 038-3315868. **Open** by appointment only.

Ikonenmuseum
Buitennieuwstraat 2. **Tel** 038-3858483. **Open** 1 Apr–1 Nov: Tue–Sat; 1 Jun–1 Sep: daily.

Religious image at the Ikonenmuseum

Environs

Five km (3 miles) south of the town, in Kamperveen, is the **Hertenhouderij Edelveen**, a working deer farm that welcomes visitors. The owners give guided tours of their farmland, explaining their jobs and allowing visitors to see their herds close up. The farmers also sell venison, paté and sausages.

Hertenhouderij
Edelveen: Leidijk 10a. **Tel** 0525-621564. **Open** by appointment only.

3 Vollenhove

Road Map D2. 71, 171. Aan Zee 2–4 (0900-5674637). Tue.

Vollenhove is a picturesque place which was once known as the town of palaces due to the many nobles who lived here. The aristocratic residences are known as *havezaten*, or manors. The large 15th-century church is known variously as the **Grote Kerk, St Nicolaaskerk** or **Bovenkerk**.

4 De Weerribben

Road Map D3.

De Weerribben is an unspoiled area of wetlands at the north-western end of Overijssel. There is plenty for cyclists, walkers and also canoeists to do in this beautiful nature reserve.

Natuuractiviteitencentrum De Weerribben
Hoogeweg 27, Ossenzijl. **Tel** 0561-477272. **Open** Apr–Oct: daily, Nov–Mar: Tue–Fri & Sun.

Water lilies in the nature reserve of De Weerribben

❺ Street-by-Street: Giethoorn

If any village were to be given the title "prettiest village in Holland", quaint Giethoorn would be the one. This well-deserved accolade is due to the village's picturesque canals which are flanked by numerous farmhouse-style buildings. A few of these buildings now contain interesting, if small, museums. The village of Giethoorn can be easily explored both by boat and by bicycle. Founded in 1230 by religious refugees, the village's distinctive form came about from peat-cutting, eventually resulting in the formation of ponds and lakes. The small canals were used for transporting peat.

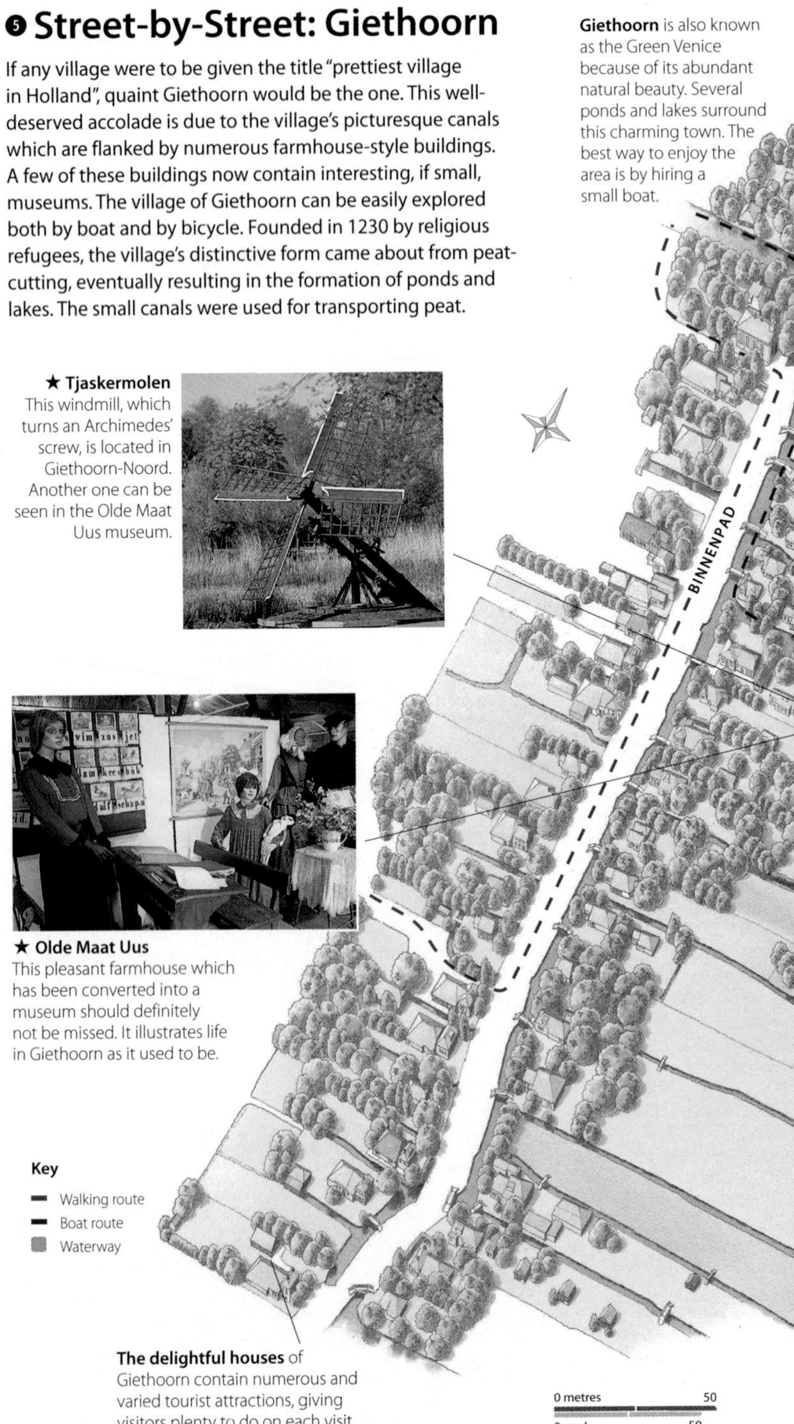

Giethoorn is also known as the Green Venice because of its abundant natural beauty. Several ponds and lakes surround this charming town. The best way to enjoy the area is by hiring a small boat.

★ Tjaskermolen
This windmill, which turns an Archimedes' screw, is located in Giethoorn-Noord. Another one can be seen in the Olde Maat Uus museum.

★ Olde Maat Uus
This pleasant farmhouse which has been converted into a museum should definitely not be missed. It illustrates life in Giethoorn as it used to be.

The delightful houses of Giethoorn contain numerous and varied tourist attractions, giving visitors plenty to do on each visit.

Islands in the area are a direct result of peat-cutting, which led to the creation of lakes and canals, giving Giethoorn its many little islands, connected by the village's characteristic footbridges.

VISITORS' CHECKLIST

Practical Information
Road Map D2.
2,500. Eendrachtsplein 1 (0521-362124). Street Theatre Festival (Jun); Rock Around Giethoorn Punt Race (Jul); Gondola Regatta (various times); Sailing Punt Race, Blues Festival, Punt Race (Aug); Slag op 't Wiede (Sep); Christmas Fair & Story Telling Festival (Dec).

Transport
70, 79.

★ Punts
Punts were formerly used to carry peat along the canals of Giethoorn. They are now used for tourist trips; one can also occasionally catch glimpses of them in the village's old ditches and channels.

Reeds
The countryside around Giethoorn abounds with lakes and ponds. The reeds which grow along their banks are used to make cane furniture and to thatch roofs.

Tourist Boats
There are many places in Giethoorn where you can hire quiet, electrically powered boats.

Deventer, larger than Amsterdam in its heyday

❻ Staphorst

Road Map D3. 15,000. 40.
Binnenweg 26 (0522-467400).
Sun. Wed am.

Staphorst is known throughout Holland as a stronghold of strict Christian beliefs. It was where the Gereformeerde Bond (reformed union), one of the strictest embodiments of Protestantism, ruled within the Dutch Reformed Church. The lovely old farmhouses, painted in a characteristic green and blue, are often monumental buildings. To get an idea of what they once looked like, visit the **Museumboerderij** (farmhouse museum).

The townspeople continue to wear traditional dress, a custom which has practically vanished elsewhere in the country. Throughout Staphorst you will see women, especially elderly women, wearing the blue and black outfits.

Museumboerderij
Gemeenteweg 67. **Tel** 0522-462526. **Open** 1 Apr–31 Oct: 10am–5pm Tue–Sat. **Closed** Sun, Mon & hols.

❼ Ommen

Road Map D3. 17,000.
Kruisstraat 6 (0900-1122375).
Tue am.

The district of Ommen lies in stunningly beautiful countryside extending from the town to nearby villages and hamlets. One-third of its total area of 18,000 ha (44,500 acres) is covered by nature reserves and forests. A former Hanseatic city, Ommen itself is home to a few interesting museums, including the **Nationaal Tinnen Figuren Museum** (national tin models museum).

Nationaal Tinnen Figuren Museum
Markt 1. **Tel** 0529-454500. **Open** Apr–Oct: 11am–5pm Tue–Sat, 1–5pm Sun & hols; Nov–Mar: 11am–5pm Sat, 1–5pm Sun & hols. **Closed** 1 Jan, 25 Dec.

Environs
To find out more about the nature reserves in Ommen, visit the **Natuurinformatiecentrum Ommen**, which houses a permanent exhibition illustrating the cultural history of the surrounding countryside. Particularly worth seeing are the typical Saxon farmhouses at Beerze, Junne, Stegeren, Besthem and Giethmen.

Natuurinformatie-centrum Ommen
Hammerweg 59a. **Tel** 0529-450702. **Open** May–Oct: 1–5pm Wed–Sun; Nov–Apr: 1:30–4pm Wed, Sat & Sun.

❽ Deventer

Road Map D3. 86,000.
Brink 56 (0570-710120).
Fri am & Sat.

The lively centre of the old Hanseatic city of Deventer features numerous medieval houses, including the oldest stone house in Holland today. Buildings worth seeing in particular are those situated on the pleasant Brink (green) and the Bergkerk. In the middle of the Brink stands the impressive Waag (weigh house) from 1528, which now contains the VVV and the renovated **Historisch Museum de Waag,** with exhibits that illustrate the town's history. On the first Sunday of August, the town holds the **Deventer Boekenmarkt** (book fair), the largest in Europe. It is preceded by a poetry festival.

A tin soldier

Historisch Museum de Waag
Brink 56. **Tel** 0570-693783. **Open** 10am–5pm Tue–Sat, 1–5pm Sun. **Closed** public hols.

❾ Nijverdal

Road Map D3. 23,500.
Willem Alexander Straat 7c (0540-612729). Sat.

The impressive beauty of the Sallandse Heuvelrug, with its fine heathland and woodland, is especially apparent at Nijverdaal. This is the last remaining breeding ground in the Netherlands for black grouse. An interesting exhibition on the Heuvelrug region can be seen at the

Flock of sheep in Sallandse Heuvelrug

For hotels and restaurants in this region see p400 and pp413–414

Bezoekerscentrum Sallandse Heuvelrug (Sallandse Heuvelrug visitors' centre), with its clever and unusual "Forester's Corner".

Bezoekerscentrum Sallandse Heuvelrug
Grotestraat 281. **Tel** 0548-612711. **Open** Apr–Oct: 10am–5pm Tue–Sun, Nov–Mar: 10am–4pm Tue–Sun. **Closed** Mon, 1 Jan, 25 & 31 Dec.

Environs
Avonturenpark Hellendoorn (Hellendoorn adventure park) *(see p426)* is great for children.

⑩ Delden

Road Map E3. 7,000. Langestraat 29 (074-3761363). Fri afternoon.

Delden is a pretty residential village, ideal for walks. This Twente hamlet has a number of attractions, including the **Zoutmuseum** (salt museum) and the 12th-century **Oude Blasiuskerk**.

Zoutmuseum
Langestraat 30. **Tel** 074-3764546. **Open** May–Sep: 11am–5pm Mon–Fri, 2–5pm Sat & Sun; Oct–Apr: 2–5pm Tue–Fri & Sun.

Environs
Some 2 km (1.2 miles) northeast of Delden are the lovely gardens of **Kasteel Twickel**.

Tuinen Kasteel Twickel (Kasteel Twickel Gardens)
Twickelerlaan 1a, Ambt Delden. **Tel** 074-3761020. **Open** May–Oct: 10am–5pm Wed–Sun.

⑪ Enschede

Road Map: E3. 150,000. Stationsplein 1a (053-4323200). Tue, Sat.

Enschede is regarded as the capital of Twente, as it is the largest town in Overijssel. It was devastated in 1862 by a fire – little of the old town survived. One of the few historical buildings that can still be seen in the otherwise pleasant centre is the **Grote Kerk** on the Oude Markt.

In addition to this centre, with its theatres, concert halls and cinemas, Enschede has a number of museums, of which the **Rijksmuseum Twenthe** should not be missed. The exhibits here range from manuscripts and paintings to modern, primarily Dutch, art.

Miracle Planet Boulevard, just outside town, offers non-stop entertainment in three mega-complexes.

Rijksmuseum Twenthe
Lasondersingel 129–131. **Tel** 053-4358675. **Open** 11am–5pm Tue–Sun & hols. **Closed** 1 Jan, 25 Dec.

⑫ Ootmarsum

Road Map E3. 4,000. 64 from Almelo. Markt 9 (0541-291214). Thu am.

The village of Ootmarsum is one of the prettiest places in all of Holland. On the map since 900, Ootmarsum was granted its town charter in 1300. It has grown little since then; indeed, not much has changed here at all, making it quite suitable

The half-timbered Stiepelhoes in Ootmarsum, dating from 1658

Stained glass in the 13th-century Catholic church at Ootmarsum

for an open-air museum. Places of interest not to be missed include the Roman Catholic church, the only Westphalian hall-type church in Holland, built between 1200 and 1300. Here you can see the burial vaults and some impressive works of art. The rococo former town hall dates from 1778 and is now the VVV (tourist) office. There are also some interesting old draw-wells.

The **Openluchtmuseum Los Hoes** (Los Hoes open-air museum) showing what life was once like in Twente is also worth a visit.

Openluchtmuseum Los Hoes
Smithuisstraat 2. **Tel** 0541-293099. **Open** 10am–5pm daily (Dec–Jan: weekends only & Christmas hols).

Environs
Nature lovers will find plenty to do in the countryside surrounding Ootmarsum, which is located in one of the finest parts of Twente. The landscape offers an ever-changing scenery, with its rushing brooks, old watermills, woodland paths, prehistoric tumuli and Saxon farmhouses.

The viewing point on the Kuiperberg affords a stunning vista over the entire Twente region and provides the place names of the various sights.

FLEVOLAND

Flevoland is Holland's youngest province, created by the Dutch entirely out of water, sandbanks and mud flats, thanks to massive reclamation schemes which created dykes and polders (reclaimed land, sometimes below sea level) from the turbulent Zuiderzee following an Act of Parliament in 1918.

This act provided funds for damming the northeastern part of the Zuiderzee and reclaiming the land behind the dykes. When the Afsluitdijk was completed in 1932, drainage works on the Noordostpolder began and, with the seawater pumped out, the islands of Urk and Schokland and the town of Emmeloord became by 1942 a part of the mainland. Further schemes to the south and southwest were completed in 1957 and 1968 respectively, and since 1986 these three new polders have officially constituted the Netherlands' newest province, named Flevoland after "Flevo Lacus", the original name given to the Zuiderzee by the Roman historian Pliny nearly 2,000 years ago.

Initially, the idea had been to use the polders as farmland only, with the occasional village here and there. However, as the built-up areas around Amsterdam and Utrecht became increasingly congested, new towns have grown up. The conurbation around Almere, with its highly impressive modern architecture, is among these. Other towns include Lelystad, with its several modern museums, and Dronten, where the Walibi World amusement park proves an irresistible magnet for younger visitors. Lelystad, whose name honours Cornelius Lely, the genius behind the massive land creation project *(see p331)*, is the provincial capital. There are many other attractions for visitors to this compact and attractive region, including a number of fascinating museums featuring subjects as varied as archaeology and World War II.

The exotic spoonbill, an icon of the new wildlife in Flevoland

◀ Farms and polder landscape in Emmeloord

Exploring Flevoland

The Noordoostpolder, which is the northern-most part of Flevoland, is distinguished by its polder landscape and its rich farmland, fruit orchards and bulb fields. There are also many young forests, which are good for walking in. Apart from the main town of Emmeloord, there are a number of small new villages, as well as the old fishing village of Urk. Oostelijk (eastern) and Zuidelijk (southern) Flevoland are relatively sparsely populated and have a lot of greenery. Between Almere, the largest town of Flevoland, characterized by modern architecture, and Lelystad, the provincial capital, there stretches a fine nature reserve known as the Oostvaardersplassen, or Oostvaarder lakes. The coastal lakes have inviting sand beaches and marinas.

The picturesque harbour of the fishing village of Urk

Sights at a Glance

1. Emmeloord
2. Urk
3. Nagele
4. Schokland
5. Swifterbant
6. Dronten
7. Lelystad
8. Bataviawerf
9. Oostvaardersplassen
10. Knardijk
11. Zeewolde
12. Almere

A fine view of Almere harbour

Markerwaarddijk
N302
Markermeer
LELYSTAD 7
BATAVIAWERF 8
Natuurpa
Lelyst
9 OOSTVAARDERSPLASSEN
Knarbos
Almere-Buiten
KNARDIJK 10
A6
ALMERE 12
Zuidelijk-Flevoland
A27
Almere-Haven
N305
ZEEWOL
Horsteru
N301

Key

- Motorway
- Major road
- Minor road
- Scenic route
- Minor railway
- Regional border

0 kilometres 10
0 miles 10

For map symbols *see back flap*

The Poldertoren in the small town of Emmeloord

The Ketelbrug bridge over the Ketelmeer

Getting Around

Flevoland has an efficient road network. All the municipalities in the region are easily accessible by car or bus. Long-distance coaches cover both the Lelystad-Emmeloord and Lelystad-Dronten routes. Almere and Lelystad can also be reached by train, and a ferry links Urk and Enkhuizen during July and August. The flat expansive landscape of Flevoland also makes exploration by bicycle ideal. Numerous excellent cycling and hiking routes have been laid out throughout the province.

Flat farmland of Flevoland

For hotels and restaurants in this region see p400 and p414

❶ Emmeloord

Road Map D2. Noordoostpolder. 24,800. De Deel 25a (0527-612000). Thu am.

When the oldest polder in Flevoland was drained, Emmeloord sprang up like a pioneer settlement. Over the years it has developed into a pleasant town. It is the main town of the municipality of Noordoostpolder, encompassing *groendorps* (green villages). Emmeloord is known mainly for its octagonal **Poldertoren**, water tower topped by a 5-m (16-ft) wind vane in the shape of an old merchant ship; the tower is 65-m (214-ft) high and was built in 1959. The carillon, one of Holland's biggest, has 48 chimes. The viewing platform (open in summer) offers a view of the polder.

❷ Urk

Road Map C3. 16,500. from Enkhuizen, summer only. Wijk 2–3 (0527-684040). Sat am.

The fishing village of Urk attracts many tourists with its sloping alleys and charming fishermen's cottages. Untilthe Zuiderzee was drained, Urk was an island. Some 1,000 years ago, the island was much larger and had five villages; flooding gradually reduced its size. The townspeople moved to the highest point on the island, a hill of boulder clay. Even after the polder was drained, Urk managed to retain its character in the middle of the new land surrounding it. Some of the older residents wear the traditional dress, though this is increasingly rare.

Beside the old village centre the fishing quay, the lighthouse (1844) and the little church (1786) are worth a look. In the **Museum Het Oude Raadhuis**, situated in the old town hall, you can find out about the history of Urk and the fishing industry.

Museum Het Oude Raadhuis
Wijk 2–3. **Tel** 0527-683262.
Open Apr–Oct: 10am–5pm Mon–Fri, till 4pm Sat; Nov–Mar: 10am–4pm Mon–Sat.

❸ Nagele

Road Map D3. 1,900. Emmeloord, (0527-612000).

This village was built in the 1950s to designs by the De Acht en de Opbouw, a group of architects which included the famous Rietveld, Van Eyck and van Eesteren, who represented the Nieuwe Bouwen movement. The flat-roofed residential buildings surround a park-like centre with shops, schools and churches. The village is surrounded by a belt of woodland. **Museum Nagele** provides information about the village's architecture.

Schokland before land reclamation

View of Schokland after land reclamation

Museum Nagele
Ring 23. **Tel** 0527-653077.
Open 1–5pm Thu–Sun. **Closed** 1 Jan, 25, 26 & 31 Dec.

❹ Schokland

Road Map C3. see museum.

Like Urk, Schokland was once an island. Archaeological finds show that the site was inhabited in prehistoric times. In 1859, the population had to abandon the island because it was disappearing into the sea. Today the "island" is so tiny that it can barely be seen.

Museum Schokland, consisting of the restored church and reconstructions of fishermen's cottages, is dedicated to geology and local history from the Ice Age up until the land was reclaimed. At the south end of the village are the ruins of a medieval church. In the Schokkerbos forest to the west is the **Gesteentetuin**, gardens featuring Ice Age boulders.

Museum Schokland
Middelbuurt 3, Ens. **Tel** 0527-251396.
Open Apr–Oct: 11am–5pm Tue–Sun; Jul & Aug: daily; Nov–Mar: Fri–Sun.
Closed 1 Jan, 25 Dec.

Cornelis Lely (1854–1929)

Flevoland has come into existence thanks largely to the plans and ambitions of civil engineer Cornelis Lely. From 1885 to 1891, as a member of the Zuiderzeevereniging (Zuiderzee Society), he was responsible for studying the possibility of closing off and draining the Zuiderzee. His appointment as minister for trade and industry in 1891 gave him the chance to convince the government and parliament how necessary it was to tame the unpredictable Zuiderzee, though it was not until his third term in office (1913–18) that the law for retaining and draining the Zuiderzee was finally passed. Apart from the Zuiderzee projects, Lely worked to improve the Noorzeekanaal. From 1902 to 1905 he was governor of Suriname. He died in 1929, but his name lives on in that of Flevoland's capital, Lelystad.

Statue of Lely

5 Swifterbant

Road Map C3. 6,500. De Rede 80, Dronten (0321-313802). Tue pm.

This young village is known primarily to archaeologists for the flint tools and earthenware of the **Swifterbant culture** that were unearthed here. The Swifterbant culture inhabited the region in the 4th millennium BC.

In spring, flower enthusiasts can enjoy the riot of vivid colour in the nearby bulbfields.

Environs

The Swifterbos forest nearby is an excellent spot for recreation. The Ketelbos is a resting place for migrant bird species.

6 Dronten

Road Map D3. 22,500. De Rede 80–82 (0321-313802). Wed.

Dronten is well-endowed with greenery and recreation facilities. The Meerpaal Complex here combines a theatre, cinema and events venue. Outside the town hall stands the Airgunnersmonument, honouring airmen who lost their lives in World War II.

Environs

Around Dronten are many pretty woods and recreation areas that offer opportunities for walking and cycling.

7 Lelystad

Road Map C3. 67,000. Bataviaplein 60 (0320-292900). Sat (Gordiaan), Tue (Lelycentre).

Lelystad, a provincial capital, has a modern centre with a number of outstanding buildings. The cylindrical **Nieuw Land Erfgoedcentrum** has models and audio-visual materials illustrating the history of the fight against the sea, of the land reclamation and of the culture of the Zuiderzee.

On the Airship Plaza is the **Zepallon** museum of balloon and airship flight. East of the town is **Natuurpark Lelystad**, where there are animals such as bison and Przewalski horses. As well as cycling and pedestrian paths, the park boasts a shipwreck and a reconstructed prehistoric village. The **Nationaal Luchtvaart Themapark Aviodrome**, at Lelystad airport, has historic aircraft, a cinema and a reconstruction of Schiphol Station from 1928.

Nieuw Land Erfgoedcentrum
Oostvaardersdijk 113. **Tel** 0320-225900. **Open** 10am–5pm Tue–Fri, 11:30am–5pm Sat & Sun. **Closed** 1 Jan, 25 Dec.

Natuurpark Lelystad
Vlotgrasweg 11. **Tel** 0320-286111. **Open** sunrise–sunset daily. by appt.

Nationaal Luchtvaart Themapark Aviodrome
Pelikaanweg 50, Luchthaven Lelystad. **Tel** 0320-289842. **Open** 10am–5pm Tue–Sun (Mon in Jul, Aug & school hols). **Closed** 25 Dec.

8 Bataviawerf

Road Map C3. Oostvaardersdijk 01–09, Lelystad. **Tel** 0320-261409. **Open** 10am–5pm daily. **Closed** 1 Jan, 25 Dec. **bataviawerf.nl**

From 1985 to 1995, a replica of the Dutch East India Company ship *Batavia* *(see p262)* was built at the Bataviawerf on the Oostvaardersdiep. The shipyard's current project is a replica of the 17th-century *De Zeven Provinciën*. Visit the sailmaking and woodcarving workshops. The entry ticket is also valid for **NISA**, the Netherlands Institute for Submarine Archaeology, with its fascinating display on shipwrecks.

The *Batavia*, which went down off the Australian coast in 1629 with 341 people on board

Observation huts on the Oostvaardersplassen lakes, situated amidst abundant bird populations

9 Oostvaarders-plassen

Road Map C3. Staatsbosbeheer, Bezoekerscentrum, Kitsweg 1, Lelystad (0320-254585).

Between Lelystad and Almere is internationally renowned marshland covering 6,000 ha (14,825 acres). The land was originally earmarked as an industrial area. When Zuidelijk Flevoland was drained, the low-lying area beyond the Oostvaardersdijk remained a wetland. Plans to drain this area were put forward but were ultimately dismissed because the place had by this time become an area of unique natural interest.

The nature reserve includes lakes, mud flats, marshes, willow thickets and grasslands and serves as a port of call for hundreds of species of birds that come here to forage and feed. Indeed, some birds which have been unable to settle elsewhere have found their place here, including the hen harrier (the symbol of Flevoland) and the great cormorant. Other birds seen here include the great bittern, the Eurasian spoonbill, heron, rail and, more recently, the sacred ibis. The many grey geese that forage here, along with the wild cattle, wild horses and red deer that occur here, have helped the region's vegetation to proliferate.

The marshland is largely off-limits to visitors, but some fine views are to be had from the edge of the swamp, the Oostvaardersdijk and the Knardijk. Additionally, the region of **De Driehoek** has a 5-km (3-mile) walking route, open sunrise to sunset. The route starts at the information centre and passes by natural woodland, lakes and observation huts.

10 Knardijk

Road Map C3. Staatsbosbeheer (0320-254585).

The Knardijk marks the border between Oostelijk and Zuidelijk Flevoland (eastern and southern Flevoland). It was built in the 1950s between the island of Lelystad-Haven and Harderwijk to enable the entire area to be placed within a polder at one time. After Oostelijk Flevoland had been dried out, it formed the south-western ring dyke of this polder. The Knardijk is of great interest to nature lovers, as it offers a fine view of the Oostvaardersplassen lakes. A great many birds live at the foot of the dyke, including hen harriers and marsh harriers. Two bird-watching huts can also be reached along the dyke. The dyke leads in a southeasterly direction along the nature reserve known as the **Wilgenreservaat**, which has evolved naturally into a mixture of woodland and clearings. Many songbirds, woodland birds, and birds of prey are to be found here, as are deer, foxes, polecats and ermines. Part of the reserve can be seen via a circular path. Nearby is the Knarbos forest, also boasting a variety of flora and fauna. A 6-km (4-mile) hiking route has been marked out.

Hen harrier

The Knardijk, looking out over a variegated natural landscape

⓫ Zeewolde

Road Map C3. 19,400.
Raadhuisstraat 1 (036-5221405).
Fri.

With its picturesque marina, this village on the Wolderwijd coastal lake is a popular recreational spot. Zeewolde is the youngest town in Flevoland, having officially become a municipality in 1984. Its youth is evident from the imaginative architecture, particularly that of the town hall, library and church. An enjoyable 7-km (4-mile) walking route has been laid out in and around Zeewolde, with landscape art along the way (for information, call De Verbeelding, 036-5227037).

Environs
South of Zeewolde is the **Horsterwold**, which is the largest deciduous forest in Western Europe.

⓬ Almere

Road Map C3. 176,000.
De Diagonaal 199 (036-5485041).
Wed & Sat (Almere-Stad), Thu (Almere-Buiten), Fri (Almere-Haven).

Almere is Holland's fastest-growing town. Its name recalls the 8th-century name for the Zuiderzee. The earliest signs of habitation date from 65 centuries earlier. Almere today consists of three centres: Almere-Stad, which is undergoing major renovation and is where all the facilities are; Almere-Buiten, which is a green suburb; and Almere-Haven, with its lovely marina. If you are interested in modern and unusual architecture, the districts to visit are Muziewijk, Filmwijk and Stedenwijk in Almere-Stad, and the colourful Regenboogbuurt (rainbow neighbourhood) in Almere-Buiten. Also worth a visit are the town hall, and the Almeers Centrum Hedendaagse Kunst **ACHK – De Paviljoens** (Almere centre for modern art), with works by late 20th-century Dutch and foreign artists.

Almere, a laboratory for modern architects

Environs
Near Almere are many recreation areas and nature reserves: the Weerwater; the Leegwaterplas lake; the Beginbos forest, with walking, cycling and bridleways; the Buitenhout; the Kromslootpark, with its polder vegetation; the lakes of Noorderplassen; **Lepelaarsplassen**, where rare wading birds occur; and the Oostvaardersplassen.

ACHK – De Paviljoens
Odeonstraat 3–5.
Tel 036-5450400. **Open** noon–5pm Wed–Sun (to 9pm Thu & Fri).
Closed 1 Jan, 25 Dec.

Landscape Art

In the countryside around Flevoland you will come across unusual and distinctive works of "landscape art". These are associated with various features of the landscape. East of Almere-Haven, for instance, is the *Groene Kathedraal (Green Cathedral)* (top photo), designed by Marinus Boezem and consisting of 178 Lombardy poplars planted to re-create the outline and pillars of Reims Cathedral. The *Observatorium Robert Morris* (bottom photo) consists of two round earth embankments, with three notches in them from which the sunrise can be observed when the seasons change. On the Ketelmeerdijk, you will find Cyriel Lixenberg's *Wachters op de Dijk (Watchmen on the Dike)*, consisting of a circle, a triangle and a square. Piet Slegers' *Aardzee (Earth Sea)*, situated between Zeewolde and Lelystad, consists of a series of elongated artificial ridges resembling waves.

GELDERLAND

Gelderland is The Netherland's largest province. Its name derives from the 11th-century county of Gelre, which was linked with the town of Geldern, just over the border in Germany. The town was the fiefdom of Gerard de Rossige, whose grandson Gerard II of Wassenberg pronounced himself Count of Gelre in 1104.

Succeeding counts skilfully expanded their territory to include the Veluwe region to the north, the Betuwe in the southwest and the county of Zutphen *(see p345)*. When in 1248 the imperial town of Nijmegen was annexed, Gelre became a power to be reckoned with. A number of its towns joined the Hanseatic League, and in 1339 the county was promoted to a duchy by the German emperor. The increasing power of the Habsburgs threatened the independence of the Gelders, eventually leading to the duke having to cede the territory in 1543 to Charles V. Gelderland thus became part of the Netherlands.

This colourful history is manifest today in the number of medieval buildings, churches, castles and fortified towns that welcome visitors throughout the province. In more recent times, the region, and especially the strategically located towns of Arnhem and Nijmegen, saw heavy fighting towards the end of World War II. The heroic action at Arnhem is remembered in the town's Airborne Museum, while the museum in Nijmegen recalls this town's long history from pre-Roman times to the tyranny of the Holy Roman Empire.

While visitors can enjoy many modern attractions, perhaps Gelderland's greatest asset is its contrasting natural scenery, which ranges from heaths and woodlands in the north to the beautiful Betuwe river valley and the pretty agricultural region of the Achterhoek.

A 17th-century granary near Winterswijk

◀ View of the old Dutch city of Nijmegen

Exploring Gelderland

Gelderland is made up of three distinct regions. In the north is the Veluwe, an extensive natural area of woodland, heaths and large tracts of drifting sand, where those looking for peaceful natural surroundings can find exactly that. To the east is the Achterhoek. This region, too, is rich in natural beauty but has a completely different character: it consists of small fields with wooden fences, old farms, stately homes and castles. In the southwest of the province, between the Rhine, the Maas and the Waal rivers, is the river-valley region with the Betuwe. This area is distinguished by its many small dykes and river banks, which offer ample opportunities for cycling and walking.

The dolphinarium in Harderwijk

ELBURG

Veluwemeer

NUNSPEET 5

Sights at a Glance

1. *Paleis Het Loo pp338–9*
2. Apeldoorn
3. Hattem
4. Elburg
5. Nunspeet
6. Harderwijk
7. Nijkerk
8. Barneveld
9. Wageningen
10. *Kröller-Müller Museum pp342–3*
11. Nationaal Park De Hoge Veluwe
12. Arnhem
13. Zutphen
14. Bronkhorst
15. Vorden
16. Lochem
17. Winterswijk
18. 's-Heerenberg
19. Montferland
20. Doesburg
21. *Nijmegen pp346–7*
22. Gelderse Poort
23. Groesbeek
24. Tiel
25. Culemborg
26. Buren
27. Zaltbommel

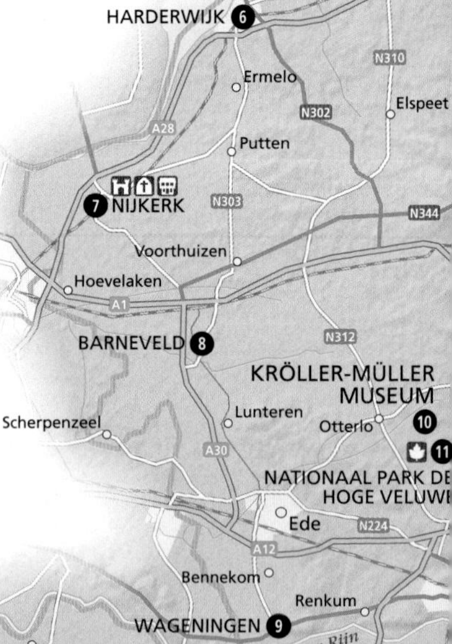

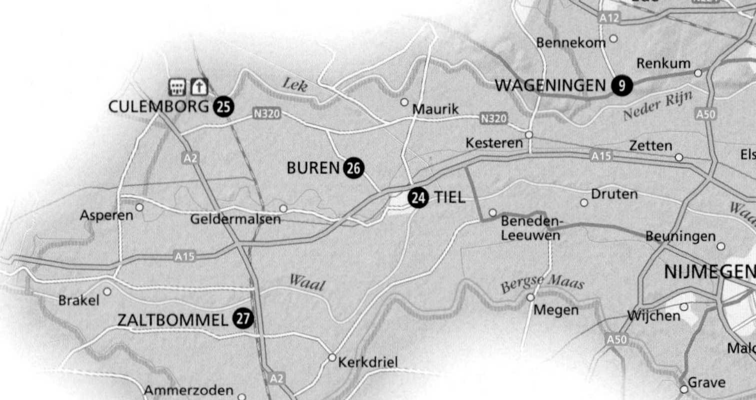

0 kilometres 10

0 miles 5

For map symbols *see back flap*

Getting Around

Gelderland has an excellent road network. A number of major motorways pass through the province, including the A2 and the A50. Public transport is also good. Many towns have rail links, and the bus will even take you deep into the Nationaal Park De Hoge Veluwe. The numerous bicycle tracks and footpaths allow the province to be conveniently explored either on foot or by bicycle. Cycling routes of varying lengths are well marked, and there are several walking routes across the province, including the very scenic Maarten van Rossum route.

The majestic red deer – king of the Veluwe

The Veluwe, characterized by large sandy areas

Bronkhorst, the Netherlands' smallest town

Key

- Motorway
- Major road
- Minor road
- Scenic route
- Main railway
- Minor railway
- Regional border
- International border

❶ Paleis Het Loo

The Stadholder William III built the elegant palace of Het Loo in 1692 as a hunting lodge. For generations, the Orange family used it as a summer residence. Its pomp and splendour have led to it being dubbed the "Versailles of the Netherlands". Its main architect was Jacob Roman (1640–1716); the interior and the gardens were designed by Daniel Marot (1661–1752). The severe Classical façade belies the ornate interior. After intensive restoration work was carried out, the palace is now open as a museum.

Coat of Arms (1690) of William and Mary, future king and queen of England.

★ Bedroom of the Stadholder William III (1713)
The wall coverings and draperies in this bedroom are of rich orange damask and purple silk.

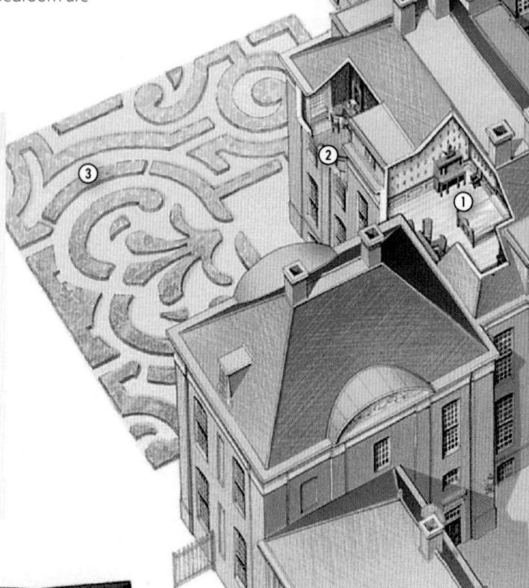

KEY

① **William III's bedroom**

② **Closet of the Stadholder William III** (1690)The walls of William's private chamber are covered in scarlet damask. His paintings and Delftware are on display here.

③ **King's Garden**

④ **Mary II's bedroom**

⑤ **Queen's Garden**

⑥ **The throne room** now contains the original designs for the gardens.

⑦ **Library**

⑧ **Picture gallery**

Vintage Cars
This 1925 Bentley, nicknamed Minerva, was owned by Prince Hendrik, husband of Queen Wilhelmina. It is one of the royal family's many old cars and carriages on display in the stables.

★ Dining Hall (1686)
The marble-clad walls are hung with tapestries depicting scenes from Ovid's poems.

VISITORS' CHECKLIST

Practical Information
Koninklijk Park 1 (Amersfoortseweg), Apeldoorn.
Tel 055-5772400.
paleishetloo.nl
Open 10am–5pm Tue–Sun & hols. **Closed** 1 Jan. gardens only.

Transport
Apeldoorn, then bus. Palace and gardens

★ The Formal Gardens
The gardens are a combination of vegetation, stone carvings and fountains in Classical style. The Fountain of the Celestial Sphere stands in the Lower Garden.

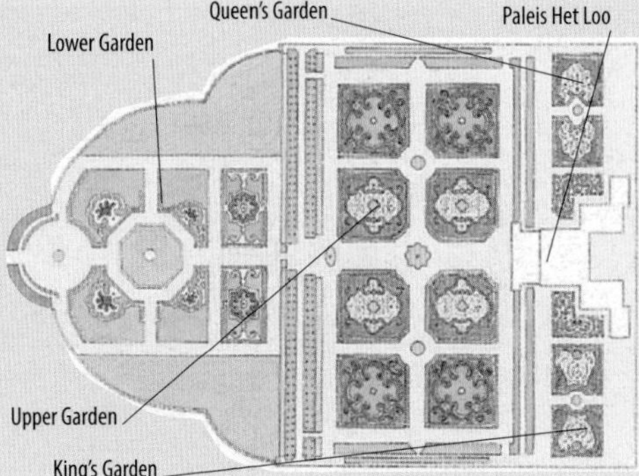

Plan of the formal gardens

The Formal Gardens

When the formal gardens on the land behind the palace were reconstructed, garden designers based their designs on old illustrations, prints, documents and plans. In the 18th century, the original ornamental gardens had been grassed over. In 1983, the intricate patterns of the original gardens were restored and planting began. The Het Loo gardens are typical of a formal garden in the 17th century in which the ideal was the harmonization of art and nature.

Stroking monkeys in Apenheul, a zoo in the Berg en Bos nature park

❷ Apeldoorn

Road Map D3. 152,000. Deventerstraat 18 (526-0200).

Apeldoorn is first mentioned as Appoldro in 793, and for centuries it was a small rural town in the Veluwe. This was changed by William III in 1692 when he built his hunting lodge Het Loo *(see pp338–9)* here. Many wealthy burghers followed William's example and set themselves up in Apeldoorn. The engaging **Historisch Museum Apeldoorn** gives a good overview of the area's history.

The **Apenheul Primate Park** is a special zoo situated in the Berg en Bos nature park, where more than 30 species of monkeys run free among the visitors. The gorillas live on wooded islands that separate them from both the monkeys and visitors.

Apenheul Primate Park
JC Wilslaan 21. **Tel** 055-3575757. **Open** Apr–Oct: 10am–5pm; Jul–Aug: 10am–6pm.

❸ Hattem

Road Map D3. 12,000. Wed pm.

The picturesque town of Hattem (first mentioned in 891) was granted its town charter as early as 1299, joining the Hanseatic League in the 15th century. Its monumental buildings, such as the house of Herman Willem Daendals, later the governor-general of the Dutch Indies, bear witness to Hattem's eventful and prosperous past. St Andreaskerk (St Andrew's Church) is particularly remarkable, its oldest part dating from 1176. The **Anton Pieck Museum** is dedicated to the Dutch painter and graphic artist Anton Pieck (1895–1987); it has been merged with the **Voerman Museum**, which showcases the IJssel painter Jan Voerman and his son, who illustrated the famous Verkade card albums.

Anton Pieck Museum/ Voerman Museum
Achterstraat 46–48. **Tel** 038-4442192 & 038-4442897. **Open** 10am–5pm Tue–Sat (Jul & Aug also open 1–5pm Sun & Mon). **Closed** 1 Jan, 9–31 Jan, 30 Apr, 25 Dec; Nov–Apr: Mon.

❹ Elburg

Road Map D3. 21,500. Jufferenstraat 8 (0525-681520). Tue.

Elburg is the best-preserved fortified town on the former Zuiderzee. The prosperity of this old town is illustrated in the 14th-century St Nicolaaskerk, with its imposing Quellhorst organ. From the 38-m (125-ft) tower you can clearly make out the medieval rectangular street pattern.

Beside the **Vischpoort** (fish gate), a former defence tower, is the oldest ropemaker's workshop in Holland. Elburg was once much nearer to the coast, but in the late 14th century the flood-plagued town was moved well away from the sea. The interesting local history museum, the **Gemeentemuseum**, is in a 15th- century monastery.

Gemeentemuseum Elburg
Jufferenstraat 6–8. **Tel** 0525-68 1341. **Open** 11am–5pm Tue–Sat.

The Oudheidkamer at Nunspeet, a town in Gelderland province

❺ Nunspeet

Road Map D3. 26,000. Stationsplein 1 (0341-274740). Thu am.

Nunspeet is a good starting point from which to explore the nearby wooded countryside. Nunspeet's history comes to life in the **Oudheidkamer**. The nearby **Veluwemeer** lake is a popular watersports centre.

Environs
Some 15 km (9 miles) south of Nonspeet is the idyllic **Uddelermeer** lake, a remnant from the last ice age.

The pleasant market square of Hattem, with its 17th-century town hall

❻ Harderwijk

Road Map C3. 38,500.
Academiestraat 5 (085-2733575).
Sat am.

The eel-smoking frames may have disappeared from the streets, but the Zuiderzee town of Harderwijk is still a pleasant place to wander around. The town has an interesting history. In the 13th century it had become so important through fishing and the trade in dyes that in 1221 Count Otto II of Gelre granted it a town charter and ordered fortifications to be built. Remnants of the old fortifications are still intact in places, including the **Vischpoort** gate. Between 1647 and 1811 Harderwijk even had a university, from which the Swedish scholar Linnaeus graduated in 1735. Harderwijk's main attraction is the **Dolfinarium** *(see p426)*, Europe's largest zoo for marine animals. Here visitors can stroke a ray or even a round fish. The **Veluws Museum** of local history in the Donkerstraat is also worth visiting.

Ray

❼ Nijkerk

Road Map C3. 27,000.
Verlaat 13 (055-5260200). Fri pm.

Nijkerk is a pleasant old town with many shops, restaurants and open-air cafés. The tobacco industry made the town rich in the 18th century. The Grote Kerk features the tomb of Kiliaen van Renselaer, one of the founders of New York. Just outside Nijkerk, on the Arkemheem polder, is the **Hertog Reijnout** *stoomgemaal*, a paddle-wheeled steam pum- ping- station, the last functioning one of its kind in Europe. Even today it is used to pump water out at times of flooding.

Environs
On the road to Putten is the **Oldenaller** estate with a castle from 1655. The cycling and walking area is open to the public. In **Putten** itself you can visit **De Gedachenisruimte** (hall of remembrance) in honour of the 600 men who in October

One of the favourite inhabitants of Harderwijk's Dolfinarium

1944 were taken from the village to the Neuengamme concentration camp, from where only 50 returned alive.

Stoomgemaal Hertog Reijnout
Zeedijk 6. **Tel** 065-3225997.
Open Apr–Sep: 10am–4pm Tue–Fri, 10am–1pm Sat, 11am–4pm Sun.
Closed Mon.

❽ Barneveld

Road Map D4. 47,000.
Langestraat 85a (0342-420555).
Thu, Sat am.

Barneveld owes its place in history books to one individual: **Jan van Schaffelaar**, commander-in-chief of the armed forces who on 16 July 1482 chose suicide rather than surrender and leapt from the tower of today's Nederlands Hervormde kerk (Reformed church). The **Nairac** museum of local history devotes considerable attention to this event. Today Barneveld is known as a poultry centre. The local **Pluimveemuseum** (poultry museum) shows how this industry has developed here.

Pluimveemuseum
Hessenweg 2a.
Tel 0342-400073. **Open** Apr–Oct: 10am–5pm Tue–Sat.

❾ Wageningen

Road Map C4. 33,000.
Wed am, Sat.

Wageningen, at the southwestern edge of the Veluwe, is a pleasant town that is home to the local Land- bouw Universiteit (agricult- ural university). The uni- versity's botanical gardens are open to the public. The town played an important role at the end of World War II; the Germans signed the official surrender in the **Hotel de Wereld**.

Hotel De Wereld
5 Mei Plein 1. **Tel** 0317-460444.
Open Call ahead to book.

The leap of Jan van Schaffelaar

⑩ Kröller-Müller Museum

This museum owes its existence above all to one person: Helene Kröller-Müller (1869–1939). In 1908, with the support of her industrialist husband Anton Kröller, Helene Kröller-Müller started to collect modern art. In 1935, she donated her entire collection to the state, and a special museum was built to house it. As well as its large collection of modern art, which includes 278 works by Vincent van Gogh, the museum is renowned for its unique sculpture garden, the Beeldentuin.

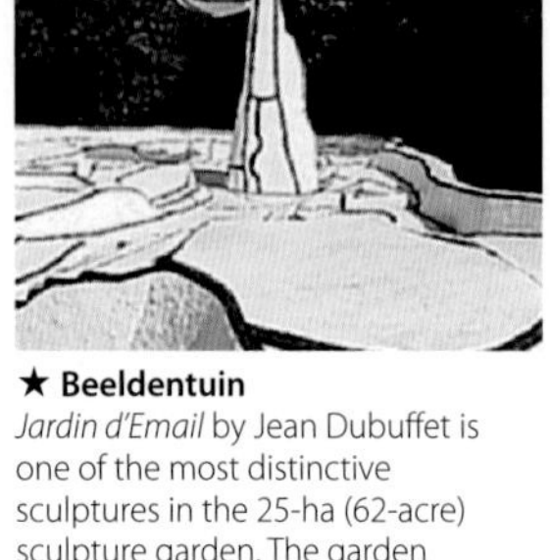

★ Beeldentuin
Jardin d'Email by Jean Dubuffet is one of the most distinctive sculptures in the 25-ha (62-acre) sculpture garden. The garden provides a natural backdrop for works by sculptors such as Auguste Rodin, Henry Moore, Barbara Hepworth and Richard Serra.

Mondriaan
In addition to old Flemish masters, the Kröller-Müller also has a major collection of 19th- and 20th-century French paintings and a dozen abstract paintings by Piet Mondriaan.

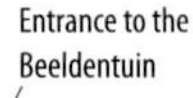

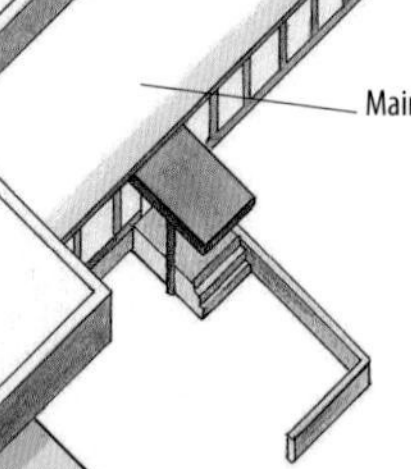

Jachthuis St Hubertus
This hunting lodge, from 1914 to 1920 by the architect HP Berlage, was commissioned by the Kröller-Müller family.

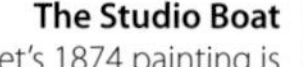

The Studio Boat
Claude Monet's 1874 painting is in the 19th- and 20th-century French collection.

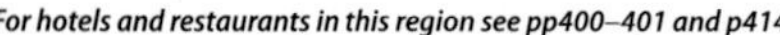

For hotels and restaurants in this region see pp400–401 and p414

estaurant

Information centre

VISITORS' CHECKLIST

Practical Information
Kröller-Müller Museum:
Tel 0318 591 241.
Open 10am–5pm Tue–Sun & public hols; sculpture garden 10am–4:30pm. **Closed** 1 Jan. Jachthuis St Hubertus: daily (Jan: open Sat & Sun only). Reserve tickets at the visitors' centre (see column at right).

★ Van Gogh Collection
Café Terrace at Night (1888). Van Gogh's huge collection of drawings, paintings and prints are the heart of the museum.

Museum Guide

The museum, together with the sculpture garden, gives expression to the notion that nature, architecture and art should be combined to form a whole.

Key to Floorplan

Exhibition rooms

⓫ Nationaal Park De Hoge Veluwe

Houtkampweg, Otterlo. Tel 055-378 8100. Ede, Apeldoorn.
Open 9am–6pm daily.

Like the Kröller-Müller Museum, De Hoge Veluwe is also the result of a collector's ambition. The Kröller-Müllers collected plots of unused land in the Veluwe until they possessed one single tract of natural land. They even bought, in 1914, the public road between Otterlo and Hoenderlo. The 5,500 ha (13,600 acres) of woodland, marshland, heath and drifting sand now make up the largest nature reserve in Holland. The park is a treasure trove for all kinds of wildlife: rare birds, butterflies, plants and fungi. Red deer, roe deer and moufflon sheep still live freely here. If you are lucky, you may be able to catch a glimpse of a wild boar or a stag (they are very shy animals). Bicycle and pedestrian paths have been laid out everywhere, and at the visitors' centre you can borrow a white bicycle free of charge.

Underneath the visitors' centre is the world's first underground museum, the **Museonder**, giving visitors an idea of what life is like below the earth's surface. You can see the roots of a 140-year-old beech tree, experience a re-created earthquake and drink ancient Veluwe groundwater. The park has two restaurants: the Rijzenburg at the Schaarsbergen entrance and the De Koperen Kop café-restaurant located in the visitors' centre.

Museonder, the world's first underground museum

⓬ Arnhem

Road Map D3. 136,500. Stationsplein 13 (0481-366250). Fri, Sat (Kerkplein).

Arnhem, the capital of the province of Gelderland, was declared the centre of the regional government back in 1544 by Charles V. In September 1944, the town suffered serious damage in the Battle of Arnhem, one of the most notorious battles of World War II. All the townspeople were forced to abandon their homes and were not able to return until 1945, when the war ended. Arnhem rose again from the ashes and is now sprucing itself up rapidly. The monuments that have been restored include the **Eusebiuskerk** from 1560, which was almost totally destroyed during the war. The tower, at 93 m (305 ft), is now taller than it ever was and has a glass lift which affords visitors a stunning view of the Rhine valley. The **Duivelshuis**, built in 1545 by Maarten van Rossum *(see p349)*, is an outstanding example of Dutch Renaissance architecture. Arnhem is also known for its monumental parks, such as the **Sonsbeek**, a romantic landscape park, and **Zypendaal**. In **Bronbeek**, a home for ex-servicemen, there is an exhibition dedicated to the former Dutch Indies. It is also worth allowing time for a visit to the **Burgers' Zoo** *(see p426)* and **Openluchtmuseum** (open- air museum), where the staff, dressed up in traditional costume, illustrate the rural way of life, handicrafts and industry in the Netherlands of the 19th century.

Traditional houses in the Openluchtmuseum

Allied troops landing in Arnhem on 17 September 1944

Openluchtmuseum
Schelmseweg 89. **Tel** 026-3576111.
Open Apr–Oct: 10am–5pm daily.

Environs

The **Posbank** at Rheden is an example of the lateral moraine landscape of Veluwe.

Arnhem Town Centre

① Koepelkerk
② Post Office
③ Eusebiuskerk
④ Sabelspoort
⑤ Provinciehuis
⑥ Stadhuis
⑦ Stadsschouwburg
⑧ Musis Sacrum

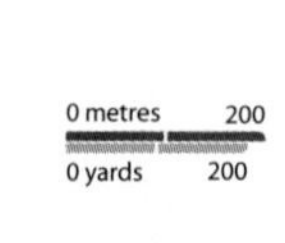

Old book at the St Walburgskerk library, built in 1564

⓭ Zutphen

Road Map D4. 36,000.
Stationsplein 39 (0575-519355).
Thu morning, Sat.

The hanseatic town of Zutphen is one of the Netherlands' oldest historical towns. One of the most distinctive features of the town, which is first mentioned in 1030, is the preserved medieval street layout. The main sights of Zutphen are the **St Walburgskerk**, the church square and the remains of the fortifications. They include the **Drogenapstoren** tower, which dates from 1444.

Zutphen has a number of interesting museums, including the informative **Stedelijk Museum** (local history museum) and the **Grafisch Museum** (graphic art museum), which is highly recommended.

Definitely worth visiting is the reading room of the unique **Librije** (library) of the St Walburgskerk. All of the 750 books in it date from before 1750 and include 80 incunabula printed before 1500. The books in the library, which was built in 1564, are chained to the desks. This is because it was a public library which was unsupervised at the time. There are only four other libraries of this kind in the world: two are in England and two are in northern Italy.

St Walburgskerk and Librije
Kerkhof 3. **Tel** 0575-514178. **Open** Jun: 1:30–4:30pm Tue–Sat; Jul–early Sep: 10:30am–4:30pm Tue–Sat.

⓮ Bronkhorst

Road Map D4. 160. 52 from Zutphen train station.

Bronkhorst's 160 inhabitants make it the smallest town in the Netherlands. The lords of Bronkhorst were granted a town charter in 1482. This very rural town, which once stood in the shadow of a castle (the castle no longer exists), never really flourished and has remained a village of farmsteads. It has many restored farmhouses, operates strict conservation rules forbidding new development and prohibits motor vehicles, which means cars must be left in a car park outside the town. All that remains of the once-mighty castle of the Lords of Bronkhorst, which had fallen into disrepair by the 17th century, is the *kasteelheuvel* (castle hill).

The Lords of Bronkhorst, together with the noble Bergh, Baer and Wisch families, belonged to the *Baanderheren*. They were nobles who were allowed to wage war under their own flag, which was an old hereditary right.

Bronkhorst, a tiny picturesque village of farmsteads

⓯ Vorden

Road Map D4. 8,400.
Kerkstraat 1b (0575-553222).
Fri morning.

There is mention of a Huis Vorden (Vorden house) as early as 1208; the first record of the family dates from 1315. The **Nederlands-herformde kerk**, which dates from around 1300, is well worth a visit. The best-known figure to come from Vorden is the poet of Achterhoek **ACW Staring** (1767–1840), who lived in De Wildenborch castle from 1791 until his death.

Environs
Around Vorden are eight castles in very picturesque surroundings. A bicycle trip of the area, passing farms and country estates, is definitely worth the effort.

An ancient watermill at Vorden, a town in eastern Netherlands

⓰ Lochem

Road Map D3. 19,000.
Tramstraat 4 (0573-251898).
Wed morning.

Lochem, one of the oldest villages in the Achterhoek to have its own parish church, was granted its town charter in 1233. During the Dutch War of Independence, the town was often besieged. It was razed to the ground in 1615. Only the **Grote kerk**, also known as **St Gudulakerk**, with its 56-m (185-ft) steeple, was spared. This 14th-century hall-type church has fine murals from Catholic times (it is now a Reformed Church). The **Stadhuis** (town hall) across from the church dates from 1615.

A charming old farmhouse near Winterswijk

⓱ Winterswijk

Road Map E4. 28,000. Mevr, Kuipers Rietbergplein 1 (0543-512302). Wed morning, Sat. **winterswijk.nl**

The 20th century was not kind to the town of Winterswijk and the grand railway station bears witness to better times. There is now only a single railway track, although it is evident that in the past the rail traffic was much heavier. The **Museum Freriks** is pleasant with its exhibits relating to the textile industry that flourished here before World War II. The museum also has prints by Pieter Mondriaan Sr, whose famous painter son Piet spent his childhood in Winterswijk.

On the outskirts of the town lies a pleasant sculpture park, **De Beeldtuin**. Set out in the shady mature orchards of an old farm, there are also meadows and wooded areas. The works of art, by contemporary, mainly Dutch sculptors, are dotted all over the grounds, and represent just about every genre, from Pop Art to traditional to highly abstract. The park also hosts changing temporary exhibitions of 3D art.

Museum Freriks
Groenloseweg 86. **Tel** 0543- 533533. **Open** 10am–5pm Tue–Fri, 2–5pm Sat & Sun.

De Beeldtuin
Steggemansweg 1. **Tel** 0543-521034. **Open** phone ahead.

⓲ 's-Heerenberg

Road Map D4. 18,000. 24. Hofstraat 1 (0316 291391). Thu.

The old castle town of 's-Heerenberg and the area surrounding it are among the prettiest corners of Achterhoek. The little town, which was granted its charter in 1379, retains its historical centre, with buildings from the 15th and 16th centuries. **Huis Bergh** is one of Holland's finest castles and houses the art collection of the textile magnate JH van Heek.

Kasteel Huis Bergh
Hof Van Bergh 8 (0314-661281). **Open** May–Oct: 12:30–4:30pm Tue–Sun. **Closed** 1 Jan, 24, 25 & 31 Dec.

⓳ Montferland

Road Map D4. Hofstraat 1, 's-Heerenberg (0316-291391).

Montferland, one of the few hilly areas in the Netherlands, is exceptionally attractive. Apart from **'s-Heerenberg** *(see above)*, there is a number of other attractions, such as Zeddam, Beek and nature reserves where you can walk, cycle, swim or even dive. The natural spring in Beek, "het Peeske", and the historic farmhouses along the Langeboomseweg in Velthuizen are worth seeing.

⓴ Doesburg

Road Map D4. 11,000. 27/29 Arnhem & 26/28 Dieren. Gasthuisstraat 13 (0313-479088). Wed am, Sat.

Doesburg is a snug Hanseatic town on the IJssel. Granted its town charter in 1237, this small town's well-preserved old town centre has had listed status since 1974. Doesburg contains at least 150 national monuments, including a late Gothic town hall, one of the earliest in Holland. The **Grote or Martinuskerk**, a Late Gothic basilica with a 97-m (320-ft) tower, is another of the town's noteworthy buildings, along with the local museum **De Roode Toren**.

De Roode Toren
Roggestraat 9–11–13. **Tel** 0313-474265. **Open** 10am–noon, 1:30–4:30pm Tue–Fri, 1:30–4:30pm Sat & Sun (Nov–Mar: pm only).

㉑ Nijmegen

Road Map D4. 152,000. Keizer Karelplein 32 (0481 366250). Mon, Sat.

Nijmegen is one of the oldest towns in Holland. Archaeological remains show that the Batavians were settled here even before

Huis Bergh, one of Holland's finest castles

the first millennium BC, while the Romans had a fort here from 12 BC. In AD 104, the emperor Trajan granted trading rights to a new settlement west of present-day Valkhof. The town's ancient name of Ulpia Noviomagus Batavorum is presumably also from this time.

Nijmegen owes its existence to its strategic position on the river Waal. A fort has stood here since early times, and even in World War II, the town was an important battle scene. The most important sights include the **Valkhof**, with its new **museum**, which stands on the spot where the fort of the Batavians, Roman engineering works and, later, one of Charlemagne's palaces stood. All that remains of the palace which was rebuilt by Frederick Barbarossa is the **St Maartenskapel** from 1155 and the **St Nicolaaskapel**, one of the earliest stone buildings in all of Holland. This chapel (part of which dates back to 1030) is a rare example of Byzantine architecture in northern Europe. Other noteworthy buildings include the St Stevenskerk, the construction of which began in 1254, the **Waag** (weigh house) and the **Kronenburgerpark**, with the remnants of fortifications (the Kruittoren tower).

A fascinating insight into the Dutch national obsession with all things two-wheeled can be found at **Velorama**, the bike museum. Spread over two floors, there are examples from the entire history of cycling, from the earliest "hobby horse"-type bikes that date back to 1817. The upstairs room is devoted to the bicycle's modern incarnation, with beautifully shiny examples of racers, recumbants and everyday bikes. Star of the show, however, is the bicycle that belonged to Queen Wilhelmina in the 1940s and 1950s.

Ruins of the Valkhof in Nijmegen, one of the oldest towns in Holland

Nijmegen's Waag, dating from 1612

Nijmegen is perhaps best known for its annual four-day rambling meet, the Wandelvierdaagse, in which tens of thousands of ramblers take part. With its many cafés, the town also has a vibrant nightlife.

Each July, **de-Affaire**, a week-long festival of music, accompanies the **Vierdaagse** long-distance marches *(see box)*. Events take place all over town, but many are focused around the Waalpark. Featuring around 100 acts, international cutting-edge rock and pop bands play alongside DJs and world musicians. There are also workshops on such activities as Latin music and dancing.

Museum Het Valkhof
Kelfkensbos 59, Nijmegen.
Tel 024-3608805. **Open** 10am–5pm Tue–Sun. **Closed** 25 Dec.

Velorama National Bicycle Museum
Waalkade 107. **Tel** 024-3225851.
Open 10am–5pm Mon–Sat, 11am–5pm Sun. **Closed** 1 Jan, 25 Dec.

Environs

Close to Nijmegen is the Ooypolder, a beautiful, relaxing oasis for nature lovers. Here you can cycle and walk.

Nijmegen's Four Days Marches

In mid-July thousands of people from all around the Netherlands (and beyond) descend on the city to take part in the annual De Vierdaagse, the Four Days Marches. This is a series of hikes in and around Nijmegen, divided into daily legs of 30 km (20 miles) to 50 km (30 miles). The walks began in 1909 as a military exercise for soldiers, who marched from Nijmegen's garrison to Breda's, where they participated in a sports tournament. In that year, 309 soldiers completed the 150 km route. After a few years, civilians began to join in, until the march became a highlight of the national sporting calendar. In recent years, the number of participants has topped 45,000. Those who complete the walk receive a commemorative medal.

Walkers tackling the Four Days Marches

Beavers introduced to the Gelderse Poort now thrive

22 Gelderse Poort

Road Map D4. Arnhem (0481 366250).

At the point where the Rhine enters the Waal, the IJssel and the Neder-Rijn (Lower Rhine) is the Gelderse Poort. This is a protected area where the flora and fauna have been allowed to grow freely. At the heart of it is the Millingerwaard, where the currents are particularly strong and where, at high water, the surrounding area regularly floods. The river banks, woodlands and marshes provide ideal breeding grounds for endangered species of birds such as the corncrake and the penduline tit.

Gelderse Poort Visitors' Centre
Gerard Noodtstraat 121. **Tel** 024-3297 070. **Open** Apr–Oct: 9am–5pm daily.

23 Groesbeek

Road Map D4. 19,000. Dorpsplein 1a (024-3977118).

Its hilly woodland surroundings make Groesbeek an attractive place for cyclists and hikers. The route of the four-day annual hike *(Wandelvierdaagse)* follows the Zevenheuvelenweg from Groesbeek to Berg and Dal, past the Canadian war cemetery. Groesbeek was subjected to heavy bombardment at the end of World War II. The **Bevrijdingsmuseum** (liberation museum) illustrates the development of Operation Market Garden (1944) and Operation Veritable (1945), which brought about the final liberation of Holland. Groesbeek has two other popular museums: the **Bijbels Openluchtmuseum** and the **Afrika Museum**.

Bevrijdingsmuseum 1944
Wylerbaan 4. **Tel** 024-3974404. **Open** 10am–5pm Mon–Sat, noon–5pm Sun & hols. **Closed** 25 Dec, 1 Jan.

24 Tiel

Road Map C4. 36,500. Plein 63 (0344-633030). Mon pm, Sat.

Tiel, situated on the Waal, is an ancient town that flourished during the Middle Ages because of its strategic location on the trading routes to and from Cologne. One of the best-preserved monuments from this time is the **Ambtmanshuis**, dating back to 1525. The town also has the oldest elm tree in the country. The local history museum, **De Groote Sociëteit** on the Plein, is worth a visit. Tiel is the centre of fruit farming in the Betuwe region. On the second Saturday in September of each year, it also becomes the centre of the **Fruitcorso** *(see p38)*, as a procession of floats

The Great Rivers

The three great rivers – the Rhine, the Maas and the Waal – have made an important mark on the history and landscape of Gelderland. The fortified trading towns that grew on the banks of the rivers brought prosperity to the region; dykes were built to protect the land from flooding.

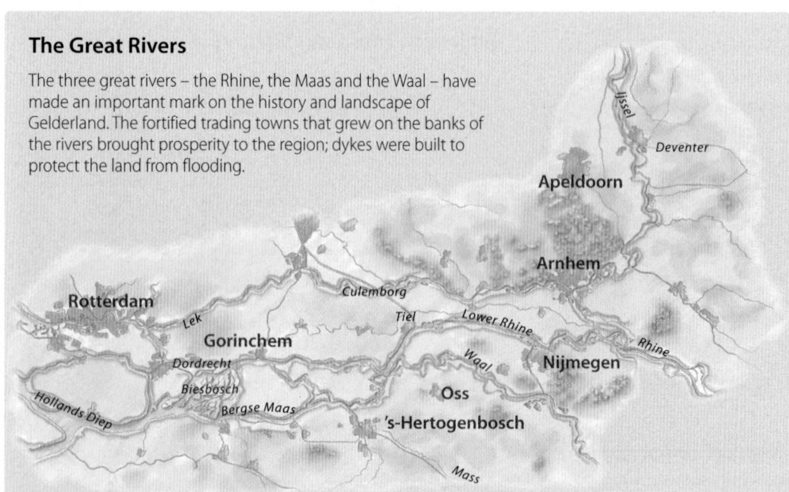

Dyke house on the Linge

decorated with fruit winds through the streets of the town. Tiel is also renowned for its tinsmith industry.

Environs

Asperen is a peaceful little town on the River Linge. On the Lingedijk is **Fort Asperen**, which is part of the Nieuwe Hollandse Waterlinie. Farther upstream is the little town of **Acquoy**, with its crooked 15th-century tower. A Lady Pisa is buried in the churchyard, but there is no connection to the Leaning Tower in Italy.

㉕ Culemborg

Road Map C4. 24,000.
Camping de Hogekuil, Achterweg 4 (0345-515701). Tue.

The old "Driestadje" (triple town) of Culemborg, formerly consisting of three walled towns, is picturesquely situated on the River Lek. It is a great place to wander around. If you enter the former fortress through the old Binnenpoort gate, you'll reach the Markt. Here is the Late Gothic Stadhuis (town hall), built by Flemish masterbuilder Rombout Keldermans for Vrouwe Elisabeth van Culemborg (1475–1555). Her estate was sufficient to finance the Elisabeth Weeshuis (1560), which is now operated as a historical museum.

Other well-preserved buildings in Culemborg are the Huize de Fonteyn in the Achterstraat and the house where Jan van Riebeeck, who founded Cape Town, South Africa, was born. The large clock in the Grote Kerk was a gift from South Africa. Even today, the "papklok" bell, which is used to announce the closing of the town gates, is tolled each and every evening at 10 o'clock.

Museum Elisabeth Weeshuis
Herenstraat 29. **Tel** 0345-513912.
Open Apr–Oct: 1–5pm Tue–Fri, 2–5pm Sat & Sun.

㉖ Buren

Road Map C4. 1,800.
Markt 1 (0344-571922). Fri.

On the main road between Tiel and Culemborg is Buren. This little town is known for its historic links with the House of Orange, and the entire town has been listed. One of the most beautiful houses is the **Koninklijk Weeshuis** (Royal Orphanage), which was built in 1613 by Maria of Orange. The late Gothic **Lambertuskerk** is also worth seeing.

㉗ Zaltbommel

Road Map C4. 11,000.
Markt 15 (0418-518177). Tue, Sat.

Bommel, as its inhabitants say, is more than 1,000 years old. During the 80 Years War *(see p53)*, it was an important mainstay of the Republiek der Zeven Verenigde Nederlanden (Republic of the Seven United Netherlands). The town is surrounded by two well-preserved sets of walls, which have now been laid out as a park. Within the town walls, the first building worth mentioning is the 15th-century **St Maartenskerk**, whose low towers give the town its distinctive skyline. The interior of the church is worth a look.

Another worthwhile stop is at the house of the Gelderland commander-in-chief **Maarten van Rossum** (1478–1555), who is known for plundering The Hague in 1528. The house is now an intimate museum with a large collection of drawings and prints from the region; it also hosts visiting exhibitions.

Maarten van Rossummuseum
Nonnenstraat 5. **Tel** 0418-512617.
Open Apr–Oct 10am–5pm Tue–Sun.

The house of Maarten van Rossum in Nonnenstraat, Zaltbommel

SOUTHERN NETHERLANDS

Southern Netherlands at a Glance

South of Holland's great rivers lie the provinces of North Brabant and Limburg, whose ambience is quite different from that of the northern provinces. The atmosphere here is more easygoing, more sociable. Both eating and drinking well are held in high regard here. Visitors to the Southern Netherlands will also find cities with historical centres, such as Den Bosch, Breda, Thorn and Maastricht; the beautiful countryside of Kempen, Peel and the hills of Zuid Limburg; thriving modern towns; and peaceful rural villages.

The Gothic Church of Sint Jan (*see pp364–65*) in Den Bosch was started in the late 14th century and completed in the 1500s.

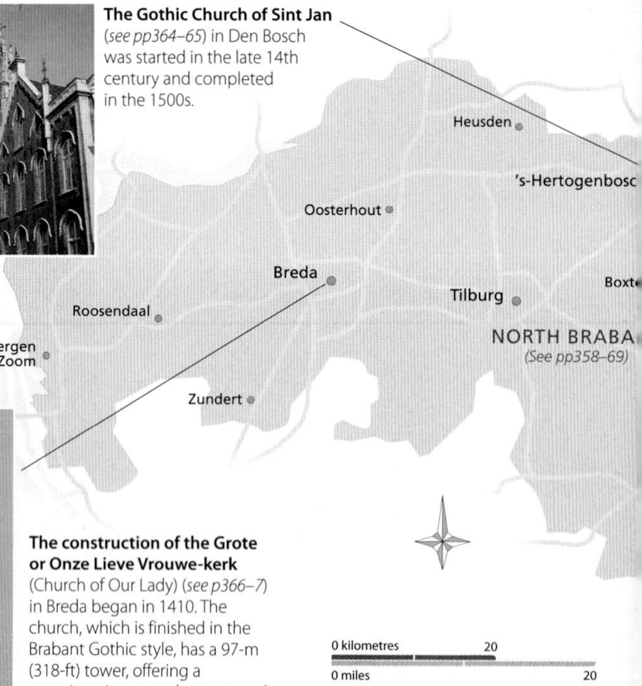

Heusden
's-Hertogenbosc
Oosterhout
Breda
Tilburg
Boxt
Roosendaal
Bergen op Zoom
Zundert
NORTH BRABA
(See pp358–69)

The construction of the Grote or Onze Lieve Vrouwe-kerk (Church of Our Lady) (*see p366–7*) in Breda began in 1410. The church, which is finished in the Brabant Gothic style, has a 97-m (318-ft) tower, offering a stunning view over the town and the surrounding countryside.

0 kilometres 20
0 miles 20

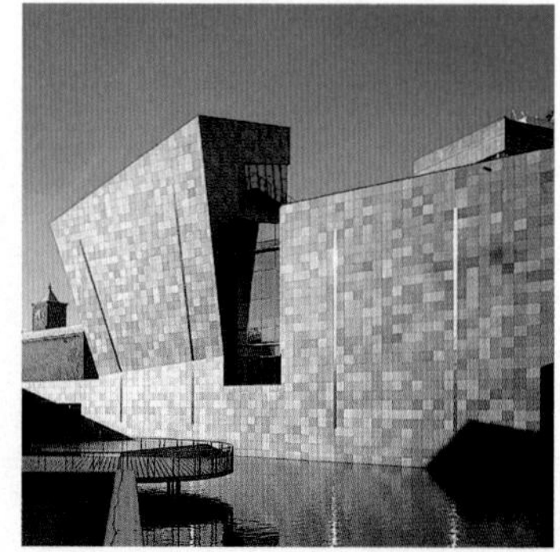

The Van Abbemuseum (*see p368*) in Eindhoven has undergone extensive renovation. Architect Abel Cahen has preserved the old builing while creating light-filled spaces in the angular, slanting new wing. A large collection of modern art, including video and other installations, is on display.

◀ Revellers take part in carnival celebrations in Den Bosch, North Brabant

The Kasteeltuinen, the gardens of the 17th-century Castle Arcen (*see p374*), in the town of the same name on the river Maas, have a lovely rose garden, as well as subtropical gardens, a forest of Scots pines and a golf course.

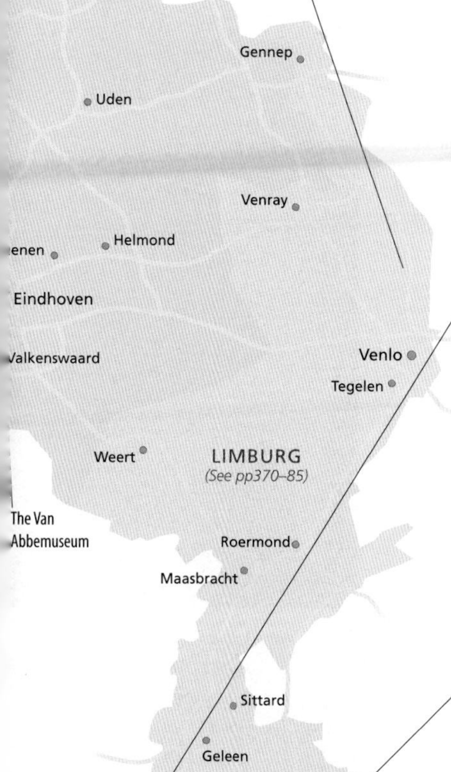

The Bonnefantenmuseum (*see pp378–9*) in Maastricht is housed in a striking building designed by the Italian architect Aldo Rossi. The collections of old works of art and contemporary international art are impressive.

The route through the Heuvelland (*see pp384–85*) passes among hills and dales and by meandering rivers, their banks dotted with old castles. Outstanding examples of these are the 17th-century Kasteel Eijsden and Kasteel Schaloen in Valkenburg.

Catholicism and Devotion

One of the main reasons for the differences between Holland's southern and northern provinces is the marked presence of Catholicism in the south, even in these secular times. Religious imagery is a common sight here. The churches in the Brabant Gothic or Neo-Gothic style are decorated flamboyantly and many host traditional processions throughout the year.

Religious images, usually of the Madonna and Child, are a common roadside sight in Limburg. This one is set into the façade of a house in Mechelen.

The Maria Magdalena Chapel (1695) in Gemert is also known as the Spijkerkapelleke ("nail chapel") because people made offerings of nails here in the hopes of having their skin disorders cured. Every 22 July, which is the day of Mary Magdalene, an open-air mass is held here.

Decorative carving

Candles abound around images of St Mary.

Detail from the retable of the Holy Family in the Basilica of the Holy Sacrament in Meerssen, Limburg. It depicts Mary, Joseph and the infant Jesus fleeing to Egypt. This fine altar is richly decorated with scenes from the life of the Holy Family. The Holy Sacrament is honoured in the church. The host is kept in the Unique Sacramentstoren (sacrament tower) in the choir. The church itself is an example of Maasland Gothic and part of it (the nave and the choir) dates from as far back as the 14th century.

This tomb in the Late Romanesque/Early Gothic Onze-Lieve-Vrouwemunsterkerk (Minster Church of Our Lady) in Roermond dates from the 13th century. Inside the tomb lies Count Gerard van Gelre and his wife Margaretha van Brabant. At the time, Roermond was part of the duchy of Gelre.

St Anna-te-Drieën – the trinity of Anna, her daughter Mary and the infant Jesus – is a familiar image in religious art. This statue from Mechelen incorporates the town's coat of arms.

The Basiliek van de HH Agatha en Barbara (Basilica of SS Agatha and Barbara) in Oudenbosch is a copy of St Peter and St John of the Laterans in Rome. The picture on the right shows the façade. The interior of the church is richly decorated, though appearances are deceiving: what appears to be marble is actually painted wood.

Statue of St Mary in the Onder de Linden Chapel in Thorn (Limburg).

Onder De Linden Chapel In Thorn

The Onder de Linden Chapel, located just outside the town of Thorn in Limburg, was founded in 1673 by Clara Elisabeth van Manderscheidt-Blankenheim, who lies buried in the parish church of Thorn. This chapel, dedicated to St Mary, is opulently decorated with carvings and Baroque paintings depicting scenes of the life of the Mother of God. Shown in the picture on the left is the Onze-Lieve-Vrouwebeeld (statue of Our Lady). St Mary's Chapel is also called the Loretokapel, after the Holy House of Nazareth in the Italian town of Loreto, on which the earlier 17th-century part of the chapel is based.

The 15th-century tower of the Michielskerk is all that remains of the North Brabant Sint-Michielsgestel. The medieval church was built in honour of the archangel Michael. The village, also named after the saint, grew up around the church. Neglect and the elements have meant that the church building itself has been levelled to the ground, but the solid tower has withstood the ages.

The church of Rolduc, a former canon's abbey at Kerkrade which today houses a Catholic middle school and a training school for priests, has a fine altar depicting the Lamb of God. The Lamb of God represents Christ, who was sacrificed in the same way as a lamb, in order to take away the sins of the world.

Carnival

Every year in February, in the week before Ash Wednesday, carnival breaks out in the towns south of the great rivers. While life goes on as usual in the north of the country, people in the south celebrate this old tradition, which is also honoured in other parts of the Catholic world. A festive mood abounds everywhere, with the best-known celebrations being held in Den Bosch, Bergen op Zoom and Maastricht. For days on end, there is drinking, singing and dancing all over Brabant and Limburg.

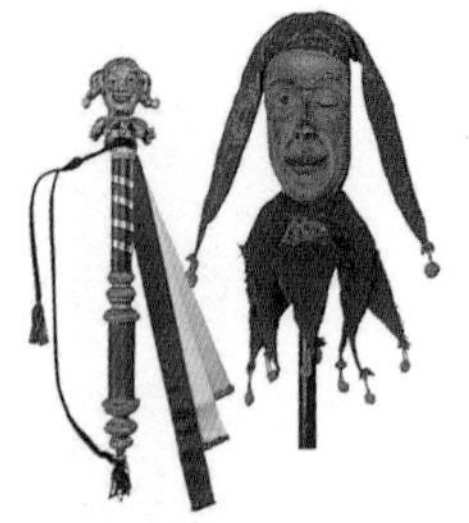

Carnavalsstokken (carnival rods) are brightly decorated. They are carried by the Prince of the Carnival when he passes through the streets on his float.

Music plays an important role at carnival time. Every year, the associations choose the official carnival anthem that will be played over and over again. The Zaate Herremienekes of Maastricht (pictured left) are among the better-known bands. Dozens of its members march through the streets blaring out enthusiastically; what their music may lack in elegance is made up for by their verve. On Shrove Tuesday they compete in the Herremienekes competition.

Although in high spirits, his question is profound (the sign on the pram reads "where are we going?")

Carnival – Putting Your Worries Aside

The carnival season officially starts on 11 November – the eleventh of the eleventh – or "day of fools", when the Council of Eleven names the Prince of the Carnival. From then on, the municipalities are busy with preparations, and on the Sunday (in many places now on the Friday) before Ash Wednesday, the festivities begin. Wild celebrations are held throughout North Brabant and Limburg, and most public institutions are closed. Long processions with floats parade through the towns. People dress up festively: the more colourful and exuberant the costume, the better. "Dansmarietjes" (dancing girls) accompany the floats in their colourful costumes, and the mood everywhere is upbeat. All the merriment comes to an end after Shrove Tuesday, the climax of the carnival.

Refreshments both indoors and outdoors at carnival time

Carnival Floats

At carnival time, long processions with extravagantly decorated floats wind their way through the main streets of towns and villages. Months of preparation often go into creating the floats, and secrecy prevails during their preparation. The decoration of the float is usually on an upbeat and amusing theme, but current events are sometimes illustrated in imaginative ways. When leading politicians are featured, they are more often than not caricatured mercilessly, and social ills are exposed, often using costumed participants in *tableaux vivants.*

A festive float

The Raad van Elf (Council of Eleven) is the central office of the local carnival organization. Every year, the council appoints a Prince of the Carnival, who holds power in a municipality on the days of the carnival. The council's ritual number is 11, which is considered the number of fools. From 11 November onwards, the Raad van Elf is busy preparing carnival events. At the lively meetings, many a beer is drunk to a call of "Alaaf!" ("Eleven!").

Silly clothes are mandatory at carnival time. In earlier times it was customary to put on masks, whereas today the trend is to dress up in as unusual a way as possible. The northerners' belief that it is enough to put on a peasant's smock to be properly dressed is a misconception.

NORTH BRABANT

The Netherland's second largest province is distinguished primarily by its natural beauty. In the south and south-east are the relatively high elevations of Kempen and the Peel; in the northwest, the watery Biesbosch. Here, arms of the Waal and Maas rivers converge through a wilderness of sandbanks.

North Brabant has been inhabited by humans since the earliest times. The Celts settled here in the 7th century BC and stayed for many centuries. They were defeated by Julius Caesar *(see p47)*, who describes them as the "Belgae" in his writings. The Rhine became the northern frontier of the Roman Empire and Roman remains have been found in the area. When the Romans left, the Franks took charge of Toxandria, as the region was known in those days. Under Charlemagne *(see p49)*, this region grew in importance as new towns expanded at points along trade routes, and in the 12th century became part of the Duchy of Brabant. The Dukes of Brabant, among them Godfried III and Henry I, expanded their territory and founded towns such as Breda and 's-Hertogenbosch. The Duchy flourished until the 16th century, when the 80 Years War left the south of Brabant under Spanish rule and the north under the rule of the Netherlands.

Although North Brabant has its fair share of commerce and industry, and Eindhoven is a major manufacturing centre, tourism has become increasingly important. The region's colourful history is evident from the medieval buildings and bastions in many of the towns, and the castles dotted around the countryside, with a range of fine exhibits in churches and museums. For younger visitors the highlight is the fairytale theme park De Efteling at Kaatsheuvel, northeast of Breda.

Het Grote Peel, an area of outstanding natural beauty in North Brabant

◀ The beautiful ceiling of the basilica in Oudenbosch

Exploring North Brabant

North Brabant's rich historic past and unspoiled countryside have given the province its unique character. The centres of 's-Hertogenbosch and Breda and the picturesque fortified towns of Heusden and Willemstad are of great historical interest. The beautiful natural areas of the Loonse and Drunense dunes, Peel, Kempen and Biesbosch areas provide opportunities for various tours. Van Abbemuseum in Eindhoven, De Wieber in Deurne and the many other museums in the region offer a great deal of cultural interest. De Efteling is one of Europe's best-known theme parks.

The Markiezenhof in Bergen op Zoom, dating from 1511

Sights at a Glance

1. *'s-Hertogenbosch pp362–6*
2. Heusden
3. Tilburg
4. Breda
5. Oudenbosch
6. Willemstad
7. Bergen op Zoom
8. Eindhoven
9. Heeze
10. Nuene
11. Helmond
12. Deurne
13. Gemert

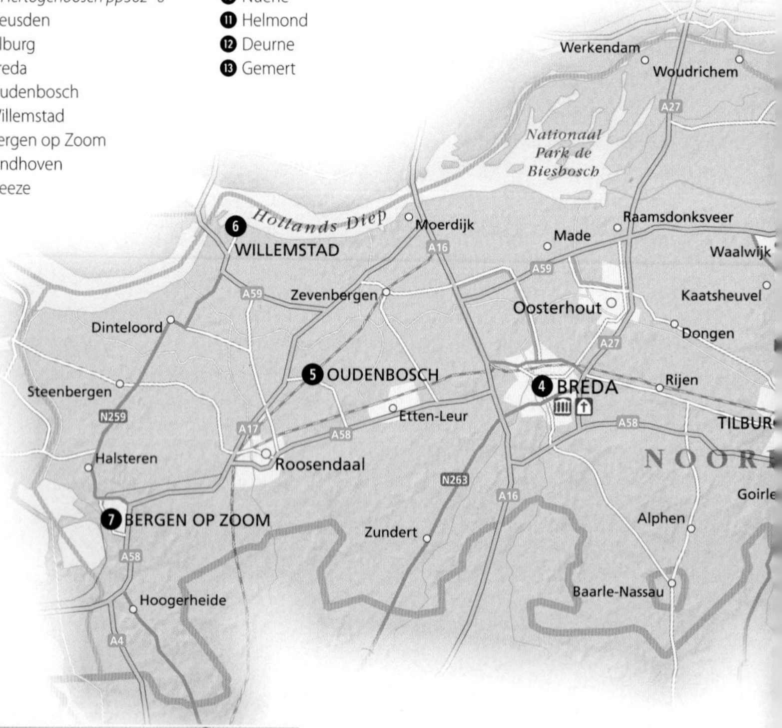

Drifting sands and conifers in the Loonse and the Drunense dunes, east of Kaatsheuvel

Key

- Motorway
- Major road
- Minor road
- Scenic route
- Main railway
- Minor railway
- Regional border
- International border

For map symbols *see back flap*

Getting Around

North Brabant has an excellent transport infrastructure. All the larger towns, as well as many smaller towns and villages, can be reached easily by train. There is an extensive network of long-distance coaches which will take you to even the smallest village. The province can be explored by car with great ease thanks to its dense motorway network, which includes the A2, and the A58, as well as its many good major roads. Areas of natural beauty such as the Peel and Kempen are ideal countryside for cycling.

The 14th-century Kasteel Heeswijk, rebuilt numerous times during its lifetime

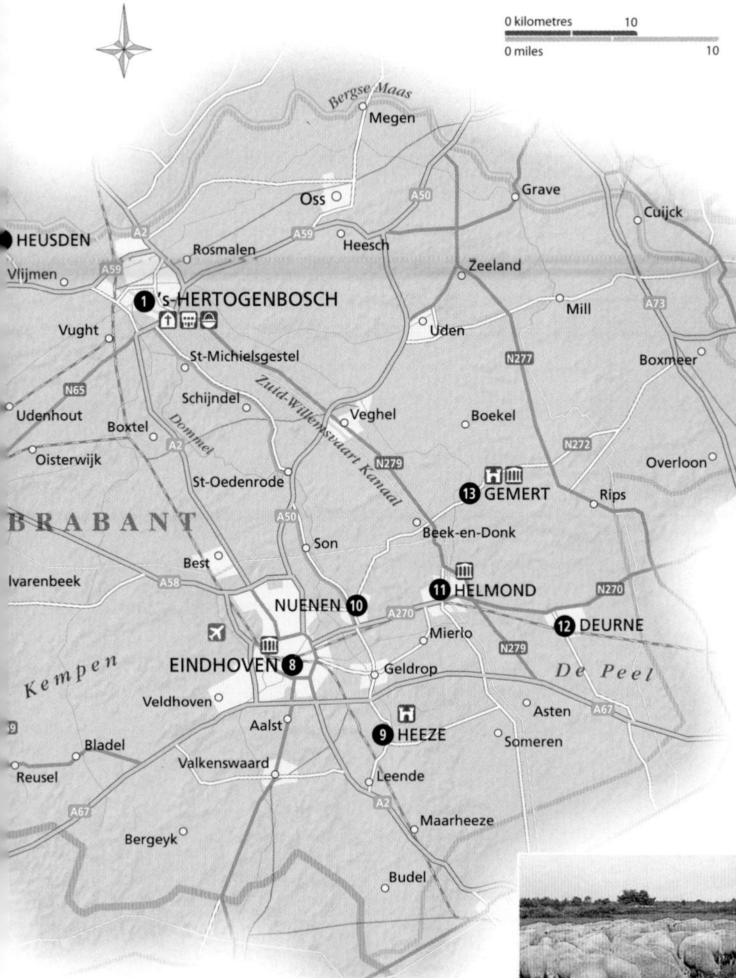

Sheep on the Strabrechtse Heide, near Heeze

❶ Street-by-Street: 's-Hertogenbosch

In 1185, Henry I of Brabant founded the town of 's-Hertogenbosch. The strategically positioned town – usually called Den Bosch – grew rapidly. From the 16th century its prosperity waned, when the States General *(see p50)* ignored Brabant and chose to favour other regions. Its prestige rose again after 1815, when it became the capital of North Brabant. Today, it is a vibrant, lively town.

Stone Plaque with Swan
Such plaques are a common sight in the city centre.

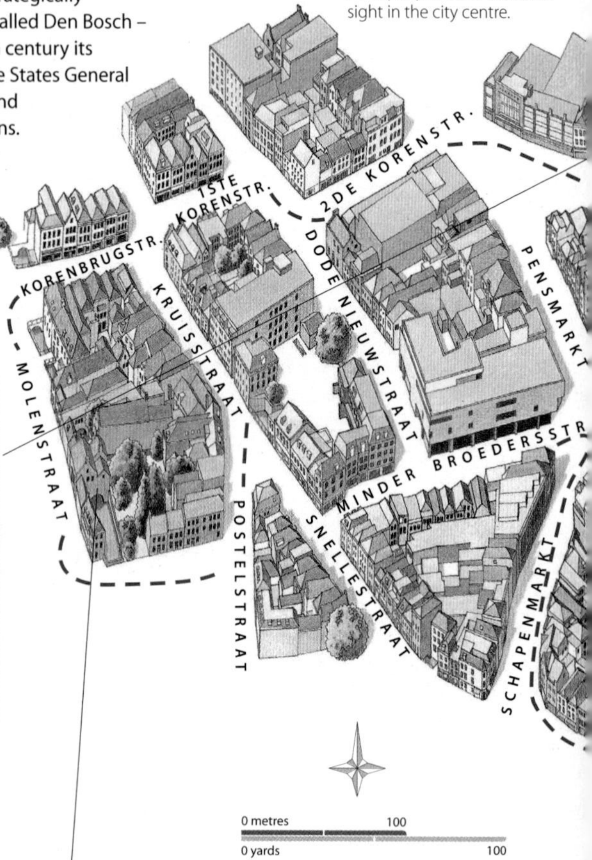

Moriaan
The medieval building known as De Moriaan, with its stepped gable, is the town's oldest building. It now houses the town's tourist office.

0 metres 100
0 yards 100

★ Binnen-Dieze
The Binnen-Dieze, the city's inner canal, runs partly underground. It is possible to make a spectacular round trip along the restored town walls.

★ Sint Jan
The flying buttresses of the Sint Jan Church *(see pp364–5)* are decorated with a variety of figures.

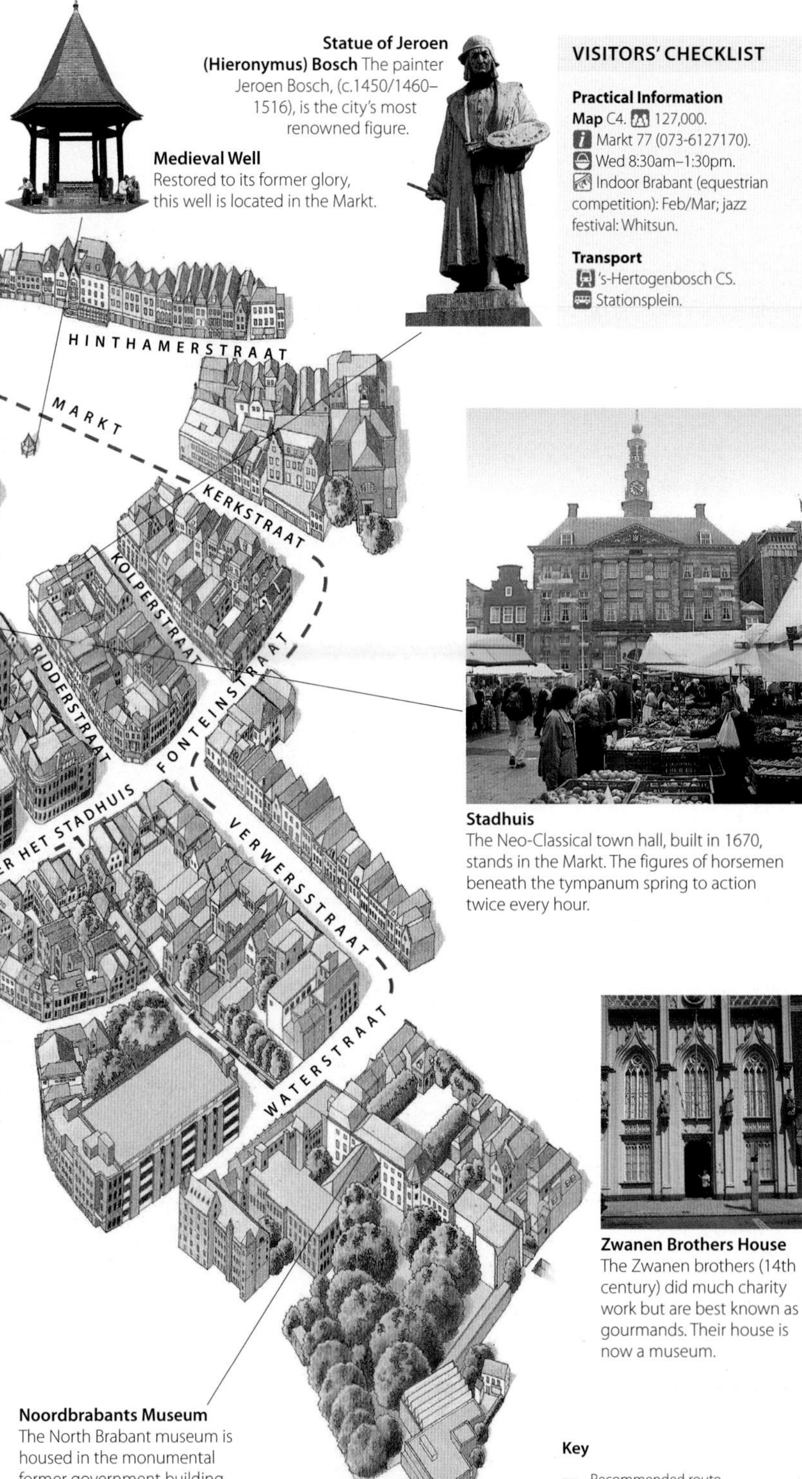

Statue of Jeroen (Hieronymus) Bosch The painter Jeroen Bosch, (c.1450/1460–1516), is the city's most renowned figure.

Medieval Well
Restored to its former glory, this well is located in the Markt.

VISITORS' CHECKLIST

Practical Information
Map C4. 127,000.
Markt 77 (073-6127170).
Wed 8:30am–1:30pm.
Indoor Brabant (equestrian competition): Feb/Mar; jazz festival: Whitsun.

Transport
's-Hertogenbosch CS.
Stationsplein.

Stadhuis
The Neo-Classical town hall, built in 1670, stands in the Markt. The figures of horsemen beneath the tympanum spring to action twice every hour.

Zwanen Brothers House
The Zwanen brothers (14th century) did much charity work but are best known as gourmands. Their house is now a museum.

Noordbrabants Museum
The North Brabant museum is housed in the monumental former government building.

Key

Recommended route

Sint Jan

There was a church of Sint Jan (St John) in Den Bosch as early as the beginning of the 13th century, although nothing of the original Romanesque church exists today. The present-day Gothic church was built from the late 14th to the 16th century. The majestic cathedral survived the iconoclastic riots of 1566 *(see p52)* and a devastating fire in 1584. The damaged building is undergoing continuous restoration.

★ Organ
The great organ (1617) was fully refurbished in 1985 and restored to its original state.

Statue of St Mary
The 13th-century miracle-working figure of the Zoete Lieve Vrouw of Den Bosch (Our Good Lady of Den Bosch) was for centuries kept in Brussels but was returned to Sint Jan in 1853.

KEY

① **The ornamental south portal** is dedicated to Saint John the Evangelist.

② **Flying buttresses** are designed to strengthen the structure of the building. They are richly ornamented with saints, angels and other figures.

③ **The gargoyles** are designed to channel rainwater pouring off the roof. Here, the drain pipes are encased by the head of mythical animals.

④ **The stained-glass window frame** depicts the woman and the dragon from *The Book of Revelation*.

⑤ **The seven radiating chapels** around the choir form an elegant crown.

Baptistery
The baptismal font in the baptistery dates from 1492. The figures on the cover depict the baptism of Jesus by St John.

For hotels and restaurants in this region see p401 and pp414–415

Baldachin
The revolving baldachin in the middle of the cathedral is ascribed to Alart Duhameel. The all-seeing eye looks down from the vaults.

VISITORS' CHECKLIST

Practical Information
Torenstraat 16.
Tel 073-6130314.
W sint-jan.nl
Open 10am–5pm daily but restrictions apply during church services.

Antoniuskapel
The Chapel of St Anthony contains a spectacular Passion altar made by a studio in Antwerp. The Church of Sint Jan managed to buy the retable in 1901 for one guilder.

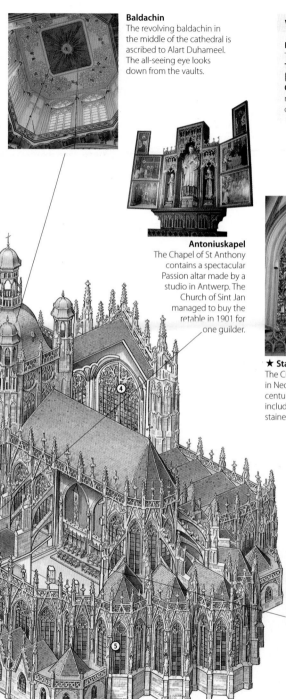

★ Stained-Glass Windows
The Church of Sint Jan was restored in Neo-Gothic style during the 19th century. A great deal was changed, including the lively and colourful stained-glass windows.

4

5

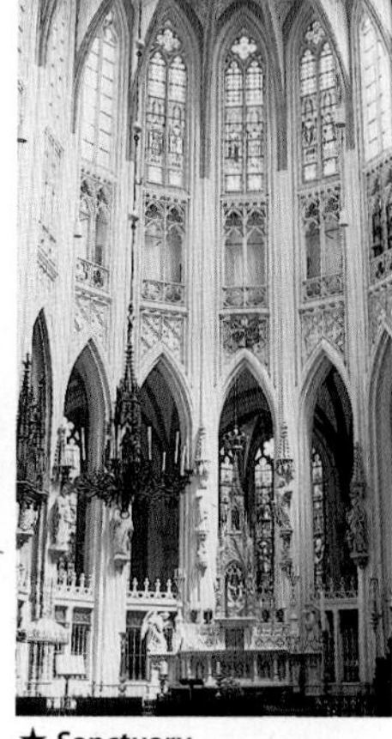

★ Sanctuary
The sanctuary was built from 1380 to 1425 by Willem van Kessel. The vaults are painted with a variety of religious scenes, among them the coronation of St Mary.

Exploring 's-Hertogenbosch

Along with a large number of historical buildings and interesting museums, the town of 's-Hertogenbosch offers a wide choice of fine restaurants. The excellent Noordbrabants Museum has an excellent exhibition of art from the Southern Netherlands from 1500 to the present. The most striking building in 's-Hertogenbosch is the majestic Gothic church of Sint Jan. The historic district of Uilenburg offers ample opportunities to while away the time with a drink or a bite to eat in a café.

The splendid church of Sint Jan *(see pp364–5)* is Den Bosch's crowning glory. In the Markt stand historical buildings such as **De Moriaan** (parts of which date back to the 12th century) and the town hall, dating from 1670. A statue of the great painter Hieronymus Bosch (c.1453–1516) stands between the two grand buildings. Born in 's-Hertogenbosch, Bosch spent most of his life here. In the town's historical district of Uilenburg, beyond the Markt, are plenty of good cafés and restaurants. The **Binnen-Dieze**, the city's inner canal, surfaces at this point; houses here stand directly in its water. Right by Sint Jan is the majestic **Zwanenbroedershuis** *(see p363)*, as well as the Museum Slager, which showcases paintings by the Slager family.

Four putti (1731) by Walter Pompe, Noordbrabants Museum

Noordbrabants Museum

Verwersstraat 41. **Tel** 073-6877877. **Open** 10am–5pm Tue–Fri, noon–5pm Sat, Sun & public hols.

The excellent Noordbrabants Museum displays art by renowned artists such as Pieter Brueghel and Teniers, as well as modern artists such as van Gogh, Mondriaan and Sluyters. The museum also features exhibits on the history of the province of North Brabant, from prehistoric times to the present.

❷ Heusden

Road Map C4. 42,000. Pelsestraat 17 (0416-662100). Thu.

After a thorough refurbishment that started in 1968 and lasted for decades, the picturesque ancient fortified town of Heusden on the river Maas has been restored to its former glory. That Heusden fell victim to the redevelopment craze of the 1960s matters little. Walls, houses, moats, the **Veerpoort** (ferry gate) and the **Waterpoort** have all been restored in the old style. As advertising is banned in Heusden, it is easy to imagine that time has stood still here, save for the fact that motor vehicles are allowed into the fortress.

❸ Tilburg

Road Map C5. 190,000. Nieuwlandstraat 34 (0900-2020815). Tue–Sat.

Tilburg, the sixth largest town in Holland, once had a flourishing textile industry. The interesting **Nederlands Textielmuseum**, which is housed in a former textile mill, illustrates the history of the country's textile industry and explains how textiles were produced. The **kermis van Tilburg** (Tilburg fair), held each year at the end of July, is the biggest fair in Holland. The entire town puts all its energy into the event, and people come from far and near to attend.

Nederlands Textielmuseum

Goirkestraat 96. **Tel** 013-5367475. **Open** 10am–5pm Tue–Fri, noon–5pm Sat & Sun. **Closed** 1 Jan, Carnival, 25 Dec.  by appointment.

Environs

Kaatsheuvel is home to **De Efteling**, the famous theme park where all kinds of fairytale personalities come to life *(see p427)*.

Mills on the bastion of the old fortified town of Heusden

❹ Breda

Road Map B5. 157,000. Willemstraat 17–19 (0900-5222444). Tue & Sat.

The Old Bastion of Breda was built at the confluence of the rivers Aa and Mark around the **Kasteel van Breda**, where the Koninklijke Militaire Academie (royal military academy) is now established. Breda was granted its town charter in 1252.

A walk through the old centre will take you to the **Grote kerk**, also known as the Onze Lieve Vrouwe Kerk (Church of Our

Lady). It is prominent on the Grote Markt and cannot be missed. Construction of this magnificent Brabant Gothic-style church began in 1410; in 1995–8 it underwent restoration.

At the Spanjaardsgat water-gate, near the castle, legend has it that in the 16th century, during the 80 Years War of independence from Spain, Adriaen van Bergen tricked his way past the Spanish with a peat barge full of soldiers and liberated the town.

Breda's Museum is housed in the old barracks of the Chassékazerne. The museum displays interesting exhibits that illustrate local history.

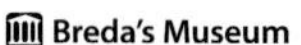

Breda's Museum
Parade 12–14. **Tel** 076-5299300. **Open** 11.30am–5pm Tue–Sun.

5 Oudenbosch

Road Map B5. 29,400 (municipality of Halderberge). Parklaan 15 (0165-390555). Tue.

Between 1860 and 1870, Oudenbosch was the point from which the Zouaves set out on their journey to Rome to defend the pope against Garibaldi. Upon their return, they had the architect PJH Cuypers *(see p375)* build a replica of St Peter's basilica in Rome, the **Basiliek van de HH Agatha en Barbara** (Basilica of SS Agatha and Barbara).

6 Willemstad

Road Map B4. 36,500 (municipality of Zevenbergen). Hofstraat 1 (0168-476055). Mon.

The Bastions of Willemstad, were built in 1583 by William of Orange. The Mauritshuis (1623), the former hunting lodge of Maurice, Prince of Orange, is today a museum. The influence of the Oranges can also been seen in the white Oranjemolen mill (1734). There is a pleasant harbour and a tree-lined "Wedding Walk", which leads to a domed church, the Koepeikerk.

The basilica of Oudenbosch, a miniature copy of St Peter's in Rome

7 Bergen op Zoom

Road Map B5. 64,000. Korte Meesstraat 19 (0164-277482). Thu.

The old town of Bergen op Zoom grew around a chapel that was dedicated to St Gertrude. In 1260, Bergen op Zoom was granted its town charter, after which it enjoyed a period of prosperity. The 15th-century **St Geertruids-kerk**, with its striking tower, stands on the site of the original chapel. The lords of Bergen op Zoom built the **Markiezenhof**, which was finally completed in 1511. The castle is today a museum, with period rooms and an unusual collection of fairground items. There are also changing exhibitions, which vary from cultural history to modern art.

Markiezenhof
Steenbergsestraat 8. **Tel** 0164-27707. **Open** 11am–5pm Tue–Sun.

The Surrender of Breda

During the 80 Years War, Breda was kept under siege by Spain for ten months, before finally surrendering to Ambrosio Spinola's troops on 5th June 1625. The moment of capitulation is captured in Velazquez's painting, known as both *The Surrender of Breda* and *Las Lanzas* – the lances – after the line of weapons that dominate the background. Velazquez, the great court painter of King Philip IV, is said to have painted the scene from memory. His picture shows the moment when the commander of the Dutch troops, on the left of the picture in a supplicating position, hands the key of the Dutch fortress to a straight-backed Spinola. The painting is famous for its composition, with the canvas divided into two balanced parts: left and right contain a group of soldiers and a horse, while the fore- and background are split into human activity and the smouldering city behind. The work is also noted for the lively way it portrays the men, several of whom look the viewer directly in the eye. The painting now hangs in Madrid's Museo del Prado.

The Surrender of Breda by Velázquez

Woman in Green (1909) by Picasso, Van Abbemuseum (Eindhoven)

8 Eindhoven

Road Map C5. 198,000. Stationsplein 17 (040-2979115). Mon–Sat.

The old market town of Eindhoven was merged with the villages of Strijp, Woensel, Tongelre, Stratum and Gestel in the 19th century. The municipality of Eindhoven grew enormously in the last century when Philips, the electronics company, sited its factory there. Philips's best-known building, the distinctive **Witte Dame** (White Lady) was built in 1922 by architect Dirk Rozenberg; it has now been sold and converted into a design college, library and centre for artists. The former Philips area in Strijp is also being developed into a residential area with shops, restaurants and theatres.

The city centre was heavily bombed in World War II and as a result very few old buildings have survived. In their place are a clutch of striking modern buildings, including the Stadhuis, an imposing structure, surrounded by a large empty space, the Stadhuis Plein, and the more appealing train station with its slender tower and glassy frontage.

The Philips Museum, in the city centre, holds a fascinating collection of electrical objects dating back to the earliest days of the company. On display are dozens of the very first light bulbs dating from the 19th century, beautiful bakelite radios and hulking cabinets from the birth of broadcasting. . Visitors can learn about the history of light-bulb making, from hand-made to mass-produced, and how the light bulb transformed Eindhoven from a small town into an industrial giant.

A rather more surprising find in the centre of this industrial city is the **Eindhoven Museum**. This open-air museum in the middle of the Genneper Park contains reconstructions of an iron-age village, a Viking settlement and a medieval town. Actors in costume people the scene, and are on hand to answer questions. There's also a restaurant where visitors can eat meals based on ancient recipes, like grain stew and lentil paté.

Looming over the railway station is the space-age **Philips Stadion**, home of the PSV Eindzhoven football team. The stadium, although ultra-modern these days, still stands in the spot where the first pitch was laid out for the team in 1913. Guided tours allow visitors to enter the players' changing rooms and to walk down the tunnel onto the pitch.

Eindhoven's most important sight, however, is the **Van Abbemuseum**, which is devoted to modern art. The original building was designed in 1936 by AJ Kropholler and has been described as a "brick castle". In the 1990s, architect Abel Cahen was commissioned to expand the museum. Cleverly integrating the existing building into a large new wing, he quadrupled the exhibition space and added a restaurant and multimedia centre. Queen Beatrix opened the museum in January 2003. The collection contains works by Chagall, Lissitzky and Beuys, and is particularly known for Picasso's *Woman in Green* (1909).

The town's fascinating Eindhoven Museum

Philips Stadion, home to the football team PSV Eindhoven

Philips Museum
Emmasingel 31. **Tel** 040-2359030.
Open 11am–5pm Tue–Sun.

Eindhoven Museum
Boutenslaan 161b. **Tel** 040-2522281.
Open Apr–Oct: 11am–5pm daily.

Philips Stadion
Frederiklaan 10a. **Tel** 040-2505505.
booking essential.

Van Abbemuseum
Bilderdijklaan 10. **Tel** 040-2381000.
Open 11am–5pm Tue–Sun.
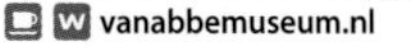
vanabbemuseum.nl

For hotels and restaurants in this region see p401 and pp414–15

9 Heeze

Road Map C5. 15,300. Schoolstraat 2 (040-2260644). Thu am.

The 17th-century castle of **Kasteel Heeze** is the centrepiece of this small Brabant town just outside Eindhoven. Designed by Pieter Post, it stands amidst lovely streams, woods and meadows. Among the many exhibits set out in the castle's 30 halls are valuable Gobelin tapestries.

Kasteel Heeze
Kapelstraat 25. **Tel** 040-2261431. **Open** May–Sep. May–Sep: 2pm Wed, 2 & 3pm Sun (Jul & Aug: also 2pm Wed).

The vast Strabrechtse Heide at Heeze and Geldrop

10 Nuenen

Road Map C5. 23,000. Berg 29 (040-2839615). Mon pm.

Nuenen, northeast of Eindhoven, is the village where van Gogh lived from 1883 to 1885. The **Van Gogh Documentatiecentrum** deals comprehensively with his time in Nuenen.

The magnificent 17th-century Kasteel HeezeL

Van Gogh Documentatiecentrum
Papenvoort 15. **Tel** 040-2631668. **Open** 11am–4pm Tue–Sun.

11 Helmond

Road Map C5. 77,600. Watermolenwal 11 (0492-522220). Wed am, Sat am.

The most outstanding feature of Helmond is the **castle** dating from 1402, today the **Gemeentemuseum** (local history museum). The museum has many historical artifacts as well as a fine collection of modern art including works by Breitner and Charley Toorop.

Gemeentemuseum
Kasteelplein 1. **Tel** 0492-587716. **Open** 10am–5pm Tue–Fri, 2–5pm Sat & Sun.

Van Gogh in Brabant

Vincent van Gogh was born in 1853 in Zundert, south of Breda. There, in the Cultureel Centrum, you can learn about his childhood. In 1883, he moved to Nuenen, where his father was rector. He stayed there until 1885, when he moved on to Antwerp. The Nuenen period was very prolific for van Gogh. Rural life in Brabant inspired him, and he painted farms, labourers and weavers in the blue and brown tones that are so characteristic of his Nuenen work. A famous painting dating from this period is *The Potato Eaters* (1885).

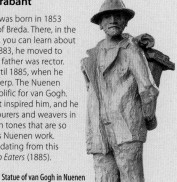

Statue of van Gogh in Nuenen

12 Deurne

Road Map D5. 32,000. Markt 14 (0493-323655). Fri pm.

The relaxing town of Deurne is an artistic centre. The house (1922) of the extravagant doctor and painter Henrik Wiedersma, who used to make house calls on his motorcycle, is now a **museum** of expressionist works by the doctor and his avant-garde friends, including Ossip Zadkine, who often stayed with him. Poets such as Roland Holst, Nijhoff and Bloem were also regular visitors to the house.

Museum De Wieger
Oude Liesselseweg 29. **Tel** 0493-322930. **Open** noon–5pm Tue–Sun. **Closed** Mon & public hols.

13 Gemert

Road Map C5. 27,300 (community of Gemert-Bakel). Ridderplein 49 (0492-366606). Mon pm.

Gemert is a town of historical importance; its nickname was once "Heerlijkheid Gemert" ("glorious Gemert"). Until 1794 it was ruled by the Knights of the Teutonic Order: their **castle** still stands and is now used as a monastery.

The **Boerenbondmuseum** (agricultural museum) is in a farmhouse dating from the beginning of the 20th century; the displays portray what rural life was like at that time.

LIMBURG

Limburg is The Netherland's southernmost province, squeezed by the course of history into its present unusual shape bounded partly by Belgium to the west and to the south and by Germany on the eastern flank. Yet its outline is not the only remarkable thing about this delightful multilingual provincc.

From a geological point of view, Limburg is much older than the rest of Holland, sitting on coal deposits that are around 270 million years old. In the mining museum at Kerkrade, east of Maastricht, you can see how coal used to be mined in this region. The caves that can be seen in many places in South Limburg are also mines, albeit for the local limestone laid down between 60 and 70 million years ago. The best-known cave systems, parts of which date from the Roman era, are at Valkenburg and at St Pietersberg near Maastricht.

The Maas river valley has been attractive to settlers since the last Ice Age. There is evidence of early nomads, followed by the remains of successive sedentary societies such as the "Bandkeramikers" and the Beaker Folk *(see p46)*. The Romans were here for around 400 years and Maastricht, which they founded, has much evidence of their impressive buildings. Heerlen was also an important Roman crossroads and the bathhouse museum here makes an excellent and informative visit. In the Middle Ages, Limburg was split up and fought over at various times by the German Empire, Gelder, Liège, Brabant and the Spanish. It acquired its present borders in the 19th century. Nowadays it has plenty to offer visitors, from historic towns with fine architecture, shops and nightlife to countryside dotted with half-timbered houses, farms, water mills in the rivers, and countless castles and country houses.

Half-timbered houses in the South Limburg town of Cottessen

◀ **Statues on the estate of one of the castles in Valkenburg**

Exploring Limburg

Noord Limburg is made up of the Peel and the Maas regions. Between the river Maas and the German border are nature reserves with fens, woodland, heathland and river dunes. The former wilderness known as the Peelgebied is on the border with North Brabant. Middle Limburg is the section from the Maasplassen lakes, which were created by the digging of gravel pits. It is now one of the most important watersports areas in the country. Zuid Limburg consists of Maastricht, the Mijnstreek (mining country) and the pretty chalk-hill landscape to the south.

Picking asparagus in Noord Limburg

National park of De Grote Peel

Getting Around

Limburg is easily reached by rail and by road, which are also the best ways to explore it. The motorways and railways invariably follow the same routes, that is to say: Nijmegen- Venlo-Roermond-Geleen-Maastricht, Weert-(Roermond)-Geleen-Maastricht and, finally, the triangle Maastricht-Geleen-Heerlen. For cyclists there are long sections of cycle paths along the Julianakanaal and the Zuid-Willemsvaart. The south of Zuid Limburg in particular is simply ideal for cycling (including racing) and rambling. The tourist railway or "environmental line" from Schin near Geul to Kerkrade via Wijlre, Eys and Simpelveld operates from April to October on Sundays and most Wednesdays and Thursdays, with two steam-trains and a "rail-bus".

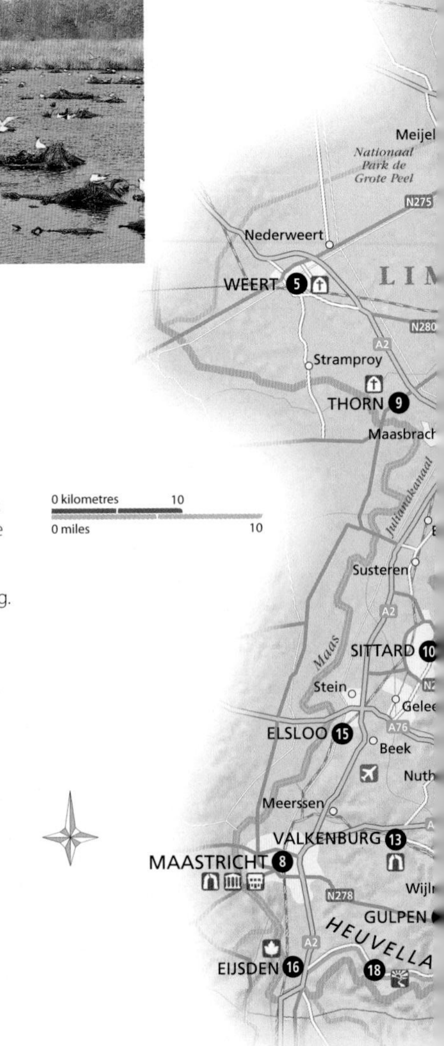

Limestone quarry with old passageways

For map symbols *see back flap*

Sights at a Glance

Tour

Field chapel in Heuvelland

Key

- Motorway
- Major road
- Minor road
- Scenic route
- Major railway
- Minor railway
- Regional border
- International border

Kasteel Schaloen at Valkenburg (13th century), rebuilt in the 17th century

❶ Mook

Road Map D4. 825. 83.
Witteweg 10, plasmolen (0900-1122344).

The village of Mook is on the river Maas in the very north of Limburg. On 14 April 1574, the Prince of Orange's army was routed on the nearby **Mookerhei** by the Spanish. The star-shaped fortifications of the Heumense Schans from the 80 Years War stand atop a 43-m (141-ft) ridge from the Saalian Ice Age. It offers a fantastic vantage point from which to view the Maas valley.

South of Mook is the recreation area of the Mookerplas lake and the fine estate of **Sint Jansberg**, where the Bovenste Plasmolen, an ancient watermill, has been restored.

The magnificent 16th-century Venlo town hall in the Markt

❷ Venray

Road Map D5. 37,000. 27, 29, 30, 39. Henseniusplein 13 (0478-510505). Mon pm.

During World War II, Noord Limburg was the scene of heavy fighting. An English and a German (at Ysselsteyn) military cemetery lie near the town. Nearby Overloon is home to the Oorlogs-en Verzetsmuseum (war museum). In 1944, Venray was largely destroyed. The 15th-century basilica of **St Petrus Banden**, with its magnificent interior, was given a new 80-m (262-ft) tower in restoration works. The Geijsteren estate on the Maas, where old Maas terraces are visible in the terrain, is an outstanding rambling area.

❸ Arcen

Road Map D5. 9,000. 83.
Nieuwstraat 40–42, Venlo (0900-0400216).

The main attraction of Arcen, picturesquely located on the Maas, is the finely restored 17th-century Arcen castle with its **Kasteeltuinen** (castle gardens). They incorporate a rose garden, subtropical gardens, Eastern gardens, a pine forest and a golf course. You can also take the waters at the **Thermaalbad Arcen** spa; its mineral-rich water is extracted from 900 m (2,955 ft) underground. Other local delights include special Arcen beer, asparagus (with an asparagus market on Ascension Day), and the drink distilled by the Branderij De IJsvogel, housed in the 17th-century **Wijmarsche water mill**. Outside Arcen is the **Nationaal Park Landgoed de Hamert**.

Kasteeltuinen

Lingsforterweg 26. **Tel** 077-4736010. **Open** May–late-Oct: 10am–6pm daily. **Closed** Rest of the year.

The exquisite gardens of the 17th century Arcen castle

❹ Venlo

Road Map D5. 60,000.
Klasstraat 17, Bookstore Koops (077-3543800. Fri pm, Sat.

The combined city of Venlo/Blerick began as a Roman settlement. In the Middle Ages it grew rich on trade. The 15th-century St Martinuskerk, a Gothic hall-type church, and Ald Weishoes, a Latin school dating from 1611 built in the Gelderland Renaissance style, are among the few historical buildings to survive World War II. The town hall was designed between 1597 and 1600 by Willem van Bommel. The local **Museum Van Bommel-Van Dam** features modern art; the **Limburgs Museum**, archaeological finds.

Museum Van Bommel-Van Dam

Deken van Oppensingel 6. **Tel** 077-3513457. **Open** 11am–5pm Tue–Sun. **Closed** Mon, 1 Jan, Carnival, 25 Dec.

Limburgs Museum

Keulsepoort 5. **Tel** 077-3522112. **Open** 11am–5pm Tue–Sun. **Closed** 1 Jan, Carnival, 25 Dec.
limburgsmuseum.nl

For hotels and restaurants in this region see p401 and p415

5 Weert

Road Map C5. 47,700. Maasstraat 18 (0495-536800). Sat.

The jewel of Weert is the **St Martinuskerk**, one of the few Late Gothic hall-type churches in Holland (in hall-type churches, the side aisles are equal in height and width to the nave). When restoration works were carried out around 1975, paintings from the 15th and 16th centuries were discovered beneath the layers of whitewash on the vaulted ceilings. Before the high altar (1790) by Italians Moretti and Spinetti lies the tomb of the lord of Weert, beheaded in 1568 on the order of Alva in Brussels. Not far from the church is the **Ursulinenhof**, an example of a new building successfully integrated into a historical centre.

Surrounding areas such as Weerterbos forest and the **Nationaal Park De Grote Peel** are remnants of a region of peat moors.

Limburg asparagus

6 Roermond

Road Map D5. 43,000. Markt 17 (0475-335847). Wed pm, Sat.

The oldest church in the see of Roermond is the 13th-century Late Romanesque, Early Gothic **Onze-Lieve-Vrouwemunsterkerk** (minster church of Our Lady), which was originally the church of a Cistercian abbey. The interior of the church is worth a visit. The **St Christoffelkathedraal**, a Gothic cruciform basilica with a gilded statue of St Christopher on the tower, dates from the early 15th century. The church's stained-glass windows are by the local glazier Joep Nicolas.

Roermond is by the Maasplassen lakes, one of the country's largest areas for watersports. The lakes cover more than 300 ha (740 acres) and have a length of approximately 25 km (15 miles). The **Maasplassen** were created through large-scale gravel quarrying in the Maas valley, which went on as far as Maaseik in Belgium.

Interior of the Onze-Lieve-Vrouwemunsterkerk in Roermond

7 De Meinweg

Road Map D6. none. 78, 79. Bezoekerscentrum, Meinweg 2, Herkenbosch (0475-528500).

The expansive national park of De Meinweg in the east of the province possesses a unique natural beauty. Six hiking routes have been laid out here. You can also tour the park by horse-drawn cart, accompanied by expert guides.

Dr PJH Cuypers

Architect Pierre Cuypers was born in Roermond in 1827. He lived and worked both in his hometown and in Amsterdam. One of Cuypers' sons and one of his nephews also became renowned architects. Considered one of the prime representatives of the Netherlands Neo- Gothic, Cuypers designed the Central Station and the Rijksmuseum in Amsterdam, and De Haar castle in Haarzuilens. He was also the architect and restorer of countless churches, including the *munsterkerk* (minster church) in Roermond.

Munsterkerk in Roermond

The 1,600-ha (3,955-acre) De Meinweg national park

❽ Street-by-Street: Maastricht

Maastricht emerged in Roman times at a point along the river Maas which could be crossed on foot (Mosae Traiectum), on the Roman road that led from Colonia Agrippina (Cologne) to Bononia (Boulogne). The founder of Christian Maastricht was St Serviatus, bishop of Tongeren, who died in AD 384 in Maastricht and was buried in the cemetery then located outside the town walls. The magnificent basilica of St Servaas was built over his tomb. In addition to the basilica, another fine church is the Romanesque Onze-Lieve-Vrouwebasiliek.

Sculpture of Pieke
This sculpture in Stokstraat is of Pieke and his dog, from a book by Ber Hollewijn.

The Generaalshuis
Now the Theater aan het Vrijthof, this Neo-Classical palace was built in 1809. General Dibbets, who succeeded in keeping Maastricht part of the Netherlands, lived here around 1830.

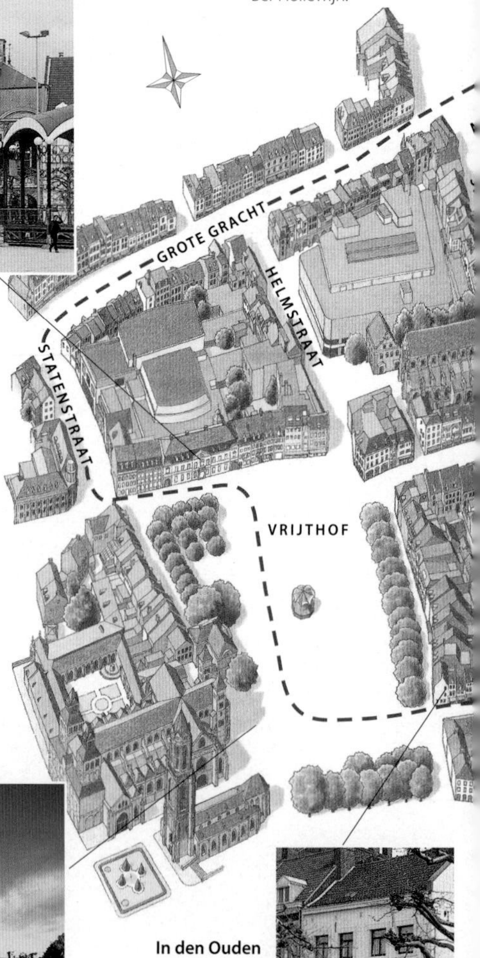

GROTE GRACHT

HELMSTRAAT

STATENSTRAAT

VRIJTHOF

Key

— Recommended route

0 metres 100

0 yards 100

★ Cemetery
Now one of the city's main squares, the cemetery was located outside the town walls when the construction of St Servaas began.

In den Ouden Vogelstruys
One of the many street cafés flanking the Vrijthof, this lively, popular spot serves a small selection of meals.

★ Stadhuis
The town hall on the Markt was built from 1559–1664 and is a masterpiece by Pieter Post of the Northern Netherlands. The lobby is open to visitors.

VISITORS' CHECKLIST

Practical Information
Road Map C6.
Kleine Staat 1 (043-3252121).
Mon–Sat. Apr: Amstel Gold Race (cycling classic); May: Vrijthof Fair; St Servaas procession; end of Aug: Preuvenemint culinary festival.

Transport
121,500. Stationsplein.
Stationsplein.

St Servaasbrug
This bridge is a solid yet elegant structure of seven semicircular arches dating from 1280. Ships can reach the Wyck side through a modern section.

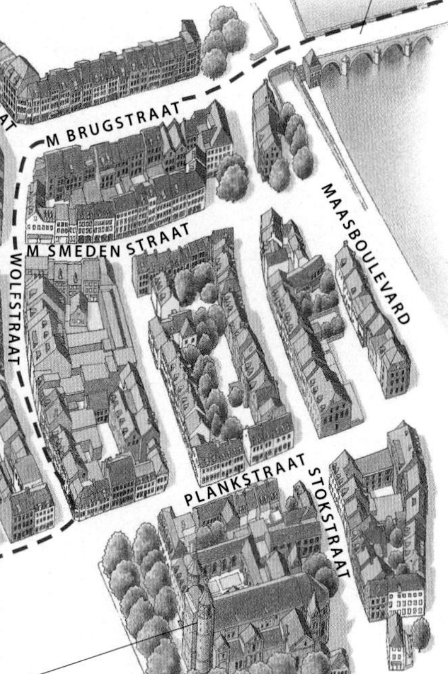

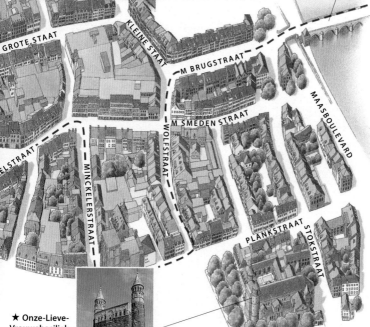

★ Onze-Lieve-Vrouwebasiliek
In one of the chapels of this Romanesque cruciform basilica is the votive statue of Our Lady "Sterre der Zee".

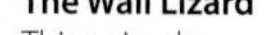

The Wall Lizard
This animal can be seen in parts of Maastricht, the only Dutch town it occurs in.

Bonnefantenmuseum

The Bonnefantenmuseum is one of Maastricht's most prominent landmarks, situated on the right bank of the Maas in a distinctive building designed by the Italian architect Aldo Rossi. The museum's exhibits include old masters, painting and sculpture from the medieval period to 1650, and a celebrated international collection of modern art.

★ Cupola by Aldo Rossi
The tower houses a restaurant and an exhibition hall.

La Natura è l'Arte del Numero
This installation designed by Mario Merz consists of tables covered with glass, branches, stones, vegetables and numbers fashioned out of fluorescent tubes.

Cimon and Pero
Peter Paul Rubens (1577–1640) depicted Pero feeding her starving father Cimon while he awaited execution in prison.

KEY

① **Plattegronden** by René Daniels (b. 1950) is a simplified re-creation of a museum hall. Daniels painted yellow rectangles over the red flat paintings, which are out of sync with the perspective of the hall, thus creating a disorienting effect.

② **Terrace**

③ **Domed hall**

④ **Inner tower**

★ Wood Carvings
The fine collection of medieval wood carvings includes *St Anna-te-Drieën*, a walnut sculpture by Jan van Steffeswert (1470–1525).

For hotels and restaurants in this region see p401 and p415

Bonnefantopia
The Rotterdam group of artists Atelier van Lieshout created this large installation in 2002. It features stylized polyester bodies hanging, squatting and lying down throughout the structure.

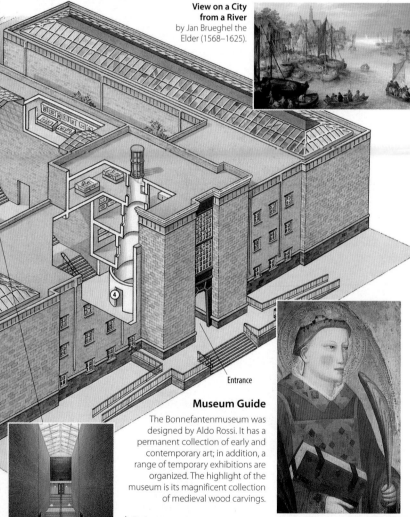

VISITORS' CHECKLIST

Practical Information
Avenue Ceramique 250.
Tel 043-3290190.
bonnefanten.nl
Open 11am–5pm Tue–Sun & public hol Mon. **Closed** 1 Jan, Carnival, 25 Dec. for temp exhibits.

Transport
1, 3, 50, 53, 54, 57.

View on a City from a River
by Jan Brueghel the Elder (1568–1625).

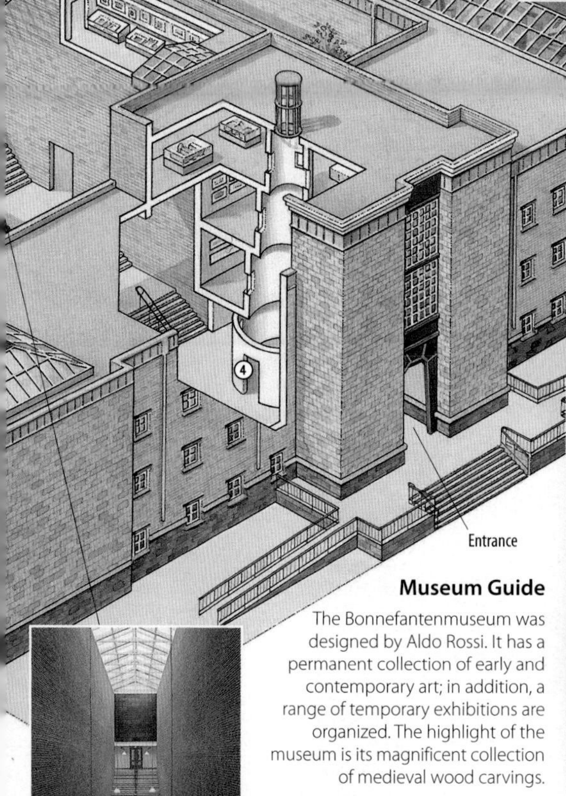

4

Entrance

Museum Guide

The Bonnefantenmuseum was designed by Aldo Rossi. It has a permanent collection of early and contemporary art; in addition, a range of temporary exhibitions are organized. The highlight of the museum is its magnificent collection of medieval wood carvings.

★ Staircase
The monumental staircase runs through the middle of the museum and leads into the different wings and floors of the museum.

St Stephen
Giovanni del Biondo (1356–99) painted this work, thought to be part of a triptych, as the panel has signs of being cut with a saw.

Exploring Maastricht

Maastricht is considered to be one of the oldest towns in Holland. It was the country's first bishopric and an impressive fortress. It has some outstanding historical monuments, including the Romanesque Onze-Lieve-Vrouwebasiliek (Basilica of Our Lady); the Romanesque St Servaas Basilica, with a very old crypt and a carved Gothic portal (early 13th century); six Gothic churches; a Baroque church formerly belonging to the Augustine order (1661); and a Walloon church from 1733. A great deal remains of the fortifications, including Roman foundations, part of the medieval wall, a 17th-century bastion, and 18th- and 19th-century fortification works.

The medieval Helpoort gate, the oldest city gate in the country

Natuurhistorisch Museum

De Bosquetplein 7. **Tel** 043-3505490. **Open** 11am–5pm Tue–Fri, 2–5pm Sat & Sun. **Closed** public hols.

This attractive natural history museum showcases the natural history of the south of Limburg through the ages. Highlights of the museum include the remains of the enormous mosasaur and giant tortoises found in the limestone strata of St Pietersberg.

Roman Foundations of the Tower

OL Vrouweplein. **Tel** 043-3251851. **Open** Easter Day–autumn hols: 11am–5pm Mon–Sat, 1–5pm Sun.

In the courtyard of the Onze-Lieve-Vrouwebasiliek you can see the foundations of a Roman tower which was once part of the Roman *castellum*. The *castellum* stood on the banks of the river Maas, just south of the St Servaasbrug bridge, where the Romans settled in 50 BC and where the district of Stokstraat, with its medieval and Golden Age buildings, now lies. The pavement of Op de Thermen, a small and peaceful square in this district where the original Roman fort once was, has been marked with the outlines of the old Roman baths. The first medieval wall around Maastricht dates from around 1229. Of these, the Onze-Lieve-Vrouwewal – which has cannons standing in front of it – and the Jekertoren tower can still be seen.

Mosasaurus hofmanni in the natural history museum, known locally as the terrible Maas lizard

Helpoort

St Bernardusstraat 24b. **Tel** 043-3212586. **Open** Easter Day–Oct, 1:30–4:30pm daily. voluntary donation.

The Helpoort gate, dating from the early 13th century, also forms part of the early medieval town fortifications. It stood at the southern end of the town and is the oldest surviving town gate in Holland, and the only one still standing in Maastricht.

Other structures from this period can be seen across the river Maas in Wyck: the Waterpoortje gate, the Stenen Wal (wall) along the river, and the Maaspunttoren. The second medieval fortifications, made necessary by the rapid growth of the city, were built around 1350. Of these, the Pater Vinktoren near the Helpoort gate, and the romantic embankment wall and the semicircular towers known as De Vijf Koppen and Haet ende Nijt continue to survive to this day.

The impressive Pater Vink tower

Museum Spaans Gouvernement

Vrijthof 18. **Tel** 043-3211327. **Open** 10am–6pm Tue–Sun. **Closed** public hols.

This museum, housed in a 16th-century chapterhouse, features period rooms from the 17th and 18th centuries, and Dutch paintings from that era.

Centre Céramique

Avenue Céramique 50. **Tel** 043-350 5600. **Open** call ahead. **Closed** public hols. **centreceramique.nl**

This information centre has a library, archive, cafés and the European Journalism Centre.

Grotten St-Pietersberg

Luikerweg. phone for details (043-3252121).

The famous St Peter's caves were created when limestone was quarried through the centuries. Eventually a maze of over 20,000 passageways came into being. Some of the inscriptions on the walls are very old indeed, and some of the miners reveal considerable artistic skills.

The Gothic Bergportaal (15th century) of the St Servaasbasiliek

St-Servaasbasiliek

Keizer Karelplein. **Tel** 043-3212082. **Open** 10am–5pm daily (Jul & Aug: 10am–6pm, Nov–Apr: 12:30–5pm on Sun). **Closed** 1 Jan, Carnival, 25 Dec.

Construction on St Servatius Basilica began around the year 1000 on the spot where the saint was buried (upon which stood an earlier church). The nave, the crypt, the transept and the chancel are the oldest parts of the basilica, dating back to the 11th century. The apse and the two chancel towers were built in the following century. The western end also dates from the 12th century. The southern Bergportaal gate dates from the early 13th century, and is one of the earliest Gothic buildings in the Maasland region. This portal is dedicated to St Mary, with representations of her life, death and Assumption in the arch. The side chapels and the Gothic transept date from approximately 1475.

Highlights of the basilica's treasury are the 12th-century reliquary containing the relics of St Servatius and St Martin of Tongeren, and the golden bust of St Servatius. The latter was donated to the town by the Duke of Parma when Maastricht was captured by the Spaniards in 1579.

During the 19th century, thorough restoration works were undertaken by Pierre Cuypers. He restored the western end to its original Romanesque splendour, as well as commissioning new murals and ceiling paintings. These were repainted during a subsequent restoration which was completed in 1990.

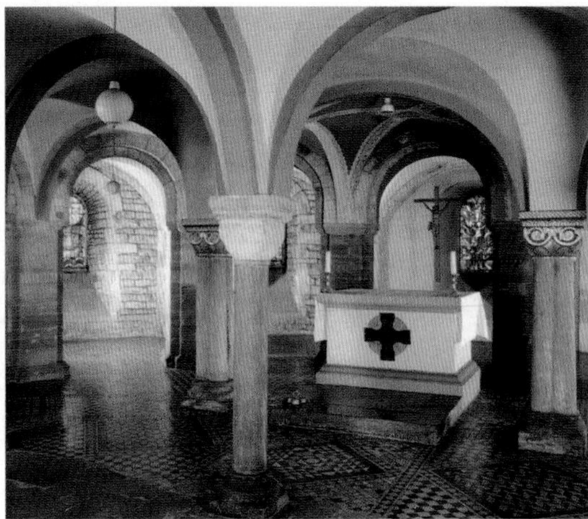

Crypt in the eastern part of the Onze-Lieve-Vrouwebasiliek

Onze-Lieve-Vrouwebasiliek

O-L-Vrouweplein. Treasury: **Tel** 043-3504040. **Open** Easter Day–autumn hols: 11am–5pm Mon–Sat, 1–5pm Sun. Church: **Closed** during services.

Construction of Onze-Lieve-Vrouwebasiliek began around 1000. The oldest part of the basilica is the imposing west façade. Once this was completed, work began on the nave and transept. The chancel followed in the 12th century, built over an 11th-century crypt. The apse pillars, made from limestone, are crowned with lavishly sculpted capitals, such as the renowned Heimokapiteel.

The Reliquary of St Servatius

The magnificent restored reliquary is a monumental shrine containing the relics of St Servatius and St Martin of Tongeren. It is made of wood covered with embossed gilded copper plate in the shape of a house. It dates from about 1160 and was built by artists from the Maasland region. The front of the reliquary depicts Christ, with the 12 apostles along the sides, and St Servatius surrounded by angels on the back. The "roof" of the "house" is decorated with scenes from the Last Judgement.

The 12th-century reliquary

The impressive medieval Kasteel Hoensbroek

❾ Thorn

Road Map D5. 2,600. 72, 73, 76. Wijngaard 14 (0475-561085).

Southeast of Weert on the A2 is the little town of Thorn, which with its picturesque narrow streets and houses, historical farm buildings and monumental **Abbey Church** looks like an open-air museum. For some 800 years, until 1794, Thorn was the capital of an autonomous secular foundation headed by an abbess. The Wijngaard, the village square, is surrounded by whitewashed houses where the noble ladies of the foundation once lived. The 14th-century abbey church with its 18th-century interior was thoroughly restored at the end of the 19th century by renowned architect Pierre Cuypers, who also added a splendid Gothic tower. Clara Elisabeth van Manderscheidt-Blankenheim, a canoness of the foundation, founded the **Kapel van O-L-Vrouwe onder de Linden** (Chapel of Our Lady under the Linden) north of the town in 1673.

A whitewashed house of Thorn

❿ Sittard

Road Map D6. 46,500. Kitzraedhuis, Rosmolenstraat 2 (0900-5559798). Thu am, Sat.

In the 13th century, Sittard was granted its town charter and built its defensive walls, of which considerable sections remain intact, including **Fort Sanderbout**. The Grote Kerk, or St Petruskerk, built around 1300, is worth a visit. The 80-m (262-ft) tower is built of layers of alternating brick and limestone blocks, or "speklagen" (bacon layers). In the Markt is the 17th-century Baroque **St Michielskerk**; Our Lady of the Sacred Heart basilica stands in the Oude Markt. The oldest house in Sittard is the half-timber house built in 1530 on the corner of the Markt and the Gats and containing the De Gats coffee house. The Jacob Kritszraedthuis, a patrician house, was built in 1620 in Maasland Renaissance style.

⓫ Hoensbroek

Road Map D6. 25,500. Bongerd 19 Heerlen (0900-5559798). Fri am.

Before the state-run Emma mine was opened here in 1908, Hoensbroek was a sleepy farming town. It subsequently grew into the centre of the Dutch coal mining industry. Its industrial importance waned with the closing of the mines.

Kasteel Hoensbroek was built in the Middle Ages. All that remains of the original castle is the round corner-tower. The wings and towers around the rectangular inner courtyard date from the 17th and 18th centuries. The castle is moated and today functions as a cultural centre.

Thermae at the Thermenmuseum

⓬ Heerlen

Road Map D6. 95,000. Bongerd 19 (0900-5559798). Tue, Thu am & Fri.

The Roman town of Coriovallum has been discovered beneath Heerlen. **Thermenmuseum** contains the foundations of the ancient *thermae* and many everyday items from Roman times. Romanesque **St Pancratiuskerk** dates back to the 12th century. In the 20th century, until 1974, Heerlen was the centre of coal mining in Limburg. FPJ Peutz built the town hall and Schunck department store (known as the *Glaspaleis*, or crystal palace) in the 1930s.

Thermenmuseum

Coriovallumstraat 9. **Tel** 045-5605100. **Open** 10am–5pm Tue–Fri, noon–5pm Sat, Sun & public hols. **Closed** 1 Jan, Carnival, 24 & 25 Dec.

For hotels and restaurants in this region see p401 and p415

⓭ Valkenburg

Road map D6. 5,500. 36, 47, 63. Th. Dorrenplein 5 (0900-5559798). Mon am, Tue am.

The old fortified town of Valkenburg, situated in an area dotted with castles, is popular with visitors. In addition to sights such as the old gates of Berkelpoort and Grendelpoort, a 13th-century Romanesque church and the ruins of a 12th-century castle, there are many new attractions, such as a casino, catacombs, the Fluweelen cave, **Gemeentegrot** (a Roman quarry and cave complex), a cable car, the Prehistorische Monstergrot and the **Steenkolenmijn** (coal mine).

Gemeentegrot
Cauberg 4. **Tel** 043-6012271. **Open** 11am–5pm daily **Closed** 1 Jan, Carnival, 25 Dec. guided tours only.

⓮ Gulpen

Road Map D6. 7,500. Dorpsstraat 27 (0900-5559798). Thu morning.

Gulpen lies at the confluence of the Geul and Gulp streams. The town's surrounding countryside, with its half-timbered houses, water mills and orchards, is probably the prettiest in Limburg. Hiking routes are marked. The 17th-century Kastell Neubourg, built on the site of a Roman temple from 2,000 years ago, is now a hotel and restaurant. Beside the castle is the Neubourgermolen mill with a fish ladder for trout. The Gulpen brewery is worth a visit. The common kingfisher, a rare bird, can be seen here.

The picturesque sloping streets of the Maasland village of Elsloo

⓯ Elsloo

Road Map D6. 8,650. 31 Kitzraedhuis, Rosmolenstraat 2, Sittard (0900-5559798).

Artifacts from the prehistoric pottery culture found at Elsloo are on display in the Maasland local history museum, De Schippersbeurs. In the Waterstaatskerk, dating from 1848, is the 16th-century **St-Anna-te-Drieën** by the Master of Elsloo. Remnants of Elsloo's earliest castle can be seen in the middle of the river at low water. Of the later Kasteel Elsloo, only one tower survives.

Limburg's picturesque countryside, with the meandering Jeker river

⓰ Eijsden

Road Map C6. 4,800. 58, 59. Diepstraat 31 (0900-5559798). Thu pm.

Kingfisher

Eijsden, the southernmost municipality in the Netherlands, is a protected rural area. There is a pleasant walk to be had along the Maas quay. Kasteel Eijsden was built in 1636 in the Maasland Renaissance style on the foundations of an earlier stronghold. The castle is not open to the public, but the park makes for a nice stroll.

⓱ Vaals

Road Map D6. 5,500. Landal Maastrichterlaan 73 a (0900-5559798). Tue am.

Vaals' wooded countryside is known for the Drielandenpunt, from which three countries are visible. At 322 m (1,058 ft), it is also the highest point in Holland. Worth visiting are Kasteel Vaalsbroek and the Von Clermonthuis; both date from the 18th century. De Kopermolen, once a church, is now a museum.

⑱ Heuvelland

In the Zuid Limburg region of Heuvelland, the hills, and the river valleys are covered with fertile loess soil, which occurs nowhere else in Holland. In the peaceful rolling countryside, with its stunning views, is a region of wooded banks, orchards and fields, dotted with picturesque villages and castles, and criss-crossed by narrow roads passing through cuttings with roadside shrines and field chapels. Heuvelland just may be one of the prettiest parts of Holland.

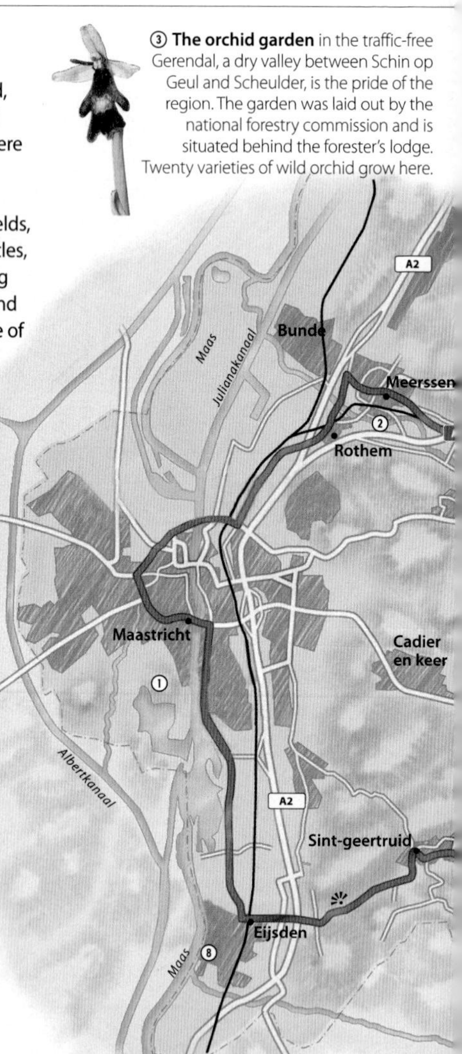

③ **The orchid garden** in the traffic-free Gerendal, a dry valley between Schin op Geul and Scheulder, is the pride of the region. The garden was laid out by the national forestry commission and is situated behind the forester's lodge. Twenty varieties of wild orchid grow here.

② **The Basilica of the Holy Sacrament** in Meerssen, built in the late 14th century of limestone in Maasland Gothic style, is one of the most elegant churches in all of Holland. The chancel features a lavishly decorated tabernacle.

⑧ **Kasteel Eijsden** was built in the Maasland Renaissance style in 1636. This style is easily distinguished by its combined use of brick and stone masonry, with stone being used to frame doors and windows.

Tips for Drivers

Tour length: 80 km (50 miles). Part of the route passes through hilly areas with narrow roads.
Stopping-off points: especially good viewing points are to be found at Noorbeek, Slenaken and Epen.

① Grape-growing in Zuid Limburg

In the past, grape-growing and wine-making was more widely practised in Zuid Limburg than it is today. For example, in the 18th century, there were at least 200 ha (495 acres) of vineyards on and around St-Pietersberg. Today, a small professional vineyards can still be found in the region, the most famous being the Apostelhoeve. On this vine-growing situated to the south of Maastricht on the Louwberg above the de Jeker valley, white wine is made from Müller-Thürgau, Riesling, Auxerrois and Pinot Gris grapes.

Grapes from Limburg

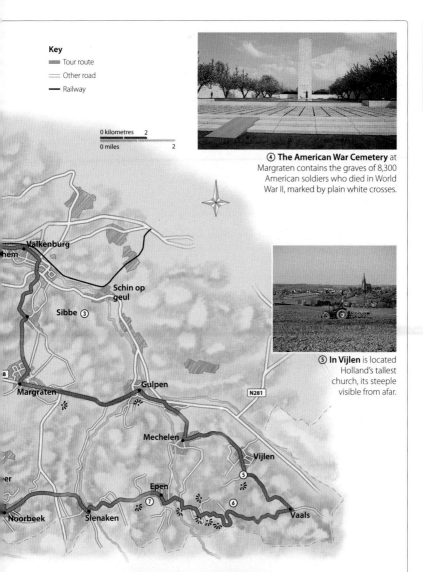

Key

Tour route

Other road

Railway

0 kilometres 2

0 miles 2

Valkenburg
Schin op geul
Sibbe ③
Margraten
Gulpen
N281
Mechelen
Vijlen
⑤
Epen
⑦
⑥
Noorbeek
Slenaken
Vaals

④ **The American War Cemetery** at Margraten contains the graves of 8,300 American soldiers who died in World War II, marked by plain white crosses.

⑤ **In Vijlen** is located Holland's tallest church, its steeple visible from afar.

⑥ **Large stretches of forest** are rare in Zuid Limburg. Exceptions are the Boswachterij Vaals with the Vijlenerbos forest, and the forests by the Brunsummerheide (Brunsummer heath). Here the woods cover the landscape and there are lots of springs.

⑦ **Rambling in the Geuldal**
At Epen, turn off towards Plaat and take the road to the fulling mill in Geul. Carry on after the bridge. A path on the opposite side follows the river upstream into Belgium. Along the Geul are poplars with mistletoe growing in the branches, which can be seen particularly well in winter. The path leads past the Heimansgroeve, a quarry for rock from the Carboniferous period.

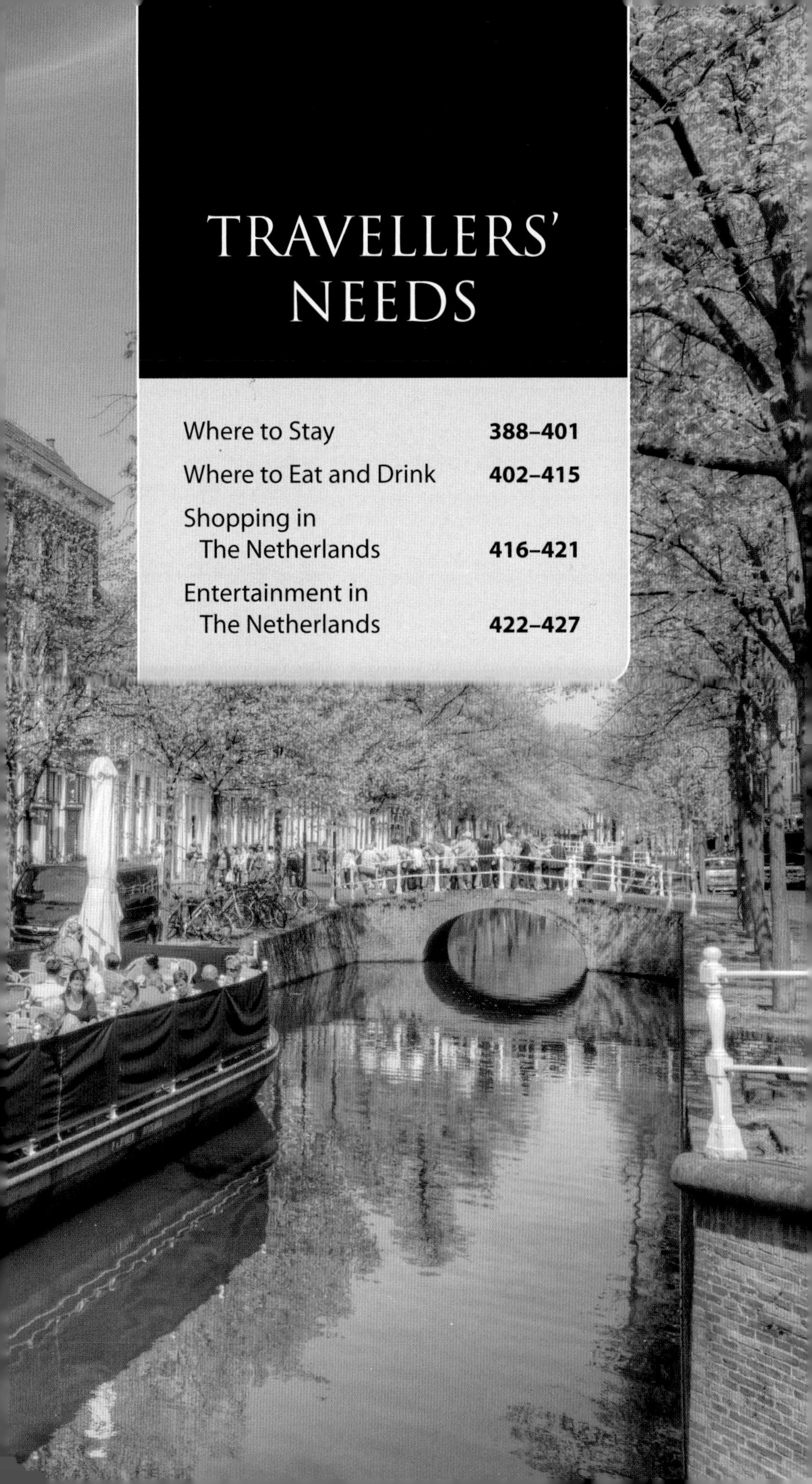

TRAVELLERS' NEEDS

WHERE TO STAY

The Netherlands offers a variety of accommodation to suit every traveller's tastes and needs, ranging from inexpensive backpacker hostels to pricey chateau living. Visitors can choose to stay in one of the luxury chain hotels here, which range from bland to spectacular, but there is also good accommodation to be found in historical castles, convents, prisons, mansions – and in one case, a harbour crane – that have been converted into hotels, hostels or B&Bs. Campers, too, will be spoiled for choice here, with numerous campsites and caravan parks, often situated in stunning locations. For those who intend to stay in a particular area over a longer period of time, camping is an especially economical option. Visitors who need more spacious or convenient accommodation can book one of the 350-odd bungalow parks in the country, or rent an apartment in one of the many coastal towns.

Hotel Types

There is a huge variation in the price, quality and facilities offered by different hotels. The choice is greatest in Amsterdam and the larger cities, where there is something to suit every traveller's pocket. There are also plenty of choices further afield, generally at lower rates. After hotels, bed-and-breakfast (B&B) accommodation has also become plentiful. As these lodgings are offered by individuals rather than by chains, this type of accommodation may vary greatly in nature and level of comfort – one night you might be staying in a family home, and the next in a chic country estate. The least expensive form of overnight accommodation is in a hostel. **Stayokay** runs 27 well-appointed hostels through the country, ranging from a house on the top of a dune to a medieval castle, and featuring dormitories or private rooms.

Hotel Chains

Most major hotel chains are represented in the Netherlands, including **Best Western**, **Golden Tulip**, **Hilton**, **Holiday Inn**, **Mercure**, **NH** and **Radisson**. Most of these can be found in the bigger cities, although some are situated in country areas also. Chain hotels range in quality from fair to excellent, and in size from large to massive, and cater to tourists and business travellers alike. Their scale, and often their internationally recognized style, mean that chain hotels are generally less personal than individually operated hotels, but when you spend the night in one of these, you are usually assured of a competitively-priced and hassle-free stay.

Stylish interiors of the Het Arresthuis, Roermond *(see p401)*

Categories

All hotels in the Netherlands are categorized according to international standards under the Netherlands Hotel Classification system, which awards each hotel with one to five stars. Hoteliers class their hotels themselves, after which an inspection is carried out by an independent organization. The number of stars awarded to each hotel depends on the facilities it offers: the more stars it has, the more luxurious it is. A one-star hotel is basic and may or may not offer breakfast. In two-star hotels, at least 25 per cent of the rooms will have their own bathroom or shower and WC. These hotels will also have a guest lounge, and a lift if they are more than three storeys high. Three-star hotels are considered middle of the range. Their rooms have central heating, and at least half have their own bathrooms. Four-star hotels will have a night bar; also 80 per cent of their rooms will have en suite bathrooms, and all of them have telephones.

Château De Havixhorst *(see p399)* in De Schiphorst

◀ A typical boat restaurant in South Holland

Colourful decor at Harbour Crane *(see p399)*, Harlingen

A five-star hotel will belong to the deluxe category, with 24-hour service, large rooms with en-suite facilities, a restaurant and so on.

Although this classification system does provide an insight into the hotel's level of amenities, it looks exclusively only at the facilities and amenities provided by the hotel.

Apartments

Staying in a self-catering apartment or holiday home is an increasingly popular alternative to hotels or hostels and can be an economical choice, particularly if you are travelling in a group. Accommodation ranges from a private room in the countryside with basic and sometimes shared facilities to a sleek city loft with five-star amenities. Some apartments might require a minimum stay, especially in high season, and it is always a good idea to inquire if there are any additional or hidden fees, such as key money or cleaning cost. On the coast and on the islands there are 'apartment-hotels', which are apartment buildings with hotel facilities, such as a reception, restaurant and swimming pool.

Prices

Room prices always include VAT ('BTW'). Tourist tax (*toeristenbelasting*) varies by municipality and is often but not always included. Breakfast is often included, but this should be specifically stated. If not, do check, as breakfast in a luxury hotel can be expensive.

Obviously, a five-star hotel is pricier than a three-star. Hotels in larger cities, in Amsterdam in particular, are relatively more expensive than those further afield, although in the city it is easier to find hotels in wider-ranging price categories and good deals can be found off-season.

As many hotels have abolished dedicated single rooms, solo travellers often end up paying only slightly less than the same accommodation would cost two people sharing. Kids under the age of 12 can usually stay free of charge or at a much reduced rate, if they share their parents' room.

Booking Accommodation

High season runs pretty much year-round in Amsterdam. In winter, with the exception of Christmas and New Year's, visitors will manage to find a room, but at all other times it is wise to book well in advance. In other major cities, high season runs from spring until autumn or further afield from late spring until early autumn. On the coast and on the islands, any month other than July or August is considered off-season.

Bookings can be made directly with the hotel by telephone or e-mail, or in person at the reception, although this often means you pay the standard room price, which is usually higher than the more competitive rates found online. Unless a hotel or chain offers a 'best rate guarantee' when booking through their website, the lowest rates are often found through dedicated hotel booking websites like Expedia.nl, Hotels.nl and Booking.com. The best way of searching for individual hotels or a particular chain is by name. The price differences found on different websites for the same room in the same hotel at the same dates can be astounding; it pays to compare prices through a meta search engine such as Travelsupermarket.com, Lookingforbooking.com or Hotelscombined.com – the latter also has a clever iPhone app.

No-frills hotels such as CitizenM, Yotel, Qbic and easyHotel that offer tiny yet smart rooms at the lowest possible price, can usually be booked only through their own respective websites.

Stayokay hostels can be booked through their own website, Stayokay.nl, while a wider choice of International Youth Hostel Federation (IYHF) and non-IYHF hostels around the country can be booked through Hostels.com, Hostelbookers.com or Hostelworld.com.

Many B&Bs can be booked through Bedandbreakast.nl. Airbnb.nl offers an equally wide range of B&Bs, plus private rooms, apartments and holiday homes.

The 'VVV' tourist information offices around the country can also assist visitors in booking all kinds of suitable accommodation.

Stempels *(see p397)* in Haarlem

The bar of the Hotel Van der Werff *(see p398)* on Schiermonnikoog

Payment

Major credit cards are accepted at almost every hotel. If you provide your credit card details at the time of booking, it is usually used as a guarantee and your card will not be actually charged until checkout. However, advance payment may be required in some cases, for example when booking at a highly discounted rate or special package, in which case your credit card will be charged immediately. Most hotels will charge a no-show fee, up to or even extending the full room rate, if you do not show up without prior cancellation. As always, watch out for any hidden charges, especially when using the 'express checkout' service that many hotels offer.

Discounts

Many hotels and chains offer 'early bird' discounts for rooms booked well in advance. Hotels that cater mainly to business travellers during the week, will often offer discounts to leisure travellers over the weekend and conversely, hotels that are usually full with tourists at the weekends may offer reductions on weekdays.

Packages

Many hotels offer special packages of one or two nights, with breakfast and dinner included. These packages are often based on a particular theme; for example, a cycling or rambling package may include cycle hire, or a wellness package may include a couple's massage at the hotel spa. Such packages can be an economical choice. Packages can be booked through the hotel booking websites mentioned in the directory. Attractive deals can also be found through group deal websites like Groupon.com and LivingSocial.com, although you need to be flexible, as the timeframes for booking and travelling are usually limited.

Travellers with Disabilities

Many large hotels are fully accessible for wheelchairs. Smaller hotels may be less accessible, particularly those in historic buildings where steps and stairs prevent this. Hotels that do have wheelchair access, but no lifts will have some accessible rooms on the ground floor. Some websites, like Hotels.com and Booking.com, allow you to search for or filter by hotels with facilities for people with disabilities. However, it is always best to consult the hotel directly before you book.

Gay Hotels

The days of Amsterdam being the 'gay capital of Europe' may be gone, according to many locals, but the city still has a lot to offer to gay and lesbian travellers. A number of hotels cater exclusively to gay guests, of which the **Amistad**, with its fresh interior and smart rooms, and **The Golden Bear**, with comfortable rooms (although some with shared facilities), are great choices.

Then there is a choice of hotels that are regarded as gay-friendly by the International Gay & Lesbian Travel Association (Iglta.org), including the hip Lloyd and the posh Grand. No hotel in Amsterdam would turn away a same-sex couple, but another particularly welcoming lodging, that is popular with women, is the **Quentin**.

At the gay tourist information centres, **Pink Point** at the Homomonument and **Gaytic** on Spuistraat, visitors can pick up a free gay tourist kit and

InterContinental Amstel *(see p397)* in Amsterdam (right), with its picturesque location

get more information on gay-friendly hotels as well as the gay scene in the city.

Recommended Hotels

The hotels listed on pages 396–401 vary significantly in both class and cost, and are considered the best choice in terms of price, charm or location. To help you find accommodation that suits your personal taste, we have divided the entries into six categories: Charming, Hotels with Character, Historic, Family-friendly, Design and Luxury. Some hotels are better than others and a few stand out for a particular reason, such as a romantic atmosphere, a fantastic spa or a stunning location. For each region we have handpicked one such exceptional lodging, ranging from an inexpensive hostel in a bunch of peculiar cube houses or a hotel that consists of individually decorated rooms spread out over several private homes, to a deluxe suite in a converted Ilyushin airliner or a room with a dazzling view in a dockside crane. Here you will not only be guaranteed a comfortable night's sleep, but also gain a memorable experience. These highly recommended hotels are marked as DK Choice. The DK Choice hotels are extra special. These hotels may have above average standards, or a breathtaking location, or they may simply have a charm that sets them apart.

Grand Hotel de Kromme Raake *(see p399)* in Eenrum, with a traditional in-built bed

DIRECTORY

Hotel Types

Stayokay
Tel 020-5513155.
W stayokay.com

Hotel Chains

Best Western
W bestwestern.nl

Golden Tulip
Tel 033-2544800.
W goldentulip.com

Hilton
Tel 0800-44466677.
W hiltonbenelux.com/nld

Holiday Inn
Tel 0800-5565565.
W holidayinn.nl

Mercure
Tel 020-6545727.
W mercure.com

NH Hotels
W nh-hotels.nl

Radisson Blu
W radissonblu.com

Booking Accommodation

Holland Tourist Information
Schiphol Airport, Arrival Hall 2.

Amsterdam Tourist Board (VVV) Offices
W vvv.nl

Local Tourist Information (VVV) offices
W holland.com

ANWB
W .anwb.nl/hotels/index.jsp

Netherlands Reservations Centre
Plantsoengracht 2,
144IDE Purmerend.
Tel 0299-689 144.
W hotelres.nl

Hotel booking websites
W hotels.nl
W booking.com
W expedia.nl

Hostel booking websites
W stayokay.nl
W hostels.com
W hostelbookers.com
W hostelworld.com

B&B booking websites
W bedandbreakfast.nl
W airbnb.nl

Compare prices
W travelsupermarket.com
W lookingforbooking.com
W hotelscombined.com

Gay Hotels

Pink Point
Homomonument,
Westermarkt
1016 DH Amsterdam,
Tel (020) 428 1070.
W pinkpoint.orgt

Gaytic Information Centre
Spuistraat 44
1012 DV Amsterdam.
Tel (020) 330 1461
W gaytic.nl

Hotel Amistad
Kerkstraat 42
1017 GM Amsterdam.
Tel (020) 624 8074.
W amistad.nl

The Golden Bear
Kerkstraat 37
1017 GB Amsterdam.
Tel (020) 624 4785.
W goldenbear.nl

The Quentin
Leidsekade 89
1017 PN Amsterdam.
Tel (020) 894 3004.
W quentinamsterdam.com

Bungalow Parks

The Netherlands has at least 350 holiday villages ('bungalowparken'), with dozens to hundreds of bungalows or cabins, many designed for four to eight persons, together with numerous facilities such as supermarkets and restaurants. They also provide many recreation facilities, some open-air and others indoors for days when the weather is not at its best. Rental is by the week, midweek or weekend, with arrival and departure on set days. The parks are often situated in areas of natural beauty and offer plenty to do in the surrounding area. A selection of the best parks in the country is given here.

Efteling Village Bosrijk
This leafy holiday park is set in woodland next to the country's biggest theme park. Cottages sleep six to eight, while apartments (in a faux manor house or gatehouse) have room for four.

Port Zélande
This Mediterranean-style CenterParcs Park at Lake Grevelingen features numerous recreation facilities and comfortable bungalows.

De Flaasbloem
The initially (and still mildly) Christian RCN recreation parks offer relatively inexpensive bungalows and plenty to do for children.

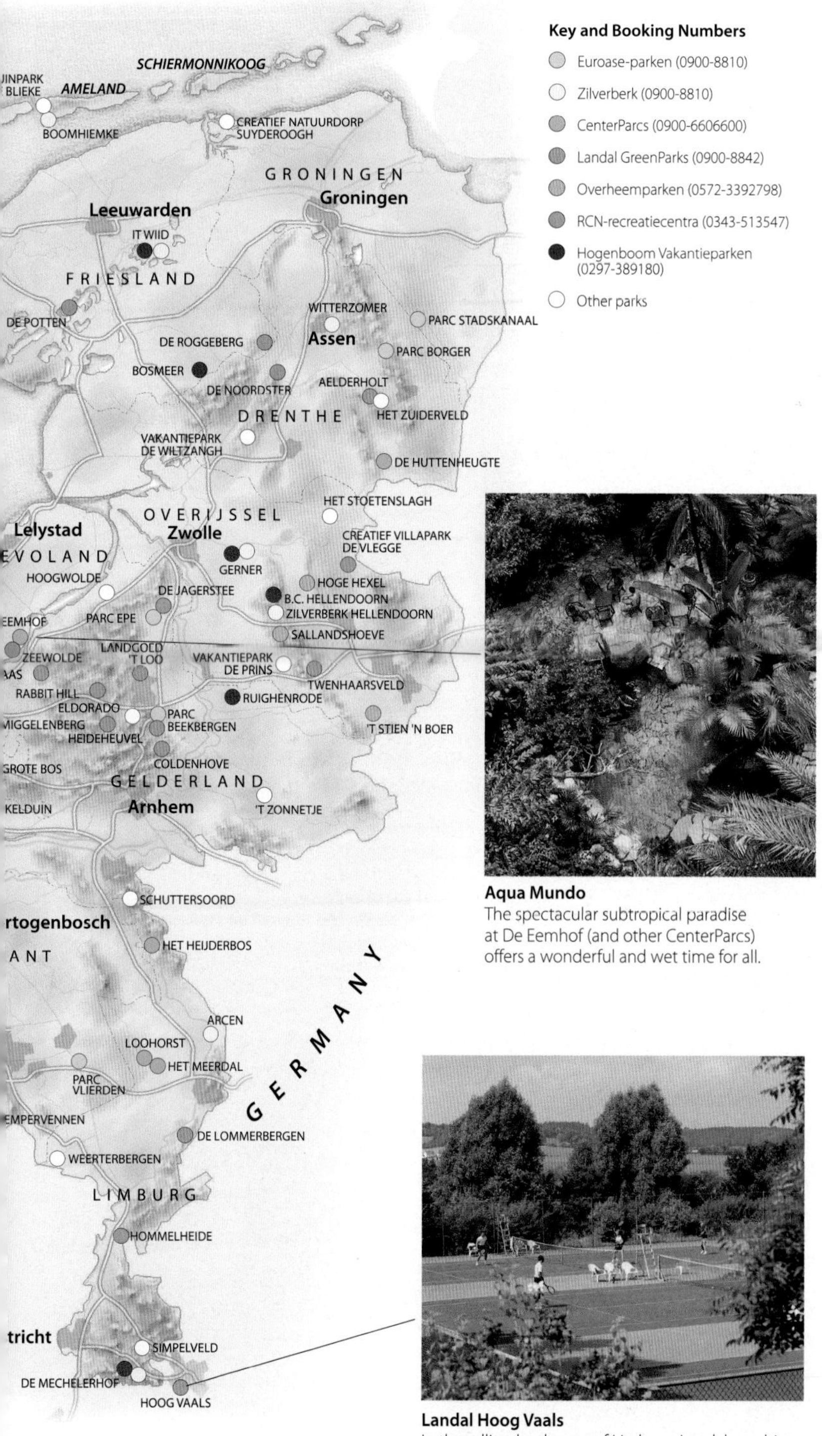

Aqua Mundo
The spectacular subtropical paradise at De Eemhof (and other CenterParcs) offers a wonderful and wet time for all.

Landal Hoog Vaals
In the rolling landscape of Limburg, Landal combines beautiful countryside with a plethora of activities.

Camping

Many people regard camping as the ideal way to take a holiday. It is inexpensive, you are out in the open air, often in beautiful natural locations. Camping comes in many shapes and sizes: settling in one place for the whole holiday or hopping from one campsite to the next; you can camp in a tent, a caravan, a tent-trailer or a camper van; you can camp in nature, on a farm or in a holiday park. The Netherlands, with its many different types of campsites, has something for everyone.

Camping at one of Holland's many nature sites

Types of Campsite

Campsites in the Netherlands fall into two main categories. There are *natuurterreinen,* (nature sites), which are small or medium-sized campsites with basic facilities, often situated in the most spectacular country-side that the Netherlands has to offer. The other group consists of larger campsites with a good range of facilities, often near recreation areas or other attractions. Both types of campsite are to be found throughout the Netherlands, and on both you can either set up your own tent and caravan or you can rent accommodation. The advantage of renting, of course, is that you travel lighter.

Nature Camping

Dutch law prohibits rough camping – i.e off designated campsites. However, there are plenty of campsites that give you a true sense of camping in nature. These natural campsites *natuur-kampeerterreinen* are small-scale and often situated in scenic locations, with plenty of countryside around for exploring on foot or by bicycle. You can pitch a tent or park your caravan, tent-trailer or camper here. There are no fixed pitches, sanitary arrangements are fairly basic but good, and there usually is a children's play area. Staying here requires a membership card from **Stichting Natuur-kampeerterreinen**, which includes a booklet listing all

De Roos campsite at Beerze, located on the river Vecht

130-plus official natural camping sites.

The campsites of the Vereniging Gastvrije Land-goederen (**LKC**) combine the attraction of natural surroundings with that of cultural history. These sites are situated on private estates, usually on the grounds of a castle or stately home. The association's 20-odd sites are distinguished by their peace, atmosphere and spaciousness, and offer abundant opportunities for rambling, cycling or horse riding.

Camping on a farm means you will be assured of a tranquil rural atmosphere. There are hundreds of **VeKaBo** farm campsites, usually small and with limited facilities, but offering a variety of

Camping in Zeeland, popular among Dutch and foreign holidaymakers alike

experiences; you will often be able to help the farmers feed the animals, milk the cows or harvest the crops.

Another excellent way of experiencing the countryside is by using hikers' cabins *trekkershutten*, designed for use by walkers on multiple-day hiking-trips. They offer basic accommodation for up to four people and are often situated at campsites whose facilities are available to the hikers. Bring your own kitchen utensils and bedding.

Hanging the laundry to dry among the fragrant blossoming trees

Large Family Campsites

Large family campsites or *gezinscampings* are popular among Dutch holidaymakers taking a break in their own country. Social life is an important aspect of these campsites, with plenty of opportunities to meet your fellow campers through an abundance of activities, such as barbecues, karaoke, games, competitions and sports events. Children also get to meet others of their age and there is plenty of room for running around and playing.

The largest campsites have extensive sanitary facilities and hot water. They also provide electrical hook-ups for caravans, as well as running water and sewage connections. Campsite shops mean that you can do most of your shopping on-site, and if you don't feel like cooking your own food, there is often a restaurant or snack bar. Launderettes and dry-cleaning services are also often available. Many have a swimming pool and other recreation facilities such as tennis courts, mini-golf and so on.

The Dutch Automobile Club, **ANWB**, has awarded the best campsites in Europe with their quality label 'Best Camping'. These offer an exceptionally great terrain with large pitches, extensive facilities and terrific service. Over thirty such campsites are located in the Netherlands, and are listed their camping guides and online, albeit in Dutch only: www.anwb.nl/verblijven/campings/home.jsf.

DIRECTORY

Nature Camping

Gastvrije Landgoederen
W gastvrijelandgoederen.nl

Karaktervolle Groene Campings
W kgc.nl

LKC
Tel 0318-578555.
W gasturijelandgoederen.nl

Nivon Naturefriends
W nivon.nl

Stichting Natuurkampeerterreinen
Tel 030-6033701.
W natuurkampeerterreinen.nl

Stichting Trekkershutten Nederland
Tel 0224-563345.
W trekkershutten.nl

SVR (Stichting Vrije Recreatie)
W svr.nl

VeKaBo (Vereniging van Kampeerboeren)
Tel 0900-3336668.
W vekabo.nl

Family Campsites

Roompot Parken
Tel 0900-8810.
W roompotparken.nl

Vacansoleil
Tel 0900-9899.
W vacansoleil.nl

Guides

ANWB online booing
W www.anwbcamping.nl/nederland.html
(Dutch only)

ANWB Campinggids 1 & 2
Both list hundreds of campsites in the Netherlands, and thousands in the rest of Europe (Dutch only).

ANWB Campinggids Kleine Campings
Lists over 1,700 small (under 40 pitches) campsites in Europe (Dutch only).

ACSI Campinggids Benelux
Almost 1,000 inspected campsites in the Netherlands, Belgium and Luxemburg (Dutch only).

ACSI Campsite Guide Europe DVD
Thousands of inspected campsites in Europe on multilingual DVD with route planner, search and comparison (Windows only).

Online camping guides
Lists over 750 campsites inspected by the ANWB.
W en.camping.info/netherlands
W alanrogers.com
W europe-camping-guide.com/en/list/netherlands
W eurocampings.eu/en/europe/netherlands

Where to Stay

Amsterdam

Oude Zijde

misc eatdrinksleep €€
Waterside **Map** 8 D3
Kloveniersburgwal 20, 1012 CV
Tel (020) 330 6241
W misceatdrinksleep.com
Six rooms, miscellaneously-themed (e.g. Rembrandt, Baroque), with rain showers, espresso machines, free minibar.

DK Choice

Droog €€€
Hotels with Character **Map** 7 C4
Staalstraat 7B, 1011 JJ
Tel (020) 523 5059
W hoteldroog.com
Droog's designers offer a hospitality experience with a twist. There's only one room here but with a few extras – an art gallery, beauty salon, fashion boutique, indoor garden, tea room/café and design store.

The Grand €€€
Luxury **Map** 7 C3
Oudezijds Voorburgwal 197, 1012 EX
Tel (020) 555 3111
W sofitel.com
Lush courtyard enclosed by a 17th century town hall. Modern decor. World Travel award nominee.

Nieuwe Zijde

Hotel Des Arts €€
Family-friendly **Map** 7 B4
Rokin 154–156, 1012 LE
Tel (020) 620 1558
W hoteldesarts.nl
Intimate single, family and group rooms; some with views. Two colourful split-level family rooms.

Hotel Sint Nicolaas €€
Hotels with Character **Map** 7 C1
Spuistraat 1A, 1012 SP
Tel (020) 626 1384
W hotelnicolaas.nl
Quirky; former harbour office and mattress factory. Outsized lift, oddly-shaped en suite rooms. Breakfast included.

DoubleTree €€€
Business **Map** 8 E1
Oosterdoksstraat 4, 1011 DK
Tel (020) 530 0800
W doubletree3.hilton.com
Large hotel with harbour views. Features 16 conference halls, free Wi-Fi, remote printing facilities, fitness rooms and a DVD library.

Western Canal Ring

The Times Hotel €€
Waterside **Map** 7 A2
Herengracht 135–137, 1015 BG
Tel (020) 330 6030
W thetimeshotel.nl
Combined canal houses dating from 1650. Blends modern comfort with old Dutch tradition.

The Dylan €€€
Luxury **Map** 1 B5
Keizersgracht 384, 1016 GB
Tel (020) 530 2010
W dylanamsterdam.com
Refined and tasteful, each room and suite is unique. Michelin-starred restaurant.

The Toren €€€
Luxury **Map** 7 A1
Keizersgracht 164, 1015 CZ
Tel (020) 622 6352
W thetoren.nl
Garden-side suites with two-person jacuzzis. Travellers' Choice award winner.

Central Canal Ring

The Golden Bear €
Historic **Map** 4 E1
Kerkstraat 37, 1017 GB
Tel (020) 624 4785
W goldenbear.nl
Famous gay/lesbian hotel, founded after World War II in two 1731 buildings. Bright and cheerful. Breakfast until noon.

Hotel Pulitzer €€€
Luxury **Map** 1 B5
Prinsengracht 315, 1016 GZ
Tel (020) 523 5235
W pulitzeramsterdam.com
Restored canal houses, dating from the 17th and 18th centuries.

Brick exterior of the Hotel Droog in Amsterdam

Price Guide
Prices are based on one night's stay in high season in a standard double room, inclusive of VAT, tourist tax and service charge.

€	**up to €100**
€€	**€100 to 180**
€€€	**over €180**

Three gardens, a restaurant, bar and wine salon. Guests can take saloon boat tours of the canals.

Eastern Canal Ring

DK Choice

Banks Mansion €€€
Waterside **Map** 7 B5
Herengracht 519–525, 1017 BV
Tel (020) 420 0055
W carlton.nl/banksmansion
This monumental former bank-cum-canal mansion is a Travellers' Choice award winner. Rooms are lovely, with Frank Lloyd Wright-inspired decor. Everything is included in the price: breakfast, movies, self-service bar, even iPad loans.

Museum Quarter

Stayokay City Hostel Vondelpark €
Family-friendly **Map** 4 D2
Zandpad 5, 1054 GA
Tel (020) 589 8996
W stayokay.com/vondelpark
Sprawling hostel offering great value. Rooms range from 20-bed dorms to double rooms.

Conscious Hotel Museum Square €€
Design **Map** 4 D4
De Lairessestraat 7, 1071 NR
Tel (020) 671 9596
W conscioushotels.com
Eco-friendly "Green Key" gold certificate holder, with an absolutely gorgeous garden.

DK Choice

Conservatorium €€€
Luxury **Map** 4 D3
Van Baerlestraat 27, 1071 AN
Tel (020) 570 0000
W conservatoriumhotel.com
Housed in a former music conservatory, the space has been imaginatively reused. It has high ceilings and a beautiful atrium designed by Piero Lissoni. Almost half the rooms are duplexes, with amazing views.

Plantage

DK Choice

Amsterdam House €€
Family-friendly **Map** 7 C4
's-Gravelandse Veer 3–4, 1011 KM
Tel (020) 626 2577
W amsterdamhouse.com
Enjoy a true Amsterdam on-the-water experience. Stay on a houseboat with a well-equipped kitchen and bathrooms. Rooms and apartment are warm, bright, modern, and great for groups.

Hermitage €€
Waterside **Map** 5 B3
Nieuwe Keizersgracht 16, 1018 DR
Tel (020) 623 8259
W hotelhermitageamsterdam.com
1733 canal house with a garden. Good for groups or families.

InterContinental Amstel Amsterdam €€€
Luxury **Map** 5 B4
Professor Tulpplein 1, 1018 GX
Tel (020) 622 6060
W amsterdam.intercontinental.com
Rock star favourite, with first class service. Michelin-starred restaurant.

Further Afield

Citizen M €€
Business
Prinses Irenestraat 30, 1077 MX
Tel (020) 811 7090
W citizenm.com/amsterdam-city
Affordable luxury with sleek techno touches. Booking online.

Lloyd Hotel €€
Hotels with Character
Oostelijke Handelskade 34, 1019 BN
Tel (020) 561 3636
W lloydhotel.com
Industrial chic, in a former borstal. Unique focus on culture, events.

North Holland

BERGEN AAN ZEE: Blooming €€
Design **Map** B3
Duinweg 5, 1861 GL
Tel (072) 582 0520
W blooming-hotels.com
Hip hotel on a beach: rooms range from tiny singles to suites.

BROEK IN WATERLAND: Inn on the Lake €€€
Charming **Map** C3
Kerkplein 11, 1151 AH
Tel (020) 331 8573
W innonthelake.nl
B&B in a former vicarage with four rooms and five-star amenities.

Simple, subtle decor at Stempels hotel in Haarlem

HAARLEM: Stempels €€
Historic **Map** B3
Klokhuisplein 9, 2011 HK
Tel (023) 512 3910
W stempelsinhaarlem.nl
Once the royal banknotes printing company, now a boutique hotel with modern amenities.

HEEMSKERK: Stayokay €
Historic **Map** B3
Tolweg 9, 1967 NG
Tel (0251) 232 288
W stayokay.com
Hostel in a medieval castle with turrets, towers, moat and gardens. Shared and private rooms.

OUDERKERK AAN DE AMSTEL: 't Jagershuis €€€
Design **Map** C3
Amstelzijde 2–4, 1184 VA
Tel (020) 496 2020
W jagershuis.com
Boutique hotel in a picturesque village on the Amstel river. All rooms are individually decorated. Suites have five-star amenities.

DK Choice

ZAANDAM: Inntel €€
Design **Map** B3
Provincialeweg 102, 1506 MD
Tel (075) 631 1711
W inntelhotels.nl
The unique building of this four-star hotel resembles the famous wooden houses of the nearby Zaanse Schans. The contemporary rooms are inspired by the town's staples or pay homage to its residents.

ZUIDOOSTBEEMSTER: Fort Resort Beemster €€
Hotels with Character **Map** C3
Nekkerweg 24, 1461 LC
Tel (0299) 682 200
W fortresortbeemster.nl
Interesting contemporary restyling of a vintage space once part of the Defence Line of Amsterdam.

Utrecht

AMERONGEN: Buitenlust €
Charming **Map** C4
Burg Jhr H v d Boschstraat 13, 3958 CA
Tel (0343) 451 692
W buitenlust-amerongen.nl
Cheerful, spacious rooms in a modern mansion near Utrechtse Heuvelrug National Park.

AMERSFOORT: Logies de Tabaksplant €
Historic **Map** C4
Coninckstraat 15, 3811 WD
Tel (033) 472 9797
W tabaksplant.nl
Spread over several medieval buildings, with a lovely restaurant and courtyard.

DOORN: Landgoed Zonheuvel €
Business **Map** C4
Amersfoortseweg 98, 3941 EP
Tel (0343) 473 500
W landgoedzonheuvel.nl
Conference hotel centred around a fairytale castle.

UTRECHT: Mary K €€
Charming **Map** C4
Oudegracht 25, 3511 AB
Tel (030) 230 4888
W marykhotel.com
Rooms of all sizes, art everywhere and breakfast in bed or in a boat.

DK Choice

UTRECHT: Dom €€€
Design **Map** C4
Domstraat 4, 3512 JB
Tel (030) 232 4242
W hoteldom.nl
State-of-the-art rooms with Auping beds, Nespresso machines and yoga mats; a coveted restaurant and a cocktail bar out of a Bond movie. Quite an experience.

ZEIST: Kasteel Kerckebosch €
Historic **Map** C4
Arnhemse Bovenweg 31, 3708 AA
Tel (030) 692 6666
W kasteelkerckebosch.nl
Castle in the woods with modern rooms and an excellent restaurant.

South Holland

DELFT: De Bieslandse Heerlijkheid €
Charming **Map** B4
Klein Delfgauw 61, 2616 LC
Tel (015) 310 7126
W bieslandseheerlijkheid.nl
Rustic B&B in a converted farmhouse close to town.

For more information on types of hotels *see page 391*

Tables awaiting diners at the lovely market cafe at Villa Augustus, Dordrecht

DORDRECHT: Villa Augustus €€
Design **Map** B4
Oranjelaan 7, 3311 DH
Tel (078) 639 3111
W villa-augustus.nl
Attractive boutique hotel housed in a castle-like water tower. Great views, huge garden and lovely 'market café' and restaurant.

ROTTERDAM: SS Rotterdam €€
Design **Map** B4
3e Katendrechtsehoofd 25, 3072 AM
Tel (010) 297 3090
W ssrotterdam.nl
Holland America Line's former flagship, now a floating hotel in fabulous 1950s style.

DK Choice

ROTTERDAM: Stayokay €
Hotels with Character **Map** B4
Overblaak 85–87, 3011 MH
Tel (010) 436 5763
W stayokay.com
In the Cube Houses built by Piet Blom in the 1980s. Distinctly quirky – try and find a straight wall! But it is comfortable, has lots of cafes and restaurants nearby, along with good transport connections.

SCHEVENINGEN: Strandhotel €
Charming **Map** B4
Zeekant 111, 2586 JJ
Tel (070) 354 0193
W strandhotel-scheveningen.nl
Small family-run hotel on the beach, with basic budget rooms and pleasant sea-view rooms. Picnic baskets available.

THE HAGUE: Mozaic €€
Design **Map** B4
Laan Copes van Cattenburgh 38–40, 2585 GB
Tel (070) 352 2335
W mozaic.nl
Boutique hotel in an elegant neighbourhood. Trendy, well-appointed accomodation.

Zeeland

CADZANDBAD: De Blanke Top €
Family-friendly **Map** A5
Boulevard de Wielingen 1, 4506 JH
Tel (0117) 392 040
W blanketop.nl
Pretty views at this resort, as well as a fine dining restaurant. Check ongoing renovations.

DOMBURG: Hotel ter Duyn €€
Charming **Map** A5
P.J. Eloutstraat 1, 4357 AH
Tel (0118) 584 400
W hotelterduyn.nl
Pleasant beach hotel with suites only, each with a small kitchen.

DOMBURG: Badhotel €€€
Luxury **Map** A5
Domburgseweg 1A, 4357 BA
Tel (0118) 588 888
W badhotel.com
Resort near the beach with all expected amenities and a library.

KRUININGEN: Manoir Inter Scaldes €€€
Luxury **Map** B5
Zandweg 2, 4416 NA
Tel (0113) 381 753
W interscaldes.eu
Relais & Châteaux member, with 12 rooms in thatched cottages, and a Michelin-starred restaurant.

DK Choice

MIDDELBURG: Aan de Dam €€
Historic **Map** A5
Dam 31, 4331 GE
Tel (0118) 643 773
W hotelaandedam.nl
Originally built in the 17th century by the same architect who designed Amsterdam's royal palace, this mansion now houses a hotel with enthusiastic staff and rooms that recall the Golden Age.

SINT MAARTENSDIJK: Kom! €
Charming **Map** B5
Markt 58, 4695 CH
Tel (0166) 663 000
W hotelkom.nl
Modern boutique hotel behind a 16th-century facade. Good low-priced restaurant.

SLUIS: Gasthof d'Ouwe Schuure €
Charming **Map** A5
St. Annastraat 191, 4524 JH
Tel (0117) 462 232
W ouweschuure.nl
Homely B&B on the Belgian border with seven rooms and a farmhouse converted into a restaurant.

West Frisian Islands

DK Choice

AMELAND: Nobel €€
Design **Map** C1
Gerrit Kosterweg 16, Ballum 9162 EN
Tel (0519) 554 157
W hotelnobel.nl
Smart contemporary hotel with futuristic-looking rooms, a fine dining restaurant, a modern take on the old brown café, a liquor store and its own distillery.

SCHIERMONNIKOOG: Van der Werff €€
Historic **Map** D1
Reeweg 2, 9166 PX
Tel (0519) 531 203
W hotelvanderwerff.nl
Legendary inn, reached by ferry and vintage omnibus, with neat, modern guest rooms.

TERSCHELLING: Stayokay €
Charming **Map** C1
t Land 2, West Terschelling, 8881 GA
Tel (0562) 442 338
W stayokay.com
Hostel on a dune top with views of the Wadden Sea. Shared and private rooms. Good for biking.

TERSCHELLING: Sandton Paal 8 aan Zee €€€
Luxury **Map** C1
Badweg 4, West Terschelling, 8881 HB
Tel (0562) 449 090
W www.sandton.eu/nl/terschelling
Four-star resort on a dune top. Pool, sauna, bike rentals.

TEXEL: Zeerust €€
Charming **Map** B2
Boodtlaan 5, De Koog, 1796 BD
Tel (0222) 317 261
W hotelzeerust.nl

Key to Price Guide *see page 396*

Up-to-date small hotel, ideally located between village, woods and beach. Fresh breakfasts.

TEXEL: Bij Jef €€€
Design **Map** B2
Herenstraat 34, Den Hoorn, 1797 AJ
Tel (0222) 319 623
W bijjef.nl
Luxurious B&B in a former vicarage with five-star amenities and fine views. Michelin-starred restaurant.

VLIELAND: WestCord Residentie Vlierijck €€€
Luxury **Map** C1
Willem de Vlaminghweg 2, 8899 AV
Tel (0562) 453 840
W residentie-vlierijck-vlieland.nl
Smart apartment hotel with a bar, restaurant, pool, sauna and balconied self-catering apartments. Close to the ferry.

Groningen

DEN HAM: Piloersemaborg €€
Historic **Map** D3
Sietse Veldstraweg 25, 9833 TA
Tel (050) 403 1362
W piloersema.nl
Well-preserved 17th-century grange. Five luxurious rooms and a Michelin-starred restaurant.

EENRUM: Grand Hotel de Kromme Raake €€
Historic **Map** D1
Molenstraat 5, 9967 SL
Tel (0595) 491 600
W hoteldekrommeraake.nl
Officially the world's smallest hotel, with only one room, but that one has hosted many celebrities.

DK Choice

GRONINGEN: Stee in Stad €
Charming **Map** D1
Floresplein 21, 9715 HH
Tel (050) 577 9896
W steeinstad.nl
Three homes in a residential neighbourhood have been lovingly converted into a characterful B&B which serves as a work project for disadvantaged people. All nine rooms (singles and doubles) have been individually decorated.

GRONINGEN: Asgard €€
Design **Map** D1
Ganzevoortsingel 2–1, 9711 AL
Tel (050) 368 4810
W asgardhotel.nl
Floor heating, rain showers and minimalist rooms in a revamped 1930s deaconess hospital.

GRONINGEN: Prinsenhof €€
Historic **Map** D1
Martinikerkhof 23, 9712 JH
Tel (050) 317 6555
W prinsenhof-groningen.nl
A 15th-century palace makes for stunning grandeur in conversion. Beautiful gardens.

LUTJEGAST: Erfgoed Rikkerda €€
Charming **Map** D1
Abel Tasmanweg 28, 9866 TD
Tel (0594) 612 928
W rikkerda.nl
Stylish B&B with spacious accomodation, stabling facilities.

WARFHUIZEN: De Theaterherberg €
Design **Map** D1
Baron van Asbeckweg 42, 9963 PC
Tel (0595) 572 742
W theaterherberg.nl
The 'Theatre Inn' houses a tiny theatre and, in the former wine barn, four literary-themed rooms.

Friesland

HARICH: Welgelegen €
Charming **Map** C2
Welgelegen 15, 8571 RG
Tel (0514) 605 050
W hotelwelgelegen.nl
A 19th-century farmhouse with a romantic bridal suite upstairs.

DK Choice

HARLINGEN: Harbour Crane €€€
Hotels with Character **Map** C2
Dokkade 5, 8862 NZ
Tel (0517) 414 410
W vuurtoren-harlingen.nl
An old harbour crane has been painstakingly converted into a hotel room: the bed is 17 metres above ground and the crane revolves 360 degrees for a constantly changing view of Friesland and the Wadden Sea.

Grand entrance to the Prinsenhof hotel in Groningen

KOUDUM: Galamadammen €€
Charming **Map** C2
Galamadammen 1–4, 8723 CE
Tel (0514) 521 346
W galamadammen.nl
Set beside the marina, this hotel calls for exploring the Frisian lakes by rental boat.

LEEUWARDEN: Grand Hotel Post Plaza €€
Luxury **Map** D1
Tweebaksmarkt 25–27, 8911 KW
Tel (058) 215 9317
W post-plaza.nl
Plush accomodation in an 18th-century former bank building with eyecatching public spaces, a spa and modern rooms.

STAVOREN: De Vrouwe van Stavoren €
Design **Map** C2
Havenweg 1, 8715 EM
Tel (0514) 681 202
W hotel-vrouwevanstavoren.nl
Swiss wine cask – complete with sitting area, private bath and twin beds. Quite extraordinary.

TERNAARD: Herberg de Waard van Ternaard €€
Charming **Map** D1
De Groedse 3, 9145 RG
Tel (0519) 571 846
W herbergdewaard.nl
An inn in an 1860s mansion, recently transformed into a boutique hotel, with rooms decorated in wood and marble. Excellent restaurant.

Drenthe

BORGER: Bed & Brood Enzo €
Charming **Map** E2
Drouwenerstraat 14, 9531 JZ
Tel (0599) 858 132
W bedenbroodenzo.nl
Rustic B&B in Drenthe's dolmen capital. One room only, with bathroom, kitchen, garden.

DE SCHIPHORST: Château De Havixhorst €€€
Luxury **Map** D3
De Schiphorsterweg 34–36, 7966 AC
Tel (0522) 441 487
W dehavixhorst.nl
Lavish suites in a romantic 17th-century manor house on an extensive estate with Baroque gardens and a fine restaurant.

GIETEN: Braams €
Charming **Map** E2
Brink 9, 9461 AR
Tel (0592) 261 241
W hotelbraams.nl
Family-run hotel right on the leafy village square. Great base for hiking and cycling trips.

For more information on types of hotels *see page 391*

NORG: De Eshof €
Charming **Map** D2
Esweg 25, 9331 AP
Tel *06 2169 0092*
W eshofnorg.nl
B&B in a converted 18th-century Saxon farm with sauna, pool and three rooms. Great for cycling trips.

DK Choice

VEENHUIZEN: Bitter & Zoet €€
Historic **Map** D2
Hospitaallaan 16, 9341 AH
Tel (0592) 385 002
W bitterenzoetveenhuizen.nl
'Dedication', 'Obligation' and 'Bitter & Sweet' – the three buildings of a monumental 19th-century hospital complex now make for a wonderful boutique hotel with stylish rooms and apartments, a sauna, restaurant and bakery.

ZEEGSE: De Zeegser Duinen €€
Charming **Map** D2
Schipborgerweg 8, 9483 TL
Tel (0592) 530 099
W hoteldezeegserduinen.nl
Four-star hotel set in a wooded nature reserve. Check in, go cycling and return to unwind.

Overijssel

BLOKZIJL: Kaatjes Résidence €€€
Design **Map** D2
Brouwerstraat 20, 8356 DZ
Tel (0527) 291 833
W kaatje.nl
Luxurious B&B with contemporary rooms on a pretty square. Michelin-starred restaurant.

DK Choice

HENGELO: Tuindorphotel 't Lansink €€
Hotels with Character **Map** E3
C T Storkstraat 18, 7553 AR
Tel (074) 291 0066
W hotellansink.com
Built a century ago as part of a garden village for Stork factory workers, this small-scale grand hotel once hosted famous (and royal) guests. Today, it has heaps of character, a fine dining restaurant and contemporary rooms.

HOLTEN: Hoog Holten €€
Charming **Map** D3
Forthaarsweg 7, 7451 JS
Tel (0548) 361 306
W hoogholten.nl
Wonderful hideaway in a former hunting lodge. Pleasant terrace, wine bar and restaurant.

Beautifully decorated interiors at Modez in Arnhem

LATTROP: Landgoed de Holtweijde €€
Luxury **Map** E3
Spiekweg 7, 7635 LP
Tel (0541) 229 234
W holtweijde.nl
Five-star resort in a tranquil setting. Suites and private cottages, spa, tennis courts and driving range.

TUBBERGEN: Droste's €
Design **Map** E3
Uelserweg 95, 7651 KV
Tel (0546) 621 264
W drostes.nl
Contemporary inn amid rolling meadows with newly decorated rooms and a restaurant.

ZWOLLE: De Koperen Hoogte €€
Design **Map** D3
Lichtmisweg 51, 8035 PL
Tel (0529) 428 428
W dekoperenhoogte.nl
Hotel in a former water tower with kitschy, but luxurious rooms and a revolving restaurant.

ZWOLLE: Hampshire Hotel Lumen €€
Design **Map** D3
Stadionplein 20, 8025 CP
Tel (088) 147 1471
W hotellumen.nl
Four-star hotel with an odd soccer stadium location, but super stylish lobby, lounge and restaurant.

Flevoland

EMMELOORD: Hotel Emmeloord €
Business **Map** D2
Het Hooiveld 9, 8302 AE
Tel (0527) 612 345
W hotelemmeloord.nl
Great value hotel beside a marina, 20 minutes from the national park.

LELYSTAD: Waterlodge de Aalscholver €
Design **Map** C3
Aalscholver 2, 8218 PW
Tel (036) 523 9273
W hajerestaurants.com
Offbeat roadside restaurant with artistic rooms in a floating 'hotel ark' on the water.

LELYSTAD: De Groene Watertuinen €€€
Luxury **Map** C3
Groene Velden 154, 8211 BD
Tel (0320) 263 310
W groenewatertuinen.nl
Set in a leafy suburb. Two suites, plus a pool, jacuzzi and sauna.

DK Choice

URK: De Roos van Saron €
Charming **Map** C3
Wijk 1–44, 8321 EM
Tel (0527) 688 115
W roosvansaron.com
Beside the port of a picturesque fishing village, this B&B has only two rooms, decorated in 18th-century style. The choice is between the stateroom and the one with the romantic bedstead. Modern amenities, like a minibar and Nespresso machine.

Gelderland

ARNHEM: Modez €€
Design **Map** D4
Elly Lamakerplantsoen 4, 6822 BZ
Tel (026) 442 0993
W hotelmodez.nl
Striking hotel decorated by 30 designers under the guidance of fashion illustrator Piet Paris.

BRUMMEN: Het Oude Postkantoor €€
Charming **Map** D4
Zutphensestraat 6, 6971 EM
Tel (0575) 566 781
W hetoudepostkantoor.nl
Village post office converted into a small hotel with authentic details.

DOETINCHEM: Villa Ruimzicht €€
Charming **Map** D4
Ruimzichtlaan 150, 7001 KG
Tel (0314) 320 680
W hotelvillaruimzicht.nl

Key to Price Guide *see page 396*

Adventurous cooking, designer furniture and art come together at this 19th-century manor.

HARDERWIJK: Harderwijk op de Veluwe €€
Luxury **Map** C3
Leuvenumseweg 7, 3847 LA
Tel (0341) 801 010
W hotelharderwijk.com
Four-star hotel in which all rooms have jacuzzis and rain showers.

NIJMEGEN: Manna €€
Design **Map** D4
Oranjesingel 2C, 6511 NS
Tel (024) 365 0990
W manna-nijmegen.nl
Stylish boutique hotel with 10 individually decorated suites.

OTTERLO: Sterrenberg €€
Design **Map** D4
Houtkampweg 1, 6731 AV
Tel (0318) 591 228
W sterrenberg.nl
A wonderful hideaway close to the Hoge Veluwe national park. Great restaurant, indoor pool, spa.

DK Choice

TEUGE: Airplane Suite €€€
Hotels with Character **Map** D3
De Zanden 61B, 7395 PA
Tel *06 1938 8603*
W hotelsuites.nl
An Ilyushin 18 aircraft that flew communist party moguls in the 1960s has been converted into a suite for two with an Auping bed, pantry, sauna and jacuzzi. The cockpit is still in perfect working condition.

North Brabant

BREDA: Bliss €€€
Design **Map** B5
Torenstraat 9–11, 4811 XV
Tel (076) 533 5980
W blisshotel.nl
Nine themed suites, with jacuzzis, fireplaces, workstations or terraces.

GELDROP: Nijver €
Design **Map** D5
Heuvel 1A, 5664 HJ
Tel (040) 286 7000
W hotelnijver.nl
Boutique hotel that pays tribute to the textile industry with its nine stylishly decorated suites.

KAATSHEUVEL: Efteling Hotel €€€
Design **Map** D5
Horst 31, 5171 RA
Tel (0416) 287 111
W eftelinghotel.com
Four-star hotel in a cloud castle near a well-known amusement park. Fairytale-themed rooms.

DK Choice

NIEUWENDIJK: Fort Bakkerskil €
Historic **Map** C4
Kildijk 143, 4255 TH
Tel *06 4593 4892*
W bakkerskil.nl
Part of the 19th-century New Dutch Water Line, this sturdy fort has now been converted into a B&B: choose between a bed in the sickbay, powder magazine or explosives storage.

OISTERWIJK: Stille Wilde €
Family-friendly **Map** C5
Scheibaan 11, 5062 TM
Tel (013) 528 2301
W stillewilde.nl
Comfortable, basic rooms with terrace or balcony. Ample recreational opportunities.

OSSENDRECHT: De Volksabdij €
Historic **Map** B5
Onze Lieve Vrouwe ter Duinenlaan 199, 4641 RM
Tel (0164) 672 546
W devolksabdij.nl
The well-appointed, modern but basic rooms of this heritage hotel occupy a former monastery, set in the middle of a nature reserve.

'S-HERTOGENBOSCH: Stadshotel Jeroen €€
Charming **Map** C4
Jeroen Boschplein 6, 5211 ML
Tel (073) 610 3556
W stadshoteljeroenbosch.nl
Stylish hotel named after painter Hieronymus Bosch. Four rooms, two spacious suites, a parlour and a terrace.

Airplane Suite, Teuge, set in an unused Ilyushin 18 aircraft

Limburg

KERKRADE: Abdij Rolduc €
Historic **Map** D6
Heyendallaan 82, 6464 EP
Tel (045) 546 6888
W rolduc.com
A 900-year-old abbey that now houses a conference centre, restaurant and hotel.

MAASTRICHT: Zenden €
Design **Map** C6
Sint Bernardusstraat 5, 6211 HK
Tel (043) 321 2211
W zenden.nl
Minimalist rooms with Auping beds, Vitra furniture, Alessi baths.

MAASTRICHT: Kruisherenhotel €€€
Luxury **Map** C6
Kruisherengang 19–23, 6211 NW
Tel (043) 329 2020
W chateauhotels.nl
Opulent design hotel with individually decorated rooms.

DK Choice

ROERMOND: Het Arresthuis €€
Hotels with Character **Map** D5
Pollartstraat 7, 6041 GC
Tel (0475) 870 870
W hetarresthuis.nl
The cells of this 19th-century prison have been converted into 'comfort cachots'. The warden's office is now a luxury suite, the yard has become a patio, and instead of roll calls, there are six-course dinners.

SITTARD: Merici €€
Historic **Map** D6
Oude Markt 25, 6131 EN
Tel (046) 400 9002
W hotelmerici.nl
A 19th-century Ursuline boarding school, now a four-star hotel.

VALKENBURG AAN DE GEUL: Dieteren €€
Charming **Map** D6
Neerhem 34, 6301 CH
Tel (043) 601 5404
W appartementdieteren-valkenburg.nl
Located beside the cable car in a picture-perfect town. Pool, garden.

VALKENBURG AAN DE GEUL: Château St Gerlach €€€
Luxury **Map** D6
Joseph Corneli Allée 1, 6301 KK
Tel (043) 608 8888
W chateaustgerlach.com
An exclusive aristocratic hideaway where the king once stayed.

For more information on types of hotels *see page 391*

WHERE TO EAT AND DRINK

The Dutch are innovative people, and this quality reflects in their cooking. Old colonial ties have long influenced Dutch cuisine and its restaurant scene, so Surinamese and especially Indonesian restaurants are aplenty. More recently, as the Dutch have been introduced to the cooking skills of immigrants into the area, Turkish snack bars and Moroccan restaurants are popping up.

The Dutch restaurant scene leans heavily on international influences. Especially in the bigger cities, visitors can choose between exotic flavours from countries as diverse as Spain, Greece, Israel, Lebanon, Sweden, Ethiopia, India, Thailand, Vietnam and Japan. A popular Dutch phenomenon is the *eetcafé*, or bar where diners can order meals from a limited menu, featuring at least one inexpensive, daily changing set menu (*dagmenu*).

Although many Dutch have forgotten there is such a thing as 'traditional Dutch cooking', this is now being rediscovered. A growing number of chefs are serving new takes on traditional Dutch fare, involving meat or fish, potatoes and more elaborate sauces. Eating out has long been considered something people hastily do in between appointments or before going to the theatre, but the Dutch are now taking it more seriously and the number of Michelin-starred restaurants is on the rise.

Eating out is an increasingly popular pastime in the Netherlands

Types of Restaurant

The Netherlands boasts a wide variety of restaurants. Amsterdam is one of the best places in Europe to try the diverse flavours of Indonesia, and Chinese restaurants and pizzerias have also spread far and wide across the country. Indeed it is difficult to find a country whose cuisine is not represented by some restaurant in the Netherlands. There is also an infinite variety in the range of dishes, ingredients, presentation and price.

Traditional Dutch cooking is best described as simple and straightforward. As a maritime nation, the Netherlands does have many fish restaurants, particularly along the coast. A large number of restaurants serve French cuisine, and their quality is consistently improving. Chefs frequently add local ingredients to French recipes, such as fennel or asparagus. This means that you can eat wild duck on endive *stamppot* (mashed potato and cabbage), a combination unheard of in France. It is in areas such as these that Dutch chefs are showing increasing inventiveness.

Eetcafés

Eetcafés (eating cafés) are a popular phenomenon in the Netherlands. The term *eetcafés* is most commonly applied to traditional brown cafés. Initially, some cafés and bars sold snacks to go with their drinks, such as an appetizer, a sandwich or a meatball. These snacks have since been refined to a growing extent. Bars and cafés have gradually evolved into *eetcafés* where diners can enjoy sandwiches at lunchtime and cheap, often very decent, meals in the evenings, usually at much lower prices than those in traditional restaurants.

Vegetarian Restaurants

Most restaurants have several vegetarian dishes on their menus. This applies both to Dutch/French restaurants and to ethnic restaurants. There is also an increasing number of restaurants that cater exclusively to vegetarian diners.

Opening Hours

The Netherlands does not have a tradition of lunching, but this is gradually changing, with more restaurants now opening at lunchtime, usually from noon to 2pm. In the evenings, the

An *eetcafé*, one of the many in Holland serving increasingly refined meals

Vibrant interiors at Eetbar Dit *(see p415)* in 's-Hertogenbosch

majority of restaurants open at 6pm and the kitchens usually close around 10pm. An increasing number of restaurants stay open all day, serving breakfast, lunch and dinner and light meals or snacks in between.

In the cities, night restaurants are on the rise, with kitchens staying open until midnight or later, allowing you to round off a visit to the theatre or movies with a late dinner.

Traditionally, many restaurants do not open on Mondays, though this is also changing.

Reservations

Anybody wishing to eat in one of the country's more renowned restaurants would do well to book, and sometimes booking a few days in advance – or weeks for the most acclaimed restaurants – is advisable. *Eetcafés* and other informal eateries can get crowded in the evenings, but reservations are usually accepted only for large groups if at all.

Tipping

It is customary to leave a tip of roughly 10 per cent by rounding up the amount. If you pay by credit card, you can either add the tip to the bill or leave change on the table. Leaving no tip at all is usually done only when you are particularly unsatisfied with the service provided. At very informal places, such as takeaways or snack bars, tipping is not expected.

Etiquette

The atmosphere at many Dutch restaurants is fairly informal, and you can generally wear what you like; smart casual dress is suitable almost everywhere. In upmarket restaurants, however, dressing smartly is appropriate. Smoking is banned in all restaurants. It is considered impolite to use your mobile phone while at the table.

Prices

Restaurants are legally obliged to display their menu outside, with prices, inclusive of VAT ('BTW') and service. Prices can vary markedly, and a restaurant can be found in each price class: you can find many establishments where you can eat for less than €25; in top restaurants, however, you should not be surprised if your bill exceeds €70, excluding wine. The cost of drinks is invariably extra and the mark-up levied by a restaurant, especially on house wine and table water, can be high.

A snack bar, ideal for a quick but satisfying bite to eat

Travellers with Disabilities

Many restaurants are accessible for wheelchairs, but even if they are, toilet facilities may still pose a problem, as they are often reached via stairs and therefore not easily accessible.

Drinks

All but the most informal restaurants will have a wine list offering a range of fine wines to accompany your meal. Although French wines are still the staple, New World wines have become increasingly popular. Upmarket restaurants will have a sommelier to help you with your choice, and many offer a wine package, serving a glass of carefully paired wine with your meal.

Typically Dutch brown cafés are making way for airy grand cafés and sleek cocktail bars, offering a long list of exotic aperitifs. However, for most Dutch, beer is still the tipple of choice, with Heineken or any other Dutch lager on tap everywhere

Recommended Restaurants

The restaurants listed on pages 406–415 have been selected not only for the quality of food served, but also on the basis of value for money, atmosphere, location and service. Obviously, some restaurants are better than others and a few stand out for a particular reason, such as their innovative chef, pleasant waterside terrace or romantic atmosphere. For each region we have have handpicked one such exceptional restaurant, ranging from a year-round beach club at the quiet end of Zandvoort beach, via a tiny Italian trattoria dishing out fantastic king crab cannelloni, to a Michelin-starred restaurant in a fairytale castle, with a terrace that seems to float in the moat. Here you will not only be guaranteed a decent meal, but also gain a memorable experience. Our highly recommended restaurants are marked as DK Choice.

The Flavours of the Netherlands

The typical Dutch menu offers good, solid fare. Pork, hams and all kinds of sausages are popular, while the North Sea provides plenty of fresh fish, especially cod, herring and mackerel, as well as its own variety of tiny brown shrimps. Leafy green vegetables, such as cabbage, endive (chicory) and curly kale make regular appearances, frequently mashed with the ubiquitous potato. Sauerkraut arrived from Germany long ago and is now considered a native dish. The world famous Gouda and Edam cheeses are sold at various stages of maturity, and with flavourings such as cloves, cumin or herbs.

Edam cheese

Sampling pickled herring at one of Amsterdam's many fish-stalls

Amsterdam's Culinary Influences

Traditional Dutch cuisine may be simple, wholesome and hearty, but the variety of food on offer in Amsterdam is huge and influenced by culinary styles from across the globe. The Netherlands was once a major colonial power and its trading ships brought back exotic ingredients, ideas and people from former colonies to settle. Dutch chefs branched out and tried new flavours, and as such, "fusion" food has long been a feature of Amsterdam's menus. From its street-corner fish-stalls to its cafés and top-flight gourmet restaurants, eating out in Amsterdam can be full of surprises. Over 50 national cuisines are represented, offering a sometimes bewildering variety of choice and good value for money.

The Melting Pot

Amsterdam has long had a reputation for religious and political tolerance. Refugees who found a safe haven there brought along their own styles of cooking. In the 16th century, Jews fleeing

Fried tofu with sambal oelek (chilli sauce)

Bami goreng (fried noodles with chicken and pork)

Steamed rice

Prawn crackers

Gado gado (vegetable salad with peanut sauce)

Satay ayam (chicken satay)

Selection of typical rijsttafel dishes

Local Dishes and Specialities

Brown shrimp

Dining out in the Netherlands is almost guaranteed to come up with some curious quirks. Cheese, ham and bread are standards at breakfast, but you may also find *ontbijtkoek* (gingerbread) and *hagelslag* (grains of chocolate) to sprinkle over bread. Ham and cheese are also lunchtime staples, often served in a bread roll with a glass of milk, though more adventurous sandwiches and salads are also common nowadays. In Amsterdam, pancake houses provide both sweet and savoury snacks throughout the day. The evening is the time when Amsterdam's eateries have the most to offer. The soups and mashed vegetables of Dutch farmhouse cooking sit alongside spicy Indonesian delights, as well as innovative cuisine from some of Amsterdam's fine chefs.

Erwtensoep is a thick pea and smoked sausage soup, which is often served with rye bread and slices of bacon.

Baskets of wild mushrooms at an organic market

persecution in Portugal and Antwerp were some of the first foreigners to make their home in the city. Today, Amsterdammers count as their own such Jewish specialities as *pekelvlees* (salt beef), pickled vegetables (often served as salad) and a variety of sticky cakes, now found mostly in the more old-fashioned tea-rooms.

The 20th century saw an influx of immigrants from Turkey and several North African countries. Large Arab and Turkish communities have become established in Amsterdam. As a result, restaurants with menus that feature Middle-Eastern style stuffed vegetables, succulent stews and couscous, are almost everywhere. *Falafel* (fried chickpea balls) are readily available from road-side take-aways and are now one of the city's favourite late-night snacks. Ethiopians, Greeks, Thais, Italians and Japanese are among other waves of immigrants to make their culinary mark, and most recently traditional British fare has become popular.

Gouda on offer in an Amsterdam cheese shop

Indonesian Legacy

The Dutch began colonizing Indonesia in the 17th century and ruled the south-east Asian archipelago right up until 1949. Indonesian cuisine has had a marked influence on eating habits in The Netherlands. Ingredients once regarded as exotic have crept into Dutch dishes. It is now commonplace to spice up apple pies and biscuits with cinnamon, which is sometimes even used to flavour vegetables. Coconut and chillis are very popular flavourings, too, and sampling a *rijsttafel* (see below) is considered one of the highlights of any trip to the country.

THE RIJSTTAFEL

Dutch colonialists in Indonesia often found that the modest local portions failed to satisfy their hunger. To match their larger appetites, they created the *rijsttafel* (literally "rice-table"). It consists of around 20 small spicy dishes, served up with a shared bowl of rice or noodles. Pork or chicken *satay* (mini kebabs with peanut sauce) and *kroepoek* (prawn crackers) usually arrive first. A selection of curried meat and vegetable dishes follows, with perhaps a plate of fried tofu and various salads, all more or less served together. A sweet treat, such as bananas fried in batter, rounds it all off.

Shrimp croquettes are shrimps in a creamy sauce, coated in breadcrumbs and deep-fried.

Stamppot is a hearty dish of curly kale or endive (chicory) and crispy bacon mixed with mashed potato.

Nasi goreng, an Indonesian-style dish of egg-fried rice with pork and mushrooms, is also popular for a *rijsttafel*.

Where to Eat and Drink

Amsterdam

Oude Zijde

Café de Engelbewaarder €
Brown Café **Map** 8 D4
Kloveniersburgwal 59, 1011 JZ
Tel (020) 625 3772
Laid back traditional Dutch pub. The menu changes every week or two, but is mostly European and seasonal. Live jazz on Sundays.

de Bakkerswinkel €
Bakery **Map** 8 D2
Zeedijk 37, 1012 AR
Tel (020) 489 8000
Try traditional English scones with cream (not clotted, sadly) or the lemon curd. Serves breakfast, lunch and has a high tea menu.

Éenvistwéévis €€
Seafood **Map** 5 C1
Schippersgracht 6, 1011 TR
Tel (020) 623 2894 **Closed** *Sun, Mon*
A paradise for fish lovers, with intimate decor and a menu that depends on the daily catch and seasons. Organic, sustainable ingredients. No credit cards.

DK Choice

Greetje €€
Traditional **Map** 8 F3
Peperstraat 23, 1011 TJ
Tel (020) 779 7450
Greetje is hailed by the New York Times as the place the Dutch go to eat Dutch. It simply doesn't get more authentic than this. Locals love the *trekdrop* (liquorice) ice cream and *bloedworst* (blood sausage) with apple compote. The menu changes every two months. The old-fashioned interior has lots of wood and traditional accents.

In de Waag €€
Fusion **Map** 8 D3
Nieuwmarkt 4, 1012 CR
Tel (020) 422 7772
In a 1488 guildhouse, on the top floor of which Rembrandt once took anatomy lessons. Informal interior lit by 300 candles. Eclectic menu, divine desserts. Book ahead.

Kilimanjaro €€
African **Map** 8 F4
Rapenburgerplein 6, 1011 VB
Tel (020) 622 3485 **Closed** *Mon*
Pan-African restaurant serving specialities from across the continent, including West-African antelope stew and Senegalese crocodile yassa. Warm decor, with African artwork. No credit cards.

Blauw aan de Wal €€€
Fusion **Map** 8 D3
Oudezijds Achterburgwal 99, 1012 DD
Tel (020) 330 2257 **Closed** *Mon, Sun*
Set in an ancient warehouse, with rustic decor, brick walls and wooden beams. Serves modern Mediterranean delights, with a menu that changes every week; outstanding wine list. Reservations essential.

Nieuwe Zijde

Catala €
Spanish **Map** 7 A4
Spuistraat 299, 1012 VS
Tel (020) 623 1141
Sample authentic Catalonian tapas in the warm rustic interior of this restaurant. Popular fish dishes include rice with shellfish, grilled swordfish and monkfish. Or, try the famous Pata Negra jamon.

Getto Food & Drink €
Cafe/Bar **Map** 8 D2
Warmoesstraat 51, 1012HW
Tel (020) 421 5151 **Closed** *Mon*
Gay, straight, mixed, anything goes bar-restaurant, offering home-style cooking. Burgers are a speciality here, and are named after famous Amsterdam drag queens, like the "Jennifer Hopeless".

Kam Yin €
Surinamese **Map** 8 D1
Warmoesstraat 6, 1012 JD
Tel (020) 625 3115
An Amsterdam institution, serving Chinese and Surinamese cuisine.

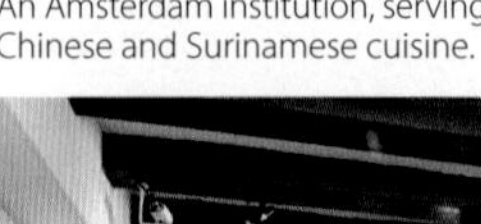

Rich decor at Visrestaurant Lucius, Amsterdam

Price Guide
Prices are based on a three-course meal per person, with a half-bottle of house wine, including tax and service.

€	up to €35
€€	€35 to 50
€€€	over €50

The extensive menu makes it a great place for quick, delicious food, despite the uninspired decor. There's an attached snackbar. Well worth a visit.

Tibet €€
Tibetan/Chinese **Map** 8 D2
Lange Niezel 24, 1012 GT
Tel (020) 624 1137
Eclectic Tibetan decor and relaxed service. Choice of Chinese Szechuan dishes, alongside staple Tibetan fare. Asian lunch (rice, noodle dishes) also served.

DK Choice

Visrestaurant Lucius €€
Seafood **Map** 7 A3
Spuistraat 247, 1012 VP
Tel (020) 624 1831
Named after the Northern pike *(Esox lucius)*, this restaurant offers delicate, delicious seafood. Dishes are cooked simply, so the fresh taste shines through. Try the "plateau fruits de mer" (large selection of lobster, crab, etc) or the North Sea sole. Very popular among the locals; French bistro decor.

ANNA €€€
European **Map** 2 D4
Warmoesstraat 11, 1012 JA
Tel (020) 428 1111 **Closed** *Sun*
Upmarket restaurant, housed in two renovated buildings. Serves European cuisine with a twist – including dishes like pan-fried corvine fillet and braised quail.

D'Vijff Vlieghen €€€
Traditional **Map** 7 A4
Spuistraat 294–302, 1012 VX
Tel (020) 530 4060
Dine surrounded by original Rembrandts and 17th century furnishings. Try lightly smoked duck breast, or the "Surprising" chef's menu.

Central Canal Ring

Goodies €
Mediterranean **Map** 7 A4
Huidenstraat 9, 1016 ER
Tel (020) 625 6122
Informal diner, serving great food. All ingredients are organic. The

ravioli is very popular, as are the meal-sized salads. The menu also includes tapas-style dishes and delectable home-made cakes.

Pancakes! €
Bakery **Map** 1 B5
38 Berenstraat, 1016 GH
Tel (020) 528 9797
Dutch and international pancakes, served in grand style. The flour is specially milled from the Dutch grain mill, de Korenmolen. Other ingredients sustainably sourced.

Balthazar's Keuken €€
International **Map** 1 B5
Elandsgracht 108, 1016 VA
Tel (020) 420 2114 **Closed** *Sun, Mon & Tue*
Personalized service, serious food in an open kitchen with hanging pans. The menu changes weekly, with only two choices, wine pre-chosen, and up to five appetizers.

Nomads €€
Arabic **Map** 1 A5
Rozengracht 133
Tel (020) 344 6401
Inspired by nomadic culture, with soft cushions and warm lighting. Live entertainment on most evenings: music, belly dancers, storytellers or masseuses.

Portugália €€
Portuguese **Map** 4 E1
Kerkstraat 35, 1017 GB
Tel (020) 625 6490
Family-run restaurant serving simple cuisine with the emphasis on fish and meat. Try the single-pan dishes *(Cataplana)*, like the smoked pork, clams, shrimp and potatoes in a cream sauce.

Struisvogel €€
International **Map** 1 B5
Keizersgracht 312, 1016 EX
Tel (020) 423 3817
In the cellar of a canal house. Specializes in unusual meats, like springbok (antelope) or wild Scottish deer. Try the apple raisin crumble with vanilla ice cream.

DK Choice

Restaurant Vinkeles €€€
French **Map** 1 B5
Keizersgracht 384, 1016 GB
Tel (020) 530 2010 **Closed** *Sun*
At this world famous, Michelin-starred restaurant, ask to be seated amid 18th-century bakery ovens, or dine on a 19th-century salon boat. Be prepared for the finest of fine dining experiences, featuring the best in French cuisine. The *anjou duif* (pigeon) is particularly recommended.

A beautifully laid table at Balthazar's Keuken, Amsterdam

Eastern Canal Ring

Kingfisher €
International **Map** 4 F4
Ferdinand Bolstraat 24, 1072 LK
Tel (020) 671 2395
Good food, ranging from snacks (goat's cheese croquettes) to lunch (club sandwich or spicy lamb burger) to a day menu (fish, meat or vegetarian). Free Wi-Fi. Excellent value.

Buffet van Odette €€
Brasserie **Map** 4 F2
Prinsengracht 598, 1017 KS
Tel (020) 423 6034 **Closed** *Tue*
Light and sunny with a great terrace. Serves breakfast, lunch and dinner. Ingredients are mostly organic and locally sourced. Popular dishes: the truffle cheese omelette and steak sandwich.

de Waaghals €€
Vegetarian **Map** 4 F3
Frans Halsstraat 29, 1072 BK
Tel (020) 679 9609 **Closed** *Mon*
Simple, modern interior. Beautifully prepared creative cuisine featuring organic produce. The menu changes twice a month and always features one international special of the month.

Le Zinc... et les Autres €€
French **Map** 5 A3
Prinsengracht 999, 1017 KM
Tel (020) 622 9044 **Closed** *Sun, Mon*
Stylish and classic, housed in a restored warehouse. Hearty, rustic cuisine. Good vegetarian options, excellent wines and sinful desserts.

Rose's Cantina €€
South American **Map** 7 B5
Reguliersdwarsstraat 38–40, 1017 BM
Tel (020) 625 9797
Established, sprawling South American restaurant. Emphasis on tacos, enchiladas, quesadilla, or try Rose's house burger. Great cocktails, and a "tequilla library". DJs on weekend.

Steakhouse Piet de Leeuw €€
Traditional **Map** 4 F2
Noorderstraat 11, 1017 TR
Tel (020) 623 7181
Open since 1949, and famous for its steaks (beef and horse) and fish (sole, salmon). Frequented by locals who praise the food as well as the brown café decor.

Sluizer €€€
International **Map** 5 A3
Utrechtsestraat 41–45, 1017 VH
Tel (020) 622 6376
Two restaurants under one roof: Specialties and Fish. Extensive à la carte and changing choice menus, with international meat, fish and vegetarian options.

Museum Quarter

Het Blauwe Theehuis €
Fusion **Map** 3 C3
Vondelpark 5, 1071 AA
Tel (020) 662 0254 **Closed** *Winter*
A 1937 octagonal concrete, steel and glass structure nestled in the park. Huge surrounding terrace. The menu is European, French or Mediterranean based.

Café Toussaint €€
International **Map** 4 D1
Bosboom Toussaintstraat 26, 1054 AS
Tel (020) 685 0737
An absolute gem. Small, charming cafe, wth an open kitchen and peaceful terrace. Emphasis on healthy, international fare: soups, sandwiches and tapas. Good range for vegetarians.

Due Napoletani €€
Italian **Map** 4 E4
Hobbemakade 61–63, 1071 XL
Tel (020) 671 1263 **Closed** *Tue*
Chic Italian cuisine served in an informal setting. The Pasta al Parmigiano is a popular dish. Staff here are so accomodating that if you call ahead, they will also open for lunch.

For more information on types of restaurants *see page 403*

Srikandi €€
Indonesian **Map** 4 E2
Stadhouderskade 31, 1071 ZD
Tel (020) 664 0408
An art gallery and music create an authentic atmosphere at this traditional Indonesian restaurant. Known for its version of a *rijsttafel* (rice table) with 18 dishes. Good vegetarian options. Book ahead.

The Seafood Bar €€
Seafood **Map** 4 D3
van Baerlestraat 5II, 1071 AL
Tel (020) 670 8355
Sleek and trendy seafood bar, open for lunch and dinner. The menu changes every three months, although some favourites remain. Popular dishes include Fruits de Mer and Fish and Chips.

Le Garage €€€
International **Map** 4 E4
Ruysdaelstraat 54–56, 1071 XE
Tel (020) 679 7176 **Closed** *Lunch on Sat and Sun*
An elegant bistro with plush red seating, in a renovated garage. French and international fare on offer, with the emphasis on organic ingredients.

The College Hotel €€€
Modern Dutch **Map** 4 E5
Roelof Hartstraat 1, 1071 VE
Tel (020) 571 1511
Renovated gymnasium in an 1895 school building, known for its classic Dutch cuisine with a modern twist, as well as the elegant dining experience it offers.

Plantage

Aguada €
International **Map** 5 C3
Roetersstraat 10-W, 1018 WC
Tel (020) 620 3782
Tiny family-run cafe restaurant that offers "home-cooked" food in an informal atmosphere. Cheese fondue is their speciality, but they also serve Dutch wild boar and Italian, Indonesian and Indian fare.

de Pizzabakkers Plantage €
Italian **Map** 5 C2
Plantage Kerklaan 2, 1018 TA
Tel (020) 625 0740
The place for authentic Italian pizza, made with locally sourced ingredients, and baked in a wood oven. Good range of antipasti, vegetarian choices and desserts.

Bloem €€
European **Map** 6 D2
Entrepotdok 36, 1018 AD
Tel (020) 330 0929
Almost all the bread, fruit, vegetables and meat served here are organic, and locally sourced wherever possible. Delicious, as well as healthy.

Meneer Nilsson €€
Mediterranean **Map** 5 C2
Plantage Kerklaan 41, 1018 CV
Tel (020) 624 4846
Think tapas, but expanded across the Mediterranean. Try grilled vegetables with goat cheese, honey/dill sauce or Black Angus steak. Fresh, organic ingredients only. Great cocktails.

Paerz €€
European **Map** 6 D2
Entrepotdok 64, 1018 AD
Tel (020) 623 2206 **Closed** *Mon (Tue in winter)*
Choose from the chef's menu with three or four courses or the à la carte menu. Both are inspired by classic French cuisine and feature seasonal produce. In summer, the seating beside the water is particularly pleasant.

Tempura €€
Japanese **Map** 5 C2
Plantage Kerklaan 26, 1018 TC
Tel (020) 428 7132 **Closed** *Mon*
Neighbourhood Japanese-style brasserie. Extensive sushi, yakatori, grilled and vegetarian menus, as well as a wide range of tempura, set menus. The squid and the St Jacques sashimi are wonderful. Credit cards not accepted.

DK Choice

La Rive €€€
Mediterranean **Map** 5 B4
Amstel Hotel, Professor Tulpplein 1, 1018 GX
Tel (020) 520 3264 **Closed** *Mon, lunch on Sat*
La Rive offers beautiful, elegant cuisine elevated to the level of art. This Michelin-starred restaurant is located in the ultra-lux Amstel Hotel, and serves dishes with inspired French and Mediterranean flavours, created using high quality seasonal produce. It also has a selection of outstanding wines. Reserve the Chef's table.

Western Canal Ring

Greenwoods €
Tearoom **Map** 7 B1
Singel 103, 1012 VG
Tel (020) 623 7071
Welcoming English-style tearoom. Serves a full English breakfast (English bacon), organic lamb burger and high tea (with real clotted cream). Its sister restaurant, on the Keizersgracht 465, also does dinner (fish and chips).

Pancake Bakery €
Bakery **Map** 7 A1
Prinsengracht 191, 1015 DS
Tel (020) 625 1333
This family-run establishment serves a variety of pancakes. Favourites include the Egyptian (lamb, paprika, garlic sauce) as well as the classic Dutch (syrup, powdered sugar or bacon). Closed for breakfast.

Piqniq €
Café **Map** 1 C3
Lindengracht 59,1015 KC
Tel (020) 320 3669 **Closed** *Tue*
Serves a selection of miniature homemade goodies: mini-sandwiches, soups, bite-sized quiches and cakes. Order a selection or try the fixed menu. High tea, gluten-free options.

Chez Georges €€
French **Map** 7 A1
Herenstraat 3, 1015 BX
Tel (020) 626 3332 **Closed** *Sun*
A must for gourmands, with a seasonal Burgundian menu. Sample the five-course set meal: salad, fish (plate combines

Elegant interiors at the Michelin-starred La Rive in Amsterdam

Key to Price Guide *see page 406*

salmon, gamba, coquille and turbot), Scottish beef with morel sauce and dessert. Fine wine selection. Book ahead.

De Bolhoed €€
International **Map** 1 B3
Prinsengracht 60-62, 1015 DX
Tel (020) 626 1803
Popular vegetarian restaurant with a canalside terrace. Serves imaginative international dishes (Mexican, Mediterranean, Asian, African) with a daily vegan choice. Mostly organic and seasonal ingredients, along with delicious desserts. Book ahead.

Stout! €€
Fusion **Map** 1 C3
Haarlemmerstraat 73, 1013 EL
Tel (020) 616 3664
International cuisine with inspired flavour combinations. "Stout Plateau" (€35) offers 10 small treats, or try the fresh "Catch of the Day". Live DJ on Saturday nights (except summer).

Christophe €€€
French **Map** 1 B4
Leliegracht 46, 1015 DH
Tel (020) 625 0807 **Closed** *Sun, Mon*
An Amsterdam institution – traditional, yet modern, offering fine French dining. Serves classic dishes with Mediterranean infusions. The "Boat Box" take-away makes for an elegant picnic.

Further Afield

Azmarino €
East African **Map** 5 A5
Tweede Sweelinckstraat 6, 1073 EH
Tel (020) 671 7587
This restaurant, with traditional African furnishings, serves a classic menu: *enjera* (pancakes), a choice of meats (mild to spicy), and some vegetarian options. Try eggs in red sauce, or *enjera* with meat or vegetable sauces. Open on weekends for breakfast and lunch.

Blauw €€
Indonesian **Map** 3 A4
Amstelveenseweg 158, 1075 XN
Tel (020) 675 5000
One of the better-known and beloved Indonesian restaurants in town. The decor is stylish and intimate, without a hint of kitsch. Order the enormous *rijsttafel*. Worth the trip.

Ciel Bleu €€€
French
Okura Hotel, Ferdinand Bolstraat 333, 1072 LH
Tel (020) 678 7111 **Closed** *Sun*
Awarded a second Michelin star in 2011, this French restaurant is renowned for its creative, innovative dishes, and terrific views of Amsterdam. The place to make an impression.

DK Choice

de Kas €€€
Organic
Kamerlingh Onneslaan 3 1097 DE
Tel (020) 462 4562 **Closed** *Sat lunch*
Dine in a lush oasis in this 1920s restaurant overflowing with plants, or reserve the frantic Chef's Table in the kitchen. The Michelin-starred chef and owner offers a fixed three-course menu (vegetarian options available) based on the seasonal produce of local growers of organic food, as well as meat and fish producers.

North Holland

BLARICUM: Tafelberg €
International **Map** C3
Oude Naarderweg 2, 1261 DS
Tel (035) 538 3975
Opened in the 1930s as a teahouse on the heath, now a full-fledged restaurant with a large terrace that serves as an idyllic resting spot after a walk in the woods. Expect the odd Dutch celebrity.

DK Choice

HAARLEM: De Jopenkerk €€
Traditional **Map** B3
Gedempte Voldersgracht 2, 2011 WB
Tel (023) 533 4114
This century-old church has been stunningly transformed into a grand café (on the ground floor) and a restaurant (upstairs) with an in-house brewery. Most of the mainly Dutch meat and fish dishes are cooked with beer, and every course comes with a beer recommendation. A favourite among locals, the restaurant can get noisy, especially on weekend nights.

HAARLEM: Specktakel €€
Fusion **Map** B3
Spekstraat 4, 2011 HM
Tel (023) 532 3841
Intimate restaurant on 'Bacon Street' that serves organic meat, fresh seafood and exotic game prepared in Japanese, Chinese, Italian or French style with Australian, African, American and Creole influences. Order the Umami menu.

Grand interior of De Jopenkerk, Haarlem, which was once a church

HAARLEM: Vis & Ko €€
Seafood **Map** B3
Spaarne 96, 2011 CL
Tel (023) 512 7990 **Closed** *Mon*
Best fish restaurant in town, in a beautifully converted warehouse. In his open kitchen, Chef Imko works with only the freshest fish, straight from the market. Pricey, but with reasonable set menus. The Sunday brunch is great value for money.

HEEMSTEDE: Southern Cross €€
Australian **Map** B3
Zandvoortselaan 24, 2106 CP
Tel (023) 521 9992 **Closed** *Mon*
There is no clearly defined "Australian cuisine", so except for the grilled crocodile and roasted kangaroo, this restaurant serves world food with a distinct Aussie touch. On balmy summer nights, book a table on the patio.

HILVERSUM: Surya €
Indian **Map** C3
Langestraat 126, 1211 HC
Tel (035) 631 9420 **Closed** *Mon*
Not your average curry house: colourful decor and long benches with lots of cushions. Serves a plethora of Indian and Nepalese specialities, such as chicken *tikka* and lamb *vindaloo*, as well as vegetarian dishes.

HILVERSUM: Rex €€
International **Map** C3
Groest 23, 1211 CZ
Tel (035) 631 9529
Former 1920s art-deco cinema turned into a hip club, lounge and restaurant, with a terrace that's popular in summer. Serves salads, pasta and fish, but is best known for the dry-aged steaks. Side dishes are extra.

For more information on types of restaurants *see page 403*

HOOFDDORP: Vork en Mes €€
Creative **Map** B3
Paviljoenlaan 1, 2131 LZ
Tel (023) 557 2963 **Closed** *Sun dinner*
Futuristic pavillion built on the lake. The chef was trained at Michelin-starred restaurants, grows his own vegetables and cooks up a changing five-course surprise menu.

MONNICKENDAM: Posthoorn €€€
French **Map** C3
Noordeinde 43, 1141 AG
Tel (0299) 654 598 **Closed** *Mon*
Old-world charm, meticulously matched with modern comforts and delicate French food, in two of the prettiest houses in this fairytale town. One Michelin star.

OUDERKERK AAN DE AMSTEL: Lute €€€
French **Map** C3
De Oude Molen 5, 1184 VW
Tel (020) 472 2462 **Closed** *Sat lunch, Sun*
Set in an 18th-century gunpowder mill, Lute makes the most of its location by the Amstel river, with sophisticated dishes served in the stables, the greenhouse or on the terrace.

SANTPOORT: Brasserie DenK €€
French **Map** B3
Duin en Kruidbergweg 60, 2071 LE
Tel (023) 512 1800
Sleek lounge bar and brasserie in an 18th-century fairytale castle-like country estate. The bar menu offers brasserie food, while the brasserie itself has a decent restaurant menu.

ZANDVOORT: Tijn Akersloot €€
International **Map** B3
Boulevard Paulus Loot 1B, 2042 AD
Tel (023) 571 2547
At the quiet end of the popular Zandvoort beach, this beach club serves sandwiches, soup and snacks by day, and stone oven pizzas, steaks and more sophisticated dishes at night.

Atmospheric interiors at Badhu, an Arabian restaurant in Utrecht

Utrecht

AMERSFOORT: De Pastinaeck €€
Traditional **Map** C4
Hof 8, 3811 CJ
Tel (033) 737 0005 **Closed** *Mon*
The parsnip that gave this restaurant its name (in old Dutch spelling) is one of many 'forgotten vegetables' featured on the menu, along with several other lovingly reinvented Dutch dishes.

AMERSFOORT: De Saffraan €€€
French **Map** C4
Kleine Koppel 3, 3812 PG
Tel (033) 448 1753 **Closed** *Sun–Mon, Tue lunch, Sat lunch*
A century-old clipper on the Eem river has been transformed into this Michelin-starred restaurant. Alfresco dining on the deck in the summer.

BAARN: Pomodori €
Italian **Map** C3
Laandwarsstraat 15, 3743 BS
Tel (035) 541 4013 **Closed** *Sun, Mon–Wed lunch*
Tiny restaurant in an even tinier back alley, featuring outstanding Italian cooking, ranging from deer carpaccio to king crab cannelloni. Recipes in the adjacent shop.

HOUTEN: Kasteel Heemstede €€€
French **Map** C4
Heemsteedseweg 20, 3992 LS
Tel (030) 272 2207 **Closed** *Sun, Mon*
Michelin-starred restaurant with a terrace that seems to float in the moat of this romantic 17th century castle. Fine dining, great service and an excellent wine list.

LEUSDEN: Bistro Bling €€
French **Map** C4
Waarden 25B, 3831 HA
Tel (033) 433 2070 **Closed** *Mon*
The interior lives up to the name with cheap chandeliers, glass curtains and baroque mirrors, but the service is friendly and the bistro fare is well done.

MAARSSEN: De Nonnerie €€
French **Map** C4
Langegracht 51, 3601 AK
Tel (0346) 562 201 **Closed** *Sat–Sun lunch*
Creative cooking and a great dining experience at this beautifully restored former nunnery by the Vecht river. The three- to five-course set menus are good value for money.

MAARSSEN: Delice €€
North-African **Map** C4
Kaatsbaan 25, 3601 EB
Tel *0346 284 4534* **Closed** *Sun, Mon*
North-African dishes, great wines, contemporary interiors and a relaxed atmosphere prove to be a winning combination. Try the lamb with apricots, sesame and seasonal vegetables.

DK Choice

UTRECHT: Badhu €
Arabian **Map** C4
Willem van Noortplein 19, 3514 GK
Tel (030) 272 0444
As befits a restaurant set in a 1920s bathhouse, Badhu's interior is inspired by the Arabian *hamam*. The restaurant is very popular and is open all day, serving Arabian breakfast, meze (small Arabian dishes to share) for lunch, afternoon chai (high tea Arabian style) and evening cocktails in a thousand-and-one-nights setting.

UTRECHT: De Keuken van Gastmaal €€
French **Map** C4
Biltstraat 5, 3572 AA
Tel (030) 233 4633 **Closed** *Sun, Mon*
Just a few tables centred around an open kitchen, in which the chef works wonders with sustainable fish, organic meat and regional vegetables. Dishes are paired with fine wines.

VREELAND AAN DE VECHT: De Nederlanden €€€
French **Map** C3
Duinkerken 3, 3633 EM
Tel (0294) 232 326
Boutique hotel and Michelin-starred restaurant set in a monumental mansion. Refined French cuisine along with a 500-bottle wine list. Fantastic terrace and kitchen garden.

South Holland

DELFT: La Tasca €€
Mediterranean **Map** B4
Voldersgracht 13B, 2611 ET
Tel (015) 213 8535 **Closed** *Sun*
Don't look for the menu – there isn't one. Guests are invited to tell the chef what they don't like, and then wait as he cooks up a three- to five-course surprise meal for them.

Key to Price Guide *see page 406*

LEIDEN: Buddhas €€
Thai **Map** B3
Botermarkt 20, 2311 EN
Tel (071) 514 0047 **Closed** *Mon*
Huge golden Buddha statues line the walls of this smart, contemporary restaurant. It may be pricey, but the extensive menu, generous portions and authentic food make up for that.

DK Choice

NOORDWIJK: Bries €€
International **Map** B3
Koningin Astrid Boulevard 102, 2202 BD
Tel (071) 361 7891 **Closed** *Winter*
This is not your average makeshift beach club, but a well-designed and spacious pavilion, fitted out with stylish furniture. There are loungers and cabanas, plus massage and yoga on the beach. The full-fledged menu leans heavily towards fresh seafood. Pick your choice of fish at the Sunday fish market. Open in the summer only.

OOSTVOORNE: Aan Zee €€
Traditional **Map** B4
Strandweg 1, 3233 CW
Tel (0181) 820 990 **Closed** *Mon, Tue*
Striking pavilion in the dunes which is truly sustainable: it is built of untreated wood, fed by solar and wind energy and uses dune water. Round off your meal with the breathtaking views from the watchtower.

ROTTERDAM: Bird €€
Italian **Map** B4
Raampoortstraat 26, 3032 AH
Tel (010) 737 1154 **Closed** *Mon, Tue*
Popular jazz stage and nightclub with the adjacent restaurant serving swinging Sicilian dishes. On the occasional culinary cinema nights, guests are served exactly what is being eaten on-screen. No à la carte; set menus only.

ROTTERDAM: Sānsān €€
Chinese **Map** B4
Hang 33, 3011 GG
Tel (010) 411 5681 **Closed** *Mon*
A favourite among Chinese locals and visitors for the quality of food and service. The traditional Sichuan fare ranges from delicate Lemon Fish to fiery Sizzling Beef.

ROTTERDAM: FG Restaurant €€€
International **Map** B4
Lloydstraat 204, 3024 EA
Tel (010) 425 0520 **Closed** *Sun–Mon*
After years of molecular cooking at Heston Blumenthal's The Fat Duck, François Geurds is now a master chef in his own right. Vegetarians get their own multi-course tasting menu. The chef's table is a coveted spot.

Tables on the beach at Bries in Noordwijk

ROTTERDAM: Zeezout €€€
Seafood **Map** B4
Westerkade 11B, 3016 CL
Tel (010) 436 5049 **Closed** *Mon, Sun lunch*
Fabled fish restaurant, situated in the fisherman's quarter of arguably the world's biggest seaport. Fresh fish only, with seasonally changing menus. Great in summer, with panoramic views over the Maas river.

SCHEVENINGEN: At Sea €€€
Mediterranean **Map** B4
Heilingweg 138, 2583 DX
Tel (070) 331 7445 **Closed** *Mon–Tue, Sat–Tue lunch*
Sleek restaurant in a rickety old fishing port, dishing out delicious seafood (but also meat and game) paired with fine wines. Order à la carte, go for the five-course Chef's Choice or choose from set menus that change daily.

SCHIPLUIDEN: De Zwethheul €€€
French **Map** B4
Rotterdamseweg 480, 2636 KB
Tel (010) 470 4166 **Closed** *Mon, Sat lunch*
Exclusive restaurant with two Michelin stars – and food, prices, ambience and service to match. Set in a picturesque house along the Schie creek. A seat at the Chef's Table includes an aperitif aboard the restaurant's own sloop.

STREEFKERK: De Limonadefabriek €€
Creative **Map** B4
Nieuwe Haven 1, 2959 AT
Tel (0184) 689 335 **Closed** *Mon–Tue, Sep–May Sat lunch*
Despite its name and appearance, this is not a lemonade factory, but a strikingly modern floating restaurant on the Lek river, serving equally modern and well-presented food. The adjacent bistro is also superb.

THE HAGUE: HanTing Cuisine €€
Fusion **Map** B4
Prinsestraat 33, 2513 CA
Tel (070) 362 0828 **Closed** *Mon*
Chinese chef Han expertly fuses traditional French cooking with oriental flavours, creating dishes that please the eye as well as the palate. The rice-paper lanterns are pretty too. One Michelin star.

THE HAGUE: Logisch €€
Organic **Map** B4
Maliestraat 9, 2514 CA
Tel (070) 363 5259 **Closed** *Sun–Mon*
Organic food that is cheerful and good value. There are salads and sandwiches for lunch, and dishes ranging from grilled duck in mandarin sauce to ricotta-filled pasta in sage butter for dinner.

THE HAGUE: The Penthouse €€€
International **Map** B4
Rijswijkseplein 786, 2516 LX
Tel (070) 305 1003
Probably the poshest spot in town, although not for those afraid of heights. Packs a terrace café, skybar, restaurant and nightclub all in one, with a smashing view from the 42nd floor of a skyscraper.

Zeeland

BURGH-HAAMSTEDE: Pannekoekenmolen De Graanhalm €
Bakery **Map** A4
Burghseweg 53, 4328 LA
Tel (0111) 652 415 **Closed** *Winter*
This pancake house in a working windmill serves pancakes in 35 sweet and savoury varieties, such as sugar and syrup, bacon and cheese or strawberries and whipped cream.

For more information on types of restaurants *see page 403*

CADZAND: Pure C €€€
Mediterranean **Map** A5
Boulevard de Wielingen 49, 4506 JK
Tel (0117) 396 036 **Closed** *Mon–Tue*
Latest venture of celebrity chef Sergio Herman, awarded a Michelin star soon after opening. Great food, relaxed atmosphere.

DK Choice

DOMBURG: Het Badpaviljoen €€€
Seafood **Map** A5
Badhuisweg 21, 4357 AV
Tel (0118) 582405 **Closed** *Mon–Wed*
In a fairytale turn-of-the-century bathing pavilion on a dune top, this fine dining restaurant has a clean-cut interior and serves anything fishy, from the freshest Zeeland oysters and mussels to North Sea crab and whole lobsters. Order a seafood plate for two and dine alfresco on the seaside terrace.

GOES: Jan Zilt Zalig Zeeuws €€
Seafood **Map** A5
Bierkade 3A, 4461 AV
Tel (0113) 219 974 **Closed** *Winter: Tue–Wed*
Fish restaurant in the old harbour with a chic interior. The chef's speciality is classically cooked shellfish: oysters, crab and clams galore. Pleasant quayside terrace.

HOOFDPLAAT: De Kromme Watergang €€€
Regional **Map** A5
Slijkplaat 6, 4513 KK
Tel (0117) 348 696 **Closed** *Mon–Tue*
Two-star restaurant in a hamlet called Slijkplaat, or 'mud plate'. Food comes straight from the silty clay of Zeeland. Adventurous cooking, emphasis on seafood.

MIDDELBURG: Scherp €€
Regional **Map** A5
Wijngaardstraat 1-5, 4331 PM
Tel (0118) 634 633 **Closed** *Sun–Mon, Apr, Jul*
Chef Scherp serves dishes such as Zeeland oysters with wasabi cream, cucumber, passion fruit foam and chardonnay vinegar. Regional delicacies, some meat and game, but mainly seafood.

OUWERKERK: De Vierbannen €€
French **Map** A5
Weg van de Buitenlandse Pers 3, 4305 RJ
Tel (0111) 647 547 **Closed** *Mon*
Striking building that houses an affordable brasserie and restaurant. It has a terrace with superb views of the surrounding polder landscape. Serves mainly seafood.

Lovely table setting at Herberg Onder de Linden, Aduard

West Frisian Islands

AMELAND: Boerenbont €€
Modern Dutch **Map** C1
Strandweg 50, 9163 GN Nes
Tel (0519) 542 293
A mix of old and new: the cuisine is traditional – with a touch of the modern – served on the classic painted crockery from which the restaurant takes its name. Old Dutch texts on the walls temper the contemporary decor.

SCHIERMONNIKOOG: Ambrosijn €€
Regional **Map** D1
Langestreek 13, 9166 LA
Tel (0519) 720 261
Intimate place serving salads and sandwiches by day, and three- to five-course set menus for dinner. "Ambro" is the name of the wild apples that grow all over the island, and which the restaurant puts in its crunchy apple pie.

TERSCHELLING: Loods €€
International **Map** C1
Willem Barentszkade 39, 8881 BD
Tel (0562) 700 200 **Closed** *Mon–Tue*
Comfort food in a light-flooded interior with an industrial feel with scaffolding wood tables, designer chairs, large metal lamps and a pleasant seaview terrace.

TEXEL: Topido €€
Regional **Map** B2
Kikkertstraat 23, 1795 AA De Cocksdorp
Tel (0222) 316 227 **Closed** *Mon–Wed*
The taste of Texel: lamb, goat and beef from the island, shrimp from the Wadden Sea and fish from the North Sea, cheese from a nearby sheep farm and locally brewed beer.

DK Choice

VLIELAND: Uitspanning Het Armhuis €€€
International **Map** C1
Kerkplein 6, 8899 AW
Tel (0562) 451 935 **Closed** *Mon–Tue*
This monumental 17th-century almshouse once sheltered orphans, the elderly, the poor, and the needy. It is now home to the island's best restaurant. A bistro by day, it serves three- or four-course set menus for dinner. Enjoy refined, classically cooked dishes either indoors or outside in the garden.

Groningen

ADUARD: Herberg Onder de Linden €€€
French **Map** D1
Burg. van Barneveldweg 3, 9831 RD
Tel (050) 403 1406 **Closed** *Sun–Tue*
The chef has kept his Michelin star rating for nearly three decades, so expect good quality and prices to match. Limited but mouth-watering set menus.

GRONINGEN: Het Goudkantoor €
Mediterranean **Map** D1
Waagplein 1, 9712 JZ
Tel (050) 589 1888 **Closed** *Sun dinner*
The 'Gold Office' is where taxes were collected during the Golden Age. It now houses a fine restaurant, serving Mediterranean fare for the local palate.

DK Choice

GRONINGEN: WEEVA €
Regional **Map** D1
Gedempte Zuiderdiep 8–10, 9711 HG
Tel (050) 588 6555
This "Living and Eating House for All" retains the atmosphere of the 1871 soup kitchen it once was, even though the clientele is greatly changed. Serves good comfort food, prepared with regional and healthy ingredients, at affordable prices – such as the dish of the day for under €10.

GRONINGEN: Flinders Café €€
International **Map** D1
Kruissingel 1, 9712 XN
Tel (050) 312 3537
Ship-shaped art deco pavilion in the Noorderplantsoen park that

serves breakfast, lunch, snacks and dinner, from soups, and salads to full-fledged meals.

NOORDLAREN: De Waterjuffers bij Vos €€
Regional **Map** E2
Osdijk 4, 9479 TC
Tel (050) 711 9310 **Closed** *Winter, Mon–Tue lunch, Mon–Thu dinner*
In a nature reserve on the banks of the Zuidlaardermeer. Serves eel and zander straight from the lake, but also vegetarian and meat dishes. Waterside terrace.

Friesland

DK Choice

HARLINGEN: Frish 'n Dish €€
International **Map** C2
Grote Bredeplaats 15, 8861 BA
Tel (0517) 430 063 **Closed** *Mon–Tue*
This modern restaurant serves some two dozen small dishes from France (smoked salmon), Spain (paella), Italy (saltimbocca), Morocco (*baba ganoush*), Indonesia (beef *rendang*), Thailand (*tom yum*), China (Peking duck) and Japan (yakitori), that can be ordered separately for lunch, or as a five-course world tour for dinner. Ten dishes come for under €30.

HEERENVEEN: Het Ambacht €€
International **Map** D2
Burg. Falkenaweg 56, 8442 LE
Tel (0513) 232 172 **Closed** *Sun–Mon, Sat lunch*
Chef Henk Markus, dubbed "the Frisian Jamie Oliver", transformed a century-old technical school into a trendy restaurant that employs disadvantaged youth. Sample local delicacies like monkfish, wagyu beef and ringneck dove.

LEEUWARDEN: Doozo Grill & Sushi €
Asian **Map** D1
Ruiterskwartier 93, 8911 BR
Tel (058) 213 6069
A hip Japanese eatery in meat-obsessed Friesland. With a Dutch celebrity chef, Doozo dishes out delicate sushi, sashimi, tempura, and other Asian and fusion dishes.

MAKKUM: De Prins €
Traditional **Map** C2
Kerkstraat 1, 8754 CN
Tel (0515) 231 510 **Closed** *Mon–Thu*
True old-fashioned Dutch dining. Established in 1760, De Prins has been run by the same family for three generations. Admire the handpainted tiles that line the walls of the historic taproom.

SNEEK: Cook & Ny €
International **Map** C2
1e Oosterkade 24, 8605 AA
Tel (0515) 433 019
A sleek interior, an international sounding name (though actually a pun on a Dutch expression) and great tapas, from *patatas bravas* and vegetable-filled filo to garlic snails and catfish *saté*.

Drenthe

ASSEN: Touché €€
Fusion **Map** D2
Markt 20, 9401 GT
Tel (0592) 769 069 **Closed** *Mon*
In the town's prettiest square. The chef cooks up modern takes on traditional dishes, like slowly braised duck glazed with hoisin sauce and star anise.

DK Choice

BORGER: Villa van Streek €€
Regional **Map** E2
Torenlaan 13, 9531 JH
Tel (0599) 657 007 **Closed** *Mon*
In the dolmen capital of Drenthe, a former Royal Marshals barracks now houses this artistically decorated eatery. Open all day for brunch, lunch and dinner, it offers a changing menu of regionally harvested dishes at affordable prices. The adjacent shop and tourist info sells maps for touring the nearby dolmens.

RODEN: Cuisinerie Mensinge €€
French **Map** D2
Mensingheweg 1, 9301 KA
Tel (050) 501 3149 **Closed** *Mon–Tue*
The coach house and stables of a 600-year-old manor tucked away in a nature reserve now house a wonderfully romantic bistro and restaurant. No à la carte at dinner.

Smoked salmon, one of the dishes that visitors can sample in Friesland

RODERESCH: Herberg van Es €€
International **Map** D2
Hoofdweg 1, 9305 TD
Tel (050) 501 2660 **Closed** *Mon*
The natural area surrounding this restaurant is popular among hikers and bikers. Extensive menus for lunch and dinner, and a game menu (in season) featuring deer, hare, boar and more.

ZUIDLAREN: De Vlindertuin €€€
French **Map** E2
Stationsweg 41, 9471 GK
Tel (050) 409 4531 **Closed** *Mon*
The Michelin-starred 'Butterfly Garden' is one of Drenthe's finest restaurants, serving refined French food with a modern twist in a 300-year-old farmhouse. Order the eight-course tasting menu.

Overijssel

DK Choice

ALMELO: Amused €
International **Map** E3
Catharina Amaliaplein 4, 7607 JP
Tel (0546) 433 974 **Closed** *Mon*
Amused lives up to its name by serving mainly *amuse-gueules*, or bite-sized appetizers on a fork or spoon, making for a tapas-like dining experience. Choose between some two-dozen hot and cold varieties, such as chicken in chilli sauce, salmon rolls or artichoke with tarragon, or order the surprise menu and be amused.

DE LUTTE: De Bloemenbeek €€€
French **Map** E3
Beuningerstraat 6, 7587 LD
Tel (0541) 551 224
In the gently rolling landscape of the Dinkel valley, Michelin-starred 'The Flower Stream' is a fine dining restaurant attached to a country house hotel. The cuisine is French, the wine, Dutch.

DEVENTER: Jackies NYCuisine €€
International **Map** D3
Grote Poot 19, 7411 KE
Tel (0570) 616 666
Contemporary eatery inspired by the style of Jackie O and the cuisine of New York City, including Chinatown. Spot on, with great food and attentive service in a stylish setting.

For more information on types of restaurants *see page 403*

ENSCHEDE: Yuen's Oriental Bistro €€
Asian **Map** E3
Walstraat 16, 5711 GH
Tel (053) 434 6042 **Closed** *Mon–Tue*
Modern Asian restaurant with an open kitchen in which the chef fuses fresh organic ingredients and Japanese, Thai, Mongolian, Cantonese and Korean flavours into an affordable surprise menu.

ZWOLLE: Librije's Zusje €€€
Modern Dutch **Map** D3
Spinhuisplein 1, 8011 ZZ
Tel (038) 853 0001 **Closed** *Mon lunch, Sat lunch*
De Librije is one of two restaurants in the Netherlands to boast of three Michelin stars, and this former prison is its little sister with two stars, and a choice of classic, modern and vegetarian dishes.

Flevoland

ALMERE-HAVEN: Bij Brons €€
French **Map** C3
Sluis 3, 1357 NZ
Tel (036) 540 1126 **Closed** *Sep–Mar: Mon*
Right in the marina, this fine restaurant has tables centred around the open kitchen. Fresh, mostly organic and seasonal ingredients. The five-course surprise menu with paired wines is a particularly good deal.

BIDDINGHUIZEN: Beachclub NU €
International **Map** C3
Bremerbergdijk 10, 8256 RD
Tel (0321) 331 629 **Closed** *Winter: Mon–Tue*
Smart beach club on a pretty stretch of sand along Lake Veluwe. Barbecue, tablegrill and limited menu in the ground floor lounge and terrace; comfort food à la carte upstairs, where lake views are an added attraction.

DK Choice

URK: Restaurant De Boet €
Seafood **Map** C3
Wijk 1–61/Westhavenkade 61
Tel (0527) 688 736
This is the smartest restaurant in the village of Urk, occupying two old harbourside buildings – an old warehouse and a steamship office. The menu changes daily and offers the freshest of seafood. Try the fried plaice, with scallops, mashed potatoes, string beans, zucchini and sweet onion sauce with mustard.

Colourful interiors at Librije's Zusje, a Dutch restaurant in Zwolle

Gelderland

ARNHEM: ZafVino & StijnKookt €€
Mediterranean **Map** D4
Zwanenstraat 22, 6811 DD
Tel (06) 5214 3150 **Closed** *Tue-Wed*
Vinoteca-style eatery with lots of atmosphere. Sit wherever there is room, including at a communal table, and choose from dishes listed on the blackboard.

BARNEVELD: De Oranjerie €€
International **Map** D4
Stationsweg 4A, 3771 VH
Tel (0342) 419 601**Closed** *Sun–Mon*
On the grounds of a mock Tudor castle, this fine dining restaurant is an accurate replica of a 19th-century greenhouse. The food, from local roe to whole lobsters, matches the ambience.

BEEKBERGEN: Het Ei van Columbus €€
French **Map** D4
Stoppelbergweg 63, 7361 TE
Tel (055) 506 1498 **Closed** *Mon–Tue*
"The Egg of Columbus" offers a limited, exquisite but affordable menu, in the midst of the leafy Veluwe nature reserve. Three-course set menu for under €30.

BERG EN DAL: Puur €€
International **Map** D4
Zevenheuvelenweg 87, 6571 CJ
Tel (024) 684 1452 **Closed** *Tue*
Stylish wine bar-cum-restaurant with a hundred wines on the list and about two-dozen by the glass, along with a plethora of starters, comparable to Spanish tapas and raciones.

ERMELO: Boshuis Drie €€
Traditional **Map** C3
Sprielderweg 205, 3852 MK
Tel (0577) 407 206 **Closed** *Mon*
A beautifully preserved thatched farmhouse in the midst of the 'Forest of the Dancing Trees'. Serves evergreen Dutch favourites, such as pancakes for lunch and shrimp cocktail, game stew or juicy steaks for dinner.

DK Choice

NIJMEGEN: De Nieuwe Winkel €€
Fusion **Map** D4
Hertogstraat 71, 6511 RW
Tel (024) 322 5093
Closed *Sun–Mon*
Radish in "edible soil" served in a flowerpot, followed by a "golden egg" filled with poached yolk – and these are only the appetizers. Besides a mad chef, "The New Shop" boasts a modern decor, friendly atmosphere, a minimal menu and food that is a feast for the eyes as much as the taste buds.

North Brabant

BERGEN OP ZOOM: Le Bouleau €€
International **Map** B5
Bemmelenberg 16, 4614 PG
Tel (0164) 258 782 **Closed** *Mon–Tue*
In a romantic spot in the woods, this restaurant serves international dishes such as garlic *gambas* and grilled ribeye. The attractively priced three-course market menu is a good choice.

BREDA: Wolfslaar €€€
French **Map** B5
Wolfslaardreef 100-102, 4834 SP
Tel (076) 560 8000 **Closed** *Sun, Sat lunch*
Michelin-starred restaurant in the converted coach house of a chic country estate. Modern takes on classic dishes using sustainable and organic ingredients, like quail with foie gras or halibut with mussels.

DK Choice

EINDHOVEN: Kreeftenbar €
Seafood **Map** C5
Kleine Berg 21, 5611 JS
Tel (040) 236 4440 **Closed** *Mon*
Discover lobster for the masses: lobster soup, lobster salad, lobster rolls and half and whole lobsters, either cooked or gratin, along with a good choice of other Asian dishes, from sushi to king crab and Peking duck. The prices here are easily affordable – the three-course lobster dinner is €25.

EINDHOVEN: Smeagol €
Argentinian **Map** C5
Kerkstraat 10, 5611 GJ
Tel (040) 737 0298
Juicy and tender steaks straight from the Argentinian pampas. Other dishes include empanadas and fajitas, garlic *gambas* and mixed grill. Modern interior.

EINDHOVEN: Piet Hein Eek €€
Creative **Map** C5
Halvemaanstraat 30, 5651 BP
Tel (040) 285 6610 **Closed** *Mon*
A beautifully revamped former Philips factory now houses Dutch designer Piet Hein Eek's flagship store, workshop, art gallery and restaurant. Design lover's paradise.

KAATSHEUVEL: De Molen €€€
International **Map** C4
Vaartstraat 102, 5171 JG
Tel (0416) 530 230 **Closed** *Sun–Mon; Sat lunch*
Expect adventurous Michelin-starred cooking at this windmill on the edge of a national park. The 10-course tasting menu is absolutely amazing.

NUENEN: Olijf €€
Mediterranean **Map** C5
Berg 18, 5671 CC
Tel (040) 291 3476 **Closed** *Wed*
In the village where Van Gogh painted *The Potato Eaters*. Serves mostly Mediterranean seafood. Affordable set menus with paired wines.

'S-HERTOGENBOSCH: Eetbar Dit €
International **Map** C4
Snellestraat 24–26, 5211 EN
Tel (073) 614 1015
Funky modern take on the old Dutch *eetcafé*. Tapas-like small dishes such as shrimp croquettes, burgers and *rendang* that are meant to be shared.

'S-HERTOGENBOSCH: De Verkadefabriek €€
International **Map** C4
Boschdijkstraat 45, 5211 VD
Tel (073) 681 8150
Former cookie factory, now houses a theatre, cinema and restaurant. Enjoy lunch, tapas and dinner in an industrial setting.

Limburg

GULPEN: L'Atelier €€€
French **Map** D6
Markt 9, 6271 BD
Tel (043) 450 4490 **Closed** *Tue–Wed, Sat lunch*
Has to be rated one of Limburg's best restaurants. Fine dining, a warm, intimate atmosphere, friendly service, and an excellent wine list.

MAASBRACHT: Da Vinci €€€
French **Map** D6
Havenstraat 27, 6051 CS
Tel (0475) 465 979 **Closed** *Mon–Tue, Sat lunch*
Not a pizzeria but a French restaurant, run by the only Dutch female chef with two Michelin stars. Expect fine French fare with meticulously paired wines, stiff linen and ditto prices.

DK Choice

MAASTRICHT: Umami €
Chinese **Map** D6
Stationsstraat 12, 6221 BP
Tel (043) 351 0006
This is one of a small chain of decidedly modern conceptual Chinese eateries (there are six other Umamis around the country), the side project of chef Han of Michelin-starred restaurant HanTing in The Hague. Michelin-star quality at bargain prices: choose seven dishes in three courses for around €20.

MAASTRICHT: SoFa €€
Mediterranean **Map** D6
Hoge Weerd 6, 6229 AM
Tel (043) 367 1337 **Closed** *Mon*
Short for 'sounds fantastic'. Located in the coach house of a 15th-century castle on a peninsula in the Maas river. Serves sunny Mediterranean food inside and out on the terrace.

MAASTRICHT: Beluga €€€
International **Map** D6
Plein 1992 12, 6221 JP
Tel (043) 321 3364 **Closed** *Sun–Mon, Sat lunch*
Star-studded restaurant, both in terms of Michelin stars (two) and visiting celebrities (many), in a striking modern building right on the edge of the Maas river. Great looks, spectacular tastes.

SLENAKEN: De La Frontière €€
South-African **Map** D6
Grensweg 1, 6277 NA
Tel (043) 457 4302 **Closed** *Mon–Tue*
A slice of South Africa in south Limburg, complete with zebra skins, pottery and colourful art, Cape wines and dishes like biltong *paté* and Kalahari kudu.

UBACHSBERG: De Leuf €€€
Creative **Map** D6
Dalstraat 2, 6367 JS
Tel (045) 575 0226 **Closed** *Sun–Mon, Sat lunch*
Fine-dining restaurant with two Michelin stars, serving creatively cooked dishes like sea urchin with avocado, and pigeon with liquid black pudding.

VALKENBURG AAN DE GEUL: Tapas BarCelona €
Spanish **Map** D6
Berkelstraat 6, 6301 CC
Tel (043) 852 4524 **Closed** *Mon–Tue*
Tiny tapas bar with Gaudí-inspired pillars, Andalusian lamps and a big Osborne bull on the wall. Serves a decent variety, from garlic bread and spicy potatoes to bacon-wrapped dates and *pata negra* ham.

VALKENBURG AAN DE GEUL: Aan de Linde €€
French **Map** D6
Jan Deckerstraat 1B, 6301 GX
Tel (043) 601 0577 **Closed** *Tue*
A brasserie by day and a restaurant in the evening, this attractive popular local eatery has taken over what was once a historic and eclectic casino hotel.

WELL: Brienen aan de Maas €€€
French **Map** D5
Grotestraat 11, 5855 AK
Tel (0478) 501 967 **Closed** *Mon*
The scenic setting of this Michelin-starred restaurant alongside the Maas River is matched by the regionally influenced cooking of its chef. The mouth-watering à la carte menu mainly focuses on seafood. Affordable set menus.

Diners at the popular Verkadefabriek in 's-Hertogenbosch

SHOPPING IN THE NETHERLANDS

Throughout the Netherlands you will find a huge range of shops and markets. Many towns will have large retail chains, but you will also find unique independent shops selling clothes, everyday goods and knick-knacks. Large specialized shops such as furniture stores, factory outlets and garden centres are usually on the outskirts of towns and sometimes grouped together in retail parks with parking facilities, child-care facilities and a cafeteria. Most are open, and at their busiest, on public holidays. Recent fashion items can often be picked up cheaply at street markets and second-hand shops.

Shop selling antiques and engrossing curios

Markets

Practically every town and village holds a general market at least once a week. There are also specialized markets, for example, the farmers' markets, where you can buy fresh farm produce, as well as antique markets and book fairs. Famous specialized markets include the cheese markets of Alkmaar, Edam and Gouda. Then there are also flea markets, where traders and individuals alike sell second-hand goods.

The Netherlands' biggest flea market takes place on Koninginnedag (Queen's Day) *(see p36)*, when practically half of the country tries to get rid of unwanted goods on the street. Fairs are also popular and are held twice a year. Most markets start at 9:30am and shut at 4pm or 5pm, while some are open either in the mornings or the afternoons only.

Antiques

Antique collectors will find plenty to occupy themselves with in the Netherlands. If you are fortunate, you may strike it lucky in second-hand shops or at flea markets, but your best bet is to go to an authentic antique dealer. Many antique dealers specialize in a particular period or a field – prints or clocks, for instance. If you prefer buying antiques at auctions, you would probably do best to visit the branches of the international auctioneers **Sotheby's** or **Christie's**. In smaller auction houses too, interesting pieces often go under the hammer. Another way of buying antiques is to visit the antique markets and fairs that are held regularly throughout the country.

Antique dealer's shop sign

Amsterdam's Nieuwe Spiegelstraat is the place for antique collectors. Vendors include antique dealers specializing in ceramics, glass, antique prints, paintings and nautical memorabilia.

Haarlem, Middelburg and 's-Hertogenbosch have large numbers of antique shops; these are often located in old farmhouses. The most common pieces on sale are pine or oak furniture. The **MECC** in Maastricht and the **Brabanthallen** in 's-Hertogenbosch are the venues of annual antique fairs, such as the renowned TEFAF, the world's biggest art and antique fair. Antique dealers from around the world come here to trade.

Fashion

The Dutch are spending more and more of their incomes on good-quality fashionable clothing. Besides internationally renowned couturiers, many up-and-coming fashion designers set up their own boutiques. Their clothes are often handmade and fairly pricey. More affordable clothes are available at the larger fashion retailers, both home-grown and international. A typical Dutch way of being fashionable is to combine a new and expensive garment with second-hand clothes. To see the designs of the most famous couturiers, it is best to go to Amsterdam. On the PC Hooftstraat you will find clothes by Hugo Boss, Armani and Yves Saint-Laurent, Classical English clothing and shoes are to be found in the shops on the Haagse Noordeinde in The Hague. Chains such as Vera Moda sell everyday and durable clothing.

One of the country's many antique and second-hand shops

A trendy clothing boutique featuring the very latest in Dutch fashion

Retail Stores and Shopping Centres

The most upmarket retail store in the Netherlands is the **Bijenkorf**, which offers contemporary furniture, the latest names in fashion, a huge book department and all major cosmetics brands. The Vroom & Dreesmann department stores are slightly smaller and offer lower prices than the Bijenkorf. One step lower on the prices scale is Hema, which offers a wide and remarkably trendy range of things such as lighting accessories and household goods. At most shopping centres you will find the same names, although some centres are reserved for more exclusive shops. One of these is the **Magna Plaza** in Amsterdam, where you will find upmarket boutiques and jewellers' shops. De Groene Passage in Rotterdam is a covered shopping centre dedicated to the environment, selling items ranging from organic meat to New Age books. **La Vie** in Utrecht has a good range of shops; in The Hague, **De Passage** is the prime shopping centre. Batavia Stad Outlet Shopping centre in Lelystad is a shopping village built to resemble a 17th-century town. Here manufacturers of expensive brands sell end-of-line products, in particular clothes, at heavy discounts. The designer outlet park in Roermond is a similar place to find bargains.

Furniture

The Netherlands' top furniture designer, Jan des Bouvrie, has his own shop in a converted arsenal in Naarden called Studio het Arsenaal. At Van Til Interior in Alkmaar you can buy designer furniture. In Amsterdam-Zuidoost, you can spend a day viewing furniture in the 75 shops of the Villa Arena. Woonthemacentrum De Havenaer in Nijkerk and Palazzo Lelystad also offer interesting collections. You will find "meubelboulevards", shopping streets of furniture stores, throughout the country.

Auction and Sales Houses

The famous British auction houses **Sotheby's** and **Christie's** have branches in Amsterdam, where international collections in particular are auctioned. The **Eland De Zon Loth Gijselman** in Diemen, deals in antiquities and art and auctions furniture and estates. **Holbein** in Rijssen sells art and antiques, the **Veilinghuis de Voorstraat** in Zwolle specializes in stamps and coins.

Magna Plaza *(see p94)*, open for Sunday shopping

Garden Centres

Dutch garden centres sell plants, seeds, bulbs, soil, compost, and garden furniture. For more unusual plants go to specialist growers, of which there are many in the Netherlands. Garden centres are usually on the edge of towns or just outside them. They are usually open for business on Sundays and public holidays.

An abundance of flowers at a Dutch garden centre

Chocolate

Verkade and Droste are the Netherlands' best-known chocolate makers, and you can find their products everywhere. Many towns now have specialized confectioners' shops. The renowned Belgian confectioner **Leonidas** has numerous outlets in the country. **Puccini Bomboni** produce exceptional chocolates, sold individually.

Tea and Coffee

The Netherlands has been a tea and coffee importer for centuries, and you can find specialist tea and coffee shops everywhere; many still roast their own coffee. In Amsterdam, **Simon Levelt** always has at least 25 varieties of coffee and 100 tea blends on sale. **Geels & Co**, an old family business, has a roasting house and museum.

What to Buy in Holland

In the cities and tourist resorts, souvenir shops are not difficult to find. But if you are looking for something out of the ordinary, either for yourself or as a gift, you can often find something in more specialized shops, or even in a supermarket. Flowers and Delftware never fail to delight. For other things worth taking home, for example, local delicacies such as Dutch cheese and *speculaas* or drinks such as *jenever* gin, see page 420.

Souvenir Dolls
Dutch national costume is hardly worn in the Netherlands any more, except by souvenir dolls such as this trio from Volendam.

Miniature Houses
Painted miniature pottery houses (often Delft blue) are a popular souvenir. Some are designed to be filled with jenever gin, while others are purely ornamental.

Painted Wooden Clogs
The traditional wooden clog has come to symbolize Holland. They can be bought in all colours and sizes. They can also be ordered via the internet at wwww.woodenshoes.com

Dutch bulbs

Flowers
Bulbs and cut flowers are available all the year round in the innumerable flower shops, flower stalls and garden centres that are easily found throughout the Netherlands.

Red Coral
Necklaces of red coral are often part of traditional costume in places such as Volendam. However, they also add a nice touch when worn with modern clothing.

Gouda Pipes
Long-necked clay pipes from Gouda, known as Grouwenaars (*see p243*), have been made here since the beginning of the 17th century and make a nice gift for smokers and non-smokers alike.

Prints of Dutch windmills

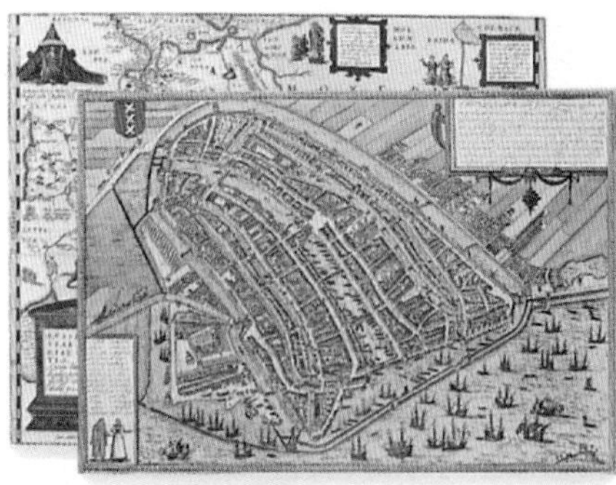

Reproductions of maps of Amsterdam and Russia

Old Maps and Prints
Amsterdam in particular has made its mark in the field of cartography. Many antique shops sell atlases and books of prints.

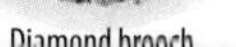

Diamond brooch

Inlaid diamond necklace

Diamonds
Diamonds were cut in Amsterdam as early as the 16th century, and the town continues to be one of the main diamond centres of the world. Many jewellers sell uncut diamonds and second-hand diamond rings.

Diamonds of different colours

Delftware mugs

Modern Delftware
Modern blue Delftware items decorated with windmills or other images of Holland are available in the form of tea sets, sculptures, vases and even royal Delft ashtrays. When buying, make sure that there is a certificate of authenticity *(see p32)* to go with it.

Makkum Pottery
This colourful earthenware, primarily tiles, plates and bowls, is still produced by the Tichelaar factory *(see p33)* at Makkum in Friesland.

Speculaas
These biscuits, flavoured with cinnamon, cloves and ginger, are eaten mainly around St Nicholas' day.

A distinctive Edam cheese

Edam Cheese
The world-famous Edam cheese *(see p178)* has an excellent taste and makes a good souvenir.

Speculaas

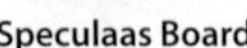

Speculaas Board
Mould your own speculaas biscuits in these biscuit moulds, or use them for attractive wall ornaments.

Haagse Hopjes
These coffee-flavoured sweets were first made at the end of the 18th century at the inspiration of a Baron Hop of The Hague.

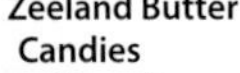

Zeeland Butter Candies
These butter-flavoured sweets from Zeeland, made of glucose sugar syrup and butter, are delicious.

Butter candies

Hopjes

Dutch Beer
The Dutch are renowned beer-drinkers. In addition to the three brands depicted here, there are countless other varieties available.

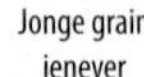

Jonge grain jenever

Sonnema herenburg

Zwarte Kip advocaat

Zaans Mustard
This coarse mustard is made at De Huisman mustard plant on the Zaanse Schans *(see p179)*.

Gingerbread

Gingerbread
This scrumptious bread comes in a variety of regional variations, and is excellent at breakfast or even as a snack – especially with a thick layer of butter.

Liquorice Drops
The ubiquitous liquorice drops are sold either salted or sweet.

Spirits
Renowned Dutch spirits include jenever, a kind of gin sold in glass or stoneware bottles (there is jonge and oude clear jenever, as well as that with herbs), berenburg *(see p301)*, the Frisian distilled herbal drink and advocaat, made of brandy and eggs.

DIRECTORY

Antiques

A Votre Servies
Vughtstraat 231, 's-Hertogenbosch.
Road Map C4.
Tel 073-6135989.

Brabanthallen
Diezekade 2, 's-Hertogenbosch.
Road Map C4.
Tel 073-6293911.
Spring antique fairs.

De Tijdspiegel
Nieuwstraat 17, Middelburg.
Road Map A5.
Tel 0118-627799.

EH Ariëns Kappers
Nieuwe Spiegelstraat 32, Amsterdam.
Map 4 2F
Tel 020-6235356.

Emmakade 2 Antiek
Emmakade 2, Leeuwarden.
Road Map D1.
Tel 058-2153464.

Jan de Raad Antiquiteiten
Postelstraat 64, 's-Hertogenbosch.
Road Map C4.
Tel 073-6144979.

Le Collectionneur
Damplein 5, Middelburg.
Road Map A5.
Tel 0118-638595.

Le Magasin Antiek & Curiosa
Klein Heiligland 58, Haarlem.
Road Map B3.
Tel 023-5321383.

MECC
Forum 100, Maastricht.
Road Map C6.
Tel 043-3838383.
TEFAF in March.

Paul Berlijn Antiques
Amsterdamse Vaart 134, Haarlem.
Road Map B3.
Tel 023-5337369.

Retail Stores and Shopping Centres

De Bijenkorf
Dam 1, Amsterdam.
Map 2 D3.
Tel 0800–0818.
Ketelstraat 45, Arnhem.
Road Map D4.
Tel 0800–0818.
Wagenstraat 32, The Hague.
Road Map B4.
Tel 0800–0818.
Piazza 1, Eindhoven.
Road Map C5.
Tel 0800–0818.
Coolsingel 105, Rotterdam.
Road Map B4.
Tel 0800–0818.
Sint-Jacobsstraat 1a, Utrecht.
Road Map C4.
Tel 0800–0818.
W bijenkorf.nl

De Passage
Passage, The Hague.
Road Map B4.
Tel 030-2565165.

La Vie Shoppingcentre
Lange Viestraat 669, Utrecht.
Road Map C4.
Tel 030-2341414.

Magna Plaza
Nieuwez. Voorburgwal 182, Amsterdam.
Map 1 4C
Tel 020-5703570.

Furniture

Studio het Arsenaal
Kooltjesbuurt 1, Naarden-Vesting.
Road Map C3.
Tel 035-6952015.

Van Til Interieur
Noorderkade 1038, Alkmaar.
Road Map B3. **Tel** 072-5112760.

Villa Arena
Arena Boulevard, Amsterdam-Zuidoost.
Tel 0800-8455227.
W villaarena.nl

Auction and Sales Houses

Christie's
Cornelis Schuytstraat 57, Amsterdam.
Map 3 4C
Tel 020-5755255.

De Eland De Zon Loth Gijselman
Industrieterrein Verrijn Stuart, Weesperstraat 110–112, Diemen.
Road Map C3.
Tel 020-6230343.

Holbein Kunst- en Antiekveilingen
Jutestraat 31, Rijssen.
Road Map D3.
Tel 0548-541577.

Sotheby's
Emmalaan 23, Amsterdam.
Tel 020-5502200.

Veilinghuis de Voorstraat
Voorstraat 23, Zwolle.
Road Map D3.
Tel 038-4211045.

Chocolates

Huize van Wely
Beethovenstraat 72, Amsterdam.
Map 4 D5.
Tel 020-6622009.
Hoofdstraat 88, Noordwijk (ZH).
Road Map B3.
Tel 071-3612228.

Leonidas
Damstraat 15, Amsterdam.
Map 2 5D
Tel 020-6253497.
Bakkerstraat 2, Arnhem.
Road Map D4.
Tel 026-4422157.
Passage 26, The Hague.
Road Map B4.
Tel 070-3649608.
Fonteinstraat 3, 's-Hertogenbosch.
Road Map C4.
Tel 073-6143626.
Pottenbakkersingel 2, Middelburg.
Road Map A5.
Tel 0118-634750.
Beurstraverse 69, Rotterdam.
Road Map B4.
Tel 010-4136034.
Oude Gracht 136, Utrecht.
Road Map C4.
Tel 030-2317738.

Puccini Bomboni
Staalstraat 17, Amsterdam.
Map 5 A2
Tel 020-6265474.
Singel 184, Amsterdam.
Map 1 4C
Tel 020-4278341.

Tea and Coffee

Abraham Mostert
Schoutenstraat 11, Utrecht.
Road Map C4.
Tel 030-2316934.

Geels & Co
Warmoesstraat 67, Amsterdam.
Map 2 4D
Tel 020-6240683.

Het Klaverblad
Hogewoerd 15, Leiden.
Road Map B3.
Tel 071-5133655.

Koffiebrander Blanche Dael
Wolfstraat 28, Maastricht.
Road Map C6.
Tel 043-3213475.

Simon Levelt koffie- en theehandel
Prinsengracht 180, Amsterdam.
Map 1 4B
Tel 020-6240823.
Veerstraat 15, Bussum.
Road Map C3.
Tel 035-6939459.
Zwanestraat 38, Groningen.
Road Map D1.
Tel 050-3114333.
Gierstraat 65, Haarlem.
Road Map B3.
Tel 023-5311861.
Botermarkt 1–2, Leiden.
Road Map B3.
Tel 071-5131159.
Vismarkt 21. Utrecht.
Road Map B3.
Tel 030 2314495.

ENTERTAINMENT IN THE NETHERLANDS

Cultural life in the Netherlands is not confined to the Randstad. Outside the big cities there is also plenty to do. There is a theatre or a cultural centre in just about every town, where theatre groups, cabaret artists, orchestras and rock bands perform. There is also a growing number of entertainment complexes, such as the Miracle Planet Boulevard centre in Enschede. You can find out what's on either by contacting the relevant venue or through the local VVV (tourist) offices; another option is the AUB Ticketshop *(see p153)* in Amsterdam. Here you can usually book tickets, or obtain more information about performances. You can also get tickets and information via the Uitlijn (0900-0191). The major national dailies publish a list of events each week. Most cities publish a weekly *uitkrant*, or entertainment guide, while the internet is another source of information.

Theatre

The Netherlands boasts a large number of theatres, concentrated mostly around Amsterdam. That city's top theatre is the Stadsschouwburg *(see p153)*, where many touring theatre companies put on performances. The Netherlands' largest theatre company, Toneelgroep Amsterdam, is based here and is now directed by Ivo van Hove.

The annual highlight for opera, theatre and dance is the Holland Festival. The best in international cultural offerings is to be had during the Amsterdam Festival. During the International Theatre School Festival in June, experimental drama is performed at venues such as **De Brakke Grond** *(see p149)* and **Frascati**. The **Soeterijn**, on the other hand, specializes in theatre from developing countries. The theatre company frequently wins prizes: the Theatergroup Hollandia has won great acclaim with its performances in large halls and aircraft hangars. The musical dramas of Orkater can be seen in various parts of the country at different times of the year, but mainly at the Stadsschouwburg and **Bellevue**. **De la Mar** stages big box-office hits, comedy and concerts by Dutch solo artists and groups. Youth-focused theatre is put on in **De Krakeling**. For years now the performances by the **Toneelschuur** in Haarlem have won critical acclaim. The De Appel group stages both experimental and repertory theatre at the **Appeltheater** in The Hague. Throughout the Netherlands there are numerous excellent theatre groups. Het Zuidelijk Toneel of Eindhoven in the south always packs theatre halls, as do the Theater van het Oosten from Arnhem in the east of the country and the Noord Nederlands Toneel from Groningen in the north.

Every year in May, the Festival aan de Werf in Utrecht presents an appealing smorgasbord of theatre and cabaret performances.

Scene from the musical *Oliver!* at the Theater Carré

Musicals and Cabaret

The Netherlands' most outstanding musical theatres are the **AFAS Circustheater** of The Hague, the **Beatrix Theater** in Utrecht and the Koninklijk Theater Carré *(see p153)* in Amsterdam. These stage Dutch versions of big box-office hits such as *Les Misérables* and *Miss Saigon*.

De Kleine Komedie *(see p153)*, a magnificent 17th-century building on the Amstel river opposite the Muziektheater, is a favourite venue for cabaret groups. Stand-up comedy has also gained popularity mainly through this venue. Other comedy venues in Amsterdam are **Comedy Café, Toomler** and **Boom Chicago** *(see p153)*.

Dance

The Netherlands is the proud home of two world-famous ballet troupes: the Nationale Ballet and the Nederlands Dans Theater (NDT). The Nationale Ballet is based in the Musiektheater *(see p153)*, which is commonly known among Amsterdam theatre-goers as the "Stopera". This contemporary building can accommodate 1,600 people and is a significant centre both for dance and for opera. The foyer affords a pleasant view of the river Amstel.

The Nederlands Dans Theater based in the Hague offers a colourful programme of modern and contemporary dance and under the direction of the present choreographers has staged sold-out performances with live music. Introdans of Arnhem performs an exciting combination of jazz, flamenco and ethnic dance. The country's biggest choreographers use the Holland Festival as a platform to present their new creations to the public. During the Internationale Theaterschool Festival, which also takes place in June, the proportion of dance performed is growing. The festival venue is the Nes, one of Amsterdam's oldest streets. Julidans is the name given to a summer dance festival in Amsterdam in which contemporary dance by various international dance companies is performed.

Noord Nederlands Toneel staging Anton Chekhov's *The Seagull*

Dr Anton Philipszaal Music Theater and Lucent Dance Opera Danstheater in the Hague

Film

Going to the movies continues to be a popular pastime in the Netherlands, and you will find at least one or more cinemas in almost every town. Amsterdam alone has more than 45 cinemas. Foreign-language films are shown in the original language with subtitles. The most magnificent cinema in Amsterdam is Tuschinski, an Art Deco masterpiece built from 1918–21, with a stylish foyer and generous seating *(see p119)*. The major premieres are held here: if you want to see famous faces, the best time is Wednesday evenings at the cinema entrance.

There is a list of all films that are showing at the box office of every cinema, and such lists are also displayed in cafés and restaurants. Cinema programmes change every Thursday, so you will find a list of films that are on in Wednesday's evening papers and in Thursday's morning papers. *De Filmkrant* is a much-respected movie magazine that is published every Monday, which in addition to the week's film listings also provides background information on major films. Major film events in the Netherlands are the Nederlands Film Festival, which is held in Utrecht in September and October, where Dutch films are premiered. The IDFA (International Documentary Film Festival Amsterdam) is the biggest of its kind, held every year in November/December. The renowned International Film Festival in Rotterdam takes place each January.

Orchestral, Chamber and Choir Music

The Concertgebouw *(see p153)* in Amsterdam is traditionally the most important venue for concert music. The Grote Zaal hall is famous for its acoustics, and its resident musicians are the Koninklijk Concertgebouworkest. During summer the orchestra puts on special concerts.

The Golden Calf

De Ysbreker is situated in a magnificent building on the Amstel, and since 1979 has been the prime venue in Amsterdam for modern classical music. An outstanding orchestra is the Rotterdams Philharmonisch Orkest, whose new conductor, the Czech Jirí Belohlávek, was appointed in 2012. The orchestra is based in **De Doelen** in Rotterdam.

The Residentie Orkest, whose history goes back almost 100 years, performs regularly at the **Anton Philipszaal** in The Hague and is not to be confused with the **Muziekcentrum Frits Philips** in Eindhoven, where the Brabants Orkest is based.

The Amsterdamse Koninklijk Concertgebouworkest performing

The Gelders Orkest makes regular appearances in the **Musis Sacrum** concert hall in Arnhem. Another venue offering a rich programme of music is the **Muziekcentrum Vredenburg**.

Church Music

Of the many organs in the Netherlands, that of the **Grote Kerk** in Elburg is probably the best known. Every year it is used in the national amateur organist competition. The instruments in the **Oude Kerk** and the **Nieuwe Kerk** are the most famous of Amsterdam's 42 church organs. Organ concerts can also be heard at the **Waalse Kerk** and also on Tuesdays at lunch time in the **Westerkerk**.

The programme of the 17th-century **Engelse Kerk** contains a wide variety of music, ranging from Baroque to modern. In the **Domkerk** in Utrecht, concerts are performed on a regular basis.

Opera

Established in 1988 in Amsterdam, the **Muziektheater** is the home of the Nederlandse Opera. One of Europe's most modern opera theatres, its stage has been graced by many established international companies, although it is also used for experimental works. The Stadsschouwburg *(see p116)* on the Leidseplein is also host to a great deal of opera, although if experimental opera is your thing, the Westergasfabriek is probably the best venue. The **Twentse Schouwburg** in Enschede, in conjunction with the Nationale Reis-opera, organizes the Twents Opera Festival each year in July and August.

Rock And Pop

Two venues in particular have established themselves as the most important rock venues in the Netherlands: **Ahoy'** in Rotterdam and Vredenburg in Utrecht, although international rock stars now perform in many parts of the Netherlands. With a capacity of over 5,000, the easily accessible **Heineken Music Hall** is Amsterdam's prime rock venue. It has been used for concerts by megastars such as the late Michael Jackson and the Rolling Stones. However, for locals, there are only two real rock venues: **Paradiso** and **De Melkweg**. Paradiso, in a former church near the Leidseplein, enjoys the greatest respect. The Melkweg (Milky Way), which is also near the Leidseplein, owes its name to the fact that the building in which it is located used to be a dairy. The programme in both of these respected venues changes constantly, and all rock and pop enthusiasts will eventually find something to their taste.

Every Sunday in summer there are free open-air concerts in the Vondelpark, often with renowned bands in the line-up. Programmes are displayed at the entrances to the park. In June the world's largest free pop festival, the Haagse Zuiderpark Parkpop, is held in The Hague. Another annual festival which attracts visitors from near and far is the Pinkpopfestival in Landgraaf (Limburg).

Hans Dulfer

Jazz

The foremost venue of the jazz scene in Amsterdam is the **Bimhuis**. Although the casual visitor might find the atmosphere a tad pretentious, the music here is of top quality, and the Bimhuis enjoys a reputation that goes far beyond the country's borders. There are good jazz cafés to be found all over Amsterdam, most of them featuring local jazz bands. Around the Leidseplein are the **Alto Jazz Café** and **Bourbon Street**, which is open until 4am on weekdays and until 5am on weekends. Alto is best on Wednesdays, when the "godfather" of Amsterdam jazz, Hans Dulfer, performs. His daughter Candy, who has gained international renown, sometimes plays in **De Heeren van Aemstel**. **De Engelbewaarder** is a venue for Sunday jazz. Meanwhile, in Rotterdam, the annual North Sea Jazz Festival takes place in the Congresgebouw. **Dizzy** jazz café has become a household name among jazz-lovers in Rotterdam, hosting over 100 jazz concerts every year.

DIRECTORY

Theatres

Appeltheater
Duinstraat 6–8, The Hague. **Road Map** B4. **Tel** 070-3502200.

Arsenaaltheater
Arsenaalplein 7, Vlissingen. **Road Map** A5. **Tel** 0118-430303.

Bellevue
Leidsekade 90, Amsterdam. **Map** 4 D1. **Tel** 020-5305301/02.

Chassé Theater
Claudius Prinsenlaan 8, Breda. **Road Map** B5. **Tel** 076-5303131.

Compagnietheater
Kloveniersburgwal 50, Amsterdam. **Map** 2 D5. **Tel** 020-5205310.

Concordia
Oude Markt 15, Enschede. **Road Map** E3. **Tel** 053-4311089.

De Flint
Conickstraat 60, Amersfoort. **Road Map** C4. **Tel** 033-4229200.

De Harmonie
Ruiterskwartier 4, Leeuwarden. **Road Map** D1. **Tel** 058-2330233.

De Krakeling
Nwe Passeerdersstraat 1, Amsterdam. **Map** 4 D1. **Tel** 020-6245123.

De la Mar
Marnixstraat 404, Amsterdam. **Map** 4 D1. **Tel** 0900-3352627.

Frascati
Nes 63, Amsterdam. **Map** 2 D5. **Tel** 020-6266866.

Orpheus
Churchillplein 1, Apeldoorn. **Road Map** D3. **Tel** 055-5270300.

Soeterijn
Linnaeusstraat 2, Amsterdam. **Map** 6 E3. **Tel** 020-5688392.

Stadsschouwburg
Leidseplein 26, Amsterdam. **Map** 4 E2. **Tel** 020-6242311.

't Spant
Kuyperlaan 3, Bussum. **Road Map** C3. **Tel** 035-6913254.

Theater aan het Vrijthof
Vrijthof 47, Maastricht. **Road Map** C6. **Tel** 043-3505555.

Toneelschuur
Lange Begijnestr 9, Haarlem. **Road Map** B3. **Tel** 023-5173910.

Transformatorhuis
Polonceaukade 27, Amsterdam. **Map** 1 A1. **Tel** 020-5860710.

Musicals and Cabaret

Beatrix Theater
Jaarbeursplein 6, Utrecht. **Road Map** C4. **Tel** 030-7990799.

Boom Chicago
Rozengracht 117, Amsterdam. **Map** 4 E2. **Tel** 020-2170400.

Comedy Café
Max Euweplein 43–45, Amsterdam. **Map** 4 E2. **Tel** 020-6383971.

AFAS Circustheater
Circusstraat 4, The Hague. **Road Map** B4. **Tel** 070-4167600.

Toomler
Breitnerstr. 2, Amsterdam. **Map** 3 C5. **Tel** 020-6755511.

Dance

Lucent Danstheater
Spuiplein 150, The Hague. **Road Map** B4. **Tel** 070-8800333.

Rotterdamse Schouwburg
Schouwburgplein 25, Rotterdam. **Road Map** B4. **Tel** 010-4118110.

Schouwburg Arnhem
Koningsplein 12, Arnhem. **Road Map** D4. **Tel** 026-4437343.

Orchestra, Chamber and Choir Music

Anton Philipszaal
Spuiplein 150, The Hague. **Road Map** B4. **Tel** 070-8800333.

Concertgebouw De Vereeniging
Keizer Karelplein, Nijmegen. **Road Map** D4. **Tel** 024-3221100.

De Doelen
Schouwburgplein 50, Rotterdam. **Road Map** B4. **Tel** 010-2171700.

De Ysbreker
Weesperzijde 23, Amsterdam. **Map** 5 C4. **Tel** 020-4681808.

Musis Sacrum
Velperbuitensingel 25, Arnhem. **Road Map** D4. **Tel** 026-3720720.

Muziekgebouw Frits Philips
Jan van Lieshoutstraat, Eindhoven. **Road Map** C5. **Tel** 040-2655600.

Muziekcentrum Vredenburg
Sint Jacobsstraat 6-8,, Utrecht. **Road Map** C4. **Tel** 030-2862286.

Church Music

Domkerk
Domplein, Utrecht. **Road Map** C4. **Tel** 030-2310403.

Engelse Kerk
Begijnhof 48, Amsterdam. **Map** 1 C5. **Tel** 020-6249665.

Grote Kerk
Van Kinsbergenstraat, Elburg. **Road Map** D3. **Tel** 0525-681520.

Nieuwe Kerk
Dam, Amsterdam. **Map** 2 D5. **Tel** 020-6386909.

Oude Kerk
Oudekerksplein 23, Amsterdam. **Map** 2 D4. **Tel** 020-6258284.

Waalse Kerk
Walenplein 157, Amsterdam. **Tel** 020-6232074.

Westerkerk
Prinsengracht 281, Amsterdam. **Map** 1 B4. **Tel** 020-624776.

Opera

Muziektheater Amsterdam
see p149. **Map** 5 B2.

Twentse Schouwburg
Langestraat 49, Enschede. **Road Map** E3. **Tel** 053-4858585.

Rock and Pop

Ahoy'
Ahoyweg 10, Rotterdam. **Road Map** B4. **Tel** 010-2933300.

Heineken Music Hall
Arena Boulevard 590, Amsterdam. **Tel** 0900-6874242.

Melkweg
Lijnbaansgracht 234 a, Amsterdam. **Map** 4 E2. **Tel** 020-5318181.

Paradiso
Weteringschans 6–8, Amsterdam. **Map** 4 3F. **Tel** 020-6264521.

Jazz

Alto Jazz Café
Korte Leidsedwarsstraat 115, Amsterdam. **Map** 1 B4. **Tel** 020-6263249.

Bimhuis
Piet Heinkade 3, Amsterdam. **Tel** 020-7882188.

Bourbon Street
Leidsekruisstraat 6–8, Amsterdam. **Map** 4 2E. **Tel** 020-6233440.

De Engelbewaarder
Kloveniersburgwal 59, Amsterdam. **Map** 2 5D. **Tel** 020-6253772.

De Heeren van Aemstel
Thorbeckeplein 5, Amsterdam. **Map** 5 A2. **Tel** 020-6202173.

Dizzy
's-Gravendijkwal 129, Rotterdam. **Road Map** B4. **Tel** 010-4773014.

Amusement and Theme Parks

The Netherlands offers a great variety of amusement and theme parks. Whether you want to see frolicking dolphins, take a white-knuckle ride, go back to Roman times or spend the day splashing in a swimming pool, there is something for everyone. And because the Dutch weather doesn't always play along, most parks have attractions indoors. Listed below is a sample of the parks to be found in the country.

Aqua Zoo Friesland

This watery domain near Leeuwarden shows beavers, minks, polecats, storks and other animals in their natural surroundings. Otters are a highlight here, having disappeared from the Netherlands due to pollution of their freshwater habitat. A path winds its way through the entire terrain, leading at one point through a glass tunnel that provides visitors with a close-up of the otters' underwater antics.

Archeon

This open-air archaeological park brings the past to life in captivating fashion. Visitors wander from prehistoric times, the Roman period and the Middle Ages, aided by the re-creations of actors. You can see how the hunter-gatherers lived and how farmers tilled their fields. You then explore a Roman town complete with bath-house, temple and theatre, followed by a medieval city with working craftsmen. The hands-on fun includes a trip in a prehistoric canoe.

Het Arsenaal

A large attraction with a maritime theme has been set up at Het Arsenaal in Vlissingen. First visitors watch a naval review with models of famous ocean liners, including the *Titanic*. For those hooked on adrenaline there is a shipwreck simulator and a scary pirate cave on a treasure island. In Onderwaterwereld you can observe sharks, lobsters and other creatures of the deep. The 64-m (210-ft) tower of Het Arsenaal gives a fine view of the Westerschelde estuary.

Avonturenpark Hellendoorn

This place offers a vast range of attractions, including the Canadian River log-ride with a 12-m (39-ft) drop in a tree trunk, the Sungai Kalimantan rafting-ride, the Tornado and Rioolrat (underground) rat ride, a monorail over a dinosaur park and Montezuma's Revenge (prepare to get wet!). Younger children will enjoy Dreumesland (Dreamland) with its play castle and much more.

Suspension bridge through the tropical rainforest in Burgers' Bush

One of the rides at the Hellendoorn Adventure Park

Burgers' Zoo

This unusual park allows you to see animals from all over the world in their natural environments, which have been carefully re-created here.

In Burger's Desert, in a vast hall with 20-m (65-ft) ceilings, you can wander through a rocky cactus desert with birds and an oasis. There is also a dense tropical jungle and a safari park with giraffes, rhinoceroses and lions. In the ocean section, you can stand on a tropical coral beach and peer through the glass at an undersea world.

Dolfinarium

Frolicking dolphins and seals always draw large crowds, but the Dolfinarium does one better with its Lagune, a large bay where dolphins, sea lions and fish live. On the Roggenrif you can mingle with the seals and stroke sharks, while in Fort Heerewich you learn how stranded dolphins are cared for. An underwater show and a 3D film provide additional excitement.

Duinrell

Nestled in the sandy woodlands of the Wassenaar region, this park has rides such as the Waterspin, toboggan runs, a frog roller coaster and a monorail. In summer there are elaborate shows such as the *Music Laser Light Show*. For the little ones there is a fairy-tale wonderland, a large playground and numerous kids' shows. A big draw is the Tikibad, an indoor pool with spectacular slides, a surf pool and a water ballet show.

Ecomare

Located on the island of Texel, this is an information centre for the tidal flats of the West Frisian islands and the North Sea. There is a display about the creation of Texel, its habitat and the local fauna. The Waterzaal is full of aquariums, plus a basin of rays for petting. There's also a centre for stranded seals and seabirds.

De Efteling

This theme park in Kaatsheuvel draws on the world of fantasy. In the fairytale forest you may bump into Little Red Riding Hood, Snow White or Sleeping Beauty. The Fata Morgana is a simplified take on the Arabian Nights; here you can view the entire park from a 45-m (148-ft) Flying Temple.

Stranded seals recovering their health in EcoMare on Texel

The splash ride in Duinrell

Extreme thrills are provided by the Python, the Pegasus and the underground Vogel Rok roller coasters and many other rides. It's worth checking the website for "busy" days.

If a day isn't enough, you can stay the night in Efteling Hotel.

Linnaeushof

This playground claims to be Europe's largest, with more than 350 different pieces of equipment, including a super slide, cable rides, a skate-rail, trampolines, a climbing wall, pedaloes and 360-degree swings. In the "spider's web", you risk tumbling into the water as you climb nets to the pirates' crow's nest. Toddlers have their own special playground with a huge sandpit and road village where they can ride tricycles and toy aeroplanes. For wet weather there's an indoor playground.

Noordwijk Space Expo

This sprawling display about the wonders of outer space is a treat for all ages. Some of its rockets and satellites are the real thing (as is the piece of moon rock 4 billion years old), but the replicas, such as a model lunar module, are convincing. You can visit a space station and watch multimedia presentations. Children will especially like the treasure hunt and weight-free simulator.

Verkeerspark Assen

This park offers an enormous circuit of roads, roundabouts and traffic lights where children aged between 6 and 12 can drive around and learn to deal with various traffic situations. Someone keeps an eye on participants from the traffic control tower. There's a play area and suitable rides for toddlers, while older children can ride motorized jeeps and "bouncy bikes".

DIRECTORY

Aqua Zoo Friesland
De Groene Ster 2, 8926 XE Leeuwarden.
Road Map D2.
Tel 0511-431214.
Open 10am–5pm daily (longer in summer).
W aquazoo.nl

Archeon
Archeonlaan 1, 2408 ZB Alphen a/d Rijn.
Road Map B4.
Tel 0172-447744.
Open Apr–Oct: 10am–5pm daily.
W archeon.nl

Het Arsenaal
Arsenaalplein 7, 4381 BL Vlissingen.
Road Map A5.
Tel 0118-415400.
Open call ahead.
W arsenaal.com

Avonturenpark Hellendoorn
Luttenbergerweg 22, 7447 PB Hellendoorn.
Road Map D3. **Tel** 0548 659159. **Open** call ahead.
W avonturenpark.nl

Burgers' Zoo
Anton van Hooffplein 1, 6816 SH Arnhem.
Road map D4. **Tel** 026-4424534. **Open** Apr– Oct: 9am–7pm daily; Nov–Mar: 9am–5pm.
W burgerszoo.nl

Dolfinarium Harderwijk
Strandboulevard Oost 1, 3841 AB Harderwijk.
Road Map C3.
Tel 0341-467467
Open mid-Feb–Jun & Sep–Oct: 10am– 5pm daily; Jul– Aug: 10am–6pm.
W dolfinarium.nl

Duinrell
Duinrell 1, 2242 JP Wassenaar. **Road Map** B4.
Tel 070-5155255.
Open Theme park: Apr–Oct: 10am– 5pm daily (mid-Jul–Aug to 6pm). Tickets: call ahead.
W duinrell.nl

EcoMare
Ruyslaan 92, 1796 AZ De Koog, Texel. **Road Map** B2. **Tel** 0222-317741.
Open 9am–5pm daily.
W ecomare.nl

De Efteling
Europalaan 1, 5171 KW Kaatsheuvel.
Road Map C4. **Tel** 0900-0161 **Open** Apr–Oct: 10am–6pm daily (later in summer).
Winter Efteling: open around Christmas.
W efteling.com

Linnaeushof
Rijksstraatweg 4, 2121 AE Bennebroek. **Road Map** B3. **Tel** 023-5847624.
Open Apr–Sep: 10am–6pm daily.
W linnaueshof.nl

Noordwijk Space Expo
Keplerlaan 3, 2201 AZ Noordwijk.
Tel 071-3646489.
Open 10am–5pm Tue–Sun (also Mon in school hols). **W spaceexpo.nl**

Verkeerspark Assen
De Haar 1–1a, 9405 TE Assen. **Road Map** D2.
Tel 0592-350005.
Open Apr–Oct: 9:30am–5pm daily. Open days vary in some weeks so check ahead.
W verkeersparkassen.nl

Sports Holidays

With its abundance of water, the Netherlands lends itself to all kinds of watersports such as boating, sailing and canoeing; however, there are also plenty of opportunities for sporting activities on dry land, whether you want to kick a ball about or play golf or tennis, or even go riding. Most *VVV-gidsen* *(see p432)* tell you where there are golf courses and tennis courts in the locality, and they give the addresses of angling clubs, stables, boatyards, sailing schools and so on.

Ramblers in the Heuvelrug of Utrecht

Holland offers much in the way of watersports, such as canoeing

Watersports

The favourite places in the Netherlands for watersports are the Frisian seas, the coastal lakes, the Plassengebied (lakelands), the southwest river delta, and the lakes of the Vechtplassen, the Maasplassen, the IJsselmeer and, of course, the North Sea. Everywhere there are abundant marinas and watersports centres, often with equipment for hire. The ANWB publishes the *Wateralmanakken*, available at ANWB and VVV offices and in bookshops, which give details of sailing regulations, bridge and lock opening times, port information and so on. The *ANWB/VVV waterkaarten* (navigation charts) are also used by many people.

You can obtain information on sailing and surfing organizations at institutions such as the **Commissie Watersport Opleidingen** (watersports training commission) and the ANWB. Surfers will find plenty to do on the North Sea and IJsselmeer coast (surfing beaches, equipment hire), and it is also possible to surf on many inland waters, including the Reenwijkse Plassen, the Randmeren and the Frisian lakes. For further information on sailing, boating and windsurfing, ask at the **Koninklijk Nederlands Watersport Verbond** (royal watersports association).

Good places for diving include the Oosterschelde and Grevelingenmeer; for more information apply to the Dutch underwater-sports association, the **Nederlandse Onderwatersport Bond**. For canoeing, your first port of call should be the **Nederlandse Kano Bond** (canoeing association). Dozens of round trips in various craft organized in lakes, rivers and the sea are also available. The local VVV tourist office will be able to direct you further.

Rambling and Cycling

Ramblers' guides and maps can be obtained in many places, including the VVV, ANWB and bookshops. The VVV also provides information on walking tours and local events. The *Er op Uit!* booklet published by the Dutch Railways contains rambling routes from one station to another. The majority of them are 15 to 20 km (9 to 12 miles), though some two-day hikes are also described. You will find route maps at the station where the hike begins. Around 30 long-distance hiking trails have been marked out in the Netherlands. These routes, which are at least 100 km (62 miles) in length, follow mainly unmetalled tracks.

Sailing

Sailing courses suitable for all ages and experience levels are widely available along the Dutch coast for practically all types of vessel. Taking lessons at a CWO registered sailing school will give you an internationally recognized CWO sailing certificate. More experienced sailors can explore the North Sea, the IJsselmeer (watch out for strong winds), the Waddenzee (where you have to watch the shallows) or the Westerschelde (which has strong tidal currents). However, you can also go for a more relaxing experience on the Vinkeveense Plassen lakes. Cruises are also widely available. Hollands Glorie (tel. 010-4156600) offers cruises on traditional sailing craft on waterways such as the IJsselmeer, the Waddenzee and the Frisian lakes.

Yachting on the Oosterschelde

Sailing dinghy

Golfers on the Lauswolt Estate in Friesland

A popular hiking trail is the Pieterpad (LAW 9), stretching 480 km (300 miles) from Pieterburen in Groningen to the Sint-Pietersberg at Maastricht.

Wandelplatform-LAW publishes guides to the routes, with and without accommodation details. Many natural areas are criss-crossed by footpaths and cycle tracks, among them the Nationaal Park Hoge Veluwe *(see p343)*. You can find out about accessibility of various areas and about enjoyable routes or excursions at VVV or ANWB tourist information offices, at the Staatsbosbeheer (forestry commission) (www.staatsbosbeheer.nl) or the Vereniging Natuurmonumenten *(see p264)*. For details on cycling, see pages 448–9.

Golf and Tennis

The Netherlands has some 160 golfing clubs, all members of the Nederlandse Golf Federatie (**NGF**). Many clubs also provide opportunities for non-members to play, although some may require proof of golfing proficiency. Many of them also offer training courses. Golf courses in the Netherlands are in dunelands, woodland and polderland.

In many areas you will find tennis clubs with outdoor and indoor courts. Most bungalow parks have tennis courts for the use of residents.

Fishing

Fishing is a popular sport in the Netherlands. In the inland waterways you can angle for bream, carp and pike, while flatfish and mackerel can be caught along the coast and in the sea. Local angling associations will give you information on when and where to fish. Don't forget to obtain a fishing permit (which is compulsory for inland waters). The permits are available at VVVs or angling associations. Sometimes you also need a permit for a particular lake or river. Along the coast, angling trips are organized on the North Sea and in the Waddenzee.

Horse Riding

There are many stables where you can hire ponies for pony-trekking. Some stables hire out horses only if you have a riding permit or if you are on a guided tour (information is available from the **SVR**). For some nature reserves which allow riding you will need to get a riding permit from the organization managing the area, and you will have to keep to the bridleways. Beach riding is an unforgettable experience, but keep an eye on the signs, because some sections of beach – especially in summer – are closed to horses.

Riding on Ameland

DIRECTORY

Watersports

Commissie Watersport Opleidingen (CWO)
Postbus 2658, 3430 GB Nieuwegein.
Tel 030-7513740.

Koninklijk Nederlands Watersport Verbond
Wattbaan 31-49, 3439 ML Nieuwegein.
Tel 030-7513700.

Nederlandse Kano Bond
Postbus 2658, 3430 GB Nieuwegein. **Tel** 030-7513700.

Nederlandse Onderwatersport Bond
Landjuweel 62, 3905 PH Veenendaal. **Tel** 0318-559347.

Walking and Cycling

Cycletours
Buiksloterweg 7a, 1031 CC Amsterdam. **Tel** 020-5218400.

Fietsvakantiewinkel
W fietsvkantiewinkel.nl.

Nederlandse Wandelsport Bond
Pieterskerkhof 22, 3512 JS Utrecht. **Tel** 030-2319458.

NTFU
Postbus 326, 3900 AH Veenendaal. **Tel** 0318-581300.

Stichting Landelijk Fietsplatform
Postbus 846, 3800 AV Amersfoort.
Tel 033-4653656.

Wandelplatform-LAW
Postbus 846, 3800 AV Amersfoort.
Tel 033-4653660. **W http://wandelnet.nl**

Golf

NGF
Postbus 8585, 3503 RN Utrecht.
Tel 030-2426370.

Fishing

Sportvisserij Nederland
Leijensweg 115, 3721 BC Bilthoven. **Tel** 030-6058400.
W sportvisserijnederland.nl

Horse Riding

SVR
De Beek 125, 3852 PL Ermelo.
Tel 0577-408365.
W veiligpaardrijden.nl

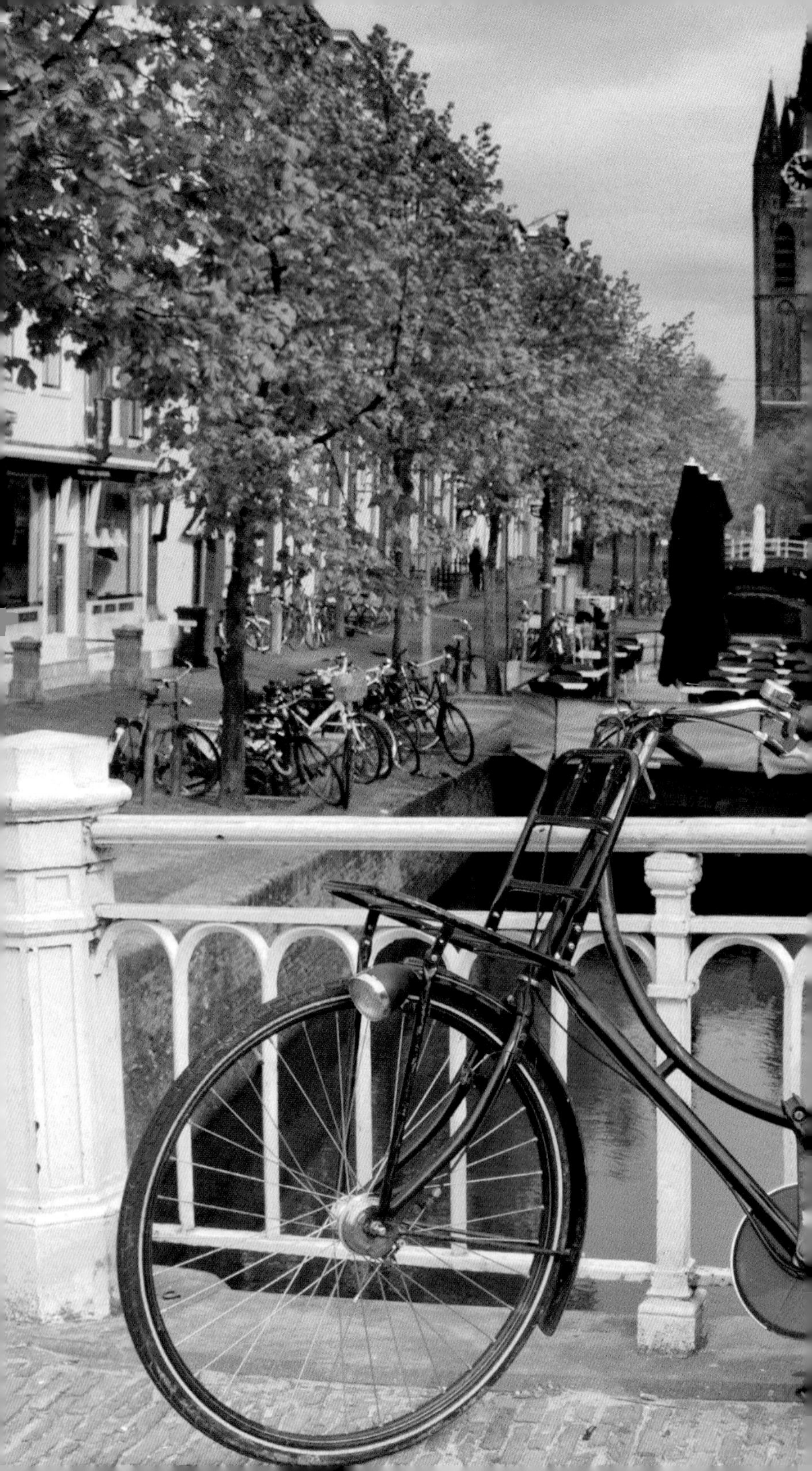

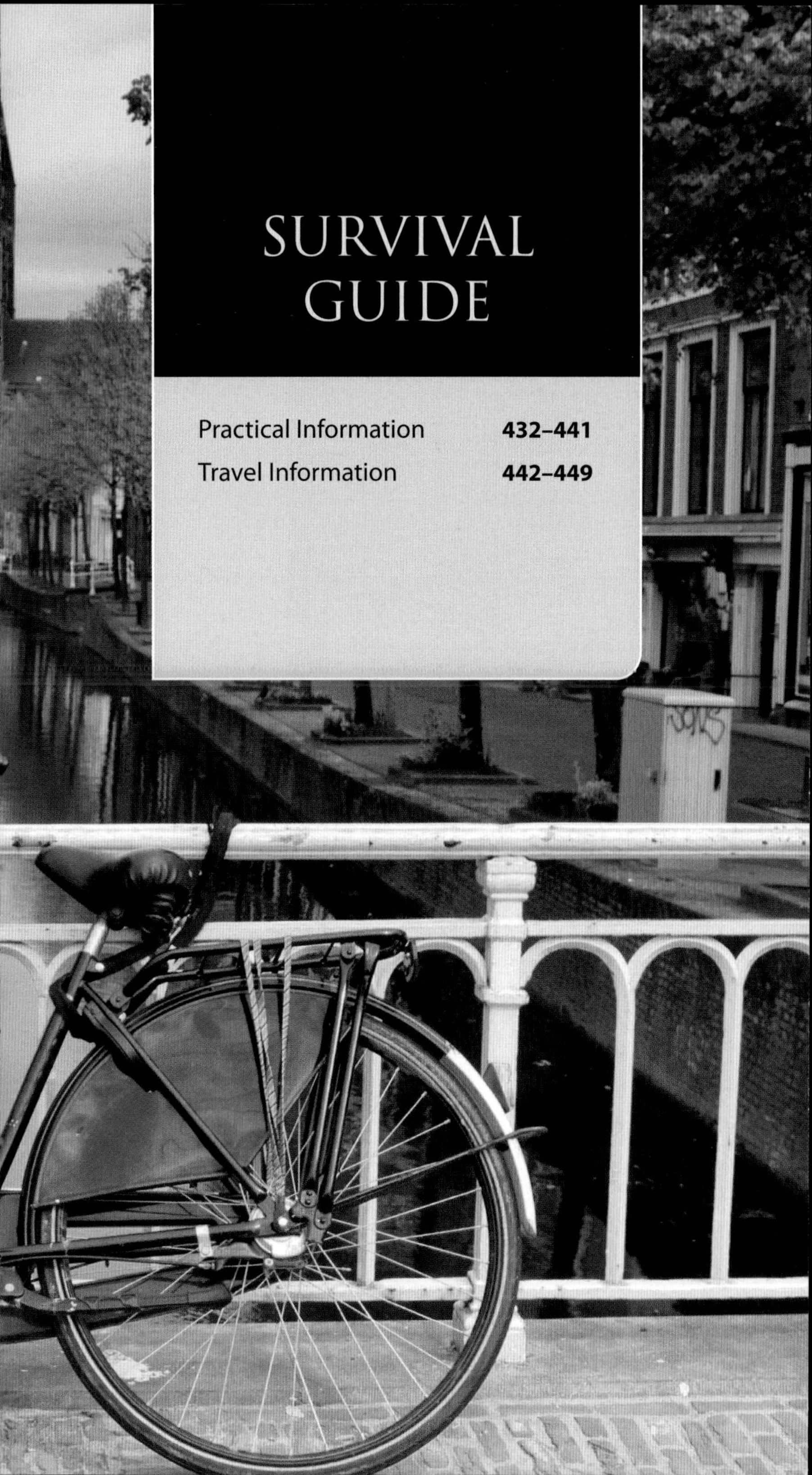

SURVIVAL GUIDE

PRACTICAL INFORMATION

The Netherlands is relatively small and has a dense road and motorway network with good public transport so getting around is quick and easy. Whether you are going to Amsterdam, the Veluwe, Maastricht or Zandvoort, you can get there from anywhere in the country very quickly by car or by train. The flat landscape with its many canals and dykes means that holidaymakers have plenty of opportunity to explore the countryside by bicycle *(see pp448–9)* or by boat *(see p447)*. Another option is to take a trip by steam train. The best place to find out what's available in your area – and in the country as a whole – is the local VVV (tourist information) office.

VVV and ANWB offices, which often share the same premises

Tourist Information

The best source of information for tourists is the local or regional **VVV** office. Many towns and places of interest have VVV offices where you can drop in and ask for advice and brochures about places of interest, local events, walks, cycle routes and excursions in the town or region. In addition, they can provide maps and books about other parts of the Netherlands. The VVV-*gidsen* series in Dutch is very practical, with information and facts about individual provinces and regions.

At VVVs you can also book domestic excursions, hotels, short breaks and theatre tickets anywhere in the country. Annual museum cards and CJPs are also on sale here. Smaller VVV outlets, although providing comprehensive information about their local area, do not provide other services.

ANWB offices in the Netherlands also have a selection of cycling, rambling and motoring guides, tickets, camping guides and road atlases. ANWB members have access to specialized membership information about various subjects and holiday offers. In many cases the VVV and the ANWB share the same premises. If you are travelling to the Netherlands from abroad you can obtain information in advance from the **Netherlands Board of Tourism (NBT)** in your own country.

ANWB logo

Language

The Dutch have been linguists for centuries, and most students learn English, some German and French. English is certainly very widely and fluently spoken in Amsterdam. However, it's always appreciated if you can handle a few niceties: greeting a Dutch person with "Dag" ("good day"), for example, before asking whether they speak English. The Phrase Book on pages 471–2 is a useful place to start.

Entertainment

Many VVV-*gidsen* guides have an annual review of events in a particular region or province. For up-to-date information on events, exhibitions, performances and films, it is worth looking in the entertainment supplements issued by daily papers *(see p150)*, or ask at the local VVV office. Plays, concerts, special events and festivals are usually advertised on billboards or in cafés. Special regional and local entertainment guides are also a good source of information; for example, the monthly *Uitkrant* tells you what's on in Amsterdam in the way of the performing arts, while the weekly *Uitloper* is Utrecht's entertainment guide. These guides are distributed at many sites free of charge.

Tickets for concerts and events are available not only at the box office of the venue itself but also via the national **Ticket Service** and at VVV offices. Some towns also have their own booking bureau; for instance, in Amsterdam you can book your tickets at the AUB *(see p153)*.

Revellers at a music festival in Amsterdam

◀ The canal with the Old Church Tower of Delft in the background

The Museum Card allows entry to a majority of museums

Museum Card

The Annual Museum Card *(Museumjaarkaart)* has quickly risen to huge popularity. It costs €49.90 for people over the age of 18, and €27.45 for under-18s. It gives the holder free entry to over 440 museums in the country. However, you often have to pay a supplement for special exhibitions. The card is available at all participating museums and at VVVs. It can also be ordered online from www.museumkaart.nl..

Travellers with Disabilities

Most public buildings have good facilities for travellers with disabilities. Museums, art galleries, cinemas and theatres generally are wheelchair-accessible. Only some establishments in very old buildings are less accessible, but there are always staff who are able to lend a hand. If you require assistance it's a good idea to phone in advance. Accessibility information for hotels is given on page 387.

In Amsterdam and other major cities, all main pedestrian crossings are equipped with sound for the blind. For disabled people travelling by train, the NS has issued a pack entitled *Gehandicapten*. This contains information on Dutch railway stations and what facilities they have, and also lists the stations (there are approximately 150 of them) where people in wheelchairs can get assistance when boarding and alighting from trains. Many trains have wheelchair-accessible doors, and most new double-decker trains have wheelchair-accessible toilets. If you need help, it's best to contact the **Bureau Assistentieverlening Gehandicapten** at least three hours before travelling.

Wheelchair-accessible tourist office

Opening Hours

Although until recently just about every shop in the country was open from 9am to 6pm, today there is an increasing variety in shop opening hours. Many retail stores and supermarkets are open until 7pm or later. In the cities, shops tend to stay open longer. Many towns have a "shopping evening" *(koopavond)* once a week, when most shops remain open until 9pm: Thursday in Amsterdam and The Hague, Friday in Utrecht. In an increasing number of towns shops open on Sundays at least once in the month. Many shops have half-day closing one day a week, usually Monday, but varying from one region to another.

Banks are usually open on weekdays from 9am to 5pm, and VVVs are also open on Mondays to Fridays from 9am or 10am to 5pm (sometimes on *koopavond* until 9pm). On Saturdays they close early or even all day, and most are closed on Sundays. Some VVVs are closed during the winter.

Many museums are shut on Mondays, and open from 10am to 5pm for the rest of the week. On Sundays and public holidays they tend to open later. Practically all museums are closed on Christmas and New Year's Day. Open-air museums and small museums tend to close for the winter.

DIRECTORY

Tourist Information

Amsterdam Tourist Board
Stationsplein 15.
Tel 020-2018800.

ANWB Main Office
Wassenaarseweg 220, 2596 EC
The Hague.
Tel 088-2692222.

Netherland Board of Tourism
PO Box 458, 2266 KA Leidschendam.
Tel 070-370 5705.
W holland.com

VVV The Hague
Spui 68.**Tel** 070-3618860.

VVV Maastricht
Kleine Staat 1.
Tel 043-3252121.

VVV Rotterdam
Coolsingel 195.
Tel 010-2710120.

VVV Utrecht
Domplein 9.
Tel 0900-1288732.

Entertainment

Ticket Service
Tel 0900-3001250.
W ticketmaster.nl

Museum Card

Stichting Museumjaarkaart
W museumkaart.nl

Travellers with Disabilities

Bureau Assistentie-verlening Gehandicapten
W ns.nl

Flower seeds and bulbs, freely exported items (with certificate)

Visas and Customs

Travellers from other EU countries can travel freely in and out of the Netherlands provided they have a valid passport or European identity card. For a stay lasting up to three months, travellers from Australia, New Zealand and North America need only a valid passport.

EU residents may bring an unlimited quantity of goods into the country provided they are for their personal use. For tobacco and alcohol, the following quantities are considered limits for personal use: 800 cigarettes, 400 cigars, 1 kg of tobacco, 10 litres of spirits, 20 litres of liqueurs, 90 litres of wine (or 60 litres of fortified wine) and 110 litres of beer. Duty will be charged on quantities exceeding these specified limits.

For travellers from outside the EU, the limits are 200 cigarettes, 100 cigarillos, 50 cigars or 250 g of tobacco, 2 litres of unfortified wine plus 1 litre of spirits or 2 litres of fortified wine or liqueur wine or spirits, 50 g of perfume, 0.25l of eau de toilette and other items up to a value of €175. Residents of other EU countries may no longer import goods on which VAT has not been paid. If you are entering or leaving the EU, you can take non-VAT paid goods with you. More details are available from the **Customs Helpline** *(Douanetelefoon)*, which gives precise information on customs regulations. Travellers from outside the Netherlands may be able to obtain information at their local embassy.

Customers showing their appreciation with a tip

Time

Like all its neighbouring countries, the Netherlands is on Central European Time, which is 1 hour ahead of Greenwich Mean Time. Daylight saving (1 hour) operates from the end of March to the end of October.

Sydney is 8 hours ahead, Johannesburg 1 hour (the same as the Netherlands), New York is 6 hours behind and Los Angeles 9 hours behind.

Tipping

Taxi drivers expect a tip of around 10 per cent. Although a service charge is included on restaurant bills, it is customary to round the bill up slightly *(see p403)*.

In hotels you may if you like leave something for the chambermaid after a longer stay, even though it is not generally the rule.

Public Toilets

There is a limited number of public conveniences in the Netherlands. In some cities you will find toilets where you have to insert money into a slot to open the door. Popping into a café to use the toilets there is accepted practice in the Netherlands; some establishments have an attendant who should be paid a small amount. Large retail stores and stations also have toilets, and you generally need to pay a small fee to use these. The latter also have nappy-changing facilities. On motorways you will find toilets at all service stations.

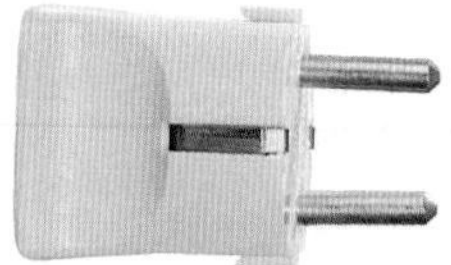

Standard continental plug

Electricity

In the Netherlands the electrical voltage is 220 volts AC. Dutch plugs are of the two-pin type, and adapters are available for visitors from countries with different plugs (for example, Great Britain).

Television and Radio

The television programmes on offer in the Netherlands are undergoing a great deal of development at the moment. The traditional system was to have a large number of broadcasting networks, each with their own political or religious leanings, being given a certain amount of air-time on each of the three public TV stations (Nederland 1, 2 and 3). More recently, however, commercial television stations have emerged to compete with Hilversum (the town where the Netherlands' main networks are based, (*see pp194–5*).

As well as national TV networks, the Netherlands has a number of regional and local providers, such as Omrop Fryslân, Omroep Flevoland, Omroep Gelderland and the Amsterdam local network AT5. In addition, large numbers of foreign programmes can be received on cable TV, the range varying depending on the local cable company.

The Netherlands has five national radio stations, each of them with their own "personality": Radio 1 deals mainly with current affairs and sport, Radio 2 broadcasts light music and various information progr- ammes, Radio 3 rock and pop and Radio 4 classical music. 747 AM is a news channel.

Cat in a travel basket

Newspapers and Magazines

The Netherlands has five national morning newspapers *(De Telegraaf, de Volkskrant, Algemeen Dagblad, NRC Next* and *Trouw)* and two national evening papers *(Het Parool* and *NRC Handelsblad)*. These tend to focus on the west of the country. Regionally the more popular papers are the *Nieuwsblad van het Noorden, Friesch Dagblad, Tubantia, De Gelderlander, Utrechts Nieuwsblad, Provinciale Zeeuwsche Courant, Brabants Dagblad* and *Dagblad De Limburger*, which contain information on local holiday activities and events. The more famous Dutch weekly news magazines include *HP/De Tijd, Elsevier* and *Vrij Nederland*.

The major bookshops in the large cities (as well as the main railway stations) sell many major international newspapers and magazines.

Pets

If you bring your dog or cat to the Netherlands from abroad, you need to be able to prove that your pet has been immunized against rabies. This is shown by a valid pet's passport provided by your veterinarian which indicates when the animal was last vaccinated.

A selection of national and international newspapers available

Embassies and Consulates

If you are visiting from abroad and your passport happens to be lost or stolen, you should report the loss immediately either to your consulate or embassy. Most embassies are sit- uated in the administrative capital, The Hague. A number of countries, including the UK, USA, France, Germany and Italy, also have consulates, and these tend to be located in Amsterdam.

DIRECTORY

Embassies and Consulates

Australia
Embassy:
Carnegielaan 4,
2517 KH The Hague.
Tel 070-3108200.
W netherlands. embassy.gov.au

Belgium
Embassy:
Johan van Oldenbarneveltlaan 11,
2582 NE The Hague.
Tel 070-3123456.

Canada
Embassy:
Sophialaan 7, 2514 JP The Hague.
Tel 070-3111600.
W canadainternational. gc.ca

France
Embassy:
Anna Paulownastraat 76, 2518 BJ The Hague.
Tel 070-3125800.
W ambafrance-nl.org

Germany
Embassy:
Groot Hertoginne-laan 18–20, 2517 EG The Hague. **Tel** 070-3420600.
W niederlande.diplo.de
Consulate:
Honthorststraat 36–38, 1071 DG Amsterdam.
Tel 020-5747700.
Fax 020-6766951.

Great Britain
Embassy: Lange Voorhout 10, 2514 ED The Hague.
Tel 070-4270427.
Fax 070-4270345.
W gov.uk
Consulate General:
Koningslaan 44,
1075 AE Amsterdam.
Tel 020-6764343.

Ireland
Embassy:
Scheveningseweg 112, 2584 AE
The Hague.
Tel 070-3630993/4.
Fax 070-3617604.
W embassyofireland. nl

New Zealand
Embassy:
Eisenhowerlaan 77N, 2517 KK
The Hague.
Tel 070-3469324.
Fax 070-3632983.
W nzembassy.com/ netherlands

South Africa
Embassy:
Wassena arseweg 40,
2596 CJ The Hague.
Tel 070-3924501.
W zuidafrika.nl

United States
Embassy: Lange Voorhout 102, 2514 EJ The Hague.
Tel 070-3102209.
W http://thehague. usembassy.gov
Consulate: Museumplein 19, 1017 DJ Amsterdam.
Tel 020-5755309.
Fax 020-5755310.
W http://amsterdam. usconsulate.gov

Customs Helpline

Tel 0800-0143.
Open 8am–10pm Mon–Thu, 8am–5pm Fri.

Personal Security and Health

If you keep to a few basic safety rules, you should have a trouble-free stay in the Netherlands. Obviously it is better not to carry large amounts of cash or valuables around, and not to keep passports, cheques and credit cards together in one place. Visitors from abroad can always insure themselves against losses of money and personal items from theft. It is also a good idea to insure yourself against medical expenses. For those who do find themselves in trouble on holiday, the country has efficient emergency services and facilities.

Emergencies

The national **emergency number** for the police, fire brigade and ambulance is 112. This number must only be dialled in emergencies. For less urgent help, it is best to contact the nearest police station, hospital or a local doctor. If your car breaks down, members of the ANWB can call out the roadside assistance service of the **ANWB Wegenwacht** 24 hours a day, 7 days a week, using the roadside emergency phones or by dialling a toll-free phone number.

Dutch police officers

Personal Belongings and Safety

It is as true of the Netherlands as elsewhere in Europe that opportunity makes the thief. When in busy shopping streets or on public transport, do not leave your wallet in your back pocket, and if you need to go to the lavatory on the train or when in a restaurant, take your handbag or wallet with you. Do not leave any valuables in your car, and always make sure it has been properly locked. Large cities, particularly Amsterdam, have a big problem with bicycle theft, so a decent lock is a good investment. Muggings are rare, but at night it is better to avoid unlit areas and parks. Women can visit cafés in the evening without risk.

Reporting Crime

If you have been the victim of theft or a mugging, report it to the nearest police station (some smaller municipalities do not have their own police station). You will need to make a verbal report describing any loss and, if necessary, injury. Many insurance companies require you to report within 24 hours of the incident taking place. If your passport is stolen, you should immediately report this to your embassy *(see p435)* as well as to the police.

Medical Treatment and Insurance

Minor medical problems can usually be dealt with at a pharmacy, though the prescription of drugs is very strict. The majority of drugs are available only on prescription. Pharmacies – which are recognizable by their snake symbol – are open on weekdays from 8:30 or 9am to 5:30 or 6pm.

If the pharmacy is closed, you will find on the door a list of the nearest pharmacies that are open. Local newspapers also give details of duty doctors, pharmacies and other health services in the town or region. In an emergency you can get treatment in hospitals, which are open 24 hours a day.

Visitors from abroad who will be carrying prescription drugs with them should ask their doctor for a medical passport. This is a document stating your condition and the medication you require for it. The passport can be shown at the customs as evidence that you are bringing the medication in for your personal use.

Travellers from European Union countries should apply for and take with them a European Health Insurance Card (EHIC). You can do this online or at post offices in the UK before you leave. It will enable you to claim for state health service treatment

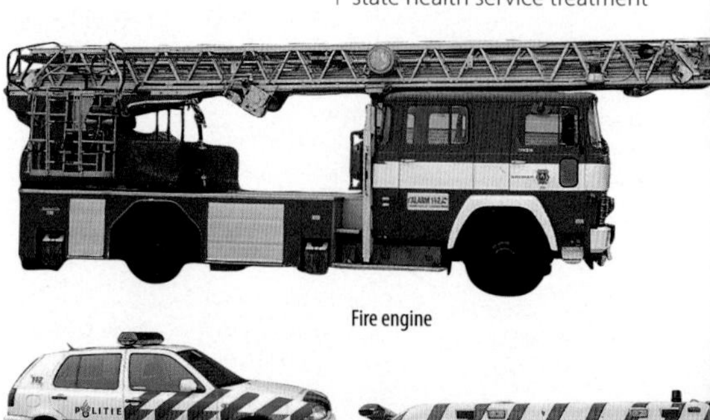

Fire engine

Police car

Ambulance

in EU countries. It is also a good idea to purchase comprehensive medical insurance if it is not included in your travel insurance.

Mosquitoes

Attracted by the canals, mosquitoes can be a real irritant. Residents and regular summer visitors deal with them in various ways. Burning coils, ultra-violet tubes, mosquito nets, repellent sprays and anti-histamine creams and tablets are available from large pharmacies and supermarkets.

A crowded street festival: a place to be wary of pickpockets

Lost Property

If you lose any valuables, you can check at the police station to see whether anyone has handed them in. Local police stations usually keep articles that have been handed in before passing them on to the central police station for the district. If you lose your passport you must also inform your consulate *(see p435)*. If you lose something on a train, inform the station first. Small stations keep lost property for one day. After that they are taken to the nearest main station, and finally to the **Central Lost Property Office** *(Centraal Bureau Gevonden Voorwerpen)* in Utrecht. By filling in a search form (available at railway stations), you can describe the items you have lost. If you lose something on a bus, tram or metro, you should contact the office of the local or regional transport organization (look for "openbaar vervoer" (public transport) in the Yellow Pages). **Schiphol** Airport has a special lost property number.

Emergency room sign

Drugs

Although the use of soft drugs is officially illegal in the Netherlands, the police will not take action if you have a small quantity of hashish or marijuana in your possession. It is worth remembering that not every restaurant or café owner will take kindly to tourists lighting up on the premises. People caught with hard drugs will be prosecuted.

DIRECTORY

Emergency Numbers

Ambulance, Fire Brigade, Police
Tel 112. For the deaf and hard of hearing
Tel 0800-8112.

Safety

Police
Non-urgent matters:
Tel 0900-8844
(you will be connected to the nearest police station). For the deaf and hard of hearing
Tel 0900-1844.

Police Amsterdam-Amstelland
Head office:
Elandsgracht 117,
1016 TT Amsterdam.
Tel 0900-8844.

Hospitals in Major Cities

Amsterdam: Academisch Medisch Centrum
Meibergdreef 9.
Tel 020-5669111.

Onze Lieve Vrouwe Gasthuis
1ste Oosterparkstraat 297.
Tel 020-5999111.

Sint Lucas Andreas Ziekenhuis
Jan Tooropstraat 164.
Tel 020-5108911.

Slotervaart Hospital
Louwesweg 6.
Tel 020-5129333.

VU Medisch Centrum
De Boelelaan 1117.
Tel 020-4444444.

The Hague: Bronovo Hospital
Bronovolaan 5.
Tel 070-3124141.

MCH Hospital Westeinde
Lijnbaan 32.
Tel 070-3302000.

Rotterdam: Erasmus Medisch Centrum
's-Gravendijkwal 230,
3015 CE Rotterdam.
Tel 010-7040704

Utrecht: Academisch Hospital Utrecht
Heidelberglaan 100.
Tel 030-2509111.

Lost Property

Central Lost Property Office
2de Daalsedijk 4, 3551 zEJ Utrecht.
Tel 030-2353923
(8am–8pm Mon–Fri, 9am–5pm Sat).

Schiphol – Lost Property
Tel 0900-SCHIPHOL / 0900-72447465.

Roadside Assistance

ANWB Wegenwacht
Tel 088-269-2888 (toll-free).

Banking and Local Currency

In the Netherlands, cash remains a popular means of payment, but credit cards and debit cards are now the norm. Almost all hotels, shops and restaurants accept major credit cards in payment. Other means of payment are traveller's cheques (with identification), and, occasionally, US dollars (particularly at antique and souvenir shops). In 2002, the Netherlands began to use the euro. The best place to change money is at a bank. You can take an unlimited amount of currency into the Netherlands, and you can withdraw limited amounts of cash at an ATM.

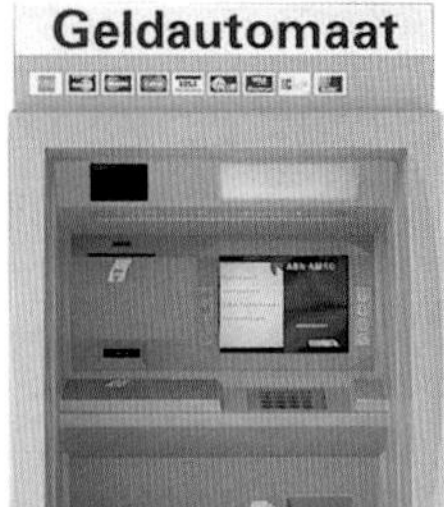

ATMs can be found outside post offices, banks and GWK offices

Bank Opening Hours

Banks are generally open on Mondays to Fridays from 9am to 4 or 5pm. Some banks remain open longer on *koopavond*, or shopping evening, often a Thursday.

These bureaux can still be found at the now unguarded border crossing points, at Amsterdam Schiphol Airport and at major railway stations. Most GWK bureaux are open daily and have extended opening hours.

GWK *(grenswisselkantoor)*, the Netherlands' official exchange bureau

Changing Money

Foreign currency can be changed at banks, post offices and American Express offices. A small commission is sometimes charged on these transactions.

In small bureaux de change (often open outside business hours), located throughout the major cities and in larger towns, you can exchange money from non-Eurozone countries, though often at unfavourable rates.

The Netherland's official bureaux de change, GWK *(grenswisselkantoor)*, is a privatized state enterprise, which gives reasonable rates of exchange and charges relatively low commissions, as well as providing various other services for travellers.

Bank and Credit Cards

You can use your bank card to withdraw money at any Dutch bank displaying your card's logo, but usually there is a substantial commission charge. You can also use bank cards to withdraw cash at ATMs 24 hours a day. These machines usually also accept Eurocard/MasterCard, American Express, Diners Club and Visa cards. When a foreign card is inserted, most ATMs will offer a choice of languages, and so should be simple to use. ATMs are plentiful and can be found outside post offices, banks and GWK offices, and within main railway stations. Shops, restaurants and hotels post signs stating whether you can pay by credit card, switch card or chipknip/chipper (top-up cards available from Dutch banks or the Postbank). Most payphones *(see pp440–41)* accept credit cards for calls.

All major credit cards are widely accepted in the Netherlands and, as elsewhere in Europe, have superseded many cash transactions, even though the Dutch have proved to be a little reluctant to abandon cash as compared to, for example, the British. Almost all hotels and hostels gladly accept credit card payments, but the position is more varied in restaurants. Clarify the situation before the bill arrives. It is normal to pay cash in bars and taxi drivers would also not want to receive credit card payments. One advantage of using a credit card is that if a purchase is contested, the credit card company will usually take up the matter on your behalf. Depending on the credit card, there are generally some attached insurances as well.

The History of Dutch Currency

Before the introduction of the guilder, the Dutch national currency unit before the euro, duiten, stuivers, rijders, schellings and ducats made out of various metals were used. Until 1847 there was a double standard where the value of the coin was equal to the value of the gold or silver in it. Silver coins were minted until 1967, when nickel or bronze coins were minted. Gold and silver coins from earlier centuries are now valuable collector's items.

The Euro

The euro (€) is the common currency of the European Union (EU). It went into general circulation on 1 January 2002, initially for 12 participating countries. The Netherlands was one of those 12 countries. EU members using the euro as sole official currency are known as the Eurozone. Several EU members have opted out of joining this common currency. Euro notes are identical throughout the Eurozone countries, each including designs of architectural structures and monuments. The coins, however, have one side identical (the value side) and one side with an image unique to each country. Both notes and coins are exchangeable in each of the participating euro countries.

Bank Notes

Euro bank notes have seven denominations. The €5 note (grey in colour) is the smallest, followed by the €10 note (pink), €20 note (blue), €50 note (orange), €100 note (green), €200 note (yellow) and €500 note (purple). All notes show the 12 stars of the European Union. Not all businesses in the Netherlands accept the €200 and €500 notes.

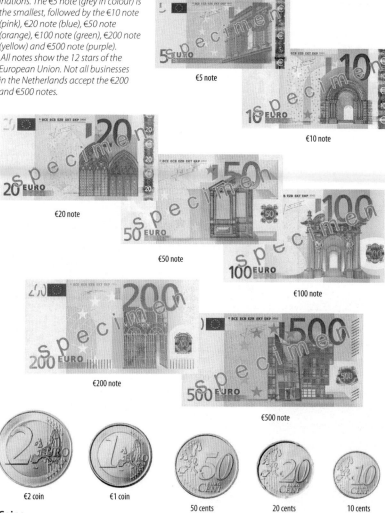

€5 note

€10 note

€20 note

€50 note

€100 note

€200 note

€500 note

€2 coin

€1 coin

50 cents

20 cents

10 cents

Coins

The euro has eight coin denominations: €2 and €1; 50 cents, 20 cents, 10 cents, 5 cents, 2 cents and 1 cent. The €2 and €1 coins are silver and gold in colour; cent coins are gold or bronze. Prices are rounded off to the nearest 5 cents; the 2- and 1-cent coins are no longer in use.

5 cents

2 cents

1 cent

Communications

Before 1989, telephone and postal services in the Netherlands were part of the same state-run company, PTT. This has now been separated into two companies – KPN Telecom and TNT Post. For some years, Telfort public telephones have also been appearing beside the KPN boxes. The Telfort telephones are mostly found at train stations.

Using the Telephone

You will find the green KPN telephone kiosks in the streets, in post offices and outside many railway stations. Most KPN telephone kiosks take both phonecards and most major credit cards (the logo on the telephone will tell you which credit cards are accepted). If you use a credit card, you need to remove it from the slot before speaking (phonecards are only removed when you have finished your call), and you have to pay a surcharge of €1.15. In KPN booths, locals can also use their bank or giro card to make phone calls, if these are fitted with a "chipper" or "chipknip" (which means you can top them up). ANWB members can also use KPN telephone kiosks to call the roadside assistance patrol *(see p445)*.

There are no longer any solely coin-operated payphones. KPN phone boxes accept only KPN phone- cards or special kiosk-cards, available at some train stations. KPN phonecards can be purchased at post offices, tobacconists, train stations and department stores, as well as at the GWK, and come in various denominations.

At train stations you will often find Telfort phone boxes, painted blue and orange. These accept Telfort phonecards, available at ticket windows and in the Wizzl station shops and also at the GWK. Telfort phones also accept coins (10, 20 and 50 cent, €1 and €2) but do not give change, credit cards (with a€1.15 surcharge) and special kiosk-cards.

Instructions on how to use KPN and Telfort telephones can be found in the booths in Dutch, English and other west European languages.

Storefront of an Amsterdam telephone shop

Mobile Phones

Mobile network coverage in the Netherlands is excellent and works on the 900/1800 MHz band. If necessary, contact your service provider for further information. Check your insurance policy to see if you are covered in case your phone gets stolen, and keep your network operator's helpline number handy.

To use your mobile phone abroad, you may need to enable the "roaming" function on it. It is also more expensive to make and receive calls while abroad, despite efforts to decrease roaming charges. A cheaper option is often to purchase a local SIM card to use in your phone. You can only do this if your handset is "sim free" or unlocked. KPN Hotspots gives Internet access for smart phones; send an SMS to: HOTSPOTS, number 4222 and you can log on for 15 minutes for a small fee, which is charged to your phone.

Finding the Right Number

- Directory enquiries for phone and fax numbers in Holland dial 0900-8008 or 118 (only one number per call on either service).
- Directory enquiries for phone and fax numbers abroad dial 0900-8418, or visit www.detelefoon gids.nl.
- National or international calls through the operator dial 0800-0410.
- Collect calls in Holland or abroad dial 0800-0101.
- National dialling codes are: Australia 61, New Zealand 64, South Africa 27, the United Kingdom 44, and the USA and Canada 1.

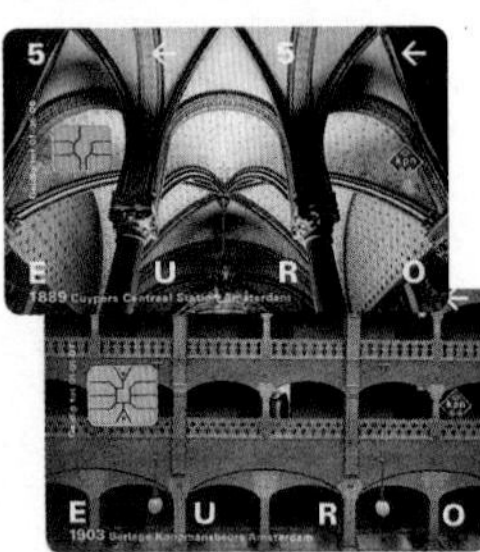

Colourful selection of Dutch pictorial phonecards

Phoning Abroad

From the Netherlands you can direct-dial almost all destinations abroad. First you need to dial the international number 00, followed by the country number, and then the local number without the first digit (usually a 0), and finally the individual number. Many country codes are listed in telephone booths. Telephone directories have more detailed lists. Directories for the whole of the country are available. Calls made from hotel rooms are usually expensive.

Internet access at OBA (Amsterdam Public Library)

Internet

Faster than a letter and cheaper than a phone call, sending and receiving email has never been easier or more convenient. As most people in the Netherlands have either ADSL or a cable connection at home, the number of Internet cafés has decreased. Also, more and more hotels offer Wi-Fi for guests with laptops, though this is not always free, so check before you run up a hefty bill.

However, in most tourist areas you'll still find plenty of places to read and send email. Most are bars, cafés and coffee (smoking) shops, offering PCs with Internet services. Opening hours vary, but cafés are often open late into the night. Not all offer headsets, so using Skype or other VoIPs to make cheap phone calls is not always possible. The website www.easy internetcafe.com has up- to-date addresses of Internet cafés worldwide, plus useful reviews from customers.

A recent development are modern and trendy coffee bar franchises, like Coffee Company and Bagel and Beans, offering Wi-Fi for customers who bring their laptop. You either buy minutes or go online for a limited time for each beverage you order, using the code on your receipt to gain access.

Visitors to Amsterdam will find www.iamsterdam.com worth a look. Financed by Amsterdam city council, it offers listings and reviews in English about cultural events in the city, plus useful information on things like doctors and dentists. It also has information for expats living in the city. *Time Out Amsterdam* is a monthly listings magazine, also in English, aimed at tourists and available from newsagents in the city centre of the capital. Apart from comprehensive listings about what's on, it also offers reviews and features.

Postal Services

Post offices in the Netherlands can be recognized by the TNT logo. In addition to buying stamps, sending telegrams and sending mail, you can also change money and traveller's cheques, make phone calls and send faxes. Larger post offices also have photocopy services and sell stationery. Smaller municipalities sometimes have only a sub post office (in a supermarket, for example) providing only basic services. There are no longer post offices in most villages.

TNT has closed many of the larger post offices and opened many smaller concerns inside shopping malls and shops.

Dutch TNT postbox

Sending Mail

Most TNT postboxes have two slots. The right slot is for local mail (post codes are given above the slot), the left one is for other destinations. A sign on the box indicates when the mail is collected (a red sign means 5pm or 6pm, a blue board means 7pm). There is no Saturday mail collection.

Postcards and letters weighing less than 20 g (1 oz) cost €0.44 (or one "Nederland 1" stamp) to send to destinations within the Netherlands; those sent to European destinations cost €0.77, or one "Europe 1" stamp; these new "standard" stamps are widely available in small shops, for example those selling postcards. For heavier letters or to post to other parts of the world, visit a post office – but be prepared for queues. Most post offices are open from 9am to 5pm weekdays; some also open on Saturdays until 1pm. Postcards and letters weighing less than 20 g (1 oz) to destinations within Europe are sent by priority mail. For other international mail which you want to send priority, pay extra for a priority sticker at the post office. Important documents may be sent by insured or registered mail. Urgent mail can be sent by TNT's courier service.

DIRECTORY

TNT
Tel 0800-1234 (customer service for domestic and international deliveries).
W tnt.com/express/nl_nl/site/home.html

TNT Post Klantenservice
(Customer service)
Postbus 99180,
8900 NA Leeuwarden.
Tel 058-2333333 (for information on postcodes and complaints).
Open 8am–8pm Mon–Fri, 9am–4pm Sat.
W tnt.com/express/nl_nl/site/home.html

TRAVEL INFORMATION

Almost every major European airport has direct flights to Schiphol, but this modern international airport southwest of Amsterdam also has direct connections with other airports around the world, including many in the United States. The Netherlands also has efficient rail links with neighbouring countries. Major stations are served by international trains, including the Thalys, the high-speed train from Paris. The country's comprehensive road network makes the Netherlands ideal for exploring by car or by public transport *(see pp446–7)*. Many packages and special-interest holidays are on offer, so it's worth shopping around.

Car-hire counter at Schiphol

By Air

Schiphol airport handles some 175,000 flights a year by many international carriers. To increase this volume further, there are serious plans to expand the airport. KLM (Royal Dutch Airlines) and its airline partners have flights to Amsterdam from over 350 cities worldwide. Northwest Airlines offers non-stop flights from Boston, Detroit and Washington, Delta Air Lines from Atlanta and New York (JFK) and United Airlines from Newark. There are many flights a day from the UK and the Irish Republic. Low-cost airline easyJet serves Amsterdam from London, Luton and several other British cities. To get the lowest fare, generally you must book well in advance.

Schiphol Airport

Schiphol has only one terminal. The airport signs are colour-coded, with yellow signs indicating transfer desks and gates, green ones amenities such as coffee bars, restaurants and shops. At Schiphol Plaza you can find shops, book hotels, hire a car or buy a railway ticket. Beneath it are the platforms of Schiphol railway station. From the car park there are transfer buses to take you to the terminal. The long-stay car park is served by an automatic bus, the Parking Hopper, that takes you to the transfer bus.

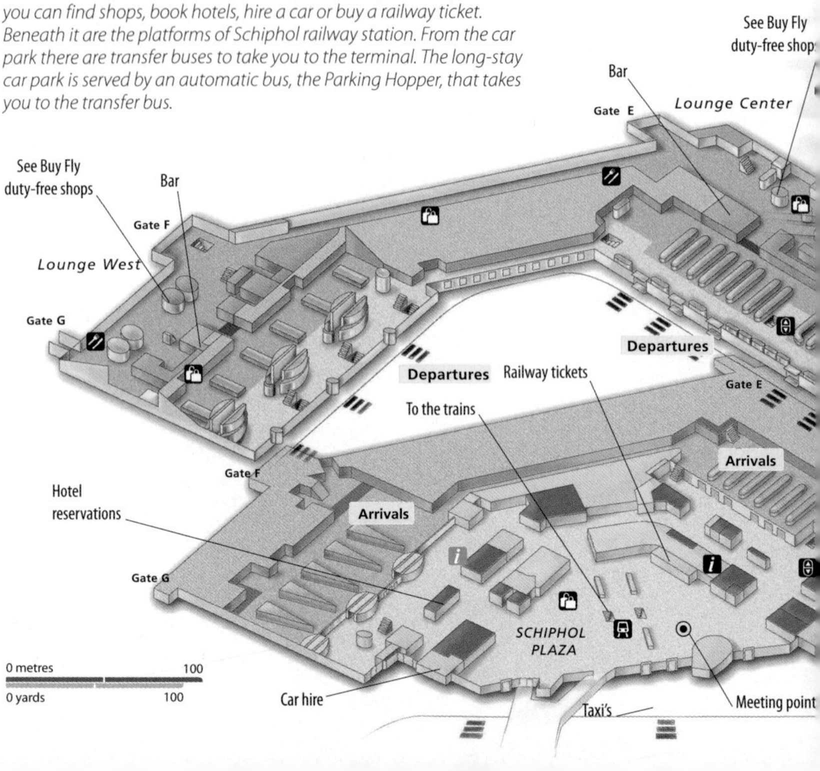

See Buy Fly duty-free shops
Bar
Gate E
Lounge Center
See Buy Fly duty-free shops
Bar
Gate F
Lounge West
Gate G
Departures
Departures
Railway tickets
Gate E
To the trains
Arrivals
Gate F
Hotel reservations
Arrivals
Gate G
SCHIPHOL PLAZA
Car hire
Taxi's
Meeting point
0 metres 100
0 yards 100

Planes at Amsterdam Schiphol Airport

Shopping

If you are leaving the country by plane, you will find the large See Buy Fly shopping centre when you leave customs control. Although travellers to other EU member states are not permitted to buy duty-free goods at the airport *(see p434)*, it is still possible to find some bargains with the low See Buy Fly prices; only alcohol and tobacco is sold here at the same price as in local shops. Passengers to destinations outside the EU can still purchase duty-free alcohol and tobacco. The centrally located Schiphol Plaza is open to everyone, but the goods stocked here are not sold at See Buy Fly prices.

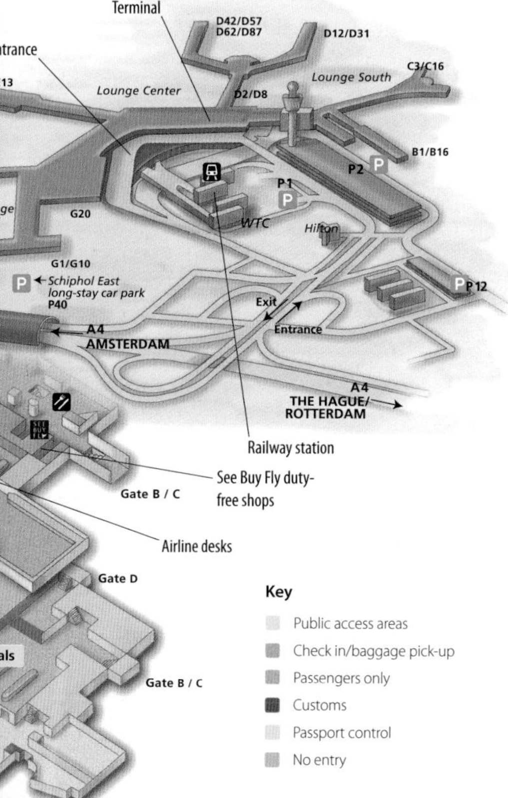

Getting to and from Schiphol

Every major city in the Netherlands can be reached by train from Schiphol Station. The journey to Amsterdam Centraal Station takes 20 minutes. Schiphol is also on the night-train network of the Western Netherlands *(see p446)*. In addition, the airport has good bus connections with many towns. KLM runs a bus service (the KLM Hotel Shuttle), linking the airport with some 20 hotels in central and south Amsterdam. There are also abundant taxis waiting at the airport. Ask for a quote before getting in as tourists are often overcharged.

Watch shop at Schiphol

Regional Airports

Eindhoven, Maastricht, Rotterdam and Groningen are all served by domestic flights, with flights between Eindhoven and Schiphol, Maastricht and Schiphol, Groningen and Rotterdam and Eindhoven and Rotterdam. There are direct international flights between Rotterdam and Eindhoven and Manchester and London, and between Maastricht and Munich, Berlin and London.

Information screens at Schiphol

By Rail

The Netherlands can easily be reached by train from most European countries, although visitors from further afield may have to change trains several times en route. Eurostar runs from London via the Channel Tunnel to Brussels, where you change for Amsterdam.

There are direct trains from a number of European stations. For example, Brussels, Paris, Berlin, Zurich, Vienna and (seasonally) Milan have direct rail links to Amsterdam Centraal Station (CS) and Utrecht CS. From Brussels and from Antwerp there are trains to Amsterdam all day, stopping at Roosendaal, Rotterdam, The Hague and Schiphol, including five journeys daily by the Thalys high-speed train from Paris.

Many other towns, particularly those in the border regions of Belgium and the Netherlands, can easily be reached by train. Hook of Holland is connected by trains which connect with ferries from the UK port of Harwich.

Special Tickets

Tourists from other EU countries can purchase cards in their countries that will entitle them to special reductions. An Interrail card for people aged 26 and under, along with a slightly dearer version for the over-26s, allows travellers to use the entire European rail network at a discount. Eurail Selectpass offers unlimited travel on the national rail networks of any three to five bordering countries out of 18 European nations, including the Netherlands.

The Thalys high-speed train

Ferries serve Rotterdam, Hook of Holland and IJmuiden

By Coach

For travellers from many European countries the cheapest way to reach the Netherlands is by coach. Most long-distance coaches have toilets and make regular stops. In summer in particular there are large numbers of coaches from other countries serving a whole range of towns in the Netherlands. **Eurolines** offers a very extensive network of coach connections. It has coaches running from many European cities to the Netherlands at least once per week. Dozens of points in the Netherlands (depending on the point of departure and route) are served by them. From Brussels and Antwerp there are coaches to places such as Breda, Rotterdam, The Hague, Utrecht and Amsterdam.

A Eurolines coach

Ferries

A number of ferry companies serve routes between Britain and the Netherlands. These include **P&O Ferries** that sail between Hull and Rotterdam/Europoort, while **Stena Line** sails between Harwich and Hook of Holland. **DFDS Seaways** serves Newcastle and IJmuiden. Other convenient ferry ports for visitors from Great Britain are Calais and Boulogne (from Folkestone and Dover) in France. Crossing times by ferry range from 16 hours (Newcastle–IJmuiden) to 75–90 minutes (Dover–Calais). Ticket prices depend on the speed of crossing. In summer it is a good idea to book in advance.

Motoring in Holland

The good system of roads in the Netherlands makes all parts of the country easy to reach by car. Beware, however, in the Randstad region: you may have to put up with traffic jams during the rush hour.

To drive in the Netherlands you need to have a valid national driving licence. In addition, if in your own car, you will need to have your vehicle log book and insurance papers with you.

Roads in the Netherlands are divided into three categories. Provincial roads are designated with the letter "N" before the road number, national motorways are designated with an "A" before the number and international highways have the letter "E" before the number. All Dutch motorways are equipped with emergency telephones from which motorists can call the **ANWB** road assistance service *(see p436)* if their car breaks down. A non-member can pay for the ANWB's services, or become a temporary ANWB member. Unless otherwise signposted, the maximum speed for cars in Holland is 120 km/h (75 mph) on motorways, 100 km/h (62 mph) on major roads, 80 km/h (50 mph) on secondary roads and 50 km/h (30 mph) in built-up areas. At unmarked junctions, give way to traffic coming from the left, except for trams, which always have right of way (except when you are driving along a road which has right of way). In built-up areas motorists must give way to buses that are leaving bus stops.

Finding somewhere to park is often a problem in the cities. As clamping is prevalent and theft rife, it is often best to look for a car park rather than to try to find street parking. When you enter a car park, take a ticket from the machine at the barrier, and pay at the payment machine before leaving. Avoid out of order street meters as you could get fined or your car clamped. You may not park on yellow lines, and on yellow broken lines you may not park even to load or unload. If you stop on a blue line, you will need to have a parking disc.

Emergency phone

Car Hire

To hire a car you need to be at least 21 years old and have a valid driving licence. Some hire companies also require at least one year's driving experience. The main international car-hire companies such as Avis, Budget, Europcar and Hertz have offices at Schiphol and in all major cities. Local car-hire firms are often substantially cheaper. When hiring a car without a credit card, you may have to pay a hefty deposit.

One way of taking your bike along is to hook it on your car

DIRECTORY

Schiphol Airport

Information and services
Tel 0900-0141
W **schiphol.nl**

Regional Airports

Eindhoven Airport
Tel 0900-9505.

Groningen Airport Eelde
Tel 050-3080850

Maastricht Aachen Airport
Tel 043-3589999/ 3589898.

Rotterdam Airport
Tel 010-4463444/ 4463454.

Airlines

Aer Lingus
Tel 020-5174747.
Tel 0818-365000 (Eire).
W **aerlingus.com**

British Airways
Tel 020-3469559.
Tel 0870-8509850 (UK).
W **ba.com**

Delta Air Lines
Tel 1-800-2414141 (US).
W **delta-air.com**

easyJet
Tel 0870-6000000 (UK).
Tel 0900-2658021 (NL).
W **easyjet.com**

KLM & KLM Cityhopper
Tel 020-4747747.
Tel 0870-5074074 (UK).
W **klm.nl**

Northwest Airlines
Tel 1-800-2252525 (US).
W **nwa.com**

Transavia
Tel 020-73654997 (UK).
W **transavia.com**

United Airlines
Tel 1-800-5382929 (US).
W **united.com**

Railways

Public transport travel information
Tel 0900-9292.
W **ov9292.nl**

International public transport information
Tel 0900-9296 (Netherlands).

In the UK:
European Rail Ltd.
Tel 020-73870444.
W **europeanrail.com**

Bus Companies

Eurolines Nederland
Amstelbusstation
Julianaplein 5, 1097 DN Amsterdam.
Tel 020-5608788.
W **eurolines.nl**

Rokin 10, 1012 KR Amsterdam.
Tel 020-4217951.

Eurolines (UK)
Tel 08717-818178 (UK).
W **national express.co.uk**

Ferries

DFDS Seaways
Tel 0870-2520524.
W **dfdsseaways.co.uk**

P&O North Sea Ferries
Tel 0870-5980333.
W **poferries.com**

Stena Line
Tel 0900-8123/ 0174-315800.
Tel 08705-707070 (UK).
W **stenaline.co.uk**

By Car

ANWB
Tel 0800-0503 (Head office).

Car Hire Firms at Schiphol

AVIS
Tel 020-6556050.

Budget Rent a Car
Tel 020-6041349.

Europcar
Tel 020-3164190.

Hertz
Tel 020-5020240.

Public Transport

The Netherlands has a comprehensive and efficient public transport system. Major cities can be easily reached by train, while towns and villages are served by local buses as well as a number of trains. The Randstad in particular gets fairly snarled up in the morning and evening rush hour. If you need to travel at that time, the best thing to do is to leave the car and take the train.

Long-distance buses cover an expanding number of routes

By Bus

The Netherlands has a good network of local buses and inter-city coaches. Booklets are available giving detailed information on routes, timetables and fares, although it is also possible to get information from **Openbaar Vervoer Reisinformatie** (0900-9292).

Operated by a number of companies, long distance buses are very comfortable. They usually follow direct routes between places and stop less frequently than local buses *(streekbussen)*. In the evenings they do not operate as late as the local buses. The timetables for buses are based on the railway timetable. Long-distance buses are green and have an information display.

By Tram

There are trams in Amsterdam, Rotterdam, Utrecht and The Hague. They generally run from 6am to midnight. On Sundays they start one or one-and-a-half hours later. Tram stops display the name of the stop, the tram numbers that stop there and show the other stops on the route. Tram shelters display maps of the tram network.

You can board or alight from any door, unless there is a conductor on the tram, when the rear door is for boarding only. Tram stops are normally announced, but if you aren't sure where to get off, you can always ask the driver to call out the stop.

By Train

The Dutch national railway company, Nederlandse Spoorwegen, or simply NS, runs a busy network which is considered one of the best in the world. Trains are clean and generally run on time, and tickets are reasonably priced. Timetables are displayed on yellow boards in stations. Rail tickets are available at ticket offices, Wizzl station shops and from ticket machines in stations, or, with a substantial supplement, from the conductor aboard the train. Dutch Railways has a wide variety of fare discounts on offer, including *Railrunner* tickets for children, and other offers for people regularly using the same route. Combined season tickets for the train and local or urban transport are also available. For information it is best to ask at ticket offices, or telephone 0900-9292.

Many railways in Friesland, Groningen and the Achterhoek are run by NordNed and Syntus. NS cards are also valid on these lines. Night trains run on the Utrecht CS-Amsterdam CS-Schiphol-Leiden Centraal-The Hague CS-Delft-Rotterdam CS lines.

Dieren–Apeldoorn steam train

Steam Trains

There are many places in the Netherlands where you can take a ride in a steam train. There is, for example, the 22-km (14-mile) Dieren–Apeldoorn line, the 16-km (10-mile) Kerkrade–Schin op Geul, (the "million line", *see p372*), the 15.5-km (9.5-mile) Goes–Oudelande, around the Valkenburgse Meer lake and through the Hoogoventerrein at IJmuiden (21 km/13 miles, departing from Beverwijk Station, *see p192*). A steam train runs the 20 km (12 miles) between Hoorn and Medemblik in summer *(see p182)*. Check with the VVV, as schedules vary.

An NS double-decker train speeding past tulip fields

Metro

Amsterdam and Rotterdam are the only towns in the Netherlands with a metro. Both networks are fairly extensive. Amsterdam's metro has three lines, two of which begin at the Centraal Station, and the third at Station Sloterdijk. They go as far as Gaasperplas and Gein. From Centraal Station there is also a suburban tram to Amstelveen. The Rotterdam metro system comprises two lines which cross one another, the north south line going from Centraal Station to Spijkenisse, and the west-east line from Marconiplein to Capelle, with a branch to Ommoord-Zevenkamp. The first metro leaves the terminus at around 6am (around 7:45am on Sundays), and the last train arrives at its destination at approximately 0:15 or 0:30am.

ov-chipkaart

Always swipe your *OV-chipkaart* to validate your journey

Tram, Bus, Metro and Train Tickets

To travel on buses, trams and metro systems throughout the Netherlands you must have an *OV-chipkaart*: a "smartcard" that works much like a pay-as-you-go phone card, deducting the cost of each trip from the available credit. OV Chipkarts are also available for train journeys. The ticketing system works via the OV Chipkaart (www.wov-chipkaart.nl). They are of two types: paper and plastic. Paper OV-chipkaarts are best used for shorter durations of travel. These can be purchased from most tram and bus drivers, many VVVs and a few hotels. They need to be checked against an electronic reader when you enter and leave the public transport system. For longer stays, purchasing a rechargeable, plastic OV-Chipkaart is advisable. It comes in two main types, personalized and anonymous and both cost €7.50. Valid for five years, these are sold at train and bus stations. Also, please note that the plastic (but not paper) OV-Chipkaart can also be used on theNS train network. In order to validate a journey, users need to hold the *OV-chipkaart* in front of the grey card reader at metro or platform gates and on boarding a bus or tram; remember to swipe again on disembarking, or you will be charged the full fare to the terminus. Children under 4 travel free; seniors and 4–11-year-olds can claim a discount if they buy their cards in advance.

A *treintaxi*

Taxis

If you need a taxi, the best thing is to either go to a taxi-stand or phone a Taxicentrale: numbers can be found in the phone directory and in the Yellow Pages. It is less common to hail a taxi in the street, although it can be done. Taxis are metered and after an initial charge, the fare depends on the distance travelled and the time. Taxis cost more at night.

Rail Taxis

Around 100 Dutch railway stations operate a rail taxi, or *treintaxi*, service which enables you to travel cheaply to a destination in the same or nearby district. A ticket costs €3.80 at the station or €4.80 from the driver and is valid whatever the length of the journey. The taxi will also take other passengers to their destinations, and so will usually take a roundabout route.

Rail taxis operate from 7am (8am on Sundays and public holidays) until just after the arrival of the last train. You can book by phoning 0900-TREINTAXI/8734682. At the station, book by pressing the button on the blue-yellow column. Information on places covered by the service is given in the NS leaflet *Treintaxi-stations op een rijtje*.

Special Outings

The Canal Bus is an excellent way to get around Amsterdam's waterways. They operate on three circular routes: the green route, the red route and the blue route, which meet at various points, which include the jetty outside Centraal Station and on the Singelgracht between the Rijksmuseum and Leidseplein. There are 17 stops in all and together they provide easy access to most major sights. During high season, boats leave from opposite Centraal Station every half an hour between 9:30am and 6pm. A day ticket for all three routes, which costs €18 per adult, and €9 for children (between 4–12 years), allows you to hop on and off as many times as you like. Another reasonable offer is the 24-hour ticket, which costs just €2 more.

The Canal Bus in Amsterdam

Cycling

The flat landscape of the Netherlands makes it a boon for cyclists. At least 85 per cent of the population has a bicycle. However, there is no shortage of maps and guidebooks with interesting cycling routes. You can use the LF-routes *(see p449)* to plan your own daytrip or cycling holiday. Another possibility is to take part in an organized cycle tour, where you are awarded a souvenir medal at the end.

Guides showing cycling routes

Road Safety

The large number of cycle paths and cycle lanes, often equipped with traffic lights for cyclists, make cycling in the Netherlands a safe and enjoyable activity. However, it's worth keeping a look-out for mopeds, which frequently make use of cycle paths. Cycling in the peaceful countryside and cycling in the busy city are two quite separate experiences. In Amsterdam particularly, the traffic is fairly chaotic – mostly because of the large number of cyclists, who tend to ignore the traffic regulations. If you are unaccustomed to this, it's worth taking extra care. Front and rear lights, a rear reflector and reflective strips or reflective circles are compulsory at night. Many cyclists ride without this equipment, often leaving them almost invisible.

Cycle Hire

There are plenty of cycle hire shops in the Netherlands. You can either go to private cycle hire places or hire a bike from some 100 railway stations with a *Rijwielshop* or *Fietspoint*. Cycle hire usually costs around €7.50 per day. Cycle hire shops also offer weekly tariffs that work out relatively cheaper. Many of them require a deposit, which can range from €30 to €145, and often want proof of identity. Tandems are also sometimes available, though they cost more, and their lack of manoeuvrability does not make them very suitable for use in city traffic.

Sign for the Rijwiel cycle hire shop, found at nearly 100 railway stations

If you are planning to make a train journey and hire a cycle from your destination, it is worth buying a *huurfietskaartje* (cycle hire ticket) when setting out. It is a good idea to reserve the bicycle by telephone in advance. The NS publishes a special pamphlet, *Fiets en Trein*, which lists stations where you can hire bicycles. The VVV and ANWB can also direct you to cycle hire shops.

An organized cycling tour on the Zaanse Schans

Security

Even if your bicycle is equipped with a rear-wheel lock, it's a good idea – particularly in the big cities – to secure your bicycle to a post or a bicycle rack by the front wheel. Cycle hire shops will often provide you with a lock for the bike, especially in cities where bicycle theft is a problem. At many railway stations you can leave your bicycle in a secure bicycle-park for around €1.00. Do not leave any luggage on your bicycle if you park it somewhere, not even in a guarded bicycle park.

Bicycles and Public Transport

For an additional payment you can take your bicycle on the train, except during rush hours (Sep–Jun: 6:30–9am and 4:30–6pm Mon–Fri). To do this, you need to buy a *Dagkaart fiets* (bike ticket) from a train or metro station in addition to your ordinary train ticket. These tickets cost €6.00 and are valid for the whole day regardless of the length of your journey. Places for bicycles on trains are marked with stickers on the carriage. Folding cycles, when folded, may be taken on trains free of charge. Bicycles may be taken on metros and suburban (fast) trams, provided that you have a bike ticket, but they are not allowed on buses and city trams.

Cycling Tours

If you want to get from point A to point B by the quickest possible route, just follow the white-and-red ANWB cycle route signposts. Maps and guides for cyclists describing routes of various lengths are available from the VVV, the ANWB and many bookstores. They often contain a variety of local background information, as well as the addresses of cycle hire shops and places to stay, such as *pensions*, camping sites and hiking huts *(see also p395)*. Useful examples are the regional *ANWB/VVV Toeristenkaarten*, which suggest some particularly enjoyable routes, and the *Dwarsstap-fiets-mappen,* which give descriptions of cycle routes, often in the area surrounding big cities, and also contain topographical maps. The regional *ANWB/VVV-fietsgidcn* have maps and provide descriptions of hundreds of enjoyable cycling trips of around 25 km (15 miles), from the *Amelandroute* to the *Maasdalroute* in Limburg. Many of these routes are marked with hexagonal signs. Around 45 railway-based routes are also offered under the name *NS-Fietstocht*. Maps of the route are on sale at the relevant railway stations. NS publishes a booklet, entitled *Er op Uit!,* describing these routes. Long-distance tours of at least 200 km (125 miles) in length (for example, the 230-km/ 143-mile *Elfstedenroute* in Friesland) are described in guides such as the *ANWB/VVV Lange Fiestronde*. These routes are also signposted. Another organization, the **Stichting Landelijk Fiets- platform**, or national cycling association *(see p437)*, has a network of some 6,000 km (3,730 miles) of numbered National Cycle Routes (*Landelijke Fiestroutes*, or *"LF"*). These often follow quiet byroads and cycle tracks and are described in two of the *LF-basisgidsen*. Some are marked with square signs, such as LF-15, which is the *Boerenlandroute* (farmland route) from Alkmaar to Enschede. Guides to individual routes are also available. The *Fietsideeënkaart*, a map available from the VVV and ANWB, also provides brief descriptions of LF and other marked cycling routes around the country. To take part in an organized cycle tour, contact organizations such as **Cycletours** or the **Fiets-vakantiewinkel** *(see p429)*, some of the main VVV offices and the ANWB (members only). These organizations can arrange cycle tour packages, including accommodation and luggage transfer. For information on cycling in nature reserve areas, see page 429.

Cycle lane sign

Cyclists on tour stopping to enjoy an ice cream

The ferry at Wijk near Duurstede, which carries bicycles

Cycling Events

Meimaand Fietsmaand is the year's biggest bicycle event: a whole month (May) packed with bicycle rides, meets and races throughout the Netherlands. In 2010, about 570,000 cyclists participated. Information on the various routes and events can be found at the national cycling association's website: www.fietsplatform.nl. Local cycle touring clubs organize regular non-competitive tours through picturesque or interesting areas, although you have to pay a fee to join. For further information, apply at the Dutch cycle tour society (Nederlandse Toer Fiets Unie, or **NFTU**, *see p429*). In addition, dozens of local tours lasting several days are organized locally, such as the *Drentse Rijwielvierdaagse* in July. Participants can often choose between routes of lengths varying from 25 to 100 km (15 to 60 miles) per day. You will find an over-view of these in the NFTU pamphlet *Fiestmeerdaagsen*, available from the VVV.

General Index

Page numbers in **bold** refer to main entries

A

B

G

H

M

N

T

Y

Z

Acknowledgments

Dorling Kindersley would like to thank the following people for their help in preparing this guide:

For Dorling Kindersley

Translation from Dutch Mark Cole (Linguists for Business)
Design and Editorial Assistance Jo Cowen, Jacky Jackson, Ian Midson, Conrad van Dyk, Stewart Wild
Dtp Designers Jason Little, Conrad van Dyk
Managing Editor Helen Townsend
Publishing Manager Jane Ewart

For International Book Productions

Proofreader Maraya Radhua

Main Author

Gerard ML Harmans graduated in biology and philosophy at the Vrije Universiteit (Amsterdam), and then chose to work in publishing. He edited an encyclopaedia for Het Spectrum before setting up an independent business with Paul Krijnen in 1989 called de Redactie, boekverzorgers.

Other Contributors

All contributors were selected from de Redactie, boekverzorgers in Amsterdam. The team of authors, translators and editors share a broad field of expertise. Every member of the team made an invaluable contribution.

Anneliet Bannier graduated in translation studies from Amsterdam University. She works as a translator and sub-editor on travel guides. She lives in Zaanstreek.

Hanneke Bos is an editor and translator in the fields of linguistics, cultural history and travel literature.

Jaap Deinema, from Eindhoven, is an expert in the field of the Netherlands. He has made numerous contributions to travel guides. He was responsible for the ATO/VVV edition Infopocket Amsterdam.

Jérôme Gommers, born in Paris, is a freelance author and lover of the Dutch landscape and its poetry. Among other things, he has conducted a comprehensive study of the construction and development of the Noordoostpolder.

Ron de Heer studied philosophy in Amsterdam. For ten years he has been working as a translator/editor, primarily of travel guides, novels and culinary publications.

Marten van de Kraats writes and translates texts in the fields of travel and automation. Every year he edits the Dutch edition of the Rough Guide Travels on the internet, the best-selling internet book on Holland and Belgium.

Paul Krijnen is a social geographer who has specialized in medieval mark organizations of the Netherlands, such as the Erfgooiers. His great passion is the Dutch borderlands.

Frans Reusink studied Dutch language. After working as a copywriter, he has been active as a photographer, written travel reports for magazines, and edited travel guides.

Theo Scholten is a Dutch scholar. He has worked on many literary publications but is currently active in non-fiction as an editor and translator. He has made previous contributions to travel guides on Belgium and France.

Ernst Schreuder, a Frisian editor, won the Elfsteden Cross for completing the Tocht der Tochten in 1986 and 1997. Travel and travel guides are his occupation and his hobby.

Catherine Smit studied Dutch language and letters at Utrecht and has contributed as editor and translator to many books, including travel guides.

Jacqueline Toscani graduated in European Studies from Amsterdam University. Since 1992 she has been working as an editor and translator of travel guides, including many titles from the Capitool and Marco Polo series. In the latest series she was co-author of the Vakantieplanner (holiday planner).

Willemien Werkman is a historian and, after studying the history of the Vecht estates, has devoted herself to translation and editing.

Additional Contributors

Paul Andrews, Hedda Archbold, Christopher Catling, Jaap Deinema, Marlene Edmunds, Adam Hopkins, Marten van de Kraats, David Lindsey, Fred Mawer, Alison Melvin, Robin Pascoe, Catherine Stebbings, Richard Widdows, Stewart Wild. Other contributions were taken from the Eyewitness Travel Guide Amsterdam by Robin Pascoe and Christopher Catling, which previously appeared in a translated and revised edition (Capitool Reisgids Amsterdam) published by de Redactie, boekverzorgers.

Additional Illustrations

Peter de Vries, Mark Jurriëns, Hilbert Bolland, Gieb van Enckevort, Armand Haye and Stuart Commercial Artists: Jan Egas and Khoobie Verwer.

Additional Photography

Max Alexander, Ian O'Leary, John Whittaker.

Editorial and Design Assistance

Louise Abbot, Willem de Blaauw, Frank Bontekoning, Lucinda Cooke, Emer FitzGerald, Willem Gerritze, Martine Hauwert, Peter Koomen, Catherine Palmi, Ron Putto, Sadie Smith, Susana Smith, Inge Tijsmans, Sylvia Tombesi-Walton, Pascal Veeger, Erna de Voos, Willeke Vrij, Gerard van Vuuren, Martine Wiedemeijer

Picture Research

Harry Bunk; Corine Koolstra; Dick Polman; de Redactie, boekverzorgers; Rachel Barber; Ellen Root

Revisions Team

Tora Agarwala, Madhura Birdi, Willem de Blaauw, Neha Dhingra, Sander Groen, Sumita Khatwani, Shikha Kulkarni, Phil Lee, Azeem Siddiqui, Ajay Verma, Gerard Van Vuuren

Special Assistance

John Bekker; Wim ten Brinke; Bert Erwich; Niek Harmans; Frits Gommers; Hans Hoogendoorn; Cathelijne Hornstra; Petra van Hulsen; Frank Jacobs; Chris de Jong; Nina Krijnen; Mies Kuiper; Louise Lang; Frank van Lier; Bas de Melker; Miek Reusink; Dick Rog; Joske Siemons; Erika Teeuwisse; Wout Vuyk, Douglas Amrine.

Picture Credits

t = top; tl = top left; tlc = top left centre; tc = top centre; tr = top right; trc = top right centre; c = centre; cl = centre left; cla = centre left above; clb = centre left below; ca = centre above; cr = centre right; cra = centre right above; crb = centre right below; bc = bottom centre; b = bottom; bl = bottom left; br = bottom right.

Every effort has been made to trace the copyright holders. Dorling Kindersley apologizes for any unintentional omissions and would be pleased, in such cases, to add an acknowledgment in future editions.

The publishers are grateful to the following museums, photographers and picture libraries for permission to reproduce their photographs:

4corners images: SIME/ Pavan Aldo 151br; VAN **Abbemuseum, Eindhoven**: © Pablo Picasso Lady in Green, 1909, 1999 c/o Beeldrecht Amstelveen 364tl; **AKG, London**: 68bl, 105tr, 126ca, 221tr; **Alamy Images**: Stephen Barnes/Netherlands 447br; Tibor Bognar 74; Bertrand Collet 405tl; Keith Erskine 150br; f1 online 10bl; GAUTIER Stephane/SAGAPHOTO.CO 72cl; Hemis 86, 294; Peter Horree 306, 423tr; Horizons WWP 14tr; Joana Kruse 16br, 196; frans lemmens 17bc, 246, 260-1, 326, 371; LH Images 125bl;

David Noble 15tr; David Noton Photography 212; Ingolf Pompe 2 152bl; PjrTravel 13tr; Peter Scholey 72clb; Paul M Thompson 368bl.
Algemeen Rijksarchief, The Hague: 61cra; **Amsterdam Tourism & Convention Board:** 111br, 114tl, 432br, 447cl; **Amsterdams Historisch Museum**: 51cra, 51crb, 68-69c, 69bl, 70cla, 96tl, 96cl, 96bc, 97tl, 97crb, 97cr, 97br, 114b, 118bl; AFF/ **Anne Frank foundation, amsterdam**: 112cl, 112b, 113br, 113cr (Miep Gies); **ANP:** 21b, 76tr, 139tl, 63cra; **ANWB audiovisuele dienst**: 27tr, 34clb, 39br, 52bl, 63tl, 142br, 145tr, 167tr, 170bl, 170br, 171b, 172bl, 173bl, 184bl, 189b, 192tl, 192bl, 195tl, 211tc, 211br, 214tr, 224c, 228t, 228br, 234tr, 234bl, 236br, 243tr, 249tr, 253br, 255tr, 255c, 255bc, 256bc, 257tl, 283tr, 293br, 319br, 336tr, 342clb, 357bl, 364tr, 365cra, 365crb, 381br, 382cr, 394cla, 394b, 432cla, 432clb, 434cr, 434bc, 435tr, 436c, 439c; **archeologisch instituut vu/f kortlang, amsterdam**: 46-47c; **The Art Archive**: Museo del Prado Madrid The Surrender of Breda (1635) Diego Velazquez 367br; **Atlas Van Stolk**: 45clb, 51bl, 52br, 56-57c, 57tl, 57cr, 58cl, 59tl. **BADHU:** 410bl; **Balthazar's Keuken:** 407tr; **B&U international picture service**: 105bl, 109br, 167br, 216cla; **aart de bakker**: 353tr, 353br, 374tr, 377tc, 377cra, 380tr, 416cla; **bonnefantenmuseum, maastricht**: 378tr, 378cl, 378bl, © Rene Daniels Platte Gronden, 1986, 1999 c/o Beeldrecht Amstelveen 378br; 379tl, 379cra, 379bl, 379br; **henk brandsen**: 49bc, 310cla, 311tl, 311tr, 311ca; **bridgeman art library**: Christie´s London, Grote Markt, Haarlem; Private collection Self-portrait © Kazimir Malevitch 133br; **Bries Noordwijk:** 411tr; **Quinta Buma**: 38t; **Harry Bunk**: 37cl, 72tr, 142clb, 143bl, 143br, 147tl, 206b, © Ossip Zadkine De verwoeste stad 1947, 1999 c/o Beeldrecht Amstelveen 234cl; 235cra, 235crb, 235bc, 241cr, © Mari Andriessen Cornelius Lely, 1983, 1999 c/o Beeldrecht Amstelveen 330bc, 417bl, 438cl, 440c; **Cees Buys**: 27tl, 51ca, 248bc, 284clb, 287c, 291b, 303c, 308cla, 319cr, 321t, 324tl, 325tr, 325bl, 329tr, 329cr, 343br, 371b, 385cra, 392clb; **George Burggraaff**: 22t, 25bl, 32tr, 36cr, 36bl, 46cl, 170tr, 172tr, 172cla, 193tl, 201ca, 204cla, 220tr, 241tl, 250tr, 250br, 253crb, 258tr, 259tr, 259br, 262cr, 264clb, 265cra, 265br, 282br, 301cr, 305cl, 318cl, 321br, 322ca, 322cl, 323cr, 323br, 329br, 337bl, 340br, 347bl, 347tr, 349br, 357tl, 357tr, 362br, 365ca.
Catharijneconvent, Utrecht: 49cra, 54bl, 56tr, 205cra, 355tl; **Centraal Museum, Utrecht**: Ernst Moritz 206br; 208cla, 208tr, 209tr, 209br; **Cleveland Museum, Cleveland**: 54-55c; **Cobra Museum, Amstelveen**: © Karel Appel Foundation, Karel Appel Questioning Children 1949, 1999 c/o Beeldrecht Amstelveen 193br. **Het Concert Gebouw**: Hans Samson 150cla; **Corbis**: Arcaid/ Alex Bartel 152tr; Dave Bartruff 404cl; Owen Franken 405c; Frans Lemmens 268; Jean-Pierre Lescourret 64-5, 83bl; Koen Van Weel/epa 350-1. **Jan Derwig**: 103tr, 145bl; **Dreamstime.com:** Rob Van Esch 38cr, 358; Patricia Hofmeester 34-5; Peter De Kievith 69cb; Ldambies 164-5; Ber Lybil 2-3; Mauvries 45br; Miv123; Neirfy 430-1; Robertlindeboom 280; Richard Semik 13bl; Pieter Snijder 334; Teo Stuivenberg 210bl; Dennis Van De Water 17tr; **Jurjen Drenth**: 32cla, 34lb, 39bl, 47crb, 57bl, 71tr, 72cla, 72br, 73cra, 73cr, 73tr, 78b, 90tr, 112tr, 122tr, 390br, 403c, © Hildo Krop Berlage, 1999 c/o Beeldrecht Amstelveen 146bl; 148cl, 149cr, 151tr, 164/165, 167 tr, 170cl, 170-171c, 173br, 175b, 177cr, 178bl, 196, 197b, 198clb, 200bl, 201b, 202cl, 202br, 203br, 204bl, 205bc, 207tl, 213b, 214cla, 214clb, 217clb, 223cr, © Peter Struycken Lichtkunstwerk NAI 1994, 1999 c/o Beeldrecht Amstelveen 237tl; 240tr, 241tr, 241br, 244tc, 247b, 250bc, 251br, 253tl, 256tl, 256cr, 263crb, 267bl, 270tr, 270br, 271tl, 271br, 274-275c, 276cra, 279br, 281b, 286b, 288tr, 288clb, 290tr, 291tr, 296tr, 296br, 301tc, 303tr, 308b, 309cr, 311cra, 314bl, 317b, 324br, 327b, 328clb, 342cla, 345tl, 349tl, 352cla, 356cl, 356bl, 357cr, 357bc, 359b, 362bl, 366tr, 367tr, 368c, 369bc, 375c, 376bl, 380cr, 384br, 390tl, 395tr, 402cl, 438cra, 438bl, 440bl; **Drents Museum, Assen**: 46br, 312bl, Badende kinderen bij stroompje c.1935 © von Duelman-Krumpelmann 315br; **Dro-vorm:** Mirande Phernambucq 146cla, 147br.

Robert Eckhardt: 292bl, 372c; **Eetbar Dit:** 402br; **Efteling Village Bosrijk:** 392cla; **Joop van de Ende Producties**: 420br; **Escher in Het Paleis, The Hague**: 222cla; **Mary Evans Picture Library**: 44bc.**Gert Fopma**: 275br, 277bl; **Foto Natura**: 168bl (B van Biezen), 295b (J Vermeer), 313tr and 314tc (F de Nooyer), 332t (J Sleurink); **Fotolia:** Jenifoto 98; **Frans Hals Museum, Haarlem**: 69tc, 190tr, 190cl, 190br, 191tl, 191tr, 191br, 191bl;

Gemeentearchief Amsterdam: 103tl, 103cl, 104clb, 105br, 106bl, 107tr, 107cr, 109r, 109tr, 109cr; Gemeentemuseum, The Hague: © Piet Mondrian/Holtzman Trust Victory Boogie-Woogie (unfinished), 1942-44, 1999 c/o Beeldrecht Amstelveen 228cl; **Getty Images**: altrendo travel 316 Hans Georg Eiben/The Image Bank 386-7; Vincent Jannink 347bl; Frans Lemmens/The Image Bank 174; Martin Rose 152cr. **Groninger Museum, Groningen**: 261tr, 288cl, 288cb, 289tl, 289cr, 289bl.**Tom Haartsen, J Holtkamp collection**: 32br, 32-33c; **Vanessa Hamilton**: 105c; **Harbour Crane:** 389tl; **Robert Harding Picture Library:** age fotostock 14br, 134; Ashley Cooper 171tc; Image Broker 16tr; Ingolf Pompe/LOOK 120; Roy Rainford 20; **Martine Hauwert**: 439tl; **Jan Den Hengst**: 95br; **Herberg Onder de Linden:** 412tc; **Het Arresthuis:** 388cr; **Hollandse Hoogte**: 307b, 420t; P. Babeliowsky 299tl, 299cra; Gé Dubbelman 300bc; B. van Flymen 36br, 304cra, 304bl; Vincent van den Hoogen 368cr; Rob Hulbers 210br; Jaco Klamer 321c; M. Kooren 22bl, 22tl, 39tr, 45cro, 45br, 63bc; M. Pellanders 63br; Berry Stokvis 185bc; Lex Verspeek 182bl; G. Wessel 278tl, 298clb, 299br; **Hortus Botanicus, Leiden**: 218cla; **Hotel Droog:** 396bc; **Hotel Modez:** 400tr; Hotelsuites.nl: 401bc; **Hulton Getty Collection**: 70t.

Iconografisch Bureau: 107tl; **Internationaal Bloembollencentrum**: 35cr, 216br, 217tr, 217clb, 217cl, 217cla, 217bl; **Internationaal Instituut Voor Sociale Geschiedenis, Amsterdam**: 59crb. **Wim Janszen**: 262cl, 266cl, 270cl; **Wubbe de Jong**: 63clb, 113tl; **Joods Historisch Museum, Amsterdam**: 71br; **De Jopenkerk:** 409tr; **Jopie Huisman Museum, Workum**: 302cla.

Hugo Kaagman: © Hugo Kaagman Delft blue plane-tail decoration 1996-1997, 1999 c/o Beeldrecht Amstelveen 33tr; **Anne Kalkhoven**: 287bl, 315tr, 348tl; **Jan Van De Kam**: 23b, 41tr, 41cra, 41crb, 41br, 173tr, 173cb, 173crb, 264cl, 264bc, 265tr, 265cr, 266cla, 266cra, 266br, 266bl, 267tl, 267cla, 267cra, 267tr, 267crb, 267cr, 267br, 272tr, 273tl, 273tc, 273tr, 273cr, 273crb, 273bc, 273clb, 273bl, 273br, 273tl, 273tr, 273clb, 273bl, 274br, 275cra, 275cra, 277tr, 278br, 282cl, 297tr, 318br, 332c, 332br, 346tl, 352br, 354tr, 354cla, 354clb, 354br, 354-355c, 355tr, 355crb, 355bl, 362tr, 362cla, 363ca, 363cr, 369cl, 372cla, 373tr, 375bl, © Joep Nicolas, Pieke 1995-1996, 1999 c/o Beeldrecht Amstelveen 376tr; 376cla, 376br, 377br, © Mari Andriessen Maastreechter Gees 1961-1962, 1999 c/o Beeldrecht Amstelveen 380bl, 381cl, 382bl, 383cr, 384tc, 384cla, 384crb, 385bc; **Klompenmusuem**: 313bl; S **Koninklijke Bibliotheek, The Hague**: 56cl; **Koninklijk Instituut voor de Tropen, Amsterdam**: 60tr, 60-61c; **Koninklijk Paleis, Amsterdam**/RVD: 69cr, 92cla, 92clb, 93crb; **Corine Koolstra**: © Suze Boschma-Berkhout Bartje, 1999 c/o Beeldrecht Amstelveen 312c; **Peter Koomen**: 182cr; **René Krekels, Nijmegen**: 27crb; **Kröller-müller Museum, Otterlo**: © Jean Dubuffet Jardin d´Émail 1973-4, 1999 c/o Beeldrecht Amstelveen 342tr; 342br, 343c.

Andries de la Lande Cremer: 269b, 282tr; **Leeuwarder Courant**: Niels Westra 298bl; **Frans Lemmens**: 34c; **Claude Lévesque**: 356-357c; **Librije's Zusje:** 414tc; **Lucius Seafood Restaurant:** 406bc.

Mauritshuis, The Hague: 8-9, 226tr, 226c, 226bl, 227tc, 227crb, 227cra, 227bc, 231tl; **Multatuli Museum, Amsterdam**: 61tr; **Musée de la Chartreuse, Douai**: 54clb; **Museum Boerhaave, Leiden**: 54bc, 55tl, 55clb; **Museum Boijmans-van Beuningen, Rotterdam**: 238-9 all; **Museum Bredius, The Hague**: 224bl; **Museum Lambert van Meerten, Delft**: 233bl; **Museum de Fundatie, Paleis a/d Blijmarkt**: Gerlinde Schrijver 320bl; **Museum Nairac, Barneveld**: 341br; **Museum Het Rembrandthuis, Amsterdam**: 79bc, 84br; **Museum Schokland**: 330tr, 330cra. **National Gallery, London**: 245tr; **Natura Artis Magistra**: 143cra; **Nederlands Architectuur Instituut**: 109cl, 146-147c; **Nederlands Scheepvaartmuseum, Amsterdam**: 136bl, 136cla, 137b, 137crb, 137t; **Niedersächsische Staats- und Universitätsbibliothek, Göttingen**: 48-49c; **Flip de Nooyer**: 272-273c; **North Sea Jazz Festival/rob Drexhage**: 37br. **Onze-lieve-vrouwebasiliek, Maastricht**: 381tr. **Paleis Het Loo, Nationaal Museum, Apeldoorn**: E. Boeijinga 338tr; A. Meine Jansen 338cla, 339tl, 338bl; R. Mulder 338cla; **Openbare Bibliotheek Amsterdam:** 441tl; **De Paviljoens, Almere**: © Robert Morris Observatorium, 1977, 1999 c/o Beeldrecht Amstelveen 333br; **Paul Paris**: 28tr, 70br, 71bl, 172-173c, 173tl, 194br, 198tr, 249br, 257br, 267cl, 272cla, 283cra, 286tr, 290clb, 292tr, 297bc, 303br, 305br, 309tr, 310clb, 311br, 335b, 352bl, 372tr; **Dick Polman**: 278c; **Robert Poutsma**: 24bl, 71tl, 146tr, 146br, 147tr, 147cr, 148cr, 148br, 166cl, 179tl, 344cr, 416br, 417tl, 418c; **Prinsenhof:** 399bc; **Projectbureau Ijburg**: 171t; PTT

Range Pictures: 52cla; **Herman Reis**: 23c, 24c, 25tr, 29cl, 56bl, 215br, 240b, 241tr, 274cla, 276br, 315cl, 323bl, **Rijksmuseum, Amsterdam**: 30tr, 30cl, 30bl, 30-31c, 31tr, 31cr, 31bl, 42, 44tr, 57t, 57crb, 61tl, 68cla, 70c, 126cl, 126bc, 127tl, 127c, 127br, 128tr, 128bl, 129tr, 129b, 199bl; **Rijksmuseum Muiderslot, Muiden**: 55cr; **Rijksmuseum van Oudheden, Leiden**: 46clb, 47tl, 47bc, 48bc, 48crb, 218tr; **Rijksmuseum voor Volkenkunde, Leiden**: 60bl, 61crb; **Rijkswaterstaat**: 250clb, 251tl, 251cr, 276tl; **La Rive:** 408bl.

Herman Scholten: 29bl, 176cla, 179bl, 182tl, 184ca, 194tl, 199tr, 203tr, 206cla, 210tr, 235tc, 244b, 250cla, 252tr, 252bl, 253cra, 258c, 258bl, 262b, 284cla, 284b, 285br, 287tr, 296clb, 300tr, 300cl, 328tr, 360tr, 361tr; 377bc, 382tl; **Schoolmuseum, Rotterdam/ Wolters-noordhoff, Groningen**: 50-51c, 53tl, 58-59c; **Science Center NEMO**: 140clb, 140cla, 140clb, 141br, 141cra; **Singer Museum**: Particuliere Collection 195bl; **Sint-jan, Den Bosch**:E Van Mackelenbergh 364cla, 364bc, 365tl; **Spaarnestad Fotoarchief**: 59tr, 61bc, 62clb, 62br, 63tc, 103bc, 147bl; **Spoorwegmuseum, Utrecht**: 205crb; **Stedelijk Museum, Amsterdam**: © Gerrit Rietveld Steltman chair 1963, 1999 c/o Beeldrecht Amstelveen 70bl; 132tr, © Marc Chagall Portrait of the Artist with Seven Fingers 1912, 1999 c/o Beeldrecht Amstelveen 132cla; © Gerrit Rietveld Red Blue Chair c.1918, 1999 c/o Beeldrecht Amstelveen 132bl; © Piet Mondrian/Holtzman Trust Composition in Red, Black, Blue, Yellow and Grey 1920, 1999 c/o Beeldrecht Amstelveen 132br; 133tl, © Karel Appel Foundation Man and Animals 1949, 1999 c/o Beeldrecht Amstelveen 133ca; © Jasper Johns Untitled 1965, 1999 c/o Beeldrecht Amstelveen 133bc; 133br, Tanzende 1911 © Ernst Ludwig Kirchner 133tl; **Stedelijk Museum De Lakenhal, Leiden**: 50cl, 108br, 220b; **Stedelijk Museum, Zwolle**: 320tr; **Stempels:** 389bc, 397tc; **Stichting Leidens Ontzet**: 39tl; **Stichting Paardenreddingboot Ameland**: 279t; **Stichting Vesting Bourtange**: 293tr; **Stichting4-Stromenland, Tiel**: 38bl; **Studio Putto, Derijp**: 22bl, 24c, 37tr, 45bl, 45crb, 48br, 88tr, 117bl, 177tr, 177cr; **Studiopress**: Guy van Grinsven 178tr.

Tony Stone Images: 104tr, 183cla; **Sven Torfinn**: 363tl, 363br; **TPG Nederland**: 440crb, 441bc; **Hans Tulleners**: 103cr, 104cr, 106c. **Van Gogh Museum, Amsterdam**: 130cla, 130clb, 131t, 131tr, 131cr; **Gerard op het Veld**: 34tr, 146c, 302tr, 340cra, 345bl, 346br, 360bl, 369tr, 372bl, 373br, 375tr, 383tr, 383bl; **Vereniging De Friesche Elf Steden** 296br; **Govert Vetten**: 22tr, 73bl, 85br, 124clb, 146-147c, 199br, 200tr, 264cla, 416c, 428br; **de Verkadefabriek:** 415br; **Villa Augustus:** 398tl; **Volkskrant**: Wim Ruigrok 26tr; **Sietske de Vries, Amsterdam**: 34cl; **Willeke Vrij**: 35tr. **Wacon-Images/Ronald Dendekker**: 151tl; **Pim Westerweel**: 166cr, 167cr, 168crb, 199cra, 263cra, 263b, 266clb, 333tr, 345cr, 353cr, 366bl; **West-Fries Museum, Hoorn**: 60cla; WL/**Delft Hydraulics**: 168br. **Zeeuws Museum, Middelburg**: Anda van Riet 254bl; 254crb; **Zuiderzeemuseum, Enkhuizen**: 169tr, photo Petra Stavast © Hugo Kaagman The Blue Fishvendor (www.kaagman.nl) stencils and spraypaint 181tl.

Front endpaper
Alamy Images: Hemis Rtc; Peter Horree Rc; Joana Kruse Lcl; frans lemmens Rcr, Rbl, Lbl; David Noton Photography Lc. Corbis: Frans Lemmens Ltc; Jean-Pierre Lescourret Ltl. **Dreamstime.com:** Rob Van Esch Lbr; Robertlindeboom Rtr; Pieter Snijder Rclb. **Getty Images:** altrendo travel Rcb; The Image Bank/Frans Lemmens Ltr.

Jacket
Front and spine - Alamy Images: Henry George Beeker.

All other images © Dorling Kindersley.
For further **information see: www.dkimages.com**

Phrase Book

In Emergency

Help!	Help!	Help
Stop!	Stop!	Stop
Call a doctor	Haal een dokter	Haal uhn **dok**-tur
Call an ambulance	Bel een ambulance	Bell uhn ahm-bew-**luhns**-uh
Call the police	Roep de politie	Roop duh poe-**leet**-see
Call the fire brigade	Roep de brandweer	Roop duh **brahnt**-vheer
Where is the nearest telephone?	Waar is de dichtstbijzijnde telefoon?	Vhaar iss duh **dikhst**-baly-zaiyn-duh tay-luh-**foan**
Where is the nearest hospital?	Waar is het dichtstbijzijnde ziekenhuis?	Vhaar iss het **dikhst**-baiy-zaiyn-duh **zee**-kuh-houws

Communication Essentials

Yes	Ja	Yaa
No	Nee	Nay
Please	Alstublieft	Ahls-tew-**bleeft**
Thank you	Dank u	Dahnk-ew
Excuse me	Pardon	Pahr-**don**
Hello	Hallo	Hallo
Goodbye	Dag	Dahgh
Good night	Slaap lekker	Slaap **lek**-kah
morning	Morgen	**Mor**-ghuh
afternoon	Middag	**Mid**-dahgh
evening	Avond	**Ah**-vohnd
yesterday	Gisteren	**Ghis**-tern
today	Vandaag	Vahn-**daagh**
tomorrow	Morgen	**Mor**-ghuh
here	Hier	Heer
there	Daar	Daar
What?	Wat?	Vhat
When?	Wanneer?	Vhan-**eer**
Why?	Waarom?	Vhaar-**om**
Where?	Waar?	Vhaar
How?	Hoe?	Hoo

Useful Phrases

How are you?	Hoe gaat het ermee?	Hoo ghaat het er-**may**
Very well, thank you	Heel goed, dank u	Hayl ghoot, dahnk ew
How do you do?	Hoe maakt u het?	Hoo maakt ew het
See you soon	Tot ziens	Tot zeens
That's fine	Prima	**Pree**-mah
Where is/are?	Waar is/zijn?	Vhaar iss/zayn…
How far is it to…?	Hoe ver is het naar…?	Hoo vehr iss het naar…
How do I get to…?	Hoe kom ik naar…?	Hoo kom ik naar…
Do you speak English?	Spreekt u engels?	Spraykt ew **eng**-uhls
I don't understand	Ik snap het niet	Ik snahp het neet
Could you speak slowly?	Kunt u langzamer praten?	Kuhnt ew **lahng**-zahmer praa-tuh
I'm sorry	Sorry	Sorry

Useful Words

big	groot	ghroaht
small	klein	klaiyn
hot	warm	vharm
cold	koud	khowt
good	goed	ghoot
bad	slecht	slekht
enough	genoeg	ghuh-**noohkh**
well	goed	ghoot
open	open	open
closed	gesloten	ghuh-**slow**-tuh
left	links	links
right	rechts	rekhts
straight on	rechtdoor	rehkht dohr
near	dichtbij	dikht baiy
far	ver weg	vehr vhekh
up	omhoog	om-**hoakh**
down	naar beneden	naar buh-**nay**-duh
early	vroeg	vroohkh
late	laat	laat
entrance	ingang	**in**-ghahng
exit	uitgang	**ouht**-ghang
toilet	wc	vhay say
occupied	bezet	buh-**zett**
free (unoccupied)	vrij	vraiy
free (no charge)	gratis	**ghraah**-tiss

Making a Telephone Call

I'd like to place a long-distance call	Ik wil graag interlokaal telefoneren	Ik vhil ghraakh **inter**-loh-kaahl tay-luh-foe-**neh**-ruh
I'd like to call collect	Ik wil "collect call" bellen	Ik vhil "collect call" **bel**-luh
I'll try again later	Ik probeer het later nog wel eens	Ik pro-**beer** het laater nokh vhel ayns
Can I leave a message?	Kunt u een boodschap doorgeven?	Kuhnt ew uhn **boat**-skhahp **dohr**-ghay-vuh
Could you speak up a little please?	Wilt u wat harder praten?	Vhilt ew vhat **hahr**-der **praah**-tuh
Local call	Lokaal gesprek	Low-**kaahl** ghuh-**sprek**

Shopping

How much does this cost?	Hoeveel kost dit?	Hoo-**vayl** kost dit
I would like	Ik wil graag	Ik vhil ghraakh
Do you have…?	Heeft u…?	Hayft ew…
I'm just looking	Ik kijk alleen even	Ik kaiyk alleyn **ay**-vuh
Do you take credit cards?	Neemt u credit cards aan?	Naymt ew credit cards aan
Do you take traveller's cheques?	Neemt u reischeques aan?	Naymt ew **raiys**-sheks aan
What time do you open?	Hoe laat gaat u open?	Hoo laat ghaat ew opuh
What time do you close?	Hoe laat gaat u dicht?	Hoo laat ghaat ew dikht
This one	Deze	**Day**-zuh
That one	Die	Dee
expensive	duur	dewr
cheap	goedkoop	ghoot-**koap**
size	maat	maat
white	wit	vhit
black	zwart	zvhahrt
red	rood	roat
yellow	geel	ghayl
green	groen	ghroon
blue	blauw	blah-ew

Types of Shops

antique shop	antiekwinkel	ahn-**teek**-vhin-kul
bakery	bakker	**bah**-ker
bank	bank	bahnk
bookshop	boekwinkel	**book**-vhin-kul
butcher	slager	slaakh-er
cake shop	banketbakkerij	bahnk-**et**-bahk-er-aiy
cheese shop	kaaswinkel	**kaas**-vhin-kul
chip shop	patatzaak	pah-**taht**-zaak
chemist (dispensing)	apotheek	ah-poe-**taiyk**
delicatessen	delicatessen	daylee-kah-**tes**-suh
department store	warenhuis	**vhaar**-uh-houws
fishmonger	viswinkel	**viss**-vhin-kul
greengrocer	groenteboer	**ghroon**-tuh-boor
hairdresser	kapper	**kah**-per
market	markt	mahrkt
newsagent	krantenwinkel	**krahn**-tuh-vhin-kul
post office	postkantoor	**pohst**-kahn-tor
shoe shop	schoenenwinkel	**sghoo**-nuh-vhin-kul
supermarket	supermarkt	**sew**-per-mahrkt
tobacconist	sigarenwinkel	see-**ghaa**-ruh-vhin-kul
travel agent	reisburo	**raiys**-bew-roa

Sightseeing

art gallery	gallerie	ghaller-ee
bus station	busstation	**buhs**-stah-shown
bus ticket	strippenkaart	**strip**-puh-kaahrt
cathedral	kathedraal	kah-tuh-**draal**
church	kerk	kehrk
closed on public holidays	op feestdagen gesloten	op **fayst**-daa-ghuh ghuh-**slow**-tuh
day return	dagretour	**dahgh**-ruh-tour
garden	tuin	touwn
library	bibliotheek	bee-bee-yo-**tayk**
museum	museum	mew-**zay**-uhm
railway station	station	stah-**shown**
return ticket	retourtje	ruh-**tour**-tyuh
single journey	enkeltje	**eng**-kuhl-tyuh
tourist information	VVV	fay fay fay
town hall	stadhuis	staht-**houws**
train	trein	traiyn

Staying in a Hotel

Do you have a vacant room?	**Zijn er nog kamers vrij?**	*Zaiyn er nokh* **kaa-mers** *vray*
double room with double bed	**een twees persoonskamer met een twee persoonsbed**	*uhn* **tvhay**-*per* **soans**-*kaa-mer met uhn* **tvhay**-*per-* **soans** *beht*
twin room	**een kamer met**	*uhn* **kaa-mer** *met*
twin room	**een lits-jumeaux**	*uhn lee-zjoo-***moh**
single room	**eenpersoons-kamer**	**ayn**-*per*-**soans-kaa-mer**
room with a bath	**kamer met bad**	**kaa-mer** *met baht*
shower	**douche**	*doosh*
porter	**kruier**	**krouw**-*yuh*
I have a reservation	**Ik heb gereserveerd**	*Ik hehp ghuh-ray-sehr-***veert**

Eating Out

Have you got a table?	**Is er een tafel vrij?**	*Iss ehr uhn* **tah**-*fuhl vraiy*
I want to reserve a table	**Ik wil een tafel reserveren**	*Ik vhil uhn* **tah**-*fuhl ray-sehr-***veer**-*uh*
The bill, please	**Mag ik afrekenen**	*Mukh ik* **ahf**-*ray- kuh-nuh*
I am a vegetarian	**Ik ben vegetariër**	*Ik ben fay-ghuh-* **taahr**-*ee-er*
waitress/waiter	**serveerster/ober**	*Sehr-***veer**-*ster/***oh**-*ber*
menu	*de kaart*	*duh kaahrt*
cover charge	**het couvert**	*het koo-***vehr**
wine list	**de wijnkaart**	*duh* **vhaiyn**-*kaart*
glass	**het glas**	*het ghlahss*
bottle	**de fles**	*duh fless*
knife	**het mes**	*het mess*
fork	**de vork**	*duh fork*
spoon	**de lepel**	*duh* **lay**-*pul*
breakfast	**het ontbijt**	*het ont-***baiyt**
lunch	**de lunch**	*duh lernsh*
dinner	**het diner**	*het dee-***nay**
main course	**het hoofdgerecht**	*het* **hoaft**-*ghuh-rekht*
starter, first course	**het voorgerecht**	*het* **vohr**-*ghuh-rekht*
dessert	**het nagerecht**	*het* **naa**-*ghuh-rekht*
dish of the day	**het dagmenu**	*het* **dahgh**-*munh-ew*
bar	**het cafe**	*het kaa-***fay**
café	**het eetcafe**	*het* **ayt**-*kaa-***fay**
rare	**rare**	*'rare'*
medium	**medium**	*'medium'*
well done	**doorbakken**	*dohr-***bah**-*kuh*

Menu Decoder

aardappels	**aard-uppuhls**	*potatoes*
azijn	**aah-zaiyn**	*vinegar*
biefstuk	**beef-stuhk**	*steak*
bier, pils	**beer, pilss**	*beer*
boter	**boater**	*butter*
brood/broodje	**broat/broat-yuh**	*bread/roll*
cake, taart, gebak	**"cake", taahrt, ghuh-bahk**	*cake, pastry*
carbonade	**kahr-bow-naa-duh**	*pork chop*
chocola	**show-coa-laa**	*chocolate*
citroen	**see-troon**	*lemon*
cocktail	**cocktail**	*cocktail*
droog	**droakh**	*dry*
eend	**aynt**	*duck*
ei	**aiy**	*egg*
garnalen	**ghahr-naah-luh**	*prawns*
gebakken	**ghuh-bah-ken**	*fried*
gegrild	**ghuh-ghrillt**	*grilled*
gekookt	**ghuh-koakt**	*boiled*
gepocheerd	**ghuh-posh-eert**	*poached*
gerookt	**ghuh-roakt**	*smoked*
geroosterd brood	**ghuh-roas-tert broat**	*toast*
groenten	**ghroon-tuh**	*vegetables*
ham	**hahm**	*ham*
haring	**haa-ring**	*herring*
hutspot	**huht-spot**	*hot pot*
ijs	**aiyss**	*ice, ice cream*
jenever	**yuh-nay-vhur**	*gin*
kaas	**kaas**	*cheese*
kabeljauw	**kah-buhl-youw**	*cod*
kip	**kip**	*chicken*
knoflook	**knoff-loak**	*garlic*
koffie	**coffee**	*coffee*
kool, rode of	**coal, roe-duh off**	*cabbage, red or*
witte	**vhit-uh**	*white***kreeft**
krayft	*lobster*	
kroket	**crow-ket**	*ragout in bread-crumbs, deep fried*
lamsvlees	**lahms-flayss**	*lamb*
lekkerbekje	**lek-kah-bek-yuh**	*fried fillet of haddock*
mineraalwater	**meener-aahl-vhaater**	*mineral water*
mosterd	**moss-tehrt**	*mustard*
niet scherp	**neet skehrp**	*mild*
olie	**oh-lee**	*oil*
paling	**paa-ling**	*eel*
pannekoek	**pah-nuh-kook**	*pancake*
patat frites	**pah-taht freet**	*chips*
peper	**pay-per**	*pepper*
poffertjes	**poffer-tyuhs**	*tiny buckwheat pancakes*
rijst	**raiyst**	*rice*
rijsttafel	**raiys-tah-ful**	*Indonesian meal*
rode wijn	**roe-duh vhaiyn**	*red wine*
rookworst	**roak-vhorst**	*smoked sausage*
rundvlees	**ruhnt-flayss**	*beef*
saus	**souwss**	*sauce*
schaaldieren	**skaahl-deeh-ruh**	*shellfish*
scherp	**skehrp**	*hot (spicy)*
schol	**sghol**	*plaice*
soep	**soup**	*soup*
stamppot	**stahm-pot**	*sausage stew*
suiker	**souw-ker**	*sugar*
thee	**tay**	*tea*
tosti	**toss-tee**	*cheese on toast*
uien	**ouw-yuh**	*onions*
uitsmijter	**ouht-smaiy-ter**	*fried egg on bread with ham*
varkensvlees	**vahr-kuhns-flayss**	*pork*
vers fruit	**fehrss frouwt**	*fresh fruit*
verse jus	**vehr-suh zjhew**	*fresh orange juice*
vis	**fiss**	*fish/seafood*
vlees	**flayss**	*meat*
water	**vhaa-ter**	*water*
witte wijn	**vhih-tuh vhaiyn**	*white wine*
worst	**vhorst**	*sausage*
zout	**zouwt**	*salt*

Numbers

1	**een**	*ayn*
2	**twee**	*tvhay*
3	**drie**	*dree*
4	**vier**	*feer*
5	**vijf**	*faiyf*
6	**zes**	*zess*
7	**zeven**	**zay**-*vuh*
8	**acht**	*ahkht*
9	**negen**	**nay**-*guh*
10	**tien**	*teen*
11	**elf**	*elf*
12	**twaalf**	*tvhaalf*
13	**dertien**	**dehr**-*teen*
14	**veertien**	**feer**-*teen*
15	**vijftien**	**faiyf**-*teen*
16	**zestien**	**zess**-*teen*
17	**zeventien**	**zayvuh**-*teen*
18	**achtien**	**ahkh**-*teen*
19	**negentien**	**nay-ghuh**-*teen*
20	**twintig**	**tvhin**-*tukh*
21	**eenentwintig**	**aynuh**-*tvhin-tukh*
30	**dertig**	**dehr**-*tukh*
40	**veertig**	**feer**-*tukh*
50	**vijftig**	**faiyf**-*tukh*
60	**zestig**	**zess**-*tukh*
70	**zeventig**	**zay**-*vuh-tukh*
80	**tachtig**	**tahkh**-*tukh*
90	**negentig**	**nayguh**-*tukh*
100	**honderd**	**hohn**-*durt*
1000	**duizend**	**douw**-*zuhnt*
1,000,000	**miljoen**	*mill-***yoon**

Time

one minute	**een minuut**	*uhn meen-***ewt**
one hour	**een uur**	*uhn ewr*
half an hour	**een half uur**	*uhn hahlf ewr*
half past one	**half twee**	*hahlf tvhay*
a day	**een dag**	*uhn dahgh*
a week	**een week**	*uhn vhayk*
a month	**een maand**	*uhn maant*
a year	**een jaar**	*uhn jaar*
Monday	**maandag**	**maan**-*dahgh*
Tuesday	**dinsdag**	**dins**-*dahgh*
Wednesday	**woensdag**	**vhoons**-*dahgh*
Thursday	**donderdag**	**donder**-*dahgh*
Friday	**vrijdag**	**vraiy**-*dahgh*
Saturday	**zaterdag**	**zaater**-*dahgh*
Sunday	**zondag**	**zon**-*dahgh*

Road Map of the Netherlands

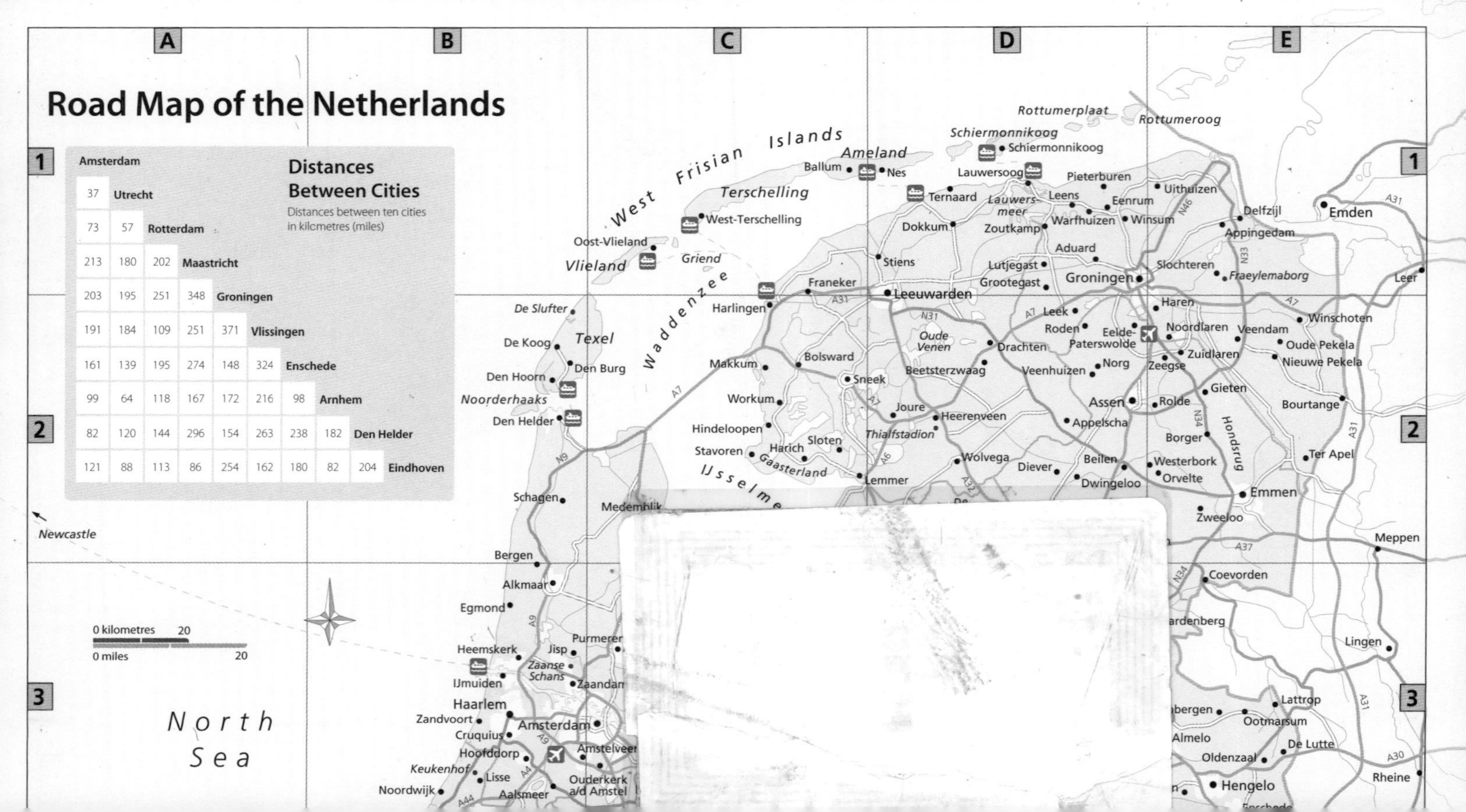

Distances Between Cities

Distances between ten cities in kilometres (miles)

Amsterdam									
37	Utrecht								
73	57	Rotterdam							
213	180	202	Maastricht						
203	195	251	348	Groningen					
191	184	109	251	371	Vlissingen				
161	139	195	274	148	324	Enschede			
99	64	118	167	172	216	98	Arnhem		
82	120	144	296	154	263	238	182	Den Helder	
121	88	113	86	254	162	180	82	204	Eindhoven